*Energy and Security*

# Energy and Security

*Toward a New Foreign Policy Strategy*

Edited by

Jan H. Kalicki and David L. Goldwyn

Published by Woodrow Wilson Center Press
Washington, D.C.

The Johns Hopkins University Press
Baltimore

EDITORIAL OFFICES

Woodrow Wilson Center Press
Woodrow Wilson International Center for Scholars
One Woodrow Wilson Plaza
1300 Pennsylvania Avenue, N.W.
Washington, D.C. 20004-3027
Telephone: 202-691-4029
www.wilsoncenter.org


Order from

The Johns Hopkins University Press
Hampden Station
P.O. Box 50370
Baltimore, Maryland 21211
Telephone: 1-800-537-5487
www.press.jhu.edu/books

2 4 6 8 9 7 5 3 1

Library of Congress Cataloging-in-Publication Data

Energy and security : toward a new foreign policy strategy / edited by Jan H.
Kalicki and David L. Goldwyn.
    p.   cm.
Includes bibliographical references and index.
ISBN 0-8018-8278-8 (hardcover : alk. paper) — ISBN 0-8018-8279-6
(pbk. : alk. paper)
    1. Energy policy—United States.   2. National security—United States.
3. United States—Foreign relations—2001–.   I. Kalicki, Jan H.   II. Goldwyn,
David L., 1959–
HD9502.U52E4543 2005
333.79′0973—dc22

                                                    2005006082

**Woodrow Wilson
Center Press**
*Washington, D.C.*

For Jan, Van, and Howard—visionaries all, in memory
For Peter and Ted, for their guidance, wisdom, and example;
for my band of brothers, for always being there;
and for Cathy, for her love and joy

Safety and certainty in oil lie in variety and variety alone.

*—Winston Churchill, 1913*

Come senators, congressmen

Please heed the call

Don't stand in the doorway

Don't block up the hall

For he that gets hurt

Will be he who has stalled

There's a battle outside

And it is ragin'.

It'll soon shake your windows

And rattle your walls

For the times they are a-changin'.

*—Bob Dylan, 1963*

# Contents

# Foreword

## *James R. Schlesinger*

Ever since the Industrial Revolution, energy and the need to secure its supply have been fundamental to any position of power in the world. More than
thirty years ago, the Arab oil embargo brought home America's (and the
industrial world's) vulnerability to disruption of that supply. Nonetheless,
OECD countries today use and import more energy than ever before, now
joined by rapidly industrializing countries such as China, India, and Brazil.

Today, supplies are more diverse than in the 1970s. America depends less
on OPEC—though its members remain major suppliers—and receives increasing imports from non-OPEC regions such as Eurasia and West Africa
(other than Nigeria). Abundant supplies of gas (liquefied or otherwise) and
coal (processed to minimize environmental impact) will provide further diversification in the coming decades, but oil will continue to be the principal
energy resource for the foreseeable future. We must recognize realistically
that wind, solar, and nuclear power remain limited alternatives, and that a
hydrogen-based economy remains at best decades away.

Two key questions arise from this assessment. The first is how best to
conduct relations with established producers, most of them OPEC states, to
ensure oil market stability and security of supply. The second is how to develop non-OPEC resources and to ensure that their production also reaches
the international marketplace. Geology and technology continue to be crucial in shaping the market—witness the remarkable progress in deepwater
exploration and the contribution of liquefied natural gas (LNG) to a new
global gas market. Still, the answers to those two questions are primarily
political and economic: the development of a foreign policy that gives sufficient priority to these objectives, and the creation of an economic environment that will ensure its success.

That is where this new book edited by Jan Kalicki and David Goldwyn on energy security for the twenty-first century is especially important. It explores how foreign policy can best advance U.S. energy interests, and how energy can be used to advance broader U.S. foreign policy interests. It does so by focusing on the main regions of energy development and supply, and then by constructing an energy security strategy that takes into account the role of strategic reserves, technology, the environment, and sustainable development.

In part I of the book, for example, Daniel Yergin analyzes the impact of supply diversification on energy security, and Edward Morse and Amy Jaffe advocate a path forward from overdependence on OPEC. In subsequent parts, the authors consider Russia and Eurasia—with Jan Kalicki and Jonathan Elkind proposing an expanding system of energy transportation, to include China and Iran, from that non-OPEC epicenter—as well as the Middle East and Africa, the Pacific Rim, and the North Atlantic and the Americas. Part VI offers creative approaches to a new energy security strategy with, for example, an assessment by Leon Fuerth on the interconnections between energy and America's national and homeland security strategy and proposals from David Goldwyn and Michelle Billig to enhance the U.S. ability to use its strategic reserves to address supply disruptions and to build cooperation for expanding global strategic energy reserves.

This book also benefits from point/counterpoint between producing-country and consuming-country perspectives—as borne out especially by commentaries from two former OPEC leaders, Alvaro Silva-Calderón and Abdullah bin Hamad Al-Attiyah, and a former Russian deputy foreign minister and energy minister, Viktor Kalyuzhny; and by chapters contributed by a former E.U. vice president and energy commissioner, Loyola de Palacio; a former Mexican energy minister, Luis Téllez; and the Australian deputy secretary for industry, tourism, and resources, John Ryan.

The analysis in this book is notable for both its regional and its global policy applications. Regionally, it is imperative to link the energy sources with the applications of wealth. In the developing world, are new energy producers doomed to repeat the mistakes of their predecessors, permitting concentrations of wealth and widespread corruption to impoverish most of their populations and destabilize their societies and political systems? Or, as suggested by Charles McPherson and other authors, can they build successfully on lessons learned and the body of experience assembled by the World Bank and other institutions? Certainly, as suggested by a task force I cochaired for the Council on Foreign Relations, the reconstruction of Iraq provides an opportunity to harness energy resources for the benefit of the many rather than the few, and to create a more stable, secure, and democratic structure that justifies the sacrifices made in two recent wars.[1]

As noted above, energy development can also contribute significantly to foreign policy objectives, and some of the most interesting examples are advanced by the authors of the chapters in the regional parts of this book. For example, the objective of a nuclear-weapons-free Korean peninsula could be advanced by regional pooling in electric power, as suggested by Keiichi Yokobori, or by gas supplies from Russia through China, as suggested by Kalicki and Elkind. The goal of greater North African stability, more integrated into the European market and less vulnerable to extremist Islamic movements, might be advanced, as Gordon Shearer notes, by greater cooperation in gas and electricity between North African producers and E.U. consumers. As Robin West recognizes, Iran presents potentially one of the most important opportunities for a new energy security strategy. If that country can engage peacefully with its neighbors and its security can be credibly assured, the objectives of nonproliferation and a more moderate and open domestic polity would be significantly advanced. Energy-related initiatives, from gas development in the Gulf to cooperation in Caspian delimitation and transit arrangements, can play a positive role in this process.

The implications are also important from a global policy standpoint. For too long, energy policy has not been sufficiently connected to foreign policy, either conceptually or institutionally. And, as made clear in an earlier study, *Strategic Energy Initiative,* the United States too often deals with energy policy in domestic rather than international terms.[2]

Jan Kalicki, David Goldwyn, and an outstanding group of contributors draw on extensive experience with energy issues in government and the private sector—including years in which Jan and I worked together on Middle East, finance, and energy issues. In my view, this book could not be more timely or important in creating a foundation for a new energy security strategy for the United States. It enables readers from government, industry, and academic institutions to analyze the most important global and regional issues from an integrated energy and foreign policy standpoint—and to develop powerful new approaches to the growing range of policy problems with an energy dimension.

## Notes

1. Thomas R. Pickering and James R. Schlesinger, cochairs, Independent Task Force sponsored by the Council on Foreign Relations, *Iraq: The Day After* (New York: Council on Foreign Relations, 2003).

2. Sam Nunn and James R. Schlesinger, cochairs, task force sponsored by the Center for Strategic and International Studies, *Strategic Energy Initiative* (Washington, D.C.: Center for Strategic and International Studies, 1999).

# Foreword

## *Bill Richardson*

American foreign policy has long been influenced by the U.S. need for energy security. As a congressman and as the permanent U.S. representative to the United Nations, I saw the United States use energy as a weapon, by sanctions that deny U.S. investors and markets to countries that threaten America or reject its values. As the secretary of energy, I saw the United States use energy as a tool for good, as America helped a newly democratic Nigeria rebuild its power grid and used the lure of energy trade and investment to help open China and Russia to Western market forces and to help secure the former Soviet Union's nuclear weapons and material.

I have seen energy advance U.S. geopolitical interests, as the nation did in pressing successfully for the construction of east-west oil and gas pipelines in Central Asia, securing political autonomy for the newly independent states of the former Soviet Union, providing economic security to the U.S. ally Turkey, and constraining Iran's ability to use its oil wealth to fund its nuclear proliferation. As the governor of New Mexico, I see every day how crucial stable energy prices are to the domestic economy and how the national economy is tied to the stability and security of oil-producing states in the Middle East, Russia and Eurasia, and Africa and Latin America. I recall all too well from my tenure at the Department of Energy how $10-a-barrel oil devastated the domestic energy industry and the economies of developing nations that rely on oil for income. I remember the impact of $35 oil prices on the U.S. and European economies, as well as on oil-importing nations such as India. In both cases, energy and economic security were interchangeable.

Yet as a nation, America has accepted for too long an ad hoc approach to energy and foreign policy. It has not used foreign policy to proactively promote the political stability of its key suppliers. It has not pressed hard enough for modernization in the Middle East. Today, the U.S. government takes its Latin American neighbors for granted, spurning its ally Argentina in its time of need, snubbing the Mexican president for insufficient loyalty to U.S. Iraq policy, and neglecting to recognize that the economic success of that region is critical to U.S. energy and economic security. The United States has failed to invest adequately in the technologies that will help it to reduce its dependency on imported oil, free the great powers of the twenty-first century from a similar path of dependency, and address the environmental consequences of U.S. consumption.

This excellent book recognizes the need to integrate America's energy interests into its foreign policy in a strategic, coordinated fashion. Though every American can make the intuitive connection between global dependence on Middle Eastern oil, dissent in Middle Eastern societies, and terrorist attacks on the United States, there is no evidence yet of a serious effort to promote open societies in that region. Though the governments of West African and Central Asian countries are clearly failing to use oil wealth to promote national development, feeding the fires of dissension and instability in those critical regions, there is no sign that addressing these root causes of instability is a key element of U.S. foreign policy. And in North Korea, where we see the most serious nuclear threat on the globe today, energy lies at the heart of the problem and the solution to that crisis; yet we see no sustained U.S. effort to use energy to forge a diplomatic resolution.

The contributors to this book present many superb proposals for restructuring the United States' energy policy and restoring strategic vision to its foreign policy. I share Luis Tellez's concern for the need for internal reform in Mexico and Venezuela and for a respectful but robust U.S. policy toward the region. I share Robin West's view that there is no foreseeable replacement for the oil reserves of the Middle East, as well as Edward Morse's judgment that America must take autonomous steps to assure the stability of global oil prices and that it cannot simply rely on OPEC's ability to manage its fractious members over the long term. I hope U.S. and Asian policymakers pay close attention to Keiichi Yokobori's creative proposals for creating a Northeast Asian power grid to denuclearize the Korean peninsula and to create incentives for better relations among North and South Korea, China, and Japan.

I very much share the concerns of many of the authors, particularly Michelle Foss, Bennett Johnston, Donald Juckett, and Shirley Neff, about the looming natural gas crisis and the need to promote both United States–

based supply and access to LNG. I strongly concur with David Goldwyn and Michelle Billig that the United States must build up its strategic reserves, modernize its reserve policy to address the threats of the twenty-first century, and empower the secretary of energy to deploy these reserves to counter serious supply disruptions, such as those in Venezuela in December 2002 and in Nigeria in 2003.

The book's editors have created an outstanding agenda for a new foreign policy strategy for the United States, which would go far to advance its national security interests. I know the editors very well. David Goldwyn was my national security deputy during my term as ambassador to the United Nations, and he led international energy diplomacy efforts for me as my counselor and as assistant secretary for international affairs at the Department of Energy. Jan Kalicki's leadership as counselor at the Department of Commerce on the Caspian Sea region, Russia, and the Middle East forcefully complemented international energy diplomacy during President Clinton's first and second terms. The editors have assembled the best and the brightest of the international energy galaxy, and together they have charted a course to a more secure, stable, and noble foreign policy for the United States. This volume should be required reading for those who make America's energy and foreign policy and for its diplomats, as well as for any serious student of national security and international affairs.

# Foreword

## *Lee H. Hamilton*

Second only to national defense, energy plays a crucial role in the survival and well-being of the United States and virtually all other countries, both developing and developed. It determines whether our lights will go on or off, our agriculture and industry will go forward or backward, our homes and offices will be habitable or become shells—and in fact whether or not we can defend ourselves. For that simple reason, energy policy must be one of the highest priorities for any White House or administration. It is a paramount consideration in developing programs for our nation's future growth, U.S. policies toward other nations, and a national security strategy for the new century.

Yet energy issues unfortunately have been debated more often in their own technical terms than in their broader policy context. Or, worse yet, they have been considered in the United States through the political optic of subsidies to producers—an unedifying spectacle brought mercifully to a temporary halt by Congress in 2003. With the exception of a few regional policy debates, however, energy has yet to be addressed in the context that I think matters most: how it can advance both U.S. and international security, and how it can be properly integrated into a foreign policy of global scope.

That is what this ambitious new volume, coedited by Jan Kalicki and David Goldwyn, sets out to do. With contributions from some of the most outstanding specialists in the field, it sets forth a new foreign policy framework focused on enhancing energy security for the United States, its allies, and its partners. After undertaking a comprehensive set of regional analyses, the book offers a new energy security strategy with both "hard" and "soft" power components. The former include securing the U.S. energy infrastructure against the increased threat of terrorism since September 11, 2001;

xxi

maximizing technology; and building a new and muscular strategic reserve policy. The latter include balancing energy and the environment, promoting transparency and good governance, and achieving sustainable development.

Just as war is too important to be left just to the generals, energy is too important to be left just to the engineers and geologists. I hasten to add that these professionals all play critical roles in their respective fields. But I think they would be the first to say that, to be effective, they must operate within a wider, agreed-on policy framework. This volume, I believe, makes a critical difference in helping America to achieve this goal.

Another key aspect of energy security is to reduce U.S. dependence on just a few, highly unstable sources of oil and gas. The obvious example is the Middle East, from the oil embargo launched in 1973 to successive conflicts in the Levant and the Gulf—including in just the past generation three excruciating wars involving Iraq, which happens to hold the world's second largest oil reserves. I would agree with the conclusion of this book that though oil trade with the Middle East is an inevitable part of the energy landscape for the foreseeable future, it is imperative to pursue policies that actually increase the stability of that region for the long term, and those policies must include the promotion of economic growth and democratic development.

But I would also agree with the editors and contributing authors that much more should be done to diversify America's sources of oil and gas, promote new technologies, and bring profligate energy consumption under control. Just to mention two examples: With one-third of the world's gas reserves and oil production that rivals Saudi Arabia, non-OPEC Russia promises to be a critical energy security partner in the future. Second, instead of debating how much pork to give U.S. industry, it is high time that automobile manufacturers be required to meet more aggressive fuel efficiency standards for all classes of vehicles. America should also finance the serious expansion of mass transit alternatives in car-clogged metropolises such as Los Angeles, and join the rest of the world in seriously combating greenhouse gas emissions.

New energy opportunities provide highly effective ways to advance U.S. foreign policy objectives. A striking example documented in this book is how the Caspian Sea region's energy development is securing the very sovereignty and independence of the newly independent states of the former Soviet Union. Other examples cited in the book—just to mention a few— are the realignment of China and the United States as the world's largest energy consumers; using Russian gas backed by Western capital as a building block (far more preferable to nuclear power reactors) for a future, nuclear-weapons-free Korean peninsula; and harnessing energy to reverse Africa's downward spiral of nation-destroying conflict, grinding poverty, and devastating epidemics.

The two coeditors are well-known practitioners and scholars who have been centrally involved in issues of energy and foreign policy for the past decade. They have worked closely with the Woodrow Wilson International Center for Scholars on a wide range of issues and programs, and it was our pleasure to publish an earlier volume coedited by Jan Kalicki on Russia and Eurasia. Now, he and David Goldwyn have made it possible for policymakers and students of policy to think and act globally about how to use energy to create new opportunities for security, peace, and development around the world. This book should be required reading for the administration and Congress entering office in 2005—and for business leaders, scholars, nonspecialists, and all others who see energy as a cornerstone for a new foreign policy strategy in the twenty-first century.

# Acknowledgments

Except possibly for the world of the divine, the act of creation is a complex affair. As coeditors, we found that we had to overcome a couple of unusual challenges. Geographically, we were located for much of this project on two American coasts, and the volume's contributing authors literally spanned the planet. Intellectually, we had to bridge the two quite distinct worlds of our contributors: the world of the foreign policy professionals and the world of the energy industry, whose paths often cross but who often keep each other at arm's length.

The challenges proved to be surmountable, however, thanks to our common outlook and experience in foreign, energy, and commercial policy work over four administrations, two Democratic and two Republican; thanks to the power of computers and technology; and thanks above all to the passion shared with our authors for securing the energy lifelines to America's future security. Moreover, though we began this journey from the perspective of U.S. interests, we quickly realized that it could not conclude successfully without adopting a thoroughly global perspective, and we are fortunate to have had the contributions of energy policy leaders from both OPEC and non-OPEC countries.

This book would not have been possible without other critical ingredients. We received support and encouragement from Lee Hamilton, Mike Van Dusen, and Blair Ruble at the Woodrow Wilson Center; from our outstanding editors at the Woodrow Wilson Center Press, Joseph Brinley and Yamile Kahn; and from our copy editor, Alfred Imhoff. We are grateful for financial support to the book project from Norwegian donors, including the Energy Policy Foundation of Norway, and for the advice and counsel of our good friend Daniel Yergin. We were assisted extremely capably by our editorial assistants in Washington, Hagit Hevron and Ricardo De Vecchi Galindo, who provided superb support from start to finish; and by Vladimir Shatilenko, who kept us analytically intact in California. And we were encouraged every step of the way by our wives, Jean and Cathy, and by Jan, Sasha, Peter (who wanted to know if there would be more pages than Harry Potter, volume five), and Benjamin (who was conceived and delivered faster than our volume, and who slept long enough in his early days to permit editing to stay on schedule). We knew we were excited about this project, but their enthusiasm made it a joy.

Our appreciation to all, and of course especially to the contributors to this book. For any errors of omission or commission, we cheerfully accept responsibility.

JHK and DLG
*San Ramon, California*
*Washington*
*January 2005*

# Abbreviations

| | |
|---|---|
| APEC | Asia-Pacific Economic Cooperation forum |
| APERC | Asia-Pacific Energy Research Centre |
| bcfpd | billion cubic feet per day |
| bcm | billion cubic meters |
| bpd | barrels per day |
| BTC | Baku–Tbilisi–Ceyhan pipeline |
| Btu | British thermal units |
| CAFE | Corporate Average Fuel Economy |
| CDM | Clean Development Mechanism |
| CPA | Coalition Provisional Authority |
| CPC | Caspian Pipeline Consortium |
| CTB | Comprehensive Test Ban |
| DOE | Department of Energy |
| EIA | U.S. Energy Information Administration |
| EITI | Extractive Industries Transparency Initiative |
| EWG | Energy Working Group (APEC) |
| GDP | gross domestic product |
| GECF | Gas Exporting Countries Forum |
| GHG | greenhouse gas |

| | |
|---|---|
| GTL | gas to liquids |
| IEA | International Energy Agency |
| IEP | International Energy Program |
| IOC | international oil company |
| IPCC | Intergovernmental Panel on Climate Change |
| LNG | liquefied natural gas |
| mmbpd | million barrels per day |
| NAEWG | North American Energy Working Group |
| NEPAD | New Economic Program for African Development |
| NGL | natural gas liquids |
| NOC | national oil company |
| NPC | National Petroleum Council |
| NPT | Nuclear Non-Proliferation Treaty |
| OECD | Organization for Economic Cooperation and Development |
| OPEC | Organization of Petroleum Exporting Countries |
| PER | Public Expenditure Review |
| ppmv | parts per million by volume |
| PRS | Poverty Reduction Strategy |
| PWYP | Publish What You Pay |
| RD&D | research, development, and demonstration |
| SPR | U.S. Strategic Petroleum Reserve |
| tcf | trillion cubic feet |
| TPES | total primary energy supply |
| UNFCCC | United Nations Framework Convention on Climate Change |
| USGS | U.S. Geological Survey |

*Energy and Security*

# Introduction: The Need to Integrate Energy and Foreign Policy

## Jan H. Kalicki and David L. Goldwyn

Is it possible for the United States to be secure without a significant change in the way it uses energy and conducts its foreign policy? This is a fundamental national security question that Americans face today, as citizens, consumers, and policymakers. Our belief is that the country cannot. America's patterns of energy consumption undermine its national and economic security. Though it can—and should—change these patterns, through the development of new technologies, and improved conservation and efficiency, the truth is that there are no quick fixes for U.S. energy dependence.

The United States and the global economy will be increasingly dependent on imported oil for at least the next two decades. This will be true even if America and its partners muster the unprecedented political will to restrain their demand for oil and gas, aggressively develop hydrogen and other less carbon-intensive technologies, and persuade rapidly developing consumer nations to adopt a similar strategy. To manage this transition to a less carbon-intensive future, the United States requires a new strategy to mitigate the foreign policy risks and dangers of continued energy dependence.

### The Foreign Policy Challenge of Energy Dependence

Energy dependence presents five new and growing challenges to U.S. foreign policy. First, policymakers must accept that for the next twenty years it will be impossible to substitute for the West's current economic and security link to the Middle East as the most energy-rich region of the world. Instead, America must work with its partners in and outside the Middle East to modify the conditions that have made the region a breeding ground of

1

al Qaeda and its terrorist copycats, which are committed to attacking the United States and its allies, and the energy infrastructure on which the region relies. Second, the United States must intensify its efforts to diversify the world's sources of energy supply to reduce the global market's dependence on energy imports from the Middle East, and thereby increase its ability to cope effectively with threats from that region.

Third, America must recognize the security and economic consequences of the so-called oil curse: the failure to translate energy wealth into long-term societal benefits, leading to poverty, conflict, and ultimately both energy and international *in*security. Fourth, America urgently requires new political and economic strategies to address these root causes of instability at a time when it must still depend on unstable or badly governed nations for oil.

Fifth and finally, the United States needs to build coalitions among nations in both the industrial and developing worlds to support a wider shared security agenda, including such issues as systemic reform in the Middle East, transparency in Africa, and the rule of law in Russia and Central Asia. And America must overcome the current policy paralysis that results from competing for access to the oil these nations produce.

## Growing Energy and Economic Vulnerabilities

The United States must pursue this unprecedented agenda for energy security at a time of growing energy and economic vulnerability—much of which is its own doing. An unintended consequence of market liberalization and oil industry deregulation in the West is that there is less excess oil capacity today than ever before. The policies of the Organization of Petroleum Exporting Countries (OPEC) also militate against surplus capacity. The productive capacity of OPEC's member states is lower today than it was two decades ago—and in 2004 their excess capacity declined to 1.2 million barrels per day, which is insufficient to protect against any major oil supply disruption.

The danger today is that there will not be enough oil to meet global demand at stable prices—not because America and the world are running out of oil, but because they are running behind on investment. After record prices, revenues, and profits for oil companies and governments in 2004, investment in new exploration and production by major oil companies is growing significantly in 2005—in contrast to relatively low investment in previous years, with many focusing on repurchasing their stock.[1]

Similarly, record revenues in 2003 and 2004 did not lead OPEC to significantly increase investment, and Saudi Arabia has kept commercial inventories at low levels.[2] But dependence on the Kingdom's preferences for global oil price levels remains central: The greatest source of new production to cool the record prices of 2004 and 2005 was Saudi Arabia, which elected to undertake new exploration and production projects starting in late 2004.

A recent study demonstrates that the world has been producing more oil than it finds to replace it. Without major breakthroughs in the technology of finding oil, non-OPEC countries will begin a steady decline in their ability to produce oil in the middle or end of the next decade. OPEC's market share will increase, but even OPEC's ability to meet demand will be challenged unless it accepts external investment in its productive capacity.[3] The results will be structurally higher prices and a long-term lack of excess capacity for oil production.

The energy sector has taken impressive steps toward increased efficiency, but "just-in-time" inventories and pressure to maximize quarterly earnings have also reduced incentives to create excess capacity. Cost-cutting measures have streamlined systems and eliminated redundant infrastructure that can serve as backup during an emergency—supertankers are unavailable should one or more be destroyed, or a crisis in the Strait of Malacca require longer global shipping routes; the refining industry is operating nearly at capacity worldwide; and in key regions the United States could face a repeat of the 2003 Northeast and Midwest power outage if it does not modernize the country's power grid and increase its reliability and capacity to meet future demand.[4]

As currently structured, the U.S. Strategic Petroleum Reserve offers only limited benefit. U.S. policy has largely refrained from using this reserve to redress less than catastrophic supply interruptions, inadvertently draining commercial inventories and allowing OPEC to deter replenishment. Although China and India have begun to create their own stocks, they will continue to be largely free riders on global strategic stocks as their consumption grows, reducing the power of the United States and others to mitigate the impact of a supply disruption. In any event, at current rates of consumption the United States, its allies, and the developing nations will need to increase the size of their existing reserves to maintain current levels of potential import replacement twenty years from now.[5]

The truth is that America is more exposed than ever to a severe disruption. Government, industry, and oil producers all share responsibility for this situation. Energy security is a public good, and the U.S. government has failed to adopt regulations or incentives to create adequate capacity, backup, or standby infrastructure. Without compensation and requirements for action, private industry has little incentive to fill the void. At the same time, OPEC's interest is to maximize U.S. dependency. Americans must hold themselves accountable as citizens for this predicament; the responsibility for not requiring our own government to act to correct this market failure lies with us.

America's economic vulnerability is worsening as well. Oil prices have moved to higher, sustained levels than ever before in U.S. history. Oil prices have been, and will remain, highly volatile; geopolitical unrest anywhere—Saudi Arabia, Iraq, Nigeria, Russia, or Venezuela—will send fuel prices surging everywhere. But in 2004, the long-feared $40-a-barrel threshold and then $50 threshold were breached—with structural changes making the prospect of restoring the $20 range highly unlikely.

The danger of an oil disruption is high and increasing, as the world grows more dependent on unstable states both inside and outside OPEC for the security of its energy supply. The once impregnable Saudi Arabia—the world's largest holder of oil reserves, its largest exporter, and the only significant holder of excess capacity to increase oil production—faces terrorist attacks on its oil infrastructure from groups seeking to overthrow the monarchy and growing pressure from those that wish to exclude influence from the West. The distribution of energy wealth is at the center of internal conflict in Bolivia, Equatorial Guinea, Nigeria, São Tomé and Príncipe, Sudan, and Venezuela—and looms in Central Asia, Iraq, and the more populous countries of the Gulf.

U.S. dependence on imported energy and on OPEC is increasing. Whereas the United States imported about a third of its oil before 1973, it now imports more than half its oil from abroad.[6] For the next decade at least, most of the incremental supplies of oil will come from countries that are for the most part unstable and undemocratic. The developing world, particularly China and India, is on the same path to dependence that the industrial world has followed. Nearly every serious energy analyst projects that by 2030 the world will still use oil for approximately 40 percent of its energy needs and that OPEC nations will control more than 50 percent of the world's supply, up from 38 percent today.[7]

Not long ago, consuming nations cooperated far more in the pursuit of energy security, creating open markets, resisting the impulse to lock up oil supplies in bilateral deals, and pooling resources to build buffer stocks of oil to combat disruption. Today, the trend is increasingly competitive, not cooperative. Beggar-thy-neighbor policies that cut off commitments to supply fuel, or efforts to lock up local supplies and lock out access for neighboring countries, have raised tensions from Argentina to East Asia.

Moreover, disputes over the exploitation of natural resources and the use of foreign capital have stalled economic development in much of Latin America, especially Mexico. The energy sector is a key instrument of government control in Russia and Eurasia and has long been so throughout the Middle East. In the Asia-Pacific region, China and Japan compete for access to Russian oil and gas. China, Malaysia, and India jockey for influence in Africa and, increasingly, in Latin America, and undermine attempts to control conflict and weapons proliferation in Iran and Sudan.

## The Need to Integrate Energy and Foreign Policy . . .

It should follow from this link between energy and security, and the world's increasingly risky sources of energy supply, that the foreign and national security policies of the United States, its allies, and its partners would be closely integrated with their energy security needs. Unfortunately, this is not the case. Despite the crucial role of energy in economic, foreign, and security policy, there has been only episodic attention to—and little change in—the interconnection among these issues in the political debate of the United States.

Foreign energy producers—particularly those in the Arabian Gulf and increasingly Russia—have been able to integrate their energy development policies more effectively with their own economic and foreign policy interests. Saudi Arabia has long traded oil for U.S. military protection and forbearance on its domestic policies. China has used the power of its enormous market to trade oil for arms and to access supply where U.S. sanctions have banned U.S. companies from operating.[8] Russia has deflected attention from its internal policies by leveraging its dominance in gas supply to Europe and its potential as a strategic oil supplier to the United States and Japan, as well as China. Yet the United States, and many other energy consumers, cannot muster the will to change the consumption or production policies of today, even if they will enhance national or economic security tomorrow. And the United States, Europe, and Asia have not confronted the connection between foreign policies that tolerate or enable repression and corruption in many oil-producing nations and the threats of terrorism, instability, and volatility they face today.

The failure of the United States to integrate energy and foreign policy is a failure of political will and leadership, not a failure of vision. Indeed, the national energy strategies of President Bill Clinton and President George W. Bush are remarkably similar. Both focus on conservation, efficiency, diversity of supply, and increased domestic production, although there are important differences over the value of drilling in environmentally sensitive areas.[9] But they—and their predecessors—have been unable to make the necessary transition from energy vision to energy security.

## . . . and the Domestic Trade-Offs

Domestically, the United States has a persistently short attention span when it comes to energy security. It focuses on conservation and stability of supply when gasoline prices are high, in times of war, or when its suffers a disruption in supply from a major producer. Once a war ends, prices drop, electric power is restored, or production resumes, attention fades. Since 1986, America's attention to energy security has not been sustained long enough to produce significant legislative or regulatory change. It treats each supply disruption—the 2003 strikes in Venezuela or Nigeria, the 1979 revolution in Iran, or the attacks on infrastructure in Saudi Arabia or Iraq in 2004—as acute problems. But the underlying illness—unchecked demand for energy, particularly for transportation fuel—is chronic and untreated.

The problem in the United States, and elsewhere, is that trade-offs between energy security and national security, energy and the environment, and energy and economic security are hard—and the politics of change is formidable. In the United States, the fault lines of energy politics follow regional boundaries more than party affiliations. The United States remains a significant producer of oil, gas, and coal. Energy taxes disfavor American energy producers, largely in the West and on the Gulf Coast (for oil and gas) and the Eastern and Western mountain states (for coal). Restrictions on carbon emissions threaten coal producers, particularly miners of high-sulfur coal. America is a nation of automobile manufacturers and consumers. Rapid changes in fuel efficiency requirements impose costs on U.S. manufacturers (which make heavier, less fuel-efficient vehicles than their Japanese or European counterparts) that can cost jobs and reduce their competitiveness.

U.S. consumers may appreciate fuel efficiency, but they also want broad choices of style, speed, and power in their vehicles.

Americans do not internalize the cost of their energy consumption in the price of fuel. Obvious externalities—such as the cost of defending the Gulf states; the health costs of carbon emissions or other pollutants; or the economic costs that volatile energy prices impose on the competitiveness of U.S. manufacturing and airline, travel, and transportation industries—are not imputed into the price Americans pay at the pump or in their electric bills. They want cheap gas and less dependence on foreign oil.

These hard trade-offs, and the disconnect between what Americans pay for energy and what it really costs them, have led to political deadlock. The United States has been unable to increase fuel efficiency standards (except raising somewhat the much lower standards for light trucks) since 1986.[10] It takes years to site refineries or liquefied natural gas facilities, even though the country needs the gasoline or natural gas supply to maintain moderate energy prices. The failure to achieve basic changes has plagued Democratic and Republican administrations alike, all of which have feared antagonizing domestic producers and manufacturers or risking consumer retaliation at even the mention of a gasoline tax. Domestic legislation has become mired in shortsighted discussions of industry subsidies or continuation of the war between the producers and the environmentalists, as in the case of the Arctic National Wildlife Refuge.

With respect to energy conservation, this deadlock is uniquely American. Europe has long had high energy taxes and experienced virtually zero growth in oil demand over the past five years. Japan has greatly diversified its sources of energy supply, also with flat growth in oil demand.[11] We believe that the prospects for serious energy security reform will remain weak, unless there is a serious shock to the international system such as a collapse of the Saudi monarchy or a major act of terrorism against its infrastructure—or unprecedented bipartisan candor about the need to curb U.S. demand by ending the day of deceptively cheap energy. The challenge of achieving domestic reform is formidable and makes the need for a new foreign policy approach more urgent.

## The Scope of This Volume

Dissatisfied by the inertia that plagues the policy debate, and prompted by the increasing importance of energy policy issues today, the editors of this book welcomed working with Woodrow Wilson Center Press to produce a volume that addresses the critical global energy challenges and proposes a new U.S. foreign policy strategy with a central focus on energy security in the twenty-first century. Although the book's perspective starts from the United States, it necessarily extends to that of all the major players in the increasingly integrated global energy system of the new century.

In this book, we seek to frame the policy debate by drawing on leading thinkers in the energy and foreign policy fields. We seek to provide first the fundamentals that any critic or serious observer must understand: an explanation of what energy security means in a liberalized market, the nature of the energy market itself, the trends of supply and demand that will drive the geopolitics of energy over the next twenty years, and the institutions and organizations that shape market behavior.

We then proceed to an in-depth analysis of energy issues in a regional context: Russia and Eurasia, the Middle East and Africa, the Pacific Rim, and the North Atlantic and the Americas. Our contributors examine each region in detail—assessing the nature and origin of political deadlock, instability, or uncertainty; and analyzing which nations will be dependent on energy supply or revenue, which have the capacity to become U.S. allies in energy security, and how U.S. foreign policy can influence these developments.

We conclude with the building blocks for a new energy security strategy, which focuses on national and homeland security, technology, transparency, governance and sustainable development, energy and the environment, global strategic reserves, and global gas resources. We then offer our own analysis of the implications of this energy security strategy for U.S. foreign policy.

We are fortunate in the book's contributors, who have made such an ambitious project possible. We were able to assemble leading experts on energy and both global and regional policy issues from think tanks, industry, and governments around the world. In addition to promoting dialogue among experts in each part of this book, we are pleased that authorities from governments and institutions both belonging to OPEC and outside it agreed to comment on each part of the book—adding, we hope, to the richness of the increasingly important dialogue between OPEC and non-OPEC states, producers and consumers, and policymakers and investors.

Other books have been written on specific dimensions of the energy security problem, energy challenges in particular regions, and new approaches to technology and transparency.[12] In this volume, we seek instead to present the issue of energy security in a uniquely comprehensive as well as authoritative fashion, with provocative and often conflicting views from the leading minds on energy and foreign policy. We also seek to build bridges between the energy and foreign policy communities, which have operated quite independently of each other despite the growing interconnections between their worlds. For those who seek to understand the intersection of energy, security, and foreign policy—the policymaker, the analyst, the student, and the consumer—we hope we have provided both a primer and a guide.

## Defining Energy Security in the Twenty-First Century

In its most fundamental sense, energy security is assurance of the ability to access the energy resources required for the continued development of national power. In more specific terms, it is the provision of affordable, reliable, diverse, and ample supplies of oil and gas (and their future equivalents)—to the United States, its allies, and its partners—and adequate infrastructure to deliver these supplies to market.

Affordable energy means the ability to buy supply at relatively stable as well as reasonable prices. Traditionally, oil prices have had a median range of $18 to $22 per barrel. However, the period from 1998 to 2005 has seen more volatile prices than at any time in recorded history—swinging from a low of $11 in 1998 to a high more than $55 in February 2005—and by mid-2004, the petroleum minister of Saudi Arabia opined that $35 per barrel was a "fair" price point.[13] More than any specific price level, however, price volatility shocks the global economy and creates destabilizing dislocations. Reducing volatility is the most important new challenge for energy security.

A reliable energy supply means predictable supplies that are less and less vulnerable to disruption. The creation of the International Energy Agency; the construction of strategic stockpiles in the United States, Germany, Japan, and other nations; and the advent of a global market together have deterred OPEC from imposing additional political embargoes in the past three decades. But in the twenty-first century, the threat to producers' stability comes increasingly from within—from revolution, civil unrest, economic collapse, and acts of terror. These threats can only be addressed by conflict prevention and diplomacy, not by deterrence.

Accessing diverse and ample supplies means ensuring that a large number of nations with hydrocarbon reserves produce them for the global market. More and more suppliers are emerging outside OPEC. But many of the nations that America hopes to rely on are unlikely to live up to this potential without assistance in stabilizing their economies or resolving internal conflicts.

Increasingly, energy security also means more than oil security—it means security of supplies of natural gas. The developing world's rate of energy consumption is rising faster than that of the countries belonging to the Organization for Economic Cooperation and Development (OECD), with consequences for the global commons as well as geopolitics. Carbon emissions from developing nations' consumption will dwarf those of OECD countries to date if current trends prevail.[14] A key path to avoiding this outcome will be the use of natural gas, not oil or wood, for power generation and for eventual transition to a hydrogen-based economy in the West. Though a global oil market has evolved—which assures that high bidders will always find physical supplies of oil, but at a price that may damage their economies—a global market is only beginning to develop for natural gas.

Rising U.S. and global demand for gas is a new and critical challenge for U.S. energy security. Today, natural gas is the fuel of choice for electric power. Gas produces far fewer carbon emissions than coal or oil, and it produces more heat per unit burned. But today, natural gas can only be transported by pipeline, or if it is liquefied for transport and regasified upon delivery. The world is awash in natural gas, but much of it is stranded far from the infrastructure needed to transport it. The political challenges that plague oil suppliers also plague suppliers of natural gas, and the risks of dependency on foreign gas are real, but for now less threatening. The United States' reserves of natural gas are dwindling or inaccessible for environmental reasons, and its demand will soon outstrip domestic supply. Security of gas supply is a new challenge that policymakers must face—and it is addressed in this volume.[15]

In this new age, energy security means both the ability to secure supplies and the ability to insulate the global economy from the effects of extreme price volatility. The internal stability of U.S. suppliers, the ways they manage their oil revenues, the influence they exercise over U.S. friends and allies, and their vulnerability to acts of terrorism all are critical factors for U.S. energy and national security. For these reasons, achieving energy security depends more than ever on the conduct of American foreign policy.

## A New Foreign Policy Strategy

Part VI of this volume describes in detail the building blocks for a comprehensive energy security policy: investment in technology, transformations in the way the United States uses energy, promoting stability of supply through enhanced transparency, and the development of natural gas as a bridge to a future hydrogen-based economy. Together, these strategies can limit dependence on oil and gas, and diversify U.S. energy sources—both in kind and in source—in the future. A comprehensive strategy can provide the assurance that America will be able to access the energy resources it requires for the continued development of its national power—the fundamental definition we advanced above for energy security.

But equally important is the need to translate such an energy security strategy into a more effective foreign policy—for the United States and its partners—in the coming century. To assure its national defense, let alone to power its multi-trillion-dollar economy, America needs to promote the stability of the oil and gas producers around the world, and that requires a policy of global engagement. We also see energy as a powerful tool of U.S. foreign policy. Alleviating energy poverty can promote economic development and provide political motivation for better governance. Collective energy security in the twenty-first century, like collective military security in the twentieth century, can transform competitors into partners and allies. Here it is useful to preview how the book's contributors apply these U.S. energy security and foreign policy principles to the world's energy-rich regions—Russia and the Eurasian states of the former Soviet Union, West and Central Africa, the Pacific Rim and South Asia, the Western Hemisphere, and the Middle East.

Energy development in Russia and the Eurasian states of the former Soviet Union has the potential to reduce Western dependence on OPEC, to contribute to their own development and political and economic independence, and to secure their positive engagement in the international system. One can expect significant oil growth coming from Russia and the Caspian Sea region—almost a 60 percent increase from 2000 to 2010. In addition, Russia can become effectively the Saudi Arabia of natural gas—holding more than 30 percent of the world's gas reserves, serving as the primary gas supplier to Europe, and becoming a major supplier of liquefied natural gas to the Pacific Rim, including the United States.[16] There are serious challenges to this vision, however. Russia's economy is still making the transition to the rules of a market economy; the state's increasing interference and its monopoly on transportation infrastructure have limited the development of new fields and may lead to a leveling off of Russian production after 2010. Russia's neighbors, particularly Kazakhstan and Azerbaijan, are increasingly important suppliers, but they must still undertake significant political and economic reforms and use their new oil wealth more effectively for development. Russia's attempts to assert economic hegemony over Caspian supplies by controlling the transportation infrastructure also raise concerns about the free flow of hydrocarbons to Western markets. In turn, the United States and its allies and partners must muster the will to use their power as consumers, investors, and developers of infrastructure to also foster democracy, transparency, and good governance in these nations as they develop, and not permit their desire to promote energy development to silence America's voice as a champion of reform.

Engagement with the energy-producing states of North and Sub-Saharan Africa can again contribute to energy diversification, but also to an expanded relationship with more moderate Islamic states and to new opportunities for development south of the Sahara that can reverse the downward spiral of poverty and disease. In North Africa, Algeria and Libya have major gas as well as oil reserves and close ties to the European market. Both countries support the United States in the war against terrorism. Algeria remains poor, repressive, and unstable, but it is seeking to develop more democratic institutions and to reengage politically and economically with partners in Europe and America. Libya remains a repressive dictatorship, but it is making significant—potentially historic—moves to eliminate weapons of mass destruction and the capabilities to produce them; and it is evolving to a more open, market-based economy. Balancing U.S. interests in promoting internal stability in these nations, countering terror, and meeting U.S. energy needs provide a challenge as well as an opportunity.

In West and Central Africa, the United States and other countries, notably the United Kingdom, have a limited window of opportunity to use their leverage to help oil-producing nations adopt transparent measures in their public finances and commit to economic development plans. Nations such as Nigeria, Angola, Chad, and São Tomé and Príncipe are poor today and saddled with debt, resettlement, or reconstruction costs. By the end of the decade, however, they will begin to earn large cash payments from exploration and production contracts that are now still recovering the costs of initial investment.[17] U.S. foreign policy must emphasize creating transparency and stability in these nations now, while they need multilateral support, or miss an opportunity to induce change. The challenge is substantial. America should find ways to persuade those that today privately profit from oil sales to open their books and share their national wealth—using the U.S. business presence, diplomacy, and shareholding in international financial institutions to create a political climate where this can be done. America also needs to find ways to influence competitors in China and India that seek access to African reserves but do so with no conditions on aid and no insistence on transparency.

The countries of the Pacific Rim and South Asia share great concern with the United States about energy dependence. Engaging these countries on alternative energy security strategies and strengthening their relations with non-OPEC producers would greatly complement regional initiatives for political and economic cooperation, for example, through the Asia-Pacific Economic Cooperation forum. China's growing energy needs present a unique and critical challenge. It is in the security interests of the United States and its allies for China to have reliable and diverse supplies of energy to avert growing competition for supply or trade in arms for oil between China and the Middle East. Helping China to use energy efficiently and access modern energy technologies may be the wisest security investment of all. In South Asia, energy integration may also provide the linkages to help knit warring states closer together, from India and Pakistan to Turkmenistan, Afghanistan, and Pakistan.

Expanded relationships in the Western Hemisphere again are compelling in the energy context, but they also can reinforce a set of positive political and economic relations, building on the United States' historic ties with Canada and Mexico and its trade relationships through the North American Free Trade Agreement and the proposed Free Trade Area of the Americas. But strides in energy security will not be achieved unless poverty and poor governance are addressed in Latin America. Trade in agriculture, job creation, and economic diversification—all needed additions to U.S. hemispheric foreign policy—can move friends in crisis such as Mexico and Venezuela away from national battles over the allocation of oil proceeds to a more modern, diverse economy that is less dependent on volatile prices and that produces more jobs for the region's growing population.

The Middle East provides the greatest challenge for U.S. foreign policy. This region holds two-thirds of the world's oil reserves, and Saudi Arabia has acted as swing supplier to the world market for decades. In times of crisis—after the September 11, 2001, terrorist attacks; in both Gulf Wars; in the Venezuelan and Nigerian oil strikes of 2002–3—it has used its costly investment in excess oil capacity to deliver supply to the world market and mitigate some of the price effects of crisis or war. But U.S. foreign policy has paid far too little attention to the failure of Arab governments to achieve equitable development for their people. U.S. efforts at fostering democracy or development have been tentative at best—although elections in Iraq, anti-Syrian protests in Lebanon, and new opportunities for Israeli-Palestinian peace offer new hope in 2005. The cost of protecting sea-lanes—repelling adversaries that threaten oil supply and stationing a military to defend global oil reserves—has been high in human and economic terms. What America should have learned from 9/11 is that unparalleled military power is not sufficient to provide for national defense. The 2003 Iraq war has taught the United States that even occupying a nation will not necessarily provide it with greater national or energy security.

Today, America needs a strong defense strategy, but it also needs a political and economic strategy that will put it and its allies—both in and outside the Middle East—on the side of the region's progress and development in a way that is forward looking and respectful of national sovereignty. If America succeeds, it can live in a world where it is seen as a force for democracy and development and not as the sponsor of oppression and corruption. In this world, America will have time to transition from oil to a diverse set of resources by promoting stability in the region. If U.S. efforts are rejected, or if America continues a policy of benign neglect, it is likely to pay a price in continued terrorism and eventually suffer the effects of destabilized governments in the Middle East.

Energy security is an important goal in its own right, but it becomes critical when viewed against the broader canvas of foreign policy and economic development. The United States must evolve from a more traditional foreign policy view, preoccupied with military security issues and relatively disconnected from the world of resources and economic forces, to a more modern view that addresses economic and political factors and recognizes that world events are determined far more by the flow of resources—human and material—than by the flow of officials and diplomats, or even soldiers.

What is needed, in our view, is a fresh engagement with the priority issues of the global agenda from the perspective of energy cooperation and energy security. At the same time, we believe that it is high time to fashion a comprehensive, global energy security strategy for the United States and all its partners. It is our hope that this volume will contribute to that crucial task for this new century.

# Notes

1. According to Lehman Brothers' exploration and production spending survey of 327 international oil companies (IOCs), IOCs will increase their spending for upstream exploration and production by about $10 billion in 2005—from $167 to $177 billion, a 5.7 percent increase. According to Deutsche Bank Equity Research, 25 IOCs spent $13.2 billion in stock repurchases in 2003 and $13.9 billion in 2004, and they plan another $7 billion in repurchases in 2005.

2. Before OPEC's July 2004 meeting, with U.S. crude oil prices near $36 per barrel, Minister Ali Naimi warned that OPEC had to be careful not to permit U.S. commercial crude oil inventories to rise above 310 million barrels: "If you're at 310 million barrels, the price is very low. . . . You have to watch it like a hawk." David Bird, "Naimi Sounds Like A Hawk on Oil Prices," Dow Jones Energy Service, March 31, 2004. When U.S. inventories exceeded 310 million barrels in July of 2002, U.S. crude prices were at $27 per barrel. OPEC's investment in new production will also fail to keep up with demand. The International Energy Agency's July 2004 Oil Market Report forecast global demand for crude oil would rise by 1.7 percent in 2005 compared with 2004, but forecast only 500,000 barrels per day growth from all of OPEC. See http://omrpublic.iea.org/omrarchive/13jul04high.pdf.

3. PFC Energy, *Global Crude Oil and Natural Gas Liquids Supply Forecast,* September 2004.

4. Global refining capacity utilization increased to 85 percent in 2004 from 83.5 percent in 2003 worldwide, but U.S. utilization has approached 95 percent as its markets require a broad variety of special clean fuels, limiting the number of refineries capable of producing supply that meets U.S. specifications. See *BP Statistical Review of World Energy,* June 2004, http://www.bp.com/statistical review2004; and U.S. Energy Information Administration refining capacity data for the United States, http://tonto.eia.doe.gov/oog/ftparea/wogirs/xls/pswll.xls. For concerns that the U.S. power grid is near capacity, see the findings at ftp://www.nerc.com/pub/sys/all_updl/docs/pubs/LTRA2003.pdf; and Barnaby Feder, "Redrawing the Power Grid," *New York Times,* June 24, 2003, http://www.nytimes.com/2003/06/24/technology/24GRID.html. See also http://www.epri.com.

5. See a fuller discussion of the need to modernize strategic reserve policy in David Goldwyn and Michelle Billig, "Building Strategic Reserves," chapter 21 of this volume.

6. U.S. Energy Information Administration, *Monthly Energy Review 2005: Petroleum Trade,* table 1.7 (Washington, D.C.: Energy Information Administration, 2005).

7. Adam Sieminski, "World Energy Futures," chapter 1 of this volume.

8. Amy Myers Jaffe and Kenneth B. Medlock III, "China and Northeast Asia," chapter 11 of this volume.

9. See President Bush's National Energy Policy Development Group report at http://www.whitehouse.gov/energy/National-Energy-Policy.pdf. See President Clinton's Comprehensive National Energy Strategy at http://www.pi.energy.gov/pdf/library/cnes.pdf.

10. The National Highway Traffic Safety Administration first established a standard of 15.8 miles per gallon (mpg) for four-wheel-drive vehicles and a standard of 17.2 mpg for 2-wheel-drive light trucks in model year (MY) 1979, which has risen to a unified standard of 21.0 mpg for MY 2005, 21.6 mpg for MY 2006, and 22.2 mpg for MY 2007. Passenger car standards, set at 27.5 mpg for 1985, have been maintained at this level since MY 1990 after being lowered from MY 1986 through 1989. See http://www.nhtsa.dot.gov/cars/rules/cafe/studies/htm.

11. However, Europe has made great strides in halting its rate of growth in oil consumption through high fuel taxes, subsidization of renewable energy, and adoption of renewable energy portfolio standards. Commission of the European Communities, *Towards a European Strategy for the Security of Energy Supply* (Brussels: European Commission, 2002); Ministry of Fuel and Energy, *Energy Strategy of the Russian Federation for the Period until 2020,* approved by Russian Government Directive 1234-r (Moscow: Ministry of Fuel and Energy, 2003).

12. See, e.g., Amy Myers Jaffe and Edward L. Morse, *Strategic Energy Policy: Challenges for the 21st Century* (Houston and New York: James A. Baker III Institute for Public Policy and Council on Foreign Relations, 2001); *The Geopolitics of Energy into the 21st Century: A Report of the CSIS Strategic Energy Initiative,* Sam Nunn and James R. Schlesinger, project cochairs, and Robert E. Ebel, project director (Washington, D.C.: Center for Strategic and International Studies, 2000); Robert A. Manning, *The Asian Energy Factor : Myths and Dilemmas of Energy, Security and the Pacific Future* (New York: Palgrave Press, 2000); John V. Mitchell, *The New Economy of Oil: Impacts on Business, Geopolitics and Society* (Washington, D.C.: Brookings Institution Press, 2001); William E. Ratliff, *Russia's Oil in America's Future: Policy, Pipelines and Prospects* (Stanford, Calif.: Stanford University Press, 2003); Patrick L. Clawson, *Energy and National Security in the 21st Century* (Washington, D.C.: National Defense University Press, 1995); and *Powerful Partnerships: The Federal Role in International Cooperation on Energy Innovation,* Report from the President's Committee of Advisors on Science and Technology Panel on International Cooperation in Energy Research, Development, Demonstration, and Deployment (Washington, D.C.: National Academy of Sciences, 1999).

13. Energy Information Administration, *Crude Oil Prices, Daily Spot WTI, Brent,* http://www.eia.doe.gov/neic/historic/hpetroleum2.htm#CrudeOil.

14. See Kevin Baumert's discussion in "The Challenge of Climate Protection: Balancing Energy and Environment," chapter 20.

15. In this volume, see Adam Sieminski's discussion of natural gas in chapter 1, Shirley Neff's discussion of North American supply in chapter 15, and Donald Juckett and Michelle Foss's recommendations for development of a global gas market in chapter 22.

16. *BP Statistical Review of World Energy,* June 2003.

17. See David L. Goldwyn and J. Stephen Morrison, *Promoting Transparency in the African Oil Sector: A Report of the CSIS Task Force on Rising US Energy Stakes in Africa* (Washington, D.C.: Center for Strategic and International Studies, 2004), 8.

# Part I

# The Global Framework

Part I sets out the global framework for understanding the intersection between energy security and foreign policy in this century. The driving forces that shape the world of energy are supply and demand, technological change, the ability of OPEC to limit supply, the effectiveness of non-OPEC producers to compete for markets with OPEC, and the power of consuming nations to undertake policies, individually or collectively through institutions such as the International Energy Agency (IEA), to shape their own destiny.

All the authors of the chapters in this part believe that despite an increase in the development of renewable energy technologies, oil and gas will remain the primary source for energy in the twenty-first century. All see the greatest growth in consumption coming from the developing world, particularly China and India. All believe that for at least the next twenty years, oil will be the dominant transportation fuel, and gas and coal will compete to be the fuel of choice for power generation. Understanding the magnitude of global demand for energy, the critical issues addressed in part I are: Where will new supplies of oil and gas come from? Will the price of energy be stable, or will it remain volatile and inflict economic pain on consumers and producers? Will consumers enjoy security of diverse supplies of energy? And will the key global energy institutions, OPEC and the IEA, adapt to assure security of supply and demand?

To assess these questions, Adam Sieminski projects world energy futures; Daniel Yergin looks at the importance of open markets, government investment frameworks, and technological change for energy security; Edward Morse and Amy Myers Jaffe cast a skeptical eye on the reliability of OPEC and stress the need for energy diversity and collective energy security; and

17

William Martin and Evan Harrje recommend new ways for the IEA to adapt to new realities.

In chapter 1, Sieminski discusses the long-term trends for energy supply and demand. He predicts that oil's share of global demand will stay the same over the next twenty years, that demand for natural gas will double, and that renewable energy supplies will grow, but only to 3 to 5 percent of global energy consumption by 2020. World energy futures will have several geopolitical implications: East Asia may compete for local supplies of oil; Europe, China, and the United States will face growing dependency; the OPEC nations are unlikely to meet demand for their oil without the help and investment of international oil companies; and dramatic strides will be required in construction of gas pipelines and liquefied natural gas facilities for global supply to meet global demand.

In chapter 2, Yergin casts his keen historian's eye on the past to assess how prepared we are to address the challenges of meeting supply and demand in the future. He concludes that we are far better equipped today to deal with oil disruptions than ever before but warns that uncertainty is the historical rule of energy markets, not the exception. Instability in the nations that supply the global market can cause disruption, but wise polices can mitigate these threats. The threat of terrorism to energy infrastructure is new. It widens the meaning of energy security beyond the flow of oil to include widely dispersed infrastructure, and it will require responses that we have yet to fully implement. Yergin recommends that U.S. policymakers focus on promoting open and attractive investment climates in Russia, the Caspian Sea region, and West Africa, fostering an open market in liquefied natural gas, and investing in the protection of critical energy infrastructure.

In chapter 3, Morse and Jaffe explain OPEC's remarkable and enduring success in managing oil prices, but they predict that this success will prove more difficult in the future. They discuss OPEC's internal dynamics and its relations with non-OPEC oil producers such as Russia, and they argue that divergent interests within and outside OPEC may lead to its weakening. Morse and Jaffe recommend that the United States, in cooperation with other consuming countries, work to break OPEC's monopoly and open the global oil trade to market forces.

In chapter 4, Martin and Harrje chronicle the IEA's ability to adapt to changes in the oil markets over time, and they set forth the challenges the organization faces in the next century. They believe the IEA must take on a range of missions, encompassing the security of natural gas supply, the vast global need for electrification, the development of environmentally friendly energy technologies (including distributed generation and advanced nuclear power systems), the reconciliation of deregulation with energy security objectives, and the expansion of strategic stocks. Martin and Harrje are optimistic that the IEA retains the flexibility to adapt and propose a comprehensive work program to meet these challenges.

In his commentary on part I, Alvaro Silva-Calderón, the outgoing OPEC secretary general, forcefully defends the role that OPEC has taken to stabilize prices and foster better cooperation with consuming nations. Silva-Calderón shares Sieminski's overall outlook on the future of oil and gas, but he projects faster growth for developing nations and even slower growth from the nations belonging to the Organization for Economic Cooperation and Development. He disagrees with Morse and Jaffe's doubts regarding OPEC's viability and their concern that OPEC can threaten the security of the United States and its allies. He counters that OPEC's price band provides stability and suggests that international oil companies can indeed play a role in exploration and production in OPEC nations, with attendant benefits in increased production, greater efficiency, and improved technology—depending on the sovereign decisions of each state. Silva-Calderón sees the OPEC member nations as evolving with the times, and he rejects the concerns of Yergin and of Morse and Jaffe that OPEC will not meet the challenge of modernizing and expanding national production. In closing, he points to the need to advance energy security on a global basis, including energy-poor developing nations, and he sees OPEC as a force for cooperation with the IEA (as Martin and Harrje also contemplate) and other consuming nations with a mission of advancing this more broadly based strategy for energy development.

# 1

# World Energy Futures

## *Adam E. Sieminski*

Understanding the implications of long-term trends in global energy supply and demand is critical to any formulation of energy policy. In the United States, much is made of the "need" for a national energy policy to steer future energy developments. In fact, a reasonably consistent set of energy policy goals has been in place in the United States for many years. These policies have deeply established trends that cannot be changed quickly or easily. These trends have shaped U.S. foreign policy, as it has sought both security and diversity of energy supply. The foreign policies of other nations, oil exporters such as Saudi Arabia and Russia, and consumers such as China, Japan, and India, have also shaped the global market and constrained U.S. policy choices. To set the context for the study in this book of the intersection of these energy and foreign policy choices—with an eye to recommending a strategy for greater U.S. and global energy security—this chapter forecasts world energy futures and projects the major trends that may shape U.S. energy and foreign policy decisions from today until 2030.

The world energy futures presented here foretell a world similar to today's in terms of aggregate consumption patterns—but quite different in terms of regional patterns of demand and supply. Oil's dominant position as the world's largest source of commercial energy is likely to remain unchallenged. Consumption of natural gas is projected to more than double by 2030, driven by the use of gas to generate electricity. Coal use overall (and especially in Asia) is forecast to continue to grow, but its market share should plummet. Nuclear power will still play a role, albeit diminishing, in supplying electricity. Both hydropower and renewable energy grow—with the growth rate of solar and wind power being the highest of all the fuels, but with renewable energy's share of global energy supply increasing only slightly. Energy use and gross domestic product (GDP) will still be closely linked, but shifts in the composition of GDP and high energy prices may be reducing the growth rate in energy use.

Regionally, the fastest growth in consumption is expected in Asia, led by China and India. In contrast, the market share that North America and Europe consume of global fuel supply is expected to continue to erode, making Asia, not the United States, the dominant driver of the global energy market. The amount of oil that nations belonging to the Organization of Petroleum Exporting Countries (OPEC) will need to supply to meet global demand (the "call on OPEC" in market parlance) will double by 2030. The question of whether OPEC will dominate the world market of 2030 is a function of global demand, OPEC's ability to attract the capital needed to meet world demand, and the policy choices made by non-OPEC suppliers. In the aggregate, however, dependence on OPEC will increase. Oil production from the region encompassing the members of the Organization for Economic Cooperation and Development, or the OECD (particularly the United States and the North Sea) will decline. There will be continued production growth in the former Soviet Union (particularly in Russia and the Caspian Sea region), but it will diminish in other non-OPEC, non-OECD areas. OPEC nations possess two-thirds of global oil reserves; they will continue to supply most of the market in the long term, if they meet the challenge to supply it on reasonable and stable terms.

World energy futures may look much like the past, at least in terms of global consumption, carbon emissions, and reliance on OPEC supply, but they can be different. Forecasts are based on educated guesses about the policy decisions of governments, the rate of technological change, and the behavior of consumers. I offer my best guesses as to these decisions in the analysis that follows. But consuming and producing governments are also capable of different choices from those they have taken in the past, with transforming effects on the global economy and international security.

The choices facing the United States and the West on energy policy, and the ability to adopt a foreign policy strategy that positively influences the behavior of other nations, are detailed in the succeeding chapters of this volume. This chapter describes the world we will see if the policy choices of the future resemble the choices we have made in the past.

## World Fuel Consumption Market Shares

To understand how the world will consume energy in the future, I examine which fuels will dominate consumption, how fast some regions will increase their rate of growth, and the aggregate amount of fuel that must be found to meet this demand. The significance of these statistics for policy-makers is understanding that even with demand restraint in populous industrial or developing nations, the aggregate amount of oil, gas, or coal that will need to be exploited during the next two decades is formidable.

As is shown in figure 1.1, in 1970, oil accounted for about 45 percent (47 million barrels per day) of the world's commercial energy consumption of 104 million barrels per day (mmbpd) of oil equivalent. Coal, which peaked in importance around 1950, was still in second place with a 32 percent global market share. The utilization of natural gas (19 percent) was gaining strength, nuclear power was just getting started, and hydroelectricity generation held a 5 percent share.[1]

By 2000, total consumption had grown to 192 mmbpd. Nuclear power provided about 6 percent of total use, and natural gas (24 percent) had managed to take market share away from both coal and oil. Nuclear power (6 percent) made clear inroads into global electricity production. Hydropower's

Figure 1.1. World Energy Consumption by Fuel, 1970–2030

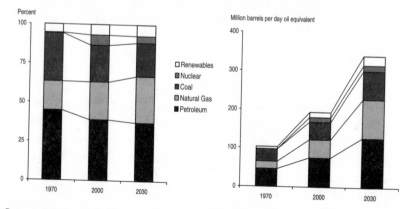

*Sources:* BP; International Energy Agency; U.S. Energy Information Administration; author's estimates for 2030.

absolute level of use had nearly doubled, but still accounted for not much more than 7 percent of consumption.

## Energy Growth by Region and by Service

Between 2000 and 2030, global consumption is expected to rise at a rate of 1.9 percent a year, a 75 percent rise over the entire period to about 338 mmbpd of oil equivalent. Regionally, the fastest growth is expected to arise in Asia. Despite the continuing problems with economic stagnation in Japan, expansion in countries such as China, India, Indonesia, South Korea, and Thailand is likely to propel strong overall energy demand in the region. Asia accounted for only 15 percent of global energy consumption in 1970 and reached 27 percent in 2000. By 2030, Asia should make up 35 percent of the global total, even as its rate of growth slows to an average of 2.7 percent from 2000 to 2030, down from 4.0 percent actual growth from 1970 to 2000.

In contrast, the amount of global energy consumed by North America and Europe is expected to decline. North American energy use grew at about 1.3 percent a year from 1970 to 2000 and will remain the same. Europe's growth averaged about 1 percent a year over the 1970–2000 period and will also remain the same through 2030. This would leave both North America and Europe with market shares of about 25 percent each in 2030.

South and Central America, the Middle East, and Africa are expected to gain market share, with energy consumption growth rates of 2.5 percent annually through 2030. However, with these regions starting from relatively low positions, their total global share together will amount to only about 15 percent in 2020.

### Petroleum

Oil's dominant position as the world's largest source of commercial energy is likely to remain unchallenged over the 2000–2030 forecast period. In spite of its relatively low growth rate of only 1.7 percent a year, oil's share of global energy use is forecast to drop only marginally, from 39 percent in 2000 to 38 percent in 2030 (table 1.1). Oil remains a nearly ideal fuel for transportation. It has a high energy density, is easily and relatively safely carried on vehicles, and benefits from a huge existing infrastructure for production and distribution. Although new vehicle technologies—such as

*Table 1.1. World Fuel Consumption and Market Share, 1970–2030*

| | Million Barrels per Day Oil Equivalent | | | Market Share (percent) | | |
|---|---|---|---|---|---|---|
| | 1970 | 2000 | 2003 | 1970 | 2000 | 2003 |
| Petroleum | 47 | 75 | 128 | 45 | 39 | 38 |
| Natural gas | 19 | 47 | 100 | 18 | 24 | 29 |
| Coal | 32 | 45 | 72 | 31 | 24 | 21 |
| Nuclear | 0 | 12 | 15 | 0 | 6 | 4 |
| Renewables | 6 | 13 | 24 | 5 | 7 | 7 |
| Total | 104 | 192 | 338 | 100 | 100 | 100 |

*Note:* Data for 2030 are author's estimates.

*Sources:* BP; International Energy Agency; U.S. Energy Information Administration; author's estimates.

electric-gasoline hybrids, or fuel cells powered by hydrogen, natural gas, or gasoline—are expected to make progress over the next few decades, momentum favors the traditional gasoline combustion engine. Pulled by transportation requirements and assisted by growth in industrial (including chemical) uses, petroleum consumption is expected to rise from about 75 mmbpd in 2000 to 128 mmbpd in 2030.

## Natural Gas

With an annual growth rate of almost 3 percent during the 1970–2000 period, natural gas was the fastest growing source of primary energy among the major fuels—easily beating coal's 1.1 percent annual rate and besting oil's 1.5 percent as well. Consumption of natural gas is projected to more than double over the 2000–2030 forecast period. Natural gas was only about 60 percent of the level of coal use in 1970, but it was nearly identical in 2000.

My projections, like those of the U.S. Energy Information Administration (EIA), show that natural gas will surpass coal consumption by about one-third by 2030. By 2030, natural gas is forecast to have a 30 percent share of total energy consumption, closing in on but not surpassing oil's 37 percent share. The projected growth in natural gas consumption is due in large part to rising worldwide demand to fuel new combined-cycle gas turbines for electricity generation.

## Coal

Unique among the major fuels, the consumption of coal actually fell in the 1990s as environmental regulations reduced demand and electricity production was augmented by substantial growth in nuclear power. During the 1970–2000 period, coal had the lowest growth rate of any of the fuels— only 1.1 percent a year. Even oil use, heavily affected by the price increases of 1973–74 and 1979–80, managed 1.5 percent average annual growth in this period.

Although coal use will grow modestly from 2000 to the end of the 2030 forecast period, at 1.5 percent a year, its share of total world energy consumption is projected to fall to 22 percent in 2030. More than half the coal consumed globally is burned in electric power plants. Air pollution and carbon regulations in many industrial countries are expected to limit coal use, pushing coal out of the market in favor of cleaner fuels such as natural gas, and "greener" fuels such as wind and solar power. Furthermore, as pointed out in the *International Energy Outlook 2004,* published by the EIA (an independent arm of the U.S. Department of Energy), the expected drop in coal's market share would be even greater without the large increases in coal use projected for China and India. Both nations have abundant domestic coal resources and above-average rates of economic growth, a combination favoring continuing coal growth in Asia.

## Nuclear Power

In 1970, nuclear power accounted for only four tenths of 1 percent of global energy consumption. Ten years later, in 1980, nuclear's share was up to 2.4 percent, and in another ten years it had more than doubled to 5.6 percent. By 2000, nuclear energy accounted for 6.4 percent of global energy consumption. By my calculations, its market share peaked at 6.6 percent in 2001, and in 2030 (barring a surprise) will be down to about 4 percent of the world's total energy use.

With current technology, the economics of nuclear power compare poorly with other methods of electricity generation. It is possible that new developments such as pebble-bed nuclear generation may improve this situation.[2] However, as the EIA suggests, "public concerns about plant safety, radioactive waste disposal, and weapons proliferation" make a near-term revival unlikely. Although nuclear power's market share is likely to decline, the absolute level of production could still climb at a likely annual rate of about 0.5 percent from 2000 to 2030. A combination of new construction (especially in Asia) and improved utilization of existing facilities is forecast to offset losses resulting from retirements.

## Hydropower and Other Renewables

Hydropower is clearly a renewable energy form but is not always considered to be a "green" category of energy. Massive new projects such as the Three Gorges Dam in China, India's Tehri Dam, and Malaysia's Bakun Dam are controversial due to the massive flooding as reservoirs are filled and are opposed because of other damage to river ecosystems. Consumption of hydroelectricity accounted for 5 percent of global energy use in 1970, and 7 percent in 2000. In 1970, commercial biofuels and other nonhydropower renewables such as wind power and solar made virtually no contribution to global consumption of energy. Even by 2000, the amount of power delivered by these sources was negligible. However, with subsidies from many governments around the globe, expansion in green energy seems likely despite the unattractive economics. By industry estimates, energy from biofuels, solar, and wind could equal the contribution from hydropower by 2030.[3] In my forecast, the use of hydropower and other renewables is estimated to grow by 2.0 percent over the 2000–2030 period, almost doubling from about 13 to 24 mmbpd.

## Energy and GDP

Energy demand and economic growth are closely linked, although not at a simple 1-to-1 ratio. Over the period from 1970 to 2000, global energy demand grew by an average annual rate of 2.0 percent while GDP measured at purchasing-power-parity[4] rates rose at a 3.6 percent annual rate. The ratio of change in energy to change in real GDP is often called "energy intensity." There is a strong correlation in the movements of energy growth and GDP growth over time. More than 70 percent of the annual shifts in energy use were explained by shifts in GDP during the period 1970–2000. Many analysts have observed that the energy intensity ratio in developing countries tends to be higher than in industrial countries—but that as incomes increase, energy consumption tends to rise more slowly.

During the past few years, oil demand has not kept its traditional rate of growth in relationship to GDP. This may have been caused by a number of abnormal factors that could abate, resulting in a return to a more normal relationship of 50 percent of GDP for oil demand growth. The surge in oil demand in China in 2004 exemplifies the potential for oil use by developing economies to provide a significant boost to consumption. Nevertheless, global oil demand may not grow as fast in the 2000–10 period as it did in the 1990s. The composition of GDP may be shifting toward less oil-intensive output (such as services) and higher energy prices may be contributing to lower GDP, but the chief reason for my concern is the impact that higher and more volatile oil prices are having on demand.

Examinations of economic and oil price data by a number of energy economists suggest that the global economy responds asymmetrically to oil price changes. Upward shocks create more harm than the positive effects of falling prices. This is because the cost of adjusting to changing prices retards economic output. When oil prices rise, growth is affected both by the higher cost of the fuel and by the cost associated with volatility. When prices fall, the volatility costs remain a drag on the system. This asymmetry is dangerous for OPEC because it means that oil demand may not grow as fast as it has previously, in reaction to volatile fuel pries, while high prices still encourage non-OPEC supply.

## Key Elements in Oil Demand and Non-OPEC Supply

Who will control the oil market over the next thirty years, OPEC or non-OPEC nations (table 1.2)? OPEC's market share of long-term oil supplies is a function of demand and non-OPEC supply. As indicated above, I believe that global oil demand will rise from 76 mmbpd in 2000 to 124 mmbpd in 2030, an increase of about 48 mmbpd. I expect that total non-OPEC oil supply will rise by about 15 mmbpd, from 46.0 mmbpd in 2000 to 61 mmbpd in 2030, leaving OPEC with control of 51 percent of global oil supply.

### Petroleum Demand

All other things being equal, the greater the rise in demand for petroleum, the more OPEC oil is needed. My forecast for 124 mmbpd of demand is based on a set of regional demand growth assumptions that estimate the world's total use of petroleum growing at about the same rate over the 2000–30 period as it did from 1970 to 2000. The basis for this development includes a number of special factors.

Table 1.2. *Who Controls the Oil Markets? (million barrels per day)*

| Producers | | Consumers | | Exporters | | Importers | |
|---|---|---|---|---|---|---|---|
| Saudi Arabia | 9.7 | United States | 20.5 | Saudi Arabia | 8.1 | United States | 12.4 |
| Russia | 9.0 | China | 6.4 | Russia | 6.4 | Japan | 5.3 |
| United States | 7.9 | Japan | 5.3 | Norway | 3.0 | China | 3.0 |
| Iran | 4.1 | Germany | 2.7 | Iran | 2.6 | Germany | 2.5 |
| Mexico | 3.9 | Russia | 2.6 | Venezuela | 2.5 | South Korea | 2.2 |
| China | 3.4 | India | 2.4 | United Arab Emirates | 2.3 | France | 1.9 |
| Norway | 3.2 | South Korea | 2.2 | Nigeria | 2.2 | Italy | 1.7 |
| Canada | 3.1 | Canada | 2.2 | Kuwait | 2.0 | India | 1.6 |
| Venezuela | 3.0 | Brazil | 2.2 | Iraq | 1.7 | Spain | 1.5 |

*Sources*: BP; International Energy Agency; U.S. Energy Information Administration; author's estimates for 2004.

First, I am assuming that the two massive oil price shocks of 1973–74 and 1979–80 are *not* repeated. In 2002 dollars, oil prices rose from about $12 per barrel in 1973 to $31 in 1974–75. The 1979–80 jump nearly doubled the price from $27 per barrel in 1978 to $50 in 1981. Oil demand in the industrial countries was significantly affected by these price disturbances. Annual growth in the OECD nations over the 1973–93 period was essentially flat. Petroleum demand did not rise in the United States, dropped in Europe, and barely increased in Japan. In the 2000–2030 period, the OECD as a whole is forecast to grow at about a 1 percent rate. Europe has the lowest rate of annual gain (0.4 percent), while the "other OECD" members, which include Mexico and South Korea, are expected to have the strongest growth (1.6 percent) among the industrial countries.

Second, I am assuming that the economic and social disruptions of the 1990s that occurred in the former Soviet Union (FSU) are not replicated—either there or elsewhere. From 1989 to 1999, consumption of oil in the FSU fell by more than 5 mmbpd as total use dropped from 8.7 to 3.6 mmbpd. The collapse of communism and subsequent economic restructuring of Russia and the other post-Soviet states reduced or simply terminated inefficient uses of petroleum. From 2000 to 2030, I expect demand in the FSU to rise by about 1.8 percent annually.

Finally, I am making the assumption (admittedly controversial) that the Kyoto Protocol will not have a significant impact on global energy use patterns over the next few decades.[5] Many energy economists believe that relying on existing technologies can only reduce greenhouse gas emissions at the expense of economic growth. With Russia's acceptance, the protocol entered into force in 2005, but there is considerable disagreement on the actual timing and extent to which the policies will affect fuel use. The EIA has analyzed the fuel implications of the treaty—if the United States were to agree.[6] Because of the higher relative carbon content of coal and oil, the use of both these fuels would be reduced. The EIA models show that there would be greater consumption of natural gas, renewable energy, and nuclear power in the United States. I believe that these findings would likely apply to most of the countries that agree to the Kyoto treaty.

I am also forecasting a slowdown in demand growth in the non-OECD countries outside the FSU. Driven largely by sizable gains in China and other Asian countries outside the OECD, the "other Non-OECD" area experienced an average annual growth rate of about 4.1 percent in demand over the 1970–2000 period. With the expectation that rates of population, GDP, and oil consumption growth are tempered over the 2000–2030 forecast period,

I estimate that oil demand will rise at about 2.5 percent yearly in this region. The highest yearly rates of regional growth are anticipated in China (3.4 percent) and "other Asia" (2.7 percent), with Latin America, the Middle East, and Africa averaging an annual increase of nearly 2 percent.

The net result of these forces is that global oil demand growth is expected to average 1.6 percent a year from 2000 to 2030, virtually identical to the 1.6 percent growth rate in the prior thirty-year period (1970–2000). The non-OECD countries grow faster than the industrial nations, but the absolute level of consumption in the OECD (65 mmbpd) in 2030 is still greater than in the developing world (59 mmbpd, including the FSU).

## The Non-OPEC Petroleum Supply

The greater the rise in the non-OPEC supply of petroleum, the less OPEC oil is needed. My forecast for 61.5 mmbpd of non-OPEC production is based on a set of country and regional supply growth assumptions showing that the non-OPEC share of output will grow during the 2000–2030 period, but at only about half the 2.1 percent annual rate of increase which occurred from 1970 to 2000. The key factors in this forecast include a decline in the OECD region, growth in the FSU (particularly in Russia and the Caspian Sea region), and a diminishing rate of production growth in the other non-OECD areas. We next look briefly at these regional patterns.

### The United States

In 1970, the United States was the largest oil producer in the world, accounting for 11.3 mmbpd out of total non-OPEC production of 25.0 mmbpd. The development of fields on the North Slope of Alaska in the late 1970s and the Gulf of Mexico offshore area more recently added significant volumes to U.S. production. Even these large discoveries were not enough to prevent a general downward drift in output, especially after the price collapse of 1986. By 2000, total U.S. oil output averaged 8.1 mmbpd. The outlook for U.S. oil production is currently being driven by the deepwater development trends in the Gulf of Mexico. Without new discoveries in the Gulf of Mexico, or the opening of new provinces in Alaska, the overall outlook for U.S. production after 2010 looks bleak. Declines are likely to be prevalent in all the major areas contributing to production (Alaska, Gulf of Mexico, other "lower forty-eight" states, as well as the natural gas liquids[7] subcategory).

Total U.S. petroleum production will fall at about a 2 percent rate over the 2000–2030 period, ending at about 5.4 mmbpd.

## OECD European Producers

The North Sea is one of the key non-OPEC producing regions, and it is responsible for nearly all the oil production in OECD Europe. I estimate that OECD Europe's oil output will fall at about a 3 percent rate over the 2000–2030 forecast period, ending at about 2.5 mmbpd.[8]

## Other OECD Producers

The remaining key petroleum provinces within the OECD are in Mexico and Canada. Both are expected to increase their contributions to global supply through 2030. Canada's conventional oil production, like the onshore lower-forty-eight states in the United States, is believed to be in a declining phase. However, the Athabasca oil sands in Alberta contain one of the world's largest petroleum accumulations of oil, with estimated proven reserves of 175 billion barrels. There will be eleven producing oil sands projects at the end of 2004, and a further fourteen projects are anticipated to come onstream by 2010.[9] Total Canadian output could reach 4.1 mmbpd in 2015, up from an estimated 3.1 mmbpd in 2003. Canadian production could be as high as 4.8 mmbpd in 2030.

Mexico's oil production averaged 0.5 mmbpd in 1970 and rose rapidly to a peak of 3.0 mmbpd in 1982, where it languished until 1990 when operating reforms at Petróleos Mexicanos (Pemex), the state-owned oil company, created an environment for further production gains. Further reforms proposed by President Vicente Fox have faced stiff resistance in the Mexican Congress. Limits on capital availability (not resources) are likely to be Mexico's greatest problem over the next twenty-five years. Demand in Mexico is rising rapidly, and Mexico's regulatory and legislative framework will have to undergo significant changes to keep the country from becoming a large importer of oil and natural gas. I expect that enough pressure exists on Pemex and the government to allow this transformation. As a result, I see Mexican oil production rising at about a 1.0 to 1.5 percent rate over the 2000–2030 period to reach 5.3 mmbpd.[10]

## The Former Soviet Union

There are three key producing countries in the FSU: Russia, Kazakhstan, and Azerbaijan, addressed in detail by Julia Nanay in Chapter 5. Since 1970,

Russian production has been on a true roller-coaster ride. Output rose from 6.5 mmbpd in 1970 to a peak of 11.2 mmbpd in 1983. From there it plummeted to 6.0 mmbpd in 1996 and stayed at about that level through 1999. In 2000, the combination of higher oil prices (greater revenues), a low ruble (reduced costs), and the election of President Vladimir Putin (political stability) resulted in the flow of cash into the Russian upstream. Production jumped to 6.5 mmbpd in 2000, and it will probably reach 9.0 mmbpd in 2005. This increase in production is due primarily to the focus of the Russian industry on enhancing production in existing fields rather than investing in new field developments.

Going forward from 2005, export capacity limitations stand more in the way of Russian growth than do upstream opportunities, natural declines, or Saudi Arabia's protestations. These limitations are addressed by Jan Kalicki and Jonathan Elkind in chapter 6. Demand growth in Russia has been flat, forcing Russian producers to maximize exports. I believe that Russian oil production is capable of rising back to its former peak by 2015. Accomplishing this will require significant new upstream investment—beyond the reworking of existing properties.

Kazakhstan is the second largest producer of oil in the FSU. Kazakhstan has the potential to produce about 2.0 mmbpd by 2007 and peak at almost 2.5 mmbpd by 2010. Reaching this level depends largely on meeting ambitious development scenarios and other factors, such as fiscal and political stability, the speed at which financing can be secured, and the building of secure exports. I believe that the technical and commercial problems can be overcome and that additional new discoveries will allow production to rise to about 2.9 mmbpd by 2030.

Oil production in Azerbaijan hovered at 0.2 to 0.3 mmbpd from 1985 to 2000. I see production leveling out at about 1.5 mmbpd beyond 2010 on the basis of the potential for exploration success in the Caspian Sea offshore area.

## China and Other Asian Economies

The remaining critical producing areas outside OPEC include a number of countries, such as Angola, Argentina, Brazil, China, Egypt, India, and Malaysia. Both China and "other Asia" are expected to increase production through 2030, although domestic consumption will absorb nearly all production in each of these countries.

China's current oil production is dominated by the onshore fields, all of which are currently operated by state-owned companies and many of which are now in decline. In contrast to the difficult onshore situation, offshore production is expected to increase significantly. Although most offshore production currently comes from the South China Sea, the Bohai Gulf will become relatively more important. Total production is forecast to peak at 3.5 mmbpd in 2005–6 and fall toward 2.5 mmbpd in 2012.

I believe that rapidly rising demand in China will ultimately create a more open and competitive atmosphere for production within China and that the vast geographic area of the country probably contains a few upstream surprises. I see production rising toward 3.9 mmbpd in 2015 and reaching 5.3 mmbpd in 2030.

The production outlook in "other Asia" is dependent mainly on developments in India, Malaysia, and Vietnam. With a bit of luck in Bangladesh and Pakistan, total "other Asian" production is forecast to reach 3.0 mmbpd in 2030, up from 2.2 mmbpd in 2000.

## South and Central America

Latin American non-OPEC oil production is driven by Brazil, Argentina, Colombia, and Ecuador. Only Brazil is likely to increase production by 2030. Brazil today is the most prolific of the producers in South and Central America. With the recent surge in foreign operators entering Brazil, many of them focusing on big exploration prospects in deep waters, I believe that production could rise above 2.6 mmbpd in 2015, perhaps sustaining at that level to 2030.

## The Middle East and Africa

In the non-OPEC Middle East, the three important oil-producing countries today are Oman, Syria, and Yemen. Production from the entire region was 2.2 mmbpd in 2000, and it is not expected to be significantly different than that over the entire 2000–2030 forecast time frame.

The two largest non-OPEC producers in Africa are Angola and Egypt. Overall oil production from Angola is forecast to continue its upward trend as a number of major deepwater developments come onstream. Output from Angola could hit 2.3 mmbpd by 2010 if the giant deepwater projects stay on track.[11] Egypt's trend is likely to be in decline. With good prospects in Sudan, Equatorial Guinea, and potentially Chad added to the region's total, overall production could grow from 2.8 mmbpd in 2000 to 4.6 mmbpd in 2010. This is a significant and powerful near-term rate of growth with effects on the producing governments that are detailed later in the book by Paul

Hueper in chapter 10 and Charles McPherson in chapter 19. Over the longer term, my forecast shows a decline to 4.0 mmbpd by 2015, with the most likely way to offset this being new discoveries, notably in the deepwater areas of West Africa, or in the relatively unexplored onshore basins of East Africa.

## To What Extent Will OPEC Dominate Long-Term Supplies of Oil?

OPEC controls the oil and gas reserves, but not necessarily production. Virtually every analysis of energy security issues begins by pointing out the fact that OPEC member states control most of the world's oil proven reserves. Six of the OPEC countries (Saudi Arabia, Iraq, the United Arab Emirates, Kuwait, Iran, and Venezuela) account for about two-thirds of the total. However, in view of the economic policies and development plans that these countries pursue, it is not surprising to find that nations with less oil reserves are capable of producing oil at significantly higher levels than many of the OPEC states. Despite OPEC's overwhelming control of reserves, this does not necessarily imply that OPEC will "dominate" the long-term supply of oil.

## OPEC Imports Fill the Gap

During the next twenty-five to thirty years, the call on OPEC's production is estimated to approximately double. OPEC produced about 28 mmbpd in 2000, and its output is expected to hold near this level throughout the decade. The recent surge in demand has enabled OPEC to recover part of the market share given up in 2000–2002 when rising non-OPEC supply growth and slow demand combined to reduce OPEC's portion. Beyond 2010, however, with demand up over 35 mmbpd and non-OPEC supply up less than 10 mmbpd, OPEC production of crude oil and natural gas liquids would have to rise by more than 30 mmbpd (roughly double today's levels) to balance oil supply and demand. Some analysts are starting to doubt that OPEC is physically, financially, or politically capable of meeting this level of demand. Clearly, this is a sizable increase, but it would still leave OPEC's global market share below the 55 percent peak reached in 1973–74 (figure 1.2 and table 1.3).

The level of expansion that OPEC would have to undertake is not impossible. Table 1.3 shows how OPEC's capacity growth could be allocated among the member states. The implied increment of about 28 mmbpd would

Figure 1.2.  OPEC's 2030 Market Share Estimated at 50 Percent

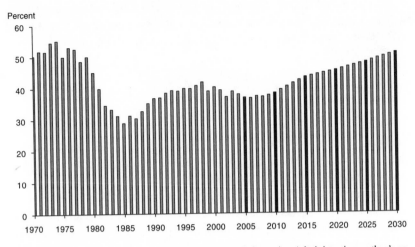

*Sources:* BP; International Energy Agency; U.S. Energy Information Administration; author's estimates for 2005–30.

*Table 1.3.  What Does It Take to Get OPEC's Oil Production Up to 54 Million Barrels per Day? (million barrels per day)*

| Country | Current Capacity | Capacity in 2030 | Growth Implied | Annual Percentage Growth Required |
|---|---|---|---|---|
| Saudi Arabia | 10.0 | 16.2 | 6.2 | 1.5 |
| Iran | 4.0 | 7.0 | 3.0 | 2.0 |
| Iraq | 2.5 | 9.0 | 6.5 | 3.0 |
| United Arab Emirates | 2.5 | 3.3 | 0.8 | 1.0 |
| Kuwait | 2.3 | 3.5 | 1.2 | 1.0 |
| Qatar | 0.8 | 2.7 | 1.9 | 5.0 |
| Nigeria | 2.4 | 6.4 | 4.0 | 4.0 |
| Libya | 1.6 | 4.1 | 2.5 | 4.0 |
| Algeria | 1.3 | 1.0 | –0.3 | 0.0 |
| Venezuela | 2.3 | 5.4 | 3.2 | 3.0 |
| Indonesia | 1.0 | 0.8 | –0.2 | –1.0 |
| Total | 30.5 | 59.3 | 28.9 | 2.6 |

*Source:* Author's estimates.

ensure capacity in 2030 of approximately 60 mmbpd, and this implies capacity utilization of about 90 percent (54/60). As the reader can see, major growth will be needed in Iraq, Iran, Libya, Venezuela, and Nigeria, all places where internal instability, restrictions on foreign investment, or U.S.

economic sanctions raise cautions about the ability of these nations to meet this growth potential. These issues are more fully addressed later in the book by Edward Morse and Amy Jaffe (chapter 3), Robin West (chapter 8), Paul Hueper (chapter 10), and Luis Téllez (chapter 16).

## OPEC's Growth and Capacity

During the past several decades, international oil companies (IOCs) have participated to varying extents in OPEC countries. The IOCs' participation is now recovering and is associated with substantial growth in both oil production and capacity.

### Achieving the Necessary Participation of the International Oil Companies

In view of the relatively high reserve-to-production ratios (the rate at which current production will exhaust known reserves) in most of the OPEC countries, the oil resources needed to achieve the implied growth do not seem to be as much of an issue as the required organization skills, technological abilities, and capital formation needs. During the past three decades, there have been very few examples of national oil companies (NOCs) making significant net increases in production capacity without some form of direct participation by the IOCs.

Using its database of global upstream projects, Wood Mackenzie Consultants recently analyzed the trends in IOC participation in OPEC countries. Before nationalization in the mid-1970s, the IOCs directly operated virtually all of OPEC's production. Company-operated production reached a low point of about 25 percent in 1986. The proportion of IOC production within OPEC began to increase again in the mid-1990s as contracts were awarded in Qatar, Algeria, and Libya. IOC production now accounts for more than 30 percent of the OPEC total and is expected to reach 40 percent by 2010.

The only country that has been able to develop major net oil capacity increases without direct participation in its upstream industry—with the exception of the partitioned neutral zone with Kuwait—has been Saudi Arabia. In the late 1990s, Saudi Aramco completed the development of the multi-billion-barrel Shaybah field in the Empty Quarter and has several development plans under implementation or consideration. Total Saudi production capacity was estimated at 11 mmbpd by early 2005, following the implementation of the Haradh-2 project last year and the successful completion of the Abu Safah and Qatif projects, brought onstream in August 2004. In contrast to oil, Saudi Arabia appears to be welcoming the participation of IOCs in the development of natural gas.[12]

## Total OPEC Oil Production:
### International Oil Company Participation Is Recovering

Where IOCs have remained, or have been allowed back into a country, both oil production and capacity have grown substantially. IOC expertise and access to capital were instrumental in most of the recent production gains, including the development of 0.5 mmbpd of Venezuelan heavy oil production brought onstream since 2001. The increases in Nigeria, Algeria, and the United Arab Emirates are also due almost entirely to the IOCs. The Northern Fields project in Kuwait and the Azadegan development in Iran are likely to be awarded to IOC consortiums. It also appears inevitable that the redevelopment and expansion of Iraq's oil industry will involve foreign companies. IOC involvement in OPEC is undoubtedly an imperative as the OPEC country asset base matures and costs rise.

In addition to the challenge of finding contractual formats for IOC participation within the regulatory framework, the potential for conflict with OPEC quotas is emerging as another theme. In some OPEC countries, rising IOC production appears to have been accommodated via a dramatic decline in NOC production. The state companies have effectively made room—or far more room than might have been expected—for the IOC output. Looking ahead, this emphasizes the importance of timing the actual IOC project approvals with regard to future estimates of OPEC capacity and quotas.

Providing the right conditions for exploration is critical. Allowing the companies into OPEC countries such as Saudi Arabia, Kuwait, Iraq, and the United Arab Emirates (and non-OPEC Mexico, as well) is "necessary but not sufficient." Another study performed by Wood Mackenzie measured and ranked more than fifty countries in terms of their relative attractiveness for oil and gas exploration. Among the winners: U.S. Gulf of Mexico deepwater, Angola deepwater, Kazakhstan, the Malaysia–Thailand joint development area, and Bangladesh. The worst places: Venezuela, Azerbaijan, and Brazil. The key characteristic of the best areas—once high success rates and large discovery sizes are established—is a fiscal regime that balances risk and rewards in the investors' favor. The key attributes of the least successful countries are an environment in which costs are not easily controlled and an excessive government take in licensing rounds. The key lesson here is that the domestic policy of OPEC nations, their stability, and their ability to attract technology and capital will determine whether they are willing and able to meet demand in the years ahead.

## What Do Growing Oil Imports Mean to the United States, Asia, and Europe?

Significantly rising imports of crude oil and products are likely to be a common theme for the United States, Europe, and China in the future. From 1970 to 2000, China was first a small exporter and then a small importer. Japan imports all of its oil consumption. During the 1970–2000 period, Europe (as a whole) saw its overall import dependency shrink as the North Sea was developed. In the United States, imports consistently climbed, but not by much. However, a clear shift in this situation is already under way as indigenous oil production in all three regions struggles while demand is forecast to inexorably climb (table 1.4).

China's attitude toward this development is already manifesting itself in plans to build strategic reserves to provide a cushion against interruptions and in support for pipeline projects from Russia, Kazakhstan, and the Middle East to reduce reliance on seaborne imports. Japan has inadvertently followed a strategy of limiting its oil imports through its passive acceptance of disappointing economic growth.

In the United States, politicians struggle to provide tax relief and credits to smaller oil producers but have failed to take the hard steps. Little effort is being made on options such as imposing a European-style gasoline tax or stricter fuel efficiency regulations to slow transportation demand growth, or

*Table 1.4. Oil Imports Likely to Rise Sharply for the Largest Consumers (million barrels per day)*

| Importer | 1970 | 1980 | 1990 | 2000 | 2010 | 2020 | 2030 |
|---|---|---|---|---|---|---|---|
| United States | 6.3 | 6.9 | 8.0 | 11.1 | 14.6 | 19.9 | 24.4 |
| Europe | 12.9 | 12.0 | 9.3 | 8.3 | 11.2 | 13.4 | 14.5 |
| China | 0.0 | −0.3 | −0.5 | 1.3 | 4.8 | 7.5 | 11.4 |
| Japan | 3.6 | 5.0 | 5.2 | 5.6 | 5.5 | 5.8 | 6.4 |

*Sources:* International Energy Agency for 1970–2000; author's estimates for 2010–30.

significantly enhancing supply prospects by opening up more federal land for exploration and development.

## The Outlook for the Global Gas Market

Gas, and particularly liquefied natural gas (LNG), has never had such a high public profile, driven by the recent U.S. gas crisis. The 2000 California energy meltdown and illegal behavior by companies such as Enron drove the 2000–2001 winter U.S. gas price spike, but a far more fundamental shift occurred in 2003. The world has seen record U.S. gas prices sustained through the summer after a global winter shortage of LNG and 2002's disappointments from U.S. domestic suppliers.

Traditionally, and in contrast to oil, the natural gas markets have been very localized. U.S. production provided most of U.S. demand. The second largest consumer, Russia, exported nearly 20 percent of its production to Europe. The United Kingdom was self-sufficient. Most of the 30 percent or so of natural gas that does move across borders has been doing so by pipeline. The exception to this has been in Asia, where producers in the south were selling LNG to users in the north. That picture is now changing—natural gas is going global.

The U.S. market is so large that to meet rising import demand, a worldwide search for supply has commenced—starting in Trinidad, and featuring Nigeria and North Africa; Qatar, Abu Dhabi, and Oman in the Middle East; and ultimately ending in Russia, Turkmenistan, Indonesia, and Australia. At the same time, there is growth in Europe, driven by the United Kingdom in the north and the Iberian Peninsula in the south. A super-hot summer in Europe in 2003 strained nuclear supply capabilities in France and emptied reservoirs for hydropower in Scandinavia—this looks like additional structural demand for gas going forward, even if a globally warm winter could send gas prices crashing. In Asia, China continues to balance how to substitute $1 per million British thermal units (Btu) of sulfurous coal with $6 per million Btu of gas against dreadful air quality in many cities. Japan also suffered a major nuclear power crisis in the summer of 2003, leading to a wave of new LNG commitments from Japan and also from South Korea and Taiwan. By mid-2004, Japan had managed to only bring about half of the seventeen shut power plants back online (table 1.5).

The gas market of the next thirty years will be global—with the increasing penetration of LNG. LNG is a more cost effective, flexible, less risky,

*Table 1.5. Key Countries in Gas: Dominant Players Include Russia, the United States, and Canada (billion cubic feet per day)*

| Producers | | Consumers | | Exporters | | Importers | |
|---|---|---|---|---|---|---|---|
| Russia | 54.2 | United States | 61.5 | Russia | 12.0 | United States | 8.6 |
| United States | 52.9 | Russia | 42.2 | Canada | 9.1 | Japan | 8.4 |
| Canada | 17.0 | United Kingdom | 10.7 | Norway | 6.8 | Germany | 6.9 |
| United Kingdom | 9.4 | Germany | 8.7 | Algeria | 6.0 | Ukraine | 5.4 |
| Algeria | 8.2 | Japan | 8.4 | Turkmenistan | 5.3 | Italy | 6.8 |
| Norway | 7.3 | Italy | 8.2 | Indonesia | 3.3 | France | 4.7 |
| Iran | 6.9 | Canada | 7.9 | Malaysia | 2.2 | South Korea | 2.9 |
| Indonesia | 6.8 | Iran | 7.5 | Qatar | 2.0 | Spain | 2.8 |
| Netherlands | 5.8 | Ukraine | 7.1 | Netherlands | 1.7 | Mexico | 0.9 |

*Sources:* BP; International Energy Agency; U.S. Energy Information Administration; author's estimates for 2004.

and comparatively less capital intensive means of bringing large quantities of gas into the U.S. market than an Alaskan pipeline, at least in the first half of the 2000–2030 period. (Shirley Neff describes the impact of this trend on North America, and gives another view of the Alaska pipeline, in chapter 15).

With demand rising and U.K. North Sea supplies peaking, the coming "U.K. gas gap" will see a rapid increase in import requirements starting in 2005 into the U.K. market—with Norway and Russia the likely sellers. Loyola de Palacio describes the European Union's planning to meet European demand in chapter 7.

Pipeline networks and LNG projects are likely to expand in Latin America, particularly as Venezuela, with its huge gas reserves, grows from its small base.

Asia provides the most interesting growth story. The Asian gas story continues to be dominated by the "hare and the tortoise." As the traditional big three Asian LNG buyers (Japan, South Korea, and Taiwan) began to slow their consumption of incremental LNG toward the end of the 1990s, the next "big thing" became the awakening of coal-burning and hydrocarbon-short China and India to the need to import natural gas. With populations in excess of 1 billion each, there was a natural excitement that demand potential was enormous.

The "hare" is sleeping India, which promised in the late 1990s to be the most dynamic new global gas market driven by a rush of LNG developments. To all intents and purposes, the epithet "developers' graveyard" has proved accurate for the Indian subcontinent. Shell's recent exit from Bangladesh and ExxonMobil's Rasgas declining to bid on Indian power giant NTPC's major LNG tender because of unreasonable conditions all point toward a momentum away from the subcontinent. This contrasts sharply with company appetites for China.

The "tortoise" is inexorably growing China, with an ongoing policy to replace high-sulfur coal supply to meet its vast demand. The issue of economics, the same that the Indian gas customer struggles with, is no less acute for Chinese gas customers who are paying about $1 per million Btu for their coal, and will struggle to pay the implied $4 per million Btu for replacement pipeline gas. The difference between India and China comes down to politics: The Chinese government is more able to enforce gas consumption at set prices within the parameters of its central planning. For example, planners can point to the indirect economic gain from health benefits of cleaner air—the World Bank estimates that China's poor air cost a staggering 3 to 8 percent of GDP a year between 1998 and 2004, totaling about $60 billion. China's massive West East pipeline, otherwise uncompetitive, fits into this picture.

Until recently, most oil producers in the Middle East tended to ignore gas development, other than Algeria, which has actively pursued gas development and LNG markets for three decades. Gas reserves in the Middle East, like oil, are enormous, and the development of LNG, gas-to-liquids, and long-distance pipeline projects will be a major factor in supply over the 2010–30 time frame.

### The Former Soviet Union

Russia is the largest gas exporter, selling about 16 billion cubic feet per day (bcfpd) in 2002, in contrast to Canada's 10 bcfpd. Its main gas export pipelines run from West Siberia through Ukraine to Europe. The Russian government is now trying to diversify away from transit dependence on the Ukraine, and new capacity has recently been built across Belarus and more is planned. Russia's expected total export capacity will be enough to sustain the envisaged increases in exports to 2020 and probably beyond.

### The Gas Alliance: Will We See a "Gas OPEC"?

The idea of organizing natural gas producers in a manner similar to OPEC has been around almost as long as OPEC itself. Although I think it is possible that producers might be able to create such an organization, I see it as less likely that a "Gas Alliance" would be capable of firm collective action. The fundamental economics of the natural gas industry argue against such activity: Too much capital is required to move gas from the wellhead to consumers, and the competition with other fuels at the burner tip is intense. Capacity issues and fleeting demand windows suggest that most of the major reserve holders are more likely to be competing with one another, but also with alternative projects such as Alaskan gas or OPEC oil. The "internationally traded" gas markets are still more in a building phase, requiring a push from gas producers to gain acceptance. If, at some point, the gas markets mature into a more dominant established stage, organizing a sellers' market becomes more realistic.

## Could the World Be Approaching a Near-Term Peak in the Supply of Oil and Gas?

If it could be shown that geological constraints signify an imminent peak in oil and natural gas production levels, the energy policy implications would be

Figure 1.3. World Crude Oil Endowment: More Left to Find than Hubbert Believed

Billion barrels

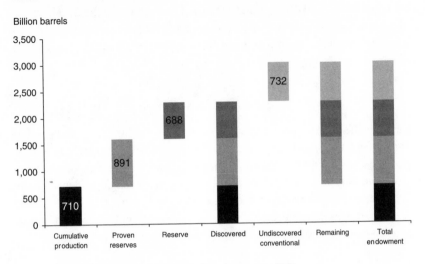

*Source:* U.S. Geological Survey, World Petroleum Assessment, 2000.

Figure 1.4. Hubbert Curve Works for 15 Years, Then Goes Seriously Wrong in the United Kingdom

Production (thousand barrels per day)

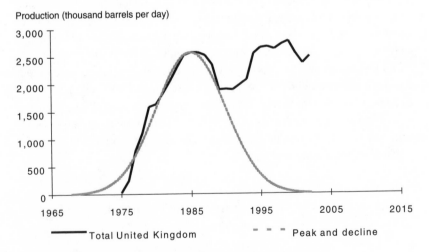

*Sources:* Wood Mackenzie historical data; author's estimates for 1995–2015.

enormous. M. King Hubbert, a geologist for Shell and the U.S. Geological Survey in the early 1960s, used a bell curve to correctly predict the 1972 peak in U.S. oil production.[13] A number of consultants and academics have recently extended Hubbert's methodology to forecast a world oil peak this decade—some claiming it has already peaked. But Hubbert models do not account for changes in technology, costs, prices, or politics—all of which can have a huge impact on the actual shape of the production curve (figures 1.3 and 1.4). Assuming a symmetric curve is critical to determining the year and amount of peak production. I think it more likely that oil and gas production will tend to follow a curve skewed to the right, which implies no immediate threat of running out of oil or gas.[14] In my view, the dynamic nature of the markets to respond to changes in prices and policies—employing the latest advances in oil exploration, development, and production—simply cannot be modeled using bell curves.[15]

## Are Alternative and Renewable Energy Supplies Commercially Viable?

Renewable energy is expected to grow rapidly over the 2000–2030 forecast period for two reasons. First, renewables are rising from a very small base that makes large annual gains possible in the early years, and second, they are benefiting from a set of regulatory mandates that are providing incentives for adoption. In contrast to the statistics available in the petroleum industry, however, problems in definitions and data adequacy have resulted in the exclusion of all noncommercial renewables from the historical data provided by most of the major statistical providers—a situation that makes tracking renewables developments a difficult task.

### Defining Renewables

The International Energy Agency (IEA) defines renewables to include combustible renewables and waste (CRW), hydropower, geothermal, solar, wind, tide, and wave energy.[16] The IEA estimates renewables accounted for about 1,374 million tons of oil equivalent (mtoe) of the world's total primary energy supply in 2000. This represents about 14 percent of the IEA's estimate for total energy use. According to the IEA data, CRW accounts for about 80 percent (1,100 mtoe) and hydropower for 17 percent (230 mtoe).[17]

From 1970 to 2000, total renewables supply experienced an annual growth of 1.8 percent, very close to the 1.8 percent calculation for yearly growth in overall energy use. The IEA estimates that the "new" renewables (geothermal, solar, wind, etc.) had significantly higher growth of about 9 percent a year, and that wind (50 percent a year) and solar (30 percent a year) were the fastest growing fuels. The keys to growth in renewables, as identified by Fereidoon Sioshansi, are regulatory mandates and goals being set in OECD countries, financial subsidies such as tax credits and research and development funding, environmental benefits, improved reliability and efficiency, and falling costs.[18]

In 2000, the United States and Europe each accounted for about 20 percent of total commercial renewables production, according to EIA data. This split is likely to change in the future, however, due to the adoption of renewable electricity targets adopted by the European Union. A new directive on "green" electricity, approved in late 2001, sets a legal framework for the future development of the renewable electricity markets in the Union. Loyola de Palacio describes this effort in more detail in chapter 7. E.U. members are obliged to establish national targets for future consumption, which are designed to increase the proportion of electricity coming from renewables from about 15 percent in 2000 to 22 percent by 2010. The European Union believes this policy will contribute to the realization of broader policies on the security of energy supplies, the environment, and competitiveness.

## Cost Reductions

Technological improvements, particularly in wind and solar applications, are reducing costs.[19] There are a number of problems to be overcome if rapid growth in the adoption of wind and solar power is to continue, as BP identified in its "Review of World Energy 2002." The intermittent nature of wind causes problems for grid operators and dispatch regimes. Some sites have been subject to disputes on environmental grounds (noise, bird fatalities, general aesthetics), and military and civilian aviation concerns over the potential for interference with radar. Solar power has been the subject of worries over the substances used in manufacturing solar panels and the impact on land use from installations. Renewables such as solar and wind are likely to grow much faster than other forms of energy, but they will still only account for 3 to 4 percent of total world energy consumption at the end of the forecast period.[20]

## Hydrogen

Hydrogen is often advocated as the paramount fuel for providing clean energy. Undeniably, there are excellent reasons for this. It has the highest energy content per unit of weight of any known fuel. When burned in an engine, hydrogen produces effectively zero emissions. When powering a fuel cell, the only by-product is water. Hydrogen is not, however, a primary fuel in the same sense as fossil fuels such as natural gas.[21]

Currently, the use of hydrogen in vehicles is primarily limited to experimental and prototype vehicles, which either burn hydrogen directly using modified automotive engines or use hydrogen in a fuel cell to produce electric power for electric motor drives. High costs are a significant obstacle to increasing the use of hydrogen, due to technological challenges in fuel generation, storage, and safety concerns. It is also fair to point out that the production of hydrogen via steam reforming is accompanied by the generation of significant quantities of nitrogen oxides and carbon dioxide.

The "end of the oil age" was recently envisaged by *The Economist* magazine, heralded by a great leap from twentieth-century crude oil to twenty-second-century hydrogen-powered fuel cells for transportation and businesses.[22] In my view, this prophecy failed to observe the reality of what is largely providing the growth in power for the twenty-first-century: natural gas. Natural gas is a hugely abundant, low-cost, clean-burning, non-OPEC commodity that counters many concerns over dependence on oil, and as a result it is witnessing significant and accelerating growth in demand and trade. The establishment of LNG as a globally traded commodity, and the promising investments in gas-to-liquids (GTL) technology that can turn methane into clean diesel, provide tangible and irrevocable evidence of a twenty-first-century megatrend.

In addition to LNG and GTL, other nonconventional natural gas technologies—such as coal-bed methane, tight sands, and gas hydrates—could be significant sources of hydrocarbons in the future.[23] Hydrogen's day will come, but the age of natural gas is likely to precede it in this century.

## Conclusion

The world energy futures projected here are not set in stone. Nations make policy changes and choices that can increase their energy security and alter patterns of supply and demand. The historical menu of policy choices is quite broad. It includes supply diversity, demand restraint, surge production, strategic stocks, international cooperation, and flexible markets (e.g., in futures and technology).

Demand restraint has typically taken the form of taxes and regulations on fuels. Consumer taxes on gasoline in Europe and Japan, as pointed out above, are extremely high compared with the cost of producing and delivering the fuel exclusive of taxes.[24] In the United States, the Natural Resources Defense Council, an environmental research and lobbying group, has proposed a set of policies designed to improve U.S. energy security that include raising fuel economy standards, requiring fuel-efficient automobile tires, enacting tax incentives for hybrids and fuel-cell vehicles, reinvesting in public transit and intercity railroads, and encouraging "smart growth" to reduce urban sprawl and the need for driving.[25]

The policy choices open to the United States and other countries are broad and challenging, and the results these choices will produce are not certain. But the results of our current path of consumption are far more predictable. It will produce a world much like today's in consumption of oil and gas— a world with higher levels of greenhouse gas emissions, that faces continued price volatility as it depends on supplies from nations that have historically been less stable, and that must overcome domestic political hurdles to create the infrastructure to deliver the energy that consumers demand.

## Notes

1. The basis for many of the statistics in this note are derived from the author's extensive and detailed calculations on global energy supply and demand performed as part of his duties with the Global Oil and Gas Equity Team at Deutsche Bank. The underlying data for these spreadsheets are drawn largely from three key sources: (1) the International Energy Agency's *Monthly Oil Market Report* and annual *World Energy Outlook* (available at http://www.iea.org); (2) the *BP Statistical Review of World Energy* (available at http://www.bp.com), a comprehensive set of downloadable data which has been published annually as a public service since 1951; and (3) the exceptionally thorough data and analyses published by the Energy Information Administration of the U.S. Department of Energy (available at http://www.eia.doe.gov). The *World Oil & Gas Review* published by Eni (http://www.worldoil&gasreview.eni.it) provides additional insight on key global oil and natural gas statistics.

2. Melanie Kenderdine and Ernest Moniz analyze the prospects for nuclear power and pebble bed reactor technology in chapter 18 of this volume.

3. Elissa P. Sterry, "Economic and Energy Outlook through 2020," in *Proceedings of the 23rd IAEE North American Conference* (Mexico City: International Association for Energy Economics, 2003); and Shell Oil Global Business Environment Department,

*Energy Needs, Choices and Possibilities: Scenarios to 2050,* and *People and Connections: Global Scenarios to 2020,* (London: Shell Centre, 2001–2).

4. To calculate global GDP, it is necessary to express the economic data for many countries in a standard currency. Using actual exchange rates when making these comparisons can understate the importance of the contribution from developing countries. Purchasing-power-parity (PPP) accounting attempts to adjust for this by calculating exchange rates based on a comparison of the cost in local currency of a standard set of goods and services.

5. Kevin Baumert addresses the Kyoto Protocol, which entered into force in 2004, in chapter 20 of this volume. The protocol established emissions targets relative to 1990 emissions levels for each of the participating countries. The targets included an 8 percent reduction for the E.U. member states and a 7 percent reduction for the United States. Developing countries (China and India, most importantly) were excluded from the protocol. In 2001, the Bush administration decided not to seek Senate approval for the treaty.

6. U.S. Energy Information Administration (EIA), *Impacts of the Kyoto Protocol on US Energy Markets and Economic Activity* (Washington, D.C.: EIA, 1998); available at http://www.eia.doe.gov/oiaf/kyoto/kyotobrf.html.

7. Natural gas liquids (NGLs) consist of products such as propane and ethane that are often produced from natural gas wells (or in crude oil refining operations). NGLs are liquid under low pressure and normal temperatures and are usually counted in barrels rather than as a gas. NGLs should not be confused with liquefied natural gas (LNG) that consists of super-cooled methane (natural gas) or the gas-to-liquids (GTL) process that converts natural gas to diesel fuel in a complex molecular rearrangement.

8. See Willy Olsen's discussion of the steps necessary to slow the decline in North Sea oil production in chapter 14 of this volume.

9. Wood Mackenzie Consultants, *Heavy Oil's Greed for Gas,* North America Upstream Insights, September 2003. With a team of more than 190 professionals and a wealth of industry and regional knowledge, Wood Mackenzie is particularly valued for its understanding of global oil and gas production activity.

10. See Luis Telléz's discussion of the dim prospects for reform of Mexico's laws governing foreign investment in the oil sector in chapter 16 of this volume.

11. Wood Mackenzie Consultants, *The Next Stage of Angola's Deepwater Development Has Begun,* Africa Upstream Insights, December 2003.

12. According to Wood Mackenzie, Saudi Arabia has the capacity to process and distribute only 9 billion cubic feet per day. The reliance on associated gas means that Saudi gas production levels are heavily dependent on the global market for oil. Reducing OPEC quotas has the effect of reducing Saudi gas production. This issue and the rapid growth of the Saudi's gas-intensive electric power, water desalinization, and industrial sectors have resulted in the Natural Gas Initiative, which aims to attract foreign investment into the upstream gas sector. The first contracts attributed with this initiative were awarded to Shell and Total in 2003 and LUKoil, Sinopec, and ENI/Repsol-YPF in 2004.

13. "Hubbert's Peak" signifies the imminent depletion of oil and gas. When analyzing the phenomenon of depletion in oil supplies, the work in the late 1950s and early 1960s of M. King Hubbert is often referenced. Hubbert, a geologist for Shell and the U.S. Geological Survey, was investigating the level of ultimately recoverable resources in the United States and concluded that the "lower-48" US states had passed their peak of

oil discoveries and that production would inevitably follow this decline. He determined that a bell curve reasonably represented the rise and eventual fall in oil production and, using the curve, he forecast that US oil production would peak in the early 1970s.

14. The Hubbert models do not easily accommodate shifts in technology or account for falling costs or rising commodity prices. They do not distinguish between demand-driven supply constraints and supply-driven demand constraints. Hubbert's model for "lower-forty-eight" oil was surprisingly accurate, but his natural gas model was less successful.

15. M. A. Adelman and G. C. Watkins, "Resource Scarcity: Evidence from Values of Oil and Natural Gas Reserves," in *Proceedings of the 26th IAEE International Conference* (Prague: International Association for Energy Economics, 2003). Adelman (of the Massachusetts Institute of Technology) and Watkins (of the University of Aberdeen) find that investment is constantly creating transitory stocks of "proved reserves," which are then depleted, and that unknowable future science and technology make any assessment of ultimate reserves an impossible task. I agree.

16. IEA Fact Sheet, *Renewables in Global Energy Supply,* November 2002; available at http://www.iea.org/leaflet.pdf.

17. Because of definitional differences, both BP and the EIA / U.S. Department of Energy estimate that hydropower electricity provided 600 mtoe in 2000.

18. "Renewables Prosper, Propelled by Regulatory Push, Financial Pull," *International Association for Energy Economics Newsletter,* third quarter, 2003.

19. Peter H. Kobos, "The Empirics and Implications of Technological Learning for Renewable Energy Technology Cost Forecasting," in *Proceedings of the 22nd Annual USAEE/IAEE Conference,* (Vancouver: International Association for Energy Economics, 2002).

20. My historical and forecast data exclude noncommercial CRW. Over the 1970–2000 time frame, I calculate that renewables (virtually entirely hydropower) grew by 2.8 percent a year from about 270 mtoe in 1970 to just over 600 mtoe in 2000. Commercial renewables (now including all grid-delivered electricity from all sources except nuclear) are expected to grow by about 2.0 percent annually in the period 2000–30, rising to more than 1,100 mtoe in 2030 and accounting for a 7 percent market share in 2030, about the same percentage share as in 2000. The 1,000 mtoe in 2030 is expected to be about half hydropower and half "green" energy.

21. Hydrogen must be produced from natural gas, coal, or biomass. Hydrogen can also be produced, at considerable expense, via the electrolysis of water. Steam reforming of natural gas is the most common way of producing hydrogen, but the quantities now generated are very small in relation to the current consumption of almost any other form of energy.

22. "The End of the Oil Age," *The Economist,* October 23, 2003; available at http://www.economist.com.

23. Timothy Collett, *Natural Gas Hydrates: Vast Resource, Uncertain Future,* U.S. Geological Survey, Fact Sheet 021-01, available at http://pubs.usgs.gov/fs/fs021-01; and Vito Nuccio, *Coal-Bed Methane: Potential and Concerns,* U.S. Geological Survey, Fact Sheet 123-00, available at http://pubs.usgs.gov/fs/fs0123-00.

24. International Energy Agency, *Oil Market Report,* table 14, September 2004.

25. *Energy and National Security: It's Time to Bring America's Appetite for Oil under Control,* at http://www.nrdc.org/air.energy.qsecure.asp (based on a Natural Resources Defense Council report prepared in January 2002).

# 2

# Energy Security and Markets

## Daniel Yergin

Energy security is squarely on the agenda again. Once more, the impact of energy on both foreign policy and the global economy is starkly clear. The problem is not one of running out. Though some worry as to whether world oil production will soon peak, the real risk to supplies over the next decade or two is not geology but geopolitics. Regional and social turmoil unsettles the Middle East, while global terrorism threatens the entire supply system. Iraq's production is more constrained than many anticipated before the Iraq War, and it remains vulnerable to sabotage and terrorism.

The risks are hardly limited to the Middle East. In the past few years, political conflicts have disrupted significant amounts of oil supplies far afield from the Persian Gulf—in Nigeria and Venezuela, both major producers. Indeed, the interruption of exports from Venezuela, considered a most reliable supplier since World War II, removed more oil from the world market than the cessation of Iraqi supplies did during the 2003 war. Consumers in the United States see the new risks in higher and more volatile prices both at the gasoline pump and in their home heating bills. China, its oil imports rising rapidly and confronting what it sees as its own "energy crisis," is seeking a new definition for its energy security that goes beyond its traditional one of self-sufficiency. Accelerating oil demand in 2004 and 2005 pushed up prices and strained the global supply system, adding to the vulnerabilities.

The issue of energy security is certainly not restricted to oil. The electric power blackout that hit the Northeast of the United States in August 2003, and the ones that followed in Europe, demonstrated the vulnerability of complex transmission systems. High natural gas prices in the United States are evidence of a tightly balanced gas market that leaves consumers vulnerable to supply disruptions or weather-driven increases in demand. This tight

51

market is driving the United States toward integration with an emerging global gas market, which, while bringing in needed new supplies, will add to the energy security agenda.

Indeed, the very concept of "energy security" is taking on wider dimensions. No longer does it mainly encompass just the flow of oil, as central as that is and as it has been for more than three decades. It now extends to the entire infrastructure of energy supply that supports both America's and the global economy—offshore platforms and pipelines and tankers as well as refineries, storage, generating facilities, transmission lines, and distribution systems. This vast network was not designed with terrorism in mind. But its operations now have to be managed with that continuing danger in view. The result is to create new and complex responsibilities for both industry and government, including communication and coordination between them. There is still much to be learned—and done—in this arena.

Yet less visible and every bit as important as the risks is a compensating reality. New sources of oil and gas, and technological advances both for energy production and for consumption—and the lessons learned and the institutional development that has come with those lessons—give policymakers the capability to manage "energy shocks" and weather whatever storms may lie ahead. Relations between producing and consuming countries are generally based much more on interdependence and cooperation than in the past, although new conflicts continue to crop up. Still, these more cooperative relations provide a crucial foundation for handling and minimizing shocks. For the longer term, a renewed commitment to new technologies and energy research and development holds promise of further diversification, although neither the timing nor the certainty is as sure as some may want to hope. At the very least, the realities—the huge scale of the energy supply system, the inevitable time lags, and the requirements for commercial proof—push off the major impact of alternatives one or two decades.

In other words, energy security requires continuing commitment and attention—today and tomorrow. Of course, energy security is hardly a new concern. It has been a recurrent issue since the rise of industrial society more than a century ago. It came clearly to the fore on the eve of World War I, when Winston Churchill, as first lord of the Admiralty, converted the Royal Navy from coal to oil. As a result, the British fleet began to shift from Welsh coal as the source of its propulsion to Persian–Iranian–oil. In addressing the risks associated with this historic move, Churchill declared, "Safety and certainty in oil lie in variety and variety alone."[1] With that, he was articulating the fundamental principle of energy security: diversification of supply.

His words are no less apt in the first decade of the twenty-first century:

Over the century since Churchill's decision, energy security has been a persistent problem. It was a critical dimension of World War II. The decades after the war saw five Middle Eastern crises that either disrupted or threatened to disrupt the world's oil supply system. The Iraq War constitutes the sixth. At the time of the Gulf Crisis of 1990–91, the imminent threat was that the "breadbasket" of world oil production—the Persian Gulf—would fall under the sway of Saddam Hussein, enabling his regime to translate oil into political, economic, and military power—and into weapons of mass destruction.

It is clear now that, with the end of the Cold War and the resolution of the 1990–91 crisis, and then with lower prices, the world passed into a decade of overconfidence about energy security—and, indeed, security overall. But turmoil in the Middle East—accentuated by demographic pressures, generational change, and the rise of political Islam; by the threat to political order and infrastructure posed by terrorist organizations; by regional conflict; and by rising demand, market pressure, and price spikes—has brought the issue into sharp focus again.

In looking anew at the issue of energy security, this chapter addresses two questions: What are the key principles for energy security? And what are the new dimensions of energy security? One critical theme recurs in both: The integrity of global markets for trade in oil and gas, and the government frameworks to attract investment for new production, are and will continue to be indispensable elements of international energy security.

## The U.S. Energy Position

America's $12 trillion economy rests on an energy foundation. Oil, natural gas, coal, and nuclear power account for 94 percent of that foundation. On a net basis (accounting for exports as well as imports), the United States currently imports almost 60 percent of the oil it consumes—or about a quarter of its total energy requirements. Oil alone makes up 40 percent of total consumption, and natural gas and coal each almost a quarter. By contrast, solar and wind, though increasingly promising, still constitute only 0.2 percent of total U.S. energy. It is often pointed out that the United States accounts for almost a quarter of the world's oil consumption, but it should also be noted that it represents almost a third of the world's gross domestic product (GDP).

Imported oil from the Western Hemisphere (primarily Canada, Mexico, and Venezuela) meets about 40 percent of total U.S. needs, whereas the Middle East (primarily Saudi Arabia) accounts for a little more than 10 percent of total consumption, as do the North Sea and West Africa combined.

At the time of the 1973 oil crisis, the United States imported about a third of its oil. How is it that, with all the attention to energy policy in the years since, the share of imports has risen to almost 60 percent—and is continuing to rise? The reason is obvious: Demand has been increasing more rapidly than domestic production. In addition to conservation, alternative sources of energy, and new technologies, the issue for the United States is how to appropriately manage such dependence and avoid being vulnerable to disruptions in supply. Unless one is able to conceive of some draconian regulations on consumption or a series of transformative technological breakthroughs, the practical question revolves not around substantial reductions in imports but rather around appropriately managing interdependence and stabilizing supply—and ensuring that there is both sufficient resilience in the system to absorb shocks and the capacity to respond quickly and effectively. That will be the challenge for at least the next decade or more.

So how does the United States make itself less vulnerable? There is no single answer or formula.

Conservation continues to have a very significant role to play. U.S. oil consumption has been partly decoupled from economic growth. As a result, the amount of oil used per unit of GDP is only half what it was in the 1970s. Conservation—energy efficiency—should be thought of as an energy source, and one with very large potential. Stabilizing domestic oil and natural gas production is also important. Continuing innovation has led to more efficient and environmentally secure production methods. But America's ability to maintain domestic production will depend, in part, on policy decisions with regard to exploration and production. The other key variable is the pace of technological advance, an often-underestimated but critical factor in oil and gas production.

A major technological revolution is unfolding with the "digital oil field of the future," or DOFF. A panoply of information and control technologies, remote-sensing mechanisms, "intelligent drilling" techniques, and highly accurate measurement tools is making exploration and production more exact and targeted. As a result, it is economically feasible to search for and extract oil and gas from reserves that were once too expensive or too difficult to reach. The impact of DOFF will be enormous: In the next ten years, DOFF could expand recoverable world oil reserves by 125 billion barrels—more than the currently proved reserves of Iraq.[2]

Research and development opens new horizons. New technologies with respect to automobiles and trucks will also contribute to energy security, but not as quickly as some might think. Only about 6 percent of the personal vehicle fleet turns over each year, while the alternative technologies still have some distance to go to be commercial. Though there has been much discussion about the fuel cell, its application on any scale to transportation still appears to be years off, with significant research and development and infrastructure obstacles to be overcome. One of the greatest effects on oil consumption over the medium term could well come from hybrid vehicles—part internal combustion, part battery-driven. Tighter fuel efficiency standards for sport utility—type vehicles, which now constitute half of the new vehicles sold, would also start to have an impact. But because of the relatively slow capital turnover, these new-technology paths to higher fleet-average fuel efficiency take time to reach their full potential. Moreover, the conundrum between fuel efficiency standards and prices at the pump, including taxes, seems to be an enduring feature of American politics.

## Principles of Energy Security

In approaching energy security, experience suggests ten key principles. First, Churchill's maxim of ninety years ago continues to hold true—diversification of supply is one of the main guarantors of security and, indeed, is the starting point for energy security. Widening the sources of supply lessens the impact of any particular disruption and provides opportunity for compensating supplies. This principle of diversification extends to energy transportation and infrastructure as well. And it also serves the interests of suppliers by creating a more stable market for their exports.

Second, policymakers need to recognize that there is only one oil market. The United States is part of a global oil market, an extraordinarily huge logistical system that moves 84 million barrels of oil around the world every day. U.S. security resides in the stability of this global market. It is not practical to consider being independent of it in the foreseeable future.

Third, security requires a "security margin." This means the availability of extra supply that can replace supplies that have been disrupted. This takes two forms. One is "spare capacity"—extra capacity above normal output levels that can be put into production quickly—that Saudi Arabia and a few other producers maintain. It was this unused but available capacity that was called into play in 1990 to replace the shutdown of Iraq and Kuwaiti oil fields in 1990 and, again, when Iraq's output was disrupted during and after the 2003 war. This spare capacity has been substantially eroded by the rapid growth in demand in 2004 and 2005; and in response, Saudi Arabia committed in 2005 to a significant increase in its capacity by 2010.[3]

At the same time, the emergency stocks, such as the U.S. Strategic Petroleum Reserve (SPR), with about 700 million barrels at this writing, and similar reserves in other industrial countries (another 750 million barrels) are the front-line defense against serious disruptions in supply. The SPR is an insurance policy against major disruptions and the resulting threat to GDP. But there is a major caveat. It should not be employed in market-management schemes to deal with temporary price fluctuations. If it is, it will be devalued as an instrument and lose its legitimacy—and, of critical importance, discourage increases in production and investment and retard markets from adjusting to shifts in supply and demand. There is an additional obvious risk: Oil released from the SPR may temporarily reduce prices. But what happens when, after the release is completed, prices revert to higher levels? The government may well find itself drawn into a much longer process of market management than was anticipated, depleting the reserve in the meantime.

Fourth, the oil market is far more flexible than it was in earlier decades. Intervention and controls can be highly counterproductive, hindering the system from swiftly shifting supplies around to adjust to changes in the market or disruptions in supply. Resisting the temptation to micromanage markets in the face of political pressures is essential. It would be well to remember that the famous U.S. gas lines that followed the 1973 and 1979 crises were largely the result of price controls and a cumbersome allocation system that prevented suppliers from moving gasoline from places where it was not needed to places it was. The negative unintended and perverse consequences of heavy-handed regulation is a searing memory for those who participated in the controls of the 1970s.

Fifth, it is critical to build cooperative relations, based on common interests, with nations that produce and export energy. Since the 1980s, most oil-exporting nations—though not all—have come to recognize the mutuality of interest between themselves and the importing nations. Though consumers need supplies at reasonable prices, producers need markets. Their national revenues depend upon this. It is in the producers' interest to be seen as credible suppliers on whom buyers can count. Thus, most exporters are deeply interested in "security of demand"—stable commercial relations with their customers, whose purchases often provide a significant part of their national revenues. This mutual interdependence helps create the framework for a continuing dialogue between producers and consumers. To be sure, when prices are high and markets tight, "security of demand" tends to recede from the minds of exporters, as we are seeing now, just as "security of supply" recedes from the minds of importers when prices are low.

Sixth, similar efforts need to go into the ongoing dialogue and coopera-tive energy relations with other importing nations. This is true whether they be the other industrial nations, the new "globalizers" like China and India whose demand for imported energy is increasing dramatically, or poorer de-veloping nations. The International Energy Agency, whose members are the countries belonging to the Organization for Economic Cooperation and Development, is a critically important bulwark for these purposes. It pro-motes cooperation, helps to coordinate energy policies, tests contingencies, develops common frameworks, and provides mechanisms for responding to energy emergencies.

Seventh, the increased interdependence requires a proactive security framework that involves both producers and consumers to prevent or re-spond to physical threats to or attacks on the entire supply chain. The elements include increased surveillance and monitoring and detection; coordination among military, law enforcement and intelligence agencies, foreign ministries, and companies; joint operational capabilities and plan-ning among the interested nations and companies; and recognition of the explicit mission.

Eighth, when markets become tight or disrupted—and inventories are drawn down and prices rise—the public's fear can, through panic buying, turn into self-fulfilling prophecies. Finger pointing, rancorous clamor, and search for conspiracies and manipulation can take over and obscure the real issues and hinder the practical solutions. Whatever the politics, the results can be bad policy. Both governments and the private sector can calm psy-chology and allay the anxieties by providing good-quality information to the public and by facilitating the exchange of information within the industry that makes possible more rapid adjustments to market disruptions.

Ninth, a healthy, technologically driven, energy industry is necessary for energy security. This means an oil and gas industry that can continue to ex-plore and produce in the United States in an environmentally sound way but that is also efficient and operates under reasonable and predictable rules. The technological leadership of the United States–based industry is also a source of strength. The power industry will require continuing innovation and diversification in the next wave of new generation capacity, including clean coal technology and potentially a new generation of nuclear power, as well as renewables and more diversified electric generation.

Tenth, a commitment to research and development and innovation across a broad spectrum is fundamental to energy security. In the long term, this is the engine both for achieving broadly based diversification and for estab-lishing the basis for a transition to new energy systems later in this century.

Much investment has already gone for this purpose. No one can be sure what will be the mix of energy sources two decades hence. How much of it will be similar to today, albeit more efficient, and how much of it will be going in new directions? To what degree will renewables and alternatives gain market share? Certainly local and global environmental concerns will loom larger. Energy security, environmental considerations, and the reality of growing world demand—these make a compelling case for significant and consistent investment in energy research and development across a broad front. Here is where commitment by the federal government is crucial, working in cooperation with both the university laboratory and the private sector, and in collaboration with other countries.

### Liquefied Natural Gas—"Gas on the Move": A New Dimension for Energy Security

Two new dimensions of energy security have come to the fore. The first concerns the emergence of a new global energy business—in natural gas. The major regional markets—Asia, Europe, and North America—will be likely be linked through an increasingly flexible liquefied natural gas (LNG) industry—"gas on the move." The world's proved natural gas reserves are as large as oil, but they have not been developed to the same degree because of the constraint of over-water transportation. Liquefying natural gas—at minus 240 degrees—has been the answer. Until recently, LNG has been largely an Asian trade, based upon highly structured long-term contracts.

But four factors are coming together to create the global market. The first is sheer abundance. Governments are keen to develop reserves within their borders to increase their revenues. Those that own or have access to "stranded" resources want to "un-strand" them and get them to market. This would not be possible, however, without the other changes. The second factor is that LNG was formerly considered a high-priced alternative—but no longer. Costs have come down 30 percent in the past few years, making it competitive with pipeline gas. The third factor is rising demand. Around the world, natural gas has become the fuel of choice in electric generation, locking in market growth. Policy in many countries is also promoting natural gas on environmental grounds.

Fourth, the reserve base in North America—which became an integrated, continental market in the 1990s (Canada supplies about 16 percent of total U.S. natural gas demand, while Mexico imports about 20 percent of its gas from the United States)—is now seen as mature. Yet demand is set to increase in the United States, owing to the huge addition of new gas-fired electric generation. Between 2000 and 2004, the United States increased its electric generating capacity by about 20 percent—almost all of it gas-fired. Mexican demand will also grow over the next ten years, as its electric generating capacity increases by 75 percent—most of it also gas-fired. LNG, along with the Alaska pipeline, appears essential to close the supply gap for the United States (and, without major exploration opportunities, for Mexico). The failure to bring in new natural gas supplies will damage the U.S. economy, hurt consumers and industry, and lead to the export of jobs. If development proceeds on a reasonable basis, the United States will overtake Japan as the world's number one importer of LNG by the beginning of the next decade. By 2020, LNG could account for 25 to 30 percent of United States total gas consumption, compared with just 3 percent in 2004.[4]

The result of all this could be a much larger, flexible, global business, with tankers responding even on the high seas to changing price signals among markets. The U.S. market, which is dominated by short-term arrangements and where producer and consumer often never meet, would be highly influential on the global business. This would contrast with the traditional "LNG Paradigm," which is governed by very long-term contracts that tightly tie a specific gas resource to a specific gas customer. Yet this is all very challenging. It means, in order of magnitude, that over eight years or so the LNG business would double in size from what it took forty years to achieve. The investment costs could well be $200 billion—or more. How this growth will be financed without the guaranteed markets under the existing LNG Paradigm is not yet clear, but certainly the role of large integrated companies that can absorb the risks and balance supply and demand on a global basis will be central.

The development of this new global LNG business has contrasting security dimensions. It contributes to further diversification of energy supply and energy sources. Yet, at the same time, it creates new global dependencies that are vulnerable to disruption.

What about an "OGEC"—an "Organization of Gas Exporting Countries"—a gas version of the Organization of Petroleum Exporting Countries of the 1970s? Some fear that a few countries could come to dominate the supply of LNG and then opt for more confrontational policies, whether for political or economic reasons. An association of LNG exporters is likely, and, indeed, already in the making. But there will be limits to how far things might go. There will be too much diversity among major suppliers to form a single bloc. Moreover, LNG suppliers will not only be competing among themselves but also with pipeline gas. Exporting countries will need to

maintain good relations with their customers in their own interest, to protect their market share and revenues, and to promote additional investment.
They will, thus, also want to protect their reputation as reliable suppliers.
For the most part, they will be very reluctant to take any actions that disrupt
the "liquidity" on which they count—the flow of revenues back into their
national treasuries.

The same energy security principles outlined above apply to natural gas,
just as to oil. The shaping of stable relationships among producers and consumers is of continuing high priority. Of particular importance are diversification and the creation of as liquid—no pun intended—and deep a market
as possible. There will inevitably be some kind of disruption of LNG exports from one country or another at various times. We have already seen
some—in Indonesia, caused by an insurgency of local separatists, and in Algeria, by an industrial accident. But the missing supplies were replaced with
other supplies, with little impact on the market.

There is one further energy security dimension to the development of the
global LNG business, and that is related to the new, wider dimensions of
energy security today.

## Energy: A "Hinge" of the World Economy

Since the rise of industrial society, the energy system has been a target in
warfare. In World War II, both Allies and Axis tried to disrupt the other's
petroleum supplies. Nazi U-boats came close to severing the flow of oil
from the Western Hemisphere to Britain and Allied forces in Europe. Later
in the war, both the Nazi-controlled Romanian oil fields at Ploesti and Germany's synthetic fuel plants were main targets of Allied bombing. By the
time the Germans developed the first jet fighter, they were so short of oil
that they had to use oxen to pull the jet onto the runway, to conserve aviation fuel.[5]

However, in the aftermath of the oil embargo of 1973 and the Iranian Revolution of 1979–80, the principal focus of energy security became somewhat
more narrow. It centered on the reliability of the flow of oil, principally from
the Middle East, and the response to and management of any disruptions.
The terrorist attacks of September 11, 2001, widened the focus again, back
to the whole system—that is, the security of the infrastructure, the entire
supply chain that stretches around the world from production and gathering
facilities to distribution to consumers.

Terrorists are not only seeking to wreak havoc and kill innocent people; they are also intent on waging economic warfare against the global economy. When Osama bin Laden threatens to attack the "hinges" of the American and world economy, he presumably means the critical infrastructures that run the modern economy—such as transportation, communications, information technology, finance, health, food—and of course energy. For terrorists from the Middle East, for whom Saudi Arabia is centrally in their sights, the energy system looms as an all-too-obvious target for disrupting both economy and society—and hitting, in the words of al Qaeda spokesmen, "the provision line and the feeding artery of the life of the crusader nation."

Tankers, which move well over half the world's oil, were already singled out as a target when a ship off the coast of Yemen was rammed by a boat filled with explosives in 2002. In addition to attacks on tankers on the high seas, there is particular concern about coordinated assaults that would scuttle ships and close down such critical shipping channels as the Strait of Hormuz and Bab el Mandeb, at the entrances respectively to the Persian Gulf and the Red Sea. The Bosphorus, running through Istanbul, is now a major channel for the export of Russian and Caspian oil to the world market. Of critical importance is the Strait of Malacca, between Malaysia and Indonesia, through which passes a quarter of world trade, including huge volumes of oil (80 percent of Japan's and South Korea's oil imports and about half of China's)—and which is already subject to continuing attacks by pirates.[6]

Much effort, in the aftermath of 9/11, has gone into addressing the security of energy infrastructure within the United States. Ports, for instance, are much better protected than previously. Still, some observers maintain that there is much more to do. The second Hart-Rudman study—following on its 2001 study that only attained the attention it deserved after 9/11—warned that the United States' energy infrastructure is "concentrated, sophisticated, and largely unprotected." Homeland security experts continue to warn that energy, along with other infrastructures, is poorly protected.[7]

While work has continued since that study, protecting energy infrastructure is not an easy job. The range is very wide—from pumping stations, gathering plants, and terminals, to tankers and pipelines, to refineries, power stations, and transmission lines, to distribution networks. And the scale in the United States is enormous—facilities to handle 14 million barrels per day of imports and exports; 4,000 offshore platforms; more than 150 refineries; 160,000 miles of crude oil pipelines; 10,400 power plants; 160,000 miles of high-voltage transmission lines and millions of miles of distribution wires; 410 underground gas storage fields; and 1.4 million miles of natural gas transmission and distribution lines. And much more. And, as it is today, some types of facilities, such as nuclear power plants, are much more secure than others.

Attacks could take the form of physical assaults on port facilities, refineries, petrochemical plants, compression stations, dams, transmission lines, and substations. These are easier to visualize. No less dangerous, however, would be another form—coordinated cyberattacks and electromagnetic attacks that would seek to break into control systems and take over control or disrupt them. There is nothing fanciful about that possibility. By one estimate, there are at least 30,000 sites on the Internet aimed at hackers. Some of them contain explicit instructions on how to launch an attack on energy and other infrastructure. Computers and notes recovered from al Qaeda operatives have included plans and diagrams for U.S. energy facilities.[8]

A study by the United States Energy Association identified three different kinds of threats. One is *attacks on energy systems.* The second is an *attack by an energy system*—for instance, using a power plant cooling tower to disperse chemical or biological agents. The third are *attacks through an energy system*—for instance, spreading chemical or biological agents through underground conduits.[9]

Not everything can be protected to the same degree. But the priorities are clear both for prevention and for recuperation. Beyond the buildup of general homeland security capabilities, they include:

- Increased personnel to guard facilities, heightened surveillance, and much-increased use of remote-sensing devices.
- Elevation of these issues in organizations, recognizing that they cut across existing organizational structure. Companies that formerly needed to think about incidents at a local facility now need to think how they fit into a national and global framework.
- Improved coordination among companies and government at all levels—and much improved coordination among federal, state, and local authorities, including clearer lines of authority both on a day-to-day basis and in an emergency.
- Stockpiling of critical components, such as transformers—in effect, strategic electric power reserves.
- Separation of control systems from the Internet, with a shift back to private networks.
- Installation of backup electric power supplies for key installations.
- Development and testing of contingency plans—including the adaptation

of contingency plans developed for environmental emergencies for security threats.
- Cooperation and training of "first responders."
- Research and development on threat detection and mitigation.

The August 2003 blackout, of course, underlined one very significant, immediate need—the urgency of upgrading and modernizing and protecting the electric transmission network.

The U.S. energy system was not designed with these new kinds of threats in mind. There is a gap, as the Silent Vector project at CSIS identified, between the traditional safety costs that the private sector internalizes and preparation for "terrorist strikes" that are "intentional and focused, designed for maximum catastrophic impact." Homeland security expert Stephen Flynn summarized the problem in simple terms: "Security is not free."[10] There is going to be a continuing cost for building a higher degree of security into the energy infrastructure, and that ultimately will need to be folded one way or the other both into the cost of homeland security that the nation bears and into the price of energy in the marketplace. That is a requirement for the enhanced energy security that America requires in this new era.

## Preparing for the Unexpected

This chapter began by quoting one British prime minister, Winston Churchill, on energy security. It ends by quoting another. When Margaret Thatcher was interviewed for *The Commanding Heights: The Battle for the World Economy,* she remarked, "Remember Thatcher's Law." She was asked what that law was. "The unexpected happens," she replied. "You had better prepare for it."[11] These days, one must be very mindful of surprises—whether in the Middle East, Venezuela, Eurasia, or Nigeria—or in places not being thought about in those terms today—or much closer to home. Thus Thatcher's Law remains a very good principle—indeed, an essential one—to keep in mind both now and in the future when it comes to the critical matter of energy security.

## Notes

1. *Parliamentary Debates,* Commons, July 17, 1913, 1474–77.
2. On conservation and energy efficiency, see the National Commission on Energy Policy, *Ending the Energy Stalemate: A Bipartisan Strategy to Meet America's Energy*

*Challenges,* December 2004, chaps. 1 and 3; Amory Lovins et al., *Winning the Oil Endgame* (Snowmass Colo.: Rocky Mountain Institute, 2004); and chap. 18 of this volume by Melanie Kenderine and Ernest Moniz. On the significance of technological change in the oil and gas industry, Cambridge Energy Research Associates, *In Search of Reasonable Certainty: Oil and Gas Reserves Disclosure,* chap. 5, "Technology: a Quarter Century of Transformation" (Cambridge, Mass.: CERA, 2005). On DOFF, Cambridge Energy Research Associates, *Digital Oil Field of the Future: Enabling Next Generation Reservoir Performance* (Cambridge, Mass.: CERA, 2003).

  3. Abdullah Jum'ah, Keynote Address, CERA Week, February 15, 2005, Houston.

  4. Daniel Yergin and Michael Stoppard, "The Next Prize," *Foreign Affairs,* November/December 2003; Robert Ineson, *On Course: North American LNG Surge Reaches the Shore,* Cambridge Energy Research Associate private report, 2005. For analysis of the safety considerations in LNG, see Sandia National Laboratories, *Guidance on Risk Analysis and Safety Implications of a Large Liquefied Natural gas (LNG) Spill over Water* (Alburquerque: Sandia, December 2004).

  5. Daniel Yergin, *The Prize: The Epic Quest for Oil, Money, and Power* (New York: Simon & Schuster, 1991), 373, 343–50.

  6. "Signs of Revived Qaeda Are Seen in Latest Strikes and New Tapes," *New York Times,* October 13, 2002; U.S. Department of Homeland Security, *The National Strategy for the Physical Protection of Critical Infrastructure and Key Assets* (Washington, D.C.: U.S. Government Printing Office, 2003). For al Qaeda spokesman, tankers, and Malacca Strait, see Gal Luft and Anne Korin, "Terrorism Goes to Sea,"*Foreign Affairs,* November/December 2004, and Henry J. Kenny, "China and the Competition for Oil and Gas in Asia," *Asia-Pacific Review* 11, no. 2 (2004), pp. 42–44.

  7. Council on Foreign Relations, *America Still Unprepared: America Still in Danger,* Report of an Independent Task Force, Gary Hart and Warren B. Rudman, cochairs (New York: Council on Foreign Relations, 2002); Stephen Flynn, "The Neglected Home Front," *Foreign Affairs,* September/October 2004.

  8. Ritchie Priddy, *Homeland Security: Protecting the Nation's Energy Infrastructure* (Cambridge, Mass.: Cambridge Energy Research Associates, 2003); Center for Strategic and International Studies, *Silent Vector: Issues of Concern and Policy Recommendations,* (Washington, D.C.: Center for Strategic and International Studies, 2003), chaps. 2 and 4; U.S. General Accounting Office, *Critical Infrastructure Protection: Challenges and Efforts to Secure Control Systems—Statement of Robert F. Dacey* (Washington, D.C.: U.S. Government Accountability Office, 2004); "Hackers Target U.S. Power Grid," *Washington Post,* March 11, 2005.

  9. United States Energy Association, *National Energy Security Post 9/11* (Washington, D.C.: United States Energy Association, 2002), 54.

  10. See U.S.–Canada Power System Outage Task Force, *August 14th Blackout: Causes and Recommendations* (Ottawa and Washington, D.C.: Natural Resources Canada and U.S. Department of Energy, 2004), 163–64; Center for Strategic and International Studies, *Silent Vector,* 17–19, 131–37; Flynn, "Neglected Home Front," 28; and 9/11 Commission, *The 9/11 Commission Report: Final Report of the National Commission on Terrorist Attacks Upon the United States* (Washington, D.C.: U.S. Government Printing Office, 2004), 397–98.

  11. Daniel Yergin and Joseph Stanislaw, *The Commanding Heights: The Battle for the World Economy* (New York: Touchstone, 2002), 105–6.

# 3

# OPEC in Confrontation with Globalization

## Edward L. Morse and Amy Myers Jaffe

Since the collapse of the Soviet Union, the United States has become, effectively, the sole world superpower, defending international peace and security and safeguarding the dependable operation of the international economic system. Michael Mandelbaum notes this in an essay on American power in *Foreign Affairs:* "It is a truth universally acknowledged that the central feature of the world at the outset of the twenty-first century is the enormous power of the United States."[1] As Mandelbaum and others have espoused, the United States plays a key role in defending, maintaining, and expanding the global system of free markets, with its military serving as the invisible hand, enforcing norms and safeguarding the system by ensuring that international commerce can proceed without the physical interdiction of international lanes of communications. The U.S. Navy's role in protecting the free flow of oil along international sea-lanes is an important example of how U.S. power protects international commerce and the global economic system.

The United States as the world's lone superpower has been evoked as evidence of, if not justification for, its geopolitical unilateralism. Liberal authors such as G. John Ikenberry have gone so far as to warn that the U.S. tendency to impose global standards and to determine and police threats unilaterally will trigger resistance, possibly becoming counterproductive over time.[2] The predominant role of the U.S. military in protecting the free flow of oil from the Persian Gulf perhaps gives the impression, not without some rationale, that America alone manages energy security both for itself and for the world community. However, managing international energy security, or U.S. energy security for that matter, is a more complicated matter of interdependencies that cannot be handled effectively either unilaterally or solely by military means.[3]

Unquestionably, there are limits to the U.S. ability to impose its vision of international peace, democracy, and free markets. When it comes to oil, the industrial democracies must import supplies from countries that remain outside the inner sanctum of the Western consensus on economic and political liberalization, democratization, and free trade. This has meant that in the area of energy security, despite three decades of trying, neither the United States alone nor the Organization for Economic Cooperation and Development (OECD) collectively has been able to counterbalance fully the monopoly power of the Organization of Petroleum Exporting Countries (OPEC). OPEC, by its very existence as a functioning, if not always successfully, commodity cartel, defies the principles of market liberalization and free trade. After 2003, world oil prices averaged their highest levels since 1981, partly as a result of OPEC's efforts to manipulate markets by artificially limiting supply.

Years of fostering supplies outside OPEC, while successful, have not changed the picture for U.S. energy security in any fundamental manner, given a comparable rise in demand for these added supplies. Today, just as in the 1970s, the U.S. oil supply continues to be highly insecure. Industrial countries have to worry increasingly about the internal stability of key oil-producing countries. New concerns have arisen regarding the threat of international terrorism to important energy targets. In some quarters, the link between oil revenues and the financing of terrorism is seen as so tight that fears have grown about the consequences of high oil prices and the flow of funds from oil revenues. There are also growing concerns about the looming competition for energy supplies from emerging economies such as China and India.

OPEC's ability to raise prices in the short run to levels damaging to the major consuming economies poses a major policy challenge to their governments.[4] Rising oil prices threaten consumer-country national interests in several ways. Oil price volatility can inhibit investment, economic growth and spur inflation.[5] Rising energy import costs also threaten social stability in such key regional consuming countries as India and Pakistan, and in Southeast Asia. Supply constraints also make it easier for governments or subnational groups with potential leverage over oil supply chains to threaten the vital interests of the United States and its allies.

Thus, consuming countries have a clear interest in undertaking policies that will undermine both OPEC's short-term and long-term ability to act as a cartel to inflate oil prices. Policy stances taken in conjunction with other consuming nations are likely to be more effective than those taken individually by increasing the strength of the so-called monopsony wedge, that is, the collective buying power of major oil using nations.[6]

The United States led the charge in this direction in the late 1970s, sponsoring the formation of the International Energy Agency (IEA) as the vehicle to foster the interests of oil-consuming countries. But in recent years, the world's superpower seems to have lost interest in fostering a long-term vision for the energy sector, favoring politically expedient, unfettered domestic consumption and rising imports over conservation and energy taxes.

The United States now stands alone among the OECD countries in key areas of energy policy. Japan and the European Union, unlike the United States, have imposed huge taxes on oil consumption of 400 percent or more, virtually halting the growth in oil demand and promoting energy-efficient technologies, including automobiles that allow drivers to travel more each year using less fuel. Japan is at the forefront of exporting energy-efficient motor vehicles. Europe is also leading the way, as a top user of renewable energy in electricity generation. The United States, by contrast, has taken a reverse course; its rising imports are now the most significant subsidizer of OPEC. U.S. oil imports represent 50 percent of OPEC's gain in market sales during the decade 1990–2000.

In 1973, the West vowed to become less reliant on OPEC. The formation of the IEA was a strong first step. In fact, the vision for the IEA remains as valid today as it did then: It is beneficial to share the burden of supply disruptions equitably, to foster diversity of fuels and of supply, to build strategic stocks to deter geopolitical blackmail, and to push for liberalized markets with open access to resource development and trade.

This chapter seeks to put such goals in perspective against the backdrop of OPEC's astonishing cohesion and endurance over the past thirty-plus years. We review the key drivers of OPEC's remarkable unity and the challenges that a globalized world poses to OPEC's future success. Finally, we explore options for the United States to creatively combat OPEC's influence, especially in the geopolitical circumstances emerging in the aftermath of the September 11, 2001, terrorist attacks. We argue that pressing a vision of a free and depoliticized market for oil should be on the top of the international agenda, with Western nations, particularly the United States, leading the charge.

## OPEC's Success, Western Losses: The $4 Trillion Transfer

OPEC has been one of the most remarkable success stories and also one of the most extraordinary anomalies in the global economy for over forty years. It is a success story because, despite persistent forecasts that it is doomed to fail, it has not simply managed to survive but can be credited with succeeding in its basic objectives: defending and supporting the income and revenue aims of its members, and forcing any burden of adjustment to higher oil prices on other countries. Yet, in an era marked by market liberalization, the retreat of the state from intervention in the economy, and the spread of the values associated with competition, OPEC remains a noteworthy exception: a persistent anticompetitive force in the world marketplace.

OPEC's remarkable endurance at the center of the global petroleum market is both an economic puzzle and an intriguing subject, even an enigma of world politics. It is an economic puzzle because it is such a striking anachronism. For the past three quarters of a century, governments have been retreating from playing more than a guiding role in their economies. They have relinquished the use of economic instruments both at home and at their borders, have fostered deregulation and liberalization, and have promoted unfettered flows of capital, goods, services, and to a substantial extent even labor. The assumption has been that free flows foster greater efficiencies and higher growth, leaving citizens at home better off.[7]

It is a political enigma and intriguing subject, for two critical reasons. First, given the differences in position, values, and objectives of the members of the producer group, it is extraordinary that they have managed to stick together for more than forty years. The variation among them includes members with extremely high reserves and a long reserve life (called the reserve-to-production ratio), as well as those with extremely short reserve lives. They have radically different political regimes, ranging from authoritarian to democratic to social democratic republics to Islamic republics and traditional monarchies. Some want high prices, others much lower prices, depending on their reserve levels; some want to cooperate closely with large oil-consuming countries, whereas others prefer confrontation; and some members have even gone to war with one another.

OPEC's endurance is also mysterious because it depends to a large degree on the willingness—even the collaboration—of key oil-importing countries, including the United States, which, when it comes to economic values, stand for a world that is radically different from the one espoused by OPEC. Why does the international community tolerate this state of affairs? Is dependence on OPEC's resources so high that the costs of lowering it are intolerable? Or are there other interests to protect at home and abroad in tolerating OPEC's market-making power?

## What Drives OPEC?

Three forces drive OPEC's origins and its continued endurance. What unites these three drivers and makes them so powerful is that they are defensive. OPEC members take action, first of all, for critical *domestic* reasons: to protect and, when possible, to increase their revenues. Second, they have a desire, in the interdependent international economy, to push the burden of adjustment to changing circumstances onto others and away from their own domestic economies. Third, they act together with the view that only through the collective action with other countries sharing a similar set of circumstances can they achieve their first two objectives.

Underlying these three drivers are geopolitical facts of life. From the time when five governments met in 1960 to found OPEC through today, the countries that make up OPEC collectively hold a disproportionate share of global oil resources as well as of the global petroleum market. The key members are also, perhaps to a greater degree than some other hydrocarbon-rich countries, uniquely dependent upon oil exploitation in their economies, which are neither diversified nor capable (at least until now) of finding means to fill government coffers other than through international sales of petroleum and petroleum products.

The essentially defensive nature of OPEC was apparent at the origins when the five founding members—Iran, Iraq, Kuwait, Saudi Arabia, and Venezuela—came together in 1960 in the face of oil price reductions.[8] These price reductions, of course, came in a context of fifteen years of frustration with respect to sharing in the profitability of oil production and the revenue received by host governments for oil produced inside their borders.[9]

The fundamental factor driving the price reductions was the decision by the United States to impose mandatory quotas on oil imports in 1958 to protect its maturing and costly production base—the quotas brought U.S. prices well above prevailing international levels and allowed U.S. producers to satisfy refinery needs, and pushed out imports from the recently discovered producing fields of what became OPEC. Thus, by 1960, U.S. domestic prices rose to an average of $2.80 per barrel, while prevailing prices for internationally traded oil fell to $1.80. The main motivation was clear:

income. The five founding members wanted to put pressure on the companies operating in their territories to, in turn, put pressure on the U.S. government to reduce, if not eliminate, the quotas. The producers also wanted to raise their revenues at the expense of the companies operating in their countries. Ultimately, the producers also hoped to raise prices.[10]

By the late 1960s, certain OPEC countries, starting with Iraq and Iran, widened their ambitions to include the nationalization of oil fields in an effort to prevent international oil companies from penalizing recalcitrant OPEC members by underproducing local oil fields to squeeze economic concessions from the OPEC host governments. In June 1968, OPEC adopted the General Declaration of Petroleum Policy, which proclaimed the "permanent and inalienable sovereignty" of the governments over their natural resources, and called on its members to acquire the greatest possible interest in existing oil concessions. Iraq began to nationalize its concessions in June 1972. Other Middle Eastern OPEC member countries followed suit, leading to a deintegration of the international oil industry during the following decade.[11]

These essentially defensive motivations for unified action have characterized much of OPEC's behavior ever since. Its unity appears strongest when its members need to work together to keep a floor under prices to prevent a collapse in income.[12] The events of 1998–99 drove this point home when a sudden drop in the price of oil below $10 wreaked havoc on the economies of OPEC members, splitting open simmering domestic political fissures and creating strong pressures on local regimes.

Unlike the 1985 oil price collapse, which convinced OPEC of the need to cooperate but was brought on by a recession in the West caused in good measure by the oil price shocks of the 1970s, the 1998 crisis drove home a new point to OPEC members: how changes in oil prices can work asymmetrically in the international economy. Relatively low oil prices hurt the economies of the OPEC countries severely through the late 1980s and sporadically into the 1990s. Middle Eastern OPEC members actually saw per capita income in their countries fall over the period. This strongly contrasts with the economic boom that accompanied low energy prices for the developing economies in Asia and Latin America, for example, where economic growth averaged in some cases more than 10 percent a year. With globalization proceeding, OPEC members became more concerned with their own economic performance relative to other nations and rejected the notion that low oil prices were good for everyone.

For key OPEC countries, whose oil revenues were critical to meeting government budgets, the impact of falling oil prices was perceived as far

*Table 3.1. OPEC Export Revenues, 1996–2003 (billions of nominal dollars)*

| Country or Group | Year | | | | | | | |
|---|---|---|---|---|---|---|---|---|
| | 1996 | 1997 | 1998 | 1999 | 2000 | 2001 | 2002 | 2003 |
| Saudi Arabia | 51.6 | 48.0 | 28.6 | 40.2 | 74.0 | 60.1 | 58.0 | 80.8 |
| Iran | 16.7 | 16.2 | 10.5 | 14.6 | 22.6 | 19.8 | 19.0 | 23.9 |
| Kuwait | 13.8 | 13.4 | 8.1 | 10.8 | 18.7 | 15.3 | 11.6 | 18.7 |
| Iraq | 1.1 | 4.9 | 6.9 | 12.9 | 20.2 | 15.9 | 12.4 | 9.6 |
| United Arab Emirates | 16.8 | 17.6 | 12.2 | 15.7 | 25.5 | 21.2 | 18.7 | 23.7 |
| Venezuela | 18.3 | 17.7 | 11.5 | 14.9 | 25.0 | 20.6 | 19.7 | 20.6 |
| Other five OPEC members | 43.1 | 41.3 | 26.7 | 36.1 | 60.1 | 51.1 | 49.5 | 62.9 |
| Total for all OPEC members | 171.5 | 166.0 | 104.4 | 145.3 | 246.0 | 204.1 | 188.9 | 240.2 |

*Sources:* U.S. Department of Energy, independent estimates.

greater than the impact of higher prices on most oil-importing countries, for which the oil import bill is a fraction of total trade. This is partly because many consuming countries followed domestic policies to diversify to other fuels or to tax oil use to hold down demand growth for oil. Key OPEC members began to resent the suffering they experienced from low oil prices, which appeared to be also providing a subsidy for growth in other countries. Hence they concluded that it was desirable to shift the burden of price adjustment onto the oil-importing community.

The critical aspects of these drivers can be seen in table 3.1, which reviews the export revenues (in the nominal dollars of the day) of OPEC countries from 1996 to 2003. Oil prices reached their highest level of the decade in 1996–97, and total export earnings for the OPEC countries hovered around $170 billion. But the next year oil prices collapsed, as export earnings plunged, in some cases by almost 50 percent. The internal pain in these countries, as well as in other oil-exporting countries, including Mexico and Oman, was comparable to the pain felt in oil importing countries in 1973–74, when oil prices quadrupled. In Indonesia, Iran, Nigeria, Russia, and Venezuela, because governments were unable to provide basic services, they lost authority and changes occurred, sometimes peacefully and sometimes not. With no help forthcoming from the industrial world, the oil producers were compelled to act together, to cut production and to shift the burden of higher prices to oil-importing countries. Adding insult to injury, the OECD countries complained about higher prices, even though world economic growth continued apace and the burden on key developing economies like China, India, and Chile appeared comparatively trivial.

The price collapse of 1998 not only drove home the need for collective action. It also prompted new politics inside the producer organization. The mid-1990s had been characterized by general OPEC disunity and over-production—so much so that OPEC members themselves questioned the future viability of the organization. Venezuela embarked on an ambitious campaign to increase oil productive capacity from 2.8 million barrels per day (mmbpd) in 1991 to 7 mmbpd by 2010. Iraq aggressively increased oil exports through the United Nations Oil-for-Food program. And Saudi Arabia, concerned with the long-range implications of Venezuela's market expansion on the Kingdom's ability to maintain its sales to the United States, increased production.[13] All these factors, combined with then-rising oil prices, made it almost impossible for the producer group to agree on a workable production-sharing arrangement.

OPEC infighting came against the backdrop of an unexpected economic meltdown in much of Asia that precipitated an unexpected drop in Asian oil use in 1997–98. In addition, two warm winters in a row had stagnated OECD winter demand. Asian oil demand fell by 1.9 percent in 1998, after a 4.5 percent rise in Asian oil demand between 1996 and 1997 (table 3.2). The slowdown in Asia contributed to a major change in the global oil supply/demand balance, limiting the growth in worldwide oil demand to 74.24 mmbpd in 1998, up only 0.5 percent from 1997. Annual growth rates averaged 2 to 3 percent in the mid-1990s.[14]

By 1997–98, the combined downturn in demand and overproduction in OPEC led oil prices to collapse below $10. This required extraordinary efforts by OPEC and non-OPEC countries Mexico and Norway, reportedly with the blessing of the U.S. government, which had become concerned about

*Table 3.2. Oil Demand by Region, 1996–98 (million barrels per day and percent change)*

| Region or Country | 1996 | 1997 | Percent Change | 1998 | Percent Change |
|---|---|---|---|---|---|
| World | 72.03 | 73.9 | 2.6 | 74.24 | 0.5 |
| United States | 18.25 | 18.62 | 2.0 | 18.7 | 0.4 |
| European Union (15 members) | 13.03 | 13.10 | 0.5 | 13.39 | 2.2 |
| Asia | 17.74 | 18.53 | 4.5 | 18.18 | –1.9 |
| China | 3.55 | 11.5 | 11.5 | 3.95 | –0.3 |

*Source:* James A. Baker III Institute for Public Policy.

the adverse consequences of extremely low oil prices on key oil-producing allies.[15] Since the 1999–2000 crisis-inspired rapprochement inside OPEC, the organization has developed a new dynamic that must be taken into account in predicting its future behavior and in developing the proper diplomatic and countermeasures to counteract its monopoly power.

OPEC's new impetus to collaboration is rooted in several factors.[16] First, political changes at the highest levels inside several key OPEC countries, such as Saudi Arabia, Venezuela, and Kuwait, have moved the agenda of the organization away from the moderate policies of the 1990s toward a more radical, confrontational developing-world approach that favors revenues over other issues, including market share. Second, a rise in democratization, freedom of the press, and political debate and a growing tide of anti-Americanism are bringing a greater concern for popular opinion inside OPEC countries, especially in the Middle Eastern Gulf. This new concern for popular sentiment is restricting the options of regional leaders to accommodate Western interests. Populations, as well as some leaders, remain bitter about the suffering that took place when oil prices collapsed in the late 1990s. Third, rapidly increasing populations and economic stagnation in many OPEC countries have meant that revenue pressures take precedence over other considerations. Fourth, a lack of investment in infrastructure and oil fields over the years due to tight state treasuries and rising social pressures has greatly curtailed OPEC's spare productive capacity, making it much easier to agree to restrain output.

In fact, OPEC's decision in 2000 to raise the target for its price band for the basket of OPEC crude oil streams within a range of $22 to $28 was more aggressive than defensive.[17] Critical to the newer OPEC consensus is the view that OPEC is in a position to stand up to the West and that it should feel justified in doing so, because the West stood by and did nothing to help ease the debilitating suffering and destabilizing consequences of the 1998 price collapse. Thus, OPEC producers became less swayed to consider boosting production or reducing prices as favors for consumer economies battling against economic slowdown and possible recession.

The producers are also more sensitive to changes in their purchasing power as the value of the dollar changes against other currencies. Their options are to change their prices from dollars to another currency like the euro, or to adjust prices to changes in the dollar's value. OPEC rhetoric has taken a turn to the left, demanding a "fair" price for OPEC oil. "Fair" generally means "high" by Western standards. The debate has become one of economic struggle for "rents" between oil producers that demand high revenues and major consumers whose economies can grow faster with low oil prices.

The OPEC countries' rhetoric is reminiscent of the 1970s, when OPEC in its infancy complained that the Western oil companies were unjustly depriving them of a fair share of the rents of their national patrimony. Today, this line of reasoning is directed not at the private international oil companies but at OECD consumer governments, which capture rents from oil sales through high national energy taxes. "People always talk about the revenues of OPEC," said OPEC president Chakib Khelil to the press following the March 16–17, 2001, OPEC meeting. "Before they point a finger at OPEC, they should probably reduce taxes in their own country."[18]

Although the antitax rhetoric is not new to OPEC, its political weight has a different, more radicalized character today and serves as a clearer justification and impetus for production restraints that do not accommodate Western interests. OPEC's antitax, anti-Western rhetoric reflects popular domestic sentiment that governments are not doing enough to deliver economic benefits to a substantial portion of the population. The leaders of OPEC countries cannot be seen as delivering benefits to Western consumers at the expense of their own citizens. Such perceptions would leave regimes more vulnerable to public attack and to the efforts of opposition groups.[19] In most OPEC countries, the press and political processes are becoming more open and therefore leaders can no longer disregard public opinion in favor of other interests. Kuwait has a strong and influential Parliament to consider in setting oil policy. Saudi Arabia must worry about an increasingly active and sometimes violent opposition with an increasingly anti-American bent.

In Venezuela, Nigeria, and Indonesia, for example, attitudes against accommodating the West with moderate oil prices are fed by years of corruption in the high ranks of government and long-standing social and economic stratification. In the Persian Gulf, economic hardship, anti-Americanism related to the Arab-Israeli conflict and the resource patrimony-style propaganda of Iraq's former Saddam regime propel similar attitudes about oil price policy in the Arab "street." Saddam had argued for years that the United States, through corrupt puppet regimes in the Gulf, exercised its global hegemony and denied the Arabs their rightful earnings from oil. He even described the Gulf War as an effort by the United States to deprive the Iraqis and other Arabs of the right to garner "fair" value for their national patrimony–oil resources.[20] Al Qaeda leader Osama bin Laden mentions low oil prices as a Western crime against the Muslim world in his treatise "Letter to the American People."

Saudi Arabia's increasingly hawkish stance, first taken during Bill Clinton's administration, has given OPEC the solidarity needed to turn idle rhetoric into political action. OPEC's more strident position would not be possible without the consent of Saudi Arabia, which suffered heavily financially in 1998. Saudi Arabia increasingly worries about internal opposition, and its authority is strained by the regime's close relations with the United States, which is increasingly viewed with hostility by the average Saudi for supporting a bellicose Israel.

But internal Saudi politics is not the only factor compelling a shift in Saudi orientation. Even before 9/11, Crown Prince Abdullah began pursuing a more regional policy focus, supporting a rapprochement with Iran and publicly expressing concerns about the fate of the Iraqi people and the Palestinians.[21] He has exhibited more reluctance to cater to U.S. wishes than King Fahd demonstrated in the 1980s and early 1990s.[22] He seems willing to test the premise that the United States has no choice but to accept less compliant Saudi positions due to the West's high dependence on Saudi oil. Cooperation is important to Saudi Arabia, but not at the expense of its own people's needs.

After 1999, while the U.S. government has been sympathetic to Saudi desires for higher oil prices, Washington has clearly been expressing a preference for prices toward the lower end of the OPEC basket, more toward $22 than to $28 a barrel.[23] The Saudis, however, increasingly looked for higher and higher effective floor prices, and for a long time OPEC, under Saudi leadership, has been able to achieve that goal. By mid-2004, Saudi Arabia unofficially was sanctioning prices in the mid-$30s. Later that year, as oil prices soared above $50, Saudi Arabia was forced to admit publicly that it had actually lost control of the market.

## Other Glues That Bind: Enforcement by a Dominant Producer

We have emphasized the communality of interests of OPEC producers as a critical driving force explaining OPEC's endurance and durability, especially after the oil price collapse of 1998. But Saudi Arabia's inclination to undertake a price war, when required, through the role it can play of swing producer that can punish uncooperative members, should not be ignored.[24]

In particular, the most important trend inside OPEC in the late 1990s, as discussed above, was the Saudi government's realization that Caracas had taken a course that put it in direct conflict with Riyadh.

In the early 1990s, Venezuela took steps to complete the internationalization program that it had embarked upon in the 1980s. The first stages of that program involved the acquisition of refining and marketing assets in Europe (Veba Oil) and the United States (a series of accords, focused on the 100 percent acquisition of Citgo). The new phase involved the reopening of Venezuela's nationalized and monopolized petroleum sector to international investment, via association agreements to rehabilitate old fields, as well as some greenfield projects. The goal was simple: increase production capacity from the range of 2.5 to 2.8 mmbpd that Venezuela had in 1990 to upward of 7 mmbpd by 2010. With higher capital expenditures by both the state-owned company Petróleos de Venezuela (PdVSA) and foreign contractors, Venezuela progressively upped its production, so that by mid-1997, the country's production capacity and its production had had both increased to 3.7 mmbpd, against its OPEC quota of 2.3 mmbpd. The relentless march to higher output would not stop.[25] In January 1997, Venezuela overtook Saudi Arabia as the number one crude oil supplier to the United States.

Concerned with the consequences of being usurped as the United States' most important supplier, the Saudi government began high-level negotiations with the Venezuelan government and quietly tried to pressure Venezuela to comply with the country's OPEC quota. Caracas ignored the Saudi efforts and persisted in its all-out production policy, continuing to ratchet up output and flaunting its defiance against the Saudis.[26] In turn, Saudi Arabia opened its own taps, raising its production from slightly above its 8 mmbpd quota in September 1996, to 8.5 mmbpd for virtually all of 1997.[27] The intention was to bring down prices to punish Caracas and induce Venezuela to cooperate. The Saudis succeeded more than they could have wished. The combined overproduction of the two countries turned out to be just about exactly the amount of extra oil inventory that built up in the world, some 400 million barrels, contributing to a price collapse from $27 a barrel (West Texas Intermediate) in the spring of 1997 to $10 in the winter of 1998–99.

This event was a stunning reminder of the special glue that binds OPEC countries together—fear that the Saudis will use their own oil weapon for punitive purposes and for discipline within the producer group.[28] In game-theoretic terms, OPEC politics involves a dominant producer—Saudi Arabia —and the peripheral countries—the other OPEC members. The dominant producer's motive is to assure itself the maximum autonomy while preventing the others from "free riding" on its efforts to manage the market.[29] It does so by maintaining its "deterrent," consisting of its shut-in production capacity, which it can use to feed the market and to discipline other producers. The peripheral countries, conversely, try to work together to prevent the dominant producer from acting on its own to produce flat out but rather offer cooperation as a means to ensure a floor under prices.

The disciplining of Venezuela has had obvious consequences: It helped usher in a regime change in Venezuela, a radical reduction of Venezuelan upstream capital expenditures, and a withering of its production capacity. This was not the first time Saudi Arabia used its oil weapon to achieve its ends. In 1985, the Kingdom rewrote the rules of oil pricing by suddenly adopting so-called netback pricing to replace administered pricing, [30] assuring itself a significantly larger market share. The kingdom increased its output from 2.3 mmbpd to more than 6 mmbpd nearly overnight and in the process of increasing its market share also brought prices down from the high $20 range to under $10 a barrel. A side benefit of the price collapse and keeping prices low was pressuring the Soviet Union after its invasion of Afghanistan, by depriving Moscow of revenues to pursue the battles there. Then, in 1988–89, Saudi Arabia turned on the taps and brought prices down at the end of the Iran–Iraq War, the very moment when the two former combatants were ready to increase output. The lesson many have drawn from that was that Riyadh wanted to make sure that neither of those fellow OPEC countries would gain the financial wherewithal to threaten the Kingdom.

There is no doubt that without the Saudi weapon, OPEC cooperation would be far shorter-lived than it has been. Other members are mindful of the damage Saudi Arabia can inflict over the short run with increased production.

## The Price of Success: Production Capacity and Market Share

A great irony of OPEC's success is that it has come at an extraordinary cost–loss of market share and a whittling away of spare capacity that could be a major long-term challenge for the organization's ability to regulate market prices at will in the future. The deterioration of OPEC's position in the oil market over the past twenty-five years is stunning. At the end of the 1970s, just before Iraq attacked Iran, OPEC production and production capacity were at their peaks. OPEC peak production hit 31.3 mmbpd in 1977, when global production reached 62.7 mmbpd. The cartel had 50 percent of the global market in terms of production. But in terms of global oil trade, it had a full 75 percent market share, because all U.S. production and almost all Soviet production (totaling 21 mmbpd) was consumed domestically.[31] Though it is hard to pinpoint total global production capacity at the time, there are common estimates that in 1979, when OPEC was producing 31.2 mmbpd (against a total world production base of 66.05 mmbd), its capacity had reached as much as 38 mmbpd. That is because until well into the 1970s, the international oil companies dominated the upstream and planned their incremental investment almost entirely within the OPEC countries, to meet global demand, which had been increasing at a brisk 7.5 percent annual rate for two decades.

OPEC adopted the strategy of withholding output and sharing production on a pro rata basis, at first informally and then more formally in the 1980s. The strategy of placing a floor under prices required giving up market share, a dramatically difficult task considering that global consumption fell from 64 mmbpd in 1979 to 58 mmbpd in 1983, a time when non-OPEC production rose from 31 to 38 mmbpd. As a result, OPEC's output was reduced from 31.3 to 16.7 mmbpd, a loss of market share of an incredible 14.6 mmbpd in a period of five years. OPEC's spare capacity, as a result, was equal to its total production, a situation that persisted for several years (see table 3.3).

With such high levels of unused capacity, and government revenues under pressure, OPEC cut back on its ongoing upstream investments. OPEC countries' decisions to limit oil field capacity investment stems, in good measure, from the nature of their incremental decision making. Underlying OPEC's ideology is the view that the future is theirs and worth waiting for. With more than 78 percent of the world's oil reserves, OPEC countries have banked their future on a combination of growth in oil demand and a presumed "natural" limit to the growth of non-OPEC production. What is more, for most of the time since 1985, "history" has appeared to be on their side. OPEC's capacity utilization was about 50 percent in 1985–87, but then it grew substantially. Starting in the late 1980s, global oil demand recovered and rose at a healthy rate of 1.5 to 2 percent a year for a long period. OPEC was able to fill much of this incremental demand, clawing back some of its market share. More important, after 1999, tightening market conditions—combined with production setbacks in Iraq and Venezuela—have meant that most of OPEC's excess shut-in capacity has been called back into use (table 3.4).

OPEC's failure to expand its capacity is not only the result of a binding strategy. A second critical factor has to do with the internal structures of the

*Table 3.3. OPEC Production Capacity, 1979–2003 (million barrels per day)*

| OPEC Member Country | 1979 | 1983 | 1990 | 1998 | 2000 | 2001 | 2003 |
|---|---|---|---|---|---|---|---|
| Saudi Arabia[a] | 10.84 | 11.30 | 8.00 | 9.65 | 9.90 | 9.90 | 10.15 |
| Iran | 7.00 | 3.00 | 3.10 | 3.70 | 3.75 | 4.05 | 3.8 |
| Iraq | 4.00 | 1.50 | 3.60 | 2.30 | 2.90 | 3.05 | 2.7 |
| Kuwait[a] | 3.34 | 2.80 | 2.40 | 2.70 | 2.40 | 2.40 | 2.5 |
| United Arab Emirates | 2.50 | 2.90 | 2.20 | 2.40 | 2.39 | 2.45 | 2.5 |
| Qatar | 0.65 | 0.65 | 0.40 | 0.71 | 0.73 | 0.75 | 0.75 |
| Venezuela | 2.40 | 2.50 | 2.60 | 3.45 | 2.98 | 3.10 | 2.75 |
| Nigeria | 2.50 | 2.40 | 1.80 | 2.30 | 2.10 | 2.30 | 2.3 |
| Indonesia | 1.80 | 1.60 | 1.25 | 1.40 | 1.35 | 1.30 | 1.15 |
| Libya | 2.50 | 2.00 | 1.50 | 1.45 | 1.45 | 1.45 | 1.45 |
| Algeria | 1.23 | 1.10 | 0.75 | 0.88 | 0.88 | 0.88 | 1.15 |
| Total | 38.76 | 31.75 | 27.60 | 30.94 | 30.83 | 31.63 | 31.20 |

[a] Saudi Arabian and Kuwaiti figures each include half the production from the Neutral Zone between the two countries.
*Source:* Data are from *Petroleum Intelligence Weekly.*

oil industry in most large producing OPEC countries. For almost all of them, reserves were discovered and developed by international oil companies (IOCs), not by the national oil companies (NOCs) that came to dominate the upstream after the 1970s. With the exception of Saudi Aramco, no NOC in any OPEC country has a good track record in exploration and development. Within OPEC, it has been difficult for NOCs to muster the capital, technology, and human resource capabilities required to find and develop significant volumes of oil. What is more, when it comes to capital, short-term financial requirements for managing the economy and maintaining public order have been so great as to limit the amount of capital the NOCs can access for development purposes.

Suspicion of the IOCs is a lingering artifact of the resource nationalism of the 1970s—suspicion of the IOCs' motivations and fear that they will earn "exceptional" profits for their endeavors. The IOCs have generally aimed to achieve returns well above 15 percent on their capital deployment, a relatively modest level considering the risks involved in exploration and production; but even that level of return has encountered political opposition in many oil-producing countries in the Middle East. Thus, for example, despite the reopening of the Iranian upstream sector in the mid-1990s to foreign investment, Iranian production continues to stagnate at a level of about 4.0 mmbpd, well under the 7 mmbpd capacity of prerevolutionary Iran. In neighboring Kuwait, political obstacles imposed by the Parliament slowed down the government's efforts, which had been under way since 1991, to

Table 3.4. OPEC Bumps against Capacity Constraints, January 1999–Mid-2004 (million barrels per day)

| Country or Group | January 1999 | | | January 2000 | | | June 2004 | | |
|---|---|---|---|---|---|---|---|---|---|
| | Deemed Capacity | Production | Spare Capacity | Deemed Capacity | Production | Spare Capacity | Deemed Capacity | Production | Spare Capacity |
| Saudi Arabia | 9.28 | 8.10 | 1.18 | 9.40 | 8.89 | 0.51 | 10.30 | 9.50 | 0.80 |
| Iran | 3.65 | 3.63 | 0.02 | 3.75 | 3.75 | 0.00 | 3.95 | 3.95 | 0.00 |
| Kuwait | 2.25 | 2.00 | 0.25 | 2.25 | 2.18 | 0.07 | 2.40 | 2.20 | 0.29 |
| United Arab Emirates | 2.40 | 2.16 | 0.24 | 2.40 | 2.35 | 0.05 | 2.50 | 2.31 | 0.23 |
| Qatar | 0.71 | 0.66 | 0.05 | 0.73 | 0.73 | 0.00 | 0.80 | 0.75 | 0.11 |
| Venezuela | 3.20 | 2.98 | 0.22 | 2.95 | 2.95 | 0.00 | 2.75 | 2.60 | 0.16 |
| Nigeria | 2.20 | 2.04 | 0.16 | 2.20 | 2.18 | 0.02 | 2.30 | 2.30 | 0.05 |
| Indonesia | 1.36 | 1.36 | 0.00 | 1.22 | 1.22 | 0.00 | 1.00 | 1.00 | 0.05 |
| Libya | 1.45 | 1.35 | 0.10 | 1.45 | 1.45 | 0.00 | 1.50 | 1.45 | 0.05 |
| Algeria | 0.88 | 0.80 | 0.08 | 0.88 | 0.87 | 0.01 | 1.25 | 1.20 | 0.00 |
| OPEC (10 members) | 27.38 | 25.08 | 2.30 | 27.23 | 26.57 | 0.66 | 28.75 | 27.26 | 1.69 |
| Iraq | 2.60 | 2.60 | 0.00 | 2.68 | 1.32 | 1.36 | 2.50 | 2.50 | 0.20 |
| Total | 29.98 | 27.68 | 2.30 | 29.91 | 27.89 | 2.02 | 31.25 | 29.76 | 2.38 |

Source: Hess Energy Trading Company.

attract foreign capital to the upstream. With the sole exception of Saudi Arabia, many OPEC countries are opting to rely again on the IOCs for capacity growth in the years ahead, a factor we will examine further below.

Philosophy aside, OPEC's success after 1999 in maintaining revenue is due in part to the limited spare capacity of its members to violate production-sharing agreements. Unlike years gone by, when the producer group had 3 to 6 mmbpd of spare capacity shut in to defend oil prices, after 1998 spare capacity fell sharply, facilitating agreements. OPEC governments, reacting to the financial suffering caused when oil prices dropped precipitously in 1998, became cautious about expanding capacity, realizing instead that greater revenue would be best achieved not by bringing new oil production capacity on line but rather by curtailing output.

The rapid deterioration of OPEC's spare capacity after 1999 has also come against the backdrop of rising global oil demand and decreased investment in oil resources, including Iran, Iraq, and Libya, due partly to long-standing U.S. unilateral and multilateral sanctions against them. U.S. sanctions policy has constrained capacity expansion to some extent in Iran and Libya, although the unilateral aspect of the U.S. action limited its impact.[32] In the case of Iraq, UN sanctions imposed as a result of the Iraqi invasion of Kuwait had a severe effect on Iraqi production—the negative impact of which still lingers, despite the removal of Iraqi leader Saddam Hussein.

Sanctions have constrained investment in several key OPEC countries and aggravated the global problem of spare production capacity by concentrating it in a much smaller pool of producers compared with the 1980s. Saudi Arabia's high and growing level of production and the lack of significant spare unutilized capacity outside the Kingdom have spotlighted that country's critical role in determining the state of current and future oil markets, in turn creating unique political pressures and augmenting a so-called terror premium onto world oil prices due to worries about the Kingdom's internal stability.

Several key producing countries remain closed to investment. Encouragement of open investment policies in these countries would greatly promote renewed competition among the largest oil producers and the advancement of oil supplies in the coming decade.

## OPEC's Dilemmas and Consumer-Country Choices

As the twenty-first century opens, critical choices confront OPEC and the industrial world, for much of the system that has been developed during the past two decades has become increasingly tenuous. Though OPEC has overcome significant challenges over the years, will new challenges pose insurmountable obstacles to OPEC's continued survival in its current form and to its successful endurance? This section reviews and evaluates some of the more significant challenges the producer group and its members confront.

## Declining Market Share and the Russian Renaissance

OPEC's experience has demonstrated the difficulty of both defending overall oil price levels and maintaining minimum market share without cooperation from other oil-exporting countries. In 1998, the producer group called for cooperation from other key oil producers—such as Russia (which has 10 percent of the world market), Norway (8 percent), Mexico (5 percent), and Oman (3 percent)—to help support prices.

But the cooperation of these non-OPEC countries has a price. For Norway and Mexico, the circumstances that gave rise to cooperation in 1998 were exceptional, because oil prices had fallen to extremely low levels and their national interests were challenged. After prices rose, several important non-OPEC producers—such as Mexico, Angola, and Russia—used their higher revenues to increase production capacity, opening the possibility of an intensification and renewal of competition with OPEC.

Garnering the cooperation from these producers poses specific problems, especially where Russia is concerned. Until 2003, when the Russian Duma (parliament) provided legislation that enabled the government to limit exports through tax policy, the government had few instruments at its disposal to restrain exports. Since then, while Moscow has centralized many controls, it also developed global ambitions as the world's largest hydrocarbon supplier and has shown little enthusiasm for joining with OPEC. As it opens up new exports routes beyond Europe, as its volumes increase, and as it integrates its oil and gas export policies into a more consistent framework, Russia will begin to define its own international interests in its own ways.[33]

Unlike the members of OPEC, Russia is not primarily an oil-resource-dependent country. It is a former and potential future superpower, with a nuclear arsenal and an ability to project force internationally in a way second only to the United States. With its growing industrial and agricultural base, it will also seek to balance its oil and natural gas objectives against those of other sectors of the economy—sectors that happen to benefit when oil prices are lower. In short, the diverging interests of evolving Russia and of OPEC as constituted today do not bode well for future cooperation between them on production restraints.[34]

## Tensions from Within

OPEC's cohesion is threatened as divisions emerging within the group distinguish the interests of some members from those of others.[35] The most important of these divisions relates to the potential divergences in interests between the countries with large oil reserve bases like Saudi Arabia and the majority of OPEC countries, which will find it difficult to increase production capacity. Disparities will also emerge between OPEC producers that become important natural gas suppliers to Western markets and those that will remain primarily focused on oil.

Glimmers of this situation were seen in 1997 at the November OPEC meeting in Jakarta. At the time, OPEC basically lifted quotas by defining them at the full capacity of most of its members. The meeting spurred speculation about the end of OPEC per se and the arrival of a new period in which Saudi Arabia together with a group of other countries, mostly Gulf Cooperation Council members, would be the swing producers, replacing OPEC.

The choices of long-term strategy are more complex for Saudi Arabia than for other OPEC members with smaller reserves. While the rest of OPEC will favor maximizing income through high prices, the high-reserve countries can opt to grow market share radically and, potentially, increase revenue through higher volume, rather than higher prices. When confronted with the problem of lower production at lower revenue, high-reserve producers may not be willing to hold up the development of the market for the benefit of all producers in the longer run.[36]

Another tension within OPEC comes from the expected quickening pace of investment by IOCs in oil fields in key member states, especially Algeria, Iraq, Libya, and Nigeria, and potentially Iran, the United Arab Emirates, and Kuwait as well. Some large OPEC countries, including Kuwait and the United Arab Emirates, have been reluctant to attract the IOCs because they have been convinced that the result will be a decline in state earnings. The rationale is simple: If oil demand is stagnating and the call on OPEC growing less rapidly than the rate of growth of oil demand (because of non-OPEC output increases), then any new share for the IOCs will require a reduction in output for the NOC.

In contrast, a number of smaller OPEC countries, faced with limitations on their own NOCs, have not been reluctant to attract IOC investment, and the results of this reopening are beginning to show.[37] For instance, Algeria is in the midst of a major drive to expand capacity. It increased its conventional crude oil output from 800,000 barrels per day in 1998 to 1.3 mmbpd in 2004, with further expansion on the horizon, but by 2004 it was double its OPEC quota. Nigeria, which is totally dependent on IOC investment, is seeing its output growing potentially by 100,000 barrels per day per year for ten years.[38] In Venezuela, IOC investment is enabling the country to hold output steady. If PdVSA is able again to increase its own capital expenditures, its capacity is expected to grow, potentially significantly, given the resource base of the country. Add to these efforts new investments in Libya, Iran, and even the United Arab Emirates and Kuwait, and the potentially higher friction within OPEC could making it difficult to secure pro-rationing agreements over time.

Finally, there is Iraq, sitting on some of the largest oil reserves in the world but producing less than 3 mmbpd in the period following the ouster of the regime of Saddam Hussein. Should stability be reestablished there, Iraq could easily restore its pre-1990, pre-Gulf War capacity of 3.5 mmbpd in two to three years. If it decides to expand capacity further by inviting IOC investment, that would have dramatic repercussions for OPEC.[39]

## Saudi Stability

Since 9/11 and the withdrawal of U.S. military forces from Saudi Arabia in 2003, attention turned toward the stability of the Saudi regime. Most analysts walked to the water's edge and stopped, partly because a disruption from Saudi Arabia would be unprecedented. There simply is no way for the world to forgo Saudi oil without an enormous increase in oil prices and untold damage to the world economy.

Needless to say, even without a massive disruption of Saudi oil, dramatic change in the Saudi regime could have a major impact on OPEC and world oil. Three critical questions must be considered with respect to a regime change in Saudi Arabia. First, would a new Saudi regime be willing to maintain spare capacity and be a swing producer? Second, what export volume would the government target? Third, depending on the outcome of a regime change, could the government maintain or expand capacity in an effective manner? These issues are obviously interrelated.

A new Saudi regime that decides not to maintain spare capacity, but either to mothball it or produce full out, would have a profound impact on Saudi

Arabia's and OPEC's ability to target a price band and to adjust output to maintain the band. But the graver issue is related to the consequence of revolutionary political change on the Kingdom's oil sector. History has not been kind to oil regimes undergoing revolutionary change. In all known cases, the result has been a precipitous decline in production capacity, which can be long lasting. Libya lost half its 3 mmbpd capacity following the revolution that brought Qaddafi to power. Iran lost half its 7 mmbpd capacity following the ouster of the shah. Neither country has been able to restore lost capacity, and in late 2004 they were producing 1.5 and 3.8 mmbpd, respectively. Venezuela lost 800,000 barrels per day of capacity after Hugo Chávez was elected.

The main reason for the decline is telling and does not bode well for a potential revolutionary change in Saudi Arabia: Revolutions are not propitious times for retaining technical capability and sustaining human resources. Modern petroleum earth science and engineering require a renewing pool of talent. When revolutions take place, those working in the petroleum sector have mobility to relocate internationally. Once they emigrate, it is extremely difficult for the new regime to maintain output at prior levels.[40] Iraq's recent experience and that of Algeria and Colombia in the 1990s highlight another potential problem: Internal political division can lead to sabotage against oil facilities.

## A Change in Demand Patterns

OPEC's most logical hope for being able to work itself out of any dilemma created by rising IOC participation and increased productive capacity is a return to the high rates of demand growth seen in the period 1986–96, when annual increments to global oil consumption were 1.0 to 2.0 mmbpd. That hope is focused on sustaining new consumption in Asia and North America.

But oil demand stagnated between 1996 and 2002. In the ten years before 1996, demand grew by 15 mmbpd, excluding the 2.5 mmbpd drop in Russian consumption due to the collapse of the Soviet Union. From 1996 to 2002, total global oil consumption rose by 3.2 mmbpd, or 600,000 barrels per day per year.[41] Demand spurted again after that, but there is an open question about the sustainability of the new growth.

Renewed stagnation in global demand growth would be problematic for OPEC, especially if non-OPEC countries increase their output rapidly through 2010.[42] Production increases from the former Soviet Union alone have exceeded 600,000 barrels per day per year for the past few years. At least for another few years, similar gains could materialize if Russia, which began major industry restructuring in late 2004, is still able to muster the investment in new export pipelines.

The changing demand situation is also reflected in the projections for demand put out by the International Energy Agency. At the beginning of this decade, the IEA projected global demand to reach 85.2 mmbpd by 2005 and 96 mmbpd in 2010. In a later and revised base case projection, global demand was expected to reach 88.8 mmbpd by 2010. Even that level could be a stretch, depending on global economic growth between now and then. If demand stagnates and reaches only 84 mmbpd by 2010, there might be no requirement for incremental OPEC output.[43]

What are the demand risks for OPEC? Aside from sustained global economic stagnation, *three critical factors could keep expected demand from materializing. These are related to enhanced efficiency gains, fuel diversification, and U.S. policies.* We conclude this chapter by assessing the options for the United States, whether its goal should be to "break" OPEC, and what aspect of the oil market it is in a position to influence—including, but not limited to, demand for OPEC oil.

## OPEC's Future and the Influence of U.S. Policy: Options for Consideration

The United States appears to be at a critical crossroads for energy policy. The status quo is increasingly untenable. Either radical change abroad, such as revolutionary change in Saudi Arabia, will impose choices on the American government, or internal pressures will result in a sharper focus on energy policy and a conscious decision on new priorities and trade-offs.

No one is satisfied with existing energy policy, but few seem willing to make the hard decisions and uncomfortable compromises necessary to depart from it. No party has sole ownership of the status quo. Current policy represents a continuity of successive administrations in Washington for more than a quarter-century in encouraging diversity of global oil production, cooperation with major oil producers—especially Saudi Arabia—to ensure stable markets, research in alternative fuels, and reliance on a robust strategic petroleum reserve for use in case of disruption.

The George W. Bush administration pursued much of this agenda after 2001, as outlined in its formal energy strategy (the so called Cheney Report). Though many of the report's domestic recommendations were controversial, most of its language devoted to the international arena could have been written under the Bill Clinton administration, or indeed under George H. W. Bush, Ronald Reagan, or Jimmy Carter.

The centerpiece of the status quo is the "special relationship" with Saudi Arabia—a strategic quid pro quo whereby the United States guarantees the security of Saudi Arabia in return for Riyadh's cooperation in keeping a reliable flow of moderately priced oil to international petroleum markets. The first pillar of the special relationship is the decisive role that Saudi Arabia plays in international oil markets; Riyadh is not only the world's largest exporter of oil but also possesses a quarter of the global petroleum reserves and, significantly, excess capacity for use in an emergency. The second pillar is the ability and willingness of the United States to intervene militarily should Saudi Arabia be threatened; Washington did so, most notably when it rushed troops to Saudi Arabia when Iraq invaded Kuwait in 1990.

But paths away from the status quo must begin by questioning whether the centerpiece of the status quo will long endure. Already, Washington and Riyadh have begun to distance themselves from one another. More might be done from the U.S. side. One step would be to recognize that Saudi Arabia uses its spare capacity not as a favor to the West but as an instrument designed to enhance its power and influence in the world. A more proactive use of the U.S. strategic petroleum reserve would enable the U.S. government to have greater control over its own policies toward the international economy and the Middle East. It would also deprive oil exporters of windfall income gains, while profitably monetizing the U.S. oil stockpile.

Here, we outline three possible paths for U.S. policy. The first is a form of preemptive engagement, using American military and economic power to change the system. The second would pursue the strength of monopsony, or buyers' power to force change among the producers. And the third path, which is by no means incompatible with either the first or the second, would involve an effort to change the rules of the game and to induce a direct integration of oil trade and investment into the Western trade rules.

The path of preemptive engagement has become appealing to many in the United States in the aftermath of 9/11. After the terrorist attacks, U.S. foreign policy became the subject of perhaps the most far-ranging reassessment undertaken since the onset of the Cold War in the late 1940s. Energy strategy is a key part of this reassessment, given impetus in large part by renewed public concerns about U.S. oil dependence on the Middle East.

The occupation of Iraq was pregnant with unstated and unimplemented options and opportunities. It is true that rhetoric about "breaking OPEC" has been more a wish list item than a practical aim.[44] That is because much of the debate about U.S. energy policy, with its stress on reducing dependence on foreign supplies through largely unilateral action in the foreign arena, flies directly in the face of harsh market realities. The foremost of those realities is the role of increasing consumption—especially in the United States —in driving petroleum markets. Accepting this reality is a vital first step in forging a practical medium- to long-term strategy to minimize the risks of severe supply disruption and skyrocketing prices.[45]

In the aftermath of 9/11, one group, loosely woven together under the neoconservative label, articulated the elements of a new policy approach of preemptive engagement. Binding these ideas is dissatisfaction with the status quo. But rather than reducing dependence on foreign oil, this approach —rather ironically—would unleash the oil potential of the Middle East through privatization and new investments.

Diversity of supply would not just be an economic end but also a strategic means. The United States would attempt to drive down the price of oil, break the ability of OPEC to set prices, and deprive uncooperative states— including Saudi Arabia—of revenue. The neoconservative approach resembles U.S. oil strategy during the Cold War, when, during the Reagan administration, Washington encouraged Saudi Arabia to suppress prices in order to cause economic damage to the Soviet Union.[46]

Neoconservative concerns (and increasingly left-of-center commentators as well) center on a belief that oil revenues permit such countries as Iran, Saudi Arabia, and formerly Libya, to sustain authoritarian regimes and promote anti-American policies. Collusion on production levels through OPEC, in turn, sustains those rents at a high level. Saudi Arabia, though nominally a U.S. ally, plays a particularly pernicious role under neoconservative ideology, by using its immense oil revenues and OPEC leadership to promote the Kingdom's own brand of fundamentalist Islam—Wahabism— in the Middle East and Central Asia.[47]

On one level, the neoconservative argument is logical: Low oil prices— in addition to providing substantial economic benefits for the U.S. and global economies—will reduce the revenue available to oil-producing states, which sponsor terrorism or pursue the acquisition of weapons of mass destruction. But it both overestimates the ability of the United States to sustain low international oil prices and underestimates the consequences of a general decline in oil prices for oil-producing allies of the United States. It assumes that the United States will be able to persuade such major producers as Russia and a postoccupation Iraq to pursue policies that are in the United States' economic interest. And, not least, the neoconservative alternative neglects the very huge risks should its approach actually succeed and prompt sufficient hardship in Saudi Arabia to cause a "regime change" in Riyadh. Indeed, recent history demonstrates that any radical domestic political change in oil-producing countries leads to suppressed output, whether that change is in an "anti-American" direction (the Islamic revolution in Iran) or a "pro-American" one (the collapse of communism in the Soviet Union).

A near mirror image of preemptive engagement is an approach that recognizes the power that comes from curtailing energy demand, and oil demand in particular. Given the sizable role of the United States in world energy consumption, unilateral steps are plausible, but multilateral steps would be even more powerful.

No one doubts that a combination of fiscal instruments and regulations can reduce the rate of increase in U.S. demand for oil as a transportation fuel. These need not include a European- or Japanese-style 400 percent tax on consumption of the fuel. They can include more modest taxes, combined with incentives to use low-sulfur diesel rather than gasoline, thus creating greater efficiencies, as well as regulations on the efficiency of sport utility vehicles, which have been largely exempt from other U.S. automobile efficiency standards. Large government fleets can be mandated to be fueled by natural gas or electric power. A sliding-scale, luxury-style tax on new vehicles based on their mileage performance would be another way to propel more efficient technologies into the marketplace without taxing gasoline per se.

Nor is there any doubt that there is considerable room for enhanced energy efficiencies. The world is currently witnessing experiments that go to the core of energy efficiency in both Russia and China. Both countries are radically changing the economic signals associated with energy costs. Indeed, when it comes to electricity generation and fuel for household heating, they are both seeing market-based pricing principles replace subsidized (and in some cases free) energy. The continued drive toward market liberalization in both countries, especially outside the transportation sector, could result in significant declines in the rate of growth of primary energy requirements.

Fuel diversification is also being accelerated, especially in East Asia after the 9/11 attacks. The key countries of Asia, beginning with China and India, have been reevaluating their plans to increase oil consumption and their reliance on Middle Eastern sources of supply. They are both looking toward gasification of significant segments of their economies and are turning toward imports of liquefied natural gas in volumes not anticipated in 2000.[48] The impact of these developments on future oil consumption has yet to be evaluated, but it certainly is not positive.

But any effective effort to weaken OPEC needs to center on the United States. Growth in U.S. oil demand has long been and remains a key driver of the international petroleum economy. In the 1990s, for example, total global trade in oil increased by 10.33 mmbpd. The United States alone, due to the decline in its production base and the increase in its appetite for oil as a transportation fuel (gasoline for sport utility vehicles), increased its net imports by 3.4 mmbpd. It imported 33.02 percent of the increment in global trade, representing 55.58 percent of OPEC's total increase in exports during the past decade. Projections are for U.S. imports to repeat this performance during the current decade. Thus, any change in U.S. policy that can significantly affect the pace of import growth could have a telling impact of OPEC's plans to increase market share.

The United States (and Canada, with a much lower consumption base) stands apart from the other OECD countries. Japan and the E.U. countries have managed, through high consumer taxes, to fundamentally end growth in oil demand. In both cases, total growth for the current decade is expected to fall in the 1 to 2 percent range, or 0.1 to 0.2 percent a year. When it comes to gasoline demand, European consumption has actually been falling as consumers opt for more fuel-efficient diesel powered vehicles.

Assuming that a U.S. government can sell such an approach at home, it would then be possible to internationalize the strategy. For example, a much more proactive stance vis-à-vis Russia and China with respect to the international energy sector could also help the United States and other IEA countries in breaking OPEC's hold. It could also help these two critical emerging energy powers to define their own goals in manners compatible with U.S. objectives, a situation that is unlikely to happen without a proactive U.S. stance. China needs to be encouraged to develop strategic stocks, and the United States can assist it, whether by sponsoring its membership in the IEA or assisting the development of new regional energy security arrangements. Either route would be preferable to sitting idle and not intervening as China stresses bilateral energy ties to individual producers in the Middle East and elsewhere. China has been slow to increase the scale of proposed strategic stocks, betting in effect that a supply crisis grave enough to merit a large stockpile is unlikely.

Finally, a third approach involves a redefinition of the rules of the game of energy trade and investment. The United States can do much to focus on market realities rather than OPEC market interventions. The one stumbling block here has been the concern that lower prices would destabilize oil-producing countries allied to the United States, with adverse consequences for U.S. national interests. The solution to that, of course, is to focus on ways to provide economic assistance to such countries if and as oil prices decline, a route likely to be far less expensive than supporting military forces throughout the oil-producing world.

But the critical element of an emerging U.S. policy is a focus on the rules that underpin the international economy, the very rules to which OPEC is an anomalous exception. At the outset of this chapter, we posited that OPEC was the main exception to the trends in today's world economy. OPEC stands apart in a world of globalization, increased international economic interdependence, and market liberalization and deregulation. There is a prevalent view that the oil sector does not involve an expanding pie from which all parties can benefit. Rather, it has been constructed as an either/or world, in which the gains of consumers are the loss of the producers, and vice versa.

The two worlds, that of the market and that of the antimarket producers, intersect every day. In paper markets, international funds daily speculate about future oil prices, based significantly on judgments about what the producers might do under different circumstances. In "real" markets in which physical commodities are traded, the fundamentals of supply and demand work themselves out through seasonal demand adjustments and changes related to evolving economic conditions, and to new supplies being brought into the market (outside OPEC) as oil supplies elsewhere undergo natural declines. In those markets, OPEC producers keep a vigilant eye on the level of inventories being built as well as on the net "short" or "long" position of speculators.

The United States and other industrial countries can do a great deal more—and indeed, in the years ahead they are likely to do much more—to enhance the institutional mechanisms that favor markets over political intervention by producers. The United States needs to show leadership by looking seriously at ways to bring the rules of global oil trade and investment into harmony with the rules governing trade in manufacturing and services. This would mean building on open trade and investment within the IEA and discriminating actively against those countries that do not permit foreign investment in their energy resources and that limit their exports to manipulate prices. This is a tough policy, but one that is essential to the counter-OPEC revolution. Liberalization and open access for investment in all international energy resources would mean their timely development rather than today's worrisome delays. Without global norms across the oil world, the world experiences capital and politically constrained limitations of supply that can cripple the global economy and perpetuate poverty in the energy-poor countries of Africa and Asia. The privatization of the Russian oil industry initially resulted in rapid growth in oil production. Although the Kremlin itself is backtracking from the benefits of such liberalization, the increase in private-sector oil output in Russia should serve as a guidepost to what could be achieved if other still-closed countries followed suit.

## Notes

1. Michael Mandelbaum, "The Inadequacy of American Power," *Foreign Affairs* 81, no. 5 (September/October 2003): 61–73.

2. John G. Ikenberry, "America's Imperial Ambition," *Foreign Affairs* 81, no. 5 (September/October 2003): 44–60.

3. For a broad discussion of case studies on the advantages of multilateral action versus unilateral action, see Daniel Yergin and Martin Hillenbrand, eds., *Global Insecurity: A Strategy for Energy and Economic Renewal* (Boston: Houghton Mifflin, 1982).

4. For a good survey of the economic literature on consuming countries and OPEC, see J. L. Plummer, ed., *Energy Vulnerability* (Cambridge, Mass.: Ballinger Publishing, 1982).

5. H. G. Huntington and Dermot Gately, "Crude Oil Prices and US Economic Performance: Where Does the Asymmetry Reside?" *Energy Journal* 19, no. 4 (2002): 107–32; and W. Gao, Kenneth Medlock III, and R. Sickles, "The Effects of Oil Price Volatility on Technical Change," forthcoming working paper, Rice University, Houston.

6. For more detailed discussion on monopsony power, see Dermot Gately, "OPEC and the Buying Power Wedge," in *Energy Vulnerability,* ed. J. L Plummer (Cambridge, Mass.: Ballinger Publishing, 1982), 37–57. Various estimates for the value of this wedge are cited on p. 46.

7. This Western liberal economic consensus was nowhere better praised than in the book by Daniel Yergin and Joseph Stanislaw, *The Commanding Heights: The Battle for the World Economy* (New York: Simon & Schuster, 2000).

8. The literature on the founding of OPEC and on OPEC behavior is rich and vast. Thankfully, Robert Mabro has provided an extraordinarily useful overview of the literature on OPEC from the foundation through the second oil price war of 1986. See Robert Mabro, "OPEC Behavior 1960–1998: A Review of the Literature," *Journal of Energy Literature* 4, no. 1 (June 1998): 3–27.

9. For interesting country-by-country studies, see Russell A. Stone, ed., *OPEC and the Middle East* (New York: Praeger Publishers, 1977).

10. For specifics on this, see Emma Brossaard, *Petroleum: Politics and Power* (Tulsa: PennWell, 1983), 63–64; and Daniel Yergin, *The Prize: The Epic Quest for Oil, Money, and Power* (New York: Simon & Schuster, 1991), 519–40.

11. Abdul Raoof, "Ideology and Politics in Iraqi Oil Policy: The Nationalization of 1972," in *OPEC and the Middle East,* ed. Stone.

12. The economic literature on whether OPEC is an effective cartel is mixed and

divisive, but it generally holds that the group, through some degree of coordination, has held oil prices above marginal costs. Leading articles that support the thesis that the cartel has been effective in coordinated strategy to lift prices include M. A. Adelman, "The Clumsy Cartel," *Energy Journal* 1, no. 1 (1980): 43–53. Adelman argues that oil prices would settle around $5 a barrel, were it not for the efforts of OPEC members to limit their own supplies. Other authors supportive to the argument that OPEC unity matters are A. F. Alhajji and David Huettner, "OPEC and World Crude Oil Markets from 1973 to 1994: Cartel, Oligopoly or Competitive?" *Energy Journal* 21, no. 3 (2000): 31–60; James M. Griffin, "OPEC Behavior: A Test of Alternative Hypotheses," *American Economic Review* 75, no. 5 (1985): 954–63; Carol Dahl and Mine Yucel, "Testing Alternative Hypotheses of Oil Producer Behavior," *Energy Journal* 12, no. 4(1991): 117–38; George Daley, James M. Griffin, and Henry Steel, "Recent Oil Price Escalations: Implications for OPEC Stability," in *OPEC Behavior and World Oil Prices*, ed. James M. Griffin and David J. Teece (London: George Allen & Unwin, 1982); and Theodore Moran, "Modelling OPEC Behavior: Economic and Political Alternatives," in *OPEC Behavior and World Oil Prices*, ed. Griffin and Teece.

13. David Bird, "Saudis Not About to Concede Any Markets," October 16, 1997, Dow Jones & Co.; "Saudis Subdue Doubters by Plowing Ahead with Crude Production," *Oil Daily*, January 8, 1998. Also see the discussion on this subject in Rapporteur's Report, Harvard University Oil and Security Executive Session, May 14, 2003, Environment and Natural Resources Program, Belfer Center for Science and International Affairs, Cambridge, Mass.

14. Amy Myers Jaffe, "The Geopolitics of Energy," in *Encyclopedia of Energy*, ed. Cutler Cleveland (San Diego: Elsevier Publishers, 2004).

15. The evidence for this shift in U.S. policy is circumstantial but powerful. During the years of struggle between OPEC and non-OPEC producers over responsibility for reversing the oil price collapse (1998–2000), the U.S. government changed its position toward an "energy dialogue," and the secretary of energy, Bill Richardson, broke tradition by attending and actively participating in the dialogue in a conference in Riyadh, Saudi Arabia on November 17, 2000. The United States also supported the establishment of a permanent secretariat for the "dialogue" in Riyadh, a decision reconfirmed by the George W. Bush administration. For a succinct statement of the change in the U.S. position and the U.S. encouragement of the floor under prices, see Antoine Halff and Manimoli Dinesh, "US: Make or Break," *Energy Compass*, March 10, 2000, 5–6.

16. From Jaffe, "Geopolitics of Energy."

17. See "OPEC Adds Micro-Control to Tight Supply Strategy," *Petroleum Intelligence Weekly*, April 3, 2000, 1.

18. For an even fuller statement, see his opening statement to that OPEC meeting, available at http://www.OPEC.org, press release 3/2001.

19. For a discussion of the impact of this trend on U.S. policy, see Amy Myers Jaffe and Edward L. Morse, *Strategic Energy Policy: Challenges for the 21st Century* (Houston and New York: James A. Baker III Institute for Public Policy and Council on Foreign Relations, 2001).

20. For a discussion of the Gulf Arab pricing policies to keep pricing artificially low, see F. Gregory Gause, "Iraq's Decision to Go to War," *Middle East Journal* 56, no. 1 (Winter 2002); and Lawrence Freedman and Efraim Karsh, *The Gulf Conflict 1990–1991* (Princeton, N.J.: Princeton University Press, 1993); as well as Michael Drew and James Schwartz, "The Rising Confrontation," *Washington Post*, January 15, 1991, A14,

which described Iraq's dissatisfaction with the Gulf Arab policy of keeping oil prices low. Also see William Quandt, *Saudi Arabia in the 1980s: Foreign Policy, Security and Oil* (Washington, D.C.: Brookings Institution Press, 1981).

21. "Saudi Crown Prince Hailed for Turning Down US Visit," Reuters, May 20, 2001.

22. For more detailed discussion on Saudi policy under Crown Prince Abdullah, see Joseph Kechichian, "Saudi Arabia's Will to Power," *Middle East Policy Council Journal* 7 (February 2000); and Nawaf E. Obaid, "Saudi Oil Politics," *Policy Watch* (Washington Institute for Near East Policy), April 6, 1999.

23. "Statement by Secretary Richardson on OPEC," NASEO Washington Update, March 29, 1999, available at http://www.naseo.org/archive/news/updates/1999_03_29 .htm. Also see "US Energy Secretary Calls for OPEC to Let Markets Set Oil Prices," *On-Line Pravda,* June 28, 2002, available at http://english.pravda.ru/comp/2002/06/28/ 31348.html.

24. For more detailed economics discussion of the Saudi role as the dominant producer, see Amy Myers Jaffe and Ronald Soligo, "Impact of the Reopening of Upstream Sectors in the Gulf," *Middle East Economic Survey* 43, no. 36 (September 4, 2000); and the longer James A. Baker III Institute for Public Policy working paper of the same title, available at http://www.bakerinstitute.org.

25. Sam Dillon, "Venezuela Again Opens to Foreign Oil Concerns," *New York Times,* March 5, 1996, section D, p. 9; Jane Knight, "3rd Marginal Round Begun by Caracas," *Platt's Oilgram News* 74, no. 214 (November 4, 1996): 7; "Venezuela Plans to Increase Output to 3.41 Million Barrels a Day in 1997," *Platt's Oilgram News* 75, no. 120 (June 23, 1997): 1.

26. Bird, "Saudis Not About to Concede Any Markets"; "Saudis Subdue Doubters by Plowing Ahead with Crude Production," *Oil Daily,* January 8, 1998.

27. For data, see *Petroleum Intelligence Weekly* / Oil Market Intelligence database, available at http://www.energyintel.com.

28. For more discussion on this topic, see Rapporteur's Report, Harvard University Oil and Security Executive Session.

29. Jaffe and Soligo, "Impact of the Reopening."

30. In 1985, Saudi Arabia stopped abiding by the official OPEC-sanctioned fixed price for its oil and began to sign contracts to sell its oil at flexible, fluctuating prices linked to the value of its oil at key refining centers around the world. This so-called netback pricing, based on the value of refined petroleum products, ensured that refiners would buy a maximum amount of oil. Refiners were offered an attractive predetermined profit margin as part of these netback-related deals, ensuring that they would have no disincentives to purchasing Saudi oil.

31. See *BP Statistical Review of World Energy,* 2003, section on oil production. The database is available in Microsoft Excel format at the BP website, http://www.bp.com.

32. See Meghan L. O'Sullivan, *"Shrewd Sanctions: Statecraft and State Sponsors of Terrorism"* (Washington, D.C. Brookings Institution Press, 2003); Also, for specifics of sanctions impact on OPEC production rates, see "Political, Economic, Social, Cultural, and Religious Trends in the Middle East and the Gulf and Their Impact on Energy Supply, Security and Pricing," James A. Baker III Institute for Public Policy, Rice University, available at http://www.bakerinstitute.org.

33. See Julia Nanay's discussion of the challenges to Russia's renaissance in chapter 5 of the present volume and Jan Kalicki and Jonathan Elkind's discussion of the challenges to new export routes for Russian oil and gas in chapter 6.

34. See Edward Morse and James Richard, "The Battle for Energy Dominance," *Foreign Affairs* 81, no. 2 (March/April 2002): 30–31.

35. An excellent essay on this subject was written by former Algerian oil minister Nordine Ait-Laoussine, "OPEC: At the Crossroads Again," *Middle East Economic Survey* 46, no. 38 (September 22, 2003).

36. There is a rich literature on the subject of the trade-offs between volume and price with respect to OPEC revenue. The most recent contributions to these debates are found in Dermot Gately's recent pieces in the *Energy Journal*. See Huntington and Gately, "Crude Oil Prices and US Economic Performance"; "How Plausible Is the Current Consensus Projection of Oil below $25 and Persian Gulf Oil Capacity and Output Doubling by 2020?" *Energy Journal* 22, no. 4 (2002): 1–27; and "OPEC's Incentives for Faster Output Growth," *Energy Journal* 24, no. 2 (2003).

37. See Adam Sieminski's discussion of growing IOC participation in OPEC countries in chapter 1 of this volume.

38. Deutche Bank Global Energy Wire, "Driving Force: The Growing IOC Role in OPEC," November 24, 2003.

39. Jaffe and Soligo, "Impact of the Reopening."

40. A. F. Alhaji, in a series of articles on this subject, argues that it takes at least three years for production capacity to be restored following regime change. His major arguments focus on Iraq. See A. F. Alhajji, "The Experience of Oil-Producing Countries with Capacity Expansion and Its Implications for the Future of Iraq," *Oil and Gas Journal* 101, no. 42 (November 2003); and A. F. Alhajji, "The Expansion of Iraq's Oil Production Capacity: Challenges Ahead," *Middle East Economic Survey* 46, no. 27 (May 2003).

41. International Energy Agency, *World Energy Outlook 1998* (Paris: International Energy Agency, 1998).

42. International Energy Agency, *World Energy Outlook 2002* (Paris: International Energy Agency, 2002).

43. International Energy Agency, *World Energy Outlook 2002*.

44. Ariel Cohen, *Energy Security at Risk,* May 23, 2003, available at http://www.heritage.org/press/commentary/ed052703a.cfm.

45. Joe Barnes, Amy Myers Jaffe, and Edward Morse, "The New Geopolitics of Oil," *National Interest,* December 2003.

46. James R. Woolsey, "Defeating the Oil Weapon," *Commentary,* September 2002.

47. Victor Davis Hanson, "Our Enemies, the Saudis," *Commentary,* July–August, 2002.

48. For a detailed discussion of the trends in Asia, see Robert Manning, *The Asian Energy Factor* (New York: Palgrave, 2000).

# 4

# The International Energy Agency

*William F. Martin and Evan M. Harrje*

Energy underpins national security, economic prosperity, and global stability. But a number of factors point to an increasingly unstable energy future: rapidly rising energy demand in Asia, growing dependence on oil from regions with less stable governments, increasing global competition for resources, and the environmental impact of rising fossil fuel consumption. Just looking at the "reference cases" for global energy supply and demand projections to 2025 from the U.S. Department of Energy's Energy Information Administration[1] and the International Energy Agency (IEA)[2] is enough to raise serious questions about the sustainability of the world's current energy policy course. In those projections, we see rising demand for oil and natural gas in particular, with growth in non–Organization for Economic Cooperation and Development (OECD) energy demand increasing dramatically over the coming decades, far surpassing demand growth in industrial countries. Pressing energy, environmental, and economic challenges await on the horizon.

These challenges cannot be addressed by national governments alone. International institutions will be called on to coordinate strategies in response to a variety of future global energy and environmental problems. The security of the natural gas supply, providing electricity to the 1.6 billion people worldwide who do not have regular access to it, the development and deployment of environmentally friendly power and transportation technologies, and the extension of strategic oil stocks are key challenges for the IEA to confront in the next century.[3] The IEA's history of flexibility can help it address these issues. The institution has had a positive influence on potential and actual energy crises, whether by avoiding their occurrence or by lessening their effects on the market. But IEA members must not rest on their past achievements. Today, energy markets are evolving far faster than the IEA's mandate. The time has come for IEA member states to muster the necessary political will and financial resources to modernize the agency and its mission.

To keep up with this evolution and anticipate new disruptions, the IEA must adopt a comprehensive and ambitious work program. The IEA should enlarge its range of actions to help ensure the security of oil and natural gas supplies, address appropriate strategies for dealing with climate change, promote efforts to "wire the world," facilitate effective consumer–producer country dialogue, examine the impact of deregulation and investment patterns on energy security goals, further develop research and development (R&D) collaboration programs, and promote closer relationships between its members and the rest of the energy world. The United States played the pivotal role in creating the IEA in response to an energy challenge that arose thirty years ago. Now the United States has an opportunity to shape the IEA's future by pledging to increase its funding and by putting significant political capital behind global energy security initiatives.

In this chapter, we describe the evolution of the IEA since its creation in 1974 and show how the institution's flexible system and adaptability have allowed it to deal with threats to its members' energy security over the past thirty years. Next, we set forth the energy security challenges the world will face in the coming decades and the role the IEA can play in addressing them. Finally, we offer specific recommendations for how the IEA can build on its historic flexibility to enhance global energy security.

## Historical Perspectives on the IEA

The IEA was formed in response to the damaging economic effects of the Arab oil embargo of 1973 on OECD countries. Although the United States and the Netherlands were the stated targets of the embargo, all oil-consuming countries suffered as a result of the oil supply disturbances. The embargo served as a stark wakeup call to the United States and its allies of a looming national security threat. Under the leadership of U.S. secretary of state Henry Kissinger, the OECD countries created the now-twenty-six-member country IEA as the oil-consuming countries' collective mechanism for responding to the energy crisis. In November 1974, the founding members produced the "Agreement on the International Energy Program" (IEP), which spelled out its responsibilities and scope of work.[4] The heart of the

IEP was a plan to share the member countries' oil supplies in the event of an embargo or other serious supply disruption that could adversely affect individual IEA countries or the group as a whole.

During the ensuing decades, the IEA's approach has shifted away from oil sharing to the coordination of collective measures emphasizing stock draw, with elements of demand restraint, surge production, and fuel switching. Such measures actually were taken at the time of the Allied attack during the Gulf War, and the IEA had plans ready to activate them for the year 2000 computer glitch popularly known as "Y2K," if needed. Since its formation, the IEA has also served as an institutional forum for sharing energy information, discussing and coordinating energy policies, and cooperating in the research and development of new technologies that can enhance national and international energy security.

## The Period 1973–74:
## Embargo, Oil Shock, and the Formation of the IEA

Any review of the effectiveness of the IEA begins with the Arab oil embargo of the United States and the Netherlands in 1973. The boycotters failed in their attempt to selectively starve two oil-consuming countries while supplying "friendly" nations and inadvertently showed that the world oil market is essentially one big pool with a variety of vulnerabilities. When supplies are withheld anywhere, the entire market is affected. The shortfall in global oil supplies during the 1973–74 shock reached about 9 percent of the global oil market and led to the worst recession among OECD countries in decades, causing significant political turmoil. For the United States, the embargo came at a time when the country was becoming more dependent on oil imports because domestic production had peaked. The U.S. gross domestic product fell by 6 percent between 1973 and 1975, while unemployment doubled to 9 percent.[5] The 1973 Arab oil embargo was the first oil supply disruption to cause major price spikes and have global repercussions. At the time of the embargo, almost all spare production capacity resided in the Middle East. When the crisis hit, there was no established mechanism to enable the OECD countries to effectively respond and limit the economic impact of the supply disruption.

On the basis of a recognition that oil supply disruptions posed a considerable national security threat, U.S. secretary of state Henry Kissinger called upon the industrial countries to meet in Washington in February 1974 to craft the beginnings of international energy cooperation. All major nations of the Western alliance participated in the conference, although French foreign minister Michel Jobert attended only with great reluctance.[6] After almost a year of intense negotiations, the IEA was born on November 15, 1974, through a decision by the Council of the OECD. The IEP was signed three days after the OECD Council's decision. The IEA was linked—for administrative purposes—to the OECD in Paris, but with France conspicuously absent from the membership.[7] The OECD had an international oil committee before the IEA's creation, and under the able direction of Hans Schneider of Germany, it had prepared a two-volume assessment of the world energy outlook to 1985, published in 1974. The report warned of rising OECD dependence on oil from the Middle East—enhancing the desirability of creating a multilateral "emergency sharing system."

Kissinger was impressed by the director general of energy of the German Ministry of Economics, Ulf Lantzke, and a consensus grew that Lantzke would become the first IEA executive director and that an American, Wallace Hopkins Jr., would serve as deputy director. A small Secretariat was formed and housed on the third floor of the OECD's new building, at 19 rue de Franqueville in Paris. The Washington conference had produced a remarkable "oil-sharing" plan, which was the centerpiece of the IEA in its formative years. The basic principle was simple: Oil sharing would occur among member nations if any country or group of countries lost more than 7 percent of its supplies. The aim was to make it impossible for the Organization of Petroleum Exporting Countries (OPEC) to embargo any country or group of countries. The system was complicated and came under close antitrust scrutiny, but its purpose was primarily to deter producing countries from withholding supplies, and to date the oil-sharing system itself has never been triggered.

In addition to the oil-sharing system, the IEA established a Statistics Office and helped formulate a system of energy supply and demand balances —a matrix-style report that remains in use today as the standard international energy reporting system. Though the IEA's main focus in its early days was the oil-sharing scheme, a division for long-term cooperation was formed. This division was responsible for conducting periodic assessments of member-country energy policies as they sought to reduce their dependence on imported oil. Policies related to resource development, conservation, fuel substitution, efficiency, and R&D were all examined country-by-country, and an overall evaluation was determined by the Secretariat. Finally, an R&D division was established to encourage cost and expertise sharing in innovative energy research and development projects.

## The Formative Years:
## The Iranian Revolution and the Iran–Iraq War

As is often the case in international relations, in developing the oil-sharing system, the IEA laid a framework for "fighting the last war." When the outbreak of the Iranian Revolution led to a tripling of oil prices in just a few months from late 1978 to early 1979, the IEA soon discovered that its emergency system was not adequate for dealing with the new crisis. Though no IEA country was the target of an embargo, the Iranian Revolution set off a worldwide scramble for oil supplies when Iran's production plummeted by about 4.5 million barrels a day over a short period of time.[8] The shortfall did not reach the IEA's 7 percent trigger, but the sudden loss created significant oil market turmoil. Instead of sharing limited supplies and drawing down stocks, concern about ongoing physical shortages of oil led to increased stock building, further exacerbating upward price pressure.

Smaller economies were driven out of the market by the purchases of the wealthier OECD economies. But ultimately all oil-consuming countries suffered. Meeting in desperation, the heads of state at the Group of Seven conference in Tokyo agreed to specific oil import targets—but the targets were inflated by the negotiators and their potential impact was weakened. The IEA agreed to reduce demand by 4 to 5 percent below normal levels, but there was little agreement on how to implement the import targets.[9] The Europeans called for conservation. The Americans tried to pump up the global oil supply—especially by urging Saudi Arabia to increase its output. The result of this beggar-thy-neighbor policy was an increase in oil prices to more than $40—plunging the world economy into recession.

Although cooperation failed to produce a notable impact on the oil price, it did strengthen the role of the IEA as a consultative body. Important lessons were learned from the Iranian Revolution—lessons that have provided valuable protection up to the present. The key lesson was that oil stocks matter. In the event of a disruption, member countries must coordinate their actions. In the end, the Iranian shortfall amounted to about 2 million barrels a day for a period of less than a year, but it was the scramble for oil and the excessive building of stocks that exacerbated the problem and kept prices high. Countries did what motorists do in the face of emergency—they panicked and rushed to fill up their tanks all at the same time, making the crisis worse.

When the Iran-Iraq War broke out in September 1980, the IEA learned from its previous experiences and was able to react more effectively. Once again, the IEA countries faced a major disruption in oil supplies from the Middle East. Within the first week of fighting, the IEA had scheduled a routine meeting of its Standing Group on Emergency Questions. An emergency Governing Board session was called the next day under the able leadership of the Japanese ambassador to the OECD, Hiromichi Miyazaki. The board agreed to coordinate a drawdown of stocks, avoid abnormal purchases on the spot market, and take such actions in a fair and equitable way. The subsequent approval of a communiqué marked a pivotal moment for the IEA, because the organization had moved away from oil import targets and demand restraint and toward the coordination of oil stock release as the central element of its cooperation—a policy that endures more than two decades later.

The IEA ministers met within a couple of weeks to confirm their decision under the chairmanship of German economic minister, Otto Lambsdorf. Prices held steady, but there was a threat of action by Japanese trading companies with Kuwait that could have spun out of control if it had not been dealt with decisively. During a late-night meeting in Lantzke's office, the Belgian director general of economics, Steve Davignon, pressured the Japanese negotiator by saying that if Japan could not stop its traders, then it could forget about selling its cars and television sets in Europe. This tactic was a bit dramatic and overstated, but it turned out to be effective in helping the parties resolve the problem. The Japanese government halted the actions of the traders, and the oil price held steady. The IEA lowered stocks, did not bid up the price, and as far as it was possible to tell did this in a fair and equitable manner.

The Iran-Iraq War erupted in the midst of the U.S. presidential election season. At the time, European countries wondered if the IEA could uphold its agreement if the challenger, Ronald Reagan, won the election. Ulf Lantzke communicated with George Shultz to find out whether a Reagan administration would back such a coordinated stock policy approach if elected. Shultz was somewhat surprised to be contacted on the issue, and he modestly replied that he did not know if he would have any role in the not-yet-elected U.S. administration, but he said the IEA's stock policy sounded reasonable to him. Lantzke had earlier befriended Shultz and invited him to participate in the IEA's Coal Industry Advisory Board. Shultz's participation in this minor board helped secure his later support (as secretary of state) of the IEA's activities during pivotal moments such as the Siberian natural gas pipeline controversy and the intensification of the Iran-Iraq War.

The period from 1974 to 1981 was a critical time for the IEA. The institution was tested by multiple oil market disruptions during its formative years, and there were often significant differences of opinion between IEA members on how best to respond. Despite these difficulties, the IEA was able to adapt to changing conditions and learn from past mistakes. It is appropriate to say that the first seven years of the IEA benefited from the exceptional contributions of State Department officials Steven Bosworth, Edward Morse, Harry Bergold, Lester Goldman, and Dean Hinton—not to mention the important appearance of James Schlesinger at the IEA Ministerial in 1979.

## The 1980s:
## The Reagan Administration, the IEA, and the Siberian Pipeline

Despite Shultz's tacit approval of oil stock policy, the Reagan administration was initially hostile to the IEA because of its oil-allocation system. This setup was at odds with the new administration's strong belief in free markets. But Cold War realities helped lessen these concerns. When controversy developed over the Soviet Union's natural gas pipelines to Europe, the IEA (along with the Coordinating Committee for Multilateral Export Controls and NATO) became an essential forum for discussing this issue. In early 1981, after the Soviets had imposed martial law on Poland, the United States insisted that Europeans not buy pipeline equipment for the long natural gas pipeline connecting the Siberian fields to Western Europe. The Americans were concerned that the Soviets could monopolize the Western European natural gas market and wanted to constrain Soviet hard currency earnings, which were being boosted significantly by natural gas export revenues.

Lantzke, once again in the center of controversy, insisted that the situation was neither "black nor white." He conceded that the Americans had some legitimate points, especially over dependence on Soviet natural gas supplies, but he also saw that natural gas offered an important energy supply alternative to Europe. With nuclear power stalling and Europe already heavily dependent on Middle Eastern oil, natural gas offered promise for European energy security and environmental quality.

Negotiations began and failed among the Group of Seven countries. Sanctions were expanded in June 1982 to cover licensees of GE turbines in Europe. British prime minister Margaret Thatcher called Ronald Reagan and voiced her concerns, saying in effect that the United States was not going to stop the Soviets, but it was going to bankrupt the British firm John Brown (a GE licensee). In the fall of 1982, Shultz had an idea. He said that the issue over the pipeline was not about gas—it was about underlying differences of view between the United States and its European Allies over East-West trade. He urged President Reagan to lift the sanctions and "study" the problem of credits, technology theft, economic security, and energy security. The president agreed, and major studies were undertaken, with the IEA becoming one of the central forums for this effort.

A critical moment came in the negotiations just before the IEA Ministerial in April 1983, when the United States insisted on limiting the share of Soviet natural gas in European markets to 30 percent and the Europeans, led by the Germans, refused. Late-night calculations revealed to the U.S. delegation that the development of Norway's huge Troll field would have a de facto effect of reducing the Soviet share of the European natural gas market below the limitation. The United States floated the idea of inserting into the communiqué the importance of developing Troll and dropped its insistence on a 30 percent numerical target. The Germans accepted the compromise. The Troll field was indeed developed and continues to produce significant levels of natural gas for the European market. Thanks in part to the discussions and decisions made within the IEA; Europe now enjoys a stable and diverse supply of natural gas from Norway, Russia, North Africa, and other producing regions.

The IEA oil stock policy agreements in 1981 at the time of the Iran-Iraq War were ad hoc in nature. In 1985, the Iran-Iraq War began to spin out of control with the targeting of oil tankers, leading to serious concerns about oil supplies and the worrisome question of "What if Saudi Arabia's oil fields are attacked?" In the White House, there was a feeling that greater preparations were necessary to formalize IEA emergency stock agreements and also to build up the defensive capability of the Arab Gulf states near Iran and Iraq. Interestingly, the Reagan administration now viewed military and political issues as very closely associated with energy and economics—a bit of a departure from its initial adherence to free market orthodoxy. There was a fundamental understanding in 1985 that oil stocks could buy time for diplomacy. They had become an essential tool of foreign policy, and there was an understanding that the tool must be implemented internationally in a coordinated manner. Recognizing this, the United States endorsed the development of a more formal system of stock usage and the need for the United States and its allies to expand their strategic oil stockpiles. As a result, the IEA undertook a major effort to formalize coordinated stock policy and to urge all member countries to build stocks. The effort successfully concluded with the 1985 agreement, which stated that "Ministers agree to a common approach whereby imported refined oil products can go to markets of different IEA countries on the basis of supply and demand as determined by market forces without distortions."

By 1985, the IEA had a new executive director, Helga Steeg, a very capable economist from the German Economics Ministry. She was insistent on the importance of market forces in the energy sector. During her tenure, the IEA made significant progress in decontrolling oil and natural gas prices and urging greater deregulation in all energy markets, including electricity. The IEA helped encourage Japan to open its previously closed products market. The Europeans made progress in developing a more competitive natural gas market and in cutting subsidies to the coal industry. However, despite the progress there were areas of considerable disagreement. Debates occurred within the IEA over the future of nuclear power, making it almost impossible to forge a common nuclear energy policy. Toward the end of the 1980s, the issue of global climate change hit the international radar screen. It appeared that a new age was dawning in which environmental concerns might overshadow oil security issues. But Iraq's August 1990 invasion of Kuwait brought oil security back to center stage at the IEA.

## *The 1990s: From the Gulf War to Y2K*

Eric Melby, a former assistant to Lantzke and Steeg, was opportunely serving on President George H. W. Bush's National Security Council when Iraq invaded Kuwait. He helped acquaint the president's national security adviser, Brent Scowcroft, with the workings of the IEA and its important role in protecting the world economy during times of oil market turmoil. In August 1990, it was essential to reassure the world market when Kuwaiti exports were halted by the Iraqi invasion and there were concerns that Saudi oil fields would be targeted next. After almost two decades of practical experience, the IEA was poised to address the impact of the supply disruption with strategic stocks, demand restraint, and opportunities to quickly draw upon spare capacity (particularly through cooperation with Saudi Arabia). Working closely with the Bush administration, the IEA developed an operation called "Black Gold," which assisted in providing clear information to the market and encouraging production increases in order to lower the upward pressure on prices. But there was no immediate need for a drawdown of the strategic reserves once the threat to Saudi oil fields subsided as U.S. and allied forces moved in to secure the area.

As the preparations for military action took place during the fall of 1990, the United States expected that the IEA, directed at that time by Steeg, would activate the automatic oil-sharing plan. But it was not until January 1991 that the IEA decided to go ahead with the use of strategic stocks. The emergency-sharing plan was composed of stock drawdown and demand restraint. The three countries that implemented measures to draw down their stocks were Germany, Japan, and the United States. The price of oil spiked for a very short period of time when the air war started in late January, but it dropped quickly thanks in part to the IEA's decision to release stocks. The markets stabilized quickly when it became apparent that Iraq was no military match for the United States and its allies. The IEA's efforts to reassure the markets by drawing down stocks, sharing information, and encouraging trans-parency helped to restore oil market stability more quickly than in the pre-IEA days of 1973 when there was no coordination. Once order was restored in the Gulf, global oil markets enjoyed a period of relative calm. Iraqi oil exports returned to the market in the mid-1990s under the auspices of the UN Oil-for-Food program, and then oil prices dropped dramatically in the aftermath of the Asian Financial Crisis, which destroyed significant oil de-mand in what had been one of the world's fastest growing economies.

The next big oil market concern for the IEA was brought on not by in-stability in the Middle East but by a computer programming glitch that threatened to create worldwide confusion when 1999 ended and 2000 be-gan (i.e., the year 2000 computer glitch, known as the Y2K problem). The IEA took a strong lead in encouraging both oil-producing and -consuming countries to audit their systems and repair any Y2K bugs that could affect the performance of energy-related systems. From December 1999 to Janu-ary 2000, based on the Governing Board's adoption of "IEA Y2K Response Plans," the IEA Secretariat maintained an emergency response team for the critical rollover period when computer problems might have led to oil supply disruptions.[10]

## Post–September 11, 2001, and the Iraq War

The terrorist attacks of September 11, 2001, reawakened many Americans to concerns about energy security. As President George W. Bush responded to the post-9/11 security reality with attacks on Afghanistan and began pressuring Iraq and Iran to moderate their behavior, it became clear that it was time to revisit the issue of oil security. Once President Bush delivered his ultimatum to Saddam Hussein to "come clean" on Iraqi weapons programs and the UN Security Council gave him a sixty-day window of opportunity to cooperate with UN weapons inspectors, the IEA was working hard to prepare for a possible oil market disruption.

In the run-up to the war, a series of unusual events conspired to raise oil prices. A strike in Venezuela crippled its oil industry and dramatically reduced export levels for several months. Iraq continued to export oil in early 2003, but the market had built a "war premium" of $4 to $6 into the average price of crude on the knowledge that Iraqi exports would end once the war started. Nigeria experienced civil unrest in key oil-producing regions, which lowered its exports. In Japan, seventeen nuclear units were shut down following a safety-data falsification scandal (requiring the use of mothballed oil generators to meet electricity demand). All these factors conspired to create a very tight oil market balance just before the war.

Amid these tense oil market conditions, the IEA made clear that it was ready and willing to use the tools at its disposal to ensure stable supplies, that is, spare capacity and strategic stocks. In close coordination with the Bush administration, the IEA plainly expressed its will to draw down stocks if conditions warranted. By announcing this possible course of action, the IEA helped to encourage OPEC countries to increase output from spare capacity and avoid the need for an IEA strategic stock drawdown. As Claude Mandil, the executive director of the IEA, has noted, strategic stocks are a very important tool of deterrence for OECD countries.[11] Mandil led efforts in the months preceding the war to increase the level of dialogue with OPEC countries, and particularly Saudi Arabia, which retains significant spare capacity.

The dialogue between the IEA and producing countries had never been better during such a time of crisis, and it helped ensure the timely cooperation of key oil producers in getting spare capacity flowing in the months before the war started. As a result of this deepening dialogue and cooperation between the IEA and oil-producing countries, there was no need to draw down IEA strategic stocks. Additionally, prices were less volatile than during previous periods of crisis in the Middle East. The IEA's response to the war in Iraq clearly showed that the OECD countries have made substantial progress during the past three decades in developing workable responses to oil market disruptions. However, though the IEA has learned from past mistakes and made some policy corrections, it remains focused on "fighting the last crisis." The institution is overdue for a twenty-first-century mandate. The following section highlights a variety of challenges that the institution must confront in the future and offers a number of recommendations.

## Current Challenges and Recommendations

Although it is clear that the IEA as an institution has had a positive impact on global energy security, there are a variety of challenges on the horizon. Unless policies and consumer habits change substantially, energy demand will continue to grow steadily, with fossil fuels continuing to dominate the global energy mix. Most of the growth in energy demand will come from developing countries. The explosive rise in Chinese energy demand during the past year and its impact on energy market dynamics dramatically illustrate this trend. Global resources are adequate to meet growing demand, but it is not clear that "business as usual" is sustainable in terms of security of supply, environmental quality, and economic sustainability.

The IEA's members currently agree on the following as their core objectives: maintaining and improving systems for coping with oil supply disruptions; promoting rational energy policies in a global context through cooperative relations with nonmember countries, industry, and international organizations; operating a permanent information system on the international oil market; improving the world's energy supply and demand structure by developing alternative energy sources and increasing the efficiency of energy use; and assisting in the integration of environmental and energy policies.[12] These objectives are highly relevant to addressing current and future challenges, but to advance global energy security, the IEA will need to go further. This section recommends ten steps for a new IEA work plan.

### Ensuring Oil Security in a Dynamic and Evolving Global Market

In the coming decades, most of the world's oil supplies will come from non-OECD countries that are typically beset by political risk and social instability. The IEA member countries are currently capable of overcoming an oil import disruption for approximately 110 days.[13] In 1986, emergency stocks held 160 days worth of supply. These numbers are important, given that the IEP agreement stipulates emergency reserves equivalent to at least ninety days of net oil imports. IEA stockpiles must be expanded to keep up with rising demand levels; otherwise, the protection they offer will erode over time. It is also important to consider the status of private stocks. Just-in-time inventory practices have meant that private stocks have steadily shrunk in recent years. At the same time, as the world oil market becomes increasingly integrated, it becomes essential that major non-IEA countries, with rapidly rising oil demand, build their own strategic stockpiles. As demand grows in non-OECD countries, the IEA system protects a declining share of oil consumers.

We recommend that the IEA (1) intensify its efforts to encourage non-IEA members to build and expand strategic stockpiles that can be utilized in concert with IEA stocks in the event of a supply emergency, (2) expand IEA member strategic oil stockpiles to meet future oil market contingencies, and (3) review and update strategic stockpile policies to account for the changing dynamics of the international oil market.[14]

## Facilitating the International Development of Secure Natural Gas Markets

With global demand for natural gas expected to grow exponentially in the coming decades, the security of natural gas supplies will become increasingly important for the IEA. The United States is now moving toward greater importation of natural gas via liquefied natural gas (LNG) as U.S. domestic gas fields mature and the growth in Canadian output slows. Europe may once again need to revisit the diversity of its natural gas supplies as North Sea production may begin to decline in the coming decade and its dependence on a potentially unstable Russia increases. The IEA needs to begin considering a strategic stockpile system for natural gas. As regional gas markets evolve toward an eventual emergence of a global natural gas market, the security of supply will become an issue of growing concern. Storage plays an important role in competitive natural gas markets, in part because seasonal swings in consumption tend to be larger than the variability in production levels. Adequate levels of storage capacity are crucial to managing price volatility and supply disruptions. As the global dependence on natural gas rises in the coming decades, it will be essential to develop an emergency response system both within the IEA and regionally.

We recommend that the IEA undertake three tasks. First, it should engage in an intensified effort of study focused on natural gas security of supply within the context of growing regional and global usage of natural gas. The study should also consider whether policies are needed to encourage more efficient consumption of natural gas (e.g., emphasizing distributed generation over central station generation). Second, it should encourage greater diversification of natural gas supply, including investments in LNG terminals to ensure competitive markets and security of supply. Third, it should encourage greater private investment in natural gas storage facilities and consider national storage facilities for the development of strategic natural gas stockpiles.

## Making a Strong Commitment to
## Improving Global Access to Electricity

Ensuring long-term global energy security requires recognition by IEA countries that more must be done to close the gap between the "haves" and "have-nots." Even in our high-technology age, close to 2.4 billion people are still relying on traditional biomass to meet basic cooking and heating needs. According to the IEA's *World Energy Outlook 2002,* roughly 1.6 billion people lack access to electricity.[15] *World Energy Outlook 2002* further notes that with a "business as usual" policy approach, 1.4 billion people (mainly in rural areas) will still lack access to electricity in 2030. Ensuring that all people have access to adequate and affordable energy supplies is beyond the scope of the IEA's mission, but IEA members must address the energy needs of the developing world to lessen global energy insecurity. The 9/11 terrorist attacks certainly showed that no country is immune to the impact of problems that emerge from a lack of economic and political development. All countries will need to work cooperatively to ensure a sustainable energy future. Though the IEA has contributed significantly to international efforts examining the linkages between energy and poverty and the transition from traditional biomass to modern energy, more help will be needed to give the entire global population access to electricity. The challenge appears greatest in Sub-Saharan Africa and South Asia, where governments are strapped and private investment is hard to come by. Greater cooperation among the IEA, World Bank, the United Nations, and other multilateral organizations could have a tangible impact on the prospects for achieving energy access for all.

We recommend that the IEA (1) intensify analytical efforts related to the electrification of developing countries through greater collaboration with international development agencies such as the World Bank and the United Nations, and (2) focus R&D efforts on identifying and deploying low-cost distributed-energy-technology solutions that can meet electricity needs in rural areas.

## Increasing IEA Action in Response
## to the Climate Change Challenge

As the implementation of the Kyoto Protocol moves forward without the participation of the United States—the world's largest emitter of greenhouse gases—a growing schism in climate change policy will lead to considerable international tension. In the midst of this policy "gap," the IEA can play an important role in harmonizing international responses to the challenge of global warming. As IEA executive director Mandil mentioned recently, its members share fundamental goals relating to the "three Es"—energy security, economic growth, and environmental quality.[16] All three are essential to assuring a stable future, but achieving balance among these three Es is not easy. The IEA has been active in examining the intersection of the three Es and finding effective balancing strategies, particularly with regard to climate change. It has been looking at the role of market-based mechanisms for efficiently reducing and managing carbon dioxide emissions. It is working to share knowledge and operational experience related to a variety of promising carbon-reduction or -avoidance technologies. It is also focusing on demand-side measures (e.g., advanced appliances) that can improve energy efficiency and reduce overall emissions. Enabling technological improvements and facilitating the transfer of knowledge and experience are core competencies of the IEA. The IEA can play an effective role in helping to "spread" key climate change policy and technology solutions.

We recommend that the IEA (1) enlarge its scope of action on climate change issues and help its members and the rest of the world move beyond the Kyoto Protocol and define a new technology and market-based approach; and (2) conduct a major study, utilizing IEA models, that soberly analyzes the strengths and weaknesses of the various technology and policy pathways.

## *Finding Strategies to Deal with Deregulation and Its Impact on Energy Security*

The ongoing deregulation of electricity markets worldwide has created a number of opportunities and challenges. For much of the twentieth century, the three major components of the electricity market (generation, transmission, and distribution) were highly regulated, with vertical utilities typically holding monopolies over all three market segments within a given service area. The traditional assumption was that electricity is not a typical commodity and does not fit neatly into a pure market economy framework. Satisfying electricity demand requires processing a complicated slate of fuels and then delivering power to every household and business. Electricity is produced in response to real-time demand and has no full-fledged substitute. It cannot be stored and can only be transported through dedicated transmission lines. Lead times for building power generation and transmission infrastructure can typically measure five years or longer. But, during the past two decades, liberalization has led to greater competition primarily in the generation sector and to a lesser degree at the distribution level. Deregulation has largely been "sold" to voters in IEA countries on the promise of lower prices; but as consumers have discovered, there is no guarantee that prices will remain low. Opening markets to increasing competition generally leads to greater efficiency and lower costs. Yet if reforms are not properly designed, market opening can also lead to greater price volatility, over-reliance on certain fuels, and reliability problems.

When implemented properly, liberalization has allowed market forces to push efficiency and cost improvements, created more choices for consumers, and put overall downward pressure on prices. However, as long as there are externalities, market forces alone cannot achieve various energy security and environmental goals. In a competitive electricity market, participants become ever more focused on the short term and look for low-risk investments with a high return. Without oversight, market participants will not ensure that adequate peak generation capacities are maintained. The market does not provide incentives for supply diversity, because short-term cost decisions trump energy security considerations.

The IEA has a significant role to play in sharing information on experiences with energy deregulation and studying the consequences of liberalization on energy security and environmental goals. The IEA's *World Energy Investment Outlook 2003* highlights the challenging investment environment for electricity and other energy projects.[17] A key challenge will be to ensure that regulatory, policy, and market barriers do not prevent timely investments that promote global energy security.

We recommend that the IEA (1) expand efforts to share information between members and nonmembers alike on experiences with electricity market deregulation and its impact on reliability and energy security; and (2) focus analytical resources on examining the intersection between deregulation, investment patterns, and energy security, with the goal of finding a balance between the short-term focus of the market and long-term energy security and environmental goals.

## *Examining R&D Priorities in the Context of Improving Global Energy Security*

Future energy R&D investments must focus on a range of energy resources, including advanced nuclear systems and small-scale renewable technologies.

Solar, wind, and biomass are likely to become cost-effective solutions for off-grid power in developing countries. A variety of innovative renewable technologies are now emerging, but they will need further R&D to improve their efficiency and ability to compete effectively in the marketplace. Though it will be imperative to develop small-scale renewable technologies, it is time to confront the wishful thinkers who believe that the rising demand for clean and affordable energy supplies in the coming decades can be met primarily through the deployment of renewable energy resources. Renewable energy holds a significant but marginal role in meeting future global energy demand.

As an energy resource that has been proven to be free of greenhouse gas emissions, nuclear power has the potential to play a major role. That said, nuclear power faces a variety of economic, technological, and political challenges that must be overcome if it is to serve as a key energy technology solution. Public concerns about safety, waste storage and disposition, and proliferation are critical areas that must be addressed. Progress is occurring in the United States with the development of the long-term waste disposition site at Yucca Mountain in Nevada and a renewed commitment to nuclear R&D. The French and Japanese have led efforts to close the nuclear fuel cycle with technologies to reprocess waste and reuse it in reactors, thereby reducing the volumes of waste for long-term disposition. These leading nuclear energy countries should be at the forefront of an IEA focus on nuclear energy development.

A cooperative international framework will inevitably be a part of this nuclear energy debate. In developing countries, modular proliferation-resistant nuclear power reactors could meet global energy, environment, and sustainable development goals. Though collaboration is occurring through international frameworks such as the United States–led GEN-IV initiative and the International Atomic Energy Agency, the IEA must help make the case that nuclear expansion will be critical to addressing future global energy needs. The IEA can also encourage advanced fusion energy research. The collaborative ITER (Latin for "the way") project was originally agreed to by Reagan and Gorbachev at the Geneva Summit in 1985, in large part thanks to the efforts of Al Trivelpiece, the former director of the Oak Ridge National Laboratory, and Yevgeny Velikhov of Russia's Kurchatov Institute. Today, the project is supported by the European Union, Japan, Canada, China, Russia, South Korea, and the United States. In the future, the IEA can play a role in demonstrating the market applications of fusion energy and encouraging other "ITER-style" long-term energy R&D efforts.

We recommend that the IEA engage in an open and productive dialogue regarding the role of advanced nuclear energy technologies (fission and fusion) in addressing global energy needs and that it support the future deployment of nuclear power.

## Improving Energy Market Transparency and the Consumer-Producer Dialogue

The IEA is the leading global consolidator and provider of energy market data and information. Nevertheless, there is a strong need for more transparency and cooperation to improve the accuracy of energy data and statistics. Deficiencies in the overall accuracy, timeliness, and transparency of global energy statistics present a significant economic cost in market efficiency. For example, data deficiencies led to a significant underestimation of second-quarter 2004 global oil demand growth, which in turn encouraged OPEC to announce a production cut.

Efforts to improve market transparency will inevitably be linked to efforts to improve dialogue between producer and consumer countries. In recent years, the IEA has attempted to cultivate closer communication with OPEC. However, fundamental areas of disagreement remain. The best opportunity for deepening this dialogue may be through the International Energy Forum (IEF), which was originally created to help facilitate periodic summits between consumer and producer nations. The aim of consumer–producer dialogue should be to improve transparency and enhance the understanding of the economic decisions made on both sides.

We recommend that the IEA (1) strengthen its existing methods of dialogue and relationship building with producers, and (2) fully develop a cooperative relationship with the IEF secretariat in Riyadh—working closely together on such multilateral transparency initiatives as the Joint Oil Data Initiative.[18]

## Reaching Out to Non-IEA Countries While Maintaining a Nimble Organization

The IEA should remain a nimble organization that can respond effectively to energy crises. In the decision-making process, the IEA Governing Board—which consists of senior energy officials from member countries—has recognized the importance of maintaining a rapid response capability. Through its Industry Advisory Board, as well as through its day-to-day activities, the IEA maintains an effective network of contacts at international organizations, universities, nongovernmental organizations, private companies, and industry associations to call upon for assistance. This network was successfully tapped during past crises and will be called upon in the future.

Yet as rapid energy demand growth shifts to the developing world, the IEA needs to reach out to nonmember countries. It is time to consider a framework for the integration of large countries, such as Brazil, China, India, and Russia, into a cooperative arrangement with the IEA. Relationships with these countries are important and cannot rely only on intermittent dialogue. The two major options are to create another parallel energy institution dedicated to developing countries in collaboration with the IEA or to define criteria that would allow these countries to enter the organization on a "partnership" basis. We recommend that the IEA move quickly to expand its framework for working effectively with non-IEA countries.

### Committing IEA Members to Addressing Global Energy Security Challenges

The challenges described on the preceding pages will require a sustained commitment from IEA members. The United States can and must lead this effort to reinvigorate the IEA's core mission and expand its vision to address global energy security. Since its rejection of the Kyoto Protocol in 2001, the United States has faced considerable criticism internationally with regard to its energy and environmental policies. America can show its commitment by significantly increasing its financial contribution to the IEA and by calling on other members to do the same. We recommend that the United States lead by example and significantly increase its financial commitment to the IEA and that it demonstrate its support for an expanded IEA role in addressing the major issues affecting global energy security.

### Conclusion

We believe the IEA has the skill and agility to take on new missions to address the threats that global poverty, political instability, terrorism, and energy price volatility may present. The United States should lead this effort to modernize the IEA's mission because improving global energy security will dramatically enhance America's own national security. Energy can be a path to bring Russia and China closer to the United States, enabling America to avoid destructive competition and better manage issues of weapons proliferation and regional security. Bringing Brazil and India into the IEA's fold will help advance free trade in energy and improve regional stability in Latin America and South Asia. Enhancing the consumer–producer dialogue will enable the United States and other IEA members to constructively engage with the energy-exporting countries of the Middle East as they undertake potentially destabilizing but essential political and economic reforms. The IEA has served its mission well for the past thirty years; the time is ripe to prepare it for the new century.

## Notes

1. U.S. Energy Information Administration, *International Energy Outlook 2003* (Washington: U.S. Department of Energy, 2004).

2. International Energy Agency (IEA), *World Energy Outlook 2004* (Paris: IEA, 2004), 25–33.

3. Strategic oil stocks under the IEA system can include "commercial stocks" held by the oil industry, "government stocks" held exclusively for emergency purposes and financed by the central government (e.g. the U.S. Strategic Petroleum Reserve), and "agency stocks" maintained for emergencies cooperatively by both public and private bodies on cost-sharing basis.

4. The full text of the "Agreement on the International Energy Program" may be found at http://www.iea.org/Textbase/about/IEP.PDF.

5. William F. Martin, Ryukichi Imai, and Helga Steeg, *Maintaining Energy Security in a Global Context: A Report to the Trilateral Commission* (New York: Trilateral Commission, 1996), 13–14.

6. Daniel Yergin, *The Prize: The Epic Quest for Oil, Money, and Power* (New York: Simon & Schuster, 1991), 630.

7. France later joined the IEA in 1992.

8. Martin, Imai, and Steeg, *Maintaining Energy Security in a Global Context,* 15.

9. Richard Scott, *The History of the International Energy Agency, 1974–1994: IEA the First 20 Years* (Paris: International Energy Agency, 1995).

10. See IEA, http://www.iea.org/about/files/factshee1.pdf.

11. Claude Mandil, "The IEA in 2003," International Energy and Environment Program seminar, Nitze School of Advanced International Studies, Johns Hopkins University, Washington, November 12, 2003.

12. IEA, http://www.iea.org/about/index.htm.

13. IEA, *Oil Supply Security: The Emergency Response Potential of IEA Countries in 2000* (Paris: IEA, 2001).

14. See a detailed discussion of this concept by David Goldwyn and Michelle Billig in chapter 21 of this volume.

15. IEA, *World Energy Outlook 2002,* 365.

16. Mandil, "IEA in 2003."

17. IEA, *World Energy Investment Outlook 2003* (Paris: IEA, 2003).

18. Participants in the Joint Oil Data Initiative, which aims to standardize and improve the accuracy of oil data collection worldwide, include such organizations as the United Nations, OPEC, IEA, the Asia-Pacific Economic Cooperation forum, and the European Union.

# Commentary on Part I

## Alvaro Silva-Calderón

Part I, "The Global Framework," gives a welcome opportunity to offer my views, as a former secretary general of the Organization of Petroleum Exporting Countries (OPEC), on its positive contribution toward stabilizing global energy markets. The organization has played a significant role in the world energy industry for more than four decades, through its direct and substantial involvement in the oil sector. I believe OPEC will continue to play this role in the decades ahead. Oil has been the leading component of the world energy mix since OPEC's inception, and I and the authors of the chapters in this part believe this will be the case for the foreseeable future.

The authors of the four chapters have handled their subject matter in a thorough and compelling manner, but their views do not necessarily match my own, nor those of OPEC member countries. With respect to the first two chapters, by Adam Sieminski and Daniel Yergin, I would disagree primarily with details and statistics, rather than with issues of substance.

There is a stark contrast in the treatment afforded by the chapters on OPEC and the International Energy Agency. William Martin and Evan Harrje's chapter on the agency is mild, as it discusses the future stability of the oil market, compared with the gloomy prospects for OPEC that are presented somewhat forcefully by Edward Morse and Amy Jaffe in their chapter. This latter chapter contains an inherent contradiction. Though it marvels at "one of the most remarkable success stories . . . over the past forty years," states that OPEC "has not simply managed to survive but can be credited with succeeding in its basic objectives" and describes OPEC as "a political enigma and intriguing subject," it nevertheless depicts a near-doomsday scenario for the organization in the not-too-distant future, something I believe flies in the face of the evidence.

117

Generally speaking, as one would expect, I am troubled when reading literature that carries—or worse still, is based upon—the assumption that the oil supply from particular regions of the world is insecure. This may not only be misrepresentative of the reality of OPEC's record and dismissive of sustained efforts by leading producers to ensure stable markets at all times, but it may also distract attention from the need to identify the essential conditions that are required for the orderly evolution of the market in the future, and to keep it in balance with the fundamentals of supply and demand.

## Energy Supply and Demand Outlook

I agree completely with Sieminski's predictions that the world will continue to need large quantities of oil and gas. And, for the foreseeable future, oil is destined to maintain its position as the world's leading energy provider. The overall picture for global oil demand growth projected by OPEC is nearly identical. Nevertheless, more significant differences exist within individual country groupings, with OPEC's *World Energy Model* figures typically projecting lower demand for the Organization for Economic Cooperation and Development, but higher demand from developing countries. From the demand perspective, therefore, despite this apparent convergence in the global outlook, there remains considerable disagreement over individual regional prospects.

Turning to the supply side, OPEC's overriding assessment is that the resource base is plentiful enough to meet the projected increases in demand. The outlook for OPEC's market share in the first decade of the twenty-first century is relatively stable. By 2020, when OPEC's share will approach 50 percent, non-OPEC production will have effectively reached a plateau. Increases in developing-country production and nonconventional oil will barely compensate for decreases in conventional production, particularly in Western Europe and North America. Russian production will stay at its peak levels. I expect only a small long-term increase in production levels from the Caspian Sea region.

## Oil Investment Horizons

The assumption has been that the key producers in OPEC will meet most of the growth in future oil demand, because the majority of the giant oil fields are located in these countries. Nevertheless, these giant fields are mature. Current OPEC producers must press ahead with new discoveries of oil and gas fields. This will require huge investments, to maintain the same level of current production, as well as to meet the growth in future demand. A steady flow of investment is essential if the world is to attain oil price stability.

Investment is also needed to maintain spare capacity, which can be brought onstream at short notice when a lack of crude in the market puts pressure on the price structure. This can be achieved by opening upstream petroleum sectors to international oil companies and assisting producers to develop their hydrocarbon resources through various types of petroleum upstream contracts, such as production-sharing agreements or service contracts. New investment will also enable producers to access new technology and increase efficiency, so they can maintain competitive, cost-effective, and successful exploration and development programs. However, the opening of upstream sectors is a sovereign issue that needs to be handled in accordance with the overall petroleum policy of each individual producing country.

In seeking to assess the full extent of investment needs, we find ourselves facing the following key challenges. The first is uncertainty over future trends in demand growth. Sound investment in the expansion of OPEC's production capacity of such magnitude, over the long term, needs to be carefully balanced against future demand trends, to ensure that the demand for OPEC's oil expands fast enough to absorb its growing future production capacity. The second is non-OPEC oil supply. Technological progress has played an important role in rendering production from high-cost oil outside OPEC economically feasible. To maintain market stability, the question is: "How much longer can non-OPEC output maintain its steady growth?" It is projected that most non-OPEC supply will begin to fall in the middle of the current decade or so, but OPEC cannot simply bank on such an eventuality. The third is the future oil price path. There is a strong relationship between investment and the perception of future prices. This is clearly evident in the most recent price decline of 1997–98 and the current projections of capital expenditure on the part of international oil companies. It will be essential to maintain a reasonable price range, both to encourage timely investment and to sustain oil demand.

Moreover, in OPEC, we believe that there should be a fair distribution of oil revenue and that the different interests concerned should be properly aligned. In other words, the various parties—natural resource-owners, investors, and consumer governments—should seek arrangements in which they can prosper together. OPEC has always acknowledged the legitimate right of investors to a fair profit. However, some investors fail to acknowledge, in turn, the legitimate right of natural-resource-owning governments to fair consideration. Fair consideration translates into a royalty representing a significant percentage of gross production. Instead, these investors insist on so-called flexible fiscal regimes, which allow costs to increase unreasonably at times of higher oil prices and, conversely, for the fiscal take of governments or national oil companies to fall disproportionately at times of lower prices.

Thus, the interests of investors and natural resource-owners are misaligned regarding price. A proper alignment requires that a guaranteed and very significant percentage of gross revenue goes to the producer governments. In this way, the latter share in the price risk. The profit risk, however, must be shouldered by the investors.

Furthermore, the situation in the oil market can easily become distorted through the imposition of high rates of taxation on petroleum products in consumer markets. The consumer government's take on oil products can be as high as 80 percent, leaving just 20 percent of the final consumer price to be shared among the producing countries and oil companies. Now, though I do not question the sovereign right of any nation to pursue its own fiscal policy, I nevertheless feel compelled to point out that such policies can have a significant impact upon fundamentals in the world energy mix, as well as compromising a fair distribution of petroleum revenue.

## The OPEC of the Future

OPEC has evolved over the past four decades, and its founding principles are as valid today as they were in 1960. They are laid down in the OPEC Statute:

> co-ordination and unification of the petroleum policies of Member Countries . . . ensuring the stabilization of prices in international oil markets, with a view to eliminating harmful and unnecessary fluctuations . . . securing . . . a steady income to the producing countries . . . an efficient, economic and regular supply of petroleum to consuming nations; and a fair return on their capital to those investing in the petroleum industry.

OPEC has additional concerns to pursue, including a balance of supply and demand, the adequacy and equity of environmental measures, trade liberalization, and the flow of investment. We believe that, if OPEC ceased to exist today, the market would soon be forced to create a substitute, because the industry and the market could not operate as smoothly without it.

Therefore, I cannot share Morse's belief that OPEC's existence, unity, and success will not continue in the future. The truth of the maxim "if OPEC did not exist or were to die, another OPEC would be invented" lies in the fact that, without OPEC's influence over supply, there could be a huge surge in oil price volatility with far-reaching adverse effects on growth in the oil industry and on the world economy at large. OPEC's quest for reasonable, stable prices means not only cutting output when prices are on a downward path but also increasing production should prices threaten to spiral out of control in the opposite direction. OPEC works for the benefit of both producers and consumers. However, to be truly effective, OPEC's market stabilization measures at all times require the support of non-OPEC producers, as well as other stakeholders.

At a more general level, OPEC seeks to create a world where energy security extends to the poorest communities across the globe. These communities have the same right as consumers in richer parts of the world to cleaner, more efficient forms of energy, which will support them on the path to sustainable development and help eradicate their chronic levels of poverty.

## Producers, Consumers, and Cooperation

Implicit in the quest for energy security is the need for cooperation at all levels of the industry, involving OPEC and non-OPEC producers at one level and producers and consumers at another, while at the same time embracing international oil companies and financial institutions. It is an evident fact of life that the more OPEC and non-OPEC producers concentrate on the partnerships they have, the more they will gain. They should try to establish joint ventures or cooperation in areas of mutual concern and provide access to their pool of technical and financial resources on the basis of fair commercial terms, consistency, and reliability. It is also vital to identify common ground for a mutually acceptable fiscal and legal framework for building new relationships between the international oil companies and OPEC member countries.

OPEC was founded on the premise of cooperation in September 1960, when five oil-producing developing countries joined forces to safeguard their legitimate national interests. This was at a time when the international petroleum industry, outside the former Soviet Union, was under the control of the established industrial powers. Other oil-producing developing countries joined OPEC in the next decade and a half. They sought to demonstrate that even developing countries had rights and that their indigenous natural resources were more than just a convenience for the rich consumer nations, to be pumped out of the ground as and when these foreign powers deemed fit.

The next major advance occurred in the late 1980s, when non-OPEC producers entered the picture. This was a consequence of, first, the gradual erosion of the oil price structure in the early 1980s and its eventual collapse in 1986; second, a significant reduction in OPEC's market influence, due to its sizable loss of market share after the late 1970s; and third, the realization by non-OPEC producers after 1986 that market stabilization measures were urgently needed and that OPEC required support in providing them.

Big strides were made in the producer–consumer dialogue in the 1990s, in tandem with the rising profile of the International Energy Forum, and it was recently agreed to establish its permanent Secretariat in an OPEC member country, Saudi Arabia. There has also been a strengthening of the relationship between OPEC and the International Energy Agency. The two groups held their first-ever joint press conference at the Seventeenth World Petroleum Congress in Rio de Janeiro in September 2002, and there was a joint workshop on oil investment prospects at OPEC's Vienna headquarters in June 2003.

There seems to be little doubt that the concept of cooperation within the world oil sector is now well established and that the industry is better off if there is an underlying consensus on the major issues that concern all parties— such as pricing, stability, security of demand and supply, investment, environmental issues, and sustainable development. I should like to conclude by thanking the editors for inviting me to contribute to this important book, on behalf of OPEC. Clearly, much effort has gone into producing a book that seeks to address issues of concern to many people today in the energy sector and to do so in a way that balances all shades of opinion. I think it will constitute an important addition to today's energy literature.

# Part II

# Russia and Eurasia

After the global framework delineated in part I, this and the following parts turn to a discussion of regional issues, and the concluding part describes a new energy security strategy. Part II discusses Russia—with the world's largest gas reserves, and whose oil exports now rival those of Saudi Arabia —and Eurasia, whose oil reserves in the Caspian Sea region are equivalent to those of the North Sea. In a turn of history's wheel, the West's former Soviet adversaries have become partners not only against terrorism but also potentially in enhancing Western energy security and reducing dependence on the Middle East. The issues for U.S. and Western policy are how best to strengthen the trade and investment relationship in oil and gas, to pursue a multiple-pipeline policy to advance that relationship and broader objectives in the region, and to coordinate with the developing European market in natural gas.

These and related issues are addressed by Julia Nanay, who considers prospects for a regional renaissance in Russian and Caspian oil and gas; by Jan Kalicki and Jonathan Elkind, who analyze Eurasian transportation futures; and by Loyola de Palacio, who focuses on reforming the gas market.

In chapter 5, Nanay argues that Russian and Caspian Sea region supplies can create diversity but cannot substitute for the Middle East. She analyzes rising oil production in the former region, comparing it with the latter, assesses the perception and reality of energy security in these two regions, and weighs the political and geopolitical risks in Russia, Azerbaijan, and Kazakhstan. Considering the United States–Russia energy relationship and the role of international and national oil companies, Nanay concludes that the long-term trend will be that, in energy security terms, Russian and Caspian supplies will be no different from other non-OPEC supplies, and that ultimately projects must stand on their own commercial merit.

In chapter 6, Kalicki and Elkind survey the basic trends and opportunities for oil and gas transportation in Russia and Eurasia in the 1990s, analyze the characteristics that define the current period, and assess the future possibilities of integrating regional energy producers with global markets through a completed array of transportation networks stretching west, south, and east, as well as north. They argue that pipeline development has contributed to an expanding energy security system providing regional oil and gas producers with alternatives to traditional pipeline monopolies in Russia, and that in the future Russians themselves will have to define the extent to which new pipelines should be developed outside state control. Kalicki and Elkind conclude with recommendations for all concerned states in the region, including an expanded transportation dialogue involving the United States, the European Union, and regional states, and new transit openings to the Middle East and Asia, from Iran to China and South Korea.

In chapter 7, Loyola de Palacio, a former E.U. vice president and energy commissioner, describes the creation of an integrated single European market for natural gas in the context of creating an enlarged European Union of twenty-five member states from May 1, 2004. She analyzes demand and supply characteristics and developments in the E.U. gas market, imports and infrastructure requirements, and the creation of a more open and competitive internal energy market through trans-European networks and the abolition of exclusive monopolies. Turning to external suppliers, she notes the continued importance of long-term contracts but also the introduction of new opportunities through spot markets, hubs, and corresponding services. She highlights Europe's key gas supply relationship and energy dialogue with Russia, additional gas supplies from Norway, Algeria, and the Caspian Sea region, and the need for a shared regulatory framework providing stability and clarity to the market—arguing that the security of supply is supported by the security of demand through a structure of complementary interests.

In his commentary on part II, Viktor Kalyuzhny, ambassador and former Russian energy minister and deputy foreign minister, notes that energy security is just as important from Moscow's perspective as that of Washington or Brussels. Russia does not expand its exports to displace those of other traditional suppliers, and its interests are determined by its dual role as a leading producer-exporter and a large consumer, where the state must strike an optimum balance. In addition, Kalyuzhny considers it axiomatic that the state must maintain control over the main oil pipelines as "the only mechanism of effective state regulation available today," while believing that multiple pipelines should continue to develop throughout the region "on strictly commercial terms," without advancing political agendas. In the gas market, he emphasizes complementary, long-term supply–demand arrangements to maintain its stability and security, with regard to both Europe and new "energy export bridges" to Asia and North America, while seeking greater understanding of Russian domestic requirements.

# 5

# Russia and the Caspian Sea Region

## *Julia Nanay*

The steady and seemingly endless increase in Russian oil production during the 2000–2003 period gave rise to the view that Russian supplies to world markets could rival those of the Middle East's top oil producer, Saudi Arabia. In particular, after September 11, 2001, when the United States was confronted with terrorist attacks that included a large group of Saudi nationals, the urgency of finding secure energy alternatives to Saudi oil pointed U.S. policymakers in the direction of Russia and also reinforced U.S. resolve to access supplies from Azerbaijan and Kazakhstan.

Years after the 9/11 attacks, the importance of Russian, Azeri, and Kazakh oil supplies for U.S. and world markets still seems clear, but the security of supply from these countries carries its own mix of risks. These are different from those of the Middle East, but they cannot be dismissed. What is more, the sheer scale of the Middle Eastern reserve base, coupled with its excess capacity, means that Russian and Caspian supplies can create supply diversity but cannot substitute for the Middle East.

This chapter sets out to assess the contribution of Russia and the Caspian Sea region, compared with the Middle East, to Western energy security. It weighs the political and geopolitical risks in Russia, Azerbaijan, and Kazakhstan, and it then considers the potential contribution of the United States–Russia energy relationship, in light of continued export constraints from Russia. The chapter also weighs competition by other importers for Russian energy resources, and the contribution of the Caspian producers to U.S. energy security in light of alternative pipelines from that region. It sets forth the close relationship between future production and export outlets and the need for a strong commercial foundation in assessing the contribution of Russia and the Caspian region to Western energy security. The challenge for

127

U.S. energy and foreign policy is to make sure that oil from Russia and the Caspian is produced in a timely fashion and flows unimpeded to world oil markets.


## Rising Oil Production in Russia and the Caspian Region versus the Potential of the Middle East

Russian oil production of 8.2 million barrels per day (mmbpd) in 2003 nearly broke even with the level of oil production in Saudi Arabia,[1] where 2003 crude oil output reached 8.8 mmbpd. Russia's growth in oil production is due to the efficiencies introduced into this industry by its private companies and the entrepreneurial class of investors that emerged in the early 1990s after the Soviet Union's breakup. It was not until the late 1990s, however, and particularly after a devastating 1998 financial crisis, that some of these privatized Russian oil companies turned more actively toward using Western service companies, Western technology, and Western business practices.

This turn toward the West for technical and business assistance resulted in rapid oil production hikes, particularly in the 2000–2003 period. Since 2000, the production increases in a high-oil-price environment have translated into a financial bonanza for a few individuals in Russia. This small group of rich entrepreneurs, referred to as oligarchs, has elicited both awe and envy, and more recently, a political backlash. Any lasting or intrusive backlash could affect the ability of some companies to meet ambitious production and export targets. Predictions of a slowdown in production growth in 2004 and beyond are now being heard.

Five key companies comprise the privatized Russian oil industry: LUKoil, Yukos, TNK, Surgutneftegaz, and Sibneft. TNK implemented a merger with BP in June 2003 to form TNK-BP, making this a formidable Russian-Western company alliance, which is now competing against the other indigenous players. Juxtaposed against the private companies are three important state-owned firms, which also occupy significant positions in the Russian business landscape. These are the oil company Rosneft, the gas company Gazprom, and the oil pipeline monopoly Transneft. In September 2004, the Russian government announced the takeover of Rosneft by Gazprom, which would essentially merge the two state companies to create an oil subsidiary within Gazprom, increasing its oil production from 121,000 barrels per day (bpd) to 550,000 bpd with Rosneft. The two major state companies at that point would be the Gazprom–Rosneft combination and Transneft. In December, Yukos's largest subsidiary, Yuganskneftegaz, was taken over by Rosneft—a move meant to create a major Russian national oil company that would rival Saudi Aramco.

In Azerbaijan and Kazakhstan, the national oil companies—Socar and KazMunaiGaz—are the dominant domestic actors. Both Socar and Kaz-MunaiGaz rely extensively not just on Western service companies but also on partnerships with Western and other foreign oil companies to attract the financial and technical muscle that they need to develop complex offshore and onshore oil fields. Azerbaijan and Kazakhstan are set to experience a spurt in production growth by 2010.

Given the anticipated output increases in Russia, Azerbaijan, and Kazakhstan, assumptions are being made about the future role of these three countries for U.S. energy security in the twenty-first century. As figure 5.1 shows, Russia, Azerbaijan, and Kazakhstan are now producing more than 10 mmbpd of crude oil and natural gas liquids (NGLs),[2] or more than half the 19.7 mmbpd of crude and NGL output in 2003 registered by the five largest Middle Eastern producers—Saudi Arabia, Iran, Iraq, Kuwait, and the United Arab Emirates.[3] In 2003, Russia, Azerbaijan, and Kazakhstan exported about 5 mmbpd of crude oil, versus estimated exports of about 15 mmbpd from the five Middle Eastern producers.

Figure 5.1. Oil Production in Russia, Kazakhstan, and Azerbaijan, 1988–2010 (thousand barrels per day)

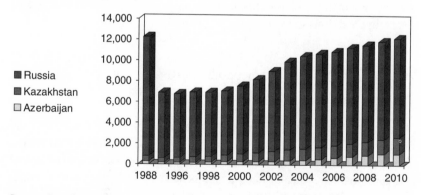

*Sources:* Data for 1988 and 1995–2003 from *BP Statistical Review;* data for 2004–10 from *PFC Estimates.*

At the same time, Russia's production today does not match the output level it experienced in 1988, when its production peaked at 11.4 mmbpd.[4] It is not even clear if Russian production can reach the 1988 level again by 2010 or even 2020. The combined production of Russia, Azerbaijan, and Kazakhstan in 1988 hit 12.2 mmbpd, a level that may not be reached again until 2010, by which time Azerbaijan and Kazakhstan should be producing significantly larger volumes.

The debate now is about how sustainable the current steady rise in oil production and exports is from these three countries, and how much this matters for U.S. energy security. Though growing volumes of oil from Russia and the Caspian region are a welcome addition to world energy supplies—and particularly to supplies not from the Organization of Petroleum Exporting Countries (OPEC)—this output can continue to supplement production from the Middle East but cannot substitute for it.

Russia and the Caspian region provide the world with access to additional oil resources and help mitigate the effects of short-term supply disruptions. This enhances supply diversity. But these countries do not provide the cushion that only the Middle East can offer in excess capacity.[5]

Middle Eastern countries adhere to quotas imposed by OPEC, which keeps some of their oil off the market. Overquota oil is either shut in, with fields producing at less than capacity, or is kept in storage. Such OPEC practices may offer the world an insurance policy against supply disruptions, if the volume of excess capacity is adequate to redress a serious disruption. Non-OPEC countries, including Russia, have no incentive to hold spare capacity, and they do not keep oil off the market. Hence, they cannot suddenly produce more oil in the event of a supply disruption. In addition, Russia's cold climate is not conducive to production fluctuations or control because of freezing conditions in its oil fields.

## Political and Geopolitical Risks in Russia, Azerbaijan, and Kazakhstan

Although Russia, Azerbaijan, and Kazakhstan are outside the volatile Middle East, they are exposed to other sorts of risks. Azerbaijan is located in the equally volatile Caucasus and depends on a stable Georgia to get its oil to export markets. Kazakhstan is a landlocked country, juggling its national interests against those of two powerful neighbors, Russia and China. Geopolitical factors are important for both Azerbaijan and Kazakhstan, because as landlocked countries, their ability to export oil hinges on the goodwill of their neighbors. The ability of all three countries to produce oil is subject to ongoing political and geopolitical shocks to their systems.

Russia has experienced a political shake-up, with President Vladimir Putin's allies gaining a majority in the December 2003 parliamentary elections, Putin's acceding to a second term as president in March 2004, and his steadily increasing dominance since then. The Russian oil industry is transitioning to tighter coordination and control, with the president playing a more direct interventionist role. The free-wheeling years that characterized the last decade in the Russian oil sector are clearly over, and Russian business-people will be more beholden to the state. How much this will affect Russian oil production growth in the future is not yet clear.

Azerbaijan recently experienced a dynastic presidential transition, as power was handed from father to son. Azerbaijan's new president, Ilham Aliyev, was formerly second in command at the state-owned company Socar, and he will keep his hand in the oil sector. Kazakhstan's presidential elections have been promised for 2006. There, too, President Nursultan Nazarbayev and his family are closely involved with the oil sector and state company KazMunaiGaz.

All elections in this region are manipulated by power brokers, who want to make sure that the levers of control over key economic sectors like oil are kept in a few hands. Only Georgia and Ukraine appear at this point able to break out of this mold but then, they are only energy transit routes and not significant producers. While the United States and European Union are working closely with these countries' Western-leaning leaders to help make their democratic transition a success, hoping that this presents an example to other countries in the region, Western intentions may backfire. Other countries in this region could crack down further on those opposing the status quo in order to avoid a fate similar to what befell the previous leadership in Georgia and Ukraine. What is more, Presidents Mikheil Saakashvili and Viktor Yushchenko may respectively define agendas for Georgia and Ukraine that sometimes conflict with Washington's goals.

Other domestic factors in all these countries that could cloud positive prospects for their oil sectors include power plays among different political groups, as well as government and private business. A number of these groups may exert pressure to divert the benefits from the petroleum sector from national interests, such as enhanced investment in new exploration or energy transportation, to their own cause. In short, by their positive or negative actions, state-owned national oil companies, domestic private oil companies, other domestic business interests, and various state-owned monopoly players and regulatory agencies can affect how much oil is produced and exported. They can determine the access that foreign companies have to upstream and pipeline investment opportunities and the economic and legal terms of access. The outcome may determine whether foreign capital flows or not and ultimately, whether the oil gets produced or not. All these risk factors militate against making clear judgments about the magnitude of the upward slope of the future production curves from these countries.

## Energy Security: Perception versus Reality

Production from Russia, Azerbaijan, and Kazakhstan accounts for about 12 percent of the 78.6 mmbpd of global oil production recorded in 2003. It is expected that these three countries will continue to increase their share of the world oil supply pie until 2010. Beyond 2010, their share may remain static or even decline, particularly because of questions relating to the sustainability of higher levels of Russian production, even without taking into account other political and geopolitical risk factors that could have a negative impact. Until 2010, these three suppliers, and particularly Russia, pose a challenge for OPEC producers, which will have to accommodate growing supplies to world markets from these non-OPEC suppliers. But given the anticipated growth in world demand, this challenge can be accommodated. After 2010, the challenge these producers pose will diminish as their combined share of global production growth is expected to decline.

As already stressed above, the role of these three countries for U.S. energy security is defined by U.S. fear of oil supply disruptions from the Middle East. This fear dictates that non-OPEC suppliers like Russia and the Caspian countries are critical to future U.S. well-being.

Because of the questions surrounding the future of Iraq and further U.S. intentions in the Middle East, there has been a frenzy of activity by the United States and other large oil-consuming nations to diversify oil supplies away from the Middle East. Oil consumers, particularly Asian ones, have responded in the same way because they have been sensitized by U.S. soundings about Middle Eastern undependability.

Japan and China are in a seemingly desperate race with each other to secure competing pipelines that direct Russian oil supplies to their markets, and they are buying growing volumes of Urals crude oil for their refineries.[6] Japan and China also compete with the United States for access to Russian and Kazakh resources. Though the United States is trying to get an expensive pipeline built to the Russian northern port of Murmansk that would feed oil from a deepwater port to the U.S. East Coast market, Japan and China are each trying to get Russian pipelines built that are directed toward their markets. In addition to securing Russian oil supplies, China is also targeting Kazakh oil with the intention of securing a pipeline dedicated to the Chinese market.

Some of the costly measures detailed above are unnecessary unless the Middle East is destabilized over the longer term. Short-term disruptions can be accommodated. Today's very efficient global crude and product trading system, combined with a surge of capacity in Saudi Arabia, has the ability to compensate for short-term supply interruptions, as numerous examples in Iraq, Venezuela, and Nigeria demonstrate.

Globally, there are more than 1 billion barrels of strategic reserves. Refiners today are able to manage on lower inventories compared with ten years ago thanks to increased efficiency, as well as flexible crude and product trading. The markets will effectively continue to manage short-term discontinuities, barring a major geopolitical crisis or highly unlikely event, such as a cutoff of Saudi oil. The fundamentals of the oil markets do not justify either the high oil prices accompanying the war with Iraq or U.S. fears of oil shortages. The problem has been one of perception, not reality—unless, of course, Saudi production is knocked out of the world's supply stream.

The longer-lasting legacy of the Iraq war is the fear of a more widespread disruption of supplies from the Middle East. Therefore, when it comes to energy security, all projects in regions other than the Middle East will now be regarded more closely as potential alternatives to the Middle East. The perception will remain that the Middle East carries both a political and a contractual risk. This may not be justified, because as the Iraq war demonstrates, the risks of depending on the Persian Gulf have been exaggerated, and billions of dollars in national product and consumer income were spent unnecessarily on war premiums.

Conversely, it is precisely this phenomenon of turning away from the Middle East because of "perceived" risk that has raised the perception of the strategic value to the United States of sources like Russia and the Caspian region. Russian oil is now being seen as a "security blanket" in case of a Saudi disruption. In 2003, the United States imported 9.65 mmbpd of crude oil, of which 4.6 mmbpd was sourced from OPEC, including 1.72 mmbpd from Saudi Arabia. Saudi Arabia accounted for 18 percent of U.S. imports. In comparison, in 2003, U.S. imports from Russia reached a mere 149,000 bpd.[7]

As pointed out above, however, the oil politics of Russia and the Caspian region bring their own uncertainties. In fact, one does not have to look too far back to understand how problematic it is to base long-term oil policy decisions on U.S. foreign policy attachments to particular regions or particular foreign leaders when the regions and leaders can undergo unpredictable transformations.

The U.S. relationship with Russia has gone from expressions of mutual support and the intent to form an energy partnership, as demonstrated in the September 2003 Saint Petersburg U.S.-Russian Commercial Energy Summit, to voicing misgivings. From the October 2003 arrest of Russian company Yukos' chief executive and leading core shareholder Mikhail Khodorkovsky to the forced auction of Yugansk amid a mountain of tax demands in December 2004, the warm ties of 2003 have given way to an uncertain view of the future. The U.S. government is unsure what to expect from President Putin. Will he extend a helping hand to mitigate U.S. energy security concerns, or will he exercise caution in the further development of the Russian energy sector? Will President Putin want Russia to become another Saudi Arabia for the United States?

## The Underlying Goals of a U.S.–Russian Energy Partnership

The United States has focused on Russia for an energy partnership because of its impressive oil production increases. No other country has made such gains during the past three years, with Russian output (crude oil and NGLs) rising from 6.8 mmbpd in 2001 to an average of close to 8.5 mmbpd in 2003. As mentioned above, this has been made possible by the efficiencies introduced into the Russian oil industry by the private Russian oil companies. Private Russian oil companies have restored order to the disarray that the Russian oil industry faced after 1991.

This is in contrast to the gas industry, where privatization was not introduced. Because Gazprom remains the monopoly producer and transporter of gas, the industry has not realized the same output gains as with oil. Yet much like Gazprom, the Russian oil companies have continued to exploit existing big fields, and the daunting task of developing large new greenfield oil and gas projects lies ahead for all parties.

The U.S. government has welcomed the growth in Russian oil output and is seeking to define a closer energy partnership, whereby U.S. oil companies would participate in the development of the expensive new fields and pipelines that will be decisive for future oil production increases in Russia. The U.S. government has also encouraged U.S. company participation in gas developments. A number of U.S. oil companies have been seeking to forge closer ties not only with some of the private Russian companies but also with Russian state-owned company Gazprom.

Just as the U.S.-Russian energy relationship appeared to be headed toward a clearer definition in 2003, the Khodorkovsky arrest has raised questions both about the stable evolution of Russia's oil sector and the legitimacy of asset ownership by all private Russian oil companies. In some respects, it was Khodorkovsky who epitomized the concrete elements of the U.S.-Russian energy partnership, with his numerous trips to Washington, his personal relationships with U.S. policymakers, and his determination to sell part of what in 2003 briefly became the newly merged company Yukos-Sibneft to a U.S. company. He was also seen as a potential presidential candidate in Russia's 2008 elections.

Khodorkovsky's abrupt removal from the world of Russian oil poses an unusual dilemma for the U.S. government and for U.S. companies. It also exposes a problem for the way the U.S. perceives its energy security, which is often based on leaders and key personalities, as well as personal relationships. This approach jeopardizes security if those leaders or personalities either act in ways the United States cannot condone or disappear from the scene.

In the case of Russia, Putin was the leader that the George W. Bush administration felt could deliver on the U.S. energy partnership and security agenda, and Khodorkovsky was the key oil personality. Putin's endorsement of the tax evasion and fraud charges against Khodorkovsky complicates the U.S. energy relationship with Russia. Some in the West see Khodorkovsky's arrest as an effort on Putin's part to eliminate a political rival. With Khodorkovsky taken out of the picture—and other key shareholders also in detention or in exile—U.S. companies suddenly had no one to negotiate with to acquire a stake in YukosSibneft. And, after the December 2003 announcement that the merger between Yukos and Sibneft would be headed for dissolution in 2004, any further action on buying into the merged company and then even its component parts had to be shelved. The difficult legal issues involved in disentangling the Yukos-Sibneft assets have been overshadowed by the rapid onslaught of back tax claims against Yukos that have ended the company's ability to function as a whole.

In a complex business environment like Russia, the arrest of Khodor-kovsky may be fortuitous because it happened before large amounts of money changed hands between a U.S. company and YukosSibneft. His arrest should give U.S. and other foreign oil companies time to pause and ponder what the best business model is when approaching oil sector investments in Russia. In the aftermath of Khodorkovsky's arrest and the assault against Yukos, the U.S.-Russian energy partnership remains undefined and without a clear sense of direction.

## A Lack of Export Pipelines Diminishes Russia's Role for U.S. Energy Security

As Russian production has risen, export pipeline and port capacities have not kept pace with the higher export expectations of the private Russian oil companies. The state-owned pipeline monopoly, Transneft, has been unable to address the multitude of export-direction demands of the private Russian producers.

Transneft's clash with private producers is largely a function of the state's determination to maintain its centralized control over exports. This provides the national pipeline monopoly with significant power and allows it to promote its own agenda, championing those pipelines and ports it wants to have built.

In addition to the export questions, Transneft's attention is absorbed by the complexities of the existing Russian domestic pipeline system, which spans a vast inhospitable territory and which requires constant maintenance. Transneft's alleged crude oil pipeline export capacity to non-CIS countries was about 3.5 mmbpd in 2004 (which also accommodates oil exports from Kazakhstan). In addition, about 900,000 bpd of crude can be exported, re-lying on rail. Rail transport is more costly, making the economics attractive only as long as high oil prices last. It is also environmentally problematic, with frequent reports of spills. Under current conditions, some private Russian oil companies are able to export more than 50 percent of the crude oil they produce (as crude and products), with the remainder of their supplies flowing to lower priced domestic markets.

Despite the desire of private Russian oil companies to build new pipe-lines and increase export outlets, their ambitions are subordinated to the state's agenda. The Russian state today is clearly not prepared to relinquish its control over pipelines and ports. Compromises between the companies and Transneft will determine export capacity for the rest of this decade.

The timing and direction of export routes will affect the private companies' production targets and exploration choices. If the private companies cannot market their oil, they will not produce it. The lack of agreement between Transneft and the Russian oil companies on export capacity and pipeline direction comes at a time when Russian companies are targeting greater supplies to Europe, the United States, and Asia, possibly at the expense of some Middle Eastern barrels. Without additional export pipelines, they will not be able to access Asian and U.S. markets with significant supplies. Foreign oil investors in Russia are also subjected to the vagaries of this centralized control over export flows. It would be foolish for any company to make major investments in oil fields on the Russian mainland without some assurance that a new oil export pipeline will be built.

Several private Russian oil companies have backed a pipeline to Murmansk, in order to create the next major deepwater port that will handle the anticipated ongoing growth in Russian oil production and exports. Tying into this deepwater port, with an estimated startup date of 2007–8, would be a 1.6 mmbpd oil pipeline that could be expanded to 2.4 mmbpd and which would cost between $3.4 and $4.5 billion to build. Because of the proximity of shipments from Murmansk to the U.S. East Coast (5,800 vs. 12,800 miles from the Persian Gulf), this is the U.S. government's favored pipeline. A possible role for U.S. companies in the pipeline was discussed during the September 2003 Saint Petersburg commercial energy summit, but these discussions have gone nowhere.

The United States and Russia have mentioned the potential for 10 to 13 percent of U.S. supplies originating from Russia by 2010, compared with less than 1 percent today. U.S. imports by 2010 of 1 to 2 mmbpd of Russian crude have been suggested, presumably displacing Saudi imports. At the same time, Russian exports of 1 mmbpd to Asia have been touted by 2010. With so many export volumes being mentioned, what is the reality?

The reality is that private company ownership stakes in Russian oil pipelines are unlikely and that new pipeline decisions will be driven by Transneft in consultation with President Putin and his circle of advisers. The decision on investing in a pipeline to Murmansk may now be indefinitely delayed. The Russian government even suggested that U.S. refiners should guarantee oil purchases from this pipeline, posing an impossible demand.

Alternative pipeline routes in Russia and the Caspian region are considered in detail by Jan Kalicki and Jonathan Elkind in the next chapter. Decisions by the Russian government on pipeline projects are dependent on a number of assumptions: about the availability of oil in the future to fill existing and new pipelines, about oil prices in the future that could affect the demand on world markets for higher-cost Russian oil from new field developments, and more generally about global oil supply and demand conditions in the future. The last thing the Russian government wants is to start building a major new pipeline project just as oil prices begin to soften—unless, of course, the buyers of the oil are offering substantial enticements. This is the case with Japan and China but is not the case with the United States.

## What Level of Russian Oil Production Is Sustainable?

Given the steady rise in Russian oil output, there has been a debate both in Russia and in the West about how much higher Russian oil production can rise given the current emphasis by private Russian companies on Western technological applications to squeeze volumes out of existing older fields. Private Russian oil companies have devoted little effort and money for exploration and new field developments. In its *Russian Energy Strategy until 2020* of August 28, 2003, the Russian government provides an estimate for the country's production outlook. In a best-case scenario, with Brent crude at $22 to $30 per barrel, Russian production reaches 9.8 mmbpd by 2010, with crude oil exports of about 5.6 mmbpd. A more conservative production outlook, with oil prices for Brent in the range of $18 to $22 per barrel, output levels off at 8.9 mmbpd in 2010 with crude oil exports just under 5 mmbpd. The best-case forecast for 2020 sees Russian production reaching 10.4 mmbpd, and the conservative case has output at 9 mmbpd.[8] Therefore, according to the Russian government's forecasts, in the period 2010–20, production will level off at between 8.9 and 10.4 mmbpd depending on the oil price. By contrast, Saudi Arabia's current production capacity is 10.5 mmbpd. What the Russian government's energy strategy outlook does not account for is the event of Brent prices in the range of $28 to $35 a barrel. If this were the best-case scenario, Russian production could reach 11 mmbpd by 2020.

Another way to address the issue of Russian oil production growth is to ask how new field developments will be financed. In its November 2003 *World Energy Investment Outlook,* the International Energy Agency (IEA) judges that Russia needs $328 billion for the development of its oil industry until 2030, most of which would be spent on replacing depleted reserves through exploration and production (E&P). This comes out to about $11 billion per year as required investment simply to replace existing capacity. As a form of comparison, ExxonMobil's annual worldwide exploration and production budget is about $11 billion.[9] The IEA considers that E&P activities will have to be directed toward Eastern Siberia, the Arctic Shelf, the Russian sector of the Caspian region, and off Sakhalin Island if Russia is to replace the resources now being produced from its mature fields in Western Siberia. Known reserves in Western Siberia can be counted on as a source of production growth until 2012–15, and after that the areas mentioned above will have to yield additional volumes through exploration.

The Russian government has several ways to approach this issue: It can decide that the private Russian companies can manage the sector without substantial foreign participation; it can decide that the TNK-BP experience should be repeated and that other large Western companies should form partnerships with Russian companies, bringing their expertise and money; or it can decide to attract Western investors into the upstream on a project-by-project basis by reviving production-sharing agreements (PSAs) for the Russian oil sector. For E&P activities in Eastern Siberia, offshore in the north of Russia, in the Caspian Sea, and off Sakhalin, PSAs would be the logical way forward for the Russian government if it is serious about maintaining its share of the global oil supply pie.

What the Russian government cannot afford is the further destruction of companies like Yukos or the TNK-BP alliance, because private companies provide the access to large amounts of capital that Russia as a sovereign state simply cannot raise. A healthy private sector is essential for the financial health of the Russian oil and gas sector and of the Russian state.[10] At the same time, what the Yukos experience has shown is that the risks in the Russian oil sector are high and that even if foreign investors succeed in accessing projects in Russia, managing the risks will pose difficult and unpredictable challenges. Accessing opportunities in a high-oil-price environment will put even greater pressure on foreign investors, and higher entry costs.

## Azerbaijan and Kazakhstan: Geopolitics as the Driver versus Energy Security

The location of the Caspian Sea, between Russia and Iran, determined the U.S. focus on this region. In part to create countries that could stand on their own without Russia and become U.S. allies, and in part to maintain the isolation of Iran, the U.S. government has devoted enormous attention to the Caspian region during recent years. One could argue that the driver here has been geopolitics, not energy security, even though one of the key manifestations of U.S. government interest has been the Baku–Tbilisi–Ceyhan (BTC) oil pipeline, which will bring Caspian oil to markets via Turkey.

## Azerbaijan

Since June 1997, when the U.S. State Department publicized very optimistic numbers on potential oil reserves in the Caspian countries, the U.S. government has focused most closely on Azerbaijan. Sitting in a key location in the Southern Caucasus and bordering on Iran, Azerbaijan became the pivotal country for the U.S. government's investment advocacy agenda. And, under the watchful eye of the U.S. government, Azerbaijan has come a long way. A large number of offshore and onshore contracts were signed in Azerbaijan during the 1997–99 period, even though the only major offshore producing oil fields—under development by the Azerbaijan International Operating Company (AIOC) consortium—are attributed to a 1994 PSA. The Azeri, Chirag, and deepwater Guneshli fields, which fall under the AIOC consortium,[11] are expected to hit peak production between 2010 and 2015 (figure 5.2). While the United States pushed and prodded to make Azerbaijan a much bigger upstream success story than just AIOC, in the end, most of the contract areas have proven disappointing and Azerbaijan's production remains concentrated offshore with AIOC.

Azeri output in 2003 reached 308,000 bpd—split as 176,000 bpd attributed to state company Socar and 132,000 bpd from AIOC. By 2007, AIOC will increase production to 440,000 bpd, with Socar's production remaining at today's level. Oil exports will rise to 490,000 bpd by 2007 from the current 182,000 bpd. The current oil export split is 50,000 bpd from Socar and 132,000 bpd from AIOC. AIOC's export share will rise to more than 1 mmbpd when AIOC production peaks.

The only other field in Azerbaijan that has demonstrated success is the huge offshore Shah Deniz gas field.[12] On the basis of Azerbaijan's one major offshore oil project, AIOC, and its one major offshore gas project, Shah Deniz, the United States set out to help provide the stable political environment necessary to create a pipeline hub in Azerbaijan, with oil and gas export routes running from there through Georgia and Turkey. The lead company in all these projects is the United Kingdom's BP, with Norway's Statoil playing a role in the Shah Deniz gas pipeline as commercial opera-

Figure 5.2. Oil Production in Azerbaijan, 1995–2033 (million barrels per day)

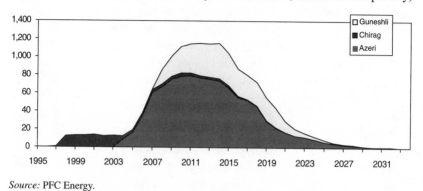

*Source:* PFC Energy.

tor. The gas pipeline will feed a small volume of gas to Turkey, with startup of deliveries scheduled for 2006, one year after oil deliveries start to Ceyhan, Turkey, in 2005. The goal is to extend the Shah Deniz gas pipeline across Turkey to Greece and then to European markets.

A cautionary note to Azeri oil plans is necessary because of recent events in the Southern Caucasus. A presidential election in Azerbaijan in October 2003 that was questioned by Western observers, followed by fraudulent parliamentary elections in Georgia in November 2003—which led to the November 23 resignation of Georgian president Eduard Shevardnadze—have highlighted the political risks in both Azerbaijan and Georgia. These two countries are the geopolitical linchpins of the U.S. government's energy evacuation plans in the Caspian region. In addition, the massive bombings in Istanbul on November 15 and 20, 2003, blamed on al Qaeda terrorists, are disturbing signposts pointing to the volatility and fragility of this Southern Caucasus oil corridor. Again, what this shows is just how difficult it is to base U.S. energy security on particular regions and leaders when the U.S. government's best laid plans are subject to potential interruptions. A transport corridor through the Caucasus will require a U.S. commitment to help with pipeline security and a constant monitoring of many complex political risks.

## Kazakhstan

To the northeast of Azerbaijan is arguably one of the most important new upstream investment frontiers since the North Sea: namely, Kazakhstan. Despite the preponderance of U.S. attention to Azerbaijan because of its

strategic location bordering Iran, it is Kazakhstan which holds the key to
the Caspian countries' oil wealth. It was here that in April 1993, Chevron
signed the region's first onshore joint venture for one of the world's giant
oil fields—Tengiz. ExxonMobil joined Chevron in Tengiz in 1996. Chevron
is also a partner in Kazakhstan's other major onshore oil- and gas-producing
field, Karachaganak. And ExxonMobil is a member of the consortium led
by Italy's Agip, which is exploring and developing the most exciting new
offshore prospect in the Caspian Sea, the Kashagan structure. Kashagan
holds many billions of barrels of oil reserves, and its size and scale will
probably exceed even that of Tengiz. Because it is offshore in an ecolog-
ically sensitive area and contains important volumes of associated high-
sulfur gas, Kashagan's development poses many difficult challenges, which
are a matter of contentious debate between the consortium and the Kazakh
government.

With a large number of already discovered and producing oil fields,
Kazakhstan's oil output keeps rising and has now exceeded 1 mmbpd (versus about 308,000 bpd in Azerbaijan). Kazakhstan's exports average over
800,000 bpd. Its prospects for increasing oil production in the 2010–20 time
frame are impressive, given the recognized potential offshore in the North
Caspian. Production estimates for 2010 range upward of 1.6 mmbpd, and
by 2020 Kazakhstan could be producing 3.6 mmbpd.

For Kazakhstan to realize its production potential, it will have to decide
what additional pipelines to use or build beyond the existing Transneft and
Caspian Pipeline Consortium (CPC) pipelines. At the end of the day, this
decision will be based on commercial considerations, including the timing
of alternative available export options and pipeline operational confidence.

Still, experience in the region has shown that politics can play an important role in pipeline commitments, but politics can be hard for companies
to predict. The U.S.–Russian relationship is a case in point here. Until 9/11,
the negatives of this relationship argued for diversifying pipelines away from
Russia. The year 2003 saw the implementation of a serious U.S.-Russian
dialogue, which by the end of the year was thrown into question. During the
Iraq war and after the Yukos controversy, the U.S.-Russian relationship has
taken many twists and turns, with the outcome still uncertain but certainly
less positive than in the first part of 2003.

One thing that is now confusing to foreign oil company producers in
Kazakhstan is the ultimate U.S. strategy there with regard to exit routes. If
the goal is to have multiple pipelines, with new pipelines bypassing Russia
and Iran, any policy that would encourage additional oil shipments from

the Caspian across Russia, beyond what an expanded CPC can carry and existing Transneft options, works against the multiple pipeline strategy and further solidifies Kazakh-Russian dependence. Given the size and scale of the Kashagan resource base, a third way, beyond Russia and BTC, would be the logical solution in the framework of stated U.S. policy, which supports multiple pipeline routes. The next route favored by many non-U.S. oil companies in Kazakhstan is Iran, but this also undermines the stated U.S. goal of pursuing projects that avoid Iran. Kazakhstan has been promoting a China pipeline option.

Some questions one could raise now include: What is the primary U.S. objective? Is it to not avoid Russia but to avoid Iran? What is the U.S. policy toward a China pipeline that orients Kazakh crude away from the West? And how can commercially driven companies rationalize U.S. policies and adjust what are long-term business decisions to changing U.S. policies? Non-U.S. companies in the Caspian region may decide to stop second-guessing U.S. policies and opt for commercial imperatives.

## International Oil Companies and OPEC versus non-OPEC in the Energy Security Equation

The Caspian region and now Russia are perceived as important for the United States because they help diversify the world's supply of oil while also being non-OPEC suppliers. Diversifying supplies is a good reason to be supportive of additional production from Russia and the Caspian. However, the "OPEC versus non-OPEC" conundrum in U.S. energy security debates is often misunderstood. Non-OPEC supplies serve as a market baseload, consistently delivering the full level of production of which those sources are capable. Clearly, diversifying and increasing these non-OPEC sources provides a more secure core of supplies for the United States and other consumers to rely upon. Non-OPEC production is growing and, according to data from the U.S. Energy Information Administration, reached 48.9 mmbpd in 2003 versus OPEC production of 26.8 mmbpd.

After non-OPEC supplies are considered, the difference between them and total global oil demand is then filled by OPEC. So the U.S. government's emphasis is misplaced. The question is not OPEC versus non-OPEC. Rather, the issue to address is how to continue encouraging non-OPEC supply growth and diversity, preferably with the involvement of international oil companies (or IOCs, including U.S. oil companies). In both OPEC and non-OPEC countries, governments determine how oil and gas reserves will be developed. The United States needs to understand that in most non-OPEC countries, governments control the resources and the way they exert their power over these resources can create enormous impediments, particularly for U.S. companies. Corruption is often endemic to the business environment in oil-producing countries. This could put a brake on U.S. companies' participation in numerous developments.

Thus, some issues to address with respect to non-OPEC countries are (1) how much access IOCs will have to support the development of these reserves and production; (2) in which countries do IOCs have this access; and (3) how stable are these countries to allow IOCs to produce and export their oil without impediments. In Russia, IOCs currently have limited access. In the Caspian region, IOCs have a great deal of access in Azerbaijan, but the prospectivity is diminishing. In Kazakhstan, IOCs have access but the investment climate is difficult. Not only are previously negotiated terms and conditions subject to reconsideration, but new contracts signed after 2003 are carrying terms that are more onerous than contracts previously in place. Moreover, the location of Kazakhstan, bordering on Russia, means that its energy future will have ties to Russia, but how strong these ties will be could be determined by the availability of export pipelines that steer oil in other directions.

## Diversity of Supply Sources Enhances Energy Security

Energy security is best enhanced by encouraging the development of diverse supply sources and not necessarily by advocating specific country investments or directing pipeline flows. Diversity of supply from countries where the U.S. government can help to create stable, long-lasting, and responsible governments would be more conducive to the sustainable development of resources than stressing target countries or pipeline routes.

Pipelines are projects with long lives and, yes, politics and geopolitics can determine whether they operate or shut down. However, over the long life of a pipeline, advocating a route one day does not mean that unforeseen political and geopolitical circumstances in the future will not alter the current judgment call. There is no predictability for long-term political and geopolitical relationships and alliances, especially in Russia and in regions such as the Caspian Sea and the Middle East.

## Conclusion

For the long term, one could argue that oil and gas supplies from the Caspian region and Russia will be no different than supplies from the North Sea or elsewhere. They will be just other sources feeding growing world demand. During the next decade, Russian production is unlikely to reach the level it attained in 1988, even with large investments in new fields. By 2020, however, production could climb significantly but only if the Russian government were to change its attitude toward foreign investors, allowing them access under PSAs. Exploration and production ventures have long lead times, are capital intensive, carry significant risks, and would need careful planning for Russia's production outlook to improve over the period until 2020.

Kazakhstan's output can continue to grow only if it gets access to more pipeline capacity beyond 2010. What is more, further significant investment by Western companies in Kazakhstan's offshore is predicated on an attractive and transparent fiscal environment. Azerbaijan is the only one of the three major regional producers that knows roughly how much production it can expect and that is also certain about the adequacy of its export routes.

In both Russia and Kazakhstan, the timing for construction and the direction of new export routes will influence the production targets of private companies. The level of oil prices will also affect the timing and direction of export routes and the ability of companies to meet their production targets. Because it is cognizant of the need to keep oil supplies in check to maintain high prices to the benefit of the budget, the Russian government is maintaining a dialogue with OPEC, while telling the United States that it has no intention of cooperating with OPEC.

Dialogue and cooperation can be construed in various ways, and dialogue may be trying to achieve the same goal as outright cooperation. Russia, in fact, is maintaining its strategic options. In an environment of high oil prices, the Russian government has calibrated its cooperation with OPEC to make sure that it continues to benefit from high prices.

Russia is not likely to try to restrain its output as a show of cooperation with OPEC unless oil prices drop dramatically. What is more, President Putin appears to see the state pipeline monopoly, Transneft, as playing the role of adjudicator of supply and demand in Russia. Transneft is the Russian government's tool for controlling Russian production and managing prices.

Looking out over this decade, how much new oil from all sources—including Russian and Caspian oil—is brought to market will have an impact on oil prices. As seen through President Putin's prism, it may not be in the Russian government's interest to allow a multitude of competing export projects to come to fruition. These projects would require enormous investments in oil development and massive new investments in pipelines and ports. Overhanging it all is the uncertain effect on prices.

Finally, one note of caution regarding U.S. support for pipelines: Pipeline projects like BTC from Azerbaijan or CPC from Kazakhstan take nearly a decade to complete, placing a particular burden on the direction of U.S. policy. The U.S. commitment to specific countries and pipelines has to last at least as long as it takes to construct these projects, but even longer if security guarantees are required. Supporting pipelines in difficult geopolitical regions demands a political and military commitment, and it costs money. Alternatively, if U.S. policy can change within the course of a decade—the time it takes to plan, finance, and build a major pipeline—why should companies be willing to invest in policy-dependent projects? What will companies do with a trade route that may last forty years if it is undercut by another more efficient route that suddenly opens up because of policy changes? Ultimately, projects must stand on their own commercial merit, because the economics of a project will dictate its success.

From a policy perspective, these regional issues of production and transportation are interwoven with U.S. strategy for global energy security. U.S. policy can and should promote increased oil and gas trade and investment with Russia and the Caspian Sea region, which will contribute to the diversity of supply and to the future economic growth and security of these countries—a result that will have considerable consequences for U.S. energy and foreign policy objectives.

## Notes

1. Saudi crude oil production was 8.8 mmbpd in 2003; Russian crude oil production was 8.2 mmbpd. U.S. Energy Information Administration (EIA), *Country Analysis Briefs,* June 2004 and May 2004.

2. Natural gas liquids include but are not limited to the following: ethane, propane, butanes, pentanes, natural gasoline, and condensate.

3. *BP Statistical Review of World Energy,* June 2004, available at http://www.bp.com.

4. *BP Statistical Review of World Energy,* 1999, shows Russian oil production in 1988 at 11.44 mmbpd; 1989, 11.13 mmbpd; 1990, 10.40 mmbpd; 1991, 9.32 mmbpd; 1992, 8.04 mmbpd; 1993, 7.71 mmbpd. The bottom was hit in 1996, when production averaged 6.115 mmbpd; available at http://www.bp.com.

5. As of April 2003, following the Iraq war, excess world oil production capacity stood at 700,000 barrels per day to 1.2 mmbpd, all of which was located in the Gulf,

according to the EIA. In an updated *Persian Gulf Oil and Gas Exports Fact Sheet,* posted to the agency's Web site on April 18, 2003 (http://www.eia.doe.gov/cabs/pgulf.html), the EIA noted the world's total reliance on spare oil production capacity in the Gulf—which normally stands at around 90 percent of the world's spare capacity. The report estimates that the oil production capacity of Gulf countries amounted to 22.3 mmbpd at the end of 2002, or 32 percent of the world's total. Proven oil reserves in the Gulf region are estimated at 674 billion barrels, which is about two-thirds of conventional global oil reserves.

6. *Petroleum Intelligence Weekly* (*PIW*), "Urals Makes First Waves in Asia," November 3, 2003.

7. EIA, http://www.eia.doe.gov/pub/oil_gas/petroleum/data_publications/petroleum_supply_monthly/current/pdf/stable3.pdf.

8. "Russia's Upside Risks Being Overstated," *PIW,* November 17, 2003. Also see Robert Ebel, "How Much Crude Does Russia Have to Offer?" *PIW,* November 3, 2003. Ebel also refers to an internal study carried out by Yukos, which found that "oil production will peak by the year 2010, somewhat exceeding 10 million b/d. Holding at that level out to the year 2015, then a very slow decline sets in, dropping production to just below 10 mmbpd by the year 2020. The two leading oil producing regions—West Siberia and the Urals-Volga—will both peak in 2010, as will Timan-Pechora. Given that, where will the growth come from? East Siberia, which produced just 40,000 barrels per day (bpd) in 2001, is to expand to 1.34 million bpd by 2020. Beyond 2010, all the growth is to be provided by undiscovered fields. The Russian Shelf, also having produced just 40,000 bpd in 2001, will also be producing in excess of 1.3 mmbpd by 2020. All of the growth beyond 2015 is to be provided by undiscovered fields. Without these two regions, Russian oil production would be around 7 mmbpd by 2020. Crude oil exports likely will expand as production expands, but, given that refining capacity likely will not be measurably enlarged, petroleum product exports could be expected to decline. Accepting either of these guidelines tells us the current decade is a decade of growth, but the next decade is part constancy, part slow decline."

9. "Robust Profits Mask Problems for Big Oil," *PIW,* November 10, 2003.

10. PFC Energy, "Russian Oil Taxes: Orders of Magnitude," *Caspian Business Intelligence Memo,* January 2, 2004.

11. AIOC is composed of the United Kingdom's BP (34.137 percent), the United States' Unocal (10.2814 percent), Norway's Statoil (8.563 percent), Japan's Itochu (3.92 percent) and Inpex (10 percent), Turkey's TPAO (6.75 percent), the United States' ExxonMobil (8.06 percent) and Devon (5.6262 percent), Saudi Arabia's and the United States' Delta-Hess (2.7213 percent), and Azerbaijan's Socar (10 percent).

12. Shah Deniz is composed of the United Kingdom's BP (25.5 percent), Norway's Statoil (25.5 percent), France's Total (10 percent), Russia's and Italy's LukAgip (10 percent), Turkey's TPAO (9 percent), Iran's NICO (10 percent), and Azerbaijan's Socar (10 percent).

# 6

# Eurasian Transportation Futures

## Jan H. Kalicki and Jonathan Elkind

As oil and gas reserves in both Russia and the Caspian Sea region come on line, they promise to increase global energy security at least as much in the next decade as the North Sea has in the last. However, the critical ingredient is the availability of pipelines to bring Eurasia's oil and gas to market. In this respect, the twenty-first century brings a new chapter to the Eurasian energy transportation scene.

In the 1990s, the issue was *whether* new pipelines could be developed around the Soviet-era monopoly; today, it is *where* these pipelines will be built, inside and outside Russia. In the 1990s, relatively limited production justified a smaller number of transportation routes; today, greater production requires greater export capacity in a larger number of routes.

With the prospect of greater production and revenues, certain questions emerge in even bolder relief than in the past: Will the governments take the necessary steps to attract the tens of billions of dollars required for developing their energy resources and transport routes? And will economies built on oil and gas diversify properly to provide broad, enduring benefits for their societies as a whole? The answers to these questions are key to the energy and foreign policy opportunities before the United States and its partners: to help develop new energy flows not dependent on the Organization of Petroleum Exporting Countries (OPEC) or the Middle East, in an environment that is secure and stable over the longer term.

In this chapter, we first survey the basic trends and opportunities for energy transportation in Eurasia in the 1990s. Next, we analyze the characteristics

The authors thank Bud Coote and Vladimir Shatilenko for their input and assistance.

that define the current period. We then assess the possibility of a further phase, one in which oil and gas producers in the region will, we hope, be fully integrated with global markets through a completed array of transportation networks that stretch to the west, south, and east, as well as the north. Finally, we offer recommendations for the United States, the European Union, and regional states.

## The Main Transportation Directions—Today and Tomorrow

Even after more than a decade of active investments, the energy transportation infrastructure of Eurasia is dominated by the pipeline architecture of the Soviet era. This means that the oil and gas pipelines, though extensively developed, still conform more to the political, security, and commercial realities of the former Soviet Union than to the needs of independent Eurasian states seeking to maximize national benefits by contributing to global energy security.

Furthermore, as will be clear from the analysis that follows—which includes brief summaries of both traditional and new export routings—export capacity will be significantly constrained for Russia and Eurasia without the creation of additional pipelines. Even with planned expansions, more than 2 million barrels per day (mmbpd) are already being forced into comparatively inefficient rail or barge traffic. Unless they are overcome, export capacity limits will retard the future contribution of this region to global energy supplies and energy security.

### Traditional Routings

*The Transneft system.* The biggest feature of the oil transportation system in Eurasia is the system operated by OAO Transneft, the Russian state-owned pipeline monopolist. Transneft's area of operations reaches across Russia's entire expanse of eleven time zones, with more than 48,000 kilometers of pipe ranging from 420 to 1,220 millimeters in diameter. Transneft has the capacity to move well in excess of its present level of 6.2 mmbpd of oil and oil products; in 1990, before the Soviet breakup, the system moved just under 10 mmbpd.

The Transneft system is thus massive in size, and it already has a high degree of intentional redundancy. Transneft's *export* capacity, however, is stretched to the limit; by late 2003, it exported approximately 3.5 mmbpd of oil, leaving an additional increment of approximately 1.5 mmbpd with no export alternative other than rail or barge traffic.[1] Moreover, it depends for most exports on transit through post-Soviet neighbors—more than 80 percent of all exports to international markets. And it has only begun to use a quality bank, of the kind adopted by the Caspian Pipeline Consortium (CPC) and Baku–Tbilisi–Ceyhan (BTC) pipelines, to allow oil producers to receive full compensation for higher-quality crude oils.[2]

*Black Sea ports and the Bosporus.* Despite these challenges, Transneft continues to dominate the Eurasian oil transport scene, feeding most of the largest export pipelines and key port terminals. First among these is the Black Sea port of Novorossiysk, which has operated at or above capacity ratings in recent years and has accounted for approximately 60 percent of Russian oil exports. The Black Sea poses two serious challenges, however. The first is the difficulty of navigating through the Bosporus to the Mediterranean—that is, through 17 miles of narrow channels and twisting shores, slicing across Istanbul, a World Heritage Site now home to more than 10 million people. The second is the frequent weather-related closures of both the ports and the Bosporus itself. In February 2003, for example, winter storms closed the Bosporus for several days and led to a backup of more than fifty vessels waiting to transit.[3]

*Druzhba pipeline system.* What Novorossiysk is to Transneft's marine export capacity, the Druzhba system is to pipeline export capacity. Together, Druzhba's two branches carry approximately 40 percent of Russian oil exports to Eastern and Central Europe.[4]

*Ventspils.* The final major element of Transneft's traditional export routings to Europe was the Baltic Sea port of Ventspils, Latvia, with a capacity of 350,000 barrels per day (bpd). Since the breakup of the USSR, however, new factors have complicated these shipments. Disputes over port fees and terms soured relations with the Latvian government and port managers. In early 2003, Transneft cut off all pipeline deliveries to Ventspils.[5]

## New Oil Exports: Projects Now Operating or under Construction

New oil exports via projects now operating or under construction include the Baltic Pipeline System, Vysotsk and Butinge, the Baku–Novorossiysk and Baku–Supsa pipelines, the Caspian Pipeline Consortium, and the Baku–Tbilisi–Ceyhan Pipeline.

*Baltic Pipeline System.* Although Transneft traditionally dominated oil exports from Eurasia using the three chief routings described above—

Novorossiysk, the Druzhba system, and Ventspils—the late 1990s and earliest years of the new century brought new pipeline capacity onto the scene to help alleviate congestion (figure 6.1). Transneft's own favorite among the new routings is the Baltic Pipeline System (BPS), internally financed by its pipeline tariffs and carrying 1 mmbpd by the end of 2004, which includes a modern new terminal north of Saint Petersburg at Primorsk and feeder lines originating in Yaroslavl'. However, BPS faces the challenge of exports through an increasingly congested Gulf of Finland and Danish straits into the North Sea. As is true in the Black Sea, the largest tankers (very large crude carriers, or VLCCs; and ultralarge crude carriers, or ULCCs) are too long and deep to move safely through the Baltic and the Gulf of Finland.[6]

*Vysotsk and Butinge.* Other new capacity has developed in recent years on Baltic shores. LUKoil converted a chemical shipping facility into an oil and refined products facility at Vysotsk, northwest of BPS's Primorsk—only for Transneft to urge the state to take it over. Yukos, in turn, now operates as an export facility the Lithuanian port of Butinge with planned capacity of 260,000 bpd—not interrupted at this writing by the Russian government's legal assault on the company—and that initially developed to allow crude oil imports to the state-owned petroleum oil company Mazheikiu Nafta.

*Baku–Novorossiysk and Baku–Supsa pipelines.* In the Black Sea, several new elements of export capacity have been developed since the mid-1990s. The Baku–Novorossiysk oil pipeline and the Baku–Supsa oil pipeline were commissioned to transport the so-called early oil from the BP-led Azeri–Chirag–Guneshli project of the Azerbaijan International Operating Company (AIOC). Baku–Supsa was significant in that it constituted the first step by Western energy companies to implement what was referred to as the Multiple Pipelines policy.[7] This policy, which was strongly advocated by Turkey, Azerbaijan, Georgia, and the United States, emphasized the need for pipeline routing choices, rather than monopoly relations. Baku–Novorossiysk also played an important role, reassuring Russia that equivalent amounts of early oil could be transported across its territory. In early years, Russia sought to facilitate this route by constructing a bypass around Chechnya, but as BTC started moving toward completion, Transneft has pressed so far unsuccessfully for a fifteen-year agreement to try to lock in Azeri oil transit at uncompetitive rates.

*Caspian Pipeline Consortium.* Another major Caspian and Black Sea development was the Caspian Pipeline Consortium system, which connected the Tengizchevroil (TCO) project in western Kazakhstan with the port of Yuzhnaya Ozerevka, just north of Novorossiysk. CPC—the first and to date only non-Transneft oil pipeline crossing Russian territory—transports approximately 560,000 bpd. Chevron, the operator of TCO and CPC, announced in October 2003 that it would increase TCO production to in excess of 1 million bpd by 2012, entailing negotiations among the partners to achieve expanded capacity for the CPC line.

*Baku–Tbilisi–Ceyhan Pipeline.* A third new oil export project, which has been the subject of intense public attention since the mid-1990s, is the Baku–Tbilisi–Ceyhan Pipeline. BTC, stretching from the Caspian to the Turkish Mediterranean coast, will avoid the transportation of 1 mmbpd through the Turkish Straits, and the deepwater port of Ceyhan will allow shippers to use VLCCs of up to 200,000 to 300,000 deadweight metric tons. BTC faces the complication of crossing three separate countries, entailing multiple legal frameworks and raising numerous questions about sovereignty issues, environmental protection, and human rights.[8]

## New Gas Export Systems Now Operating or under Construction

As we have seen already, Eurasian oil exports have been constrained by the availability of pipeline and port capacity. Gas exports are much less susceptible to alternative modes of shipment such as barges and railcars, so options for gas exports have been even more constrained. As described in the next chapter, gas demand is skyrocketing in western Europe, and it is projected to continue rapid growth into the foreseeable future.[9]

*Gas exports through Ukraine and Belarus.* This European demand translates into strong markets for Eurasian gas exporters, as well as competitors in North Africa and the Middle East. In response to this demand, Gazprom has embarked on a series of new gas export projects, and other gas producers are also pursuing new possibilities. Gazprom's first focus has been to stabilize, regularize, and then increase gas transit through Russia's two key post-Soviet neighbors in Europe, Belarus and Ukraine.

About 80 percent of Russia's gas exports transit Ukrainian territory en route to consumers in Turkey, the Balkans, Central Europe, and the European Union. Belarus, in turn, is the routing for the major new Yamal–Europe line, which plays a key role in Gazprom's development plan for the next decade. Both Ukraine and Belarus have struggled to find a new equilibrium in gas relations with Russia since the Soviet breakup. Instead of enjoying any form of energy security, these two post-Soviet states have become increasingly dependent on Russian supplies and, thanks to their accumulated gas debt, vulnerable to Russian pressure.

Figure 6.1. Map of Eurasian Energy Export Pipelines

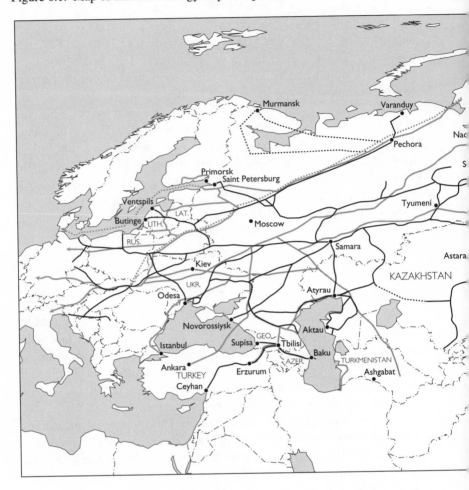

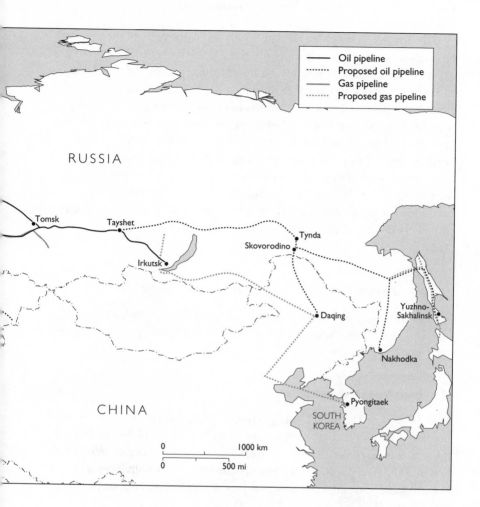

*Blue Stream.* Throughout the late 1990s and early years of the new century, Gazprom officials frequently observed that Russia needed to have gas export routings that did not rely on intermediate parties, such as Ukraine and Belarus, which might either divert gas or seek higher transit fees. The company sought to develop ambitious new pipeline projects, and the first was the Blue Stream line to Turkey under the Black Sea, brought into operation in early 2003 after overcoming formidable challenges as the deepest underwater pipeline in the world. However, concerns over alleged corruption issues, high pricing, and volume commitments erupted into public disputes in the Turkish press, requiring renegotiation of the terms by the two sides—with deliveries interrupted for most of 2003 but now resuming shipments far less than the planned throughput of 16 billion cubic meters (bcm) per year.[10]

## Future Eurasian Oil and Gas Export Expansions

With energy demand growing rapidly in Western Europe and, increasingly, in Asia as well, new export proposals have materialized in all directions—west, north, south, and east.

### New East-West Developments

*Shah Deniz gas.* The Shah Deniz gas project in Azerbaijan—with its planned South Caucasus Pipeline across Georgia to Turkey—will be the first significant non-Gazprom export line from Eurasia when it comes into operation in 2006. As a result, Azeri gas will compete directly with Russian gas in both the Georgian and the Turkish markets, and potentially onward to southeast Europe.[11]

*Bosporus oil bypasses.* In relation to oil, the period ahead offers opportunities for decisive steps to implement one or more long-standing ideas for pipelines that would further reduce the need for tanker passage through the Bosporus. There are numerous proposals for Bosporus bypasses, perhaps the best-known routings being Burgas (Bulgaria) to Alexandropolis (Greece), Burgas to Vlore (Albania), Constanta (Romania) to Trieste (Italy) or Omisalj (Croatia), Odessa to Brody (Ukraine), and possibly onward to Plock or Gdansk (Poland);[12] and an interconnection of the Druzhba and Adria pipeline systems. In addition, there is growing discussion in Turkey of a possible in-country bypass, either immediately north of the Bosporus or extending from Samsun to Ceyhan. With encouragement from a Kremlin frustrated by Bosporus bottlenecks, Transneft itself has explored such a bypass, but routing, land-use issues, financing, and tariffs have yet to be resolved.[13]

Prospects for all these projects are hampered by a "free-rider" problem related to the Bosporus. All parties recognize that the Bosporus is a hazardous waterway, that accidents are a distinct possibility, and that a major accident might result in significant, expensive new operational requirements for shippers. Until such time as a catastrophic accident occurs, however, there is little incentive to expend the capital for a bypass pipeline. Once such a catastrophic accident were to occur, there would be greater demand for any existing alternative routings—the BTC pipeline (if it is operating and has excess capacity at the time), the Druzhba system, and BPS—as well as one or more bypasses.

### Proposed Northern Export Projects

*Murmansk oil terminal project.* One of the highest-profile new proposals for Russian oil export enhancements has been the idea of a new oil export terminal at Murmansk. This concept gained prominence starting in late 2002, particularly in light of the George W. Bush administration's interest in developing sources of oil supply for American consumers that are not from the Persian Gulf or OPEC. Murmansk would offer numerous benefits as an oil export terminal: deep water suitable for year-round use of VLCCs, proximity to markets on the East Coast of the United States, freedom from navigational choke-points such as those that afflict Baltic and Black Sea ports.[14]

*North European Gas Pipeline.* The Murmansk pipeline is not the only dramatic new export proposal under consideration in Russia's north. In 2003, Gazprom started active discussions of a proposed North European Gas Pipeline, a new mega-project costing anywhere from $5.7 to $7 billion, which would deliver gas to European customers without traversing any post-Soviet neighbor. The line would run along the seabed of the Gulf of Finland and the Baltic from Vyborg to Germany, with possible deliveries to buyers as far away as the United Kingdom. The cost-effectiveness of the project remains manifestly unclear, but Gazprom has begun active discussions of the project with Ruhrgas, Shell, Total, BP, and other possible partners, and then–prime minister Mikhail Kasyanov signed a decree in January 2004 approving construction of this pipeline with an estimated capacity of 20 bcm per year.

Proposed Eastern Export Projects

*Kazakhstan–China oil line.* Since the 1990s, Kazakhstan has favored its own version of multiple pipelines, supporting the CPC line as well as continued oil and gas exports in the Transneft and Gazprom systems. One long-discussed project that may finally come to fruition would connect several existing pipelines to create a system that would run from Kazakhstan's oil-producing western regions to its industrial areas in the east and then over the Tien Shan Mountains into northwestern China. In October 2003, Kazakhstan's state-owned energy company KazMunaiGaz announced that the China National Petroleum Company (CNPC), which has invested in Kazakhstani oil fields, had agreed to finance an initial segment of this project.[15]

*Taishet–Nakhodka and/or Taishet–Daqing.* An active debate has been under way in Russia on whether to expand east Siberian oil exports by constructing a line from Taishet (previously Angarsk) to the Pacific port of Nakhodka, to the northeastern Chinese city of Daqing, or both. Transneft and state-owned Rosneft have been proponents of the 4,000-kilometer line to the Pacific coast. They have stressed that this line would help develop the Russian Far East and would be able to sell oil to numerous Pacific Rim buyers. In October 2003, the Japanese government offered to support the Nakhodka project by providing $7 billion in low-interest loans—$5 billion for the pipeline and $2 billion for upstream development in eastern Siberia. The possible competitor for Taishet–Nakhodka would be a shorter (2,400-kilometer) and less expensive line to Daqing. That line, advocated by the Chinese government and Yukos in its heyday, would connect with the Chinese oil pipeline system and thus create a dedicated link between producer and consumers—the line's chief selling point and its chief liability simultaneously. By 2004, the Russian government was favoring Nakhodka on both strategic and regional development grounds, while continuing to support supplies to China by rail and eventually an additional spur in the pipeline. However, Transneft's sharply higher cost estimate of $16.2 billion for Nakhodka in 2004 may shift the balance once again, or simply result in deferring a decision and defaulting to Transneft's favorite BPS.[16]

*Sakhalin.* Another critical area for expanded eastern oil and gas exports is the series of Sakhalin Island oil and gas projects. The Sakhalin-1 project, led by ExxonMobil, will expand the existing port of DeKastri on the Russian mainland. The Sakhalin-2 project, which is led by Royal Dutch/Shell and is already producing, will export oil and liquefied natural gas to Japan,

South Korea, and the Pacific Rim from the Prigorodnoye terminal, now under construction at the south end of the Island.

*Kovykta gas export line.* One other major pipeline project that would add capacity to Eurasian exports in the east would be a line from the Kovykta gas condensate field, northwest of Lake Baikal, to the Chinese and South Korean markets. In November 2003, license holder Rusia Petroleum (in which TNK-BP has a controlling interest) signed a preliminary letter of intent with CNPC and Korea Gas Corporation to supply 600 and 300 bcm of gas, respectively, to these two markets, based on a feasibility study they submitted to the three governments. This massive project would have throughput of up to 30 bcm per year, but the project's proponents still need to resolve licensing issues and define the extent of Gazprom's partnership.

### Possible Southern Export Expansions

*Trans-Afghan gas pipeline.* In the mid-1990s, potential investors engaged in active discussions of a southern gas pipeline from Turkmenistan across Afghanistan to South Asia. The concept of a trans-Afghan pipeline fell out of favor with the progressive destabilization of Afghanistan, but after the fall of the Taliban, the idea reemerged, despite enormous remaining complications: chiefly, instability in Afghanistan; the conflict (now lessening) between Pakistan and India; gas supply competition from Iran and Qatar; and finally, the discovery of gas reserves in Pakistan itself.[17]

*Iranian oil swaps and pipeline.* Iran has long pressed for another option to the south of the Eurasian region: trans-Iranian swap deals possibly growing into an oil pipeline project. Though U.S. companies continue to be barred from this option by both legislation (the Iran-Libya Sanctions Act) and executive order, national, Russian, and Western European companies have pursued such swaps, which are likely to increase as Iran expands its Neka to Tehran pipeline and moderates its commercially aggressive negotiating tactics. The French company Total is engaged in active discussions with Kazakhstan, Uzbekistan, and Turkmenistan to construct over the longer term a north–south oil pipeline to Iran. In addition, Turkmenistan can be expected to continue to ship gas to the neighboring Iranian market.

## The Opportunity Ahead: An Expanding Energy Security System

It is clear, then, that multiple oil and gas transport routes have been developing not only in but around Russia in the wider Eurasian energy space. The result is that more alternatives are developing which reflect today's requirements; thus the export systems can compete with each other more strictly on commercial terms, rather than being dictated on political terms. This competition is especially clear in oil transportation, where the CPC, Baku-Supsa, and soon BTC pipelines will provide alternatives for non-Russian production—and to a limited extent Russian production—to Russia's state company Transneft. Conversely, Transneft is clearly keeping the upper hand in the debate over future oil pipelines *within* Russia: Despite efforts by Russian oil companies to develop privately funded and operated pipelines, it is clear that the Russian government favors at a minimum an exclusive operating role for Transneft in any new pipeline arrangement.

During President Vladimir Putin's second term, Transneft's hand will likely be further strengthened by the growing power of conservative statists (e.g., close presidential associate and Rosneft chairman Igor Sechin), including those who argue that Russia should conserve its oil resources rather than maximize exports and those who believe that oil and gas are strategic resources governed by state interests rather than private-sector considerations. Countering the statists will be some strategists and economic reformers (e.g., the minister of economic development and trade, German Gref), including those who argue that economic growth and diversification and Russia's global economic and political influence depend on a continued high level of oil and gas exports into the international market.[18]

In addition, competition is even more prospective than real in the case of natural gas. Gazprom—expanding to include Rosneft, Zarubezhneft, and possibly Yukos's main subsidiary, Yuganskneftegaz—continues to monopolize the Russian gas pipeline network and to dominate Eurasian gas supply arrangements through long-term contracts and control of infrastructure. This has become clear in the evolving network of Russian gas agreements with the states of Central Asia, including a thirty-year gas supply contract concluded with Turkmenistan in 2002. Moreover, following an October 9, 2003, meeting with German chancellor Gerhard Schröder in Yekaterinburg, President Putin made the flat statement that Russia would not relinquish control over gas pipeline infrastructure in the former Soviet republics. That system was built by the Soviet Union, he said, and only Russia is in a position to keep it in working order, "even those parts of the system that are beyond Russia's borders." Putin added that Russia will maintain state control over the pipeline network and over Gazprom. "We will not split up Gazprom, and the European Commission should have no illusions about that. In the area of natural gas, they will deal with the state."[19]

In reality, the degree of Gazprom's control in the gas sector may indeed vary from relatively subservient states such as Turkmenistan to relatively independent states such as Azerbaijan. Over time, Gazprom's dominance may also level off as new gas supply arrangements come on line, notably the pipeline from the Shah Deniz gas field to the Turkish and ultimately the European markets. Ultimately, such control will only lessen markedly as more gas transportation alternatives emerge, analogous to those that have emerged in the oil sector, and as Russia itself recognizes that its interests will be better served by more open access and competition in its gas sector. For example, Russian legislation already provides for third-party access to gas pipelines on nondiscriminatory terms, but Gazprom has continued to fight a successful rearguard action against transportation of gas produced by Russian and foreign oil companies.[20]

It is therefore clear that the battle between the Russian state monopolies —Transneft and Gazprom—and private companies and transportation systems continues both inside and outside Russia. In commercial terms, companies and governments alike will be better off to the extent that the region's energy development rests on multiple, reliable oil and gas transportation alternatives in the future. Competition will lead to more attractive transportation conditions—for example, Transneft's belated acceptance of the quality bank concept—and lower transportation costs, increasing the revenues to be shared between governments and investors in energy projects.

In security terms, increased transportation alternatives translate into reduced reliance on any single route. This in turn means that oil companies and their host governments face less vulnerability to political pressures or, for that matter, physical interruption by regional and local forces, possibly including terrorists.[21] We would argue strongly, therefore, that an expanding energy security system, predicated on increasing numbers of oil and gas transportation routes, is in the interests of all countries as well as outside investors working in the region. Such an expanding system can be described in terms of three phases: one in the late 1990s, one from 2000 to 2005, and one from 2005 to 2010.

## The First Phase, the Late 1990s

*Breakout.* The first phase of the Eurasian security system was characterized by a breakout, in the latter 1990s, from Transneft's oil transportation monopoly by both the CPC and BTC pipelines. As might be expected, Transneft strenuously opposed these independent oil pipelines and, in the earlier years, persuaded the Russian government to oppose them as well. Political arguments weighed even more heavily in the early days after the end of the USSR, as Moscow recognized that alternative oil routes would give the Caspian states a measure of independence never before enjoyed since at least the Bolshevik Revolution.

The U.S. government played a critical role in countering this opposition —recognizing the stakes involved for the future independence of the Caspian states, the contribution that the Caspian could make in reducing dependence on OPEC oil, and the reality that future Western energy investment in the region would depend crucially on reliable oil transportation to international markets. Many of the early debates in Washington revolved around whether to engage the Russians in discussion of Caspian pipeline development or— in a Cold War overhang—to disregard Russian concerns or even seek to isolate Russia in pursuing multiple pipelines from the Caspian. The strategy of engagement prevailed.[22]

In fact, active engagement with Russia on Caspian energy was the only appropriate strategy. The route of the CPC pipeline, after all, crossed southern Russia to the Black Sea. Over time, this engagement also proved extremely helpful in alleviating Russian concerns about the Baku–Supsa and BTC pipeline projects from Azerbaijan. The United States consistently supported the other "early oil" route carrying oil north from Azerbaijan across Russia to the Black Sea, and it was able to point to both that northern route and the CPC as counterbalances to the routes being constructed to the West.[23]

*Iranian routing.* The other big strategic question during this first phase was whether Eurasian oil producers could or would transport their Caspian output through Iran—either through a new north-south pipeline or by delivering Caspian oil to Iran's northern coast and swapping it for equivalent volumes exported from Iran's southern ports on the Persian Gulf. Confrontation with Iran—exacerbated by its support of terrorism, opposition to the Middle East peace process, and pursuit of weapons of mass destruction —led the United States to oppose any form of economic cooperation with Tehran. In addition, the United States urged the Caspian states not to exchange old reliance on a regional energy competitor, Russia, for new reliance on another competitor, Iran. The consequence was the denial of swap proposals by U.S. companies, but even leaving the United States aside, Iranian delays in constructing a pipeline from the port of Neka to Tehran refineries and hard-nosed commercial negotiating tactics limited Iran's imports of Caspian oil and gas during this period.

*Caspian delimitation.* In the meantime, another breakpoint developed between Iran and its Caspian neighbors, as Tehran refused to moderate its insistence on a 20 percent share of Caspian waters for exploration and development of energy resources. Under painstaking leadership from the first deputy foreign minister (and former energy minister), Viktor Kalyuzhny, Russia, Kazakhstan, and Azerbaijan agreed to delimit the subsea surface based on modified midlines drawn from their respective shorelines. The fourth Caspian littoral state, Turkmenistan, hesitated because of its proximity to Iran; but Iran remained adamantly opposed. To date, as a consequence, impasse prevails; Russia has concluded bilateral treaties with its own Caspian neighbors, Kazakhstan and Azerbaijan, using the modified median-line approach. Iran's rigidity in these Caspian delimitation negotiations simply reinforces the interest of the Caspian producers not to depend on it for energy exports.

## The Second Phase, 2000–2005

*New options for Azerbaijan and Kazakhstan.* The new Eurasian energy security system was at a very early stage, however. Only one small-volume oil pipeline, Baku–Supsa, operated completely separate from Russian territory, and no separate gas transportation existed at all. However, Azerbaijan's "main" oil pipeline, Baku–Tbilisi–Ceyhan, was finally approved by BP and its fellow shareholders. Construction commenced in 2003, and the line is to begin operation in 2005.

Kazakhstan will face similar challenges and opportunities as other fields are developed onshore and the giant Kashagan structure and related fields are developed by an ENI-led consortium offshore. The United States and more recently Azerbaijan have made sustained efforts to encourage Kazakhstan to export a significant share of its new offshore production across the Caspian and through the BTC, and the latter two countries are concluding an intergovernmental agreement to facilitate this transportation link. Russia has countered with offers of expanded Transneft capacity, including increased barging to Makhachkala and pipeline shipment through the Dagestan bypass.

*Options on all sides.* Kazakhstan's oil transportation choices are not limited to the north and the west, however. From the south, the Iranians have continued to press for oil swaps, and the French company Total is undertaking a feasibility study for a north–south pipeline consisting of both upgraded and new pipelines across Turkmenistan and Iran to the Persian Gulf.

Finally, as noted earlier in this chapter, China and Kazakhstan have agreed to start initial construction in 2004 on one small segment of the routing that may eventually link various pipelines and reach from CNPC-operated fields in western Kazakhstan to a refinery in western China. The very fact of these transportation choices *a toutes azimuthes* has put Kazakhstan in a position of greater strategic flexibility than ever previously imagined. Kazakhstan is exploring each of these opportunities and—to the consternation of the suitors—declines to rule out any option.

*Commercially driven decisions.* To facilitate the prompt development of an efficient Eurasian energy transportation infrastructure, commercial factors should guide investments—not political pressures. As this second phase continues, we expect that oil pipeline alternatives will develop not only in the Caspian but in the neighboring Black Sea. Steadily more oil will be exported through Novorossiysk and adjoining ports, and steadily more must find its way through or around the Bosporus to the Mediterranean.

The BTC pipeline will represent a significant reduction in this pressure on the Bosporus. In addition, any of the proposed Bosporus bypasses would reduce the pressure on the straits, and although the bypasses should properly be considered on commercial grounds, governments can and should do more to help expedite their consideration. For example, the European Union, and particularly Slovakia, the Czech Republic, and Poland should move proactively to support Caspian oil exports through Odessa–Brody into the European market, rather than Russian shipments to the Black Sea and the Bosporus.[24] As another example, Turkey and the United States are in a good position to facilitate the negotiation of the more cost-effective bypasses, given that the Turkish Straits will otherwise become increasingly congested even after BTC enters operation.

*Little gas export diversification.* The major exception to this trend of expanding energy transportation in this second phase is gas. Russia has moved strongly to assert its gas dominance in the Eurasian region. State control has been strengthened over Gazprom—including a welcome cleanup from much of the asset stripping in the mid-1990s—and over Gazprom's gas pipeline system. As noted above, no private gas producer has yet achieved significant access to the gas pipeline network. Rather, Gazprom has negotiated long-term gas contracts with the Central Asian suppliers, which continue to be paid at prices far below world market levels and effectively to backstop Gazprom's supply commitments to its European and other international markets.[25]

By the end of the second phase of energy security development, Eurasia will have achieved a range of viable transportation options for oil, but we do not expect that the same will be true for gas. These new oil transport options will have provided, in turn, the prospect of greater access to the international market and lessened significantly the dependence of the major oil producers, Azerbaijan and Kazakhstan, on Russia. From the international energy security perspective, Russia can be expected to produce more than 9 mmbpd and the Caspian states more than 2 mmbpd—with a resulting contribution of more than 11 mmbpd to the world energy balance, more than that of OPEC-constrained Saudi Arabia, if export capacity is increased to make this possible.

## The Third Phase, 2005–2010

In its third phase, we can expect decisions on whether the energy security system in Eurasia can cross several thresholds. The first is to decide whether it can achieve the full potential of a diverse system of oil export routes. The second is to determine whether gas exports will continue to be controlled by Russia, or will be subject increasingly to the diversification and competitive pressures experienced in oil exports. The third is to translate the potential into the reality of non-OPEC energy production contributing to the global security of energy supplies.

Political as well as economic factors inevitably come into play as these thresholds are approached. In Russia as well as the Eurasian states, market-oriented reformers must overcome the objections of those who advocate state control. Thus, altering the current roles of Transneft and Gazprom is not simply a question of energy economics; it is a more fundamental expression of state power in the most lucrative sector of the economy. Against this backdrop, oil and gas export decisions entailing significant policy struggles can be expected in the years ahead. At least for the remainder of the second Putin term, it appears likely that Russian state control of export pipelines will continue along with increased control of the country's oil companies (and continued control of gas through Gazprom). At a minimum, the consequence will be delayed decisions on increased export capacity—with corresponding limits on Russia's contribution to global energy security.

*Oil exports—significant incremental changes ahead.* First, Russia itself will face important decisions on its future oil export routes. It is already clear that Russian oil companies have lost in their advocacy of privately funded and privately operated oil routes to accommodate their growing exports, which the national energy strategy released in 2003 projects may exceed 6 mmbpd by 2010.[26] Transneft is riding the wave of state control, and the only possible concession (for projects such as the Murmansk terminal and the Nakhodka and/or Daqing lines) may be Transneft-operated pipelines that receive some measure of private funding in return for access rights or reduced tariffs, with a limited return on investment. Russians will have to wait a much longer period of time for the role of Transneft to diminish significantly; the issue will be, as economic reforms continue, whether the government comes to recognize it can exert control through regulation rather than ownership, and competition may then increase in the Russian pipeline network. Russian economic and political interests will play the preponderant role in this debate, but in turn the Kremlin's perception of these interests can be influenced significantly by its energy partners—including economic incentives from Japan, Europe, and the United States for the creation of additional pipeline and port capacity on terms that help reform Russia's energy system.

Beyond Russia comes the likelihood of the full operation of the BTC pipeline, the expansion of the CPC pipeline to 1.3 mmbpd, and the construction of at least one other bypass around the Bosporus. The Odessa–Brody pipeline also came into operation. In July 2004 President Kuchma decided it would carry Russian oil to the Black Sea—which would only increase the congestion through the Bosporus. In March 2005 his successor Viktor Yushchenko canceled that decision. More commercially competitive conditions and more concerted efforts by the European Union, Turkey, and Caspian producers such as Kazakhstan will be required for this pipeline to fulfill its initial intent of transporting primarily Caspian oil to the Central European market—and possibly to the Baltic, if it is extended across Poland to Gdansk. In the latter part of the decade, we expect that Kazakhstan will transport additional volumes west to the BTC and possibly Transneft lines, as its offshore oil comes online, and will export additional oil volumes to China and likely Iran.

*Gas exports—only slow change.* By contrast, gas exports will continue to be much more constrained in the region. We expect that Russian economic reformers such as German Gref will continue to press for restructuring of the Russian gas industry, but that will prove to be a lengthy and difficult process, and the earliest that unbundling or privatization of Gazprom could be achieved would be in a post-Putin era in Russian politics. The Central Asian states will already have been bound by long-term supply contracts to Gazprom and the Russian market.

In this third phase, we believe there will still be limited breakout from the gas monopoly in Eurasia. In Azerbaijan, the BP-led Shah Deniz gas consortium plans to build the South Caucasus Pipeline from Azerbaijan to Turkey, supplying modest volumes initially in 2006, with the potential to increase volumes to 7.3 bcm per year or more and perhaps even ship gas onward to Europe by the end of the decade.

In Asia, the newly merged TNK-BP venture will seek, together with CNPC and Korea Gas, to build a pipeline from the huge Kovykta field near Irkutsk to transport and sell gas to the Chinese and South Korean markets. The critical issue there will be whether and to what extent companies outside Gazprom are permitted to sell Russian gas outside the domestic market, and it is hardly surprising that TNK-BP is negotiating a substantial Gazprom role in this project. Gas production from the Sakhalin projects will represent another major export flow, in which Gazprom will now participate as a result of its acquiring Rosneft's share in these projects. The negotiations for the north European pipeline could provide leverage for European investors and governments to encourage a more competitive environment in Russia as well.

*New openings with Iran?* From the policy perspective, Iran will present another challenge and possible opportunity. Unlike the 1990s, there will no longer be concern about Iranian competition undercutting an east—west energy corridor. Instead, the issue will be limited to whether the United States should continue to oppose oil and gas transportation through Iran, and whether there are conditions under which the United States should at least acquiesce in a southern route. We believe that, in the third phase of Eurasian energy transportation, the entire system will be sufficiently well developed that the United States should review its Iran oil and gas transport policy. In our view, if Iran were prepared to offer meaningful compromise on issues of central concern to the United States—including its support for terrorist organizations, its development of weapons of mass destruction, Caspian delimitation, and adoption of a more cooperative policy toward its Caspian neighbors—allowing even U.S. companies to engage in new oil and gas exports, including swaps, would be a natural component of a package of "carrots" that Washington could use to help facilitate a new set of bilateral relations with Tehran.

*Other Eurasian export options.* Over the longer term, there is the prospect of further expansions of the energy security system as well. The most important—and quite possibly the most complicated—of these is the export of gas across Afghanistan to South Asia. In the event that the three major external challenges—stability in Afghanistan, stability in Pakistan, and relations between Pakistan and India (which are now improving)—could ultimately be addressed, this project could afford Ashgabat a belated second chance to end its disadvantaged monopoly relationship with Gazprom.

*Eurasia's role in global markets.* By 2010, the potential prize is clear: the establishment of a multiple and secure oil transportation system in Russia and Eurasia and at least the beginning of similar options for the transportation of gas. Not only will this enhance energy security in Russia and Eurasia, but it will make a potentially important contribution to market development and energy security in other parts of the world. In the Far East, Russia, and to a lesser extent Kazakhstan, could become major oil and gas suppliers to China, Japan, and South Korea. In South Asia, Turkmenistan as well as Uzbekistan and Kazakhstan could conceivably become longer-term gas suppliers.

Even more immediately compelling may be the North American connection. LUKoil has already acquired Getty's downstream assets and established a significant presence in the United States. Yukos has shipped oil directly to U.S. refineries. With a new pipeline, Murmansk could be a major new outlet of Russian oil to the United States. In 2003, President Putin suggested that Russia could supply as much as 10 percent of American oil by the end of the decade. Furthermore, Gazprom is engaged in negotiations with a number of international oil companies to develop the giant Shtokman gas field and create liquefied natural gas facilities, which could supply gas to the American and other markets.

Thus, in a sense, energy security will have moved full circle through these three phases, in the short space of about fifteen years. Initially, the United States and its partners, particularly Turkey, strongly supported energy development in both Russia and the Caspian states, including the creation of multiple export routes, in the sure knowledge that energy security would contribute to their national independence. At the end, it is Russia and the Caspian states that are contributing increasingly to U.S. energy security, and its ability to depend less on OPEC states for its energy requirements. There is a certain beauty in this historical moment.

## Recommendations for the United States, European Union, and Regional States

The United States and the European Union can play an important role in encouraging more open oil and gas pipeline access and greater competition in the Russian and Eurasian energy transportation sector. Both the United States and the European Union have ongoing energy dialogues with Russia, which has a strong desire to attract increased investment and to promote increased oil and gas exports to their markets. This gives the United States and the European Union a logical basis to promote open and competitive energy investment environments—at the same time as they both share with Russia a desire to reduce global dependence on OPEC oil supplies and to increase global energy security.

In particular, both the United States and the European Union should acknowledge the fact that Russia faces domestic political challenges in removing obstacles to the export of energy. In the case of oil exports, as noted above, they as well as Japan can provide export credits and other incentives to promote additional pipelines and port terminals. In the case of gas, today's export limitations assure inexpensive supply for Russia's domestic market, and Western decision makers should recognize the inherent political volatility of policies that would lead predictably to energy price hikes. Through careful dialogue between and among the governments of Russia, the United States, and the European Union (and/or some of its key member states), all sides might succeed in identifying sectoral reform approaches that have worked elsewhere in international practice and that might provide useful ideas or tools for Russia.[27]

Beyond this, the United States and the European Union would be well advised to expand their direct energy consultations and cooperation with their Eurasian counterparts, from Turkey and Ukraine to the Caspian states. With Turkey and Ukraine, they share an interest in pursuing alternatives to exports through the Bosporus. They also share with those countries as well as Russia and the Caspian states an interest in ensuring shipping safety through the Bosporus as well as the physical security of shipping lanes and pipeline routes against future terrorist acts.

Ultimately, the goal of the United States and the European Union should be to engage Russia and all Eurasian states to create a stable and reliable energy security system for the entire region. That also entails, in our view, the progressive engagement of Japan, China, South Korea, Iran, and southern Asia in developing an oil and gas transportation system in which all share a strong interest. We believe that such a goal is not unrealistic. Japan is already a major investor in Sakhalin and has offered to finance a new pipeline to Nakhodka. China is already investing significantly in Kazakhstani fields and has shown it will help develop pipelines from Kazakhstan and Russia to reach the Chinese market. Because a Russian oil pipeline to Daqing appears questionable in the near term, China has moved to promote even more actively the oil pipeline from Kazakhstan. Yet a gas pipeline from Russia to China and on to South Korea does appear achievable, if the issue of Gazprom participation noted above can be resolved. In such an event, the gas could be transported undersea from China to South Korea—or it could also be supplied to North Korea as part of a denuclearization accord.

With respect to Iran, the United States and the European Union can support the Caspian littoral states as they seek Tehran's agreement to a modified median-line delimitation, and in turn agree not to oppose exports to and through an Iran that chooses to cooperate in the region. These steps could make positive contributions to energy security in the Caspian region as well as broader efforts to encourage moderation in Iranian policies and ultimately integration of a postrevolutionary Iran in the international system.

In all these matters, the governments can play a significant political and economic role. Wherever possible, commercial considerations should determine new investments in energy fields and pipelines. But in those cases entailing a powerful public good, where private investment is insufficient, governments should also contribute. For example, intergovernmental cooperation is clearly desirable, indeed essential, to assure the safety of the shipping lanes and the security of pipelines. In addition, governments can play a significant role in organizing and providing political risk insurance, and in providing financing both bilaterally and multilaterally through such institutions as the International Finance Corporation and the European Bank for Reconstruction and Development.[28]

Last but not least, both governments and private investors need to pay attention not only to the immediate energy security challenges and opportunities but also to the chance to strengthen fundamental security in the Russian and Eurasian region. Energy investment can and should go hand in hand with the stability and long-term development and growth of energy-producing states. For this to happen, investment revenues must enter national economies on a transparent basis, and effective and accountable mechanisms must be instituted for the long-term benefit of the economies. Azerbaijan and Kazakhstan have made a start in this direction by creating national petroleum funds, and Russia has also moved positively in a broader context by creating a new stabilization fund.[29] The prospect of increasing energy wealth should be converted into long-term national wealth, for the benefit of future generations, and into true long-term energy security for Russia and Eurasia.

## Notes

1. U.S. Energy Information Administration (EIA), *Russia Country Analysis Brief* (Washington, D.C.: EIA, 2005), available at http://www.eia.doe.gov/emeu/cabs/russia

.html. Transneft disputes the idea that its pipeline system provides capacity insufficient to meet the needs of Russian oil producers. It claims that it is rapidly increasing capacity and that certain elements of its system are not used fully at present. We view Transneft's statements with respect but skepticism. Pipeline systems, in our view, provide a utility service. They exist only for the purpose of connecting reserves and end users. If the prime customers (the oil companies) are unsatisfied because the pipeline system does not provide service where, when, and with what capacity the customers wish, then the service is by definition lacking in some measure.

2. EIA, *Russia Country Analysis Brief,* 99. Virtually all the oil in the Transneft system is blended together into a crude that is frequently referred to as "Urals blend" and that trades at a discount by comparison with industry benchmarks such as dated Brent. Sweeter (lower-sulfur), lighter oils, such as some of those found in the Caspian Sea region, lose substantial amounts of value when blended into the Transneft system. A good quality bank would provide a system for compensating shippers for the value of the oil that they put into the system, with higher prices paid to the shippers that ship higher-quality crudes. After long delays, Transneft began to introduce quality banks in its system in 2004—a goal recognized in Russia's new energy strategy. See Ministry of the Russian Federation for Fuel and Energy, *Energy Strategy of Russia for the Period to 2020,* Document 1234-r (Moscow: Government of the Russian Federation, 2003).

3. At the end of that same month, 24 tankers were queued up at Novorossiysk waiting to receive shipments of crude. Demurrage charges for these delays cost shippers from $30,000 to $50,000 per day or even higher. See Poten and Partners, *Tankers in World Markets* (New York: Poten and Partners, 2003), available at http://www.poten. com/attachments/tiwmsample.pdf. In early December 2003, when Turkey introduced new safety regulations for the Turkish Straits, as many as 100 vessels queued to pass through the Bosporus. See *Lloyd's List,* December 1, 2003.

4. The northern Druzhba runs from Russia into Belarus and then southern Poland and operates at or near its 700,000 bpd capacity; the southern Druzhba cuts from Belarus to Ukraine before entering Slovakia and (as of fall 2003) operates at approximately 60 percent of its capacity of 500,000 bpd.

5. Transneft shipments that had averaged around 350,000 bpd dropped to zero, only partly replaced by non-Transneft shipments that reached the port by rail. See "Transneft on Ventspils," *Moscow Times,* October 13, 2003. The official explanation for Transneft's cutoff is a lack of capacity to make deliveries to the port. See Ilya Khrennikov and Yuliya Bushuyeva, "Ventspils Nafta gotovit k prodazhe" [Ventspils Nafta prepares for sale], *Vedomosti,* October 16, 2003.

6. Although the Danish straits are a wider waterway than the Bosporus, the Oeresund and the Store Belt (Great Belt) have shallow waters and narrow navigation channels that require heavily laden tankers to maneuver in close proximity to other vessels. Author's interviews with commercial shipping safety experts.

7. The authors both participated actively in the development of U.S. policy in support of Multiple Pipelines during their government service in the Clinton administration. For more on Multiple Pipelines and the development of an East-West Energy Corridor serving the Caspian region, see Jan H. Kalicki, "Caspian Energy at the Crossroads," *Foreign Affairs,* September/October 2001, 120–34.

8. BP, the largest investor and operator of the BTC pipeline, mounted a substantial consultation and communications effort designed to address these elements of controversy. See BP, *Regional Review: an Economic, Social, and Environmental Overview of*

*the South Caspian Oil and Gas Projects,* and other documents available at http://www.caspiandevelopmentandexport.com.

9. The EIA projects that by 2015 Western European gas demand will grow by more 33 percent over 2001 levels, nearly doubling from 1990 levels. It lists Western European (not inclusive of Turkey) demand as 10.1 trillion cubic feet (approximately 286 bcm) for 1990, 14.8 trillion cubic feet (tcf) (419 bcm) for 2001, and 19.7 tcf (558 bcm) for 2015. See EIA, *International Energy Outlook 2003* (Washington, D.C.: EIA, 2003), available at http://www.eia.doe.gov/oiaf/ieo/pdf/appa1_a8.pdf.

10. Blue Stream deliveries began at 2 bcm a year and planned, too ambitiously for currently projected demand, to ramp up to planned throughput of 16 bcm a year by 2010.

11. Even in the face of considerable political tensions over the fate of Cyprus, the Turkish and Greek governments have cooperated to assess the feasibility of cooperation on gas supplies from Turkey to Greece and onward into southeast Europe. In February 2003, the two parties agreed to build a 350-kilometer pipeline to connect their gas systems. See Andrei A. Konoplyanik, "Compromise Is Best Course for Russia, EU in Protocol Negotiations," *Oil and Gas Journal,* October 27, 2003, 68. For general background on the Greek–Turkish cooperation, and especially on the support from the European Union's INOGATE program, see http://www.inogate.org/html/resource/resource4.htm. For more information on the Shah Deniz and South Caucasus Pipeline projects, see the common project Web site that covers all the BP-led Caspian projects, http://www.caspiandevelopmentandexport.com.

12. In July 2004, President Leonid Kuchma decided as part of a realignment with Russia to permit TNK-BP and other Russian oil companies to transport up to 200,000 bpd through Odessa-Brody to the Black Sea In March 2005, his successor Viktor Yushchenko decided to restore the pipeline's planned flows from south to north.

13. This Bosporus bypass would extend from Kiyikoy on the Black Sea coast to Ibrikbaba on the Aegean, less than 200 kilometers away. It would require only a short construction period, but as of 2004, outstanding project issues have not been resolved. See "Transneft Looks to the Bosporus," *Petroleum Argus/FSU Energy,* December 19, 2003.

14. Several of the largest Russian oil companies—LUKoil, Yukos, TNK, and Sibneft—proposed in 2002 to build the Murmansk pipeline system and feeder pipelines that would transport 1.6 million bpd of oil, or more, from western Siberia. When Transneft objected, the Russian companies suggested some form of compromise—e.g., private financing and priority access, with Transneft operation—and Transneft reluctantly agreed to conduct a feasibility study.

15. Many observers have regarded the idea of an oil pipeline from western Kazakhstan to China as a not very commercial—indeed fantastical—undertaking. In fact, because this routing can be covered by the interconnection of several existing lines, the connection to China is substantially better grounded than many believed when the idea was first broached in the mid-1990s. It is also viewed increasingly by both the Kazakhstani and Chinese governments as a strategic priority.

16. In the near term, however, a pipeline to both Daqing and Nakhodka would face high hurdles in terms of cost and available supply. Again, feasibility studies are under way, and the Russian government will face a choice replete with economic and political implications for its relations with China and Japan. Bayan Rahman and Andrew Jack, "Japan Offers Russia $7bn to Build Oil Pipe," *Financial Times* online edition, available at http://www.ft.com.

17. The presidents of Afghanistan, Pakistan, and Turkmenistan have expressed sup-

port for the trans-Afghan pipeline proposal, but it has yet to garner the necessary commercial support and market assurances.

18. Cf. PFC Energy, "Russia: Transport Debate Leads to Oil Policy Clash," PFC Memorandum, August 6, 2004.

19. Dmitriy Simakov and Yuliya Bushuyeva, "Nedelimiy 'Gazprom': Putin ostanovil gazovuyu reformu" [Indivisible "Gazprom": Putin stops gas reform], *Vedomosti*, October 10, 2003.

20. The first contract to assure pipeline access for independently produced gas was finally agreed in late October 2003, between LUKoil and Gazprom. Under the terms of their initial 14-month agreement, in 2006, Gazprom will buy 8.75 bcm of gas from the Nakhodkinskoye field at a price of not less than $22.5 per thousand cubic meters, with the actual price to be determined according to an agreed algorithm. Aleksandr Tutushkin, Irina Reznik, and Vladimir Karpov, "Lukoil pristroil gaz" [Lukoil places its gas], *Vedomosti*, http://www.vedomosti.ru, October 22, 2003.

21. Historically, Russia itself demonstrated this advantage when it constructed a bypass to transport Caspian oil (from Azerbaijan as well as eastern Caspian suppliers through the port of Makhachkala) through Dagestan rather than embattled Chechnya. It also demonstrated it in seeking to build the Blue Stream and Baltic Pipeline systems, which helped Russia reduce its own reliance on transit countries.

22. Russia was encouraged to become the single largest government shareholder in CPC, alongside the U.S. company Chevron, which is the single largest private shareholder. To achieve a large Kazakhstani share within a 50–50 government–private structure, the U.S. government quietly encouraged Oman to reduce drastically a large share it had obtained through agreeing to finance an earlier, failed CPC proposal. The largest Russian company at the time, LUKoil, became a shareholder in CPC as well as the Tengiz and Karachaganak fields in Kazakhstan and AIOC. (LUKoil also became a shareholder in the Shah Deniz consortium, but it later divested its holdings in both Shah Deniz and AIOC.)

23. Discussions with Russian officials on development of energy transportation from the Caspian region took place in a variety of settings and circumstances, including small-format discussions between Vice President Al Gore and Prime Minister Victor Chernomyrdin on the margins of the United States–Russia Binational Commission (the "Gore-Chernomyrdin Commission"), and meetings between the energy ombudsmen of the two countries, first deputy minister Anatoly Shatalov and Jan Kalicki. The discussions were not always easy, but they became more businesslike over time.

24. See note 12.

25. The example of Turkmenistan is especially striking. In a strategic error of historic proportions, President Saparmurat Niyazov refused in the late 1990s to accept the proposal of the PSG consortium, supported by the United States and Turkey, to build a gas pipeline under the Caspian to join with the planned pipeline from Shah Deniz to serve the Turkish and then the European markets. Left virtually without options, Niyazov then committed to sell Turkmenistan's gas to Gazprom for thirty years at $44 per thousand cubic meters—half for cash and half for goods of questionable value and quality. In 2005, Turkmenistan was able to negotiate higher price levels—still well below Gazprom's gas sales to Europe at $80 per tcm, though the delivery point is hundreds of kilometers to the west, and there are transit fees that are subsumed in this higher price.

26. Ministry of the Russian Federation for Fuel and Energy, *Energy Strategy of Russia for the Period to 2020,* fig. 8, p. 51.

27. In 2004, Russia agreed to additional liberalization of its energy prices as part of

its negotiations with the European Union on Russian accession to the World Trade Organization. However, much more progress will be needed to equalize gas prices between Russia's domestic and external markets.

28. In November 2003, the International Finance Corporation approved $310 million and the European Bank for Reconstruction and Development another $300 million in financing—half from their funds and half on a commercially-syndicated basis—for the BTC main export pipeline. These loans serve as the keystone for financing to cover the total project cost of $2.95 billion.

29. External analysts have offered a mix of praise and criticism of Azerbaijan's and Kazakhstan's efforts to deal transparently and effectively with energy revenues. For an example that contains criticism and some praise, see Svetlana Tsalik, ed., *Caspian Oil Windfalls: Who Will Benefit?* (New York: Open Society Institute, 2003).

# 7

# Reforming the Gas Market

## *Loyola de Palacio*

The years 2003 and 2004 will be seen as a landmark in the history of the European Union. For the first time in modern history, almost the whole of Europe is now unified under one flag and shares the same values and objectives. Enlargement represents a huge step towards a peaceful and stable Europe based on the largest integrated economic area in the world.

Energy policy will play a key role in ensuring that Europe's integration benefits its citizens and its neighbors. Its economic welfare and societies depend on the secure, reliable, and economic supply of energy as a fundamental precondition for economic development. Guaranteeing the competitiveness of the European market will enhance Europe's energy security, but pressing its suppliers to maximize competition in meeting its energy needs will promote global energy security.

Creating an integrated single European market for natural gas is a key component of this effort. Opening Europe's markets to competition will lead to more economic prices for consumers of natural gas, thus promoting the competitiveness of European industry. A relatively clean fossil fuel, natural gas, will rise in attractiveness to consumers, replacing more polluting fuels.

Secure and reliable gas supplies are the second key component of such a policy. In the longer term, a well-functioning internal market for gas will only be sustainable if the market remains liquid and is based on robust and stable security of supply from sources in Russia and Eurasia, North Africa, and the Middle East, as well as other regions.

Conservation will play a third, critical role. Europe's energy security depends on conservation and efficient fuel use, which has been promoted by relatively higher taxes in E.U. countries than in the United States or elsewhere.

175

And it depends, in my opinion, on a more proactive policy to strengthen petroleum reserves in Europe and other regions, to make their use more flexible, and to strengthen cooperation of consumer countries regarding future contingencies.

In this chapter, I focus exclusively on natural gas, to show how Europe has transformed its gas market, how it has worked with its neighbors to assure competition and adequate infrastructure, and how it can use the power and example of an open competitive market in energy to promote its foreign policy interests in the stability and prosperity of its neighbors.

## The European Gas Market—Today and Tomorrow

The importance of natural gas for the European Union is growing (figure 7.1). Though it accounted for a market share of 22.8 percent in 2000 for the enlarged union with twenty-five member states (hereafter, the E.U. 25), the European Commission's data suggest that it will rise to 32 percent by 2030. Our estimates project a 67 percent growth in consumption of natural gas for the E.U. 25 during the next thirty years.

Given the projected considerable decrease of domestic production of natural gas in the European Union (for the E.U. 25 in 2000, 216 billion cubic meters, or bcm; in 2030, 129 bcm), imports from external suppliers will have to rise considerably, in order to match demand and supply (figure 7.2). Though current imports account for approximately 44 percent of total gas

Figure 7.1. Market Share of Gas in E.U. Member States, 2000–2030

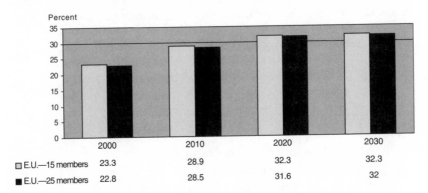

*Source:* European Commission.

Figure 7.2. Demand and Supply Developments, European Union, 2000–2030

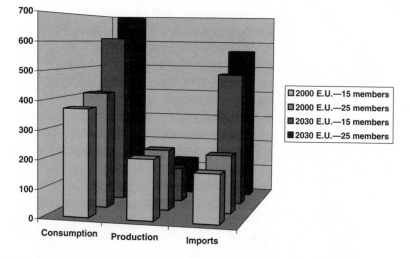

*Source:* European Commission.

consumption by the Union's fifteen member states before enlargement (hereafter E.U. 15), this figure would go up to almost 80 percent by 2030.

One of the main driving factors behind this development is electric power generation. On the basis of European Commission scenarios, 65 percent of the additional E.U. gas demand between 2010 and 2020 will go to this sector. While gas is expected to maintain its relative share of E.U. energy use by 2030, total consumption implies that power generation alone will consume 281 bcm in 2030.

The European gas market is not a monolithic bloc but is made up of fifteen, and prospectively twenty-five, national gas markets with very different characteristics. Some states are major users of natural gas, while others are just beginning to introduce this fuel into their consumption mix. Figure 7.3 indicates the share of natural gas in total primary energy consumption.[1] The same range of diversity exists, when considering the importance of domestic production. Some member states are net exporters of gas, and others consume all their reserves or hold none at all.[2] Although the large consuming countries, such as Germany, Italy, and France, utilize a very diversified supply that include both E.U. and non-E.U. sources, a large number of member states have to import their total supplies only from countries outside the European Union.

Figure 7.3. Share of Gas in Total Primary Energy Consumption, European Countries, 2003

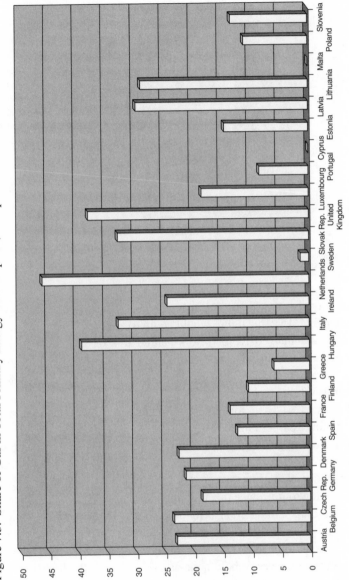

*Source:* Cedigaz.

## Imports and Infrastructure Requirements

In light of the rising demand for natural gas, will gas arrive in sufficient quantities to the European market? Up to now, natural gas demand has been matched by contracted supplies. However, a gap will emerge in 2005–8 between projected demand and contracted-for supplies, which by 2020 will amount to approximately 130 bcm for the E.U. 15 (no figures are available for the E.U. 25). This is not unusual and should not create concern, because gas supply contracts are usually concluded on a rolling basis in line with market developments. However, it highlights the need for new contracts, new capacity, and new infrastructure.

Industry estimates suggest that several hundred billion euros in investment will be required to match demand and supply over the years to come. This enormous sum may also indicate that supply costs (production and transportation) are set to rise due to new fields, which may be more remote from the market and more difficult to develop.

Today, Russia is the most important external supplier of natural gas to the European Union. It accounts for about 50 percent of total E.U. gas imports, or 25 percent of total E.U. 25 gas consumption. Russian gas exports to Europe (including Turkey, Switzerland, and nonacceding countries in Southeast Europe) in 2002 amounted to more than 127 bcm, or a quarter of all gas consumed in Europe. Algeria and Norway hold shares of 23 and 22 percent of total E.U. gas imports, respectively, while the balance is made up by liquefied natural gas (LNG) imports from the Middle East, Trinidad and Tobago, and African countries.

Moreover, Russian supplies of gas—as well as oil—will make it possible for E.U. member states to rely less on countries belonging to the Organization of Petroleum Exporting Countries for their energy imports. In addition to gas supplies across Central Europe, the future may bring Russian gas across the Baltic Sea as well—contributing to increased gas trade between Russia and Europe through multiple routes. Although Russia will likely remain the European Union's most important supplier of natural gas, Algeria, Norway, and a number of new suppliers are expected to increase their market share in the European Union in the decades to come (figure 7.4).

In any case, however, new gas supply projects will be necessary to make sure that the demand for and supply of natural gas can be matched in the European Union over the next twenty to thirty years. In its Communication titled *Development of Energy Policy for the Enlarged European Union, Its Neighbours and Partner Countries*,[3] the European Commission listed new

Figure 7.4. Import Shares of External Suppliers, Selected Countries, 2003

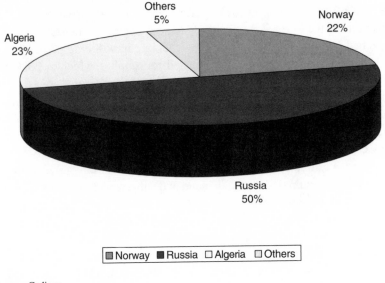

Norway ■ Russia □ Algeria □ Others

*Source:* Cedigaz.

planned supply projects that would increase the import capacity of the European Union by 192 bcm per year. The list includes pipeline projects from Russia, Norway, Algeria, but also from the Caspian Sea region and Libya. In addition, a number of LNG projects are planned that would almost double current LNG import capacity to 43 bcm per year by 2020.

Therefore, it is safe to say that, provided the regulatory and economic conditions are right, the rising demand for natural gas in the European Union will find its supply. The European supply portfolio is likely to be more diversified, but it will continue to attribute a very important role to existing non-E.U. suppliers.

## Trans-European Networks:
## Vehicles for Market Reform and Energy Security

In acknowledging the role and importance of infrastructure for energy and transport, the founding treaty of the European Union (the Maastricht Treaty) established a policy for trans-European networks in these sectors. Since then, considerable achievements in the energy and transport sector through this policy have led to increased investment and improved infrastructure across the European market.

In response to rising import requirements and a more open and competitive internal energy market, the European Union adopted new infrastructure policies in November 2003, including guidelines for trans-European energy networks. These guidelines streamlined and updated the trans-European energy policy and called for pursuing two key objectives: first, effective operation of the internal energy market; and second, strengthened security of energy supplies, including enhanced relations with non-E.U. states in the energy sector. The guidelines identify so-called axes for priority projects— that is, projects considered very important for the operation of the internal energy market and/or security of energy supply, and which in turn will have priority for receiving E.U. financial aid.

Trans-European networks can be expected to serve as vehicles for gas market reform and energy security. E.U. guidelines are specifically designed to promote these objectives, and to assign the priority and the funding that they require to be achieved throughout the E.U. area.

## The Single Market for Natural Gas: Ending the Monopolies

In August 1998, the first Internal Gas Market (IGM) Directive entered into force. Member States were granted a period of two years to transpose it into national laws. The directive is based on the principles of nondiscrimination, transparency, and the introduction of competition. It abolished all exclusive rights on the internal market for gas, such as import and supply monopolies.

To allow the European gas industry—which had been used to operating under monopoly conditions—to adapt to the new market environment, the IGM Directive provided for a gradual market opening, defining so-called eligible customers entitled to choose freely their suppliers. Markets had to be opened in three steps from 20 percent of total consumption in 2000 to 28 percent in 2003 and 33 percent in 2005. Third-party access to the networks of the incumbent companies could be organized either by negotiation between the parties concerned or on the basis of regulated access conditions including tariffs. Vertically integrated companies had to unbundle their accounts, in order to provide transparency and nondiscriminatory treatment of third parties.

Following the IGM Directive's entry into force, the European Commission carried out benchmarking reports, which demonstrated some progress but also a huge diversity among member states with respect to key elements of the liberalization process: market opening, unbundling, network access, and regulation.[4] Recognition that it was not possible to create a fully operational internal market for gas through the first IGM Directive led to a series of actions—by the European Commission, the European Council,[5] and the European Parliament—to amend the directive and speed up the liberalization of European energy markets.[6]

The new IGM Directive will complete the single European market for natural gas. It provides for full market opening by July 2007, while all non-household customers are already eligible as of July 2004. Though many other reforms are still needed, the market-opening provisions of the new IGM Directive represent a tremendous step toward the European Union's declared objective of becoming the most competitive economic area of the world.

Third-party access to transmission and distribution systems will be permitted on the basis of published tariffs, which are applicable to all network users supplying eligible customers. They have to be applied objectively and without discrimination between system users, improving transparency, nondiscriminatory treatment, cost-effectiveness, and the reliability and predictability of behavior of grid operators.

Moreover, both transmission and distribution system operators, usually considered to be natural monopolies, will have to be legally unbundled, with implementation demonstrated in an annual compliance report. The unbundling provisions of the new directive will contribute significantly to achieving a well-functioning internal market. It will be in the interest of all parties—the legally separated entities and member states' regulatory authorities—to improve access conditions to the networks to ensure transparency and nondiscrimination.

A very important function in monitoring competition has been assumed by the E.U. Gas Regulatory Forum, which meets biannually in Madrid ("the Madrid Forum"). Chaired by the European Commission, the forum gathers representatives of member states, national regulatory authorities, the European gas industry, and the gas consumers. Its objective is to agree on a voluntary basis by involving all relevant parties to the European gas market on technical measures that will contribute to creating a well-functioning internal market for gas. Following long negotiations, the forum accepted a new set of guidelines for transmission systems which, while legally nonbinding, can be expected to shape access conditions for network operators.

Their implementation would ensure a big improvement in access conditions across the European Union, including the ten new member states.

The second Internal Gas Market Directive and the new set of guidelines will therefore set and define an excellent regulatory framework for the European market to develop in a competitive and efficient manner—to the benefit of European consumers and European industry.

## The Impact on External Suppliers

This new European market environment will require new market strategies—and both countries and companies will have to adapt. Indeed, European gas companies are not only focusing on their national markets but are increasingly eyeing the markets of other member states. Spot markets and hubs are developing, along with corresponding services, and will open up new market opportunities. The duration of long-term contracts may be shortened with more flexibility built in to enable market participants to react quickly to market developments. However, this does not mean that the role and importance of long-term contracts will be undermined or even questioned. On the contrary: Long-term contracts will continue to play an important role in delivering the bulk of European gas supplies. Their adjustment to the new market requirements will not change this.

With respect to destination clauses in such contracts, tremendous progress has been achieved. In October 2003, Russia's Gazprom, Italy's ENI, and the European Commission reached a settlement that will reinforce the necessary certainty and stability required for investors in gas-producing and -transiting countries, in order to both cope with the challenges ahead and also benefit from the opportunities offered by the new market environment.

In this new environment, there are no exclusive monopolies in the European Union. Every company can compete for customers. Gazprom, for example, has already set up a large number of joint ventures in almost all member states of the pre- and post-enlargement European Union; concluded strategic agreements with companies on the internal market, such as Gasunie and Wingas; and made important strategic investments in the past (e.g., the United Kingdom–Continent Interconnector). In addition, it is about to take the initiative for new important gas supply projects, which will reinforce its importance and position on the European market.

Companies from other non-E.U. countries have also undertaken or are considering moves to reinforce their position on the integrated natural gas market of the European Union. Thus, it can be assumed that all players in the European market for natural gas will benefit from the new opportunities emerging from market opening.

## The Impact on Neighboring Countries

An enlarged European Union should be seen even more as a source for political and economic stability in Europe and in the world. The attraction of the European market can be a force for promoting open economies and open societies in its neighbors, if pursued through dialogue and mutuality. Such a strategy should spread the benefits of political and economic stability to the neighboring countries and help reduce prosperity gaps where they exist. The European Commission seeks to achieve this, in part, by offering access to the European market to its neighbors in return for concrete progress in demonstrating shared values and the effective implementation of political, economic, and institutional reforms, including aligning legislation with the *acquis communautaire*, that is, the total legislative achievements of the European Union. All the neighboring countries should be offered the prospect of a stake in the E.U. Internal Market and further integration and liberalization to promote the free movement of persons, goods, services, and capital (i.e., the four freedoms).[7]

With respect to energy, the full integration of these countries into the E.U. energy market—both gas and electricity—will require compatible and interconnected infrastructure and networks as well as harmonized regulatory environments. The European Union's trans-European networks policy will accordingly lead to the drawing up of strategies for its eastern and southern neighbors. The regional program for the Middle East and North Africa has produced blueprints for infrastructure interconnection and regulatory harmonization in, among other things, energy. These blueprints are intended to be implemented with loans and risk capital from the European Investment Bank through the Facility for Euro-Mediterranean Investment and Partnership.[8]

Russia figures prominently among the European Union's neighboring countries. With respect to gas, a long-term vision would include a regulatory system for gas in Russia that is not only compatible with that of the Union but also based on the same principles and mechanisms. Of course, it goes without saying that any regulatory system would have to protect the specific needs of Russia. Today, the two sides are far apart from such a harmonization, but it will be a central focus of the E.U. dialogue with Russia. It is clear that a common regulatory space, to accompany the common economic space, would both contribute to energy security and increase business opportunities for all participants in both markets.

Southeast Europe, an immediate neighboring region of the European Union encompassing, among others, actual and future member states, is not only crucial for political stability in Europe but will also play an increasingly growing role as a transit region for natural gas. As a consequence, the European Commission brought forward proposals for the creation of a regional electricity market in Southeast Europe in 2002, followed by a gas plan in 2003. The process will soon be institutionalized and is expected to lead to an integrated market for gas and electricity in the near future.

The Caspian Sea basin will in the future contribute to security of supply in Europe. Abundant natural gas reserves in Turkmenistan, Kazakhstan, and Uzbekistan reveal a huge export potential. More immediately, a planned pipeline will transport gas from Azerbaijan to Turkey and then potentially to Southeast Europe and the E.U. market.[9] In the case of each of these countries, the key will be to facilitate the transportation of Caspian resources toward Europe. Indeed, secure and safe export routes for Caspian gas will be important for the European Union's security of energy supply as well as crucial for the economic, but also social and political, development of the Caspian region.

Finally, the Middle East and North Africa will continue to provide substantial energy resources to the European market. In gas, Algeria in particular but also Libya and Egypt are significant suppliers, which will add to the diversity of supply and in turn the energy security of the European Union. European energy trade will complement other trade, investment, and development assistance urgently needed by North African states for their future economic and political stability.

## The European Union–Russia Energy Dialogue

Russia is the most important external supplier of natural gas to the European Union. In 2002, more than 50 percent of the E.U. 25 total gas imports came from Russia. Therefore, it is important for the Union to maintain and enhance Russia's role as a supplier of gas and to strengthen Russia as a secure and reliable supplier of gas through technology transfers and investments to upgrade Russia's energy infrastructure. However, both the European Union and Russia have also recognized the importance of giving a new political impetus to this relationship by working together toward a strategic European Union–Russia energy partnership, given the importance of ensuring adequate energy supplies and appropriate prices for economic development across the whole of the European continent, as well as the long-term nature of investments in energy production and transport.

Recognizing this mutual dependence in the energy sector, the October 2000 European Union–Russia summit in Paris agreed to institute an energy dialogue to define and create a European Union–Russia Energy Partnership. As noted in the Joint Declaration,

> this will provide an opportunity to raise all the questions of common interest relating to the sector, including the introduction of co-operation on energy saving, rationalisation of production and transport infrastructures, European investment possibilities, and relations between producer and consumer countries.[10]

In the three years of its existence, the Energy Dialogue has assisted in developing trust and a better understanding of policy objectives in the energy field and has made significant progress on a number of the issues, paving the way for a long-term institutionalized partnership. These include, among other things, the identification of energy infrastructure projects of common interest; a noncommercial risk guarantee fund; the central role of long-term gas supply contracts in securing the conditions for the Internal Energy Market by facilitating investments; and the legal framework in Russia.

## Energy Security and Interdependence

Besides market opening, the European Union's main concern is security of supply. In this respect, the main issue concerns ensuring that appropriate market conditions and, where necessary, incentives exist to ensure the construction of new gas production capacity and pipelines to supply growing European gas requirements.

Russia, Algeria, and Norway are and will continue to be the principal suppliers of natural gas to Europe. The development of new supply sources and the construction of pipelines to bring this gas to the European Union will require the investment of many billion euros. To permit financing for these investments—which are often characterized by a significant level of commercial and in some cases political or regulatory risk—the European Community must demonstrate its commitment to these projects. The different policies conceived and implemented by the European Union (including the European Union–Russia energy dialogue and neighboring countries) provide important mechanisms to alleviate and even resolve problems that may arise.

In addition the European Commission, recognizing the importance of long-term contracts, has proposed the creation of a safety net for long-term contracts, which is to be set up in the framework of the draft directive for the security of gas supplies under consideration by the European Council. This safety net allows taking measures aimed at ensuring an appropriate minimum share of new gas supplies from external suppliers to be based on long-term contracts. Although the natural desire of a competitive company to secure long-term reliable and fair-priced supplies should ensure the continued existence of long-term contracts in any case, the Commission also wishes to get the message across to the external partners of the European Union and investors alike that long-term contracts are needed both now and also to secure European gas supply in the decades to come.

One may argue that the European Union ought to take measures to avoid too much dependence on natural gas delivered from external sources. Though it cannot be refuted that the diversification of supply sources and routes is necessary, in most cases there is in fact a mutual dependence. Not only is Europe dependent on gas supplies from non-E.U. producers, but the producing countries depend also very much on the revenues gained through gas exports.

In my view, such a complementary structure of interests provides a solid basis for the whole of Europe to cooperate and promote political stability and economic welfare. The emerging interdependence could expand in the longer term into a broad range of political and economic interests accruing from a parallel economic development in a wider Europe encompassing Russia and the other former Soviet republics. Such a development would indeed represent an excellent foundation for not only the most efficient allocation of economic resources for the benefit of our population but also the most stable and reliable political environment in Europe in many centuries.

In line with the findings resulting from the debate on the Green Paper titled *Towards a European Strategy for Security of Energy Supplies,*[11] the European Union is trying to broaden its overall gas supply base. As mentioned above, a considerable number of projects diversifying supply routes and linking new gas fields to the internal market are planned or under construction.

In this respect, the reserves in the Caspian basin (e.g., Azerbaijan) are of particular interest. In addition, new LNG projects in Italy, France, Spain, and the United Kingdom will further contribute to a more diversified gas supply for the European Union.

Conversely, LNG may also serve as a trigger for competition between the United States and Europe across the Atlantic. As a matter of fact, Russia has repeatedly shown its interest in diversifying its export markets. In view of the vast Russian gas reserves, estimated at one-third of global gas resources—and in light of the rising demand for natural gas in the United States, which, like Europe, will have to increasingly import its supply from non-American sources[12]—Russian reserves, if economically exploitable in the form of LNG, may become attractive for the North American market.

However, I do not believe that such a development would jeopardize the security of supply in Europe. It just proves the fact of a global market and that there is no reason for complacency, but a constant need to deal with the challenges arising from security of supply.

## Conclusion

To ensure a well-functioning internal market including security of supply, new investments upstream and also downstream are inevitable. The European market for natural gas will remain attractive, because it is a strongly growing market and it will be, even more in the future, a fully open market, offering a range of business opportunities to the gas-supplying and -consuming industry.

However, it is of utmost importance to set up the right regulatory framework providing stability and clarity to the market. The second Internal Gas Market Directive will bring about such a framework for the single E.U. gas market.

As for producers and suppliers of gas outside the European Union, the newly developed policy vis-à-vis neighboring countries and the concept of a "wider Europe" described above prove that the Union is taking account of the increasing importance of the external dimension for its gas supply. Russia and the Eurasian area, but also Africa and the Middle East, are obviously very important partners in this respect, and they have to be addressed in a differentiated manner adapted to the needs and interests of each individual region.

I believe these policies will enable the European Union to cope with the challenges appearing in the twenty-first century, not only to secure gas supplies but also to further the integration of neighboring energy markets with those of the European Union. In turn, this will promote economic growth and political stability, as well as the energy security of a wider Europe.

## Notes

1. Although some E.U. member states, such as the Netherlands (but also Hungary and the United Kingdom), are well above the E.U. average market share of 22 percent with natural gas accounting for up to 47 percent of primary energy consumption, others, such as Sweden (below 2 percent), Portugal (8 percent), and Greece (6 percent), make only minor use of gas. The latter two introduced the first gas fewer than ten years ago.

2. Denmark, the Netherlands, and still the United Kingdom are net exporters. The Baltic states, Belgium, Finland, Luxembourg, Portugal, Slovenia, and Sweden consume all their reserves. Austria, the Czech Republic, France, Greece, Hungary, Ireland, Slovakia, and Spain have modest or no reserves and import their total or a huge part of their consumption.

3. European Commission, *Development of Energy Policy for the Enlarged European Union, Its Neighbours and Partner Countries,* Document COM (2003) 262 final of 13.5.2003 (Brussels: European Commission, 2003).

4. Whereas some member states opened their market fully, others just stuck to the minimum market-opening requirements. In terms of unbundling, a considerable number of member states decided to go further than unbundling of accounts, which is the weakest form of unbundling and opted for management or even legal or ownership unbundling. With respect to access regimes to the network, regulated access proved generally to be more effective than the negotiated approach. Set up by most—but not all—member states, regulatory authorities contributed to the proper application of the principles of nondiscrimination, transparency, and competition.

5. The European Council is composed of heads of state and government and decides on the main policy directions of the European Union.

6. Pursuant to the so-called Lisbon strategy adopted in March 2000, the Commission submitted a set of new proposals to the European Parliament and the Council in March 2001 with a view to completing the European internal energy market. The package contained, among other things, a proposal to amend the Gas Directive, in order to remedy the most obvious shortcomings emerging from the implementation of the first Internal Gas Market Directive. Following the opinion of the European Parliament on its first reading and discussions at the energy Council, a revised proposal was submitted in July 2002 and this paved the way for a political agreement in the Council in November 2002. Following the second reading in the European Parliament, the directive was finally adopted in June 2003 and entered into force in August 2003. Member states were given until July 2004 to transpose the provisions of the directive into national laws.

7. See European Commission, *Development of Energy Policy for the Enlarged European Union, Its Neighbours and Partner Countries.*

8. The Commission has set out such a strategy in its 2003 Communication titled *Wider Europe–Neighbourhood: A New Framework for Relations with Our Eastern and Southern Neighbours,* Document COM (2003)104 final of 11.3.2003 (Brussels: European

Commission, 2003). Its objectives are twofold: first, working with partners to reduce poverty and create an area of shared prosperity and values based on deeper economic integration, intensified political and cultural relations, enhanced cross-border cooperation with shared responsibility for conflict prevention between the European Union and its neighbors; and second, anchoring the E.U. offer of concrete benefits and preferential relations within a differentiated framework that responds to progress made by the partner countries in political and economic reform.

9. Gas reserves for Turkmenistan are estimated at 2,900 bcm; for Uzbekistan, 18,500 bcm; for Kazakhstan, 1,900 bcm; and for Azerbaijan, 1,370 bcm.

10. European Union, "Joint Declaration by the President of the European Council, J. Chirac, with the Assistance of the Secretary-General of the Council/High Representative for the Common Foreign and Security Policy of the EU, J. Solana, by the President of the Commission of the European Communities, R. Prodi, and by the President of the Russian Federation, V. V. Putin, Paris, October 30, 2000," Press Release 405, 12779/00; available at http://ue.eu.int/newsroom/.

11. European Commission, *Green Paper: Towards a European Strategy for the Security of Energy Supply* (Brussels: European Commission, 2001), available at http://europea.eu.int/comm/energy_transport/doc-principal/pubfinal_en.pdf.

12. Cf. various International Energy Agency reports, e.g., *World Energy Outlook Insight* (Paris: International Energy Agency, 2001) on global energy supply.

# Commentary on Part II

## Viktor I. Kalyuzhny

Because the preceding three chapters bring an American and European perspective to issues of energy security for Russia and Eurasia, I welcome the opportunity to provide a corresponding perspective from within the region—drawing on my responsibilities at both the Ministry of Fuel and Energy and the Ministry of Foreign Affairs of the Russian Federation. It is certainly the case that the problem of energy security is no less important a subject for Moscow than for Washington and Brussels. Russia's people and industry, located as they are on an enormous continent reaching up to the far north, depend on secure and affordable energy supplies for their very livelihood. With record production in oil and gas in this new century, Russia cannot only be self-sufficient but also must contribute to the energy security of its neighbors in Europe and North America. Thus it can only welcome the establishment of energy dialogues with the European Union and the United States, and it expects these dialogues to become even more profound in coming years.

As Russia expands its exports to Europe and increasingly to the United States and other markets, it does not do so to displace the exports of other traditional suppliers at all. Indeed, if existing forecasts are correct, future projected global demand will require imports from OPEC and non-OPEC states alike. As Julia Nanay points out in her chapter, most Western oil imports continue to come from OPEC, but Russia and other suppliers can add significantly to that supply, and such diversified sources will be indispensable in developing global energy security. However, I would differ frankly with her emphasis on maximizing exports from Russia. Russia's interests are determined by its dual role as a leading producer-exporter and, simultaneously, a large consumer of hydrocarbons. Today, Russia's task is to

191

double its gross domestic product, which requires steady increases in its economic potential and the strengthening of its domestic industry, defense complex, and social sector. Increasing oil and gas volumes will be needed to achieve these goals. In these circumstances, it is extremely important to find an optimum balance between internal consumption and the export of hydrocarbons produced in Russia—a balance that should be established by the state.

I am convinced that, for Russia, oil and gas exports are both important and profitable, but the country should not rely on these exports as an economic panacea. It does not suit Russia to be a raw materials appendage to Western economies.

In the particularly sensitive domain of transportation, it is quite natural that state-owned companies—Transneft and Gazprom—are responsible for oil and gas transit under the regulation of the Federal Energy Commission. For me, it is axiomatic that the state needs to maintain control over the main oil pipelines. In fact, because most of Russia's oil industry is privatized, the control of the main pipelines is the only mechanism of effective state regulation available today. Conversely, privatized oil companies attract significant volumes of foreign investment and make substantial contributions to Russia's energy capacities and to the socioeconomic development of the country as a whole—assuming, of course, that they do not fall prey to corporate egoism and pay their taxes properly.

Russia welcomes the use of its pipelines by its neighbors for the transportation of oil and gas. Significant quantities of oil and gas come to and through Russian territory from Azerbaijan, Kazakhstan, Turkmenistan, and Uzbekistan. Both Transneft and Gazprom are engaged in the expensive expansion of their pipeline system to accommodate growing volumes of hydrocarbons from both Russian and Eurasian sources. At the same time, Russia understands that for European markets—and probably also Asian markets—additional pipelines will be required in the due course of time. In that sense, I would agree with Jan Kalicki and Jonathan Elkind that a pipeline network should include not only traditional but also new supply routes—north, west, east, and south. But these routes should be developed on strictly commercial terms.

As President Vladimir Putin stated at the first Caspian Summit in Ashgabat in April 2002, "Russia does not have any allergy to the idea of multiple pipelines. It is important only that decisions about pipeline routes are not driven by politics, and are justified from the economic and environmental points of view." In other words, external forces should not use pipelines to advance political agendas, or worse yet to seek to isolate one or another state in Russia's region. Unfortunately, the politicization of pipeline issues does occur.

I welcome Kalicki and Elkind's suggestion of a broadened transportation dialogue involving the regional states and others with commercial interests in pipeline development, and their view that barriers should be removed to energy trade with Iran. I also support the idea that only the constructive engagement of all coastal states in the Caspian in the resolution of regional problems will help to increase security in all spheres, including energy, and create the framework for increased economic development. It was precisely this premise that led to the delimitation agreements for the Caspian seabed achieved (with my participation) among Azerbaijan, Kazakhstan, and Russia. I expect that similar agreements ultimately will be reached by Azerbaijan, Iran, Kazakhstan, and Turkmenistan.

More broadly, I believe too many analysts underestimate the increasing interdependence of interests between suppliers and consumers. For that reason, I note with satisfaction Loyola de Palacio's emphasis on "a complementary structure of interests" for security of supply versus security of demand. Just as Europe gained confidence in the reliability and security of Russian gas exports since 1968—and I appreciate Loyola de Palacio's recognition of this fact—so Russia needs to be assured of the reliability and security of the European gas market. Gas, in particular, involves very substantial and long-term investments, and it calls for a community of interests between consumer and supplier. From this point of view, to put it mildly, attempts to achieve diversification of supply into the European market by inherently unilateral acts are not welcome. Taking into account Europe's growing dependence on gas imports, many experts believe that inadequate diversification is fraught with risks and may have a boomerang effect. Long-term export contracts should and will play an important role in maintaining the stability and security of the gas market.

While ensuring that it meets growing domestic demand, Russia is ready at the same time to supply gas to new markets. With the help of liquefied natural gas (LNG) terminals in Sakhalin and prospectively the far North, it can build energy export bridges to the Asian and North American markets as well. In 2003, both the U.S.-Russian commercial energy summit in Saint Petersburg and the LNG summit in Washington significantly advanced the prospects for both bilateral and global cooperation in creating a new LNG marketplace. In this context, the creation of a Eurasian gas alliance— formulated conceptually in the joint statement of the presidents of Russia,

Kazakhstan, Uzbekistan, and Turkmenistan in Almaty on March 1, 2002—is also very promising.

At the same time, Russia hopes for greater understanding from its Western and particularly its E.U. friends on the requirements of its domestic gas market. Though a unified gas price is a desirable longer-term goal, in the near term the lower domestic price is essential to Russia's economic growth and the success of its economic reforms. International trade purists tend to overlook these immediate, compelling requirements.

In my energy and foreign ministry experience, I have found that energy specialists often do not take into account the foreign policy implications and that diplomats often do not take into account the energy and economic implications of their work. But they should. Russia and Eurasia, the United States, and Europe need to think much more seriously, together, about both energy and foreign policy—how to advance their shared energy security agenda. This probing, forward-looking book will help them do this.

# Part III

# The Middle East and Africa

Part III turns to the Middle East, which has most of the world's oil and gas resources, and to Africa, which will produce substantial supplies in the future. From the oil boycott to the second Iraq war, oil-consuming countries have experienced deepening concerns about their dependence on the world's most unstable region, and these concerns are compounded by renewed questions about the stability of Middle Eastern governments in the face of military conflict, fundamentalism, terrorism, and the revolution of rising expectations. The stability of African governments is also at issue, as is the question of whether newfound oil revenues will sink in military and showcase spending along with widening corruption or will swim to the long-term, transparent development of the continent. For U.S. and Western policy, key issues arise about reducing dependence on unstable supply sources while encouraging more stable development with more widespread benefits in both the producing and consuming countries.

Addressing these and related issues are J. Robinson West, who focuses on Saudi Arabia, Iraq, and their impact on both Gulf and global oil market dynamics; Gordon Shearer, who considers North Africa and the Mediterranean; and Paul Hueper, who writes about Sub-Saharan Africa.

In chapter 8, West examines Saudi Arabia's future as a stable supplier in light of the recent turbulence in the Kingdom and concludes that no other country in the world will be able to maintain excess production capacity and act as a swing producer to the same extent. Looking beyond the immediate economic and energy sector crisis in Iraq, he argues that, over the medium term, the principal challenge for OPEC will be to manage Baghdad's return to the market; quota reallocation pressures and eventually dangers of a price crash will increase as Iraqi oil comes online, with a likely adverse impact on future non-OPEC energy investment. The longer-term question is whether the United States can and should seek to substitute this country, with the world's second largest oil reserves, for Saudi Arabia in oil market primacy and energy security—and to this question, West's answer is negative for both feasibility and desirability. The challenge for U.S. policy is to ensure the cooperation of Saudi Arabia and other leading producers, both OPEC and non-OPEC, in stable and secure markets over the longer term.

In chapter 9, Shearer describes a transformation of the Mediterranean energy picture, with large natural gas reserves in North Africa becoming integrated through new pipelines and liquefied natural gas terminals into Europe and eventually North America. He considers the positive trade-off between security of supply and security of markets, and he addresses the need to translate increased energy wealth into improved economic performance in North Africa. After analyzing each of the producing countries as well as Turkey, he calls for a more direct U.S. engagement that takes into account the region's greater interdependence and growing diversity.

In chapter 10, Hueper describes how Sub-Saharan Africa will play a growing and critical role during the next two decades. Even in the more mature oil provinces to the west, he demonstrates that there is a significant upside for oil exploration and development, particularly in deep offshore waters. He then outlines how technological advances have begun to show significant oil and gas potential in additional countries not only in the west but in the south and east of the continent. He argues that ensuring the political and economic stability of these producing countries is vital to global energy security, and that this in turn will require increased attention to transparency, eliminating bribery and corruption, and resolving civil wars and conflicts in the region. Hueper analyzes both national and international initiatives (including those of the World Bank) to increase the likelihood that their energy revenues will be used for economic development.

In his commentary on part III, Abdullah bin Hamad Al-Attiyah, Qatar's deputy prime minister and minister of energy and industry, highlights the interdependence of energy producers and consumers, describes his country's important and growing role in the global gas market, and underlines the need for strategy of cooperation rather than confrontation in the energy field. He welcomes growing regional energy cooperation in both the Mediterranean and Gulf regions, and he emphasizes the need to ensure that both long-standing and new energy sources contribute to a healthy energy market and global economic growth. In defending a record of reliability by both gas producers and OPEC, which he has served several times as president, Al-Attiyah calls for maintaining prices "within a predictable, acceptable, and fair range, taking into account the interests of both producers and consumers."

# 8

# Saudi Arabia, Iraq, and the Gulf

## J. Robinson West

The U.S. invasion of Iraq and rising levels of unrest in Saudi Arabia both have enormous potential to change global oil market dynamics. These trends will almost certainly change the current political and economic circumstances of the Gulf states at both the domestic and regional levels. The unrest in Saudi Arabia has led some to raise serious questions about the Kingdom's ability to function as a stable supplier, and to propose that a rehabilitated Iraq might be able to take Saudi Arabia's place. Relations between the United States and some of the region's largest oil producers could also be altered by the consequences of the U.S. invasion, and a clear shift in the pattern of alliances is already developing. This chapter examines Saudi Arabia's future as a stable supplier; whether a "New Iraq" can replace Saudi Arabia; and the implications for the other Gulf states, energy security, and U.S. foreign policy. U.S. policymakers must be cognizant of these issues when developing policies toward the region, as the consequences for U.S. and Western energy security are of vital importance.

## Saudi Arabia: The Question of Regime Stability

Somewhat lost in the hectic atmosphere of the run-up to the Iraq war was the fact that the U.S.–Saudi relationship has undeniably changed, and not for the better. Saudi Arabia's role as a "breeding ground" for the September 11, 2001, hijackers and its subsequent foot-dragging in the U.S. "war on terror" has earned it few friends on this side of the Atlantic, even now that the regime itself is under attack. The questions surrounding Saudi Arabia's continuation as a stable supplier essentially fall into one of three

197

categories: (1) regime stability, which covers political legitimacy, the economic situation, and the rising wave of terrorist attacks; (2) production capabilities, which encompass reserve and capacity issues; and (3) foreign policy and external alignment.

In the short term, the Saudi regime appears to have achieved a stable and secure status quo, but some clear long-term risks remain. Since May 2003, the regime and its security forces have been locked in an ongoing battle with various militants who have taken to targeting Westerners and oil infrastructure. Though the direct threat to the regime is thus limited, these attacks are an attempt to undermine the foundation upon which the regime bases its rule. The regime's legitimacy stems from its ability to maintain high levels of oil revenues, and to distribute these earnings in the form of social services to its constituents. Another, no less important, component is the regime's ability to provide security, especially in its role as the Custodian of the Two Holy Places of Islam, Mecca and Medina. Failure to fulfill either of these functions will lead to a loss of legitimacy for the regime, with potentially dire consequences. It appears that the regime will be able to deal with these issues in the short term and is already looking for ways to address them in the long term as well.

The murder of nearly thirty U.S. and European foreign workers in Saudi Arabia in 2004 sent shock waves through global oil markets, with fears that oil output from the Kingdom might drop precipitously if foreign workers fled. Moreover, worries mounted over the possibility that interruptions in critical social services would destabilize the economy and exacerbate the country's social and economic problems. While the lives of foreign workers have certainly been disrupted, with many moving their families to Bahrain or other Gulf countries, there has not been the mass exodus feared in the immediate aftermath of the attacks. Security in housing and work compounds has been increased, and provisions made to allow foreign security personnel to be armed. Saudi Aramco has also beefed up its security, allocating extra funds to protect its infrastructure, and assured markets that even though there are likely to be some future attacks on facilities, there are sufficient redundancies in the entire system that exports will not be disrupted even in the event of a serious attack. The amnesty offered to militants in July 2004, following the beheading of Paul Johnson, a longtime resident contractor, seems to have yielded some high-value individuals, despite clear divisions within the Royal Family about the desirability of such a program. This division in turn mirrors a deeper divide within the family, between the full brothers and half brothers of King Fahd, between those who want to engage in dialogues on reform and those who do not.

The issue with the militants is the most pressing and glaring one, and the one with the most significant short-term implications. The Soviet withdrawal from Afghanistan led to thousands of Saudi citizens who had fought alongside the *mujahedeen* flooding back to their homeland. During the 1990s, these militants kept a low profile and did not threaten the government, which in turn allowed them freedom to organize and fund external operations. The 9/11 terrorist attacks set off a change in this coexistence, with the United States placing great pressure on the Saudi government to crack down not only on the militants but also on the religious schools and mosques that provide both ideological support and sources for new recruits. However, even in the face of this pressure, the ruling family negotiated with a number of Saudi members of al Qaeda seeking to return home from Afghanistan to avoid capture by the United States. The government offered these returnees jobs in the public sector and sought the help of local relatives and tribes to integrate them back into their societies.

All this changed with the attacks on Saudi Arabian citizens and facilities in the Kingdom in May and December 2003, persuading the government that a more aggressive policy was needed. However, even then members of the Interior Ministry continued to negotiate with some of the militants, including Abdul Aziz Al-Mukrin, the alleged head of al Qaeda in Saudi Arabia. The ministry, which is headed by Prince Nayef, a full brother of the king, wants to balance any nonterror policy with stringent curbs on liberal reformers, thereby securing the support of nonviolent Salafi clerics who have issued declarations in support of the regime and against al Qaeda and Osama bin Laden. These curbs on liberal reformers would obviously have a detrimental effect on Crown Prince Abdullah's reform agenda, which he is holding out as his way of bringing long-term stability and security to the Kingdom.

In January 2003, Abdullah called for reform across the Middle East in a major speech that many interpreted as a call for reform at home. This prompted a series of petitions, beginning with one from a group of 104 liberal reformers, titled "A Vision for the Present and Future of the Homeland."[1] The petition called for broad reforms to the Saudi political system based on Islamic principles, which included elections to the national consultative council, the expansion of civil rights (freedom of speech, assembly and, association) together with the creation of appropriate human rights organizations to monitor the change, and finally an independent judiciary. In September 2003, Sunni and Shia secularists submitted another petition titled "In the Defense of the Nation," which contained many of the same demands. In yet another petition in 2003, reformers reiterated these principles but went further by calling for limits on the monarchy, embodied in a constitution that would be submitted to the popular vote—in effect, a constitutional monarchy.

At first, the ruling family embraced the reformers, despite their calls for political change. Crown Prince Abdullah met with them several times. In the name of Islamic unity, the crown prince hosted a gathering of religious leaders representing various Salafi factions, but also Shias from the eastern province, and even Ismailis from Najran, as well as other scholars representing the Maliki and Shafi'i schools in Islamic jurisprudence. This National Forum for Dialogue discussed the forces threatening national unity, the centrality of Islamic law and the clergy, diversity of thought, the rights and responsibilities of women in society, and freedom of expression.[2]

This was significant for several reasons. For one, it brought the various factions together to discuss deeply divisive issues. Second, it brought different Saudi citizens together and notably placed the Shia on the same footing as Wahabi Sunnis and Sunnis from other schools of thought. Third, it signaled how much the various factions, ethnic groups, and regional blocs actually wanted to work with the ruling family to bring about change, and it underlined the critical role of the ruling family as political brokers.

The bombings in May and December 2003, the killings of foreign workers thereafter, and the attack on the U.S. consulate in Jeddah in late 2004 unsettled the Al Sauds and threatened their ability to manage all the factions. It also reopened the rivalry between members of the ruling family on how best to deal with the violence. At the heart of this rivalry is the power struggle mentioned above. It appears Nayef's stance has won the day within the family, because police have so far arrested 4 out of the 104 liberals who signed the January petition, expelled 2 senior journalists sympathetic with the liberal Salafis, and jailed other liberal reformers for short periods. Reflecting this rift within the family, one of the journalists, Jamal Khassoggi, ended up working for Prince Turki Al-Faisal, who is the former Saudi intelligence chief, Saudi ambassador to the United Kingdom, and part of a faction of the ruling family that supports Crown Prince Abdullah's reforms. Since this spring, the liberal Salafi reform movement's momentum has been checked, and the ruling family has largely counted on the more conservative Salafis for support in fighting the militants.

The Saudi family's control over political power in the Kingdom is not, however, in any serious danger of being lost in the short run. The ruling family has secured some support among its previous critics, the conservative Salafis, who are seen by a large part of the core Sunni constituency as legitimate and credible. Their support among the establishment clergy is also secure and has been used to undermine clerics who went over to the side of the militants. They have sacrificed the support of the liberals, but this signifies more than ever that liberal Salafis have nowhere to go and can only hope to further their agenda through the sufferance of members of the ruling family. The loss of support from within the ruling family has stalled the reform agenda.[3]

The ruling family also secured the support of the Shia but is unlikely to take their demands very seriously. It is true that Crown Prince Abdullah had started a slow process of allowing greater freedoms to the Shia. The National Forum for Dialogue gave them an unprecedented place at the national table. In April 2003, 450 Shia men and women signed a petition titled "Partners in One Nation," which affirmed national unity and support for the ruling family, while also calling for reform along the lines of the January 2003 petition and an end to religious discrimination. These moves deeply troubled the conservative Salafis, whose opposition means that any movement toward greater religious tolerance and equality is unlikely for now.

The end to serious political reforms does not necessarily mean that elections on a provincial level will be disallowed, and in fact they have been held in 2005, after repeated rescheduling. However, elections for half the seats of an assembly hardly count as a serious exercise in popular sovereignty. Educational reform appears to be stalled as well. There was a purge of some radical teachers and clerics with the help of the establishment clergy and the conservative Salafis, but there is no sign that positive reforms, including moves toward a more liberal and economically useful curriculum, are imminent.

All in all, the reform agenda has stalled in the Kingdom. Economic reform has made greater progress, although in critical areas—particularly the hydrocarbons sector—state institutions remain paramount. New laws have been instituted to encourage foreign investment, but given the current political climate and threats to foreign workers, it is unlikely that Saudi Arabia will soon become a significant target for foreign investment. The liberalization of prices so necessary to attract domestic investment in infrastructure has not advanced in the past few years. The government, flush with cash in a high-oil-price environment, can afford the subsidies for now.

Besides the political legitimacy of the regime, the other pillar of support lies in the economic well-being of the Kingdom, and how that is managed through times of low oil prices. Saudi Arabia has worked very hard in the past ten years to stabilize its budget and lay the groundwork for renewed growth in its economy. This was achieved through three means. First, the Kingdom, particularly after the accession of Crown Prince Abdullah in 1995, changed its oil price policy from favoring low to moderate prices to one that favored moderate to high prices. Whereas in the past the Kingdom had erred on the lower side of a notional price band and allowed prices to float downward, now it and the rest of the Organization of Petroleum Exporting Countries (OPEC) aggressively defend against weaker prices and prefer to see prices overshoot OPEC's price band of $22 to $28 a barrel. Indeed, their actions suggest the Saudis are now more comfortable with a range from $35 to $40, not the declared $22 to $28. As a result, it has earned record oil revenues in the past several years, amounts unseen since the early 1990s. In effect, then, it has temporarily solved the chronic revenue shortfalls that plagued its finances in the early 1990s. Although the government has done very little to reduce its dependence on oil, small nonoil revenue changes—including the imposition of service fees and higher utilities prices—did add modest amounts to the government's revenues.

Second, the Saudi government has cut expenditures, especially on arms purchases. This has completely undermined the large weapons buying program from the United States. The Saudi government has also frozen increases in current spending—wages and salaries, goods and services—and stabilized capital spending on major projects. It has also "privatized" some services—extracting greater efficiencies.

Third, with the budget no longer seen as the main engine of growth in the economy, the Saudi government has moved to put in place a set of institutional and economic reforms. These reforms have included initiating the process to join the World Trade Organization and attract foreign direct investment in a variety of sectors. The National Gas Initiative was to be the signal to foreign investors that Saudi Arabia was open to the foreign private sector, and even though it failed initially, it clearly helped attract attention to the reforms the government was attempting to pursue.

In the event of a price crash, Saudi Arabia has shored up its finances, whereby it could take substantially lower prices for a period of one year to eighteen months. Its foreign assets now stand at well over $100 billion, having been rebuilt from a post-oil-price-crash low of about $45 billion in the late 1990s.[4] Its foreign debt is negligible and owed mainly by public enterprises such as Sabic, which borrowed to fund economically viable export-oriented petrochemical projects. The government's domestic debt—currently estimated at about 85 percent of gross domestic product ($160 billion)[5]—is a problem in the long run because most of the debt is owed to the social security fund. Given that the population is skewed toward the youth, however, funding retirement schemes will not be a material problem for some years to come. A series of virtually balanced budgets since the late 1990s, the stabilization of debt, and increases in foreign assets together have given the Saudi state enough of a cushion to weather lower oil prices for a limited period. With oil prices having definitely moved into a higher price range for the foreseeable future, Saudi planners can now look beyond simply balancing the budget and providing minimum social spending commitments. Saudi Arabia now has an opportunity to begin implementing structural economic development programs, and there is evidence that some steps are already being taken toward the goal of developing a functioning productive sector in the long-term.

## Saudi Arabia: The Question of Oil Supply Security

Having established that the Saudi regime is fairly well positioned politically and economically, at least in the short to medium terms, the next question that arises is whether Saudi Arabia can sustain its dual roles of dominant oil producer and swing producer. As the largest oil exporter in the world, with a current production level of more than 9 million barrels per day (mmbpd), Saudi Arabia is by far and away the dominant producer of oil as far as world markets are concerned. Added to the daily production and exports is the fact that Saudi's reserve base also far exceeds that of any other nation, and the reserve/production ratio (the measure of how long a given country can keep producing oil at its current rate) extends to well over a hundred years.

Although some analysts have raised questions about the integrity of the limited data Saudi Aramco has provided on its reserves, it appears from the vast majority of accounts, whether compiled by international oil companies like BP, government organizations such as the U.S. Energy Information Administration or various geological experts, that Saudi Arabia has proven reserves of almost 300 billion barrels. At one of the first public disseminations of Aramco proprietary data, executives from the Saudi oil company pointed out that this number encompassed strictly "proven" reserves, or those that can be extracted with a greater than 90 percent probability.[6] This number therefore does not include those reserves that have been located and identified but that are given a slightly lower extraction probability and thus fall into the category of "possible" reserves. Because these are reserves that have already been identified, and ever-improving technologies are allowing for much higher recovery rates, it is likely that Saudi Arabia will be able to substantially increase its recoverable reserve base without even having to tap the large unexplored desert areas of the Kingdom.

Yet will having ample reserves be enough for Saudi Arabia to maintain its role as strategic supplier into the future? Saudi Arabia's importance stems not only from the fact that it is the single largest supplier to oil markets but also from its ability to serve as the "swing producer," as the producer of last resort. The Kingdom can fill this role because it maintains roughly 2 mmbpd of idle capacity, meaning capacity above and beyond its daily production needs. This capacity can then be brought on to substitute for the loss of any other production on the world markets.

In 2003 alone, the world witnessed significant outages from three major producers: Iraq, Nigeria, and Venezuela. Saudi Arabia's ability to immediately step in and make up this loss of supply, thereby preventing an imbalance that would have rapidly driven up the price of oil to untenable levels, ensures that it maintains the dominant role in world oil markets. Two unique features give Saudi Arabia strategic significance as a crude oil supplier (as distinct from purely its commercial importance). The first is its willingness and ability to maintain substantial excess production capacity, and the second is its willingness and ability to swing production to meet changing market conditions. No other country in the world can perform these two roles to the same extent as Saudi Arabia. In the twelve months leading up to the U.S. invasion of Iraq, Saudi Arabia increased its crude output from 7.3 to nearly 9.4 mmbpd, an increase of nearly 2.1 mmbpd.[7] This increment is substantially larger than the combined production of Kazakhstan and Azerbaijan, which average approximately 1.3 mmbpd.[8]

As with oil reserves, recent trends in oil markets have called into question Saudi Arabia's ability to function as the swing producer for the indefinite future. No other country in the world, of those with sufficient reserves, maintains the level of spare capacity that Saudi Arabia does, simply because it is prohibitive on a cost basis to do so. The recent surge in demand stemming from China and to some extent the United States is beginning to put the current market dynamics under pressure. China's rapid growth and resultant energy demands grew at an unprecedented level in 2003 and 2004, accounting for about 40 percent of the growth in total world oil demand by some estimates and catapulting it into the world's second largest consumer of oil after the United States. The United States has also seen an increase in demand, especially in the transportation sector, mainly as a result of the gradual shift of automotive sales toward sport utility vehicles. Saudi Arabia appears to be up to the supply challenge, however, announcing in mid-2004 that it was increasing its production capabilities to well over 11 mmbpd. That they were able to bring this capacity online much sooner than anticipated speaks to the fact that the Saudis are both cognizant of the need to increase supply and able to do so at relatively short notice.

## The Return of Iraqi Oil, Saudi Oil Market Primacy, and U.S. Energy Security

In dealing with the complex interactions between Saudi Arabia, Iraq, and the United States, an underlying question needs to be answered: Can and should Iraq replace Saudi Arabia's oil market primacy and, if it could, would it enhance U.S. energy security? The short answer to this very important and complicated question is "no" on all three counts.

The ability of the global oil sector to deal with major supply disruptions is not accidental. It derives from a complex set of interactions and developments in and among producing countries, consuming countries, traders, and the industry. Thus, the realities that have reduced the world's vulnerability to oil supply disruptions have a permanence that will keep them relevant and effective in the foreseeable future.[9]

One of the most basic features of this dynamic is the divergence between the degree of dependence of oil-importing and oil-exporting countries on oil. In the past thirty years, while the industrial countries successfully diversified their sources of crude oil imports, established substantial strategic reserves, and greatly reduced their relative dependence on energy, the major oil exporters remained dependent on oil revenues. Today, oil exporters have much more reason to worry about the security of their markets than importers have reason to worry about the security of their supplies. This persistent dependence on oil revenues has meant that the major exporters—largely the member countries of OPEC—have had to constantly balance between two conflicting interests and needs: their short-term financial requirements and their long-term market share interests. The former calls for relatively higher prices, which jeopardize the latter. The latter requires relatively low oil prices, which jeopardize the former.

So it is not a coincidence that price moderation and stability have been the key policy objectives of the major exporters for the past quarter of a century. They pursue this objective, because it is the only way to optimize the balance between their revenue and market-share requirements. When oil prices rise too high, the industry and the world economy strike back through both reduced demand and higher non-OPEC supplies, eroding the producers' market share and revenue base. When oil prices fall too low, the industry and the world economy respond with higher demand and lower investments in exploration and production, eventually curtailing the rise in non-OPEC output and sometimes even causing a reduction in mature, high-cost production areas. Though this helps to eventually turn around the eroding market share of the exporters, it does cause considerable short-term financial pain and economic and budgetary instability in the major producing countries.

This has led to an alignment of interests between major exporters and the United States. The United States has itself opposed both very low (single-digit or low teens in terms of dollars per barrel) and very high (more than $30 a barrel) crude oil prices. Thus, the producers have tried to manage crude oil market supplies, sometimes successfully, to achieve a price range over $21 a barrel since 1991. This price is high enough to continue encouraging substantial investment in the global upstream sector as well as in technology, but not so high as to cause any major economic dislocations in the industrial economies.[10]

Diversity of supply enhances security of supply, but by itself is not sufficient to guarantee security of supply. It is important to distinguish between crude oil suppliers of commercial significance and suppliers of strategic or security significance. Size and growth potential are important and generally sufficient determinants of the former. They are not sufficient determinants of the latter. To qualify as a strategic supplier, a producing country also needs to have the capability to cause large swings in its production at very short notice in order to compensate for a disruption elsewhere in the world.

Since September 11, 2001, there has been growing skepticism toward the Kingdom of Saudi Arabia, not only as an ally that does not share the United States' goals and values but also as a key supplier of crude oil. Although 9/11 did not change the below-ground realities of oil reserves, it did change above-ground perceptions enough to challenge Saudi Arabia's continued role as a strategic supplier of crude oil. The central concern that has been raised in the United States is that if Saudi Arabia is unreliable as an ally in the fight against terrorism, it may also be unreliable as an ally in providing energy security, regardless of the record of the past twenty-five years. To reinforce this position, some critics have maintained that the United States will soon not need Saudi oil, and that the Kingdom's role as supplier of last resort can be replaced by new energy from the countries of the former Soviet Union—Russia and the other Caspian Sea region states—and Iraq. This reasoning is flawed and could have catastrophic consequences if turned into the bedrock of a new energy security policy.

Saudi Arabia has been a reliable supplier of oil for more than a quarter-century. The consuming world will need as much Russian, West African, Caspian, Latin American, and European oil as it can get. As argued already, such diversity of supplies enhances security. But it is a simple fact that the Middle East in general, and Saudi Arabia in particular, will continue to be the keystone of the oil markets as long as the industrial world relies on petroleum. The size and nature of their resource endowment, the commitment of the Saudi government to play this role, the unrelenting dependence of the region's governments on oil revenues, and the negative consequences of their own past experience with politically interrupting oil supplies will almost guarantee this.

## Iraq: Where to from Here?

There is no question that Iraq, with its massive proven oil reserves and vast potential, will be a major player in world oil supplies for decades to come. To take its rightful place as a major player, however, Iraq needs to overcome a number of issues. In the near term, the country needs to come to terms with the aftermath of the 2003 war, the ongoing insurgency with its attacks on oil infrastructure, and what will be a politically testing change to first a transitional and then a permanent government. This will lay the foundations for the longer term, when the postwar oil administration structure and foreign investment will be crucial to establishing Iraq's future role in global oil markets.

The success of the present and future Iraqi governments will depend on a number of factors. First and foremost is ensuring security and stability on a day-to-day basis, and providing Iraqis with the jobs and services they demand. Managing relations with the United States, introducing effective governance, combating regionalism and the accompanying threat of violence or civil war, and establishing true legitimacy in the eyes of the Iraqi people will all be part of this process of meeting domestic expectations.

## Security

Despite the handover to an Iraqi government and a concurrent reduction in U.S. troop visibility in Baghdad, violent attacks continue throughout Iraq, ranging from suicide bombings against police stations to assassination attempts on senior government ministers. Hampering the interim government's ability to bring stability to the country is the fact that, with the army disbanded in May 2003, there was no longer an Iraqi military to speak of; the police force and the National Guard in whose hands the United States–led Coalition Provisional Authority (CPA) chose to place responsibility for restoring and keeping order are large in number but poorly-trained and equipped, and often lacking in morale. The task of the police has not been helped by the fact that they have been singled out by the insurgents, who view such individuals as traitors for helping the American cause.

The security issue is likely to be a long-term concern, with low-level insurgency on a constant simmer until a fully functional police force backed by a true security apparatus can be deployed—a process that could take years. This means the likely continuation of attacks on oil facilities and infrastructure that have dogged the sector since late 2003. Coalition initiatives, combined with the guerrilla nature of the attacks, have ensured that there have been no long-term shutdowns of oil production. Instead, even the worst incidents have led to no more than one- or two-day interruptions, and there were signs in the autumn of 2004 that preventative security measures were beginning to work.

Yet for the Iraqis themselves, attacks on infrastructure are of less concern that the rise in violent crime that they have faced on a daily basis since the end of the war. This, more than the insurgency, is what Iraqis fear most. Quelling the rise in kidnapping, armed robbery, and a sense of general lawlessness that has been witnessed since then is crucial to build public confidence in the Iraqi government and the new order in the country—Iraqis have consistently signaled in public and in private that it is the measure by which they judge the effectiveness of their political leaders and the new institutions of state, and the country will struggle to regain a sense of normalcy without it. This does not mean that the broader trends threatening to divide the country are not the cause of public fear. Indeed, these challenges will require adroit maneuvering from the central government and its representatives in the provinces to strike a balance between reaching out to groups disenfranchised politically and economically since the end of the war without exacerbating fear among the Kurds and the many Shia groups that faced the harshest repression under the old regime that a Baathist or Saddamist revival is at hand. Finding a national formula that is acceptable to all Iraq's traumatized communities is crucial. Otherwise, instability is bound to persist, and there is a danger that a future government, whether elected or not, will lack the broad legitimacy necessary to restore order through anything but violence. Alternatively, a narrowly supported government could be forced to retreat behind security barriers that leaves it as isolated as the CPA had become in its final months, or creates a situation similar to Afghanistan, where the government controls the capital and little else.

## Regionalism

Engaging Iraq's disparate communities will require addressing the growth in regional sentiment that threatens to divide the country into a patchwork of conflict zones. During the period of direct rule by the CPA, it was possible to defer the most difficult questions about the future form of the Iraqi state, although a need for federal government was emphasized in the Transitional Administrative Law and in the CPA orders that governed the country under occupation. A nationally elected government will have no such luxury, and it will be immediately faced with the challenges of how to reconcile the conflicting pressures of demands for greater autonomy in parts of Iraq with the desire to ensure the cohesion of the state and the equitable distribution of its resources. Indeed, just as these questions dogged the negotiations of the Transitional Administrative Law, so they are likely to be a central and contentious issue for the transitional government that follows the first set of elections, and whose task will be to draw up a permanent constitution for the country.

The problem of Kurdistan was always going to be the most difficult, and has already raised tensions within the Iraqi political elite and the interim government. With the parts of northern Iraq governed by the militias of the Kurdistan Democratic Party and the Patriotic Union of Kurdistan having enjoyed de facto independence since 1991 (if not harmonious relations), and with functioning administrative institutions and security that the rest of Iraq currently lacks, the Kurds are loathe to agree to anything that would weaken their autonomy. The combined forces of the two Kurdish militias, the Peshmerga, are thought to number about 70,000, and these together are by far the most competent security force in the country, with more actual combat experience than Iraq's other militias, to say nothing of the new Iraqi army and security services. Moreover, few younger Kurds speak Arabic, and there is very broad support for the idea of full independence, tempered only at the senior leadership level by an understanding of the internal and regional political realities that make that a dangerous option at present. An open breach between Arab and Kurdish Iraq would be a potential calamity for both sides, leaving a landlocked Kurdish state with at best disputed oil resources as its principal revenue source bordering a resentful Arab Iraq that is unlikely to come around quickly to the notion of reconciliation with its former compatriots. However, this outcome will take enormous skill and patience to avoid.

Regionalism is not only a challenge in the Kurdish region, however. In the south, political leaders in Basra have called for the creation of a regional government modeled on that of the Kurds that would encompass the three provinces of Basra, Maysan, and Dhi Qar. At the same time, the CPA, and since transition the interim government, have faced consistent challenges to its authority from local militias, warlords, or mafias, whether in Nasseriyah, Kut, Najaf, or most notoriously Fallujah. Militias and armed criminal gangs have attempted to establish themselves in local fiefdoms, and often it was only the CPA's provincial authorities that stood in the way. With the CPA's local offices gone, a greater power vacuum has emerged, especially if the lack of strong government institutions means that the connection between center and periphery breaks down.

## Governance

Going into Iraq, the George W. Bush administration assumed that it would be able to decapitate the Saddam Hussein regime—to remove the top layer of government—but carry on administering Iraqi with the existing state institutions. However, the collapse of public administration in the anarchy that followed the war, combined with the CPA's decision to enforce rigid de-Baathification in the public service and to assume direct control over Iraqi ministries, ensured the collapse of Iraq's administrative infrastructure. The challenges to fully reestablishing a working government proved beyond the CPA's abilities, and remain daunting for Iraqi governments. Because holding almost any position of any real importance or weight under Saddam Hussein's regime required relatively senior membership in the Baath Party, some of the country's most able technocrats have been removed from the mix. The judiciary, though now nominally independent, was neglected to a large extent by the CPA and was asked to perform in an utterly changed legal and political context. Moreover, there are already clear signs that it is susceptible to political pressure, and its members face the threat of violence.

The obvious risk is that this administrative confusion will complicate the delivery of badly needed public services and the administration of the state. The big question is: Can Baghdad maintain administrative control over the far-flung provinces of the country when capacity building has been ignored? Of equal concern is the possibility that frustration with poorly functioning government institutions will cause Iraq's new leadership to take shortcuts to dealing with instability and impose a more authoritarian style of rule. For ordinary Iraqis at the other end of the chain of command, administrative failures are likely to produce an increase in corruption, and an environment in which government services can only be obtained with bribes.

## Legitimacy and Weakness

To appreciate the scale of these challenges, it helps to bear in mind that the interim Iraqi government and its successors are being asked to succeed where the CPA failed, despite the might of the U.S. and U.K. governments behind it, namely to establish security and provide basic services on a reliable basis. Moreover, the present and future Iraqi governments will have fewer resources, both security and financial, and they face difficult political challenges from a plethora of parties and groups that all still look at government as a zero-sum game.

Of course, the interim government will still be able to call on the coalition forces for help, but that raises a paradox. The more any Iraqi government is seen to be reliant on U.S. military assistance, the less legitimacy it will have—indeed, the reversal of the CPA's original postwar transition plan and the decision to transfer at least nominal sovereignty to an Iraqi authority in June was essentially an acknowledgment that only a homegrown government that might be accepted as legitimate had any hope of establishing security. In a sense, the interim government represented a gamble that security could be substantially improved simply by putting forward a new, more legitimate administration—a gamble that has yet to pay off, in part because the Ayad Allawi government has increasingly come to be seen as a U.S. puppet with little real power. After a brief honeymoon period, the government looks to be increasingly discredited by its inability to provide security and by its reliance on foreign military support, and it has struggled to reach out to supporters of the insurgency and disgruntled elements of the former regime and its security forces. Its hopes of bringing about national reconciliation, while unbowed, have dimmed over time.

Under these circumstances, holding genuinely free and representative elections in 2005 poses a daunting challenge. A national vote is seen as vital to bolstering the legitimacy of a government in Baghdad; it has been a central demand of influential figures and groups among the Shia and the Kurds, not least Ayatollah Ali Sistani, who—like many Iraqis—regarded any institution selected by the United States–led coalition as suspect and unrepresentative of popular sentiment. And given the prevailing circumstances, it is unlikely that any election would be perfect. However, the dangers in having an election in which large proportions of one part of the population do not or cannot vote because of violent opposition to the new system carries with it dangers of its own. Far from eventually coming to terms with reality and acquiescing to the new order over time, as some in the Bush administration believe they would, a vote that excluded significant portions of the Sunni population along with secular nationalists who oppose the U.S. military presence in Iraq and what they see as the sectarianization of politics could further destabilize the country and fan the flames of the insurgency. Nor is the poll an end in itself. The resulting government will have the task of laying down a permanent constitution for the state, and thus it will be forced to tackle the key issues that have dogged the country since is modern inception, such as regionalism, the role of Islam and the rights of minorities and majorities. To have a chance of lasting success, participation in this process will need to be as broad as possible. Otherwise, the future state will face many of the violent challenges of its prewar predecessors.

## Iraq's Oil Sector

The U.S. administration's call for Iraq's oil sector to be run for the benefit of the Iraqi people is critical, especially if the democratic process is to be nurtured and the issues outlined above are to be overcome. Iraqis have demanded that they should retain sovereign ownership of the country's principal national resource, and that credible and competent Iraqi professionals, not foreign nationals, should run Iraq's oil and gas sectors. Nonetheless, the participation of foreign capital and technology in the sector through production-sharing agreements is broadly accepted—indeed, it was a strategic decision that Iraqi technocrats made in the 1990s. However, transparency and accountability will be crucial, not only to ensure that the oil sector is in fact being run for the benefit of the Iraqi people but also to provide a level playing field for the international oil and gas companies to compete in Iraq and to successfully bring capital and technology to maintain and increase Iraq's production. This can be achieved through scrutinizing the oil revenue flows, not controlling the physical oil assets or running the sector.

But even if such a system is put in place and Iraq's oil production capacity increases, Iraq cannot act as a strategic alternative to Saudi Arabia. First, the financial pressures that a new government will face over the next decade or more will be tremendous. Iraq may produce below capacity as part of OPEC policy, particularly in the latter half of this present decade, but it will not be able to afford keeping spare capacity simply to play the role of swing producer.

Second, with significant additional production capacity increases being dependent on foreign investment, Iraq would be forced to decide whether idled production capacity should be at the expense of international oil companies operating in the country or the Iraqi people. Neither Iraq's finances nor its reliance on foreign investment bodes well for its emergence as a new swing producer.

Third, it is worth recalling here that the excess capacity in Saudi Arabia was developed a long time ago, not from the Saudi government budget but by the former American partner companies of Aramco. Saudi Arabia compensated these companies when it nationalized Aramco through the huge oil surpluses accumulated in the 1970s. It would be next to impossible for any government today to allocate billions of dollars from its current budget to build substantial production capacity for the intention of keeping it idle.

Policymakers in Washington are grappling with the reconstruction of Iraq. Oil will play a critical role in the recovery of the Iraqi economy. The United States is very sensitive to the charge that the invasion was to seize, or at least control, Iraqi oil. U.S. policy emphasizes that the Iraqis must control the petroleum sector. Any investment by international oil companies would be at the discretion of the Iraqis. Foreign capital will be critical to increase production, and the Iraqi government will be unable to finance its own needs for national infrastructure and social development as well as the requirements of the petroleum sector. International oil company investment will be inevitable. The issue will be when, and under what terms. At the same time, U.S. policymakers and their Iraqi counterparts will keep a close eye on the issue of corruption, and technocrats in the Oil Ministry are already endeavoring to make the sector as transparent as possible to ensure that the problems faced by other petroleum-producing states are avoided as much as possible.

## U.S. Policy

The U.S. government has many significant policy changes to consider in the Gulf. After 9/11, the view of many in Washington changed dramatically toward Saudi Arabia. Where it had been seen as the closest U.S. ally in the region, after 9/11 it became viewed as the main source of terrorism, or at least its funding and inspiration. Dramatic reform, if not regime change, was urged. Some poorly informed commentators suggested that Russia, or a liberated Iraq, could replace Saudi Arabia. Cooler heads, including some senior officials in the Bush administration with experience in the Gulf, recognized that this was not realistic.

Saudi Arabia was alarmed by the dramatic change in U.S. opinion, and it undertook an extremely ineffectual public relations offensive and little else. After some internal threats and bombings in the Kingdom in 2003, the Saudi Royal Family reached a consensus on how to respond. A tough crackdown has been undertaken, terrorists arrested or shot, funding to potential al Qaeda sympathizers cut off, and extremist clerics pressured to moderate or reverse their position. Saudi Arabia is now seen in Washington as a better partner in the war on terrorism, although many Americans continue to find the social and religious values and political structure of the Kingdom to be extremely distasteful.

The difficulty now comes with formulating a new U.S. strategy to engage Saudi Arabia and to promote positive change. Saudi Arabia cannot be ignored or marginalized, either as an oil supplier or in its role as the region's most important political force. U.S. policy following the 9/11 attacks has been to simultaneously attempt to ignore Saudi Arabia and focus on the smaller Gulf states, and to call vociferously for rapid and complete change at all levels. Neither of these strategies is a winning one, or even a viable option. The attacks of May and December 2003, not the 9/11 attacks, woke up the Saudis to the fact that changes are required, some at the most fundamental levels of society.[11] External pressure cannot, however, be called upon to bring about these changes, and indeed will have the opposite effect by hardening internal resistance. This is not to say that other countries cannot assist Saudi Arabia in its transition, but rather that attempting to implement a predetermined set of initiatives will be viewed as a move to enforce compliance with a list of demands. Also, the current U.S. policy of calling for "regime change" will in fact hinder its attempts to bring about positive change in the country and indeed the region.

The strategy the United States needs to adopt instead is one of engaging the political elites of Saudi Arabia and the other states it is targeting for change. Without the buy-in and participation of these elites, nothing concrete will be accomplished in these countries. In fact, simply haranguing these regimes from the outside will merely serve to strengthen them, because they can point to these efforts as an attempt by a hostile power to infringe on their national sovereignty. This ploy has so far been successful, especially when played in conjunction with the religious card, allowing the regimes to paint U.S. efforts in the light of a new "crusade," aided by incautiously worded comments from U.S. officials themselves.

What U.S. policymakers thus need to realize is that trying to bypass these elites by either working with "exile" groups or by trying to provoke the masses to rise up and overthrow the regimes is not going to work. Neither will the threat of economic sanctions or "soft initiatives," such as creating media channels or funds to promote democracy. What is needed is a concerted, considered, and nuanced policy to engage the ruling elites in a progressive dialogue. The Euro-Mediterranean Partnership, while falling far short of a number of its stated goals, at least provides a starting model of how such a process might work. This partnership began not with the issuing of a list of conditions which need to be changed, as did the U.S. Greater Middle East Initiative, but rather by bringing together all the relevant foreign and finance ministers of the countries involved on both sides. A series of meetings then produced a comprehensive framework outlining initiatives and desired changes in the political, economic, and cultural arenas. U.S. policymakers, instead of trying to bring about rapid "regime change," should thus focus on adapting some of the best-practices of the Euro-Mediterranean Partnership process in engaging the Arab elites, and making them willing agents of change rather than obstacles to be overcome.

## The Smaller Gulf States

The smaller Gulf States—Kuwait, Bahrain, Qatar, the United Arab Emirates, and Oman—play different roles. The country that has transformed itself from a sleepy backwater into a modern, albeit small, state is Qatar. This change has been fueled by the rise of gas exports coupled with political leadership eager to engage change. In the past decade, Qatar has become the home of the largest U.S. military installation in the region. Foreign investment has been welcomed, and more capital from the international oil and gas companies has flowed into Qatar than the whole rest of the Gulf combined. The country and its economy are booming.

The basis for Qatar's economic transformation is the North Field, an immense natural gas field. Two large liquefied natural gas (LNG) export projects, Qatargas and RasGas, are moving 12 million tons of LNG, largely to Asia.[12] Given the growing demand for gas worldwide, substantial expansion and at least one new LNG project are expected. Qatar, a modest oil producer, is rapidly becoming one of the leading gas exporters in the world.

Bahrain has limited petroleum resources, and thus it seeks to play a commercial role as a banking center. Its young king successfully responded to political challenges by introducing democratic institutions. The country is now stable with a growing economy.

Oman, with modest oil resources, now exports roughly 750,000 barrels per day,[13] and it has developed an LNG export facility, directed primarily to Asia.

The United Arab Emirates, primarily Abu Dhabi, with enormous reserves and a small population, will continue its production of 2.2 mmbpd.[14] Abu Dhabi now generates more income from its financial investments than from petroleum. Dubai has aggressively developed itself into a commercial center, successfully becoming the first significant tourist and conference destination in the Gulf.

Kuwait, no longer threatened by Iraq, will continue to be a significant oil producer with the ability to produce more than 2.1 mmbpd.[15] With the exception of the Neutral Zone with Saudi Arabia, no foreign petroleum investment has been made in Kuwait, although extensive discussion has been ongoing for a number of years with international companies.

Ironically, it is the two smallest Gulf countries, Bahrain and Qatar, that have moved with the times. Both have created representative institutions with political accountability and have welcomed foreign investment. Of particular importance, the rulers of both countries are relatively young, better educated, and more comfortable with Western values. Alone in the Gulf, they are leaders of the new successor generation to those who have led the region since the 1960s. Their people have prospered, and both countries appear quite stable in the face of challenges confronting some of their neighbors. Qatar and Bahrain have become the strongest allies of the United States in the region.

## Conclusion

Energy security is only achievable for the United States and the West on the basis of a realistic recognition of the continuing role of Saudi Arabia as a swing producer in the global oil market. It is illusory to believe that Iraqi capacity will displace that role in the foreseeable future. Rather, the challenge is to manage Iraq's return to OPEC and the future balance between OPEC and non-OPEC oil in such a way that energy security can be achieved and maintained over the long term.

This goal is made more achievable by the alignment of interests between the United States and major oil producers on oil price—with both sides seeking to avoid either prices that are too high, with their destabilizing economic effects, or prices that are too low, with their negative impact on oil production. It is also enhanced by the growing contribution of non-OPEC producers as well as key gas producers in the Gulf (Qatar and Iran) and Eurasia (including Russia). The constructive role of smaller Gulf states should also be factored into the equation.

## Notes

1. Toby Jones, "Seeking a 'Social Contract' for Saudi Arabia," *Middle East Report,* Fall 2003.

2. Jones, "Seeking a 'Social Contract' for Saudi Arabia."

3. Toby Jones, "Violence and the Illusion of Reform in Saudi Arabia," http://usa.mediamonitors.net/content/view/full/2091/.

4. International Monetary Fund data; Saudi Arabian Monetary Agency data; PFC Energy internal estimates.

5. Statement by Saudi Arabian finance minister Ibrahim al-Assaf, December 21, 2003.

6. Statement given by Mahmoud Abdul-Baqi, vice president for exploration, Saudi Aramco, at a Center for Strategic and International Studies conference titled "Global Oil Supply: Are We Running Out?" Washington, February 24, 2004.

7. Saudi Arabia Ministry of Petroleum and Mineral Resources Quarterly Statistics Bulletin.

8. PFC Energy, "OPEC Crude Supply."

9. Testimony of Vahan Zanoyan, president and chief executive of PFC Energy, "Global Energy Security Issues," before the U.S. Senate Committee on Foreign Relations, Subcommittee on International Economic Policy, Export, and Trade Promotion, April 8, 2003.

10. Testimony of Zanoyan.

11. Jones, "Seeking a 'Social Contract' for Saudi Arabia."

12. PFC Energy estimate based on existing LNG supply contracts, using data from Qatar Petroleum, available at http://www.qp.com.qa/qp.nsf.

13. Ministry of National Economy, Sultanate of Oman, *Monthly Statistical Bulletin* 14, no. 10 (October 31, 2003).

14. PFC Energy, "OPEC Crude Supply."

15. PFC Energy, "OPEC Crude Supply."

# 9

# North Africa and the Mediterranean

## *Gordon Shearer*

Large and growing energy resources within the countries of North Africa and rising European gas demand continue to drive a transformation of the Mediterranean energy picture. At the same time, unstable social and economic conditions within the North African nations will continue to play a role in the development and security of the world's energy supply. With limited or underexploited oil reserves, the North African story is primarily one of natural gas, and its unique opportunities and challenges.

This chapter considers the progression of these energy markets, keeping in mind that the potential outcomes described here will change with evolving diplomatic, social, economic, and political dynamics. In particular, the gas resources of the Maghreb (the North African countries of Algeria, Libya, Mauritania, Morocco, and Tunisia) and Egypt create a nexus of interests among the countries bordering the Mediterranean Sea. Increasingly, these markets and suppliers are becoming integrated through the development of new gas pipelines and liquefied natural gas (LNG) export and import terminals.[1]

A growing pipeline infrastructure should see Europe's natural gas supply from this area increase.[2] Expanding pipeline connections should also lead to increasing supply security, tempered to some degree by the continued political tensions within North Africa. Pipeline development will also secure Europe's access to the region's natural gas resources in competition with North America. The United States and Canada are predicted to become major importers of LNG during the coming decades, offering the Maghreb nations an almost unlimited market and the hope of high prices as a result of falling domestic gas production.

As pipeline and LNG import capabilities expand, and natural gas makes its way from the Middle East and Central Asia to southern Europe, North African LNG supplies will to some degree be pushed west to the North American East Coast and the Gulf of Mexico. These trends should create increased interaction between the European and North American gas markets, spur the development of new sources of gas supply, and in general support the creation of a more diverse and active global gas industry. A more global gas market should, in turn, bring consuming countries greater security of supply and producing countries greater security of markets.[3]

From a policy perspective, long-term contracts, most likely containing take-or-pay clauses or similar provisions, will likely continue to characterize the gas supply relationship, because these contracts provide the underpinnings for both seller and buyer to justify the necessary investments in natural gas infrastructure with their long lead times, high capital intensity, and relatively slow payback period. Given the scale of their reserves and their proximity to the market, the North African producers should be well positioned as the lowest cost suppliers to the Mediterranean European markets, allowing them to increase market share even in the face of growing competition. Access to North America will allow these suppliers to diversify their sales portfolios and expand volumes without risking the same downward price pressures that might occur if all their gas exports were concentrated on the smaller European market.

Growing volume and higher prices should bring substantial economic benefits to the exporting countries. If handled properly (unlike the experiences with the oil revenue windfalls of the 1970s), improved economic performance could relieve the social tension in the region and permit the continued move toward democratic forms of government. Harder will be moves toward a stronger role for the private sector in the exporting countries' economies, as export revenues will be largely concentrated in the hands of the state or the state-owned oil companies. The track record in this regard has been problematic during the past decades; national oil companies have dominated oil and gas production in Libya and Algeria, with host governments highly dependent on hydrocarbon revenues to fund government budgets. Political support from the West for continued political and economic reform will be essential to secure and build on the fragile progress that has been made recently and to ensure these countries share a common interest with their Western customers in a stable and secure energy future. A laissez faire attitude on the part of the West could see a repeat of the previous pattern of government-controlled economies that collapse when energy prices fall from their present levels. A future economic collapse could have grave consequences for Europe and ultimately the entire West if social upheaval became more closely coupled with religious intolerance and an emergence of a hostile front on the southern Mediterranean coast.

## The Mediterranean: Energy and Political Economy

The Mediterranean region offers in microcosm many of the issues facing the global energy market (see figure 9.1 and table 9.1). On the southern coast of the Mediterranean Sea, the energy "haves," Algeria, Libya, and Egypt, are or will become more important suppliers of energy to the Mediterranean and Atlantic markets.[4] Along the northern Mediterranean coast lie some of the major consuming countries of Europe, the energy "have-nots" of France, Italy, and Spain. The eastern end of the Mediterranean has its own special problems rooted in the continuing tensions between Israel and its Arab neighbors, while Turkey has created a small energy crisis with broader regional implications.

The north/south divide also reflects strong political and economic differences. Although Algeria, Egypt, Libya, and Tunisia are not democratic societies in the Western sense of the word, neither are they Islamic societies in the sense of the countries of the Middle East. Though acknowledging their Islamic religion and heritage, the political systems of North Africa are more secular. In spite of their great oil and gas wealth, the North African countries have in general experienced poor economic performance during the past two decades (although Tunisia witnessed strong economic growth during most of the 1990s), coupled with rapidly growing populations. Their governments have been unable to satisfy the expectations for improved economic and social conditions, leading—in Algeria, Egypt, and to a lesser extent Morocco—to social and political unrest. There is a significant risk that a windfall of energy revenues could simply allow the energy-exporting countries to "buy time" by underwriting major social welfare programs, rather than tackling the economic reforms which could bring long term stability and prosperity to their populations.

In Libya, the political dynamic had been compounded until recently by the imposition of economic sanctions against the country in light of its apparent support for and involvement with acts of terrorism against the West. Although the United Nations lifted the sanctions on Libya in 2003, the United States has not yet formally ended sanctions. General commerce is permitted, other than in aviation. Libya remains on the terrorism list, restricting the

Figure 9.1. Map of Mediterranean Gas Infrastructure

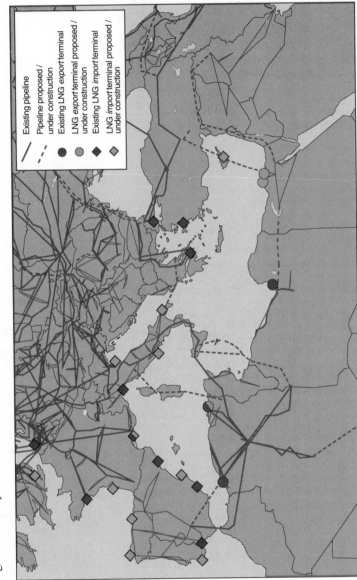

*Note:* LNG = liquefied natural gas.
*Sources:* European Union; Poten and Partners.

Table 9.1. Key Economic and Energy Statistics for the Maghreb, 2002

| Country | Population (millions) | GDP (billions of dollars) | Percent of GDP Energy | Percent of Revenues from Energy | External Debt (billions of dollars) | Oil Reserves (billion barrels) | Gas Reserves (trillion cubic meters) | Oil Production (thousands of barrels per day) | Gas Production (billion cubic meters) |
|---|---|---|---|---|---|---|---|---|---|
| Algeria | 32.8 | 167 | 30 | 60 | 21.6 | 9.2 | 4.52 | 1659 | 80.4 |
| Libya | 5.5 | 41 | 25 | N.A. | 4.4 | 29.5 | 1.31 | 1376 | 5.7 |
| Egypt | 74.7 | 268 | N.A. | N.A. | 30.5 | 3.7 | 3.51 | 751 | 22.7 |
| Tunisia | 9.9 | 63 | N.A. | N.A. | 13.6 | 0.3 | Minor | 76 | Minor |
| Morocco | 31.7 | 115 | N.A. | N.A. | 17.7 | Minor | Minor | Minor | Minor |

Note: N.A. = not available.
Sources: U.S. Central Intelligence Agency; BP.

export to Libya of certain items and barring U.S. companies from deducting taxes paid in Libya. If Libya continues its cooperation against terrorism, the removal of these sanctions is probably only a matter of time. Moves by Libya to renounce its weapons programs should, over time, lead to a full normalization of political and commercial relationships with the West.

Historic ties have tended to strain the relationships between Maghreb nations and the countries that previously colonized them. Algeria was incorporated into France and achieved its independence only after a long and bitter civil war. Both Tunisia and Morocco were French protectorates. Libya was an Italian colony. The tensions between the north and south today are also influenced by the immigrant influx from North Africa to southern Europe. France today is home to a large Muslim population, and legal and illegal immigration from North Africa and Turkey to Europe may have the potential to further complicate relationships within the region.

Another element causing difficulties in the energy relationships between these countries is the role of the individual states in their domestic energy markets. The oil- and gas-producing sectors of Algeria and Libya have long been characterized by the domination of their state-owned oil companies, Sonatrach and the Libyan National Oil Company. Egypt has had a state oil and gas company, but the sector has traditionally been more open to foreign investors.

In Europe, state-owned companies have also dominated oil and gas transmission until relatively recently. Though many of these companies have been fully or partially privatized in recent years, tensions remain between the desire of producers to gain price certainty to finance infrastructure development and the European desire to promote competition and control the rents from gas once it reaches national borders.[5] Without the historical "baggage" of the European countries, the United States is uniquely positioned to engage with the North African states. In Algeria, French companies dominate the economy, but U.K. and U.S. companies have made great headway in energy. In Morocco, French companies also hold sway, but U.K. and U.S. companies are making inroads. Egypt has long been open to U.S. upstream producers. Libya today strongly seeks U.S. investment for political as well as commercial reasons. U.S. companies may face challenges in expanding their position. The United States carries a different burden, given its support for Israel and the backlash in the Arab "street" against its direct confrontation with fundamentalist Islam through its military engagements in Afghanistan and Iraq. However, this does not appear to have influenced the willingness of the North African governments to encourage participation by

U.S. companies in energy development. Solutions to these concerns are beyond the scope of this analysis, but these issues cannot be ignored in the coming interactions with these countries.

## The North African Producers

Algeria and Libya have been producers and exporters of oil for many years. Egypt has moderate oil production and exports, but because the Egyptian oil fields are located to the south of the Suez Canal, they might be more appropriately considered as a part of the Middle Eastern oil-producing region. As oil producers, these countries do not rank in the highest tier of global oil standings. However modest the volumes, their light, sweet crudes command premium prices in the world market for the lighter product slate they can yield.

It is rather in their role as natural gas producers and exporters that these countries will have the greatest influence on the dynamics of the global energy markets. Algeria has very significant reserves of natural gas; Libya less so. Tunisia has modest natural gas resources, but only enough to satisfy its internal market needs (Tunisia remains a net importer of energy). Morocco has discovered modest reserves and is promoting the search for more. Mauritania holds the promise of developing a significant natural gas resource base within the next decade.

Egypt is the surprise. From a modest start that provided enough gas resources to satisfy internal demands, Egypt has almost overnight emerged as a potential major player in the gas export market. Israel and Gaza have also been the site of new gas discoveries in the offshore Mediterranean, but the exploitation of these reserves has been entangled in Palestinian–Israeli politics and security concerns. Each country will now be considered in more detail.

### Algeria

Algeria is an important oil producer and influential within the Organization of Petroleum Exporting Countries (OPEC), but its future significance is as a strategic supplier of natural gas to Europe and major player in the global LNG trade. Its growth demonstrates how a state-owned company can work with foreign investors to develop the reserve base and compete for a share of the economic rent in downstream markets.

Figure 9.2.  Shares of Mediterranean Natural Gas Reserves, 2003

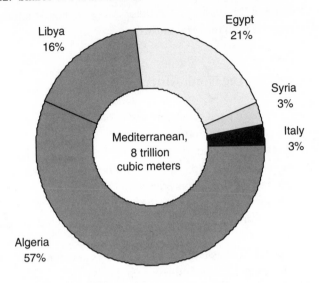

*Source: BP Statistical Report, 2003.*

Algeria exports about 900,000 barrels of oil a day, a figure that is expected to grow to 1.3 million barrels in the next few years. This growth is being driven by the new oil discoveries that followed the partial opening of the Algerian upstream sector to outside participation since the early 1990s. As a member of OPEC, Algeria has traditionally been a proponent of prices supported by market intervention rather than based on market economics. Because Algeria has historically been unable to raise its oil exports much beyond its OPEC quotas, and with a significant condensate, liquefied petroleum gas, and natural gas exports (which were traditionally indexed to oil prices but are excluded from OPEC quotas), it had every reason to support high oil prices. With growing oil exports and a need to satisfy the expectations of the foreign companies who have now entered the oil sector, Algeria may experience a shift in its OPEC role.

In natural gas, Algeria is a world-class player, and it is the dominant gas resource holder in the Mediterranean (figure 9.2). Algeria is the third largest exporter of natural gas in the world, behind Russia and Canada. It is in this role that Algeria will have its strongest influence on global energy security.

Algeria was the world's first LNG exporter, commencing with sales to the United Kingdom in 1964. By the mid-1970s, Algeria was the largest LNG producer in the world, with four liquefaction complexes producing about 27 billion cubic meters (bcm) of LNG a year. Algeria fought for many years to earn what it viewed as a fair rent for its LNG, manifest today in its struggle to control the ultimate marketing of its gas. In the very early stages of the commercialization of LNG, prices, especially in the sales contracts with the United States, were tied to a formula indexed to the fixed costs of the plants and inflation. After the energy crisis of the 1970s, the national hydrocarbon company, Sonatrach, began a campaign to shift all its LNG pricing to parity with crude oil (without taking into account the sharply higher costs of shipping, terminaling, and distributing LNG as compared to oil and its derivative products). This strategy was successful in Europe, where Sonatrach's buyers were more readily able to absorb these price increases (and had fewer alternatives to choose from), but it failed miserably in the United States, which would not agree to the new prices and where subsequent price decontrol and regulated "open access" on U.S. pipelines produced a sharp and sustained fall in the price of natural gas and undercut the economic terms of the remaining Algerian LNG contracts. Imports of LNG from Algeria fell to zero by 1986.

Sonatrach subsequently used infrastructure development to ensure security of gas demand. Sonatrach constructed the Trans-Mediterranean Pipeline in partnership with SNAM, the principal Italian gas transmission company and gas purchaser, and over the next twenty years expanded pipeline sales of gas to Italy and Spain. Despite a strained political relationship between Algeria and Morocco over the Western Sahara, the two countries were able to put their differences aside to make the Greater Middle East (now Pedro Duran Farell) pipeline a technical and economic success. These pipelines provided Sonatrach with a secure market outlet—something it had been unable to achieve with LNG sales to North America. Sonatrachs's participation as an equity shareholder in these pipeline ventures also reinforced their commitment to supply.

By the late 1980s, Sonatrach revived its LNG sales to the United States, entering into a series of innovative contracts based on netback price formulas, which for the first time took into account conditions specific to the U.S. gas markets, which by then had been deregulated and largely decoupled from oil.

In the early 1990s, a combination of price hawkishness on European gas pricing and operational problems in its liquefaction plants had saddled Sonatrach with a reputation of being a problematic supplier. This perception was reinforced by the turmoil that accompanied the country's moves toward democracy, culminating with the Algerian Army canceling general elections in 1992 after an apparent victory by the main Islamic party. An Islamic insurgency followed, which launched the country into civil war between 1992 and 1998. Since 1998, the insurgency has largely been brought under control. While Algeria has an active press and has a declared commitment to democratic, free elections, it has some way to go in addressing economic distribution, transparency, and the development of a civil society free of military control. Yet there are real signs of progress, including close cooperation with the United States on counterterrorism and the conduct of its 2004 presidential elections with little military interference and more widespread participation by the electorate.

The technical problems at the LNG facilities were addressed through a massive revamping program, which was completed in 1999. Sonatrach has also adopted a more cautious approach to sales of LNG, not placing all its volumes under long-term fixed-obligation contracts, but keeping a portion back for short-term sales. This more cautious approach was underscored in the aftermath of the accident that destroyed part of the Skikda LNG plant in early 2004, when Sonatrach was able, through a combination of increased pipeline deliveries, LNG swaps, and other measures, to meet its delivery obligations to its firm customers with minimum disruption. By the summer of 2004, Sonatrach had resumed spot deliveries to U.S. LNG terminals (table 9.2 and figure 9.3).

In the mid-1990s, Sonatrach took the first steps to opening its natural gas

Table 9.2. Algeria's Exports of
Liquefied Natural Gas, 2000
(billion cubic meters)

| Country | Exports |
|---|---|
| Belgium | 4.2 |
| France | 10.9 |
| Greece | 0.54 |
| Italy | 28.1 |
| Portugal | 2.35 |
| Spain | 10.33 |
| Turkey | 3.45 |
| Slovenia | 0.36 |
| United States | 1.25 |
| Tunisia | 1.2 |
| Total | 62.68 |

Figure 9.3. Algeria's Exports of Liquefied Natural Gas, 2000

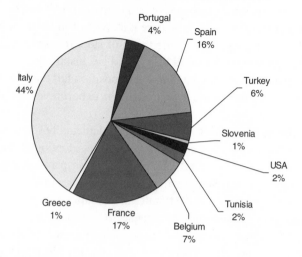

*Source:* Cedigaz, 2000.

resources to foreign participation, though limiting this initially to pipeline-focused projects and retaining tight control over the marketing of the gas to avoid undercutting its own market share. Subsequently, Sonatrach has offered, for competitive bid to foreign participants, a new integrated LNG project, Gassi Touil, including the right to participate in the liquefaction plant and LNG marketing. At the same time, Sonatrach, in partnership with BP, announced that it had taken all the available capacity at the United Kingdom's new Isle of Grain LNG terminal being developed in the River Thames estuary. This complements earlier decisions by Sonatrach to seek equity participation in new terminals being developed in Spain. Stepping further afield, Sonatrach has also taken an equity interest in the Camisea gas fields in Peru and is likely to also assume a shareholding in the proposed Peru LNG project, which will export to the markets of the North American West Coast. With increased foreign participation in the upstream and Sonatrach's participation in the downstream, the result should be stronger links throughout the gas-delivery system.

Although the political situation in Algeria remains somewhat unsettled, the experience during the Islamic fundamentalist insurgency demonstrated some valuable lessons for the market. At no time during a sustained period of extreme violence and terror did terrorists succeed in disrupting the flow of gas exports, with one brief exception following an attack on the Trans-Mediterranean Pipeline, which was quickly repaired. This can be attributed to the fact that the producing fields are hundreds of miles from populated areas, and protected by the so-called ring of steel security measures imposed by the government around the oil and gas installations. It may also be the case that even the fundamentalist opposition left these installations alone because they too would have needed the export revenues if they had prevailed.

Today Algeria can be viewed as a more fundamentally sound and secure supplier of LNG and natural gas, in part due to its adoption of market pricing, openness to foreign capital, and enhanced transparency in bidding in the upstream gas sector. Sonatrach faces a more sober future, with rapidly expanding competition in the Atlantic and Mediterranean markets from existing and new suppliers, and this appears to be gradually bringing a more "commercial" approach to LNG sales on the part of Sonatrach. These factors hold for pipeline sales to a lesser degree, because the physical connections ensure that buyer and seller are bound together for a long period of time, and neither can readily suspend deliveries or seek new suppliers or customers if either becomes dissatisfied with the relationship.

As a strategic matter, it appears that Sonatrach will concentrate on marketing natural gas in southern Europe by pipeline, expanding the Trans-Mediterranean and Greater Middle East pipelines, and through developments such as the new MEDGAZ line to northeastern Spain. LNG appears to be increasingly reserved for diversion to more distant markets, such as northwest Europe and the reemerging North American market. Unlike the earlier model of rigid long-term sales and purchase commitments, new LNG supply agreements would appear to incorporate increased flexibility, allowing both parties to the transaction to exploit price differentials between geographically disparate markets through physical and financial arbitrage.

With increased foreign participation in the upstream, growing investments in the downstream, and a foothold in the world's two largest gas markets, Sonatrach is well positioned to be the first state-owned oil company to take on the appearance of an integrated gas major with a clear stake in demonstrating that it can be a source of secure and competitively priced energy. Politically, Algeria has probably made the greatest advances in democratization of any of the Maghreb countries during the past decade. The continued encouragement of both these trends by the West will serve to further reinforce Algeria's and position as a reliable and competitive supplier of energy, not just to Mediterranean Europe but also to North America.

Figure 9.4. Shares of Mediterranean Oil Reserves, 2003

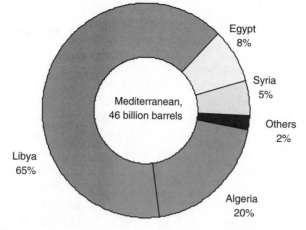

*Source: BP Statistical Report, 2003.*

## *Libya*

Just as Algeria dominates gas resources in the region, the same holds true for Libya with respect to oil, where the country controls more than 65 percent of the region's reserves, though its production potential has not been fully realized (figure 9.4). Libya, in contrast to Algeria, had long welcomed international oil company participation (including several U.S. oil companies) in its upstream industry. This lasted until sanctions against Libya forced these companies to suspend operations in the country in 1986. It was Libya's pressure on the U.S. companies in 1971 that broke the then-established pattern of oil pricing and demonstrated the political leverage that oil producers later exerted on consuming countries through OPEC. Just as OPEC has matured and become less radical in its rhetoric and expectations, so too has Libya.

Libya had been punished harshly by the international community for President Mu'ammar Gadhafi's past support for terrorism. However, after it complied with long-standing UN demands to acknowledge responsibility for the bombing of Pan Am Flight 103, cooperate in the trial of the perpetrators, and offer compensation to the victim's families, on September 12, 2003, the United Nations Security Council formally voted to lift the UN sanctions against Libya. Though Libya remains on the U.S. list of countries supporting terrorism, its decision in December 2003 to renounce its nuclear, chemical, and biological weapons programs following negotiations with the United States and the United Kingdom appears to be a precursor to the normalization of relationships between Libya and the West, and the United States in particular.

The sanctions have impaired Libya's ability to develop its oil and gas resources, though much less in the oil sector, where the needed technology was more readily available without raising issues of sanctions violations, and the financing was less demanding. For gas, the same analysis does not hold. Much of the technology and finance for sophisticated natural gas projects comes from the West and had been largely blocked. Libya's access to capital has been limited and in the face of such circumstances, upstream oil projects tended to win out over gas projects. Finally, markets for gas, either as LNG or pipeline gas, are much less fungible than oil markets, and Libya's attempts to come to terms with Western buyers would have drawn international attention and probable political pressure to block the consummation of such arrangements.

These obstacles have begun to fall away. In 2000, ENI signed a contract to supply 4 bcm per year of Libyan natural gas to Edison Gas in Italy. Gas will be transported through Green Stream, a pipeline linking Libya to Sicily, which is due to be completed in 2004. The project had moved slowly because Italy has been addressing the restructuring of its gas market in line with E.U. directives. However, Libya faces growing competition in this market. The Trans-Mediterranean Pipeline from Algeria is potentially undergoing a further expansion, bringing more volumes to southern Italy. New LNG terminal projects and suppliers are targeting Italy. Increasing competition in the Italian market may force Libya to either settle for reduced value for its gas or to look for alternative markets, which would need to be supplied by LNG.

The LNG option is an intriguing one. Like Algeria, Libya was also an early pioneer of LNG exports, completing the small Mersa El Brega LNG plant in 1970, which today still ships modest volumes of LNG to Spain. Throughout the period of sanctions, Libya has preserved the rights of the U.S. companies that were present in the country before sanctions went into effect. Today, many of these same companies are now looking for the opportunity not only to regain their position in the oil sector but also to grow their reserve and production bases by entering the LNG business. Libya may eventually emerge as an LNG supplier to Europe and North America.

From a policy perspective, the lifting of U.S. sanctions would be a major step forward in allowing the return of the U.S. companies to Libya and permitting the more rapid development of the upstream resource base. However, Libya will also need to be encouraged to drop the anti-Israeli boycott requirement, which has remained in place as a condition to obtaining oil and gas contracts. U.S. companies cannot legally enter into contracts containing this provision. Libya will also need to persuade U.S. authorities that it has permanently renounced terrorism. Allegations that Gadhafi financed an assassination attempt against Saudi Crown Prince Abdullah in mid-2003, while still claiming to the United States an end to its support of terrorism, cloud Libya's removal from the U.S. terrorism list.

## Egypt

The Egyptian upstream has long been open to foreign participation, with companies like BP (previously British Petroleum and Amoco), Apache, and British Gas among the major players, generally through production sharing contracts in partnership with the Egyptian General Petroleum Company (EGPC). Egypt produces about 750,000 barrels of oil per day, much of which is used domestically. This production is centered in the area of the Red Sea, giving it more of the characteristics of Middle Eastern supply in its position in the global oil market.

It is in the area of natural gas where Egypt is showing evidence of becoming a world-scale energy producer. Gas was first discovered in Egypt in the 1970s. Egypt's gas reserves were initially developed to serve the domestic market, with one objective being to displace fuel oil from power generation to free oil for export. EGPC essentially adopted the role of aggregator, purchasing gas production from the upstream producers and remarketing the volumes domestically. As exploration expanded, substantial quantities of additional reserves were discovered, especially offshore in the Nile Delta and the Western Desert.

In the late 1990s, with growing gas reserves and a limited domestic market, Egypt looked to its neighbors for markets. At the same time, reacting to changing conditions in the Spanish market, Union Fenosa, a large Spanish power producer, approached Egypt to develop an LNG export plant at Damietta that would supply Fenosa's power plants as well as support its efforts to enter the Spanish wholesale and retail gas market. Fenosa was also developing LNG import terminals in Spain. Following immediately behind Fenosa, British Gas launched another LNG project, Egypt LNG, to exploit the offshore Nile Delta reserves, which it had discovered together with its partner, Edison of Italy. (Edison has since sold its position to Petronas, the Malaysian state-owned oil company.) Both the Damietta and Egypt LNG plants are being developed as "tolling" facilities, following a model developed at the Atlantic LNG project in Trinidad. This model would allow other gas producers in Egypt to propose processing their gas reserves into LNG at these plants, taking advantage of the existing infrastructure and economies of scale to lower the costs of liquefaction. By 2006, Egypt will be producing about 17 bcm of LNG annually. With continuing exploration efforts, this figure is expected to grow significantly in the future.

Egypt has sought export markets not only for LNG but also for pipeline gas. On several occasions, discussions began with Israel for the purchase of Egyptian gas, but each time they were derailed by events in the Middle East. Egypt has reached an agreement with Jordan, and pipeline deliveries from Egypt to Jordan will be used to fuel new gas-fired power projects. Egypt has also looked at an offshore, eastern Mediterranean pipeline that would supply Lebanon, Cyprus, and possibly Turkey, but these markets have more cost-effective alternatives. It would appear that this project is moribund, leaving LNG as Egypt's only export vehicle.

## Israel and Gaza

British Gas has also found gas reserves in the offshore Mediterranean, roughly on the boundary of Gaza and Israel. Though Israel has been looking for many years to develop gas supplies, whether through pipeline gas from Egypt or LNG from other destinations, the discovery of gas on its own doorstep would seem to present Israel with an opportunity.

However, the development appears to be in suspension. Because most of the gas lies within the boundaries of Gaza, the upstream value would flow to the Palestinian Authority. Israel has so far refused to discuss purchases of gas from the Palestinians in the absence of assurances as to how the revenues received by the authority would be used. Although it makes obvious economic and commercial sense, this project remains a hostage of the larger Israeli–Palestinian problem.

Israel remains a potentially attractive natural gas market. However, not only is the supply picture very unclear, but the Israeli government also has had a hard time establishing the rules for the development of the market. The largest consumer is likely to be the Israeli Electric Power Authority, which would prefer to retain its own gas development, while the government has been seeking to bring in third parties to build an Israeli gas network. This combination of factors leaves Israel on the side of the regional gas market for the time being.

## U.S. Policy toward Exporting Countries

From the perspective of U.S. policymakers seeking to enhance the security of the energy supply, and especially expanding LNG imports, expanding the production potential of the Maghreb countries makes good energy and foreign policy sense. Ensuring that Europe diversifies and expands its supplies of natural gas from multiple sources is sound policy. As an overall proposition, the more gas delivered to Europe by pipeline, the more should then be available to deliver to other markets (including North America) in the form of LNG.

The United States should take every opportunity to encourage the expansion of additional trans-Mediterranean pipelines as a way to further this objective, as well as encourage the construction of gas pipelines from the Central Asian republics to Turkey and beyond, to provide Eurasian suppliers with security and diversity of demand and Turkey and southeastern Europe with security and diversity of supply.[6] The presence of U.S. producers in the upstream in Egypt and Algeria and the return of U.S. companies to Libya should also lead to positive developments in the expansion of gas and oil production. In addition to supporting the continued expansion of the Mediterranean pipeline grid, the United States should encourage the development of additional LNG projects, such as Algeria's Gassi Touil, which can be directly marketed to North America.

The continued availability of funding from U.S. institutions such as the U.S. Export-Import Bank and Overseas Private Investment Corporation should also be encouraged as a means of giving U.S. interests a competitive edge. Linking this funding to energy-export projects specifically targeted at the U.S. market should also be given consideration.

Encouraging the exporters to participate in downstream opportunities is also a way of tying them more closely to the markets, encouraging them to remain engaged even when market conditions (e.g., prices) are less than ideal. Recent policy initiatives that allow U.S. LNG import terminals to be developed with reduced economic oversight should make foreign producers more willing to participate in LNG import terminals. Because most exporters are probably unfamiliar with U.S. regulations, a program of education on these issues might prove helpful. So too would any policy moves to reduce the uncertainties surrounding the permitting on new U.S. LNG terminals, which can put the United States at a comparative disadvantage to other importing countries with less adversarial permitting regimes. The United States will need access to Middle Eastern LNG supplies as well as North African production, and it should work to remove any obstacle that can be reduced or eliminated to accessing these supplies, including ensuring that LNG tankers have ready access through the Suez Canal.

Finally, the United States should work to promote political stability in the Maghreb for energy and foreign policy reasons. The Maghreb nations, which are more secular than those in the Middle East, are already partners with the United States in the Pan Sahel counterterrorism initiative. U.S. policy can promote the development and diversification of Maghreb economies to reward cooperation and encourage their steady but challenging path to more open societies. The United States does not have an especially active dialogue with the Maghreb countries outside the issues related to the Israeli–Arab conflict or terrorism. Prior initiatives, such as that undertaken by Stuart Eizenstat during Bill Clinton's administration, have generally petered out due to a lack of follow-through. Recommitting to this dialogue and to its maintenance and elevation will provide the United States with a more secure political relationship, and one that would likely be welcomed by the countries of the Maghreb as a counterweight to their European relationships.

## The European Markets

Because Loyola de Palacio addresses the European market in chapter 8 of this book, this chapter only considers the impact of E.U. policy on North African development. By far the greatest source of tension between the European Union and North Africa (and with Russia) are Europe's attempts to place limitations on long-term gas contracts, and especially its prohibition of "destination clauses."

The European Union determined by directive of the European Commission to require the elimination of "destination clauses" in long-term gas contracts—that is, contract provisions that limit the right of resale of the natural gas to the country in which the buyer was located. (In the "old" model of the European market, where each country had essentially a single supplier, these had the effect of supporting limited competition within the Continental market.) These clauses were designed to protect the gas sellers (primarily Russia and Algeria) from competing against their customers reselling the gas outside their own territories, thereby reducing the risk of "gas-on-gas" competition and a decoupling of gas prices from alternative fuels.

The European Union sought to have the destination clause provisions dropped without offsetting considerations. The producers tried to retain a profit interest in onward sale of the gas, which the Union saw as indirectly inhibiting competition. Russia has agreed to drop these clauses, but Russia has been more active in competing on the liberalized open market and is aggressively seeking to expand its share of European sales. Algeria has been more reluctant to settle, colored perhaps by its experiences with the liberalization of the U.S. market in the 1980s. Algeria is expected to reach a settlement with the European Union in 2004. To protect itself, it has been moving to make more of its LNG sales on a delivered basis (controlling the shipping of the LNG to the delivery port) and expanding its participation in the downstream markets, as described above.

The result is a less predictable and orderly progression of the market than would have been the case under the old order. In the short-to-medium term, at least, the traditional concern of security of supply on the part of the importing countries may be replaced by a new concern over security of markets on the part of the supplier countries, even if the broad indicators for gas market growth seem to be almost entirely positive. There have been clear signs of oversupply in the Spanish and Turkish markets (where Turkey appears to have contracted for gas deliveries well in excess of its needs), and a similar trend could be emerging in Italy. These trends feed a fear on the part of the suppliers that prices will drop, which is, naturally, the European Union's objective. Turkey has pressured its suppliers to reduce both prices and volumes of deliveries. Algeria, ironically, has benefited by diverting LNG deliveries away from Turkey toward the more lucrative U.S. market. Similar trends have also emerged on the Spanish market.


## The Competition for Market Share

Europe, especially Southern Europe, represents a growing market for natural gas. The North African producers are ideally positioned to access this market. Notwithstanding the increasing competition within the European market, the prospects for growing gas demand appear secure, driven by gas-fired power generation. These trends do not appear likely to be halted or reversed.

In competing for these markets, Algeria and Libya are expected to be the lowest-cost pipeline gas suppliers to Western Europe by 2020. Algeria,

Egypt, and Libya are projected to be the lowest-cost LNG suppliers. For the Mediterranean European countries, the North African suppliers can offer even lower costs given their geographic proximity.

However, changing E.U. energy policies create some degree of uncertainty in these markets. Though it appears that the producers can and will compete successfully for the markets, the impact of deregulation on natural gas prices may be another matter. For the foreseeable future, long-term contracts are likely to characterize the market, underpinning the financing of infrastructure of upstream and downstream facilities.

The challenge will be to find mechanisms that permit suppliers and buyers to adjust prices that no longer follow the "classical" model indexed to crude oil or oil products but are more reflective of supply and demand for natural gas on its own, giving rise to gas-on-gas competition. The producers' fear is that at least initially, gas-on-gas competition will drive down gas prices to their detriment and undermining the viability of the infrastructure investments. The increased use of gas in power generation brings gas into direct competition with other fuels, such as coal and nuclear, in competitively priced power pools, and with this a market regime where gas pricing and delivery volumes may have to adjust rapidly.

Interestingly, this challenge may be addressed in some measure by the changing North American market. For Algeria and Egypt certainly, and for Libya at some point in the future, the ability to export gas in the form of LNG could provide a measure of protection against falling European prices, as well as allowing the producers more flexibility in their supply offerings. North America has the ability, within the limits of LNG shipping and import capacity, to act as a "shock absorber" for the European market. The end of the destination clauses in LNG contracts will almost certainly be replaced by new, more flexible arrangements which will permit buyer and seller to agree to shift LNG to other higher-priced markets. Though not a perfect response to gas-on-gas competition, these features offer the North African LNG producers choices that their pipeline-dependent Russian, Iranian, and Caspian Sea region counterparts do not have. If designed appropriately, these more flexible arrangements may prove to be as or more robust as the historical arrangements.

Finally, Algeria is expanding its presence into the downstream markets as a means of further securing outlets for its gas as well as ensuring that it is positioned to secure margins that might otherwise accrue to the buyers. Sonatrach has taken minority positions in LNG import terminals in Spain, committed to long-term capacity at a proposed new terminal in the U.K. in partnership with BP, and entered into joint marketing arrangements with Gaz de France and CEPSA. These moves bind the suppliers' interests more closely to the market position. Other producers may be expected to follow this example.

## Conclusion

From the perspective of U.S. policy, the continuing development of North Africa as a major gas-supplying region will be critical. As North America becomes a major importer of LNG on the Atlantic and Gulf of Mexico coasts during the next decades, access to Mediterranean supplies and to LNG shipped through the Mediterranean will be important. Although the United States may find itself in competition with Europe for these supplies, the lower costs associated with pipeline deliveries to Southern Europe will favor expanded pipelines as the preferred means of delivering gas to the European market. The increasing flexibility associated with LNG will provide producers and consumers with access to gas supplies that can react more favorably to high prices in regional and local markets, thereby lowering prices and price volatility.

Unlike the 1980s, when the United States opposed the expansion of Russian gas exports to Western Europe, the United States has been more muted in its views on the expansion of Libyan exports to Italy and Iranian exports to Turkey. The implications of pressuring Iran by opposing its exports to the West will have an impact on the United States as it becomes a net gas importer itself, a circumstance that did not enter the policy considerations in the 1980s. Expanded U.S. gas imports from North Africa will place those countries in a more direct trade relationship with the United States, one that it appears would be welcomed by the exporters.

The energy picture, especially for natural gas, that is emerging in the Mediterranean is a more diverse, more complex one than has prevailed during the past two decades, but it is characteristic of trends observed in gas markets globally. The result will be more, not less, security of supply for the importing nations of the Mediterranean and North America, along with a greater measure of interdependence.

The larger question that remains is whether the growing opportunity for the exporting countries in the world market can be converted into improved economic conditions for their broader populations. Without growing employment opportunities (which are not usually a direct by-product of capital-intensive energy extractive industries), these social tensions may continue to build and might erupt, threatening the otherwise optimistic picture painted in this chapter. Encouraging the North African countries to adopt appropriate economic and political policies to achieve improved standards of living for their general populations will be a major challenge for Western countries and may prove decisive for the degree to which the West can rely on supply from these gas-rich nations.

## Notes

1. Poten & Partners, "Atlantic Basin LNG: A New Vista for the Industry," October 2002, updated as of October 2003.

2. Observatoire Mediterraneen de l'Energie, "Future Natural Gas Supply Options and Supply Costs for Europe, and the Role of the Mediterranean Both in Terms of Supply and Transit," paper presented at Conference on Natural Gas Transit and Storage in Southeast Europe, May 31–June 1, 2002.

3. See Donald Juckett and Michelle Foss's discussion of the prospects for a global gas market in chapter 22 of this volume.

4. U.S. Energy Information Administration, *Country Analysis Briefs* (Washington, D.C.: U.S. Energy Information Administration, various years).

5. See Loyola de Palacio's discussion of European Union energy competition policy in chapter 7 of this volume.

6. European Economic and Social Committee, "Opinion of the European Economic and Social Committee on Trans-Euro-Mediterranean energy networks," October 29, 2003.

# 10

# Sub-Saharan Africa

## *Paul F. Hueper*

Africa will play a growing and critical role in global energy supply during the coming decades. From the perspective of the United States and Europe, it will be increasingly important to engage in bilateral and multilateral dialogues with African oil producers in an effort to ensure the security of oil and gas production and exports, the expeditious use of export revenue streams by host governments, and the transparent relationship between these governments and private companies involved in extractive industries.

Because of widespread political instability, civil wars, and geographic remoteness, much of Sub-Saharan Africa remains unexplored, and large amounts of investment by multinational companies will be necessary to tap the subcontinent's undiscovered oil and gas resources. Sub-Saharan Africa contains roughly 180 recognized geological provinces, and although more than 2,500 oil and gas discoveries have been made so far, all have been in just three dozen of these regions. On the basis of industry estimates, the subcontinent holds about 35 billion barrels of proved, probable, and possible reserves and 151 trillion cubic feet of natural gas.[1]

When assessing the future security of world oil supplies, undiscovered resource potential, not just currently producible reserves, is also important to consider. According to U.S. Geological Survey estimates, Sub-Saharan Africa could hold 72 billion barrels of undiscovered oil resources. If calculated on a barrel-of-oil-equivalent basis, the subcontinent's total mean undiscovered hydrocarbon endowment, including natural gas and all liquids,

The opinions expressed in this chapter are solely those of the author and do not necessarily reflect the official policy of the U.S. government.

is about 121 billion barrels. This is roughly a fifth of the Middle East's undiscovered potential, and it surpasses that of North America, Europe, the Asia-Pacific region, and South Asia.

Even in Sub-Saharan Africa's mature oil provinces—Nigeria, Angola, Gabon, and Congo (Brazzaville)—significant growth potential exists for the discovery and development of new oil resources, especially in those countries' deep offshore waters. Recent estimates suggest that this region could export up to 2.5 million barrels per day (mmbpd) to world markets during this decade and account for 15 to 20 percent of oil imports by 2020.

The commercialization of gas resources in the West African oil-producing states, through liquefied natural gas (LNG) exports and gas-to-liquids conversion, also will be an important source of energy supply for world markets. Elsewhere across the continent, recent exploration efforts—utilizing technology only newly available—have begun to identify significant oil and gas potential both onshore and offshore countries such as Côte d'Ivoire, Ethiopia, Guinea-Bissau, Kenya, Liberia, Madagascar, Mauritania, Mozambique, Niger, Sierra Leone, Somalia, South Africa, Tanzania, and Uganda.

The key questions for U.S. national and energy security will be whether African nations will use their oil wealth to foster democratization and sustainable economic development, or whether current patterns of corruption and rent seeking will create even greater instability, with adverse consequences for regional security, terrorism, the spread of HIV/AIDS, and ultimately the ability to produce oil and gas. Guiding the region's governments toward better governance will require creative diplomacy. But if such initiatives succeed, and African nations invest in gas and electric power systems, there could be substantial economic, security, and political benefits for Africa and the West.

Indeed, political and economic stability are critical issues to be considered when assessing Sub-Saharan Africa's energy security. The subcontinent has experienced some of the most brutal examples of civil war and strife in the history of the world. Tribal and ethnic rivalries—many of which predate the colonial period—have exacerbated many conflicts. Regime instability, dictatorial rule, rampant bribery, corruption, and opaque handling of oil revenues and national expenditures are commonplace. Even with the support of international financial institutions, blatant economic mismanagement and the squandering of oil resource wealth seem to be the norm in West Africa.

Because oil export revenues account for a majority of the gross domestic products of several key West African oil producers, it is important for the international community to assist these nations in properly managing these funds. Not only does such management contribute to the welfare and development of these countries, but it also helps to ensure the security of oil and gas supplies from these countries to world markets. After decades of ineffectual action, international efforts to assist West African governments in revenue management—and to obtain their firm commitment and willingness to submit to oversight—only recently have begun to gain traction. As new African countries become oil exporters, following the examples of Chad and Sudan, broader efforts to engage these new producers will become equally important.

## Assessing West Africa's Oil Production and Revenue Potential

In any discussion of energy security in Africa, it is important to understand both the true potential for the subcontinent to supply world oil markets as well as the scope of the oil revenue windfall that will be reaped during the coming decades. West Africa is the subcontinent's main oil-producing region —except for limited volumes from Sudan, Chad, and South Africa. It consequently has the most influence in the region on future global energy security as well as the continent's own economic development. In 2003, West Africa accounted for about 6 percent of global oil supplies and about 3 percent of the world's proved oil reserves, according to the U.S. Energy Information Administration's estimates. In addition, more than 10 percent of U.S. crude oil imports originated in West Africa, with Nigeria and Angola both ranking among the top ten oil suppliers to the United States. Also in 2003, Nigeria and Angola earned revenues from oil production of $19 billion and $9 billion respectively.

Current oil output from West Africa's main oil producers—Nigeria, Angola, Gabon, Congo (Brazzaville), and Equatorial Guinea—of about 3.5 mmbpd will grow significantly during the coming decade. Most of this production capacity, about 2.8 mmbpd, is located in the Niger Delta and the area offshore from the Angolan enclave of Cabinda. Since the early 1990s, exploration in deeper waters offshore from Nigeria, Angola, and Equatorial Guinea has resulted in oil field discovery rates unmatched elsewhere in the world.[2]

West Africa's five most important oil-producing countries could produce a peak of roughly 6.7 mmbpd, according to the base-case scenario of an analysis that assumes a continued trend of deepwater and ultra-deepwater discoveries, optimization of overall reserve development and production

Figure 10.1.  West African Oil Production, Base Resource Case, 2003–20

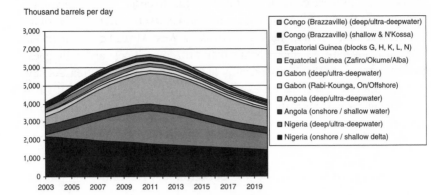

Thousand barrels per day

Legend:
- ▨ Congo (Brazzaville) (deep/ultra-deepwater)
- ■ Congo (Brazzaville) (shallow & N'Kossa)
- ☐ Equatorial Guinea (blocks G, H, K, L, N)
- ▨ Equatorial Guinea (Zafiro/Okume/Alba)
- ☐ Gabon (deep/ultra-deepwater)
- ☐ Gabon (Rabi-Kounga, On/Offshore)
- ▨ Angola (deep/ultra-deepwater)
- ■ Angola (onshore / shallow water)
- ▨ Nigeria (deep/ultra-deepwater)
- ■ Nigeria (onshore / shallow delta)

scenarios, and sufficient levels of investment in maintaining production from mature fields, especially in the Niger Delta and offshore Cabinda (figure 10.1). Two alternative scenarios suggest that West Africa's key oil producers could achieve peak outputs of anywhere between 5.9 and 7.6 mmbpd, depending on production decline rates at existing fields as well as the rate and extent of future offshore discoveries (figures 10.2 and 10.3).

It is important to note that in any of three scenarios, regional offshore production declines begin soon after 2010, primarily because by that time, there will be few large undiscovered fields left offshore. If the rate of ultra-deepwater discoveries—in water depths of more than 1,500 meters—offshore West Africa does not parallel that of the shallower deepwater finds in Angola and Nigeria, inevitable oil production declines could be steep.

The ability of West Africa's key oil producers to explore for and develop their offshore oil resources under these three scenarios will be tied directly to investment levels. Under a base-case production scenario, the finding and development costs for new deepwater and ultra-deepwater developments would total $106 billion between 2003 and 2020 (figure 10.4). In all three scenarios, Nigeria and Angola will require ten times the investment— a cumulative total ranging from $17 billion to $23 billion in both of these countries—as that needed by Gabon, Equatorial Guinea, and Congo (Brazzaville) during the forecast period.

Assuming that the forecast investment levels are realized, however, West Africa's producers will reap extensive rewards from their oil production.

Figure 10.2. West African Oil Production, High Resource Case, 2003–20

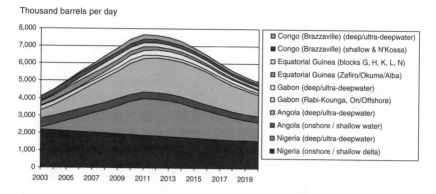

Thousand barrels per day

Figure 10.3. West African Oil Production, Low Resource Case, 2003–20

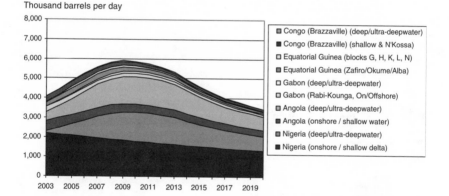

Thousand barrels per day

Under the base-case production scenario, West Africa's five key producing states would earn almost $800 billion—about $360 billion in 2003 dollars, assuming a 10 percent discount rate—from oil produced in their countries between 2003 and 2020 (figure 10.5).[3]

Under the high-case scenario, revenues would reach $905 billion, or almost $400 billion in 2003 dollars. Nigeria and Angola would earn roughly

Figure 10.4. Present Value of West African Offshore Finding and Development Costs, 2003–20

Billions of 2003 dollars

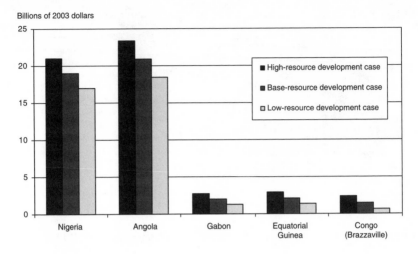

Figure 10.5. Present Value of West African Oil Production, 2003–20

Billions of 2003 dollars

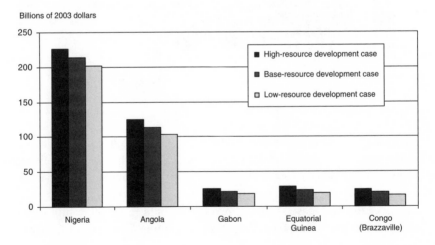

$200 billion and $120 billion in 2003 dollars, respectively, or 80 percent of the total. Under the low-case scenarios, earnings would total $690 billion, or $325 billion in 2003 dollars. Under all three production scenarios, Nigeria would earn about half the region's revenues, with Angola accounting for roughly 30 percent of the total.

Under any of the above production scenarios, West Africa will remain an important oil supplier to world energy markets during the coming two decades. However, the degree to which key producers such as Nigeria and Angola remain among the world's top oil suppliers will depend not only on the favorableness of their ultra-deepwater geology but also on foreign investment for exploration and development. West African oil-producing countries also must implement political agendas and economic policies conducive to ensuring the maintenance of attractive investment environments. This is especially important as the region competes with other newly developing frontier oil and gas provinces around the world.

## The Role of Natural Gas

Although the region has played an important role in global oil markets since the 1960s, it has been only in the past decade that the commercialization of West Africa's sizable natural gas resource base has occurred. As the world's energy consumption profile begins to favor natural gas, the exploitation of these reserves will ensure that West Africa and other countries in Sub-Saharan Africa will play an even more important role in global energy supply and security than today.

Nigeria, in particular, has world-class gas reserves estimated at about 124 trillion cubic feet. With the start-up of both the Escravos gas plant in 1997 and the country's first LNG export terminal in 1999, Nigeria finally has infrastructure in place to begin commercializing this resource. It also is making considerable progress in reducing flaring, which is expected to end in 2008. In addition to the LNG export terminal, two new LNG export schemes have been proposed in addition to the planned West Africa Gas Pipeline, which would export associated gas from Nigeria to consumers in Benin, Togo, and Ghana. Excellent prospects also exist for gas-to-liquids projects, which convert natural gas into middle distillates such as gasoline and diesel.

Additional greenfield LNG projects have been proposed in Angola and Equatorial Guinea, highlighting the reality that the export of natural-gas-related products will be a major contributor of revenues for key West African governments. Increased gas utilization in regional economies also will be a catalyst for spurring economic growth and stability through its use in industrial development and electric power generation. For these reasons, revenue management and the oversight of gas sales will become as important as that of oil sales.

## Energy Supply and Security beyond West Africa

New frontiers are opening up for modern oil and gas exploration all across the subcontinent, with substantial potential for large discoveries. Technological advances and reevaluation of geological prospects, particularly in East Africa, mean that a decade from now, there could be a half-dozen or more new oil-producing countries outside the core West African region. Will these new producers fall into the same resource exploitation pattern as nations in West Africa? Or will the United States and other countries seek to engage and support these governments in managing their newfound oil and gas wealth? The engagement efforts that the United States and Europe make now with respect to helping African countries implement sustainable development strategies will have direct consequences for long-term global energy security.

In the near future, what are now considered "frontier" oil and gas exploration provinces in western, southern, eastern, and central Africa may become the lynchpins of regional geopolitics and stability, based in part on their possible role as oil and gas exporters. A cursory look at the subcontinent's broader resource potential is revealing. Unexplored areas such as offshore Liberia, Sierra Leone, Mauritania, and other West African countries hold good prospects for small and medium-sized oil discoveries, most likely in the range of 50 to 300 mmbpd. The geology offshore from southern Africa is only recently being understood, but the deep waters offshore South Africa are thought to hold good potential for oil, most likely in medium-sized volumes. Offshore Namibia, exploration of large geological structures that have been identified on seismic surveys may result in the discovery of giant natural gas fields.

East Africa holds some of the greatest and most exciting exploration potential on the continent. With the gradual development of the region's economy as well as containment and resolution of many of its security issues, a number of groundbreaking oil and gas developments are under way across the region. Commercial gas production is set to flow next year in both Tanzania and Mozambique, oil has been discovered in Uganda, and several recent geophysical surveys have indicated that there are good oil and gas prospects offshore portions of East Africa.[4]

In addition to East Africa, the interior rift basins of Central Africa also hold interesting prospects. These basins extend through portions of Niger, Chad, the Central African Republic, and Sudan. Despite high prospectivity for oil and gas, this rift system has remained relatively unexplored—civil war and conflict have precluded oil sector investment in many of these countries. Even the little exploration done so far in Sudan and Chad have proved up more than 2 billion barrels of oil reserves, and the upside potential of the oil resources in these two countries is very significant.

Fostering political and economic stability in these important frontier regions of Africa is a prerequisite to creating an investment environment conducive to oil and gas exploration. For countries such as Chad, the continuation of oil exploration is critical to providing it with the revenues needed to spur sustainable long-term economic development. Under the Chad Export Project, the country will achieve a peak production plateau of 225,000 barrels per day during only the first four years after the start of production. Oil production and exports will decline rapidly after this time, falling to less than 100,000 barrels per day after 2012. Ensuring political stability in N'Djamena, encouraging proper oil revenue management, managing expectations by the local population, and limiting the spread of banditry and rebel activity in the southern and northern parts of the country, respectively, will be important factors in the degree to which oil companies invest in future oil sector activities in Chad.

## Revenue Management and Stability

Motivating the governments of oil-exporting regimes in Sub-Saharan Africa to use their oil and gas export revenues to further economic growth and prosperity remains an important and unmet challenge. Oil export revenues account for a large proportion—ranging from about 40 percent in Nigeria to more than 85 percent in Equatorial Guinea—of the gross domestic products of most of the region's oil-producing countries. In Sub-Saharan Africa, as in many of the world's other oil-producing regions, the windfalls created by oil wealth have led to widespread corruption and abuse.

In West Africa, numerous cases of corruption, bribery, theft, embezzlement, and kickbacks have occurred since oil production began a half-century ago. In Nigeria, an estimated $10 billion of oil revenues were siphoned off by the country's former leader, General Sani Abacha, in the 1990s. In Angola, the International Monetary Fund and nongovernmental organizations such as Global Witness and Human Rights Watch have cited the recent "disappearance" of more than $1 billion in oil export receipts from government coffers since 2001 and an estimated $4 billion in revenues since 1999. Transparency and bribery issues exist in a host of countries in former French West Africa, as exemplified by the recent court cases of former Elf Aquitaine executives who were involved in corrupt oil-related dealings with regional government officials.

Efforts by Western governments and nongovernmental organizations to hold African governments accountable for wealth generated from the oil and gas sector show promise, but achieving the goals sought by such disclosure- and transparency-related efforts will be difficult. In 2003, the United Kingdom's Department for International Development began direction of the Extractive Industries Transparency Initiative (EITI), which seeks to promote good governance and transparency in the extractive sector, not only in Africa but also elsewhere in the world's resource-rich developing countries. Other efforts, such as Transparency International's "Publish What You Pay" campaign, seek similar goals. The Group of Seven's 2003 Evian Declaration placed emphasis on the transparency of expenditures as well as revenues. Using leverage such as offering or withholding debt relief and international funding programs may provide the impetus needed to encourage governments in the region to comply with the goals of these initiatives.[5] Vested personal interests and decisions by countries' leaders about what they believe is best for their respective countries, however, may preclude progress with respect to improving transparency. In the case of Angola in 2003, after significant pressure was applied by international lenders, the government finally agreed to commit to improve the transparency of its oil deals and to disclose how oil export revenues are used.

In 2003, Nigerian president Olusegun Obasanjo also committed to publishing what revenues the government receives from the oil industry. Additionally, under the Abuja Joint Declaration signed jointly by President Obasanjo and São Tomé and Príncipe president Fradique de Menezes in June 2004, both countries agreed to disclose publicly the revenues earned from oil developments in the Joint Development Zone. Another related initiative begun by President Obasanjo is the creation of an Economic and

Financial Crimes Commission. Investigations by the commissions have resulted in the firing of a number of top military officers and civil servants who were involved in illegal oil bunkering activities that typically siphon off hundreds of millions of dollars each year from government coffers. Time will tell if pledges by Angola, Equatorial Guinea, and Nigeria to participate in EITI will be fulfilled. One key question for Nigeria is whether it will make transparent not just its revenues from the oil industry but also from LNG and other natural gas export projects. Because these will rival oil export revenues in size during the coming decades, any effort to achieve transparency without their inclusion will be seriously flawed.

## Broader Security Issues a Concern

Besides transparency, corruption, and bribery issues, a broader dimension exists with respect to the appropriate use of oil export revenues by Sub-Saharan African countries. Since the continent's countries attained independence from colonial European powers, many have been racked by civil war and conflict. Some governments have used oil export revenues to strengthen their military, paramilitary, and law enforcement capabilities, which in turn have been used to fight civil wars, repress local opposition, and commit human rights violations.

Such actions have broad implications for regional stability and the security of energy exports to the United States and Europe. Lengthy civil wars in Angola and Sudan have been directly affected by the availability of oil export revenues. In Angola, interruptions to oil production by the National Union for the Total Independence of Angola (UNITA) and the Front for the Liberation of the Enclave of Cabinda have been only sporadic during the past two decades, mainly because the country's oil fields are predominately offshore. Beginning in 1999, the Angolan government undertook licensing of four ultra-deepwater exploration blocks. The signature bonuses paid by the oil companies that won these blocks have totaled in excess of $1.4 billion, according to a variety of independent sources. This windfall received by the government was used to boost the military's capabilities and to enable the government to force UNITA to the negotiating table, especially after the Lusaka Peace Accords fell apart at the end of 1998.[6]

Sudan's road to becoming an oil exporter also has not been without controversy. Between 1985 and 1991, civil war forced all foreign oil companies with onshore concessions either to withdraw or to suspend activities. In the mid-1990s, Canadian independents Arakis and subsequently Talisman led plans to export oil from fields found in southern Sudan by Chevron in the early 1980s. As work progressed, the Sudan People's Liberation Army (SPLA), the primary insurgent group fighting the government for independence, warned that any oil export revenues Sudan received would be used by Khartoum to strengthen the country's military forces. The SPLA then declared foreign companies to be military targets, and it stated that all oil production activities in southern Sudan would be forcibly shut down. The SPLA was unable to stop the export project, however, and after the 1999 start-up of the country's export pipeline, Khartoum received a sizable revenue windfall. Before the peace accord in 2004, the government's military activity had greatly increased in the oil-producing regions, reportedly financed by these new oil revenues, prompting outside observers to raise concerns of alleged human rights violations and leading the United Nations Security Council to condemn Khartoum's actions and the United States to impose unilateral sanctions on Khartoum and additional measures under the Sudan Peace Act.

The resolution of decades of civil war in both Angola and Sudan are worthy goals that have not been easy to achieve; in Sudan, the resolution is deeply uncertain. In Angola, the funds used to make the military purchases necessary to bring UNITA to the negotiating table would not have occurred without the windfall created by signature bonuses on ultra-deepwater offshore license blocks and the ongoing ramp-up in offshore oil production. In Sudan, limited oil exports since late 1999 created a small, but still critical, discretionary windfall for the government of this impoverished country.

Despite the apparent and near resolution of these conflicts, ensuring peace in Sub-Saharan Africa—where national borders were drawn arbitrarily across tribal and ethnic lines by colonial European powers—will be difficult to maintain. This especially is true in oil-producing countries in which equitable distribution of oil revenues has been problematic. In Angola, UNITA draws support from Ovimbundu and Bakongo ethnic tribal groups located in the northern, central, and southern parts of the country. The Popular Movement for the Liberation of Angola—the party largely in power—has its Kimbundu power base located along the coast. In Sudan, a stark contrast exists between ethnic groups, tribal practices, and religion in Saharan Sudan and the Sudan of the Sahel. Sustaining equality in the economic and social development and treatment of disparate peoples within national borders remains a challenge in Sub-Saharan Africa.

Nigeria's main oil-producing region, the Niger Delta, also has been the site of ethnic clashes, civil strife, disruptions to oil production, kidnapping, extensive environmental damage, and human rights abuses by the military and law enforcement organizations. The human cost of the Nigerian government's attempt to control the region has been well documented.[7] A prime case is point is the Ogoniland situation and the 1995 execution of Ken Saro-Wiwa, an act that provoked international condemnation. Continuing ethnic clashes in Warri and the Western Delta are unlikely to end without proactive and effective efforts by the government to resolve the region's underlying political and economic problems. Abuja's apparent willingness to let the Delta remain unstable—seemingly in perpetuity—does not bode well for the future of one of the world's most important oil-producing regions.

In Nigeria, the role of foreign oil companies with respect to human rights abuses requires cautious examination. In many cases, oil companies confronted with a hostage situation or a takeover of oil production infrastructure (e.g., drilling rigs, flow stations, or wellheads) have learned that the best way to respond to such situations is through negotiations with tribal leaders rather than by force. But companies are obliged at a certain point to seek government assistance, especially when employees' lives are at risk, and there have been numerous cases where the overreaction of government forces has led to civilian deaths. This in turn has fomented animosity in various Niger Delta communities, particularly among the Ijaw and Itsekiri, toward foreign oil companies.

Corruption, graft, and poor oil revenue management in the Niger Delta also have promoted feelings of distrust and dissent among local communities. In the 1990s, the government's suspension of its constitutionally mandated requirement to give 13 percent of all oil revenues earned back to communities in the Niger Delta's six states also was an example of how oil development and revenue management can be detrimental to a country's social well-being.

For new oil-producing governments that are inexperienced with oil wealth, the risk of long-term societal destabilization is a concern, as in the Niger Delta. In Chad, ensuring the proper management of future oil revenues has been a persistent and controversial issue. Reports that the Chad government had used monies derived from the oil export project to purchase arms in 2000 raised concerns about oversight and the government's priorities, which many outside observers believe should be poverty alleviation. The World Bank's support for the project also has stirred considerable controversy, especially by human rights groups, which are concerned that President Idriss Deby, a northerner, will exclude communities in Chad's southern oil-producing region from the financial benefits that will occur in the future.

A promising solution that has been developed is the creation of a Special Oil Revenue Account, that will be under direct World Bank oversight and the accounts of which will be periodically published. A Petroleum Revenue Oversight Committee, composed of government officials and nongovernmental organization representatives, also has been established to oversee the management of revenues, which will be spent in predetermined allocations to projects in various sectors, such as public health, education, and agriculture, as well as for infrastructure development. Finally, a Future Generations Fund has been set up and will be funded with 10 percent of the project's earnings.

Concerns still exist, however, over the relatively small share of oil wealth —only 4.5 percent—that will be reinvested in local communities in southern Chad's oil-producing region. A key driving force behind the urgency and importance of instituting controls over the repatriation of a portion of Chad's oil income back to the oil-producing region has been the experience of Nigeria. It is too soon to judge whether Chad's revenue management model will be an example that can be applied in other future oil-producing countries in Sub-Saharan Africa.

## Multilateral Engagement: The Time Is Now

Sub-Saharan Africa contains considerable oil and gas resource potential, but geopolitical challenges will affect the timing and extent of the development of these economic assets. Sudan and Chad are examples of countries whose sizable oil resource potential has been known for decades, but where civil war and instability have precluded their development. When it does finally occur, the development of Madagascar's enormous heavy-oil resources, the suspected giant gas fields offshore East Africa, and the medium-sized oil and gas fields located on the continent's western, southern, and eastern margins will have great impact on regional and global markets during the coming decades.

It is important to emphasize that the entire continent's anticipated and hypothesized future oil revenue windfall—particularly that in Nigeria, Angola, and Equatorial Guinea—is inextricably linked to both geology and private-sector investment. It is in the best interest of the international community—as well as of the region's governments—to manage oil and gas development in a fiscally responsible and transparent way. For West Africa's key producers, prospects for a sustained, but finite, period of oil export revenues mean that it is critical to immediately institute revenue management and oversight processes in these countries.

Assistance in governmental capacity building as well as charting a viable path toward economic diversification and growth also will be essential in assisting these countries to achieve their economic and social goals, before oil revenues begin to decline at the end of the next decade. From U.S. national and energy security perspectives, especially when the specter of global terrorism is considered, it is not too soon to ensure the underlying political and economic stability—as well as the security capabilities—of both current and future oil producers throughout the continent.

Sudan, Chad, and Niger—after more comprehensive exploration efforts are mounted—are in the position of having highly prospective, relatively unexplored oil basins that will require capital-intensive and labor-power-intensive efforts to develop. Due to the inherently poor security situation in this part of Central Africa, the stark divide between the Sahara and Sahel, ethnic and tribal differences, and the risk that human rights abuses will occur if political stability deteriorates, the exposure that foreign oil companies face through their investments in these countries is significant. It is unclear what kind of role that the international community would, or even could, play during adverse circumstances in these countries, but it is an issue that should be further addressed.

## Fueling Growth, Stability, and Economic Integration

It is equally important to look at the impact of future oil and gas discoveries, not just in terms of their potential to export energy to world markets but also because of the effect they will have in promoting the small- and medium-scale economic development that will lead to greater integration of this region's countries into the global economy. Natural gas discoveries, if sizable enough, have the potential to make a much greater impact on economic growth because they encourage fuel switching and the development of natural-gas-based industry. Two cases in point are the recently completed natural gas pipeline projects in Mozambique and Tanzania. The use of natural gas for power generation is an important precedent in East Africa and elsewhere in Sub-Saharan Africa, where less than one quarter of the populations of many countries has access to electric power. Electricity is the key driving force behind the development of industry and modern service-oriented economies, and natural gas provides the opportunity to supplement existing large hydroelectric and coal-fired power plants that exist throughout Sub-Saharan Africa.

Within the past decade, the rehabilitation and construction of key transmission and distribution links between southern African countries have allowed for a sizable increase in regional power trade, and this activity is likely to expand. As links between the national grids in Southern African Development Community countries expand, "wheeled" power—exports across third countries—becomes a critical new sourcing option for member countries. Since 2002, governments in East Africa and West Africa have progressed toward creating their own regional power pools, modeled after the southern African experience. The development of regional power pools in Sub-Saharan Africa will be influenced heavily by natural gas finds and development across the continent. During the next two decades, natural gas finds across Sub-Saharan Africa likely will reshape regional electric power markets and trade as well as boost industrial output and economic efficiency throughout the region.

As regional power grids grow and become more reliable through the use of gas, ultimately a trans-African power grid will take shape. Although it will be decades in coming, this grid will have far-reaching and lasting geopolitical implications for Europe. Proposals for a "Cape to Cairo" transmission system—supplied in part by the DRC's Inga hydroelectric power site—would have the potential to link permanently the energy markets of Africa and Europe. Realities prohibit the realization of such a vision at the present time. But perhaps in two or three decades, and with the establishment of political and economic stability across Sub-Saharan Africa, the investment environment may be conducive to undertaking this endeavor.

At present, it is oil and gas development that will provide the export revenues necessary to spur sustainable economic growth and to fuel industrial development and power generation. In doing so, it will play an essential role in promoting the political and economic stability needed in the continent. The participation and engagement of the international community in persuading oil- and gas-producing governments to govern transparently and invest wisely in their own development will be vital in this process and beneficial for all.

# Notes

1. See T. Hemsted, "Second and Third Millennium Reserves Development in African Basins," in *Petroleum Geology of Africa: New Themes and Developing Technologies*, ed. T. Arthur, D. S. MacGregor, and N. R. Cameron (London: Geological Society, 2003).

2. Roughly 80 deepwater exploration wells drilled between southern Congo and central Angola yielded more than fifty discoveries, most of which are considered commercially feasible to develop. Success rates in the deep waters offshore Nigeria also have been impressive. The development of these newly found oil fields offshore West Africa will result in a sizable boost in output through 2010, and these additions will more than offset natural declines in the mature producing areas of the Niger Delta and offshore Cabinda.

3. This scenario assumes that real oil prices remain relatively flat, in accordance with recent U.S. Energy Information Administration projections.

4. More specifically, these assessments have shown significant potential for oil-prone source rocks in the deep waters offshore from East Africa—extending from Somalia to Mozambique—as well as the potential for multiple petroleum systems located offshore from Mozambique and Madagascar that each could hold a billion barrels under the right circumstances. This is in addition to already-known sizable oil resources: Madagascar holds the world's largest heavy oil and tar sand deposits outside Canada and Venezuela. The country's Tsimiroro field holds between 1.5 and 2.2 billion barrels of heavy oil, and the Bemolanga deposits hold and an estimated 20 billion barrels of tar sands. Despite their immense size, these resources have remained fallow for decades, partly because of the lack of a commercial market.

5. Examples of proposals to leverage diplomatic or financial incentives to promote transparency are offered by Ian Gary and Terry Lynn Karl, *Bottom of the Barrel: Africa's Oil Boom and the Poor* (Boston: Catholic Relief Services, 2003), and David L. Goldwyn, "Extracting Transparency," *Georgetown Journal of International Affairs,* Summer/Fall 2004.

6. According to Human Rights Watch's *The Oil Diagnostic in Angola* (New York: Human Rights Watch, 2001), about $870 million in funds generated by signature bonuses for blocks 31, 32, and 33 were used by the government to purchase weapons.

7. Human Rights Watch, *The Price of Oil: Corporate Responsibility and Human Rights Violations in Nigeria's Oil Producing Communities* (New York: Human Rights Watch, 1999).

# Commentary on Part III

## Abdullah bin Hamad Al-Attiyah

From my vantage point in Qatar and the Arabian Gulf, I am impressed most of all by the interdependence of producers and consumers in the energy market. It is this interdependence that made possible the more than 600 percent increase in Qatari gas sales from 2.2 million metric tons in 1997, when the production of liquefied natural gas (LNG) began, to 16 million metric tons in 2003. Moreover, by the end of the decade, Qatar hopes to export about 65 million metric tons per year—as a result of several more projects agreed on or under negotiation.

This extraordinary growth is the consequence, I believe, of three main factors. The first is the very positive investment environment in Qatar, which has led to the major, long-term capital commitments for gas production and LNG terminals by foreign companies, working with Qatar Petroleum. The second is the growing international demand for energy in general and gas in particular, with its environmental benefits and its contribution to diversified energy use. The third factor is the set of close economic, political, and security relationships between Qatar and the United States as well as other key countries in Asia and Europe, which reinforce the specific ties these nations enjoy in energy trade and investment.

This interdependence is not limited to gas. My own view is that producers and consumers must reach greater mutual understanding and cooperation in crude oil as well. During the terms that I have served as president of the OPEC Conference, I have seen increased producer–consumer dialogue, and also an increased desire to coordinate between OPEC and non-OPEC members.

This cooperative perspective leads me to share Robin West's view in his chapter that OPEC will manage successfully increased exports from Iraq,

259

which are essential to that country's postwar reconstruction and recovery. He points out that it is neither realistic nor desirable to rely primarily on projected increases in Iraqi exports in preference to those from Saudi Arabia. Moreover, a strategy that suggests it is somehow in the West's interest to pit one oil producer, whether an OPEC member or not, against another is highly objectionable. Its inevitable consequence will be confrontation and retaliation, when the real goal should be to develop cooperative measures that promote increased energy and economic security for both producers and consumers.

The benefits of cooperation are clearly demonstrated in Gordon Shearer's account of the growing interdependence of producers and consumers in the Mediterranean market. The parallel with the experience of Qatar is striking: North African gas producers are demonstrating the security of their supply, and European consumers are demonstrating the security of their markets. As Shearer points out, it is to be hoped that the gas revenues will result in additional economic growth—in short, that energy security will result in economic security in this region. I believe this will be accomplished not only through LNG projects but also through gas pipelines that connect the North African and European markets. Regional gas pipelines are developing in the Arabian Gulf as well, with important benefits for the countries in the region, and in the longer term for other markets further afield.

Sub-Saharan Africa also promises exciting developments in oil exploration and production. In his chapter, Paul Hueper makes it clear that this is the case not only for existing oil producers—such as Nigeria and Angola, whose onshore production will be increased by new deepwater offshore development—but also for additional producers across the continent.

I believe that these additional energy sources will be vital to African development, but they also will be needed for ever-increasing worldwide demand. Therefore they are only to be welcomed, and the test of leadership will be to make sure that interested nations expand the circle of energy cooperation to ensure that both long-standing and new energy sources contribute to a healthy energy market and global economic growth.

These three chapters represent together a sensible view of the Middle East, Africa, and the broader issues of energy security and the energy markets. It is to be hoped that they will help to bring greater understanding and more balance to Western policy debates. Too often, Western commentators seem to assume that existing energy producers are unreliable or simply wish to maximize prices. That simply is not borne out by the record. As a whole, OPEC has acted responsibly to compensate for the unavoidable shortfalls resulting from strikes or conflicts, and to maintain prices within a predictable, acceptable, and fair range, taking into account the interests of both producers and consumers. In gas, the record of producers is one of unbroken reliability—which has been indispensable to the development of the global gas market.

Moreover, I would ask our Western friends to consider whether criticism has not been directed unfairly to the Middle East as a region. Qatar and other countries have been close and reliable partners in economic, political, and security affairs. Economic, social, and educational opportunities are key to the region's development, as is greater public participation in decisions affecting the future of its countries. The Middle Eastern nations are proud of their traditions, culture, and religion—but these can and should be pillars of peaceful development and cooperation across regional lines.

Thus, this book is required reading in more ways than one. I believe it will make an important contribution to mutual understanding not only in energy but also in the broader realm of energy security and foreign policy.

# Part IV

# The Pacific Rim

Part IV assesses the trends and challenges for energy security in the countries of the Pacific Rim, where the rate of growth in energy demand is the fastest in the world. The conduct of the nations of this region will have a heavy impact on the geopolitics of energy worldwide. China's national policies to manage energy demand, control greenhouse gas emissions, compete for regional energy supply, and relate to its neighbors in North Korea and Japan will have national security implications for the United States. Japan's wide use of nuclear energy and its decision whether to seek its future energy security through bilateral or collective arrangements will affect the ability of the United States to form a partnership with Japan on global security issues. The decision by the rest of the Asia and Pacific region to seek energy security through the integration of oil and gas pipelines, the collective pursuit of strategic reserves, or efforts by each nation to seek its own path to self-sufficiency may determine whether the region is truly pacific over the next century or becomes embroiled in destructive competition. In each case, U.S. policy and U.S. commitment to global energy security can play a major role.

This part includes chapters by Amy Jaffe and Kenneth Medlock on China and Northeast Asia, by John Ryan on the Asia-Pacific Economic Cooperation forum's (APEC's) multilateral approach to energy security, and by Keiichi Yokobori on Japan. The authors point out that the greatest challenge for policymakers is how to expand the circle of cooperation, avoid declining into destabilizing competition in a region whose nations (other than South Korea and Japan) lack strategic reserves, and promote the development of cross-border pipelines and transport.

In chapter 11, Jaffe and Medlock point out that as China grows and moves from oil self-sufficiency to net importer, its foreign policy priorities are changing. They argue that China can continue to assure its own security of supply by pursuing bilateral deals and competing with U.S. geopolitical interests or, with a more enlightened U.S. policy, can become an ally in promoting energy security by developing strategic reserves and investment in energy efficiency, conservation, and renewable energy technologies. Jaffe and Medlock conclude that current U.S. policy does not adequately promote cooperation, and they suggest alternative steps, including incorporating trade in energy and energy services into the global free-trade network, that the United States should take to advance its interests in the region and strengthen its energy security.

In chapter 12, Ryan observes that energy security is a driver of closer foreign policy cooperation and economic integration among the APEC member countries. He describes how APEC's voluntary, consensus-based approach has succeeded in securing the adoption of a regional strategy to address the challenges of energy security. APEC's Energy Security Initiative includes measures to address temporary disruption, long-term policy goals, improved data collection, and sustainable development. Ryan concludes that APEC's approach to regional cooperation on energy security issues can be a global model for enhancing global energy security.

In chapter 13, Yokobori points out that Japan's main issues of concern are (1) its lack of energy resources coupled with a projected increase in demand and insufficient transport infrastructure; (2) increased competition for energy resources with its neighbors, notably China, which also lack strategic reserves; and (3) the need to address global greenhouse gas emissions and the impact and implementation of the Kyoto Protocol. He calls for closer regional cooperation as the best approach for Japan to meet these concerns. And he suggests that the United States and Japan can cooperate, together and with APEC, in developing strategic reserves for Asia, along with gas and power infrastructure that can bind the Asian economies together. He highlights a creative approach to North Korea, suggesting ways to use its need for energy to support a diplomatic resolution of the nuclear issue. And he also suggests a fresh U.S. approach to the Kyoto Protocol that would enhance U.S. cooperation with Japan and U.S. influence in the region.

In his commentary on part IV, J. Bennett Johnston, a former U.S. senator (and chairman of the Senate Committee on Energy and Natural Resources), shares the view of Jaffe, Medlock, Ryan, and Yokobori that the key to the Asia-Pacific region's energy security and stability is China's relationship with the United States and its own neighbors. Johnston calls for strong leadership to draw China closer to the United States, through cooperation on strategic reserves, energy efficiency, research and development, and the peaceful use of nuclear energy. He lauds Japan's example in diversifying its energy supply by expanding safe nuclear power and urges more research on nuclear safety and waste disposal. Johnston shares Ryan's view that stronger regional cooperation, through APEC, will create a system of collaboration rather than divisive competition for energy. Finally, Johnston foresees that closer cooperation on energy can pay great dividends for U.S. national security by creating a platform on which the United States, Japan, China, and Russia can pursue peaceful solutions to nuclear proliferation worldwide, but most urgently in North Korea.

# 11

# China and Northeast Asia

*Amy Myers Jaffe and Kenneth B. Medlock III*

Economic growth in Asia—where Asia is defined to include the Indian subcontinent, Southeast Asia, East Asia, Australia, and New Zealand but exclude the countries of the former Soviet Union and Middle East—will result in a substantial increase in energy demand in the coming decades. China, in particular, as home to more than 1.2 billion people, will shape the future of the Asian energy balance as its economy develops. Because of resource constraints in China and in the rest of Asia, increased demand will result in significant increases in energy imports. Consequently, there will be dramatic changes in the geopolitical landscape as new relationships are forged between Asian countries and both major energy-exporting nations and other energy-importing nations, such as the United States.

China's energy sector is one of the key areas where dramatic change can be expected in the coming years. Inexpensive, readily available energy resources will be critical to future economic growth in China, just as was seen during industrialization and development in the West. Already, China's economic expansion is being accompanied by a strong increase in demand for energy, and this can be expected to continue into the near future. Since 1990, Chinese oil demand has risen from 2.1 million barrels per day (bpd) to more than 5 million barrels per day (mmbpd), and the Baker Institute projects Chinese oil use will continue to grow to around 7 mmbpd by 2010.[1] China's domestic oil output averaged about 3.4 mmbpd in 2003 and, by most projections, is likely to remain flat to slightly lower in the coming years. Therefore, China's oil imports can be expected to grow significantly in the coming decade after nearly decades of complete self-sufficiency. This change has important implications for Asian energy security and oil geopolitics.

Concerns about oil security are increasingly influencing China's diplomatic and strategic calculus, extending China's foreign policy concerns beyond its traditional focus on its border areas to global interests that extend as far away as Eurasia, the Middle East, and Africa. During the past few years, China has demonstrated a willingness to deepen its oil trading relationships with countries whose ties to the United States are strained, such as Iran, Sudan, and Libya, taking advantage of U.S. sanctions policy and leading to fears that Beijing will form oil-for-arms, military–client relationships with nations under boycott by the United States.[2] This has put China into a position of geopolitical rivalry with the United States.

As China continues to pursue bilateral oil diplomacy, political pressures will build for Beijing to back positions popular with particular oil producers in forums such as the United Nations. This could pose new challenges for the West on a variety of issues, in much the way that Russian and French political opposition to military strikes against Iraq hurt U.S. efforts to create UN support for a "coalition of the willing." The diplomatic, strategic, and trading focus of emerging Asian states such as China can be expected to shift in light of growing energy import requirements, leading to a strengthening of economic and political ties with major Middle Eastern oil-exporting countries and African oil states.[3] U.S. policy must recognize this possibility and become more engaged in efforts to bring China into the fold of Western energy consumer cooperation. China, as a growing oil consumer, has concrete strategic interests that coincide with the United States. To date, however, the United States has failed to effectively promote common interests and goals such as energy supply diversification, research and deployment of energy-efficient technologies, and promotion of alternative energy.

The geopolitical fallout of rising energy demand in Asia will depend on the policy choices made by the key players in the region and by the United States. Territory and nationalism remain defining issues in Asian interstate relations.[4] This means that energy security for all concerned must be managed carefully, lest other pathologies spread into deliberations in the energy area. Environmental concerns could exacerbate energy security fears, as regional powers share concerns about future emissions from the increased use of fossil fuels in emerging economies like China.

Despite the apparent need for policy initiative, China has yet to seriously consider activities involving multilateral alliances on oil issues with other important oil-consuming countries. For example, China has not yet joined in any international or regional emergency stockpiling systems or other energy policy groupings. Moreover, Western interests are only now beginning to make significant efforts to transfer new, cleaner, more energy-efficient technologies to Chinese industry, and they have only just begun to involve China in multinational energy research initiatives. Energy cooperation could be key to bringing China into closer relations with the United States and its allies.[5] Such cooperation could smooth the way for better coordination on weapons nonproliferation and environmental protection.

## Trends in Asian Energy Use: The China Factor

Economic development, in general, is correlated with increased urbanization and electrification, and growth in the use of private automobiles. The Asian experience will be no different, and without significant growth in renewable energy supplies and/or new energy technologies, the consumption of crude oil and natural gas should rise substantially in the coming years. In fact, Asian energy use is expected to expand significantly as the twenty-first century progresses. By 2020, Asian energy consumption is projected to account for more than one-third of global energy use, rivaling that of North America and Europe and likely resulting in large increases in an already substantial dependence on imported energy.

More than half the future growth in energy demand in Asia is expected to come from the transportation sector, where—barring a technological breakthrough—increased reliance on crude oil and crude oil products will be unavoidable. Per capita income growth in developing countries in particular, such as China, India, Indonesia, Malaysia, and Thailand, will account for an increasing proportion of energy demand through an increase in automobile ownership and a corresponding rise in motor fuel demand.[6] Asian oil demand averaged about 21.5 mmbpd in the first half of 2003 while local oil production totaled only around 6.2 mmbpd, leaving a deficit of more than 15.3 mmbpd that was met by imports from the Middle East and Africa.[7] To put this into perspective, total oil demand for the region is already larger than that of the United States,[8] and oil imports, which are already above 70 percent of total consumption, have risen substantially in recent years.[9] Given the inadequate resource endowment of the region, this trend is unlikely to change as Asia becomes increasingly dependent on oil and gas supplies from the Middle East and Russia. According to the "business as usual" forecast by the International Energy Agency,[10] oil demand in all of Asia is expected to grow two to three times faster than in the industrial West, reaching 25 to 30 mmbpd by 2010.[11]

## China in Focus

China's total energy use has increased steadily from 14.08 quadrillion British thermal units (Btu) in 1975 to 43.18 quadrillion Btu in 2001, according to official government statistics. Though the bulk of total Chinese energy demand will continue to come from industrial activities for the foreseeable future, the transportation sector is beginning to represent an increasing share of total energy use. In fact, at a per capita gross domestic product (GDP) growth rate of 5 percent, the Baker Institute projects that energy demand in the transportation sector could triple by 2015, fueling a sharp increase in oil and petroleum product use.[12]

Figure 11.1 illustrates the share of the world total primary energy supply (TPES) in 1980 and 2000 for developing Asia (exclusive of China), China, the rest of Asia, the United States, and the rest of the world. It is apparent from figure 11.1 that TPES in the countries in Asia, in particular developing Asia, is growing relative to the rest of the world. In 2000, developing Asia (including China) represented approximately 46 percent of the total world population, and roughly 21 percent of the total world output (measured as GDP). During the same period (1980–2000), energy use in developing Asia rose from about 9.5 to 18 percent of the world total. This rising share

Figure 11.1.  Share of World Total Primary Energy Supply by Selected Regions, 1980 and 2000

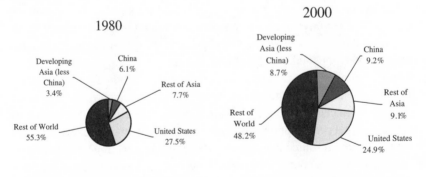

*World TPES = 285 quadrillion Btu*          *World TPES = 397 quadrillion Btu*

*Note:* TPES = total primary energy supply; Btu = British thermal unit.
*Source:* U.S. Energy Information Administration, *International Energy Annual, 2002* (Washington, D.C.: U.S. Energy Information Administration, 2002).

of total world energy use is correlated to the tremendous economic progress in developing Asia, and energy use is expected to increase further as the economies and populations of key Asian countries continue to expand.

Chinese energy consumption is almost nine times that in Australia and almost twice that in Japan. However, energy use per person in Australia is almost ten times that in China, and Japanese energy use per person is almost seven times that in China. Population and the level of economic development (measured as real GDP per capita) are the two primary factors that account for this disparity. China's population is approximately sixty-six times that of Australia and ten times that of Japan, while China's GDP per capita (in 1995 purchasing-power-parity dollars is roughly 14 percent of Australia's and 15 percent of Japan's. According to work by Medlock and Soligo, a 5 percent per capita GDP growth rate in China to 2020 (which is modest by most accounts) will result in an increase in per capita energy use to about 61 billion Btu per person.[13] Assuming an annual population growth rate of 0.7 percent, and ignoring the effects of price and new technology, this translates into an energy consumption of about 88 quadrillion Btu, or an increase of about 4.4 percent a year.

However, in an attempt to avoid becoming highly susceptible to political instability in oil-producing regions and other geopolitical forces, it is possible that China will adopt aggressive policies to prevent such an unfettered expansion. China has long prided itself on its past ability to maintain self-sufficiency for most primary materials needed for its economy, and it will be inclined to pursue strategies that can minimize its exposure to forces outside its national control. It is likely to pursue policies that will support a reduction in its energy intensity (defined as energy use per unit of economic output). Economic liberalization has and will continue to contribute to reductions in energy intensity by encouraging higher efficiency in production. In the 1990s, the Chinese government encouraged larger-scale production in energy-intensive industries, contributing to higher output per unit consumption of energy (or lower energy intensity) in certain industrial sectors.[14] As David Fridley and his colleagues note in a recent article, "Such self-reliance has involved the production of domestic resources regardless of cost, the artificial suppression of demand and the promotion of investment in overseas resources by state companies."[15]

China's intense state-led restructuring of key industries as China prepared to join the World Trade Organization—in textiles, building materials, ferrous and nonferrous metals, and coal mining—led to a decline of 79 million metric tons in coal consumption in those industries from 1996 to 1999.[16]

More recently, China has been preparing to impose strict minimum fuel economy standards for new cars by 2005. The move is aimed to enhance the country's energy security, according to senior Chinese officials.[17] In other such efforts, voluntary agreements are being considered between industry and government in such sectors as iron and steel to implement targets from improvements in industrial efficiency.[18] The country is also encouraging higher standards for new plants in important sectors like petrochemicals, and it is promoting the development of standards and certification programs for appliances and industrial equipment.

Furthermore, the Chinese government has embarked on programs to enhance the sale of vehicles that are operated with either liquefied petroleum gas or compressed natural gas. To the extent that new automobile technologies replace existing traditional combustion engine systems, projections for large rises in oil use in Asia beyond the period 2010–15 could be overstated. Nevertheless, despite the promise of these efforts, internal political hurdles remain as witnessed by the fact that a recent proposal to raise the level of the country's gasoline sales tax has failed to be passed by the National People's Congress.

## A Case for Natural Gas: An Issue of Environment

Carbon emissions in Asia are disproportionately high, primarily because of the large share of coal in total energy consumption. In fact, much of this can be tied to China. In 2000, Chinese carbon emissions accounted for almost 40 percent (775 million metric tons) of total Asian emissions, and 76 percent of carbon emissions in China were from coal use. Per capita emissions in China are far below the world average, standing at 0.61 metric tons of carbon. Nevertheless, economic growth and the accompanying increase in energy use per person will lead to large increases in total carbon emissions. In fact, gross carbon emissions in China will most likely exceed those in the United States by 2010, making China the single largest emitter of carbon in the world.[19] China's per capita carbon dioxide emissions could rise from 2.44 to 3.77 metric tons by 2010. To put this in a regional context, a Baker Institute study indicates that the region's three most populous countries, China, India, and Indonesia, could produce up to 2.0 billion tons of carbon annually in 2010.[20]

Cleaner, more efficient emerging technologies in the fields of transportation and power generation could play a positive role in reducing emissions in emerging economies where major infrastructure investments remain to be made. In the United States, the George W. Bush administration has invited China to participate in its carbon sequestration pilots and to join in multinational hydrogen research initiatives as part of an effort to address the problem of emissions on the global level.[21] These policies, which have room for expansion, could make a constructive contribution to reduce pending energy rivalries between China and the United States and its allies as well as lessen environmental tensions.

The effects of transnational pollution could be a source of instability in Northeast Asia but will be hard to tackle, according to some analysts.[22] Given the other pressing social, economic, and health challenges facing China, its leaders are unlikely to make the control of greenhouse gases a major priority. For developing countries like China to take effective action on global warming, they will need to be compensated until the net cost is acceptable. However, localized pollution resulting from the heavy use of coal, such as the emissions of sulfur oxides and nitrous oxides, may force China to switch to other resources where possible. In fact, domestic pressures already exist to reduce these types of emissions, as well as other pollutants associated with the burning of coal and other fossil fuels. Though international pressures to reduce carbon emissions have not yet played a major role, tensions over environmental issues are likely to influence Asian politics in the future. The development of additional hydroelectric or nuclear facilities remains an option for the leadership in China but carries a host of problems, including a lack of capital funding in the case of hydropower or, in the case of nuclear power, uranium supply and waste disposal issues and negative public sentiment. Thus, increasing natural gas consumption is a popular alternative now being pursued, not only in China but in other Asian countries as well.

Natural gas has tended to be underutilized in the Asia-Pacific region, despite its economic and environmental benefits. As of 2000, the share of natural gas in the region was only 10.2 percent of primary energy supply, compared with the world's share of 22.7 percent.[23] Asian natural gas market development has been held back by geography where prolific regional gas resources were distant from key end-user markets and in many cases were separated by an ocean or other major waterway. But increasingly, liquefied natural gas (LNG) projects are being organized to bring gas to consumers in southern China and coastal India, and massive cross-border natural gas pipeline projects are under consideration.

China has targeted natural gas use to expand from 3 percent in 2000 to

10 percent by 2020.[24] In India, natural gas supplies constituted about 7 percent of total energy consumption in 2000, but this could double in the coming decade as gas use in the electricity sector rises rapidly.[25] Furthermore, new LNG terminal facilities and pipeline projects aimed at bringing Russian, Australian, and other international supplies are under implementation in Japan, China, and India. Among China's most ambitious natural gas projects is the development of domestic resources in the Tarim Basin of Xinjiang Province and the construction of a 4,000-kilometer pipeline that would carry 1.2 to 1.9 billion cubic feet a day of natural gas from these Western Chinese fields across the country to Shanghai.

## Oil Geopolitics and Asia

In the 1970s, as the West struggled with the near insurmountable challenges presented by two successive Middle Eastern oil crises, the problem failed to grab the attention of Asian elites, with a few exceptions, such as Japan. Many Asian powers, notably India, China, South Korea, and Indonesia, were energy self-sufficient during that period and thus were naturally shielded from the economic and political dislocation associated with the West's first big policy lessons in the imperative of energy security strategy.

Thirty years later, Asian leaders are suddenly facing the same dilemmas seen in the West three decades earlier. Strong economic growth—led by industrialization and the rise of a large middle class clamoring for consumer goods—has dramatically increased oil use in the region, converting major regional powers, previously self-sufficient in energy supply, to oil-importer status. As Asian oil imports have grown and with it, vulnerability to short-term supply disruptions, energy security concerns have moved to the forefront of policy focus in such capitals as Beijing, New Delhi, and Seoul. This trend is likely to accelerate in the coming years as oil becomes an increasingly important fuel for local economies.

As energy security has moved to a first-order priority around Asia, worries about competition or even confrontation over energy supplies and lines of transport have gained prominence in policy deliberations. In his 1997 book *Asia's Deadly Triangle,* Kent Calder warned that "expansionist, confrontational strategies, not to mention the acquisition of nuclear weapons, offer some attractive prospects of gain to regional powers, such as preferential access to energy resources and sea-lanes in the South China Sea."[26] In an analysis that became common wisdom among China watchers, Calder noted that this strategic rivalry, if unchecked, represents "a recipe for disaster" and will increase the likelihood of conflict in Asia. Calder's view, however, implies a certain worldwide scarcity of energy resources that might not actually materialize.

The reopening of areas in the Middle East and former Soviet Union to Western investment and technology—combined with technological advances in oil and gas exploration and recovery methods and improvements in energy efficiency in the transport and power sectors—could mean that world oil markets might just as easily be grossly oversupplied ten years hence as starved for supply.[27] Notes Michael May, "China's growing need for oil need not roil oil markets nor drive up oil prices beyond where they would go anyway . . . when present conventionally recoverable oil reserves run low, which may happen before the middle of the next century, the very large higher priced oil resources available put a lid on oil prices."[28]

Under a scenario where oil consumers face diverse, ample supplies and substitutes, more congenial policies such as energy market deregulation and regional integration, cooperative infrastructure and stockpiling ventures, and joint investment in technological innovation might be enough to assuage Asian security analysts, thereby tempering the impulse toward more competitive, warmongering-style solutions. Daniel Yergin and his colleagues argue that in the future, "stresses can be resolved not through massive armies and blue-water navies, but through markets and investment within the ever-denser web of international commerce."[29] Yergin's vision rests on the reality that the massive energy infrastructure investments required throughout Asia will require cooperation between neighboring and distant powers, superseding nationalistic or ideological urges.[30]

## The Case of China

The premise that a hegemonic China will act with aggressive military force to grab needed energy supply is not supported by recent experience. As Felix Chang points out, the long-standing border dispute between China and Vietnam in the Gulf of Tonkin was settled in late 2000 with a political accord, not a naval battle, despite brief armed clashes in the Paracel and Spratly Islands in 1974 and 1988.[31] Still, though unlikely to prompt military conflict, the geopolitical implications of China's shift to a world energy importer will be significant. Over the next ten to twenty years, China will have to participate in international energy trade on a substantial and sustained basis, forming alliances for energy supply and transportation and making security and environmental choices about fulfilling its future burgeoning energy needs.

Chinese security and foreign policy analysts are debating such changes from a variety of perspectives. Wu Lei of Yunnan University posits that China opposed the U.S. 2003 military campaign in Iraq in part because of its strategic interest in Middle Eastern oil:

> Oil price rises related to Middle East tensions inevitably lift China's oil import bill. According to customs statistics, China witnessed its first trade deficit in its foreign trade history in January 2003 due to the rise of the oil price. In January, China's import of crude oil amounted to 8.36 million tons, up 77.2 percent from the corresponding period last year, with an average import cost up by 51 percent resulting in a net import cost increase of $1.10 billion. The rapid growth of oil imports and the rise of oil prices are the major elements behind the trade deficit.[32]

He adds that U.S. victory over Iraq gives it a "tighter grip" over Middle Eastern oil, a development that causes "worry and concerns" in China.

Other Chinese analysts discuss other strategic problems created by the U.S. military dominance of oil sea-lanes of communications. A military analyst, Wang Haiyun, argues that in light of American dominance of Asian sea-lanes, an overland source of oil, such as pipeline supplies from Russia or Central Asia, could be critical to China in the event of a future conflict with the United States over the status of Taiwan.[33] But others note that if China's military power was not strong enough to prevent a U.S. blockade of oil routes by sea, then it would be equally hard for China to avoid the destruction of domestic energy infrastructure, including cross-border pipelines, by war.[34] The United States would have difficulty enforcing a full physical blockade of China's coastline, but it could try to orchestrate an international oil trade embargo under certain extreme conflict scenarios, combined with air attacks on shipping into China's main ports and other energy infrastructure. The reality of U.S. power could create an opening for it to encourage China to explore joint energy strategies that would reduce Beijing's need for oil imports, lessening fears China might have of U.S. blockage and easing future rivalry for oil supply from the Middle East.

As its security literature demonstrates, China's expected import dependency has left it with some tough choices. These choices remain an opening for a shrewd U.S. initiative but so far have not been well-tapped, with China focusing instead on improved relations with oil-exporting countries rather than alliances with major consumers. Many Chinese analysts recognize that U.S. and Chinese energy interests are converging. "Both countries hope for a stable supply and price in international markets. The two countries have a lot in common in terms of maintaining a reliable, safe and constant oil supply globally and preventing international oil supply from being disrupted and oil prices from going up too sharply."[35]

Beijing appears to be resisting the tendency to focus solely on increased purchases from the Middle East, though its policies also acknowledge that increases in oil imports from that region will be unavoidable. In 1986, China's State Planning Commission, acknowledging that its domestic oil industry could not maintain oil self-sufficiency in light of the country's growing energy demand, officially gave the go-ahead to allow foreign crude imports.[36] By 1996, squarely facing the emerging trend of rising oil imports and flagging domestic oil production, China unveiled a plan to attain about a third of its energy needs through international exploration and acquisition activities.[37]

The impetus for the internationalization program was created by a sudden surplus of cash within the 1996 budget of the China National Petroleum Corporation (CNPC)—which it feared would be diverted if CNPC did not utilize the funds rapidly. Thus, CNPC quickly initiated investments in international oil fields in 1996–97 in such countries as Sudan, Venezuela, Kazakhstan, and Peru—which all had existing exploration rights tender rounds and with which CNPC stood a good chance of winning acreage quickly (table 11.1). China also pursued oil deals with Iraq and Iran.

China made its first investment in Central Asia in June 1997. CNPC agreed to purchase 60 percent of Kazakhstan's Aktyubinsk Oil Company for $4.3 billion and announced plans to build a $3.5 billion, 3,000-kilometer pipeline linking western Kazakhstan with its own Xinjiang region.[38] In announcing its investment, China said it hoped to secure significant, long-term supplies of crude oil. This project, however, has yet to develop.

China is faced with the same endemic problems that have prevented the building of significant pipelines proposed by other countries and consortiums in Central Asia. Not only are the economics of the pipeline projects tenuous, mainly due to the lack of proved reserves in the region, but there are also other matters, such as ethnic and social unrest, in almost all the newly formed states. Accordingly, it remains unclear whether China will be able to acquire major oil imports from Central Asia in the coming years. Attempts to purchase a stake in the large Kashagan field in 2002 were rebuffed by the field's

*Table 11.1.  Chinese Oil Foreign Direct Investment Projects, 1997*

| No. | Country and Projects | Year Signed | Contracted Investments (millions of dollars) | |
| | | | Total Value | Foreign Inputs |
| --- | --- | --- | --- | --- |
| 1 | Sudan, 1/2/4 blocks | 1996 | 187.37 | 105.38 |
| 2 | Sudan, 6 blocks | | 3.02 | |
| 3 | Sudan refinery | March 1997 | 56.20 | 28.11 |
| 4 | Kazakhstan, Arkbinsk | 1997 | 91.33 | |
| 5 | Kazakhstan, Uzen | September 1997 | 64.08 | 44.16 |
| 6 | Venezuela | 1997 | 82.59 | |
| 7 | Peru, 6/7 blocks | 1997 | 6.14 | |
| 8 | Iraq, Al-Ahdab | MOU[a] 1997 | Survey work | |
| 9 | Nigeria | | 26.09 | 13.04 |
| 10 | Canada, JV | | 1.80 | |
| | Total | | 518.8 | |

[a]MOU = memorandum of understanding.
*Source:* China National Petroleum Corporation, *Statistical Report.*

existing stakeholders, and CNPC's existing fields at Uzen and Aktyubinsk have yielded disappointing production rates.

Given the competition China has faced from American, European, and Japanese firms in acquiring acreage in countries of the former Commonwealth of Independent States, some Chinese researchers have also remarked that China should focus its international exploration drive on countries where Western firms cannot impede its activities, perhaps demonstrating that such competition has proven counterproductive. Chinese oil industry sources say CNPC's lack of legal and financial deal-making expertise compared with the international oil majors has made it difficult to acquire acreage, prompting CNPC to investigate countries where it might have a competitive advantage. Countries under unilateral U.S. oil sanctions are considered a prime investment target for this reason, as are countries from the former Soviet Union that are less receptive to U.S. influences.

"Western monopoly capital, with the support and assistance of their governments, has scrambled and seized the main oil and gas resource markets in all parts of the world. Almost all good resources markets in the world have been occupied and possessed by them," notes Xia Yishan. "There is intense competition among different groups of Western monopoly capital. All of them will certainly try even harder to impede Chinese companies from obtaining these oil resources. This will cause certain obstruction to our implementation of the 'going out' strategy."[39]

The possibility that China could be more successful in places where U.S. sanctions are blocking competition finds its roots in China's strong success in Sudan. CNPC signed an exploration and production agreement with the Sudanese government for blocks 1, 2, and 4, and CNPC agreed to finish a 1.54-million-kilometer pipeline, which was completed in May 1999 to the Port of Sudan. Sudan is now exporting 260,000 bpd of oil, with China holding a 40 percent stake in operations there.

The China Petroleum Engineering Construction Corporation and the Great Wall Drilling Company (GWDC) have several services to support CNPC's exploration and development efforts in Sudan, and they also have plans to expand activities elsewhere in Africa, including Nigeria, Chad, and possibly Niger and Equatorial Guinea. The GWDC has contracts in Sudan and Egypt, among other countries. China has also begun expanding arms trade and cooperation in Africa in many of the same countries. CNPC is also looking at acreage in Algeria, Tunisia, and Libya, according to interviews with its officials.

China's activities in Africa and North Africa have geopolitical overtones as well as commercial roots.[40] First, China has been working steadily over the years to enhance its relationships with African and other states to garner more support in international forums such as the United Nations for its positions, especially on the question of the status of Taiwan. In addition, China would also like to enhance its leadership role in the developing world to build up its superpower global stature. Chinese trade and military delegation visits to Africa are often accompanied by statements regarding Taiwan by the host African states, and it is clear that China would like to enlist as many countries as possible to support its position on "one China." China has also shown an inclination to counterbalance oil trade deficits with sales of Chinese goods, in many cases also including the sales of military equipment. This trend is already emerging in West Africa, potentially introducing a further destabilizing feature to that region.

The Chinese energy literature has also pointed out the benefits of expanding relations with oil-producing states that have troubled relations with the United States. China may see such ties as an important protection against any U.S. attempt to implement an oil embargo against China. Relations with producing countries that are not "friendly" with the United States would ensure that China has access to oil from some producing nations that would be unwilling to support American-imposed sanctions.[41]

China's efforts to increase its imports from Russia have put it in direct competition with Japan. Before its tax problems surfaced, the large Russian oil firm Yukos signed with CNPC, on May 28, 2003, a general agreement outlining terms for the export over twenty-five years of up to 600,000 bpd via a pipeline from Angarsk to Daqing. The Yukos project, however, met resistance from the Russian state-owned pipeline monopoly Transnft and the well-connected firm Rosneft, which favored the construction of a longer, more expensive $6 to $8 billion Angarask–Nakhodka route across Eastern Siberia to the Pacific Ocean that would allow shipments to Japan, South Korea, and possibly the U.S. West Coast. While noting that the Nakhodka route might incur losses at its initial stage, advocates for the longer pipeline in the Russian state-owned firms warned against a China route that would allow CNPC to dictate purchase terms because it would be the line's sole consumer. Russia recently suffered a setback when Turkey cut purchases from the newly built Blue Stream line. The Nakhodka route, it is argued, would allow Eastern Siberian crude exporters to capture the pricing of the international market.

The Kremlin has shown its inclination toward the Nakhodka routing, and Japan has offered billions of dollars in soft loans to help finance the pipeline, which has been proposed to carry 1 mmbpd through very challenging terrain. There has also been other evidence of Moscow's reservations regarding long-term energy relations with China since Moscow banned CNPC from bidding to purchase Russia's eighth largest oil company, Slavneft.[42] Proposals exist to build both lines to Asia or to construct a compromise route that would fork at the Chinese border to serve both destinations, but Russian officials have warned that continued delays in Asian-bound pipeline projects are probable. Russian prime minister Mikhail Kasyanov, following his September 2003 visit to Beijing, noted that the pipeline might not be built until 2013, citing four reasons for delay: environmental concerns, a lack of confirmed oil resources, the need for further technical study, and Moscow's strategic concerns about maintaining control over developing East Siberia.[43]

In fact, the timing of most of Russia's Far Eastern and East Siberian projects have been put at risk by the emerging battle between Russia's government and state-controlled monopolies on the one hand and its private oil firms on the other. Russian oil supplies to East Asia from the Sakhalin fields could reach as high as 500,000 bpd in addition to significant natural gas exports, but these will depend on the pace and level of investment that can move forward.

A Chinese failure to line up alternative supplies from Russia and Central Asia will mean that Beijing, like its other East Asian neighbors, will face increased reliance on Persian Gulf oil. Such reliance seems to imply that

China will suffer the same negative consequences as Japan, the United States, and Europe if the military equipment it, or others, pass to regimes such as Iran is used to interdict the free flow of oil from the Middle East or elsewhere.

However, it remains to be seen if China's energy interests will be enough to alter its military's perceptions of its own more general strategic interests, particularly on the issue of weapons nonproliferation. China may continue to perceive a benefit in diverting U.S. strategic engagement away from Asia. China's leaders may view larger strategic interests in Asia—beyond the energy sector—as better served by diverting U.S. diplomatic attention and military assets away from the Asian theater to places like the Middle East. This latter interpretation of Chinese interests will depend greatly on Beijing's perceptions of U.S. intentions—both in the short and in the long terms—and their potential risk to China.

China views the possibility of access to Iranian oil and gas, through a continental pan-Asian energy land bridge, as a fundamental, strategic attraction.[44] China made a written pledge to refrain from engaging in new nuclear cooperation with Iran and agreed to halt cruise missile sales during a visit by Chinese leader Jiang Zemin in 1997. Nonetheless, some analysts cite reports that China has continued to help Iran build a missile factory at Isfahan and improve its Zelsal-3 missile program, providing guidance and other advanced technologies.[45]

However, it is important not to overdraw the case of a link between China's rising need for oil and its military sales. That link was particularly weak in the 1990s, when Chinese arms sales generally fell from $2 billion to $500 million, with a markedly abrupt decline in sales to the Middle East.[46] The drop is thought to be related to the poor quality of Chinese technology when compared with other suppliers rather than Chinese restraint, but China did agree to bring its missile export policy in line with the Missile Technology Control Regime in 2000. The Chinese decision has been linked with publicly announced declaration of concerns for the strategic stability of the Middle East so as to assure no disruptions in oil supply,[47] boding well for joint strategic interests in nonproliferation to the region between China and Western industrial countries.

Still, China's inclination to pursue bilateral oil relationships rather than join in consumer-country strategies remains a possible challenge for the West. As long as China stresses bilateral arrangements, it will be more vulnerable to pressure from energy regions, including those seeking sensitive military equipment not being made available by the West. China's military will also be called upon for light arms that might fuel regionalized conflicts and civil wars such as that in Sudan in 2004.

Already, the thirst for oil has convinced Beijing of the concrete benefits that could be reaped by taking advantage of U.S. sanctions policies. China's oil industry is reaping spoils in the Sudan, has planted its flag in Iran (and in Iraq, before the U.S. military campaign there) and dabbled with overtures to Libya. China is also courting other potentially unstable oil-producing countries in North and West Africa, and it is bringing a political as well as economic agenda to bear on these new relations.[48] Beijing's agenda will also include the development of stronger ties with the largest oil power, Saudi Arabia, potentially offering the Saudis an expanding alternative market to the United States and Japan.

The challenge for the United States and its allies will be to convince an ambitious, energy-hungry China that a secure energy supply for all concerned will depend on a cooperative foreign policy that seeks to minimize geopolitical rivalry and lessen the chances for disruptive armed conflict in oil-producing areas. Bilateral approaches during periods when oil markets are tight, such times of civil wars and Middle Eastern conflict, can lead to increased pressure from oil suppliers for political concessions in exchange for a stable supply. The United States and Europe have faced similar problems, especially in the 1970s, and have taken certain unified policy steps, such as membership in the International Energy Agency (IEA) to lessen exposures. China has announced plans to have a twenty-day oil reserve at four sites by 2010, with the first oil in place by 2006.

China has yet to seriously consider a multilateral alliance with other oil-consuming countries. Instead, China has reached out in greater measure to individual oil-exporting countries. This presents new challenges for the United States as it seeks to forge constructive approaches to a China on the rise. Energy cooperation, initially greeted merely as a possible ice-breaker toward warmer relations between Washington and Beijing, might actually be an important element in a stable United States–China relationship. Moreover, it might be a necessary ingredient for an effective bilateral United States–China weapons nonproliferation agenda.

Perhaps not coincidentally, China's approaches are beginning to be mirrored in Indian energy policy. India's state-owned concern, the Indian Oil Corporation, buys about 70 percent of its oil under long term contracts, mainly from the Middle East, Nigeria and Malaysia. The Indian Oil Corporation is reported to have set aside $1 billion for an upstream oil field acquisition program abroad.[49] Indian state-owned oil concerns purchased

Canadian Talisman's 25 percent stake in the Greater Nile Petroleum Operating Company of Sudan, in which China's CNPC is a partner. The Indian Oil Corporation is also negotiating for exploration acreage in Qatar and pursuing an investment in the Farsi block in Iran. Indian firms have also staked out post-UN sanctions exploration arrangements for blocks in Iraq's western desert as well. Still, while holding well-established military ties with Saudi Arabia, Iran, Qatar, Oman, and Israel, India has not sold significant arms or military technology to the Gulf states—consistent with its general track record of restraint on exporting sensitive nuclear and missile technologies.

## India and Japan

India, like China, has also engaged in discussions with the IEA, but so far no coordination has been agreed on. Until recently, India held only very small oil stocks, but it has been forced to enhance oil security measures in light of escalating tensions with Pakistan. For example, India reportedly built an oil storage depot at Leh in Kashmir in September 2003. The depot also holds extra supplies of jet fuel, allowing for refueling of war planes. A plan is now circulating in New Delhi to build strategic oil reserves that could supply up to sixty days of India's demand. India's existing storage capacity at domestic refineries is inadequate to hold extra stocks of this size.[50] Previous discussions of a national strategic oil reserve have been stalled by the costs of storage and transportation infrastructure.

India and China are by no means the only countries pursuing a bilateral foreign investment approach to energy security. The state-owned Japan National Oil Corporation has spent billions of dollars trying to amass profitable equity oil to import back home. Japan has utilized its diplomatic muscle to lobby for a share of the giant Azagadan oil field in Iran and has substantial investments abroad, including shares in fields in Russia and the Caspian Sea Basin. In fact, Japan is now the largest bilateral aid donor to each of the major prospective energy producers of the Caspian region.[51]

## Rivalry and Energy Cooperation

It is feared that this pursuit of individual country investments abroad by the Asian powers will fuel geopolitical rivalry and potentially raise regional tensions, in contrast to more constructive (and probably more effective) strategies such as joint stockpiling. Though equity oil is attained at prices competitive to spot market cargo levels, oil production "owned" in the Middle East can be just as easily disrupted as oil exports to be purchased as a third party. And as the international oil companies have learned the hard way, foreign equity oil can become arbitrarily subject to the individual country production restraints of the Organization of Petroleum Exporting Countries, denying its owner the right to export barrels home. Moreover, regular equity oil shipments offer only minor assistance in bringing down overall market prices in times of crisis, leaving Asian consumers almost unprotected from disruption-inspired price gyrations, despite the billions of dollars that might have been invested in oil fields in the Middle East or elsewhere. In the global, deregulated marketplace, oil export prices will clear to the highest bidder, regardless of how much money or how many arms a particular client may have invested in any given oil-producing country. By contrast, jointly held, strategic stocks can actually be used to lower prices during a supply emergency, providing Asian consumers with greater security and "public goods" at a smaller initial investment.

The link between Asian oil stockpiling and the continued effectiveness of the IEA system will become increasingly important in the coming years as Asian oil use grows. The IEA's member countries now represent a smaller portion of the oil market than they did at the time of its formation in 1977. As oil demand growth in Asia expands in the coming decade, new strains could come to the international system if new policies are not put in place. The omission of key consumer countries from Asia into the global emergency stockpiling system will increasingly put pressure on the effectiveness of limited, existing stocks in the Organization for Economic Cooperation and Development (OECD) countries. Moreover, tensions created by Asian "free riding" or possible Chinese or Indian "hoarding" actions during a crisis could hinder the IEA's ability to stabilize international oil markets in the future.

The OECD countries making up the IEA represented 42.3 mmbpd out of a total world oil use of 60.6 mmbpd in 1977, or about 70 percent of world oil demand. The United States alone consumed 30 percent of the world's oil used in 1977. The Asia-Pacific region's demand at that time was a less critical component of the world oil use situation at 10.1 mmbpd, or roughly 16 percent of world oil demand.

By 2001, the OECD's oil use had declined to 62 percent of total world demand, while the Asia-Pacific region's use had grown to 28 percent, overtaking the U.S. share of 25 percent. Japan, South Korea, Australia, and New

Zealand are OECD members and now part of the IEA system, but other key Asian oil consumers such as China, India, Taiwan, Thailand, Philippines, and Pakistan are not. As their share of world oil demand grows, the disconnect between Asia's size and importance as a consumer region and its lack of energy policy coordination with other large oil-consuming countries (and/or the IEA) will create new problems and challenges for international oil markets and the international economic system. Thus, pulling major Asian developing countries into a formal role in the global oil emergency stockpiling system should be a priority for energy cooperation in Northeast Asia and an important element of U.S. diplomacy toward the region.

## Conclusion: Options for the United States

No matter how bright the prospects for cooperation on energy could be in Asia, the policy responses from each individual Asian player will in the end determine whether such joint efforts produce the desired fruits of energy security and diversification. The United States has a critical role to play in helping shape an energy future for Asia that is in line with its own interests in oil supply and price stability, energy diversification, and crisis management. By harboring inclinations to "contain" China's energy influence abroad and block their investment and infiltration in Central Asia, the actions of Russia and certain countries in the Persian Gulf have had the counterproductive result of fueling geopolitical rivalry and prompting China to countermand U.S. economic sanctions. China has assisted countries with hostile or tense relations with the United States, including oil-exporting countries under unilateral U.S. economic trade sanctions such as Iran.

Still, despite emerging geopolitical and diplomatic rivalries, a Chinese military challenge to the United States in the Middle East or other key oil-producing regions seems remote. Analysts of Asian energy security should make no mistake that China has concrete strategic interests in Asian sea-lanes linked to energy concerns, among other issues, as well as a major commitment to its own military strength. In light of the limitations on China's own force-projection capabilities, these interests will be best served, at least for many years to come, through cooperation and strategic partnerships. It is precisely the U.S. guarantee of equal access to all Asia's sea-lanes that allows China to fulfill its strategic energy requirements. A U.S. military asset drawdown in the Pacific, which might open space for security competition—for example, between China and Japan—to fill the vacuum would be far more dangerous to Asian stability than the potential for a Chinese challenge to the status quo.

The United States presently has a window of opportunity to pursue cooperative energy policies that will help China feel more secure about its energy security, thereby reducing the stimulus to conflict. U.S. political and military leaders should communicate clearly with their Chinese counterparts about areas of emerging mutual interest, particularly regarding energy security issues in the Persian Gulf. Discussions of weapons proliferation should be broached in the context of converging geopolitical interests related to oil. China should also be engaged at the highest level to participate constructively and collaboratively with the United States in Middle Eastern diplomacy, including the Arab-Israeli peace process and the reconstruction of Iraq.

Initiatives that assist China in developing cleaner energy sources can also enhance Western environmental goals. Funding and research for alternative energy and development of joint strategies for conservation, stockpiling and the enhancement of energy-efficient technologies will be more effective if taken together rather than alone.[52] In the interest of energy security and the environment, the United States should continue to support, and even expand, multilateral efforts to bring China into programs for the research, development, and deployment of energy-efficient technologies, alternative fuels, and carbon sequestration, including through existing and potential new programs at the World Bank, U.S. Export-Import Bank, and Asian Development Bank. The Chinese government should also be encouraged to increase transparency in its energy statistics, analysis, and collection as an aspect of its participation in multilateral programs and institutions. By sharing resources and information in a coordinated fashion, major oil-consuming countries garner great protection against would-be oil-producer monopoly power and exposure to supply disruptions or political instability.

Despite recent resistance, the United States should continue to press China to create a strategic petroleum reserve capable of covering ninety days of imports, which is the same level as required in the IEA, and to convince China of the benefits of coordinating actions with the IEA in case of an international oil supply disruption. Beyond the co-optation of China into the multilateral emergency response system of the IEA, the United States should find other ways to encourage China to develop its trade relations with oil-exporting countries on a nondiscriminatory, nonspecial case basis. The best vehicle for accomplishing this is the World Trade Organization, by developing universal trade rules in the organization that will impede members from politicizing energy relations.

The United States should also encourage and assist China in enhancing its natural gas industry as a means of diversifying its energy portfolio and reducing its heavy reliance on coal. This could also serve to enlarge the international energy supply pool and contribute to stated international environmental goals. To accomplish this, several measures could be pursued. The U.S. Department of Energy could be supported strongly in its efforts to provide information and assistance about natural gas market regulation, operation, and development. Western government support and trade credits could be provided to energy companies that invest in major natural gas infrastructure projects in China. And the United States could communicate its support of Chinese imports of Russian gas.

## Notes

1. Kenneth B. Medlock III and Ron Soligo, *The Composition and Growth in Energy Supply in China* (Houston: James A. Baker III Institute for Public Policy, 1999).

2. Amy Myers Jaffe and Steven W. Lewis, "Beijing's Oil Diplomacy," *Survival,* Spring 2002, 115–33.

3. See Qiang Wu and Xuemei Xian, "China's Energy Cooperation with the Middle East," *Strategy and Management,* no. 2 (1999): 51; John Calabrese, "China and the Persian Gulf: Energy and Security," *Middle East Journal,* Summer 1998, 351–66; Sergei Troush, *China's Changing Oil Strategy and Its Foreign Policy Implications* (Washington, D.C.: Brookings Institution, 1999), available at http://www.brookings.org/fp/cnaps/papers/1999_troush.html.

4. For detailed discussion of such issues, see Robert A. Manning, *The Asian Energy Factor* (New York: Palgrave, 2002); Michael T. Klare, *Resource Wars* (New York: Henry Holt, 2001); and Kent Calder, "Asia's Empty Tank," *Foreign Affairs,* March/April 1996, 55–69.

5. See testimony by Amy Myers Jaffe, Guy Caruso, and Edward Morse before the Commission on U.S.–China Economic and Security Relations, Hearing on China's Energy Needs and Strategies, October 30, 2003.

6. Medlock and Soligo, *Composition and Growth in Energy Supply in China.*

7. Oil Market Intelligence Database, *Petroleum Intelligence Weekly* (2003).

8. Energy Intelligence Group, Oil Market Intelligence Database, July 2001.

9. Energy Intelligence Group, Oil Market Intelligence Database.

10. International Energy Agency, *World Energy Outlook 1998* (Paris: International Energy Agency, 1998).

11. Authors' projections; for a more detailed forecast, see International Energy Agency, *World Energy Outlook 1998* and *World Energy Outlook 2000* (Paris: International Energy Agency, 2000).

12. Medlock and Soligo, *Composition and Growth in Energy Supply in China;* and

Kenneth B. Medlock III and Ronald Soligo, "Economic Development and End-Use Energy Demand," *Energy Journal,* April 2001.

13. This calculation is made using the results derived in Medlock and Soligo, *Composition and Growth in Energy Supply in China.* Specifically, they show the income elasticity of energy demand to be a decreasing function of income per capita. Thus, given any level of per capita income, a corresponding elasticity can be calculated. A 5 percent growth rate would lead to a Chinese per capita income of close to $10,000. According to the work of Medlock and Soligo, this growth path means that China's long-run midpoint income elasticity of energy demand would be about 0.75, approximately 0.2 for Japan and Australia, and 0.16 for the United States. Note that the formula in that paper is contingent on GDP per capita denominated in 1985 purchasing-power-parity (PPP) dollars, whereas the GDP per capita values quoted here are denominated in 1995 PPP dollars. Therefore, a conversion must be made prior to calculation.

14. David Fridley, Jonathan Sinton, Joanna Lewis, and Phillip Andrews Speed, "China," *Oxford Energy Forum,* issue 53, May 2003.

15. Fridley et al., "China."

16. Fridley et al., "China."

17. Keith Bradsher, "China Set to Act on Fuel Efficiency," *New York Times,* November 18, 2003.

18. Fridley et al., "China."

19. Peter Hartley, Kenneth Medlock III, and Peter Warby, *First Things First: Development and Global Warming* (Houston: James A. Baker III Institute for Public Policy, 1999), available at http://www.bakerinstitute.org.

20. Hartley, Medlock, and Warby, *First Things First.*

21. Presentation by Robert Manning at a conference titled "Pipelines Fault Lines: The Geopolitics of Energy Security in Asia" organized by the Asia Pacific Center for Security Studies, Honolulu, October 21–23, 2003.

22. Michael M. May, *Energy and Security in East Asia* (Palo Alto, Calif.: Asia-Pacific Research Center, 1998).

23. U.S. Energy Information Agency, *International Energy Annual, 2002* (Washington, D.C.: U.S. Energy Information Agency, 2002).

24. Xiaojie Xu, *The Gas Dragon's Rise: Chinese Natural Gas Strategy and Import Patterns,* Baker Institute Working Paper, May 1998, available at http://www.bakerinstitute .org.

25. U.S. Energy Information Agency, *India: Country Analysis Brief,* available at http://www.eia.doe.gov/emeu/cabs/india.

26. Kent E. Calder, *Asia's Deadly Triangle* (London: Nicholas Brealey, 1996), 136.

27. Amy Jaffe and Robert Manning, "Cheap Oil," *Foreign Affairs* 79, no.1 (2000): 16–29.

28. May, *Energy and Security in East Asia.*

29. Daniel Yergin, Dennis Eklof, and Jefferson Edwards, "Fueling Asia's Recovery," *Foreign Affairs* 77, no. 2 (1998): 34, 36.

30. See John Ryan's description of the Asia-Pacific Economic Cooperation forum's efforts to foster regional infrastructure in chapter 12 of this volume.

31. Felix Chang, "Chinese Energy and Asian Security," *Orbis* 45, issue 2 (Spring 2001): 211.

32. Wu Lei, "Oil: The Next Conflict in Sino-US Relations," *Middle East Economic Survey* 46, no. 21 (May 26, 2003): supplement.

33. Wang Haiyun, *China's Energy Security and Energy Strategy,* China Institute of International Studies, 2001, as cited in the doctoral dissertation of Erica Downs, Princeton University.

34. Li Junfeng as quoted by Erica Downs.

35. Wu Lei, "Oil."

36. Gaye Christoffersen, "China's Intentions for Russian and Central Asian Oil and Gas," *NBR Analysis* (National Bureau of Asian Research), no. 2 (1998): 6.

37. "China's CNPC Leaps on to Global Oil Production Stage," *Petroleum Intelligence Weekly,* June 9, 1997, 3.

38. Tony Walker and Robert Corzine, "China Buys $4.3bn Kazak Oil Stake," *Financial Times,* June 5, 1997, 9.

39. Xia Yishan, "My View of China's Energy Situation and Energy Strategy" *People's Daily,* Beijing Renmin Ribao, August 10, 2001 (FBIS translation article CPP20010811000000052, Ogi5tx100hn9r2).

40. Jaffe and Lewis, "Beijing's Oil Diplomacy."

41. Wu Lei, "Middle Eastern Oil and China's Future Oil Supply and Demand Balance," *World Economics and Politics,* no. 3, 1997.

42. Bernard Cole, "China and Japan Compete for Russian Energy Supplies," paper presented at a conference titled "Pipelines and Fault Lines: The Geopolitics of Energy Security in Asia" organized by the Asia Pacific Center for Security Studies, Honolulu, October 21–23, 2003.

43. Alena Kommersant, *Mikhail Kasyanov Deprived China of Russian Oil,* FBIS-CEP20030926000227.

44. Troush, *China's Changing Oil Strategy.*

45. Chang, "Chinese Energy."

46. Philip Andrews-Speed, Xuanli Liao, and Roland Dannreuther, *The Strategic Implications of China's Energy Needs,* Adelphi Paper 346 (London: International Institute for Strategic Studies, 2002), 90.

47. Andrews-Speed, Xuanli Liao, and Dannreuther, *Strategic Implications of China's Energy Needs.*

48. For more details, see Jaffe and Lewis, "Beijing's Oil Diplomacy."

49. "Free Market Realities Drive IOC Shake-Up," *Petroleum Intelligence Weekly,* June 17, 2002.

50. "India Revives Plan for Strategic Reserve as Tensions with Pakistan Mount," *International Oil Daily,* May 23, 2002.

51. Kent E. Calder, "Japan's Energy Angst and the Caspian Great Game," *NBER Analysis* (National Bureau of Asian Research) 12, no. 1 (March 2001).

52. Jaffe and Manning, "Cheap Oil"; also see the detailed discussion of the benefits of multilateralist cooperation as consumers in Dermot Gately, "OPEC and the Buying Power Wedge," in *Energy Vulnerability,* ed. J. L. Plummer (Cambridge, Mass.: Ballinger, 1982), 37–57.

# 12

# APEC's Regional Approach to Energy Security

## *John Ryan*

The Pacific Rim region encompasses a significant proportion of the world's population and contains some of its most dynamic economies. Its economies have generally performed well in economic growth and in raising the standard of living of their citizens, despite weathering some significant economic events over the past thirty years. These include the oil price shocks of the 1970s, conflict in the Middle East, the bursting of the Japanese economic bubble, the emergence of strong economic growth in China, and more recently the East Asian economic crisis of 1998 and the instability of the international economy caused by the ongoing conflict in the Middle East. Ironically, it is the economic success of the Pacific Rim, and the increase in energy demand that this growth portends, that has led to the emergence of energy security as a significant foreign policy issue for the region's economies.

In discussing energy security in the Pacific Rim, this chapter focuses on the emerging cooperative approach to security undertaken by the economies that constitute the Asia-Pacific Economic Cooperation forum (APEC).[1] This diverse group of economies covers a wide geographic area across Southeast Asia, North Asia, the Americas, and Oceania. The economic and political linkages among APEC economies have given rise to a focus on energy

The author acknowledges the contribution of Wayne Calder in developing this chapter, and he thanks Vicki Brown, Chamandeep Chehl, Rick Miles, Aidan Storer, and Michael Whitfield for their valuable comments and Melanie Maclean for her research assistance. The views expressed in this chapter are those of the author and do not necessarily represent the views of the Australian government or its Department of Industry, Tourism, and Resources or the members of the Asia-Pacfic Economic Cooperation Energy Working Group.

security across the region and enabled the forum to engage constructively and collectively on this issue.

APEC is unique in that it is based on voluntary, nonbinding commitments among member economies, open dialogue, and consensus-driven decision making. This may appear to make APEC an unlikely choice for a discussion of a new foreign policy direction to address the growing concerns about energy security. However, APEC, through its Energy Working Group (EWG), has successfully developed a regionally based response to the challenges posed by this issue to APEC economies that has produced concrete results. Australia has taken a lead role in chairing the EWG since its inception and has provided the guidance necessary to develop the APEC Energy Security Initiative.

The Energy Security Initiative comprises a set of measures to address short-term disruptions to energy supplies. It also includes longer-term policy responses to ensure that APEC economies have access to the energy needed to meet the rapid economic growth and rising living standards that are forecast to occur in the next twenty to thirty years.

The Energy Security Initiative also demonstrates how energy security can be flexibly addressed within a framework of voluntary, nonbinding commitments to accommodate the legitimate national interests of member economies, rather than with the traditional model of treaties and mandatory obligations. It demonstrates how, within a such supportive framework, energy security can become a force for closer foreign policy and economic integration of economies instead of increased political and economic tensions. In short, APEC's regionally based response to the challenges of energy security represents, in my view, a new foreign policy prescription to address energy security in the twenty-first century.

To understand the power of APEC's example of a multilateral approach to energy security, this chapter examines APEC's unique diplomatic approach, the critical role its economies play in the future of energy demand, the energy security challenge facing APEC economies, and how APEC's EWG is addressing the issue of energy security through cooperative measures such as the APEC Energy Security Initiative.

## The Asia-Pacific Economic Cooperation Forum

APEC is the premier forum for facilitating economic growth, cooperation, trade, and investment in the Asia-Pacific region. APEC was established in

1989 to further enhance economic growth and prosperity for the region and to strengthen the Asia-Pacific community.[2]

APEC has twenty-one members—referred to as "member economies"—which account for more than a third of the world's population (2.6 billion people); approximately 60 percent of global gross domestic product, or GDP ($19,254 billion); and about 47 percent of world trade. It also represents the most economically dynamic region in the world, having generated nearly 70 percent of global economic growth in its first ten years.

Unlike the World Trade Organization or other multilateral trade bodies, APEC has no treaty obligations required of its participants. Despite being based on voluntary commitments, APEC has successfully promoted its key goals of economic growth, cooperation, and trade and investment in the Asia-Pacific region. APEC has focused on reducing nontariff trade barriers, promoting exports, and encouraging economic reform in member economies. Indeed, the open, consensus-driven approach of APEC is a strength in achieving real outcomes.

APEC's open dialogue nature gives it the flexibility to focus on the concerns of members and to meet changing regional and global circumstances. A rules-based framework requiring mandatory commitments could easily have been less successful in drawing together the interests of the culturally and economically diverse member economies that are represented by APEC.

This flexibility in addressing the divergent concerns of member economies has proven valuable in addressing the rising challenge of energy security in the APEC region. The individual circumstances facing APEC economies in relation to their endowments of energy resources, and their stages in the economic development cycle, are quite divergent. Some member economies have significant reserves of energy, while others have little or no indigenous supplies of key energy commodities. The capacity of APEC, through its EWG, to draw together the common energy security concerns of member economies demonstrates a capacity for an outcomes-oriented, multilateral approach to foreign policy.

The EWG is a subforum within APEC that works cooperatively to maximize the energy sector's contribution to the region's economic and social well-being, while mitigating the environmental effects of energy use and supply. It brings together some of the world's largest producers and consumers of energy at a governmental level, and it also includes dialogue with the business community within the APEC region. The EWG plays an important role in fostering capacity building throughout the region, both in terms of the physical infrastructure required to support economic growth and by strengthening economic and political institutions. The common objective is to promote economic and social development, leading to rising standards of living in member economies.

## The Energy Security Challenge for APEC Economies

Energy security poses several challenges for APEC's member economies. One challenge is the emergence of significant political and security issues on the global stage that can threaten the stability of energy supply to APEC economies and create volatility in the price of energy. A more direct challenge is the rapid pace of economic growth in the region and the likely increase in dependency on imported oil for the APEC economies as a whole, particularly the Asian APEC economies. For APEC economies, these factors have focused attention on the importance of foreign policy to energy security and how multilateral approaches can enhance energy security by providing a framework for economies to collectively develop responses to the challenges they are facing while recognizing their shared future.

To meet their long-term energy needs, APEC's member economies have pursued security of supply by undertaking national strategies, but they have also engaged multilaterally through the EWG to develop cooperative regional responses. A significant reason for this multilateral engagement is the economic interdependence of APEC economies.

To set the context for why energy security has become a dominant foreign policy concern for APEC economies, it is useful to consider the economic imperative that is driving these concerns. APEC member economies as a whole experienced strong economic growth in the 1990s and are projected to outpace global GDP growth through 2020.[3] Table 12.1 contains a breakdown of the forecast growth in GDP by APEC economy regional grouping. Figure 12.1 provides a comparison of the GDP growth rates of the APEC regional groupings over the period 1990–2000 and the forecast period compared with that of the forecast for world GDP growth.

APEC economies are forecast to experience 1 percent population growth during this projected period of strong economic growth. The rapid economic growth rate, coupled with moderate population growth, suggests that per capita incomes will rise in the APEC region, creating the opportunity for increased standards of living and consumption throughout the region, and an increase in per capita consumption of energy. Figure 12.2 provides

*Table 12.1.  Gross Domestic Product by APEC Regional Grouping, 1990–2020*

| Grouping | Gross Domestic Product, 1990 (billions of dollars) | | | | Average Annual Growth Rate (percent) | |
| --- | --- | --- | --- | --- | --- | --- |
| | 1990 | 1999 | 2010 | 2020 | 1990–99 | 1999–2020 |
| North America | 6,388 | 8,397 | 11,592 | 16,209 | 2.5 | 3.2 |
| Latin America | 319 | 436 | 742 | 1,057 | 2.9 | 4.3 |
| Northeast Asia | 3,538 | 4,243 | 5,407 | 6,889 | 1.7 | 2.3 |
| Southeast Asia | 338 | 519 | 866 | 1,422 | 4.0 | 4.9 |
| Oceania | 352 | 477 | 692 | 979 | 2.8 | 3.5 |
| China | 388 | 943 | 2,111 | 4,049 | 8.4 | 7.2 |
| Russia | 454 | 275 | 492 | 803 | –4.4 | 5.2 |
| APEC total | 11,777 | 15,291 | 21,901 | 31,409 | 2.4 | 3.5 |

*Note:* APEC = Asia-Pacific Economic Cooperation forum.
*Source:* Asia-Pacific Energy Research Centre, *Energy Demand and Supply Outlook 2002* (Tokyo: Asia-Pacific Energy Research Centre, 2002).

Figure 12.1.  Gross Domestic Product Growth Rate of APEC Regional Grouping and World (percent)

Percent

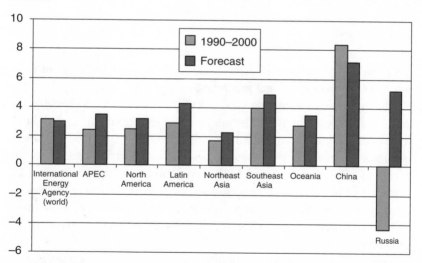

*Note:* APEC = Asia-Pacific Economic Cooperation forum.
*Sources:* Asia-Pacific Energy Research Centre, *Energy Demand and Supply Outlook 2002* (Tokyo: Asia-Pacific Energy Research Centre, 2002); and International Energy Agency, *World Energy Outlook 2002* (Paris: International Energy Agency, 2002).

Figure 12.2.  Gross Domestic Product and Population Growth by APEC
Regional Grouping

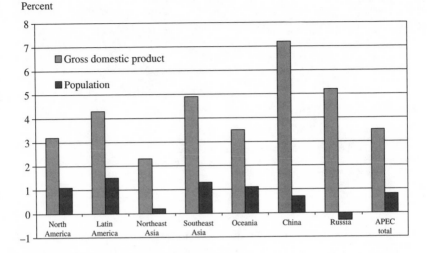

Percent

*Note:* APEC = Asia-Pacific Economic Cooperation forum.
*Source:* Asia-Pacific Energy Research Centre, *Energy Demand and Supply Outlook 2002* (Tokyo: Asia-Pacific Energy Research Centre, 2002).

a comparison of the forecast growth rates of GDP and population through-out APEC economy regional groupings.

This increase in economic growth and the concomitant increase in the demand for energy by APEC economies will exacerbate the already high level of dependency on imported oil. This dependency for APEC as a whole is forecast to increase from about 36 percent to almost 55 percent over the period to 2020. For the Asian APEC economies, this figure will reach 80 percent.[4] Given the global geopolitical environment, reliance on imports from the Middle East raises the possibility of significant supply disruptions, and the attendant economic and social dislocation that such events could precipitate.

The coalescence of rapid economic growth and rising dependency on imported oil raises national security and foreign policy issues for all APEC economies. An increased dependency on energy imports increases the vulnerability of economies to temporary supply disruptions. However, given the increasing economic integration of APEC economies, disruptions to energy supplies will have a broader impact than just on those economies with limited indigenous energy supplies; they will affect regional trade flows, growth rates, and prosperity across the region. This provides a strong impetus for APEC economies to engage multilaterally to address energy security challenges.

## The APEC Energy Working Group:
## A Multilateral Approach to Energy Security

Although there is no doubt that energy security is primarily a policy concern of sovereign governments, regional cooperation undertaken within the voluntary framework of APEC has proven to be an effective mechanism for addressing energy security issues and, more broadly, the sustainable use of energy. This type of foreign policy engagement provides an additional security dividend to APEC member economies by lowering potential tensions over energy supplies.

The potential for competition over energy supply is strong, particularly in Asia. As noted by Kent Calder:

The deadly triangle of growth, energy shortage and armament, in the context of fluid post–Cold War geo-strategic alignments, threatens to destabilise Asia, and indeed the whole Pacific. Energy shortage, the deadly but little known link in this equation, provokes turbulence by deepening the nuclear bias of Northeast Asia, by provoking new naval rivalries centering on emerging Chinese blue-water capacity, and by deepening tensions over offshore reserves such as those in the South China Sea.[5]

Such concerns are heightened by increasing oil import dependency, forecast to occur for the APEC economies. In this worldview, increases in import dependency exacerbate the vulnerabilities of economies to disruptions in energy supplies, and they create an environment whereby political tensions between neighboring economies can rise. These heightened sensitivities have typically been seen as a source of potential conflict in an environment where a number of economies are striving to achieve rapid advances in economic development, which is evident particularly within Asian APEC economies. APEC economies will pursue their own national interests in securing access to energy supplies, APEC's EWG provides the framework for these economies to also engage constructively to reduce political tensions and engage in collective action.

A number of factors have interacted to reduce the potential conflict over the availability of energy resources. The world does not face an immediate shortage of energy resources; data on proven reserves suggest that there is little prospect of an immediate shortage of oil and gas. Technological change is also likely to have a substantial impact on the supply side through the development of better exploration and extraction techniques, and on the demand side through greater energy efficiency and the development of new and renewable energy technologies. Finally, the development of international markets has given greater confidence to policymakers and consumers that commodities such as oil can be obtained even in times of crisis.

This has shifted the primary focus of energy security to addressing the potential for temporary but significant disruptions in the flow of energy supplies and ensuring that the investment in energy markets is able to support the forecast economic growth across APEC economies. The core of APEC's energy security challenge is to maintain access to sufficient energy and to attract investment for energy infrastructure to sustain strong regional economic growth. These common objectives of economic growth and prosperity have given birth to a cooperative approach. The approach developed through the EWG recognizes that though nations will pursue their own energy security strategies, an integrated strategy can prevent scarcity, or the fear of scarcity, from becoming a cause of rising tensions and conflict. As noted by Robert Manning:

> Precisely because of the strategic economic and national security implications of energy, the willingness of a nation to voluntarily link its energy fate to others in the form of a pipeline or other form of interdependence requires a certain modicum of trust and confidence. . . . In some respects, this positive national security—enhancing dimension of energy security is already beginning to be visible.[6]

## APEC's Energy Security Initiative

In recognition of the importance of ensuring reliable and cost-effective access to energy to support economic growth and development, APEC's EWG has responded proactively, under Australian leadership, to develop the Energy Security Initiative. The initiative comprises measures to respond to temporary energy supply disruptions and longer-term policy responses to address the broader challenges facing the region's energy supply. It is an example of how energy security has become a driver for the development of a new foreign policy strategy and how energy security can be a driver for cooperation and integration.

The Energy Security Initiative includes five elements addressing different aspects of the energy security challenge confronting APEC: sea-lane security, real-time information sharing, the Joint Oil Data Initiative, energy emergency response arrangements, and longer-term responses (each of which is described in detail below). The Energy Security Initiative was designed to be both practical from a policy context and politically acceptable, and it addresses sustainable development issues by strengthening the security and reliability of affordable energy.

APEC leaders endorsed a detailed implementation plan for the Energy Security Initiative, with firm time frames, at their meeting in Bangkok in October 2003. This is the first time that an APEC forum has agreed to short-term time frames for implementing activities, and it thus demonstrates the degree of commitment that exists to ensure regional energy security.

This commitment was further reinforced at the Sixth Meeting of APEC Energy Ministers on June 10, 2004, in Manila. The theme for this meeting was "Energy Security in APEC: Cooperation for a Sustainable Future," noting the dominance of energy security as an issue for APEC economies and acknowledging that cooperation throughout the region is necessary to achieve the objectives of energy security and sustainable economic growth.

As noted just above, the activities that are being undertaken as a part of the Energy Security Initiative include

- *Sea-lane security:* The Asia-Pacific Energy Research Centre (APERC)[7] hosted a sea-lane security simulation exercise in 2002 to test the effects of a major disruption to oil supplies passing through the Strait of Malacca. This is the second largest choke point in the world, with about 25 percent of world oil trade. About 10.3 million barrels per day of oil are carried through these straits, which span only 500 meters at their narrowest point. The outcome of this exercise has been the development of greater links to other relevant international groups, such as the International Maritime Organization and the APEC Transportation Working Group, to share information, expertise, and technical assistance to strengthen sea-lane security.

- *Real-Time Information Sharing System:* APEC's EWG endorsed for implementation a real-time information sharing system for oil emergencies to act as a market-calming mechanism during a crisis. This system was tested by several member economies in February 2004 and previously had operated on an informal basis during the 2003 conflict in Iraq. The Real-Time Information Sharing System is now in permanent operation.
- *Joint Oil Data Initiative:* This initiative was developed by APERC and aims to improve the transparency of global oil data in cooperation with a range of international organizations, including the International Energy Agency (IEA), the Organization of Petroleum Exporting Countries (OPEC), the European Union, the Latin American Energy Organization, and the United Nations Statistical Division. As a part of the Joint Oil Data Initiative, APEC's EWG is seeking to undertake further capacity building to develop data collection skills in APEC economies.
- *Energy emergency response arrangements:* This initiative aims to encourage all member economies to implement appropriate energy emergency response arrangements. All APEC members have agreed to develop and present their emergency response arrangements through the EWG. A range of activities in relation to managing oil emergencies and oil stockpiling have also been undertaken.[8] The EWG has developed a set of best practice principles for oil stockpiles, which will inform interested member economies in building strategic stockpiles. In addition, the EWG completed the third phase of the Earthquake Response Cooperation Program for Energy Supply Systems in 2003.

APEC's EWG is also focused on the long-term policy considerations that are essential elements of regional energy security, such as investment in energy infrastructure and the development of the region's significant reserves of natural gas. The interconnection of energy systems between economies will add to energy security by promoting increased production, distribution, and supply of energy. In addition, investment in diversifying energy supplies through alternative energy sources and improving energy efficiency will also have a major impact on energy security.

The APEC economies can unlock the full potential of their gas reserves by considering steps to promote greater interconnection among natural gas networks. Australia has developed and presented to the EWG a project to develop a best practice approach to addressing barriers to the cross-border interconnection of natural gas in APEC member economies, encompassing

both cross-border pipeline interconnection and the transportation of liquefied natural gas. APERC estimates that APEC-wide investment in natural
gas projects is approximately $70 billion, with an additional $90 billion
committed or planned.[9]

Cross-border natural gas pipeline development is at the forefront of this
investment. The major developments that are taking place include the Arctic–
Canada–United States pipeline interconnection, the Trans-ASEAN Gas
Pipeline, the West Natuna–Peninsular Malaysia project, the Sumatra–Batam–
Singapore project, the West–East project in China, and the Sakhalin project.

Interconnection of gas pipelines will increase the economic integration
between economies. This will in turn reduce the potential for conflict over
energy resources.

Although existing investment commitments are significant, they are
dwarfed by the total energy investment needs of the APEC region. In total,
it is estimated that APEC will require $3.4 to $4.4 trillion of investment in
the energy sector over the period to 2020.[10]

APEC energy ministers have tasked the EWG with increasing energy investment flows to the regions economies. To ensure that adequate investment capital is available, it is essential that the EWG engages effectively
with the private sector and international financial institutions. It is unlikely that most APEC economies will be able to fund all the required investment in the energy sector in the absence of private-sector financing.
This investment will need to compete with the plethora of demands on funds
facing governments and communities. In addition, the APEC economies
will be competing for investment against other regions and economies.

The EWG Energy Business Network, a group of company representatives from APEC economies who provide the EWG with a business perspective on energy issues, is working to promote closer linkages with international financial institutions. In March 2004, the Energy Business Network
hosted a workshop drawing together relevant energy sector participants to
develop closer linkages with international financial institutions. The workshop sought to enhance the understanding of future investment needs in the
region and to facilitate linkages among government officials, financial sector representatives, and energy business representatives. A key outcome of
the workshop was the principle that energy infrastructure projects need to
be consistent with an economy's specific energy security and sustainable
development objectives, again recognizing the importance of energy security to the future development of APEC economies. This workshop was one

of three held in the first half of 2004 under the auspices of APEC's EWG that explored ways to facilitate energy projects, including infrastructure, energy efficiency, and new and renewable energy technologies.

The EWG also has developed a framework for the discussion of nuclear energy, recognizing that nuclear energy is an option for some member economies but not others. The EWG is also undertaking a range of information-sharing activities to develop capacity in relation to a hydrogen-based economy and potential relationships with the International Partnership for the Hydrogen Economy.

Finally, through the commitments made at the World Summit on Sustainable Development, the EWG is developing a work program that focuses on the sustainable use of energy. This program encompasses issues such as impediments to the exploration and development of energy resources, energy efficiency and conservation, the development of new and renewable energy technology, alternative fuels, and measures to mitigate the growing demand for oil in the region. This work will focus on producing tangible outcomes for people and improving the standard of livings of all member economies.

The EWG's focus on energy security reflects the fact that long-term policy responses to the challenges of energy security will ultimately have the greatest impact. Though responding to temporary disruptions in energy supplies is essential, energy security can only be guaranteed through sustainable long-term policies that create an environment that supports investment and economic development and improves living standards.

Although all APEC economies are committed to the implementation of the EWG's Energy Security Initiative, this does not constrain their ability to engage in other activities, either individually or in cooperation with other economies, to address their individual energy security concerns. For example, some economies that are highly dependent on oil imports have developed stated-owned oil stockpiles, and some have industry-based oil stockpiles, while other economies are net oil exporters and have developed national policies in this context. The EWG is supporting these efforts by identifying best practice principles for establishing and managing strategic oil stocks.

The capacity for individual economies to develop responses that are tailored to their individual circumstances, while at the same time participating in the APEC-wide Energy Security Initiative, illustrates one of the key strengths of APEC's EWG—its flexibility in meeting the challenges facing a diverse group of economies that are spread over a wide geographic area and have different histories and cultures.

As can be seen from the discussion above, the APEC Energy Security Initiative is a multifaceted response to the energy security challenge. However, the initiative's most impressive achievement is the level of commitment and trust that has developed among member economies as they seek to address the challenges of energy security. The concept of joint oil stockpiles, for example, could not even be considered within many international forums, let alone be pushed forward as a mechanism to address legitimate national security concerns.

## Conclusion

The APEC member economies encompass a significant part of the Pacific Rim, and energy security is one of the most pressing policy concerns they face. A lack of sufficient energy resources to support the continued economic growth and social development of the APEC economies would have the potential to destabilize not only individual economies but the region as a whole. The development of the APEC Energy Security Initiative needs to be recognized as a major foreign policy accomplishment in that it provides a framework for regional economies to engage in ongoing dialogue and activities related to energy security and to reduce the potential for conflict throughout the region. Other than the IEA, which does not include seventeen of the twenty APEC member economies (Australia, Canada, Japan, and the United States are IEA members), no other forum delivers such effective cooperation between consumers and producers. The Energy Security Initiative is not an end in itself, but just the beginning of a major program of work for the EWG, and the APEC economies, in achieving long-term energy security.

Much work remains to be done. Future challenges include ensuring that measures to address the potential of temporary disruptions in energy supplies are continued; mobilizing the investment required in energy infrastructure across the APEC region; diversifying energy supplies; building strategic stocks commensurate with regional demand; using energy more efficiently; and capitalizing on the emergence of new energy technologies.

To meet these formidable challenges, the APEC economies—through APEC's EWG—must maintain their commitment to cooperation. To continue to attract the private capital that will be needed to finance new investment, the APEC region as a whole must demonstrate that it is politically and economically stable. In a region where competition could easily create political tensions that could threaten investor confidence, the APEC approach to energy security offers a practical alternative to destructive beggar-thy-neighbor policies.

By undertaking tangible activities and delivering real outcomes to member economies, APEC's EWG demonstrates how energy security can become an integrative force rather than a source of political and economic competition. The success of the EWG—addressing the issue of energy security within a framework of consensus-based regional cooperation and mutually beneficial outcomes—bodes well for a multilateral foreign policy strategy for energy security in the twenty-first century.

## Notes

1. The APEC member economies are Australia; Brunei Darussalam; Canada; Chile; China; Hong Kong, China; Indonesia; Japan; Republic of Korea; Malaysia; Mexico; New Zealand, Papua New Guinea, Peru, the Philippines, Russia, Singapore, Chinese Taipei, Thailand; the United States; and Vietnam. These economies represent the majority of the population and economic activity of the Pacific Rim.

2. See the APEC Web site, http://www.apecsec.org.sg/.

3. In the period 1990–99, the average annual growth rate of GDP for APEC was 2.4 percent. According to the Asia-Pacific Energy Research Centre (APERC), economic growth is expected to grow at an average annual rate of 3.5 percent through 2020, compared with global GDP growth of 3.0 percent. APEC, *APEC Energy Supply and Demand Outlook* (Manila: APEC, 2002). The IEA's projections of world GDP of 3 percent from 2000 to 2030 are at International Energy Agency, *World Energy Outlook 2002* (Paris: International Energy Agency, 2002), 37.

4. APEC, *APEC Energy Supply and Demand Outlook.*

5. Kent E. Calder, *Asia's Deadly Triangle* (London: Nicholas Brealey, 1997), 200.

6. Robert A. Manning, *The Asian Energy Factor* (New York: Palgrave, 2000).

7. APERC is overseen by the Expert Group on Energy Data and Analysis, one of the five expert groups established to support the work of the EWG. The other expert groups are Expert Group on Clean Fossil Fuel, Expert Group on Energy Efficiency and Conservation, Expert Group on New and Renewable Technologies, and Expert Group on Minerals and Energy Exploration and Development.

8. EWG, "Energy Security Initiative: Emergency Oil Stocks as an Option to Respond to Oil Supply Disruptions," 2002; EWG, "Energy Security Initiative: Some Aspects of Oil Security," 2003; and workshops on Oil Emergency Response Arrangements, 2003, and Joint Oil Stockpiling, 2003.

9. APEC, *APEC Energy Supply and Demand Outlook.*

10. Masaharu Fujitomi, president of APERC, "APEC Energy Outlook and Security Issues," speech at the Sixth APEC Energy Ministers' Meeting, Manila, June 10, 2004.

# 13

# Japan

## *Keiichi Yokobori*

Concern for the security of its energy supply will dominate Japan's energy policy debates for the foreseeable future. Japan's flexibility in its energy supply choice will be constrained by its lack of energy resources to meet energy demand and by inadequate energy delivery networks, including both a power grid isolated from the Asian continent and insufficient oil and gas pipelines. These constraints will limit, in turn, the country's ability to compete in the global economy. Japan's obligation to reduce greenhouse gas emissions under the Kyoto Protocol and subsequent international commitments to combat climate change will only further compound its difficulties. Japan should consider supporting greater regional energy cooperation, which will provide it with greater flexibility in securing energy supplies and enhance its political relations with its Asian neighbors.[1]

## What Will Japan's Future Energy Demand and Supply Look Like?

Japan's energy demand will increase by about 20 percent during the next two decades. Its total primary energy supply (TPES), or total primary energy demand, is projected to grow from 10.3 million barrels per day of oil equivalent (hereafter expressed as "mmbpd oil equivalent") to 12.5 mmbpd oil equivalent from 1999 to 2020, at an average annual growth rate of 0.9 percent (table 13.1).[2] However, this increase will be much smaller than those of other Northeast Asian economies such as China, Russia, and South Korea in both absolute amount and growth rate. In particular, China's added energy demand alone will be larger than Japan's projected total energy demand in 2020 by nearly 40 percent.

*Table 13.1. Japan's Total Primary Energy Demand Outlook, 1999–2020 (million barrels per day of oil equivalent)*

| Energy Source | 1999 | 2005 | 2010 | 2015 | 2020 | 1999–2020 annual percentage change |
|---|---|---|---|---|---|---|
| Coal | 1.74 | 1.80 | 1.80 | 1.83 | 2.06 | 0.8 |
| Oil | 5.33 | 5.34 | 5.54 | 5.67 | 5.77 | 0.4 |
| Gas | 1.24 | 1.36 | 1.57 | 1.67 | 1.72 | 1.6 |
| Hydropower | 0.15 | 0.17 | 1.18 | 1.18 | 0.18 | 1.0 |
| Nuclear | 1.64 | 1.80 | 1.98 | 2.26 | 2.41 | 1.8 |
| NRE[a] | 0.19 | 0.24 | 0.30 | 0.12 | 0.35 | 3.0 |
| Total | 10.3 | 10.71 | 11.38 | 11.96 | 12.49 | 0.9 |

[a]NRE: new and renewable energy resources.
*Source:* Asia-Pacific Energy Research Centre, *Energy Balance Tables for the APEC Energy Demand and Supply Outlook 2002* (Tokyo: Asia Pacific Energy Research Centre, 2002).

By fuel, oil will remain dominant during this forecast period, still accounting for 46 percent in TPES in 2020, compared with 52 percent in 1999. Despite the declining share, the volume will stay relatively flat. As a result, China will overtake Japan by 2020 as Asia's leading oil consumer and importer. Japanese gas consumption will increase at a modest rate, so China will also catch up with Japan during the forecast period.

Japan is expected to increase its nuclear power generation by nearly 50 percent. Its ability to grow its nuclear power sector will be a major factor in moderating its demand for hydrocarbons. In 2003, the Tokyo Electric Power Company (TEPCO) dealt with some safety problems. If the projected nuclear power construction and operation materialize, Japan will remain the largest nuclear power operator in the Northeast Asian region.

By sector, industry will remain the largest energy user in total final energy consumption (TFEC), namely, total energy uses other than transformation. However, industry's demand growth will remain stagnant, while other sectors, particularly commercial use, will increase at a much faster pace.[3]

In the energy transformation sector, power generation constitutes a major energy user. Japan is counting on nuclear power to fuel incremental demand for power generation fuel inputs with modest incremental contributions from coal, gas, and new and renewables. Oil is expected to decline in its contribution. Nuclear power is expected to expand in spite of the TEPCO incident and other project downgrading. The recent cancellation or freeze in construction of nuclear power plants results from the current reduction in the rate of growth for power rather than public opposition to nuclear energy.[4]

Japan will also continue to depend heavily on imports for its energy supplies. Fossil fuels will still dominate its energy supply structure due to its limited indigenous sources. Energy imports will account for 78 percent of TES in 2020, slightly lower than 82 percent in 1999. This minor reduction will largely result from the modest size of import increases (1.38 mmbpd oil equivalent, or 16 percent from 1999 to 2020) and the nuclear power expansion.

However, other Northeast Asian economies will increase their energy imports at a much faster pace. Total energy imports in Northeast Asia will grow by nearly 30 percent from 1999 to 2020, from 14.44 to 20.44 mmbpd oil equivalent, or by 6 mmbpd oil equivalent. Although Japanese energy import demand may marginally increase, the competition for fuel supplies will become more intense in this region, and, consequently, globally.

Combined Northeast Asian oil net imports, encompassing Japan, China, South Korea, and Taiwan,[5] will surpass those of the United States in the middle of the 2010s. Similarly, natural gas net imports, already exceeding U.S. imports, will increase in the Northeast Asian region. But Japan will still be the major regional importer of natural gas for the next two decades.

The Asia-Pacific Energy Research Centre's (APERC's) *Outlook* does not take into account the impact of policy measures that Japan would take to comply with its obligation to reduce emissions of carbon dioxide and other greenhouse gases (GHGs) to a level 6 percent lower than its 1990 level by the First Commitment Period (2008–12) under the Kyoto Protocol to the United Nations Framework Convention on Climate Change (the UNFCCC, which in 1997 led to the Kyoto Protocol). The protocol was agreed on at the third Conference of Parties to UNFCCC in Kyoto in December 1997. Japan is expected to increase its energy-related carbon dioxide emissions from 1,171 to 1,246 million tons, or by 6.4 percent between 1999 and 2020. Compliance with the Kyoto Protocol would require significant emission reductions that could severely damage Japan's economy. Northeast Asia will see a large increase of carbon dioxide emissions during this period, reflecting higher energy demand growth in other economies. China will increase its emissions both in absolute size (by 2,379 million tons) and by rate of increase (by 83 percent). As a result, total emissions from Northeast Asia will exceed those from the United States by 2020.

Expanded energy demand and supply will require significant additional investment to cover the construction of energy supply infrastructure for production and domestic and cross-border transportation of coal, oil, gas, and electric power. Japan will require $163 billion in cumulative investment between 1999 and 2020. However, the corresponding amount of investment covering Japan, China, South Korea, and Russia will amount to $2,355 billion, which is equivalent to 63 percent of Japan's gross domestic product in 1999.[6]

In July 2004, the Ministry of Economy, Trade, and Industry (METI) published two sets of provisional energy outlooks, one for a short term up to fiscal 2010 and another for a long term covering the period to 2030.[7] Both were posted on its Web site for public comments.[8] These provisional METI outlooks present a more modest energy demand picture than APERC's, based on estimates for a decline in Japan's population and consequently lower demand for energy growth.[9] Even with its modest energy demand perspective, the METI draft outlook shows a need for additional policy measures to achieve the Kyoto Protocol target.

The difference between the METI and APERC outlooks does not alter Japan's future energy challenges. Japan's expected high reliance on foreign sources of oil and natural gas and faster-growing energy demand and import requirements in other economies in the region will make energy supply security an even more important issue for Japan than it is today. At the same time, Japan will face a tremendous challenge in meeting its Kyoto Protocol target for carbon dioxide emissions because these emissions are likely to increase.

## Key Factors Affecting Japan's Future Energy Security

The future course of energy supply security of Japan will be affected by the way its policymakers respond to several key factors, including its compliance with the Kyoto Protocol, the vulnerabilities revealed by the temporary closure of TEPCO nuclear power reactors between 2002 and 2003, the impact of high domestic electricity prices on its economic performance, the cost of the Asian oil premium, the need for increased oil stockpiling in the Asian region, and the challenges and opportunities presented by the North Korean energy situation.

### The Kyoto Protocol's Implications

Japan's compliance with the Kyoto Protocol could impose high economic costs and increase its reliance on nuclear power. Japan formally accepted the protocol in June 2002. The protocol's entry into force is secured by the ratification by Russia in October 2004, which satisfies the requirement for the inclusion of Annex I Parties accounting for 55 percent of that group's carbon dioxide emissions in 1990.[10] in order to implement its treaty obligations, Japan plans to meet the Kyoto target by limiting GHG emissions of energy origin at a 1990 level in the First Commitment Period, offsetting the remainder with other measures including carbon sequestration by reforestation. The emphasis on energy related measures reflects the fact that about 90 percent of GHG emissions originate from energy uses and supplies in Japan.[11]

Although the reduction of Japanese emissions by 6 percent could appear much easier to achieve than those of the European Union (8 percent, including the United Kingdom, France, and Germany), and the United States (7 percent), many Japanese energy experts consider this target to be very difficult. European Union members would benefit from the E.U. bubble or intra–European Union emission trading and the high coal dependency that existed in the United Kingdom and Germany in 1990.[12] The United States will escape the obligation, because the U.S. government has declared that it will not ratify the protocol. But more important, the costs incurred to Japan would be higher than in other industrial countries. The result of the Modeling Forum Simulations, reviewed for the Third Assessment Report of the Intergovernmental Panel on Climate Change, shows that in nine out of twelve models, which compare Japan and other regions, marginal emission reduction costs are the highest in Japan.[13] The simulations also show a large emission-reduction cost-saving potential from emissions trading. Thus, Japan would gain much in cost savings arising from emission-trading regimes.[14]

## TEPCO's Nuclear Reactors Closure

TEPCO, the largest vertically integrated power company in Japan, temporarily closed all seventeen of its nuclear reactors from autumn 2002 to the middle of 2003. Although much-feared blackouts were avoided, the closure of the nuclear plants revealed Japan's vulnerability to an internal energy disruption, the need for reserve capacities of electric power in the future, and the critical role that safe nuclear power will play in Japan's economic security.

The plant closures did not result from any serious nuclear plant accidents releasing high radioactive substances; but they responded to public criticism against the falsified reports concealing scars on the shrouds or supporting devices of fuel rods inside the reactor (which were unique to the boiling water reactors). Although safety and security requirements were not violated, the situation suggested a risk of negligence on safety and security by TEPCO. As a result, TEPCO's top executives resigned and all TEPCO nuclear reactors were shut down temporarily to avoid unsafe operation. Subsequently, safety regulations were revised to address public concerns, clarifying that those scars would not affect the safe operation of nuclear power reactors. However, public outcry can result in stricter regulations, which could increase the cost of nuclear power generation and damage the economics of future generation.

TEPCO's nuclear power plant closures unmasked Japan's vulnerability to a power disruption. The closed plants contribute more than 45 percent of TEPCO's power generation and caused a risk of blackouts in the Kanto area, including the Tokyo metropolitan area, which of course constitutes the economic and political gravity center of Japan.[15] Although the power transmission network is well developed in Japan, the frequency of electricity differs in the west (60 cycles per second) and the east (50 cycles per second) of the Mainland, which in turn constrains electricity supplies from the western regions. Japan avoided power outages during the nuclear plant shutdown primarily because of cooler-than-normal summer weather in 2003 and the stagnant economy. If there had been an outage, it would have constituted a major case of energy supply disruptions caused by a domestic origin, similar to the blackouts in New York State in July 2003.

The plant closures also showed that Japan is as vulnerable to an internal energy disruption as it is to an external disruption. This would suggest that Japan should rethink its traditional assumption of energy security risk arising only from an interruption of foreign sources of oil. Japan should therefore consider the cost of enhancing the reliability of domestic energy sources and the degree to which it needs domestic emergency response measures.

The TEPCO nuclear power plant closures affected the regional oil and natural gas markets through Japan's fuel switching.[16] This suggests that the security of the electric power supply is a regional as well as a domestic issue. TEPCO tried to offset the resulting supply losses by running natural gas and other fossil-fuel-fired power plants. The overall capacity utilization of TEPCO's fossil-fuel-fired stations exceeded 60 percent between January and April 2003, rising from below 40 percent before July 2002. This fuel shift affected the fossil fuel market on a regional level. Imports of low-sulfur crude oil as well as heavy fuel oil combined from the fourth quarter 2002 to the first quarter 2003 surpassed those in the corresponding periods of the previous year by 30 to 40 percent, which raised spot prices for Minas and

Tapis crude and low-sulfur waxy residue from about $25 per barrel before June 2002 to above $30 between October 2002 and April 2003. Japan's imports of liquefied natural gas (LNG) were increased by 2.4 percent in the fourth quarter 2002 and by 8.1 percent in the first quarter 2003. Average prices of LNG rose from about $210 per ton in June 2002 to $250 in March 2003. Fearing reduced oil and natural gas supply availability for meeting winter demand, South Korea also increased its imports by 15.8 percent in LNG and by 9.5 percent in heavy fuels in late 2002 and early 2003, also causing higher import prices.[17]

In short, the TEPCO incident presents the complexity of energy security: a risk of unexpected supply cost increases arising from popular emotional reactions, a possibility of supply disruptions of domestic origin, a need for more widely conceived emergency response options, and a cross-border impact of supply disruptions or their response actions.

## High Electricity Prices in Japan

Electricity prices in Japan (measured in dollars per kilowatt hour, or kWh) are among the highest (about twice as high as the average for the member countries of the Organization for Economic Cooperation and Development, or OECD) for both household and industrial users in the industrial and Asian countries.[18] High electricity prices have not only handicapped the ability of Japanese industry to compete in a globalizing market but have also impaired Japanese consumers' purchasing power and thus Japan's economic growth potential. With this concern, the Japanese government has begun a program of regulatory reform in the electricity sector to enhance competition in the power sector.[19] In the power industry's view, higher electricity prices largely reflect Japan's higher performance (e.g., lower rates of blackouts), higher environmental performance (e.g., lower emissions of sulfur oxides and nitrous oxides from fossil-fuel-fired power plants) and other factors (e.g., higher land prices). Japan's primary goal in power-sector regulatory reform, as in other countries, is to promote efficiency improvements. As of April 2004, about 40 percent of retail markets, which cover "high-voltage" customers with contracts of 500 kilowatts (kW) or more, have been open for competition. Electricity retail prices have declined by about 7 percent since 2000. Another opening, accounting for 13 percent of retail markets, is planned for April 2005. Thus, it still remains to be seen how far electricity prices to both industrial and household users can be reduced in Japan.

## The Asian Oil Premium

Since the early 1990s, Japanese, Korean and Chinese energy experts and policymakers have noted that East Asian oil importers are paying a $1 more per barrel premium than oil prices paid by Europeans and North Americans (particularly for crude oil coming from the Gulf region).[20] They reason that East Asia's excessive dependence on the Gulf oil and, to a certain extent, the diminishing role of Dubai crude oil as a regional marker for Asia, have led to the higher oil price. But there are few good candidates to replace Dubai crude oil as a marker among types of crude traded in East Asia. The heavy dependence on Gulf oil is difficult to reduce, and though oil imports from other regions such as West Africa have commenced, their volume remains low.

Somewhat similar to this, many Northeast Asian LNG importers now consider the contractual take-or-pay clause as inflexible and expensive. With the emergence of spot LNG trading, this clause will become more contentious between the supplier and the customer of LNG.

## Oil Stockpiling in East Asia

Japan holds a fairly high level of emergency oil stocks, but the stock level in neighboring Asian economies is relatively low or even nonexistent. Japan's oil stocks are equivalent to approximately 120 days of net imports in accordance with the International Energy Agency (IEA) formula, which requires its members to hold oil stocks at least equivalent of 90 net oil import days.[21]

The IEA's calculation of stocks is rather complex and hides real supplies. For example, IEA calculations exclude 10 percent of stocks as "technically unavailable,"[22] which is no longer justified, because oil is well mixed in tanks and today nearly every last drop can be extracted. Naphtha for chemical feedstocks is also excluded in calculating both the amount of consumption and the volume to be stored.

A simpler yardstick, which uses unadjusted oil stocks and oil consumption or imports, indicates that the Japanese oil stocks can cover about 160 days of imports.[23] This level could respond to a fairly wide range of possible oil supply disruptions facing Japan. The government's emergency stocks alone would account for nearly 90 days of inland consumption (virtually equal to imports for Japan), and they could roughly satisfy the IEA requirements.[24] However, in globally integrated oil markets, any significant supply disruption in any regional or economy market could affect other parts of global markets. Currently, Japanese emergency stocks can be used only to replace domestic supply losses. Thus, Japan would be adversely affected by any panic buying behaviors of other importing countries with low emergency-stock levels, but Japanese emergency stocks could not be released to offset their supply loss.

In addition, Japanese oil emergency stocks would be more effective with some other improvements. For example, Japan requires its industry to hold up to seventy oil import days of oil. These mandated stocks make up 46 percent (as of March 2003) of Japanese emergency reserves. Industry has no incentive to distinguish stocks needed for operational purposes and those needed in case of supply disruptions. It would be more preferable to replace industry stocks with government stocks. Government stocks can be managed directly and the cost of government stocks still charged to industry.

In Northeast Asia, China, South Korea, and Taiwan have small or little emergency oil stocks. Korea joined the IEA in 2001 and thus needed to satisfy the IEA's stock requirements of ninety days of oil imports. However, the Korean stocks do not cover imports of naphtha for petrochemical feed stocks. The unadjusted level would be much lower. The Korea National Oil Corporation is thus striving to achieve a government target level of stockpiling to cover consumption of sixty days by 2006. China plans to establish a state oil stockpile. The Energy Research Institute, which reports to the National Development and Reform Council, proposed to have a state oil stockpile of 8 million kiloliters (50 million barrels), equivalent to thirty days of oil imports, by 2005 and then to increase the level to cover fifty days of imports by 2010.[25] In Taiwan, there is an emergency stockpile held by the China Petroleum Corporation, but most of the stockpiles are considered to be working stocks, which would amount to only thirty to forty days.[26]

With regional stocks well below IEA equivalent levels, Japan's own stocks could offer a considerable degree of security coverage for Northeast Asian economies by 2010, if Japanese policy permitted drawing down these reserves under more flexible circumstances.

### *The Korean Peninsula Energy Development Organization's Nuclear Power Project*

North Korea faces enormous power shortages. Even in the event that energy becomes a useful tool for the resolution of the Korean nuclear issue, a new solution for North Korea's energy deficit will need to be devised because the arrangements provided by the Framework Agreement do not match North Korea's energy needs.

The Korean Peninsula Energy Development Organization (KEDO) was created in March 1995 to support the construction of two light-water nuclear reactors (pressurized water reactor type) of 1 gigawatt each. KEDO was a product of the Framework Agreement between the United States and North Korea, under which North Korea agreed to freeze and ultimately dismantle its nuclear program in exchange for the construction of two light-water reactors and the delivery of heavy oil for current energy needs. The construction of these power reactors has been delayed for various economic and political reasons, and in 2003 North Korea suspended its adherence to the framework and resumed reprocessing its nuclear fuel. The original 2003 target date for completion of the reactors was not met. However, besides its delayed schedule of completion, there are three major problems associated with the KEDO nuclear power project.

First, the proposed size of the nuclear power capacity, 2 gigawatts, appeared to be too large for an area with a currently low level of power consumption. Although no official or credible estimate is available, the IEA estimates that North Korea's total primary energy demand was 0.41 mmbpd oil equivalent (or 0.02 barrel per day of oil equivalent per capita) and electricity consumption was 17.01 terawatt hours (760 kWh per capita) in 2001. Assuming 80 percent of capacity utilization, more than 80 percent of the additional power provided by the proposed reactors would be available. Even if the current power shortage is severe, this huge increase will pose a tremendous challenge for the North Korean power supply.

Second, it is not a secret that the North Korean power transmission and distribution network has deteriorated due to a lack of proper maintenance. Thus, even if the KEDO project becomes operational, power could not be safely sent to the needed population in the country. No financial or technical arrangement has been made to repair and upgrade the power transmission infrastructure.

Third, the KEDO project was not well conceived in terms of North Korea's or the region's energy needs. Completing the construction of the power plants will not make a meaningful contribution to the improved living standards and economic development of the country. North Korea will need improved power delivery infrastructure before it can operate the nuclear power plants.

## Japan's Energy Policy

The Government of Japan released its Basic Energy Plan (the "plan") in October 2003 as a response to the concerns and challenges mentioned previously.[27] The plan reconfirmed the three basic objectives, namely: securing stable energy supply through energy conservation, supply diversification, and emergency stocks; pursuing compatibility with environmental concerns through energy conservation; utilizing nonfossil fuels and gasified energy sources, and developing and deploying cleaner fossil fuel utilization technologies; and making greater use of market mechanisms through schemes appropriate for Japan.

The issue of energy supply security received top priority, reflecting, particularly, the TEPCO nuclear power plant problems and the large-scale blackouts in North America in 2003. The Basic Energy Plan also recognizes the importance of environmental concerns in energy policy debates, because energy uses and supplies are principal sources of GHG emissions in Japan. The plan proposes a wide range of energy efficiency and conservation measures encompassing all energy use sectors, such as an exemplary efficiency appliance and vehicle standard setting called the "top runner method," promotion of energy service corporations activities in all end-use sectors, introduction of hybrid cars, and promotion of intelligent transport systems. Although energy intensity in Japan is relatively low, the plan calls for further efficiency improvements in sectors other than industry.

On supply, the Basic Energy Plan confirms the role of nuclear power, despite some antinuclear views expressed in public comments, and it urges further nuclear safety efforts by electric industry and the government. The plan commits Japan to pursue the use of plutonium in light-water reactors, although this issue remains under heated debate.[28] The plan intends to promote nuclear power generation in a manner compatible with retail liberalization in the power sector.

The Basic Energy Plan gives renewable energy sources a supplementary role in energy supply and places strategic importance on fuel-cell development. It intends to monitor the implementation of renewable portfolio standards, introduced in April 2003, to enhance the further use of renewables for electricity generation.

The Basic Energy Plan pursues greater use of gaseous energy, natural gas, and liquefied petroleum gas (LPG) for reducing emissions and increasing efficiency by developing natural gas pipeline networks; diversifying supply sources; lowering LNG import prices; promoting gas-to-liquids (GTL), dimethyl ether (DME), and methane hydrate technology; and establishing a national LPG emergency reserve by fiscal 2010. The plan also supports the use of coal, hydropower, and geothermal energy with appropriate environmental considerations.

The Basic Energy Plan expects oil to play an important role in Japanese energy supply. This could be a departure from the past "policy away from oil." It advocates the value of government stocks with better management and calls for greater regional cooperation to increase oil stockpiling. The plan supports cooperation with Russia for resource development in the Russian Far East and Siberia and for oil pipeline construction to Nakhodka.

The Basic Energy Plan advocates gradual steps toward retail liberalization in the electricity and gas sectors, and it is cautious on unbundling the supply services of the incumbent utilities for the sake of energy security. The plan stresses expanded regional interchange arrangements to enhance power supply security. It promotes research and development of relevant technologies for energy efficiency.

The Basic Energy Plan favors greater international cooperation, specifically Japan's positive role in global energy issues, through active participation in international energy and environment organizations and the dissemination of energy efficiency technologies in Asian economies. It concludes that Japan should strive for balancing energy demand and supply and respond to environmental issues, taking account of energy demand trends and their implications for energy supply and the environment in the Asian region as a whole.

Thus, the Basic Energy Plan addresses many of the policy issues presented by the APERC *Outlook*. Subsequent to the adoption of the plan, METI's advisory groups have started elaborating on many of these issues. The remainder of this chapter addresses several key areas of concern, which might not be fully discussed in the plan, particularly how Japan should engage its regional partners in ways that would enhance its energy and national security.

## The Case for Regional Cooperation

Greater regional energy cooperation, including the joint use of emergency oil stockpiles and energy infrastructure connections, would enhance Japanese energy supply security at a lower cost and help Japan achieve the other energy policy goals given in its Basic Energy Plan. Some of the relevant suggestions are presented here in more detail.

## The Joint Use of Oil Stockpiles

Oil stockpiling is used to fill missing supply in the case of a significant oil supply shortfalls and to minimize adverse economic and social effects. Originally, the emergency oil stocks held by IEA countries were intended to protect IEA countries from such oil supply (especially import) shocks. In 1973, when the first oil crisis hit, OECD member countries accounted for 75 percent of the globally traded crude oil (according to UN Statistics). In a world where OECD nations dominated consumption, an IEA system that used its member countries' oil stocks to protect them from global oil disruptions was effective. However, the OECD share in global oil traded declined to less than 70 percent by 1998.[29] The U.S. Energy Information Administration's *International Energy Outlook 2004* projects industrial countries'[30] share of the world's petroleum imports to decline from 65 percent in 2001 to 55 percent in 2025.

The globalizing oil markets reduce IEA oil stocks' effectiveness in responding to supply disruptions. Further, the IEA emergency stocks' coverage in terms of days of net imports of its members is declining.[31] Some new members have low emergency stock levels. Also, oil stock levels held by many East Asian economies other than Japan remain low despite their rapidly increasing oil imports. Oil importers in these economies are prone to panic buying of oil in the case of supply disruptions. But Japan holds a high stock level sufficient to counter such a panic. Thus, Japan should consider releasing its oil stocks to other East Asian economies in the case of supply disruptions. Open access to the Japanese oil stocks could be made as an incentive in return for those economies' commitments to gradually introduce and increase oil stocks over a span of time (e.g., by 2010).[32] The effects of such measures could be enhanced globally if the United States and key European oil importers followed suit in their respective regions. Japan would also benefit from the improved oil supply security that would result from neighboring economies' higher oil stockpiling. Further closer regional cooperation could evolve, if the joint use and management of stockpiles is developed.

## *Energy Infrastructure Connections: Oil, Natural Gas, and Power*

The lack of major cross-border energy transport infrastructure in the Northeast Asian region has been considered one of the major obstacles to improving energy security in the region. The region's dependence on tanker transport for crude oil and natural gas tends to limit the scope of supply sources and use. Furthermore, it puts Asian energy buyers at a disadvantage, as seen in the case of the Asian oil premium issue and rigid LNG contract conditions known as a take-or-pay clause. On electricity, Japan's sole reliance on the domestic generation option limits supply flexibility as seen in the TEPCO nuclear power plant closure in 2002 and 2003.

Pipelines from Russia

Noting these problems, interest in regional energy cooperation is growing in Japan and its neighboring countries. Untapped energy resources in Russia attract interest in Japan, Russia, and other countries. Russia wishes to develop its East Siberia and Far East regions, which have historically been energy importers and lack developed infrastructure (roads, rails, etc.). Russia seeks to reduce its reliance on Western Europe for energy exports. Table 13.2 summarizes the views of experts with respect to the relative strengths and weaknesses of some countries and regions in Northeast Asia.

Several steps have been already taken on the development of oil and gas resources in Russia and the construction of pipeline transport infrastructure. Japan plans to import natural gas from Sakhalin in the form of LNG or by pipeline. A feasibility study is under way to assess a pipeline from Sakhalin to near Tokyo. Further, the idea of constructing a regional gas pipeline network has been proposed and studied by China, Japan, Russia, and South Korea.[33] Difficulties arise from conflicting priorities and interests and from differing situations. For example, China completed its domestic trunk pipeline from Lunnan, Xinjiang Province, to Shanghai (the Transport-West-Gas-to-East Project) in 2004, and its commercial operation started from January 1, 2005. Proposed pipeline routes through Mongolia to China or through

Table 13.2. Energy Strengths and Weaknesses of Selected Countries and Region

| Country or Region | Energy Resources | Population | Energy Market | Technology | Fund |
|---|---|---|---|---|---|
| Eastern Russia | +++ | + | + | ++ | − |
| China | + | +++ | ++ | ++ | + |
| South Korea | − | + | ++ | ++ | ++ |
| Japan | − | ++ | +++ | ++ | +++ |

Source: Mitsubishi Research Institute, Inc.

Figure 13.1. Map of Proposed Cross-Border Natural Gas Pipeline Network in Northeast Asia

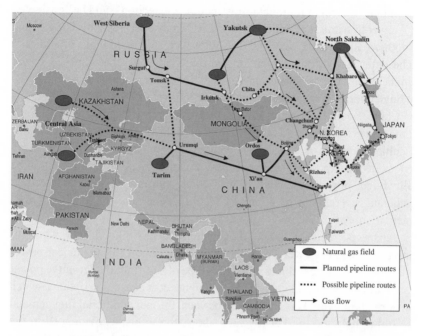

*Source:* S. Abe, "The 3 E Target in the Context of Northeast Asia," presentation at Meeting with Practitioners organized by the Economic Research Institute for Northeast Asia (ERINA) and Northeast Asia Economic Forum, Tokyo, October 10, 2003.

North Korea to South Korea would entail geopolitical considerations (figure 13.1). As noted above, Japan is handicapped by its own lack of a domestic trunk pipeline for gas. It is unclear whether Russia's resource base can support all the Asian pipelines that Asian importers desire. Japan's Basic Energy Plan makes oil exports from Siberia by extending pipelines to Nakhodka a priority, and Russia agreed to make Nakhodka the final destination for the Siberian pipeline. This project competed with a project to export oil to China. Despite these problems, the emergence of new supply sources and routes would enhance the flexibility in energy supplies and introduce elements of competition. They could alleviate or eliminate the contract rigidity and the higher premiums imposed. In addition, environmental gains could also result.

A Regional Power Grid?

A similar concept of regional infrastructure connection could be considered in power transmission. Indeed, an APERC study addressed this issue,[34] and another APERC study discussed its relevance with natural gas pipelines.[35] The latter study finds, depending on the conditions, that regional power connections could reinforce energy security and environment concerns. Although interest in regional power connections is fairly strong among experts in China, South Korea, and Russia, little interest has been observed among Japanese counterparts so far, perhaps due to the possible technological difficulties such as losses in long-range transmission and the frequency differences inside Japan. However, if these technological difficulties could be alleviated, power transmission grid connection across the border could generate several benefits in energy security, economic efficiency, environmental improvement, and regional security.

Japan's isolated electricity grid constrains its flexibility in energy switching in the case of power shortage inside Japan. The TEPCO nuclear power plant closure only exhibited one of this type of shortfall. If alternative power generation were provided inside Japan, higher cost generation options, which in normal times are kept idle, could be used. Further additional fuel demand would tighten the market for such alternative fuels, as evidenced in the TEPCO case. If imported power supplies could offset some of the lost power supply, impacts on other energy markets would be smaller. The reliance on domestic energy supply would not always provide relief in energy security.

Second, as noted above, electricity prices in Japan are very high. However, as long as Japan continues to rely on domestically produced electricity, its scope for electricity price reductions will be very limited, even if drastic regulatory reform to encourage competition is introduced. Domestic producers are compelled to generate electricity at high costs due to high land prices, tighter environmental standards, and other conditions prevailing in Japan. A lesson could be learned from a history of the interconnection between France and the United Kingdom with direct current transmission, which forced U.K. producers to face competition from low-priced French electricity. This eventually resulted in the U.K. power sector's deregulation.

Third, Japan would also benefit from power grid connection environmentally. Though the Kyoto Protocol provides for flexible schemes called "Kyoto Mechanisms" to achieve emission reductions at a lower cost, various conditions attached to their use would make it pragmatically difficult, if not impossible, on a large scale. As noted above, Japan would benefit from the use of these measures. However, many conditions attached would require prior screenings of projects or posterior verifications, whose compliance alone could be costly or cumbersome enough to offend possible users. This risk was evidenced by a decision on the Clean Development Mechanism and Joint Implementation to exclude nuclear options in the Marrakech meeting of the UNFCCC Conference of Parties. With the interconnected transmission lines with other Asian economies, Japan could get electricity without emitting more GHGs or with even lower emissions. This could be achieved without using the Kyoto Mechanism.

A North Korean Connection?

In addition, if the North Korean grid rehabilitation could be made in conjunction with the regional grid interconnection project, North Korea—as well as South Korea, China, and Russia—would benefit from the more efficient use of power stations and development of environmentally benign power generation, such as hydropower in Russia. At the same time, the KEDO nuclear power plant might be used to export electricity to South Korea, China, or Russia to raise income for North Korea. With the extension of the power grid from Korea to Japan, Japan could be integrated into power markets in Northeast Asia, which are lower-cost power producers. Any grid rehabilitation of North Korea requires political stability and diplomatic openness in that country as a precondition, but the potential for regional integration and hard-currency income could be a powerful tool in current conflict-resolution efforts.

## Obstacles to Overcome

Certainly, there remain other hurdles for realizing the regional cooperation suggested here, such as adherence to the rule of law across the region; harmonization of technical, institutional, and legal systems; and most important, the economic feasibility of those potentials. However, economic feasibility sometimes depends on institutional factors as well as technological ones. Serious considerations for regional cooperation would be merited to ensure Japan's future energy security.

Perhaps, the most difficult hurdle is related to political conflicts often associated with territorial claims. China's claim over the Spratley Islands and its conflicts with neighboring economies are well known. Early in July 2004, in the East China Sea, Japan started a geological survey inside the Exclusive Economic Zone demarcated by Japan, in response to Chinese hydrocarbon exploration activities in the adjacent area. China has been reported to ignore Japan's request for joint development, which appears to be motivated by China's desire to monopolize energy resources.[36] However, heightened political tensions could discourage needed capital and technology inflows to China from abroad. An attempt for energy self-sufficiency would not work if the quality of hydrocarbons produced did not fit China's needs. In the long run, China will have to find a mutually acceptable solution with other nations.

## Regional Cooperation and Globalization

These proposals for active Japanese participation in regional energy cooperation should have positive effects on global energy cooperation. To succeed, Japan's contributions would require support and cooperation from other economies in Asia but also from other partners such as the United States. Japan has pursued a policy of support for global welfare and institutions for more than half a century. One such example was its participation in the creation of the IEA in 1974, despite its heavy dependence on oil imports from the Middle East, which might have considered it "provocative." The IEA has evolved into an important energy forum and provides a variety of international public goods, including oil supply emergency response mechanisms, energy data and information dissemination, and technological development and deployment cooperation. Japan has actively participated in most, if not all, IEA activities, and it maintains dialogues with oil-producing countries and their organizations such as the Organization of Petroleum Exporting Countries. Japan has been a strong advocate for an energy consumer–producer dialogue to facilitate stable energy flows at an acceptable price level between producers and consumers and encourages its industries to invest in both energy (e.g., upstream hydrocarbon development) and non-energy-related (e.g., petrochemicals) projects in Middle Eastern countries. The peaceful economic development of this region remains of vital interest to Japan. Saudi Aramco's 15 percent participation in Showa–Shell Oil, a Japanese subsidiary of Royal Dutch Shell, which was reported in July 2004, has been favorably received in Japan as a way for ensuring supply security.[37] Similarly, Japanese participation in the Azadegan oil field development in Iran is considered to help expand the global oil supply base.[38]

Japan's active role in regional cooperation will have many benefits for global energy security. First, its more flexible policy for the maintenance and use of oil emergency reserves would discourage neighboring economies from panic buying in the case of significant supply disruptions and encourage them to introduce or strengthen their emergency stockpiles. If the United States and the E.U. partners take similar initiatives, oil supply emergency responses would be enhanced globally.

Second, the construction of cross-border energy transport infrastructure, pipelines and power grids in particular, will connect hitherto isolated or segmented energy markets and expand both suppliers and customers and, thus enhance both intrafuel and interfuel competition. Oil and gas markets in Europe and Asia would be interlinked (together with other regional network developments), unjustified price disparities would disappear, and more reasonable or innovative contract conditions would emerge. For such purposes, the expansion of the Energy Charter Treaty or the creation of its clone would deserve consideration. Some public investment may be needed in parallel with efforts to create an adequate institutional framework to encourage private capital flows. The issue of the KEDO nuclear power plant could be examined in this context of infrastructure development and the future energy demand supply trend in Northeast Asia.

Third, regional cooperation in Northeast Asia will also provide environmental benefits. Greater use of natural gas and hydropower resources and safely operated nuclear power plants would reduce emissions of air pollutants (which also cause acid rain) and of GHGs as well as enhance economic well-being in the region. Furthermore, such attempts as regional emission trading could be tested because of the diverse backgrounds of China, Japan, Russia, South Korea, and Taiwan in resources, including technologies, human resources, and capital. The loose form of cooperation inside the Asia-Pacific Economic Cooperation forum (APEC), of which both China and Taiwan are members, would facilitate such flexible approaches. They would also bear the global benefits.

It is often argued that the costs of the creation, maintenance, and operation of regional or international public goods will require larger contributions from leading countries. Though Japan should share an appropriate burden on this account, the United States and the other industrial partners should do the same in accordance with their capacity. The developing economies should do similar things within their ability. In particular, the United States is expected to play an exemplary role. The United States could lead the expansion of the Energy Charter Treaty or the creation of a similar scheme in Asia.

Furthermore, the United States could suggest an alternative form of the Kyoto Protocol for the GHG emission reduction commitment beyond 2012. The protocol's first commitment period is only an intermediate point for an eventual GHG concentration reduction, at which the UNFCCC aims. Another open question is whether and which of the Annex B countries will meet the Kyoto Protocol target. If an alternative emission reduction regime is developed, it may well be acceptable to South Korea and Mexico, two other OECD countries that do not accept the GHG emission reduction obligation. On the exemplary effort, one small area where the United States could perform such a function would be to internalize (monetize) externalities, such as charging the cost of U.S. strategic reserves to oil product consumers or charging the environmental cost of emissions to hydrocarbon consumers, which Japanese and European counterparts practice. Charging security and environment costs to the ultimate consumers with higher energy prices certainly entails political difficulties in any democratic country. This small step would eventually enhance global energy security and moderate environmental stresses.

## Conclusion

With growing energy demand in neighboring nations and intensifying environmental concerns, Japan will continue to face significant challenges in securing energy supplies despite its prospect for lower energy growth. Though its Basic Energy Plan addresses many issues to be considered in taking domestic actions, Japan should also take steps to actively participate in creating regionally integrated energy markets, especially by contributing to regionally connected energy infrastructure. This would include the use of oil stockpiles for regional oil supply disruptions on a nondiscriminatory basis and facilitating the energy infrastructure connections with other Northeast Asian countries.

Regional interconnections will also provide economic and environmental benefits as well as energy security benefits for Japan over time. The United States could encourage such undertakings inside the APEC framework, which will also serve its energy and foreign policy interests. At the same time, there would be global benefit if the European Union and the United States coordinated efforts in oil stockpiling and considered the extension to Asia of the Energy Charter Treaty (or the creation of a similar agreement). Further, the United States could suggest an alternative GHG emission reduction path beyond 2012. As an exemplary effort for global energy security, in particular, the United States could internalize the cost of oil security and other externalities in the prices of oil products and other energy uses.

## Notes

1. This chapter relies on the energy outlook published by the Asia-Pacific Energy Research Centre's (APERC's) *APEC Energy Demand and Supply Outlook* (Tokyo: APERC, 2002); hereafter, *APEC Outlook.* APERC, a part of the Institute of Energy Economics, is an energy research arm of the Energy Working Group of the Asia-Pacific Economic Cooperation forum (APEC). Though *APEC Outlook* is largely consistent with other global energy forecasts, such as the International Energy Agency's *World Energy Outlook* and the U.S. Energy Information Administration's *International Energy Outlook (IEO),* it allows an economy-by-economy comparison in the APEC region.

2. The original outlook uses "million tons of oil equivalent," or mtoe, for calorific value. But this chapter uses "million barrels per day of oil equivalent," or mmbpd oil equivalent, assuming 50 mtoe as equal to 1 mmbpd oil equivalent. Japan's annual growth rate of TPES is much lower than that of APEC average at 2.1 percent (1999–2020).

3. The industry sector will grow from 2.9 mmbpd oil equivalent in 1999 to 3.12 mmbpd oil equivalent in 2020 (by 7.6 percent), while commercial energy use will grow from 0.88 to 1.2 mmbpd oil equivalent (by 36.4 percent) during the same period. The transport and residential sectors will grow, respectively, from 1.88 to 2.4 mmbpd oil equivalent (by 27.7 percent), and from 1 to 1.26 mmbpd oil equivalent (by 26 percent). Other uses will remain flat at the level of 0.2 mmbpd oil equivalent through this period. The industrial use share will decline from 42 to 38 percent of TFEC, while transport and commercial uses will expand from 27 and 13 percent to 29 and 15 percent, respectively, and residential use will remain at 15 percent.

4. On December 5, 2003, the Chubu, Kansai, and Hokuriku Electric Power Companies decided to freeze their jointly developed project of a nuclear power plant at Suzu, Ishikawa (total planned capacity of 2.7 gigawatts, or GW), due to the lower electricity demand prospect. On December 24, 2003, the Tohoku Electric Power Company declared the cancellation of its nuclear power plant project (planned capacity of 825 megawatts) at Maki, Niigata, after its failure to obtain the site from the local community of Maki. However, Tohoku's decision also resulted from its pessimistic view on power demand in future. With these downward changes, additional nuclear power capacity by the end of fiscal 2012 is expected to amount to nearly 20 GW, with 15 units. The current nuclear power capacity is 45.7 GW, with 52 units.

5. The author uses the terms *Republic of Korea* and *Chinese Taipei* following the practice used by the Asia Pacific Economic Cooperation (APEC) and the World Trade Organization (WTO) to name these two economies. However, throughout this book the terms *South Korea* and *Taiwan* are used.

6. APERC, *Energy Investment Outlook for the APEC Region* (Tokyo: APERC, 2003).

7. Japan's fiscal year starts in April and ends in March of the next year.

8. The two outlooks were contained in a document titled "Energy Demand and Supply Outlook for 2030 (Interim Draft Report)," drafted in the name of the Demand and Supply Working Group of the Advisory Committee for Natural Resources and En-

ergy, one of the METI advisory bodies (available at http://www.meti.go.jp/feedback/data/ i40705aj.html). Because projections of energy demand and supply figures as well as carbon dioxide emissions are presented in different forms from those of APERC, only percentage changes are shown in this text.

9. Industrial energy use is projected to decline from fiscal 2000 to fiscal 2010 by 4 percent in the METI reference case. Accordingly, oil demand is also expected to decline by 6 percent, while natural gas is projected to grow by 15 percent during the same period in the reference case. In the long term, TFEC is projected to grow by 5.3 percent between fiscal 2000 and fiscal 2021 to reach a peak and to decline by 4.2 percent by fiscal 2030, whose level will be about 3 percent above fiscal 2000's. Energy-originated carbon dioxide emissions will remain flat between fiscal 2000 to 2010, then rise to a peak at around 2020 by 2 percent and decline by 4 percent by fiscal 2030 to a level that is 9 percent higher than its fiscal 1990 level. The eventual decline of energy demand and carbon dioxide emissions follows the pattern of population, which will grow from 126.9 million in 2000 to a peak of 127.7 million in 2006 and decline to 117.58 million, close to the 1980 level, in 2030.

10. Before the Russian ratification, carbon dioxide emissions from the Annex I countries that had ratified the protocol accounted for 44.2 percent of this group's emissions. The Russian Federation accounts for 17.4 percent, while the United States accounts for 36.1 percent. Other Annex I countries that have not yet ratified are Australia (accounting for 2.1 percent), Liechtenstein (0 percent), and Monaco (0 percent). Thus, Russia's ratification was a must for the protocol to enter into force. See United Nations Framework Convention on Climate Change, *Kyoto Protocol Thermometer* (Bonn: United Nations Framework Convention on Climate Change, 2003), available at http://unfccc.int/ resource/kpthermo_if.html.

11. In fiscal 2001, Japan emitted GHGs amounting to 1,299 million tons of carbon dioxide equivalent ($Mt/CO_2$), of which energy-related $CO_2$ accounted for 87 percent (1,139 $Mt/CO_2$). Energy use and production also emits methane and other GHGs. Thus, energy use and production related GHG emissions would account for about 90 percent. See Ministry of the Environment, Japan, *The GHGs Emissions Data of Japan (1990– 2001)* (Tsukuba: Ministry of the Environment, 2003), available in English at http:// www-gio.nies.go.jp/library_j/lib.

12. The lower the use of carbon-intensive coal, the lower the carbon dioxide emissions. Coal consumption in Germany declined by 35 percent between 1990 and 2002, while its share of the total primary energy supply shrank from 37 to 26 percent. In the United Kingdom, coal use was reduced by 44 percent, and the U.K. share of TPES declined from 31 to 17 percent during the same period. See BP, *BP statistical Review of World Energy 2003* (London: BP, 2003).

13. Intergovernmental Panel on Climate Change (IPCC), *IPCC Third Assessment Report: Climate Change 2001,* Working Group III: Mitigation, Technical Summary (Geneva: IPCC, 2001).

14. See also Kevin Baumert's discussion of the challenges on implementing the Kyoto Protocol in chapter 20 of this volume.

15. Nuclear accounted for 47.3 percent of TEPCO's power generation (with 121 terawatt-hours) in 2001, namely before the plant closure. The closure took place in the later part of 2002, and the nuclear contribution declined to 36.2 percent in 2002. Tokyo Elec-

tric Power Company, *TEPCO in Figure* (Tokyo: Tokyo Electric Power Company, 2003), available in English at http://www.tepco.co.jp.

16. J. Odawara, *Impacts of Nuclear Power Plant Closure in Japan on the International Energy Market* (Tokyo: Institute of Energy Economics of Japan, 2003).

17. Odawara, *Impacts of Nuclear Power Plant Closure.*

18. International Energy Agency, *Energy Prices and Taxes* (Paris: Organization for Economic Cooperation and Development and International Energy Agency, 2002).

19. See Loyola de Palacio's discussion of the European Union's program to reform the E.U. power sector in chapter 7 of this volume.

20. Y. Ogawa, "Proposal on Measures for Reducing Asian Premium of Crude Oil," a presentation made at the 375th Regular Research Meeting, Institute of Energy Economics of Japan, Tokyo, November 27, 2002.

21. The Agreement on an International Energy Program (as Amended) (IEP) obliges its participating countries to "maintain emergency reserves sufficient to sustain consumption for at least 90 days with no net oil imports" (article 2). The original level was, however, set at 60 levels (article 2, paragraph 1), but it was subsequently raised to 90 levels (article 2, paragraph 2). See International Energy Agency, *The Agreement on an International Energy Program (as Amended)* (Paris: Organization for Economic Cooperation and Development and International Energy Agency, 1974), available at http://www.iea.org/about/iep.pdf.

22. IEP Annex article 1 defines "total stocks," from which its paragraph 2 excludes "those stocks which can be technically determined as being absolutely unavailable in even the most severe emergency." The same paragraph further states: "The Standing Group on Emergency Questions shall examine this concept and report on criteria for the measurement of absolutely unavailable stocks." In addition, its paragraph 3 states, "Until a decision has been taken on this matter, each Participating Country shall subtract 10 per cent from its total stocks in measuring its emergency reserves." No such a decision has been made.

23. Not only Japan, but also the United States and Germany, among others, hold emergency stocks well above the IEP requirement. This is partly because the ninety-day level cannot be lowered unless emergency stocks are released in accordance with the activation of the emergency measures under the IEP (chapter IV). However, the emergency measures as defined in the IEP are unlikely to be activated. Since 1984, the IEA has developed a more flexible mechanism, which is called "Coordinated Emergency Response Measures" (CERM), which rely more on flexible use of emergency stocks. However, in this situation, the maintenance of a ninety-day stock level is required. Thus, many IEA participating countries are encouraged to hold emergency stocks well above the minimum ninety days. See International Energy Agency, *Oil Supply Security: The Emergency Response Potential of IEA Countries in 2000* (Paris: International Energy Agency, 2001).

24. The government stock was held by the Japan National Oil Corporation (JNOC) until January 2004, when JNOC was disbanded. Since February 2004, the Japan Oil, Gas, and Metals National Corporation has been contracted to manage the emergency stocks.

25. X. Liu and Y. Zhang, "China Petroleum Security and Regional Cooperation," a presentation made at the International Workshop on Cooperative Measures Enhancing

Oil Security in Northeast Asia organized by the Korea Energy Economics Institute, Seoul, September 6, 2003.

26. APERC, *Emergency Oil Stocks and Energy Security in the APEC Region* (Tokyo: APERC, 2000).

27. Japan's Basic Energy Policy Law (enacted in June 2002) required that the government present its plan to the Diet. The Cabinet adopted the plan after the draft had undergone a public comment process. Agency for Natural Resources, *Energy Basic Plan* (Tokyo: Agency for Natural Resources, 2003).

28. *Nihon Keizai Shinbun* reported in its October 7 issue that the Nuclear Power Commission's Expert Subcommittee disclosed that the cost of the spent fuel reprocessing and recycling would be 80 percent higher than that of the once-through ¥15 trillion and that the household electricity consumer would pay an extra amount of ¥600 to ¥840 per year for the recycle option. But it also reported that the commission would pursue spent-fuel recycling for the sake of a stable power supply, while making a once-through option a matter of further study.

29. The OECD membership has increased since 1975, but it is not clear whether the United Nations has adjusted the OECD coverage. But because the new members could have been mostly small importers, their omissions or inclusions would have a small relevance to the current argument.

30. The coverage of "industrialized countries" in *IEO 2004* is almost identical to the OECD member countries. But among some other new OECD member countries, the *IEO* includes South Korea in "Developing Asia" and Poland in "Eastern Europe and the Former Soviet Union." For further information, see U.S. Energy Information Administration *International Energy Outlook 2004* (Washington, D.C.: Energy Information Administration, 2004).

31. APERC, *APEC Outlook.*

32. APERC, *APEC Outlook.*

33. APERC, *Power Interconnection in the APEC Region, Current Status and Future Potentials* (Tokyo: APERC, 2000).

34. APERC, *Power Interconnection in the APEC Region.*

35. APERC, *Energy Supply Infrastructure Development in the APEC Region* (Tokyo: APERC, 2001).

36. In the past, Japanese hydrocarbon development companies, which are qualified for tax relief, were required to ship oil produced to Japan. Some part of such oil did not meet Japan's domestic needs. Later, this requirement was dropped and such oil could be exported to appropriate markets.

37. *Nihon Keizai Shinbun* reported in its July 6, 2004, issue that the deal would be mutually beneficial for the Japanese (with supply source diversification) and the Saudis (with greater access to the Japanese market).

38. Despite Iran's problems with the International Atomic Energy Agency, there is no strong view in Japan opposing energy development and other economic cooperation with Iran. Unlike North Korea, which is considered a potential security threat to Japan, based on kidnappings and missile proliferation, Iran simply does not look harmful to Japan.

# Commentary on Part IV

*J. Bennett Johnston*

This volume highlights the ways in which U.S. energy policy can advance America's foreign policy and national security interests. The authors of the chapters in this part, "The Pacific Rim," paint these intersections in sharp relief. In my view, the United States can increase its share of global trade, maintain its security umbrella for Asia, forge partnerships to address complex issues such as North Korea's nuclear proliferation, and advance American values in the region through creative partnerships with the great powers of Asia, such as China and Japan, and through cooperation with multilateral organizations like the Asia-Pacific Economic Cooperation forum (APEC). Energy can be one of America's most powerful tools in crafting these new relationships.

As the authors of the chapters in part IV point out, energy insecurity in China and Japan, and national policies that seek self-sufficiency rather than regional cooperation, can cause serious tensions. There is a tendency for Americans and various Asian nations to see China as a competitor for oil and to fear its growth and appetite for energy as a threat. As Amy Jaffe and Kenneth Medlock rightly state, China is today seeking to act on its own to achieve energy security. China's actions are quite progressive in some respects. China is curbing demand by raising fuel efficiency standards, redressing adverse environmental effects by closing inefficient mines, developing its own resources both by modernizing its national oil companies and by inviting partial foreign ownership in them, and actively planning to build strategic reserves.

But China is also seeking security by bilateral means that put it at odds with U.S. policy. Jaffe and Medlock point out that China seeks access to reserves in places like Sudan and Iran, where the United States has deep security and humanitarian concerns. China exchanges arms for oil with Middle East suppliers, where China can tip the balance of power in ways that could compromise Western security interests. China has also sought to compete with its neighbors for deepwater reserves in contested waters.

In my view, America can use shared U.S. and Chinese interests in energy security to forge a relationship of cooperation that will allow China to have greater investment in their common concerns than in divergent interests. The United States can cooperate on new energy efficient technologies with China, to help it curb demand. It can help China learn how to develop strategic stocks and how to manage them in a way that does not disrupt the global market. It can exchange information on clean coal and gas utilization strategies, which would advance shared environmental and energy security objectives. It can share its global energy market data with China in exchange for transparency with respect to China's energy demand and supplies. This kind of cooperation will put United States–China discussions on North Korea, Southeast Asia, and global security issues on a more secure footing.

Another component of a wise U.S. Asian policy should be to link China closely to its neighbors and the international system through multilateral organizations that share a common mission to promote trade and investment and energy security. John Ryan highlights the utility of APEC as a voluntary, consensus-building organization. His discussion of the evolution of the APEC Energy Security Initiative highlights the promise of multilateral cooperation. An Asian emergency response system that can address oil shocks, cooperation on oil spills, and regional planning on the delivery of natural gas to fuel power plants will give all nations a sense of interdependence and collective will. Ryan points out that APEC's gas reserves, including Russia, are more than adequate to fulfill regional demand. I would suggest that APEC take its energy planning a step further and seek to fashion a regional gas and power system that will address the needs of all nations.

Transportation arrangements present opportunities for cooperation and competition. On the one hand, Russia, China, and South Korea are negotiating a possible pipeline to carry east Siberian gas to these two Asian markets. On the other hand, one of the sharpest competitions bruited today has been between China and Japan over the direction of a new oil pipeline from Russia. Russia has decided that, initally the pipeline will go to Nakhodka. The opportunity is still there to make sure that cooperation prevails in the energy relationship between these major Asian powers. In turn, APEC and the United States should find a more comprehensive solution for the region that promotes the development of sufficient infrastructure to avoid harmful competition.

Keiichi Yokobori's comprehensive, insightful look at Japan's energy policy points out both challenges and opportunities for regional cooperation. He reminds us that Japan, America's closest ally in Asia, faces complete energy dependency and seeks security both by cooperation with multilateral forums such as the International Energy Agency and APEC, and through bilateral agreements that give it access to oil fields in the Middle East and gas from Sakhalin as well as potentially east Siberia, in Russia. Japan's energy insecurity presents some tensions with U.S. policy, particularly because the United States seeks to deter Japan from cooperation with Iran. But Japan's diversification strategy bears emulation. Japan is pursuing nuclear energy as well as renewables, diversifying its sources of supply at all costs. Japan's pursuits make it a leader in the deployment of energy-efficient technologies and in the diversification of energy supply. Japan can continue to share this expertise with others, directly or through APEC. Yokobori chronicles Japan's recent setback in nuclear energy. The United States and APEC should find ways to learn from Japan's lessons and pursue joint research in nuclear safety and the storage of nuclear waste.

Yokobori's most insightful contributions are his proposals for developing regional energy reserves, regional infrastructure, and an energy solution for the North Korean crisis. The idea of regional strategic reserves (proposed in detail by David Goldwyn and Michelle Billig in chapter 21) can provide an Asian energy security umbrella. If China can join in a strategic reserve, without bearing the full cost of the oil and the storage, it will see a real and dramatic security dividend for cooperation. If that umbrella covers other Asian nations such as Vietnam and its neighbors, regional tensions will decrease. Likewise a regional plan for gas and liquefied natural gas infrastructure, with nations helping to assure long-term demand at market prices, could accelerate gas transportation development and boost the regional economy.

Yokobori's North Korea proposal is intriguing. He suggests that by connecting the North and South Korean power grids, as well as the Japanese and Russian grids, the region could enjoy greater electrification, lower power prices (in Japan), and reduce greenhouse gas emissions by allowing the use of cleaner fuels. The political benefits of such integration would support significantly the development of linkages between North Korea and South Korea, as well as linkages among North Korea, South Korea, and Japan.

The key to the advancement of any of these bold ideas depends on the leadership of the United States. The U.S. role as investor, bridge builder, and facilitator of multilateral organizations is a historic one. U.S. leadership has been indispensable for lasting peace and security in the Pacific. For America to sustain this role in the coming decades will require that it to return to those roots, and invest its diplomacy in building a true Pacific community.

This forward-looking book makes clear the dividends of a new energy strategy for U.S. national and economic security. The authors have provided a concrete vision of how energy can support regional and global cooperation instead of conflict in the new century.

# Part V

# The North Atlantic and the Americas

Part V discusses the challenges facing the oil-producing countries of the North Atlantic region and Latin America, with chapters by Willy Olsen on the North Sea, Shirley Neff on North America and the U.S. West Coast, and Luis Téllez Kuenzler on Latin America. These regions face serious challenges to their ability to contribute to global energy security in the twenty-first century. The United States and the North Sea region are mature geological provinces. Social and environmental opposition to opening remaining areas rich with hydrocarbons will limit the contribution these regions make to the diversity of the global energy supply. The United States and Europe face growing demand for natural gas, but their ability to meet demand with domestic supply is uncertain, without new investment in gas importation infrastructure. The nations of Latin America face a different challenge. The region is rich in reserves, but political resistance to the use of foreign capital has made Mexico a gas importer rather than exporter and has impaired its ability to serve the global oil market. In Argentina, Bolivia, and Venezuela, the development of energy is fraught with deep nationalistic political meaning, slowing economic development in the region as well as the development of energy supplies.

In chapter 14, Olsen describes Norway's efforts to maintain production levels in the North Sea, and he addresses the implications of declining production on global energy security and Norway's economy. He observes that technological innovation, favorable government policies such as tax incentives and improved fiscal terms, and cooperation among the United Kingdom, Russia, and Norway can help increase production in the North Sea and enhance global energy security. In addition, he argues that the Norwegian model for managing oil revenues, which includes an oil fund, can be emulated by other producers to ensure the effective use of natural resources for economic development.

In chapter 15, Neff argues that a stable supply of natural gas will be crucial to U.S. and Mexican economic growth. She indicates that the major advances in regional integration and cooperation forged in the 1980s can serve as a foundation for meeting the challenges facing the United States and Mexico as a result of a looming shortage. She argues that common policies on energy efficiency, the real integration of a North American power grid, and a rapid and strategic decision on natural gas infrastructure will help preserve jobs and industries in North America and reduce price volatility. She also suggests that an enlightened U.S. foreign policy, which works with Canada and Mexico on gas and power issues, can promote economic development and job growth.

In chapter 16, Téllez argues that the United States should give more attention to Latin America, and through a noninterventionist strategy help the resource-rich countries maximize the productive value of their oil and gas reserves. He argues that outdated fiscal and legal regimes are the main obstacles to the development of Latin America's natural resources and to the development of their economies. He recommends that the United States help Latin American countries reform their energy sectors and realize the full benefit of their resources. He urges Latin American governments to maximize production now, and to invest in the health, education, and economic infrastructure of the current generation, rather than simply husband resources for future generations. Téllez concludes that a U.S. foreign policy emphasizing cooperation, trade, and a reasonable migration policy will not only enhance the region's energy security but also help to ensure its political and social stability.

In her commentary on part V, Michelle Michot Foss cautions that there is more to the security of supply than access to oil and gas resources. Investors need an institutional framework that attracts investment, and government institutions must have the managerial capacity and political will to implement that framework. She assesses the different models that nations have used to balance the desire to retain sovereignty over national resources with the need to compete globally for capital. Noting the success that Norway, the United Kingdom, Canada, and the United States have had in adjusting their fiscal regimes, reviving investor interest in dormant sectors, and creating employment, she provides useful insights for the nations in Latin America that are still searching for investment frameworks to satisfy their development needs within a political culture that still fears foreign capital.

Foss shares the view of each of the authors in this part that the surest path to energy security lies in integration. She notes that the United States and Mexico, the United Kingdom, and Norway have each faced challenges balancing their differing investment frameworks, and she highlights the need for nations to make the harmonization of legal regimes a foreign policy priority if they intend to provide their citizens with energy security. As nations seek to create competitive power markets—a growing concern for the United States, Mexico, and an expanding European market—foreign policymakers will need to assure that there is competition for supplying natural gas, as they fashion the intergovernmental agreements needed to encourage a diversity of supply.

# 14

# The North Sea

## Willy H. Olsen

For the past thirty years, the North Sea oil and gas industry has been at the forefront of global oil and gas developments. At their peak, the offshore areas in Northwest Europe produced more than 6 million barrels of liquids per day. As a result, the North Sea has been important in providing diversity in supply for the past two decades.

The region has now entered a more mature stage of life. The days of the big discoveries may have passed in the North Sea, on both the U.K. and the Norwegian continental shelves, but the large unexplored frontier areas in the northern part of Norway can still yield significant oil and gas discoveries. Norway, however, is at a crossroads. Either it will create the terms and conditions to extend its role as a key exporter of oil and gas, sustaining its role as a major source of diversity of supply other than the Organization of Petroleum Exporting Countries (OPEC), or its stature will recede, diminishing its constructive role as a supplier, technology leader, interlocutor with OPEC, and leading example of a prudent model for balancing the role of government and market forces, and energy and environmental concerns, in oil-producing economies.

This chapter addresses Norway's and the United Kingdom's role in energy geopolitics, Europe's growing dependency on oil and gas imports, the decline of U.K. and Norwegian continental shelf production, and Norway's challenges and choices with respect to sustaining oil and expanding gas production. It provides a brief history of the Norwegian policies that originally attracted capital and technology to the nation, as a template for the kind of policies that other countries may follow to continue to compete in a globalized world. It describes the Norwegian model for revenue management and concludes that Norway's internal energy policy choices will shape its geopolitical relations with Russia, Europe, and the United States. Competitive Norwegian energy policies will enhance global and particularly European energy security and bind Norway and Europe closer together through economic integration.

## Key Challenges

The energy policy choices Norway and the United Kingdom face today will determine whether they will continue to be important sources of energy supply tomorrow, with three main geopolitical implications for the global oil market. First, will they provide access to unexplored frontier acreage in Norway, the United Kingdom, and the Faeroe Islands, and will that acreage deliver what geologists hope for? So far, the exploration has been disappointing, with the exception of the Ormen Lange gas discovery. Second, will the governments provide competitive terms to allow companies to squeeze the last remaining drops of oil from the mature fields and stimulate exploration in deeper waters and sensitive environment? Third, will the Norwegian politicians of the future have the same political courage as their predecessors in the 1970s—and take the steps required to sustain Norwegian oil and gas policies, or will the world lose a major source of supply stability?

Nearly 40 percent of estimated European oil and gas resources are still either undiscovered or unappraised. On the Norwegian continental shelf (NCS), less than a third of the potential hydrocarbon resources have been produced. Norway may therefore still be a major producer for decades to come, but its oil production has peaked and the decline curve in the most pessimistic scenario is dramatic. Natural gas production will continue to grow, however, and by 2006 liquefied natural gas (LNG) will be exported to the United States from the Arctic Snøhvit field.

Technology has been the major success factor in developing oil and gas reserves in the North Sea. The development of offshore discoveries has depended on bold construction initiatives undertaken in a difficult and hazardous environment. The challenges have inspired enormous advances in science and technology of offshore exploration and production. The cost of finding, developing, and producing oil has been dramatically reduced. Technology has increased the recovery of oil from existing fields and added several million barrels of oil to production. Technology has also made it possible to meet stricter environmental requirements—like the carbon dioxide sequestration projects on the NCS.

The maturity of the U.K. continental shelf (UKCS) and the NCS is bringing new blood to the region, in the form of new players. Medium-sized and smaller oil companies are looking for finds too small to be of interest to the very large firms known as "super majors." The British and Norwegian governments are now actively stimulating new entrants to boost the activity level and to produce to the last drop. Norway is still lagging behind the United Kingdom, but changes introduced into the Norwegian system are now resulting in more investments.

## The Geopolitical Perspective

Energy transformed Europe's role in energy geopolitics, providing both wealth and security during the Cold War. But declines in energy production could significantly affect Norway, the United Kingdom, and Europe as a whole. Norway's importance as a supplier of natural gas to Europe and the United States will grow, while other European nations, and particularly the United Kingdom, may see increasing dependence on imported oil and gas color their relationships with Russia and North Africa.

Oil and gas were the most important natural resources to be discovered in Europe during the twentieth century, providing energy and essential chemicals for transport, industry, and commercial and residential uses. The Netherlands, Denmark, the United Kingdom, and Norway became major oil and gas producers. The discovery of oil transformed Norway into one of the world's richest countries, while the United Kingdom became self-sufficient in oil and gas.

However, Europe is now facing increasing dependency on energy imports, which makes the security of its supply one of the key aims of energy policy in the European Union. According to current forecasts, the dependence of the European countries belonging to the Organization for Economic Cooperation and Development on imported energy will grow from about 36 percent in 2000 to 69 percent in 2030. As a result, Europe is becoming more vulnerable both to physical disruptions in energy supply, whether permanent or temporary, and to economic disruptions in energy markets. This situation creates a major challenge for European policymakers, because stable, secure, and affordable energy supplies are of fundamental importance to the future of Europe. The U.K. government made energy security one of its strategic priorities in its foreign policy document in 2004.[1]

Europe is also keen to implement the Kyoto Protocol and meet its targets.

It has therefore been vital for the European Union to develop a strategy that can reconcile security of supply with other objectives such as competitiveness and sustainable development.

## Europe's Growing Import Dependency

Continental Europe's dependence on oil and gas imports is not a new phenomenon. Europe has been dependent on oil imports for decades, but its degree of dependency is projected to rise dramatically in the medium to long terms as UKCS and NCS production decline further. This will require a new look at the need for building strategic storage facilities, not only for oil but also for gas. As Loyola de Palacio notes in chapter 7 of this volume, this will also require more harmonization of energy policy in Europe, and increase the importance of energy in the European Union's dialogue with Russia, North Africa, and the Middle East.

The new market situation in Europe offers fresh opportunities for Russia, Algeria, and other gas-producing nations. Seventy percent of the world's gas reserves are estimated to lie within 5,000 kilometers of Europe.[2] The challenge is therefore not the lack of resources, but the producing countries' ability to exploit their gas reserves and deliver that gas at minimum cost to the market.

The market will provide some of the response to European demand. Gazprom is planning a new pipeline to Europe. The pipeline has been a key feature of the Russia–European Union energy dialogue. Algeria is expanding its capacity to deliver gas to Europe. Natural gas from the Caspian Sea region, North and West Africa, and the Middle East may also be imported into Europe. But Europe will also have an interest in the political stability and economic productivity of these producing nations.

### A New Situation for the United Kingdom

The largest European gas market, the United Kingdom, is the fourth largest gas producer in the world, supplying more than 100 billion cubic meters per year of gas from its offshore fields. Gas production peaked in 2003 and is slowly declining. The United Kingdom will probably be a net importer of gas by 2005.[3] Imported energy could account for three-quarters of the country's total primary energy needs by 2020. Figure 14.1 illustrates the future development of the U.K. gas market.

Figure 14.1. Demand for Gas in the United Kingdom, 1990–2012 (billion cubic meters)

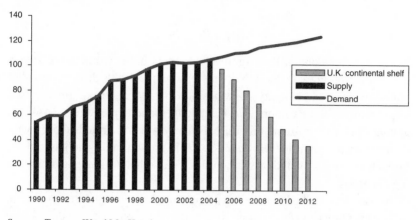

*Sources:* Transco; Wood MacKenzie.

The new focus in Britain will therefore be the country's ability to secure reliable energy supplies. The need for additional import infrastructure is acute if the country is to avoid a very tight supply and demand position by fiscal 2005/06, especially in the event of an extremely cold winter. The British government is taking steps to foster long-term commercial and political relationships with exporting countries. Industry has also responded quickly to the new market situation, and a number of new import schemes are moving ahead.

## Norway's Role in Gas

Norway's influence as a major exporter of natural gas will continue to grow. The country already has a significant market share in continental Europe, above 20 percent in large markets like Germany. In the next decade, the United Kingdom will emerge as the fastest growing market for Norwegian gas. By 2006, Norway will also deliver natural gas for the first time to the U.S. East Coast.

The Norwegian gas regime has changed as a result of both the European Union's gas directive and intense pressure from Brussels. The directive is applicable because of Norway's membership in the European Economic Area. As a result, the producers on the NCS are now able to sell their gas directly to customers in Europe. More than 60 percent of Norway's gas, however, is marketed by Statoil, the Norwegian state-controlled oil and gas company.

## Norway's Role in Oil

Norway became one of the largest oil exporters in the world in the 1990s. Oil production grew faster in Norway through the 1990s than in any other non-OPEC country. Norway's new position as a global oil exporter exposed its government to new international challenges, and to pressure from OPEC to contribute to stabilizing oil prices. Norway's historic role had been with the consuming countries. However, its rapid growth in oil and gas exports through the 1980s altered its relationship with both consuming and producing countries.

Norway has worked to balance consumer and producer interests in stable oil prices. On various occasions since 1986, the country has reduced production to support oil prices. The Norwegian government has always emphasized, however, that production regulations were introduced on the basis of an independent assessment, which took into consideration the benefit of a production cut for the domestic economy, and the activities on the NCS. E.U. officials in Brussels are increasingly vocal, however, in their criticism of Norway's willingness to reduce oil production to help stabilize oil prices.

Within OPEC, Norway is viewed as having the same objective as OPEC: to maintain stable oil prices at "a reasonable level." For Norway, that has meant a price of about $20 to $22 per barrel, even as oil prices increased in 2003–5. In recent years, Norway has developed closer relations with some of the key OPEC countries, like Saudi Arabia, Venezuela, and Iran, and has worked to foster a more formal consumer–producer dialogue. However, Norway has never contemplated joining OPEC.

Although Norway's role in the global oil markets will be significantly reduced in the next decade, the country will still export close to 2 million barrels per day (mmbpd) until 2015. Not many emerging producers will export similar volumes. Norway should retain its influence with OPEC; the leading OPEC countries will be keen to maintain close relations with Norway in case they again need its cooperation to stabilize future oil prices.

## A Basis for Future Norwegian-Russian Cooperation?

Norway's desire to explore its Arctic region to sustain oil and gas production could provide a basis for cooperation or tension with Russia. Statoil believes that the Arctic region, including the Russian sector of the Barents Sea, may become a core growth area in the future. Norway and Russia have been in close discussions for many years on cooperation in the Barents Sea, but they have not been able to solve their boundary dispute. Several large structures have been mapped in the dispute area—and a solution to the boundary dispute could lead to an active exploration program, with positive political benefits.

Commercial cooperation may help to drive political cooperation. Currently, both Statoil and Norsk Hydro are aiming for a stake in Gazprom's giant natural gas discovery in the Far North. Gazprom initially planned to develop the Shtokman field as piped gas to Europe. An LNG plant is now considered as an alternative or as an additional option.

The developments in the Russian Far North are of fundamental importance to Norway—including from an environmental point of view. The increased Russian transport of oil from the Far North along the Norwegian coastline is a major concern for coastal societies and the fishing industry, which fear a major disaster. A potential large export terminal for oil at Murmansk is adding to this concern. Cooperation with Russia on exploration could provide a stronger basis for negotiations on environmental and commercial concerns.

## Maintaining Competitiveness:
## The U.K. Continental Shelf Challenge

The United Kingdom and Norway achieved their prominent role in energy geopolitics by adopting competitive energy sector policies. This historical success offers a model for the future, as existing fields decline. The ability of North Sea producers to stay competitive will be key to their energy as well as national security.

The UKCS is past its peak. Oil production reached almost 3 mmbpd in 1999, but it had declined to 1.8 mmbpd in 2004. Natural gas production—which exploded in the 1990s as Britain converted from coal to gas—is still at its peak, above 100 billion cubic meters per year in 2003, but is now entering rapid decline.

The two main objectives for British energy policy are to make sure that UKCS oil and gas reserves are exploited fully and effectively and to maintain Britain's position as an oil and gas center of expertise.[4] Despite the maturity of the UKCS, it still holds considerable future potential. Its exploration potential is estimated at between 5 and 11 billion barrels of oil equivalent. New fields are, however, expected to be smaller, geologically more complex, remote, and difficult to exploit.

The British government and industry realize that tax revenues, profits, and opportunities will eventually start to dry up if structural changes are not introduced. Closer dialogue and closer cooperation between government and industry is essential to maintaining the same level of activity. The main forum for this cooperation is PILOT.[5] The vision for PILOT is a production level of 3 million barrels of oil equivalent per day in 2010. It is an ambitious target.

The government is giving a high priority to attracting new investors to boost the activity level and stimulate new exploration. A number of new policies have been introduced to encourage the development of otherwise redundant fields and prospects and to increase exploration in the mature and frontier areas of the UKCS.

The government has also been pressing the oil companies to release licensed but unexploited fallow areas to those prepared to exploit them. In addition, the government is cutting red tape and improving the taxation system to accelerate activities, secure smooth transfer of North Sea assets, and pave the way for the new entrants, and it has had excellent responses to licensing rounds in 2003 and 2004.

Although industry and the British government are working hard to achieve their production ambitions, it is obvious that the United Kingdom has to look well beyond the UKCS to meet its future oil and gas needs. The U.K. supply gap has led the country to seek the security of its gas supply both by pipeline and by an increased emphasis on LNG. The country has negotiated at least three new pipeline projects and three new LNG terminals. The capacity in the pipelines linking the United Kingdom and continental Europe will be substantially expanded, and Norway will add a new export pipeline to the United Kingdom. BP and Sonatrach will bring LNG from Algeria to the United Kingdom, while Exxon Mobil is looking at the possibility of substantial LNG exports from Qatar.

## U.K. Energy Diplomacy:
## New Cooperation with Norway and Russia

Norway was a major natural gas exporter to the United Kingdom in the late 1970s and early 1980s, but relations have alternated between competition and cooperation. The British government's decision to cancel the agreement for gas deliveries from the Sleipner field to the United Kingdom in the mid-1980s led to the rapid rise in domestic British gas production. Today, Norwegian companies are ready to develop new gas reserves to fill the U.K. supply gap. A new pipeline will be built from the large Ormen Lange gas field in mid-Norway to Easington in England.

There has been considerable exchange of experience over the years between the United Kingdom and Norway. A few fields are even shared between the two countries, but cooperation has still been limited. Trust has not always been present. The operators and governments in both countries have more recently agreed to strengthen their ties. The prize is high—improved cross-border cooperation has a possible payoff of about $2 billion.[6]

Russian gas can also play an important part in securing supply to the United Kingdom. This was evident during President Vladimir Putin's state visit in 2003, when he and Prime Minister Tony Blair agreed on closer energy cooperation, with a view to increasing security, improving the investment climate, preserving the environment, and tackling climate change. The two countries also signed a memorandum of cooperation on a North European gas pipeline between them. Both documents recognize the value of Russia as a future energy partner for the United Kingdom.

The discussions with Russia demonstrate that Britain wants to strengthen its ties with key energy-supplying nations. This cooperation will have an impact on the United Kingdom's foreign policy with Russia. Though U.K. or Norwegian industry has the technical and commercial expertise to purchase or help develop Russian gas, it is the government's function to ensure that Russia's markets are open and that the necessary political, economic, and legal conditions are created to ensure long-term investment in supplies. These conditions need to be backed by official agreements and regulations that will allow industry to fulfill its role. The United Kingdom–Norway experience suggests the challenges the United Kingdom and the European Union may face similar negotiations with Russia.

## Maintaining Competitiveness:
## The Norwegian Continental Shelf Challenges

Norway became the world's third largest exporter of crude oil and natural gas in the 1990s. Oil production peaked at 3.4 million barrels of liquids per day in 2002. Natural gas production is still growing, and in the next decades it could reach 120 billion cubic meters per year (figure 14.2).[7]

Figure 14.2. Norway's Oil and Gas Production History, 1970–2000 (million barrels per day oil equivalent)

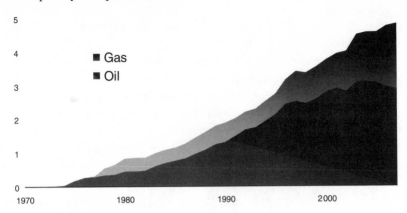

*Source:* Norwegian Petroleum Directorate.

The key goals for Norwegian oil and gas policies since the early 1970s have been national management and control, and building a Norwegian oil community with competitive national companies and active state participation. Emerging oil powers and OPEC nations looking to sustain job creation and manage oil wealth more productively regularly look to the Norwegian model.

Why has Norway succeeded when so many other resource-rich countries have failed? Three main factors contributed to Norway's success. First, visionary politicians were in power when oil was discovered in 1969. Their objective was to develop a strong oil and gas industrial base, but also to avoid becoming too dependent on oil and gas revenues. Their perspective was long term. They wanted Norway's oil and gas era not to be an episode but an epoch.

Second, a strong and highly competent civil service ensured long-term planning, continuity, and stability in the decision-making process. New institutions were transparent and accountable. Stakeholders, local communities, and academics were involved from the beginning of the oil era. Third, management responsibility for the energy sector was clearly divided among Parliament, the government, the regulatory body (the Petroleum Directorate), and the national oil company, Statoil.

Statoil was established with the objective of becoming a fully integrated oil and gas company. Statoil was an instrument in implementing the government's policies, but it had no role in the development of the government's oil policy. The government's control of the new national oil company was important, but the company was also allowed operational and commercial freedom and could make its own decisions without interference from the minister in day-to-day operations, which is so common in most national oil companies. The minister or other government officials were not allowed to serve on the company's board.

The role of Statoil evolved over time. Parliament restructured the role of Statoil in 1985 after a long political debate. A major part of the company's cash flow was transferred to a new nonoperating entity, the State Direct Financial Investments (SDFI). SDFI was managed by Statoil, but invested directly in projects on the NCS and received the returns on the investments. Today, SDFI is the major revenue earner on the NCS.

In the past decade, Statoil has expanded its activities internationally, and in 2001 it was partly privatized. However, the Norwegian government remains the main shareholder, controlling 70 percent of the shares.[8]

Norway tried from the beginning to find "the right balance between foreign participation and Norwegian interests." The government was keen to attract highly competent companies that were strong financially and were at the leading edge technologically. At most, about 25 foreign oil companies were active in Norway, while around 100 companies were involved in the United Kingdom. Norway was seen as a place for the "big boys." The government gave priority to oil companies with a long-term perspective and willingness to transfer technology and competence to Statoil, to Norsk Hydro, and to the Norwegian offshore industry, which were awarded the most attractive acreage and service opportunities.

Many oil- and gas-producing countries are looking at the Norwegian way of managing its oil and gas sector to learn from its experience. Many would like to build a strong domestic oil industry with a high "local content." Norway has therefore initiated an extensive program of assisting emerging producers in establishing the legal framework and institutions required to manage the oil and gas sector. The message delivered is to develop an oil policy based on resource management; value creation; high standards for health, safety, and the environment (e.g., no gas flaring); transparency; and accountability. Norway has in recent years signed cooperation agreements with Angola, Nigeria, Mexico, and Venezuela, as well as Iran and East Timor.

## Norway: At a Crossroads as an Oil and Gas Producer

The petroleum sector is Norway's largest and most important economic activity. As the country faces a gradual reduction in the activity level, its

Figure 14.3. Two Scenarios for Petroleum Production on Norway's
Continental Shelf, 2012–50

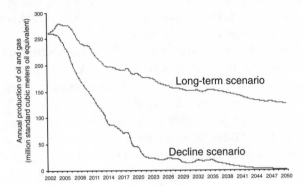

*Source:* Norwegian Ministry of Petroleum and Energy.

government has therefore launched initiatives aimed at increased exploration
activity, increased oil and gas recovery from existing fields, and reduced
costs.[9]

The government's ambition is to implement a policy that will ensure that
the country avoids the decline scenario (figure 14.3), which is based on
harvesting existing discoveries and not finding new fields. The government
has introduced measures to increase exploration activity, and it promises to
continue with a flexible policy to obtain faster and more efficient exploration.

In Norway, as in other countries, the heart of the debate is over the economic framework. The oil industry accepts the government's diagnosis of
the health of the oil and gas sector, but the industry is not happy with the
medication. It sees the fiscal regime (primarily a special oil tax that makes
returns on investment in Norway less attractive to investors) as the main
problem, and it believes that the government's unwillingness to improve
fiscal terms will lead to a slowdown in activity. The government does acknowledge that Norway has to offer terms that are competitive to attract
investments, but it advocates a new tax regime for exploration to reduce the
risks for new oil companies entering the country.

Access to attractive fields is another factor in Norway's ability to attract
investment and sustain production. Oil companies have also emphasized
that they must be provided with prospective acreage to drill. Pressure to
open up more of the environmentally sensitive Norwegian and Barents seas
has been mounting. Environmental lobby groups are arguing, however, for

keeping the oil industry out of some of the most sensitive environmental areas, and the issue has become very politically charged. The government struck a balance, deciding in 2003 to allow drilling in the Barents Sea but not to accept exploration south of the Lofoten Islands due to the environmental risks. In 2004–5, a program to allow exploration in previously defined areas drew a positive response.[10] Future choices will involve access in the northernmost part of the NCS in the Barents Sea (where only one discovery—the Snøhvit field—has been declared commercial), the rest of the Barents Sea (where the large accumulation of petroleum that once was present seems to have migrated out of the trap), or the barely explored acreage toward the Russian border. Most geologists see higher potential to the east.

## The Future of Norway's Energy Sector

Norway faces significant choices that will affect its role in the global energy market for the next century. The key factors will be policy decisions made with respect to the role of technology, the development of new projects, the role of gas, the balance between environmental and development concerns, and incentives for new exploration and development players.

### *The Role of Technology*

So far, the development of Norway's oil and gas industry has been associated with the development of large fields that have justified high investment costs. Future development projects may consist of significantly fewer large fields, while small field development is expected to progress rapidly, as has been the case on the UKCS.

The Norwegian oil industry sees technology as the single most important factor in recovering more oil and gas, reducing costs, and strengthening competitiveness. The Ministry of Petroleum and Energy therefore initiated in 2001 a new technology program, $OG_{21}$.[11] The program is an illustration of the close links between the government, industry, and the research community in Norway.

The Norwegian government is also strengthening its ties with other oil- and gas-producing nations on technology. In 2004, the Norwegian minister of petroleum and energy and the U.S. secretary of energy signed a memorandum of understanding between their two countries on long-term energy research and technology.[12]

The two countries share a common interest in energy-related research and technology, which may be strengthened through focused and intensified bilateral effort in several areas of research and development, such as oil and gas exploitation, carbon sequestration, hydrogen research, and new renewable energy.

Two large gas projects demonstrate the impact of technology on both exploration and the environment. The Snøhvit development—operated by Statoil—is the first Norwegian and European production and export facility for LNG, with deliveries scheduled to start in 2006.[13] The field lies 140 kilometers from the coast off northern Norway. It is the first field to be developed in Arctic waters. The production will be piped to a receiving and liquefaction plant on a small island outside the city of Hammerfest.

After processing and liquefaction, LNG will be shipped to markets in Europe and the United States. Total investment in the project is put at about $7 to $8 billion, making this the largest industrial development in north Norwegian history. The development has been hit by a series of cost increases due to its complexity.

Snøhvit represents the first major Norwegian offshore development with no surface installations. It is also setting a standard for future developments in the Barents Sea. As an operator, Statoil has had to incorporate high environmental standards in the development solution. The carbon dioxide in the well stream will be separated out in the receiving plant and piped back to Snøhvit for storage below ground.

The other complex and advanced project on the NCS is the Ormen Lange development in the Norwegian Sea.[14] The field will be developed by Norsk Hydro with sea floor production facilities at about 3,000 feet of water depth, connected to an onshore processing and exporting plant. No installation will be visible on the sea's surface above Ormen Lange when it starts operating. The subsea solution is not just a technological leap but also a highly competitive economic solution. This $10 billion project is aiming at first production in 2007.

## The Environmental Challenge

One current dominant feature of the Norwegian oil and gas sector is the potential for conflict between environmental concerns and continued active hydrocarbon development on the NCS. Environmental groups are arguing in favor of introducing "petroleum-free zones" along the coastline.

The basic philosophy behind Norway's oil and gas policies since the commencement of petroleum activities can be summarized in one word: co-existence. This coexistence is now under severe strain. As petroleum activities are moving further north and into coastal areas, there is the ever-present need to balance the interest of the petroleum sector with other industries, such as fisheries, and to preserve the environment.

Another environmental issue of high importance to Norway is global climate change. The Norwegian government is actively seeking to reduce offshore emissions through a broad set of policies and measures. Norway has had an extensive carbon dioxide tax in place for a decade in the oil and gas sector, greenhouse gas emissions from the NCS are well below the global average, and Norway has become a pioneer in introducing carbon dioxide sequestration at two offshore gas fields.

The policy line Norway has taken regarding climate change differs from those of many other petroleum-producing countries. Norway tries to combine its interest as a petroleum-producing country with its ambitions to be an active participant in reducing greenhouse gas emissions.

### *Attracting More Players: Maintaining Strong State Participation*

Statoil, Norsk Hydro, and a few large foreign oil companies have traditionally been the dominant players on the NCS. In the new mature environment, with smaller discoveries and increasing tail-end production from older fields, Norway has to attract a new breed of companies. However, companies that can undertake demanding and capital-intensive projects like Ormen Lange will still be of great importance.

The Norwegian government sees the need to bring in new independent firms to increase competition, to stimulate exploration, and develop smaller discoveries. Talisman has already acquired a small BP field, while Paladin, Revus, and others are expanding their involvement. The fiscal framework will be changed in 2005 to reduce the exploration risks for new companies.

Even though a new breed of companies is entering Norway as an addition to the existing foreign players, Statoil and Norsk Hydro will continue as key players, but it is likely that the balance between Norwegian and foreign participation will be adjusted in favor of the foreign oil companies. In all circumstances, however, the Norwegian state will be heavily involved in petroleum operations on the NCS.

## Norway's Petroleum Fund

Norway's Petroleum Fund is often-cited as a model of transparency and effectiveness in oil revenue management. The fund is important to Norway's national economy and to the national consensus with respect to the energy industry. Those who look to Norway as a model should understand how the fund is structured and how it interacts with national economic policy.

The petroleum sector is very significant for Norway. It plays an important part in the national economy, and it has made a big contribution to the development of the Norwegian welfare state. The sector represents more than 40 percent of export revenues and about 20 percent of gross domestic product and state revenues, contributing to the government's solid financial position. The people of Norway are in a unique position. For most Norwegians, life in material terms has never been better, and the last couple of generations have experienced an unparalleled rise in prosperity. Norway is now at the top of the UN Human Development Index. However, the prosperity enjoyed by present generations carries obligations. Because the oil and gas resources are limited, the widely held view is that these riches should not only benefit a few generations but must also be safeguarded for future generations.

The Government Petroleum Fund was established in 1990.[15] The first transfer from the state budget to the Petroleum Fund was made in 1996. At the end of 2004, the fund amounted to more than NOK 1,000 billion—about $153 billion. Projections indicate that the fund will grow substantially in the next decade. The fund is intended to serve as a tool to help the management of fiscal policy, by making the spending of petroleum revenues more visible.

The Petroleum Fund had two main purposes. First, it was seen as a buffer to smooth short-term variations in the oil revenues. The objective was to make the Norwegian economy more robust and allow greater room to maneuver on economic policy. The stabilization role is now of limited importance. Second, it was seen as a tool for coping with the financial challenges associated with an aging population and the eventual decline in oil revenues, by transferring wealth to future generations.

The income of the Petroleum Fund consists of the net cash flow from petroleum activities plus the return on the fund's capital and net financial transactions related to petroleum activities. The Ministry of Finance is responsible for the fund because the fund is an integrated part of government finances, but the fund's day-to-day management is delegated to the Norwegian Central Bank. Most of the revenues are saved in the fund, but the annual budget allows for a modest use of petroleum revenues. The fund can only invest *abroad* for the following reasons:

- The need to maintain and protect the Fiscal Budget as a management tool. If the Petroleum Fund were used to finance domestic investments such as infrastructure, know-how, and businesses, it would become a supplementary source for financing government expenditures. This would undermine the position of the Fiscal Budget as a political management tool and weaken the budget process.
- The need to stabilize the Norwegian economy. By investing the Petroleum Fund directly abroad, the central government contributes to the capital outflow needed to match current account surpluses. This dampens the pressure for a stronger exchange rate and/or lower interest rates, and shelters the domestic economy from the effect of high petroleum revenues.

The Petroleum Fund is well diversified. The fund was a minority shareholder in 2,900 companies in forty-one countries worldwide in 2004. The fund is not allowed to invest in companies that contribute to unethical actions or omissions, such as violations of fundamental humanitarian principles, gross violations of human rights, gross corruption, or severe environmental degradation.[16] At the same time, the debate on how much oil revenue to spend in Norway is steadily growing with the increasing size of the fund. The pressure to spend more is increasing.

The Norwegian Petroleum Fund is one of many similar funds in the world. The Permanent Fund in Alaska and the Heritage Fund in Alberta, Canada, are other examples. Establishing a petroleum fund has become part of the policies for many of the new emerging oil and gas producers. Kazakhstan's new Petroleum Fund is based on the Norwegian Fund, while Azerbaijan has many of the same principles in its fund. The advantage of the funds is to provide more transparency—one of the most important factors to ensure that oil and gas production does not become a curse but rather a blessing.

## Conclusion

The largest value creation in the Norwegian oil and gas sector may still lie ahead. The remaining resources can provide the country with large revenues for a long time to come, but this will require willingness to consider a broad range of measures to secure the competitiveness of the Norwegian continental shelf.

The industry's message to the politicians has been loud and clear. It is high time to adopt measures that can increase the level of profitable activity on the NCS. Tax changes are a necessary instrument for achieving this.

The Norwegian Sea and the Barents Sea have prospects of becoming significant European petroleum provinces in the future. Norway is in an excellent position to become a key player in the Arctic—not only on the NCS but also in the wider region, including Russia. Norway has the technology and expertise that could allow Norwegian companies to take an active role in the future development of the region, which might accelerate in the years to come.

In these efforts, Norway's energy policy and foreign policy will be closely interrelated. Diplomacy will enhance Norway's integration with the U.K. gas market, the rest of Europe, and the U.S. gas market. Norway's relations with Russia will have an impact on the development of the Arctic Sea and the management of delicate environmental issues. Norway's relations with new oil exporters will, it is to be hoped, enhance their transparency and stability. If Norway sustains its role as an important oil producer, it can be a continuing voice for price moderation with OPEC. These energy developments should also pay national security dividends for Norway, through closer ties with Europe and the United States, cooperative relations with the OPEC nations, and stronger integration between Russia and Europe.

## Notes

1. See the 2004 strategy document at http://www.fco.gov.uk/.

2. UKOOA Offshore Operators' Association Limited, *UK Security of Gas Supplies,* November 11, 2003.

3. Multiclient studies by Wood MacKenzie, 2003.

4. U.K. energy minister Steven Timms at Offshore Technology Conference, May 2004.

5. More information on the PILOT initiative can be found at http://www.pilottask-force.co.uk/. PILOT brings together industry and government to find solutions from maintaining activity on the UKCS.

6. The report was launched at the Offshore Northern Seas Conference in Stavanger in August 2002 by the two ministers, Brian Wilson and Einar Steensnaes.

7. The production outlook can be found on the Norwegian Petroleum Directorate Web site at http://www.npd.no.

8. More information on Statoil's privatization and ownership can be found at http://www.statoil.com.

9. Ministry of Petroleum and Energy, *White Paper no. 38, 2001–2002, Oil and Gas activities,* and *White Paper no. 38, 2003–2004,* available at http://odin.dep.no/oed. An unofficial English translation is available at http://odin.dep.no/archive/oedvedlegg/01/01/Srepo067.pdf.

10. Knut Evensen, "Norwegians Spice Up Mature Menu," *Upstream,* February 4, 2005, 16.

11. For more information, see http://www.og21.org/.

12. See http://odin.dep.no/oed and press release, June 2004.

13. See updated information on the project at http://www.statoil.com.

14. For updated information, see http://www.hydro.com/en/.

15. For more information, see http://odin.dep.no/fin/engelsk/p10001617/p10002780/007051-990004/index-dok000-b-n-a.html.

16. The report from the government commission, *The Petroleum Fund: Management for the Future: Proposed Ethical Guidelines for the Government Petroleum Fund,* is available at http://odin.dep.no/fin/engelsk/p10001617/p10001682/006071-220009/index-dok000-b-n-a.html.

# 15

# North America

## *Shirley Neff*

The future of North America's energy security lies in greater continental integration of energy markets and infrastructure, coupled with increased energy efficiency. The symbiotic relationship between Canada, Mexico, the United States with respect to oil and gas markets has provided a modicum of security for all three countries—with Canada and Mexico providing significant supplies of oil to the United States, and Canada providing the balance of natural gas supplies to the United States and enabling some gas export support for Mexico.

Prospectively, the rate of demand growth for energy in the United States and Mexico is forecast to continue at a significantly higher rate than continental production, requiring the United States to seek greater oil supplies from outside North America, reducing Mexico's oil export potential and requiring both the United States and Mexico to seek new suppliers of natural gas.[1] Though Canadian oil sands could provide an important opportunity to expand continental oil production, tight natural gas supplies and high natural gas prices could restrain exploitation. As a result, the continent will rely increasingly on imports of not only oil from outside the region but natural gas as well.

Accessing reliable supplies of natural gas to supply power generation will be important for economic growth in the United States and Mexico, in particular. The current and projected natural gas supply situation has serious implications for the United States if it does not create the infrastructure for increased piped gas or liquefied natural gas (LNG) import capacity. Natural gas prices will remain high, industries reliant on natural gas will move overseas, power prices will rise (or utilities will seek to use cheaper but less environmentally friendly coal supplies), and growth could be impaired.[2] These changes in the North American market are having an impact on global oil and natural gas markets today and will continue to do so as import dependency grows.

The United States, Canada, and Mexico will all require new supplies of oil or natural gas from different supply sources, necessitating new pipeline and import infrastructure expansion in all three countries. Managing these changing markets will require increased efficiency of energy use, overcoming political obstacles to infrastructure development, and mustering the political will within the three governments to implement effective new measures, especially providing access to the ample gas resources on the North American continent.

An important part of the solution lies in new energy investment policy and legal frameworks in the United States, Mexico, and Canada, and, more critically, in forging better integration of policies, infrastructure, and energy trade among the three. Stronger continental energy ties would also pay national security dividends by fostering political and economic stability in Mexico. Finally, deepening cooperation between the United States and Canada to support the construction of pipeline capacity from the Arctic regions of both countries would have an appreciable impact on U.S. self-sufficiency in natural gas.

The irreversible decline of continental U.S. oil and gas production is addressed by Adam Sieminski in chapter 1 of this volume, and the need for Mexico to adopt a new legal framework to promote its own oil and gas production is detailed by Luis Téllez in chapter 16. This chapter focuses on the dramatic changes in the natural gas market in North America, the prospects for greater oil supply from Canada's tar sands, and the possibility for U.S. policymakers to help slow the rate of decline for U.S. production, while balancing energy and environmental concerns. The chapter reviews the status of the integration of energy markets in North America; the drivers of its oil and natural gas markets; challenges to accessing continental gas supplies, including competing pipeline options for Arctic gas; and a menu of solutions for balancing the North American gas market and opportunities to increase continental oil and gas production.

## A History of Successful Market Integration

The integration of North American energy markets has been increasing steadily since the 1980s. The most important transformation has occurred in natural gas, but crude oil, refined products, and power markets have evolved as well. According to a report by the North American Energy Working Group (NAEWG),[3] a panel established as a result of a 2001 agreement between the three nations, North America constitutes the largest single energy market in the world. In 2000, the three countries combined were responsible for 31 percent of total world oil demand and nearly one-third of world natural gas consumption. The continent produced 60 percent of the oil it consumed and all but 1 percent of natural gas consumption. Canada supplied 27 percent of total U.S. net energy imports, and Mexico another 9 percent.[4]

During the past two decades, U.S. and Canadian natural gas markets have undergone dramatic restructuring, moving from overt regulation to reliance on market forces. Those market-oriented policies, incorporated into the Canada-U.S. Free Trade Agreement, have resulted in a more than doubling of trade in natural gas as the necessary infrastructure has expanded. In the 1990s, the implementation of the North American Free Trade Agreement (NAFTA) reinvigorated the natural gas trade between northern Mexico and the United States, pulling Mexico into the booming continental market. As the Mexican economy continues to grow, its demand for natural gas, particularly as feedstock for electric power, will grow rapidly.

## Oil Market Prospects

Net continental oil imports are forecast to increase significantly during the next decade. Whereas Canada and Mexico are expected to maintain or increase oil production, all forecasts assume U.S. demand will continue to dramatically outstrip production.[5] While Canadian conventional oil production is projected to decrease by as much as 0.5 million barrels per day between 2003 and 2015, production from unconventional sources could dramatically increase to more than offset the loss.

After years of uncertainty about economic viability, Canada now touts its oil sands resource base in the western province of Alberta as second only to the supply potential of Saudi Arabia. "Oil sands production has surpassed one million barrels per day and with 175 billion barrels of reserves in the ground it is one of the few basins in the world with growing production. Companies expect to produce 2.9 million barrels per day of bitumen and synthetic light crude oil by 2015."[6] While the resource potential is unquestioned, cost is another matter as extraction of oil sands requires steam production to stimulate oil flow. Optimistic projections could be tempered by high natural gas prices without either additional gas supplies from the Arctic or the development of Canadian coal-bed methane resources or alternatives, such as burning bitumen, to hold down costs.

The United States and Canada are mature oil provinces with only relatively high-cost and unconventional resources remaining in significant quantities. Unlike Mexico, with its national oil company subject to political drivers and constraints, exploration and production activity in the United States and Canada is driven by the capital expenditure decisions of the private sector. To encourage investment, both countries have provided various tax and royalty incentives to encourage oil and natural gas development. The most significant in recent years was the U.S. Outer Continental Shelf Deep Water Royalty Relief Act, a major incentive for deepwater development in the Gulf of Mexico, enacted in 1995.[7]

The downturn in the oil market in 1998, which occurred at the same time the rest of the economy was booming, was an inflection point for the industry. The annual average wellhead price for U.S. oil production in 1998 was $10.87, down from $17.23 the year before.[8] Relentless pressure from Wall Street analysts to meet annual, even quarterly, return on investment targets has made the companies extremely conservative with respect to increasing capital expenditures.[9]

The major oil companies base capital investment decisions on a ranking of international opportunities for resource quality, cost of development, and political risk. The Lehman Brothers 2004 midyear survey found capital expenditures up 4.3 percent in the United States and Canada versus 11.9 percent outside North America.[10] The factors motivating investment in exploration and production are complex. Though the industry cites access limitations in the United States as the single most important constraint on investment, less than 25 percent of the federal acreage currently under lease is actually in production.[11] In the deepwater Gulf of Mexico, with some of the best fiscal terms in the world, development has been increasing significantly but considerable leased acreage has yet to even be explored.

Industry analysts argue that as long as a large portion of the remaining prospective areas in the offshore United States—the East and West coasts and offshore Florida—and all of Mexico remain off limits, the major oil companies will likely to continue to favor capital investments outside North America. Such U.S. policy changes that industry might favor, however, are unlikely without a real change in the public perception of security risks, a change that has not occurred even in the aftermath of the terrorist attacks of September 11, 2001.

Supply, however, is only one side of the oil market equation. Rhetoric aside, U.S. policymakers and the public's vehicle-purchasing decisions demonstrate a lack of real concern about oil imports and "security." Even the prospect of head-to-head competition with China for oil supplies has not registered sufficiently as a concern with consumers or policymakers to produce changes in fuel economy or consumption in the face of the growing maw of U.S. fuel demand.[12] The only opportunity may be the result of policies to address air emissions responsible for excessive levels of ground-level ozone pollution and climate change. Some states, led by California, are looking to use the regulation of greenhouse gases from motor vehicles as a way to restrict emissions and, indirectly, increase vehicle fuel efficiency.[13] Though the U.S. federal government has abdicated its policy role, these states are stepping up with creative policies that could ultimately affect consumer choices as well as the automobile industry's manufacturing and marketing strategies. Complex state and federal jurisdictional authorities could stymie such efforts, but these proposals offer the only real prospect for any course correction in U.S. oil demand.

## Fundamental Change in Continental Natural Gas Markets

Although dependence on global oil supplies has long been a reality, the North American natural gas market has until now been supplied almost exclusively with continental production. Today, however, current and projected continental demand for natural gas is outstripping production. The U.S. Energy Information Administration (EIA), in its *International Energy Outlook 2004,* projected continental gas demand to increase an average of 1.6 percent a year through 2025. Mexico's demand growth, driven primarily by the industrial and electricity generation sectors, is projected to average 6.1 percent a year. At the same time, production in the United States and Canada is expected to remain relatively flat as the maturity of the resource base compounded by access restrictions have limited supply growth potential. Future real production growth in Mexico is less predictable and not forecast by the EIA.

For years, the United States benefited from the integrated continental market to supply growing natural gas consumption. While U.S. demand for the environmentally preferred fuel has been growing at near record rates, the same has been happening in Canada and Mexico as all three countries have been experiencing a major conversion to natural gas as the fuel of choice for power generation. After more than a decade of continental gas prices averaging $2.00 to $2.50 per million British thermal units (Btu), in the winter of 2000–2001 prices spiked to over $10.00 per million Btu, only to have settled at a new average of $4.00 to $6.00 per million Btu.

In 2002, citing projections of a 50 percent increase in consumption over the next twenty years, the U.S. secretary of energy requested a comprehensive natural gas review by the National Petroleum Council (NPC).[14] The report, issued in September 2003, concluded that higher gas prices were the result of a fundamental shift in the supply and demand balance. Further, that production from U.S. and Canadian supply basins had reached a plateau and North America would no longer be self-reliant in meeting its natural gas needs.

The report's recommendations included a balanced portfolio that includes all the following elements: increased energy efficiency and conservation; alternate energy sources for industrial consumers and power generators, including renewables; gas resources from previously inaccessible areas of the United States; LNG imports; and gas from the Arctic.[15] The NPC supply scenario is shown in figure 15.1.

## Natural Gas Demand Pressures and Prices

Under the NPC's most optimistic scenarios, the price of natural gas would remain in the range of $3 to $5 per million Btu in constant 2002 dollars, double the level of the 1990s. The more pessimistic, but possibly more realistic scenarios, suggest a range of $5 to $7 per million Btu. These projections are for average prices, although the study predicts increasing price volatility.

This deterioration in the supply situation has occurred just as the entire continent has turned to natural gas as the source of most new power generation. Virtually all new capacity in the United States in recent years has been gas-fired—increasing gas use by 30 percent in the electricity sector over ten years, 2000–2010, and doubling by 2025. Canada is projecting a threefold increase in gas-fired power generation in the coming decade. Mexico is experiencing growth in power demand of 6 to 7 percent annually at the same time it is implementing a policy of converting existing oil-fired generation to cleaner natural gas.

The impact is being felt economy-wide as the power sector, the most rapidly growing component of the gas market, competes directly with the other

Figure 15.1. U.S. and Canadian Natural Gas Supply, 1990–2025

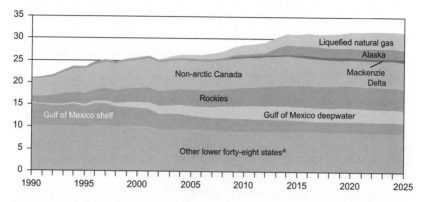

*Note:* Production from traditional basins remains strong but has reached a plateau; the Rockies and the deepwater Gulf of Mexico offset declines in other areas. Growth is driven by imports of lique-fied natural gas and Arctic supply.
[a]Includes production in the lower forty-eight states, ethane rejection, and supplemental gas.
*Source:* National Petroleum Council, *Balancing Natural Gas Policy: Fueling the Demands of a Growing Economy* (Washington, D.C.: National Petroleum Council, 2002), vol. 1, 7.

long-established industrial, commercial, and residential uses. The high prices of the 2000–2004 period have already caused the loss of upward of 40 percent of U.S. fertilizer production capacity, most of which depends directly on natural gas as a raw ingredient.[16] Beyond the fertilizer industry, the impact on energy-intensive industries in the United States, Canada, and Mexico is not yet well understood. Though additional chemical capacity has been shut down as well, it appears likely that gas prices were only one factor. The industrial sector, increasingly under competitive pressure from China, has voiced strong concerns that gas prices will drive manufacturing out of Mexico. Industrial groups in the United States, Canada, and Mexico have mounted high-profile campaigns calling for policies to mitigate elevated natural gas prices. Users in the United States have been arguing for policies to ensure diversity in the electricity sector, including more coal-fired generation and a requirement that new gas-fired generation be limited to highly efficient combined heat and power technologies.[17] These users all argue that current policies rely on demand destruction to balance the market.

## Challenges to Expanding Supply

The greatest challenges to increasing North American supplies of hydrocarbons are access to the remaining resource-rich areas, the high cost of
exploiting frontier areas, and the political challenges of siting energy infrastructure. These challenges have proven to be enduring and make significant
supply expansion unlikely in the near term.

### Access

In the United States, access to resources has been limited by public opposition to drilling offshore and on public lands. Since the Ronald Reagan and
George H. W. Bush administrations in the 1980s, the United States has had
nearly complete moratoriums on exploration and development off the East
and West coasts and in the eastern Gulf of Mexico off Florida. Onshore,
conflicts between surface owners and other surface users, where public land
is involved, have led to controversy, litigation, and withdrawals of prospective areas from potential exploration and development. Beyond the offshore
moratoria, the Alaska National Wildlife Refuge, federal land on the North
Slope of Alaska, is the most celebrated area off limits to oil and gas development. In spite of the bleak supply picture detailed by the NPC, efforts by
Congress to even reconsider offshore moratoriums were squarely defeated
during consideration of comprehensive energy legislation in 2001–2.

Canada has similar, although less extensive, limitations on access. Recent settlements of long-standing disputes on aboriginal lands have created
new access opportunities. British Columbia has initiated a review of prohi-
bitions on drilling off the West Coast to increase supply. At the same time,
in other areas once thought promising, the Atlantic Coast off Newfoundland
and Nova Scotia, recent exploration results have been disappointing.

Opposition to private-sector investment in the upstream oil and gas sector in Mexico has severely limited production for years. Since Mexico nationalized the oil industry in 1938, Petróleos Mexicanos (Pemex) has been
imbued with nearly mythic importance as a symbol of national sovereignty.
As the single most important contributor to the federal treasury, Pemex's
capital available for development is severely constrained by the government's annual cash call of more than 50 percent of revenues. As a result,
only 22 percent of the Mexican onshore and 4 percent of the offshore has
been explored. The tight supply and high natural gas price environment has
spawned a campaign by Mexican industrial users to press for reform.[18] The

group has called for opening exploration and production of natural gas to private capital investment similar to the regime in Canada. Mexican waters of the Gulf of Mexico, adjacent to highly prolific areas of the U.S. continental shelf, could be developed efficiently and at low cost under a reformed upstream sector. The illogic of the current regime has led to plans to site LNG import facilities above what may be some of the most prolific natural gas fields left in the Gulf of Mexico.

## Unconventional and Frontier Resources

Maintaining even a flat level of production in the United States and Canada will depend on increasing production from higher-cost "unconventional" and frontier supplies. To meet demand growth at a "reasonable" price, significant expansion in the development of gas from tight sands and coal-bed methane formations, deep gas wells (15,000 feet and more), and Arctic resources will all be required. In addition, imports of LNG from other areas of the world will have to be increased significantly.

Technological progress, coupled with high prices and additional fiscal incentives, can work to increase production from unconventional formations. The natural gas resources that exist in significant quantities on the North Slope of Alaska and in the Canadian Arctic have not yet been developed due to the lack of transportation infrastructure. The State of Alaska has more than 36 trillion cubic feet of natural gas that have been produced as part of normal oil operations over the past thirty years and then reinjected back into reservoirs. In 2001, the major Alaska producers conducted a joint feasibility study on natural gas pipeline options from the North Slope of Alaska. The study evaluated a route along the Trans-Alaska Highway into Canada, referred to as the "southern route," or the "Alaska Gas Pipeline," and another through the Beaufort Sea north of Alaska connecting with a proposed "Mackenzie Valley Pipeline" in Canada. This option was dubbed the "northern route" (figure 15.2). (Estimates for the northern route included the Mackenzie Valley Pipeline portion expanded to encompass Alaska gas via a leg through the Beaufort Sea from Inuvik to Prudhoe Bay on the North Slope of Alaska.) Either route would take eight to ten years from the initial permitting stage to first volumes.

The companies' evaluation concluded that, although the northern route would be shorter, the environmental and physical challenges of underwater construction made the two routes roughly comparable. A pipeline, with a capacity to deliver 4 to 6 billion cubic feet per day (bcfpd) would require

Figure 15.2. Map of Arctic Gas Delivery Pipelines

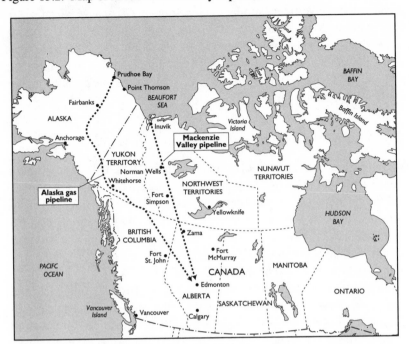

*Source: Oil and Gas Journal.*

an investment of $17 to $20 billion, which if built would be the largest single infrastructure project in North American history.

Alaska's gas is critical to the overall North American supply outlook. Potential Alaskan volumes were assumed in the NPC supply cases and in all forecasts of the EIA. The three companies concluded that neither route was economic in the absence of significant risk mitigation by the State of Alaska and the U.S. government, especially with respect to commodity price risk.[19] Legislation to create a special office to expedite and streamline the permitting of an Alaska pipeline and to provide certain fiscal incentives, pending in the U.S. Congress since 2001, was finally passed late in the congressional session in 2004.[20] At the insistence of members of the Alaska delegation, the legislation was specific to a southern route.

The U.S. focus on a southern route through Alaska caused concern in Canada that gas resources in the Mackenzie Delta in the Northwest Territories would be stranded. While gridlock in the U.S. Congress on broader energy legislation held up action for more than three years, a separate proposal for a standalone Mackenzie Valley pipeline proceeded with permitting and engineering design. The base capacity of that pipeline is planned at 1.2 bcfpd, expandable to 1.6 bcfpd. How much of that gas might be available to the continental market is uncertain. As noted above, Alberta has the largest oil sands deposits in the world, which if economically recoverable, would put Canada in the same league as Saudi Arabia as a long-term oil producer. Under current development plans, there is a direct energy trade-off because the extraction of bitumen from oil sands requires significant amounts of water and natural gas for steam injection operations and onsite power generation. A recent Lehman Brothers report suggests that most, if not all, of the gas from a Mackenzie Delta pipeline would be committed to oil sand production because plans for incremental bitumen production of 1.1 million barrels per day by 2012 would require 1.2 to 1.5 bcfpd of gas.[21]

A possible extension of the Mackenzie Valley line through the Arctic to Prudhoe Bay was adamantly opposed by the State of Alaska.[22] The state insisted that the Alaska gas, most of which would be produced from state and aboriginal lands, should traverse the state to provide local economic development opportunities. With passage of the federal incentives and streamlined permitting authority for construction of a pipeline, the project appears to hinge on negotiations over fiscal terms between the state and the three major companies. Those negotiations have included the state possibly taking an equity position in the pipeline.[23]

## LNG Imports

The United States currently imports roughly 15 percent of its natural gas in the form of LNG—primarily from Trinidad and Tobago, Algeria, and Nigeria. Neither Canada nor Mexico currently imports any LNG. Having been commissioned during the 1970s, three of the four existing LNG regasification facilities in the United States were mothballed for most of the 1980s and 1990s as market reforms in the United States and Canada led to a dramatic decline in natural gas prices. Only the Boston terminal has remained in continuous operation. As the market has tightened in recent years, the Cove Point (Maryland), Elba Island (Georgia), and Lake Charles (Louisiana) terminals have been brought back into full operation with plans for expansion.

The NPC study concluded that even with relatively robust gas development in the United States and Canada, imports of LNG would have to increase to 14 to 17 percent of U.S. natural gas supply by 2025. Under the more pessimistic scenario, which assumed that Arctic supplies from Alaska and the Mackenzie Delta would reach the market by 2012–13, U.S. imports of LNG would eventually rise to above 20 to 25 percent.[24] The construction of seven to nine new regasification terminals and expansion of three of the four existing terminals would be required.[25]

Proposals for new facilities are at various stages in the United States and in Mexico, but active community opposition due to security concerns has slowed progress. Though there have been some inflammatory arguments put forward against the possibility of dependence on an LNG "OPEC," policymakers seem to accept that the diversity of LNG suppliers and the very nature of LNG trade mitigate against such a possibility.[26] The primary caution has been related to ensuring siting in locations where security and safety considerations in a post-9/11 world can be best managed. Given the political difficulties, it appears increasingly likely that most additional regasification capacity in the United States will have to be built in or near existing terminal and refining centers, mostly along the Gulf Coast or totally offshore.

## Options to Balance the Natural Gas Market

Policymakers have several effective options that can reduce the imbalance between projected natural gas supply and demand. Improved efficiency in energy consumption, better integration of North American electricity markets, and harmonization of regulatory frameworks are the first steps.

### Efficiency

As the NPC study concluded, increased efficiency is the single most significant mechanism, and the only option in the short run, to mitigate the tight natural gas supply situation. A recent study by the American Council for an Energy Efficient Economy indicated that a concerted national campaign "reducing demands for electricity and natural gas, especially during peak periods, and increasing the share of renewable energy" would have long-lasting benefits.[27] Lagged utility billing hinders the user response to price signals that can happen with other commodities, like gasoline. A coordinated education campaign, coupled with consumer incentives, could be deployed to encourage the public as to the benefits of increasing energy efficiency.

Proactive policies in all three countries to replace older gas-fired electricity generating plants with modern combined-cycle units have increased the average efficiency, but at a much lower rate than could be achieved with the use of integrated combined heat and power (CHP) systems. Newer central-station, combined-cycle power plants can achieve generating efficiencies of 45 to 50 percent, whereas a CHP system that captures the waste heat from the generation of electric power for district heating and cooling can achieve output efficiencies of 90 percent.[28] The amount of CHP in the United States increased fivefold during the past two decades, but it still accounts for barely 7 percent of electric generation capacity.

Existing market structures, outmoded regulatory regimes, and the conservative technology preferences of incumbent utilities work to limit the penetration of these highly efficient systems in the United States, Canada, and Mexico. Elsewhere, the efficiency and environmental benefits of CHP are widely recognized. District heating systems combined with local distribution of electricity are common in many European cities and are a major part of the European Union's energy and environment agenda.[29] In Denmark and the Netherlands, more than 40 percent of electricity is obtained from CHP systems. The amount has doubled in the United Kingdom during the past decade, with additional growth targeted by the government.

## Improved Coordination and Market Integration

The United States, Canada, and Mexico all have a wealth of energy resources, but historical policy decisions and resource concentrations have resulted in differing mixes of domestic production and consumption. These differences create opportunities for synergies, expanded trade, and market arbitrage. Expanding electricity integration would create greater flexibility and opportunities to increase efficiency and thereby reduce natural gas use in power generation. Significant improvements in the efficiency of power generation and dispatch can be achieved in the United States and across the continent with more rapid integration of the interstate and international grid.

At the time NAFTA was negotiated in the early 1990s, it was posited that gas-fired power plants would be built in Mexico to supply the high-growth border region and southwestern U.S. markets. Though facility siting in northern Mexico may be easier than in some areas of the United States, tight gas supplies in the region have hindered such development. The potential for such transborder efficiency improvements still exists, however, with more creative proposals using renewable technologies alone and in combination with other conventional fossil-fueled technologies. Northern Mexico has very-high-quality solar and wind resources that have not begun to be developed. Hydro Quebec is moving aggressively to augment its vast hydropower resources with wind generation. In 2003, the company issued a call for tenders to build 1,000 megawatts of wind power generation capacity between 2006 and 2012.[30] The combination of wind and hydropower provides an interesting opportunity to provide a highly reliable power supply using wind when available while conserving water for low wind periods. Utilities in the Pacific Northwest are looking at using the same strategy.

The NAEWG provides a framework for U.S., Canadian, and Mexican coordination on these policies. The 2002 NAEWG reports on efficiency standards and labeling[31] and the regulation of electricity trade[32] are strong evidence of the commitment of the three countries to jointly address current and future energy challenges. First steps have been made in the area of harmonizing efficiency standards and test procedures for a number of appliances. This effort will have long-term benefits for energy users and help reduce natural gas prices. The enhanced trade opportunities are an ancillary benefit.

The work on electricity trade has only begun with the joint study titled *North America: Regulation of International Electricity*. The NAEWG has a timely opportunity to use the nascent efforts to create continental electric reliability rules as an opportunity to truly expand policy and market integration, with an emphasis on diversity in the electricity sector. However, simply expanding the domestic and transboundary transmission grid is not enough. The fundamental question of how a continental electricity market can meet expected demand growth, while protecting the environment, requires a more complex answer. Consistent with the findings of the NPC, the first option should be the development and promotion of coordinated policies to promote optimal efficiency from generation to end use.

## Expanding the Production of Continental Natural Gas Supplies

Despite President Vicente Fox's best efforts, reform proposals to increase Mexican production of natural gas have met with limited success in the Mexican Congress. Though the natural gas market circumstances in the United States and Canada were different in significant ways, the political difficulties of implementing reforms were equally complicated. Interparliamentary exchanges to share that experience could provide an opportunity to reinforce the economic case being made by Mexican industry. The Mexico–United States Interparliamentary Congress should make natural gas production a priority item at its future meetings.

How and when Alaska's natural gas will be brought to market is an issue of importance for the entire continent, but most important for the United States and Canada. A pipeline from Alaska along the southern route would provide a transit opportunity for supplies from the Yukon, as well as production from areas in Alaska south of Prudhoe Bay. During the 1970s, the United States and Canada agreed on a transboundary natural gas pipeline framework that was embodied in the Alaska Natural Gas Transportation Act. At that time, the two countries agreed, for political reasons, on a legal framework for a pipeline along the southern route. The southern portion from Alberta into the United States was built and has been in operation since the 1980s, but the leg north to Alaska was never built due to poor economics. Now that development of a Mackenzie Delta pipeline is well under way and the regulatory framework is in place for an Alaska pipeline, a mechanism to reengage federal, state, and provincial governments, producers, and other interested parties should be established to ensure the timely development of the infrastructure to move the Alaska and Canadian Arctic gas to market.

Another significant, but longer-term, opportunity lies with the unconventional resources in western Canada. According to a report by the Canadian Gas Potential Committee, "there is long-term potential for unconventional sources such as coal-bed methane (CBM) and gas hydrates, but work on these is still in the initial stages. It reckons that commercial CBM production could be as much as a decade away for potential reserves located in Alberta and British Columbia."[33]

On the subject of increasing LNG imports, recent changes in global LNG markets, including reduced costs and increased flexibility coupled with changes to U.S. regulatory policies, have improved the investment opportunities for LNG import terminals. Canada and Mexico have both been moving forward with the permitting process for facilities under their respective domestic siting frameworks. As the United States seeks to double its LNG imports during the next decade, ensuring reliability from a diversity of sources will be a top energy security priority for the United States. Timely expansion of LNG receiving and regasification terminals will be important for the development of those supply arrangements in a competitive global market. A well-functioning, integrated market will maximize the benefits of LNG imports by providing optimal market flexibility. Such options can be smoothly accommodated with the existing regulatory framework under NAFTA and through continued efforts under the NAEWG.

## Conclusion

Delivering natural gas to the North American market at a competitive, affordable price will be equal to oil supply as an energy security challenge for the twenty-first century. Gas-dependent industries are already fleeing the United States and Mexico for countries with cheaper supplies. Mexico's ability to continue to industrialize, produce jobs, and control migration is already threatened by manufacturing flight to Asia; failure to ensure competitively priced natural gas will only exacerbate that trend.

Natural gas supplies are critical to maintaining environmental quality in the United States, Canada, and Mexico. The trend to gas-fired power generation will be difficult to slow or reverse in the short to medium term, even if natural gas prices remain high, without deliberate policy changes to emphasize the need for fuel diversity and to drive deployment of more efficient technologies such as CHP in the power sector. The integration of the natural gas market resulting from several decades of market reforms and the implementation of NAFTA has created the platform for joint solutions. The policy and institutional mechanisms are in place for such collaboration, if the political will to act in an effective manner can be found. The North American Energy Working Group provides an excellent forum for continuing progress, but its mandate must be far more ambitious and its timetable for action more swift. It needs to undertake four primary tasks.

The first task should be a regional efficiency program to control the rate of demand growth, with enforcement of higher building and appliance efficiency standards and the promotion of combined heat and power at the top of the agenda. The second task should be development of an acceptable regulatory and fiscal framework, supportable by U.S. and Canadian interests, to ensure that the pipeline infrastructure is built to move Arctic gas to market within the 2012 time frame.

The third task must be to promote closer communication between the legislatures of the United States and Mexico (and Canada) to speed Mexico's restructuring to support competitive gas development. And the fourth task should be to devise a true integration of the North American power grid, maximizing efficiency through trade in energy in the form of natural gas and power and enhancing the continent's aggregate energy security through common reliability standards. These solutions are good energy policy, good economic policy, and good foreign policy.

## Notes

1. See Adam Sieminski's projections for U.S. demand and supply in chapter 1 of this volume and Luis Téllez's projections for Mexico's increased need for oil and gas in chapter 16.

2. See remarks by Chairman Alan Greenspan at the Center for Strategic & International Studies, Washington, April 27, 2004 (http://www.csis.org/energy/040427_greenspan.pdf): "These elevated long-term prices, if sustained, could alter the magnitude of and manner in which the United States consumes energy. Until recently, long-term expectations of oil and gas prices appeared benign. When choosing capital projects, businesses could mostly look through short-run fluctuations in prices to moderate prices over the longer haul. The recent shift in expectations, however, has been substantial enough and persistent enough to influence business investment decisions, especially for facilities that require large quantities of natural gas." Also see testimony of Robert C. Liuzzi, president and chief executive of CF Industries of Long Grove, Ill., on behalf of the Fertilizer Institute before the House Committee on Energy and Commerce, June 10, 2003 (http://energycommerce.house.gov/108/Hearings/06102003hearing944/Liuzzi1521print .htm). Liuzzi told committee members that the natural gas crisis is responsible for permanent closure of almost 20 percent of U.S. nitrogen fertilizer capacity and the idling of an additional 25 percent of production capacity.

3. North American Energy Working Group (NAEWG), *North America: The Energy Picture,* June 2002, available at http://www.eia.doe.gov/emeu/northamerica/engnaewg.htm.

4. NAEWG, *North America.*

5. U.S. Energy Information Administration, *International Energy Outlook 2004* (Washington, D.C.: U.S. Energy Information Administration, 2004), available at http://www.eia.doe.gov.

6. Canadian Association of Petroleum Producers, Canadian Crude Oil Production and Supply Forecast, 2004–2015, available at http://www.capp.ca; and U.S. Energy Information Administration, *International Energy Outlook 2004.*

7. Under the Outer Continental Shelf Deep Water Royalty Relief Act, Public Law 104-58, no royalties will be charged until the respective volumes have been produced: 17.5 million barrels of oil equivalent in water depths of 200 to 400 meters, 52.5 million barrels of oil equivalent in 400–800 meters of water, and 87.5 million barrels of oil equivalent in water depths greater than 800 meters. The royalty waiver applies unless the annual average closing prices on the New York Mercantile Exchange for light sweet crude oil exceeds $28.00 per barrel or $3.50 per millions of British thermal units for natural gas, in which case any production of oil or gas will be subject to royalties at the lease stipulated royalty rate. The threshold prices are adjusted for any calendar year after 1994 by the change in the implicit price deflator for the gross domestic product. For a detailed description of the act as implemented, see http://www.gomr.mms.gov/homepg/offshore/royrelief.html. For a detailed account of the political process to pass the legislation, see Randall Davis and Shirley Neff, "Anatomy of a Legislative Victory: Deepwater royalty relief product of 3 1/2 year U.S. political effort," *Oil & Gas Journal,* April 1, 1996, available at http://ogj.pennnet.com/.

8. U.S. Energy Information Administration, *Annual Energy Review 2002,* table 5.16, "Crude Oil Domestic First Purchase Prices, 1949–2002," available at http://www.eia .doe.gov/emeu/aer/pdf/pages/sec5_39.pdf.

9. Lehman Brothers' regular surveys of worldwide exploration and production spending have consistently shown company conservative exploration and production budget planning assumptions are West Texas Intermediate and natural gas prices at Henry Hub that are at least 20 percent lower than actual market prices. According to "Lehman Bros. Midyear Survey Shows Increased Worldwide E&P Spending," *OGJ On-*

*line,* June 30, 2004, "Reflecting much stronger commodity prices, 2004 E&P budgets are now based on an average oil price of about $28.44/bbl (West Texas Intermediate). This price compares to $25.29/bbl in our yearend survey. Natural gas price assumptions also have risen to approximately $4.76/Mcf (Henry Hub) currently from $4.17/Mcf in December. http://ogj.pennnet.com. These prices are compared with the EIA's recent forecast prices of $36.90 for West Texas Intermediate and $6.12 for Henry Hub. Energy Information Administration, "Short-Term Energy Outlook," July 2004, table A4; "Annual Average U.S. Energy Prices: Base Case," http://www.eia.doe.gov/emeu/steo/pub/pdf/a4tab.pdf.

10. "Lehman Brothers Midyear Survey Shows Increased Worldwide E&P Spending," *OGJ Online,* June 30, 2004.

11. Statistics from the U.S. Minerals Management Service, the Bureau of Land Management, and the Forest Service.

12. See Amy Jaffe and Ken Medlock's projections in chapter 11 of this volume, and the regional and Japanese policy responses to Chinese demand in chapters 12 and 13, respectively.

13. See California Air Resources Board (ARB), http://www.arb.ca.gov/cc/cc.htm. "The historic regulation sets limits on the amount of greenhouse gas emissions that can be released from new passenger cars, SUVs and pickup trucks sold in California starting in model year 2009. The new regulation is based on a state of the art assessment of the various technologies and fuels that can reduce motor vehicle global warming pollutants. According to ARB staff, the average reduction of greenhouse gases from new California cars and light trucks will be about 22 percent in 2012 and about 30 percent in 2016, compared to today's vehicles." Press release dated September 24, 2004, available at http://www.arb.ca.gov/newsrel/nr092404.htm.

14. Letter from Secretary of Energy Spencer Abraham to Mr. William A. Wise, Chairman, National Petroleum Council, March 13, 2002. In *Balancing Natural Gas Policy: Fueling the Demands of a Growing Economy,* ed. National Petroleum Council, vol. 1, Summary of Findings and Recommendations, appendix A, available at http://www.npc.org/.

15. National Petroleum Council, *Balancing Natural Gas Policy.,* Executive Summary, 5.

16. Testimony of Robert C. Liuzzi.

17. Letter from the Industrial Energy Consumers of America, dated June 23, 2003, to Secretary of Energy Abraham outlining "thirteen short-term recommendations to deal with the natural gas crisis that is dismantling the nation's manufacturing base," available at http://www.ieca-us.com/issunatgas.html.

18. Jose de Jesus Valdez, "Perspectives of Natural Gas in Mexico," presentation by Grupo Alvero to the IAEE North American Conference, Mexico City, October 2003, available at http://www.iaee.org/en/conferences/2003-mexico.aspx.

19. All current forecasts project natural gas prices at a level above $3.50 per million British thermal units in 2010 and later. However, a similar outlook prevailed in the middle to late 1970s, when the natural gas industry committed billions of dollars to construct LNG receiving terminals. By the time the terminals were in operation, demand destruction and fuel switching had wiped out more than 27 percent of the market, driving prices to dramatic lows. Before committing to constructing a pipeline, two of the producers, ConocoPhillips and BP, have insisted on some risk sharing on the part of the government in the event of an extreme decline in the price of natural gas realized at

the North Slope of Alaska. The experience of gas market restructuring during the 1980s and 1990s has made the industry wary of optimistic projections for the North American gas market. The wellhead price of natural gas fell from a high in 1983 of $3.76 per thousand cubic feet to $1.58 by 1995 (in 1996 dollars). Available at http://www.eia.doe.gov/emeu/aer/pdf/pages/sec6_17.pdf.

20. See "Gas line provisions a go," *Petroleum News* 9, no. 42 (October 17, 2004), http://www.petroleumnews.com/pntruncate/363998029.shtml.

21. Robert E. Snyder, "What's New In Production," *World Oil* 224, issue 10 (October 1, 2003), available at http://www.worldoil.com.

22. Alaska has insisted that the gas traverse the state so that it will be available for economic development. Aboriginal groups have opposed this disruption of the Arctic Ocean.

23. Susan Warren and John Fialka, "Alaska May Take a Stake in Pipeline," *Wall Street Journal,* October 18, 2004.

24. Discussions with the major companies have confirmed that the Arctic supplies from Alaska are not economical as LNG due to the need for pipeline infrastructure from the North Slope to southern Alaska. Once that investment is made, it is more economical to transport the gas by pipeline to interconnect with the existing North American grid than to liquefy and ship the gas.

25. National Petroleum Council, *Balancing Natural Gas Policy,* vol. 1, Summary of Findings and Recommendations, 63.

26. See Adam Sieminski's skepticism regarding the effectiveness of a "gas" OPEC in chapter 1.

27. American Council for Energy Efficient Economy, *Natural Gas Price Effects of Energy Efficiency and Renewable Energy Practices and Policies,* December 2003, available at http://www.aceee.org/pubs/e032full.pdf.

28. Tom Casten, "Thinking Outside the Box: Economic Growth and the Central Generation Paradigm," presentation by the chair and chief executive of Primary Energy, LLC, to the North American Conference of the International Association for Energy Economics, Washington, July 2004, available at http://www.iaee.org/documents/washington/Tom_Casten.pdf.

29. See Euroheat & Power Web site, http://www.euroheat.org/, which is maintained by Euroheat & Power in cooperation with several European District Heating and Cooling associations; also see http://www.chp-info.org.

30. See http://www.hydroquebec.com.

31. NAEWG, *North American Energy Efficiency Standards and Labeling,* December 2002, available at http://www.eere.energy.gov/buildings/appliance_standards/pdfs/naewg_report.pdf.

32. NAEWG, *North America: Regulation of International Electricity Trade,* December 2002, available at http://www.fossil.energy.gov/programs/electricityregulation/pdf/electricitytraderegulation.pdf.

33. As reported in "Canada's Huge Gas Potential Challenged by Cost, Price, Pipeline Transport Issues," *Oil & Gas Journal,* January 20, 2003, available at http://ogj.pennnet.com.

# 16

# Latin America

## Luis Téllez Kuenzler

Energy is the lifeblood of an economy. From moving a car, to heating a house, to turning on a personal computer, energy is found in every single aspect of modern society. This is especially true for the United States, and being a net energy importer represents a huge challenge in terms of energy security. This threat is magnified when considering the high dependence of the U.S. economy on imports from politically unstable Middle Eastern countries.

When recognizing the difficulties in reducing U.S. dependence on foreign oil, it makes economic and political sense to have Latin American countries as major suppliers. Latin America has more than 110 billion barrels of proven reserves,[1] and it could increase its oil production capacity from 10.6 million barrels per day (mmbpd) in 2001 to 17.1 mmbpd by 2025.[2] Latin America's reserves are equivalent to thirty-one years of oil production, as opposed to only eleven years in the United States and in Canada.

Latin America's potential for supplying energy to the U.S. market can also be appreciated by comparing Latin American oil production-to-reserve (P/R) ratios to other oil and natural gas net exporters, such as those of Russia, Norway, and the United Kingdom. While Latin America had a P/R of 30.8 years at the end of 2003, Russia, Norway, and the United Kingdom had 22.2, 8.5, and 5.4 years, respectively. The same trend can be seen in the natural gas industry (with an exception of Russia, which exceeds the Latin American ratio).[3]

At present, the countries of Latin America do not fully exploit their

The author thanks José Carlos Fermat for his invaluable insight on this chapter.

Figure 16.1. Mexico's Demographic Structure, 2000–2025

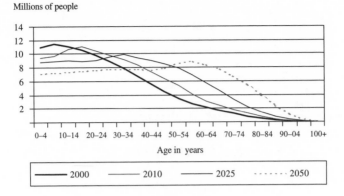

Source: Consejo Nacional de Población, *Población de México en cifras.*

resources for the benefit of their people. In Mexico, the government will need to develop its energy resources at a higher rate to be able to finance education, job training, health care, and general social programs. The government should use the country's resources now and not leave the majority of its reserves for future generations. Mexico's government should use its oil reserves to empower its human capital now—for the largest cohort of population the country will have in the coming decades (figure 16.1).

Although the Latin American region is not exempt from economic and political problems—as evidenced by the social uncertainties in Venezuela, and the 2004 strikes, protests, and changes in government in Bolivia focused on natural gas exports—it is in the interest of the United States to promote the region's development and support an improved distribution of economic growth, as the most effective vaccine against social and political instability. In this context, larger energy exports from Latin American countries to the United States will contribute to the achievement of these goals while improving the United States' energy security.

## Energy Resources within the Region

Despite high levels of government taxation, oil production from Latin America's major producers is expected to rise by the end of the decade. Political resistance to foreign investment may slow the rate of increase in many countries. The region's demand for natural gas for power generation will rise as well, with liquefied natural gas (LNG) providing diversity of supply. Though the hemisphere's natural gas resources are plentiful, here again, national economic frameworks that resist foreign investment will hinder the hemisphere's potential.

## *Oil*

According to the U.S. Energy Information Administration (EIA), worldwide oil demand is projected to grow from 76 mmbpd in 2001 to more than 123 mmbpd in 2025.[4] Though OPEC is expected to lead the respective increase in production, other producers from the Caribbean Basin and the countries of the former Soviet Union are also expected to augment supply.

Within Latin America, Venezuela, Mexico, Brazil, Argentina, Colombia, and Ecuador are expected to increase oil production in a significant way as a result of policies directed at facilitating and financing investments in the energy sector. Venezuela has the greatest potential for capacity expansion and could increase its production capacity by 2.4 mmbpd from the 2001 level (3.2 mmbpd) to 5.6 mmbpd by 2025. However, it remains unclear whether the political climate in the country will be adequate to support any local or foreign investment to finance this increase in production.[5] Despite President Hugo Chávez's victory in the August 2004 presidential recall referendum, the country is likely to remain polarized. As a result, social unrest and political instability will act together with tight legislation to keep investment in the country at low levels.

Although in Mexico private direct investment, be it foreign or domestic, is restricted, it is expected that the Mexican government will adopt a series of energy policies to foster the efficient development of the country's energy sector. Among these is the unavoidable revision of Petróleos Mexicanos' (Pemex) fiscal regime and, given legal constraints, the Multiple Service Contract program.[6] Numerous taxation schemes make analysis of Pemex's fiscal regime quite complex. However, the following taxes can be clearly identified: (1) the Hydrocarbon Extraction Duties (which represent Pemex's most important contribution to government revenues); (2) the Hydrocarbon Income Tax (equivalent to the income tax applied to all other Mexican corporations); (3) the ARE, or Aprovechamientos sobre Rendimientos Excedentes (which are collected from higher-than-expected oil prices); (4) the IEPS, or Special Tax on Production and Services; (5) the value-added tax; and (6) Pemex's direct contributions as determined by the federal government.[7]

Figure 16.2.  Effective Tax Rate as a Percentage of Revenues, Mexico, 2001

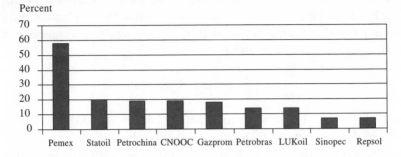

*Source:* Morgan Stanley, 2003.

All in all, the various taxes and duties levied on the company make its effective rate tax one of the highest among emerging market oil and gas companies, as can be seen in figure 16.2. Despite having one of the most levied oil and gas companies in the developing world, Mexico is expected to increase its oil production to 4.2 mmbpd at the end of this decade, and to 4.8 mmbpd by 2025, which is a significant increase when compared with its current level of 3.8 mmbpd.[8]

It is expected that Brazil, Argentina, Colombia, and Ecuador will increase their oil production in the next few years. Although Brazil became a 1.0 mmbpd producer in 1999, it is thought to have a considerable potential, especially after the opening of the oil sector to private investment. It is forecast that Brazil might produce 3.9 mmbpd in 2025. Argentina, a country that has also successfully opened up its oil sector, could become a 1.0 mmbpd producer by the end of the decade. Although Colombia's economic downturn and political unrest have delayed the development of its oil sector, this is changing; and with a new fiscal regime, it is expected to produce as much as 0.7 mmbpd by 2013 and to show a modest decline toward 2025. It is considered that Colombia as well as Brazil could benefit significantly from improving their investment climate. Finally, Ecuador could, once its political transition settles, increase its production by as much as 0.4 mmbpd in the next ten years.

## Natural Gas

According to the EIA, natural gas is expected to be the fastest growing source of world primary energy demand between 2001 and 2025, increasing from 90 trillion cubic feet (tcf) in 2001 to 176 tcf in 2025.[9] Natural gas demand in North America (Canada, Mexico, and the United States) is estimated to grow at an average annual rate of 2.2 percent between 2001 and 2025. The United States alone would account for two-thirds of the total North American increase in consumption, mainly driven by natural-gas-fired combined-cycle electricity generating plants.[10]

In Mexico, demand for natural gas is expected to grow at an average annual rate of 6.1 percent throughout 2025, reaching 5.7 tcf. Most of the increased consumption will also be driven by the electricity industry.[11] Mexico is currently a net importer of natural gas and according to the Ministry of Energy (Secretaría de Energía, or Sener), demand over the period 2001–11 will grow at an average annual rate of 7.4 percent while supply will grow at rate of 5.9 percent.[12] Overall, the country will remain a net importer of natural gas during this decade. As in the case of the oil industry, the restriction on private investment in the natural gas sector is a major impediment for its development, and it represents a major challenge for Mexico's energy policy.

Considering the financing restrictions that Pemex will face, the LNG market is expected to play a major role in the future as an alternative gas supply source. This will help to diversify Mexico's hydrocarbons supply sources and reduce the country's dependence on the United States for natural gas.

In the long-term, it is likely that the United States will not be able to provide Mexico with all the natural gas it needs for its economic development. This is mainly because domestic demand in the United States will outpace local production and thus, the United States will have to rely even more on imported natural gas to fill the gap. However, if the Mexican Congress lifted the restrictions on private investment, Mexico could become self-sufficient and eventually even turn into a net exporter of natural gas, which could be a major stimulus for growth in the region. Nevertheless, it is my impression that the necessary political conditions for this important step do not exist in Mexico today.

Although natural gas markets in Central and South America accounted for 3.9 percent of the world's gas consumption in 2001, demand has been growing at a strong pace in the region. In the period from 1990 to 2001, consumption increased by 73 percent, and it is expected that demand will keep growing at an average annual rate of 5.2 percent to 11.7 tcf a year by 2025. Except for LNG exported from Trinidad, all Central and South America's consumption is produced within the region, so local production is enough to meet regional demand. Given Bolivia's geographic position and plentiful gas reserves (after Venezuela, it has the second largest volume of reserves in the region), President Carlos Mesa's administration wants the country to become a regional gas hub. Apart from its neighbor countries (Argentina and Brazil), two other prospects for expanding its natural gas exports are Mexico and the United States (via Chile). President Mesa's victory in the July 2004 referendum authorized new export negotiations within the region, thus renewing the ideal of becoming a regional gas hub but making it difficult to continue the export projects to these other countries. President Mesa tendered his resignation in March 2005 to test the confidence of the Bolivian Congress in his strategy. The congress did not accept his resignation, but continuing political polarization over gas exports makes Bolivia's goal of becoming a regional gas hub more an ideal than a reality.

## Trade

The hemisphere's rich natural resource base of oil and natural gas provides an opportunity for greatly increased trade with the United States. It is in the United States' interest to promote policies that will permit it to diversify its supplies of oil away from the Middle East and to create the potential to import natural gas from the region.

### Oil

North American imports from the Persian Gulf are expected to almost double by 2025, reaching 5.7 mmbpd (from 2.9 mmbpd in 2001),[13] making the region even more vulnerable to the political instability of the Middle East. U.S. dependence on Middle Eastern oil highlights the U.S. vulnerability to future oil supply disruptions and high world oil prices. This dependence is not a reliable strategy and could endanger the energy security of the United States.

In this context, the United States should seek to exploit resources in Latin American countries, because the region has vast hydrocarbon reserves and a potentially large export capacity. Though the region's oil production accounted for 9.5 mmbpd in 2001, 7.1 mmbpd were consumed in the region, leaving an export capacity of 2.4 mmbpd (figure 16.3).

Of this oil export capacity, Venezuela contributes the largest share (52 percent), followed by Mexico (26 percent), Colombia (8 percent), and Argentina (6 percent).[14] Together, Mexico and Venezuela have more than three-fourths of the region's oil export capacity, estimated at 3.0 mmbpd. A large

Figure 16.3. Crude Oil Production and Consumption, Latin America, 1992–2001

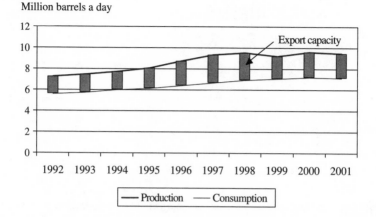

Million barrels a day

*Sources:* U.S. Energy Information Administration and International Energy Agency, 2001.

share of these exports goes to the United States. In 2001, Latin America contributed approximately a quarter of U.S. imports (figures 16.4 and 16.5).[15]

Currently, the international oil markets are very tight. The December 2002 oil strike in Venezuela, which resulted in a loss of almost 3 mmbpd of crude oil production, brought about a sharp increase in world prices of crude oil that had not relented by 2005. Because Venezuelan production accounts for a little more than 4 percent of the world's production, a sudden reduction in output can have major effects worldwide. Apart from social unrest and the economic downturn of the Venezuelan economy, the effects of the cri-

Figure 16.4. Latin American Export Capacity, 2001 (share of region's total capacity)

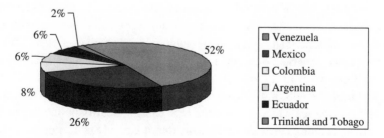

*Sources:* U.S. Energy Information Administration and International Energy Agency, 2001.

Figure 16.5. U.S. Oil Imports by Country of Origin, 2001

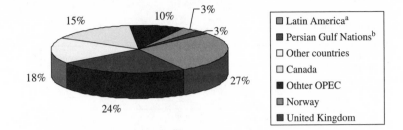

*Source:* Annual Energy Review, U.S. Energy Information Administration, 2001.
[a]Columbia, Mexico, and Venezuela.
[b]Bahrain, Iran, Iraq, Kuait, Qatar, Saudi Arabia, and United Arab Emirates.

sis postponed, to some extent, the projections for an economic recovery in the United States. Furthermore, considering the importance of the U.S. economy to the global economic market, the strike indirectly delayed recovery in other countries.

A projected increase in oil demand in the United States will exacerbate energy security concerns. The U.S. Department of Energy estimates that total U.S. oil imports are expected to increase from 9.3 mmbpd in 2001 to 13.1 mmbpd by 2025.[16] Out of this total, imports of light crude oil are expected to more than triple by 2025 to 5.3 mmbpd. Most of this increase would come from refineries located at the Caribbean Basin, North Africa, and the Middle East, where refining capacity is likely to increase. Because a dynamic growth for lighter petroleum demand in developing countries is foreseen, U.S. refiners are likely to import relatively smaller volumes of light, low-sulfur crude oils,[17] opening the doors to the heavy, sour-quality crude oil imports, the kind Venezuela and Mexico sell to the United States markets that are located at the Gulf Coast.[18]

All capacity additions in the United States are projected to occur on the Gulf Coast,[19] where existing refineries are designed to process heavy oil. This opens a major new opportunity to expand the exploitation of oil reserves in the Latin American region. Geographical location gives a clear advantage to Latin America; Venezuela has only a five-day travel distance; while Middle East oil is thirty to forty days away from the U.S. markets.

In summary, U.S. policymakers should consider three elements regarding Latin America when determining U.S. energy security policy: (1) Latin American countries provide nearly a quarter of United States' imports of oil

Figure 16.6. U.S. Natural Gas Net Imports, 2000–2025

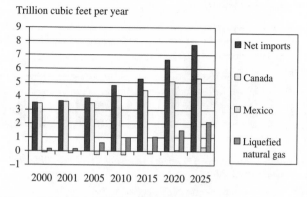

Trillion cubic feet per year

Source: U.S. Energy Information Administration, 2003.

and have major potential at current exploitation ratios; (2) considering the pressure that the changing demographic structure is creating in the Latin American region, in terms of job creation and economic growth, Latin America has a need to increase the rate at which it is exploiting its reserves; and (3) given the tightness of oil markets, it is in the United States' best interest to promote, through a noninterventionist strategy, the stability and economic development of the Latin American region.

## Natural Gas

Opportunities for near-term increases in gas trade from Mexico to the United States are limited. Natural gas imports from Canada and the Scotian Shelf in the offshore Atlantic would cover most of the projected increase in U.S. natural gas imports. Although Mexico has considerable natural gas resources, it is currently a net importer from the United States and will be until 2019, when the United States could be importing as much as 0.3 tcf of natural gas from Mexico on an annual basis,[20] as can be seen in figure 16.6.

## Capacity Expansion Limitations within Latin America

The capacity expansion of Latin American energy sectors, particularly those related to hydrocarbons, is considered to be limited, because the region's

Figure 16.7. Shares of Refined Product Imports and of Natural Gas Imports on Total Demand, 1993–2001

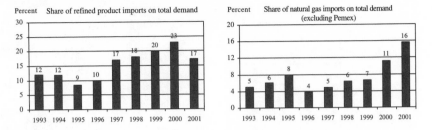

*Sources:* Secretaría de Energía (Sener), *Prospectiva de petrolíferos 2002–2011 and Prospectiva del Mercado de gas natural 2002–2011.*

greatest exporters—Mexico and Venezuela—face budgetary and legal constraints as well as an adverse political climate, such as in the case of Venezuela. With regard to Mexico, despite being a net exporter of crude oil, it is a net importer of refined products and natural gas, due to financial constraints facing Pemex and legal restrictions on private investment (figure 16.7).[21]

This heavy dependence on imports of refined products in Mexico is more noticeable in the gasoline market, where almost a third of total demand is met with imported products. It is clear that Mexico's energy policy faces an important challenge: If the hydrocarbons sector of the economy is opened to private investment—with the proper regulatory framework—a source of wealth for Mexico and the Mexican people would be tapped, having an important impact on welfare (figure 16.8).

## Politics and Energy in Latin America

The development of solid institutions in Latin America is directly related to the changing social and political history of each country. Latin America's institutional framework was the result of several circumstances: (1) internal wars (to impose a model of state and working government); (2) the imposition of the tradition of the predatory Spanish empire's institutional framework; (3) the influence of the United States and Europe as sources of constitutional and political knowledge; and (4) the omnipresent threat of an invasion from Spain, France, and the United States, which spurred the cre-

Figure 16.8. Contribution of Gasoline Imports to Total Supply, Mexico, 1994–2001

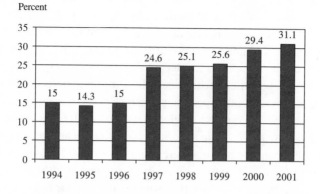

Percent

Source: Sener, *Prospectiva de petrolíferos 2002–2011.*

ation of a working and legitimate government to respond in case of international aggression or a civil war.

Both Mexico and Venezuela view natural resources as a political expression of their sovereignty. This concept of sovereignty has been used over time by different political factions to provide political and social movements with a specific identity. The most salient example is the Mexican nationalization of the oil industry in 1938, with its "historical connection" with La Revolución—the civil war of 1910—in search of political and social legitimacy. One interesting historical question is why in Mexico economic institutions that were created in the 1930s, like the monopoly of oil exploitation by the state, did not evolve over time. Mexico's institutions, in a sense, were no different than other economic institutions created by Leon Blum's France, the Soviet Union, or even New Deal institutions under Franklin Roosevelt. It is possible that Mexico's institutions did not change while institutions in other countries did because of the effects of World War II.

"Sovereignty" was understood as the utmost defense of a paternalistic and overwhelming state composed of monolithic and unmovable institutions, whereas a "modern" conception of sovereignty would encompass the ability of people to self-determine their future, which implies the notion of being able to select the best route of action for the community or society. However, in Latin America when the process of "historical connection" to the revolution took place, public policies adopted in areas such as natural resources reached the category of a "fundamental political decision"[22] at the political arena, and of an "institution" in public ordinary life.

This category could only be modified by the "national sovereignty" represented by the federal congress and local legislatures. The implication of this "national sovereignty" as a political actor represents clear evidence of the limitations of the Latin American political system to assimilate, improve, and modernize those new institutions that could maximize the natural resources to the benefit of its people and establish the necessary viability of their economy in the context of globalization and the integration of new geopolitical arenas.[23] If Latin American countries are not capable of understanding that being the monopolistic providers of energy does not intrinsically lead to the maximization of natural resources wealth, and if they do not integrate a "modern" concept of sovereignty to their basic institutions, they are running the risk of letting opportunities pass, having done nothing but leaving their "sovereignty"—whatever it means—intact.

Mexico, together with Bolivia and Venezuela, seem to continue defending their "resource sovereignty." The new hydrocarbons law submitted to the Bolivian Congress on July 2004 (which contemplates giving the state greater control by strengthening the state-owned oil company), the 2001 Hydrocarbons Law in Venezuela (which restricted private participation, particularly in exploration and production), and the failure of the energy sector restructuring process in Mexico are good examples of governments retaining or regaining state control over natural resources.

These inconsistencies are further aggravated when it is considered that almost all governments in the region must deal with strong unionism, a strong bureaucracy, and a divided public opinion that is not well informed about the national economic and energy realities and the possibilities of implementing a different set of public policies that would help maximize the rational exploitation of national energy resources. Even raising these subjects in public discussions, when proposing even modest reforms, can invite criticism that the proponents lack an understanding of nationalism.

In the case of Mexico, an elemental energy security policy analysis must consider the implications of the inefficiencies and risks related to the exclusive operation of Pemex in the energy sector. Having only one participant in certain activities makes it difficult to establish comparative analysis and induce efficiency. There are clearly economic inefficiencies related to any monopoly, whether it is private or state owned. Also, a state-owned company usually faces politically motivated demands, such as price subsidies and special treatments. Furthermore, both in Mexico and in Venezuela, the high dependence of fiscal revenues on income from the oil sector (a third and close to half, respectively) makes their economies more vulnerable to oil price changes, which represents a serious macroeconomic risk for these countries. For example, the Venezuelan nationalization of the petroleum and gas industries in 1975 was designed to provide the state with more financial resources to accomplish the normative functions of the government and take advantage of the 1973 crisis and the need of liquid money in order to reduce the burden of public debt.[24]

In both cases, the need to find a political solution to alleviate the inefficiencies and risks derived from the monopolistic control of energy extraction by the state—the gridlock imposed by the paternalistic conception of sovereignty, the lack of competition within the countries, and the perpetuation of operational inefficiencies in state-owned companies—is quite urgent. If this is not achieved, such Latin American countries as Mexico and Venezuela will find it difficult to maximize the benefits of a more efficient exploitation, production, and distribution of oil-related resources.

## The Need to Find a Solution

For the above reasons, there is an urgent need to find a solution that contributes to accomplishing a dual objective: (1) an energy security agenda for Latin America and the United States, and (2) the sustainable development of the energy sectors in Latin America.

Norway's Statoil may provide a model that Mexico can adapt as a potential solution. Several examples can be analyzed whereby governments have introduced competition and implemented corporate best practices in state-owned monopolistic enterprises responsible for oil and gas activities. Although no two countries have exactly similar political and social contexts, and every oil and gas industry is unique, international experience can provide valuable guidelines for designing and implementing strategies aimed at increasing efficiency.

Recently, Norway adopted a strategy to increase the overall efficiency of its oil and gas industry, which is a majority state-owned enterprise.[25] Just as in many Latin American countries, the Norwegian oil and gas industry plays a very important role in the economy and in the society in general.

Norway is the third largest oil exporter in the world after Saudi Arabia and Russia. In 2000, the oil industry in Norway represented more than 25 percent

Figure 16.9. Oil Industry Participation in Gross Domestic Product, 1990–2020

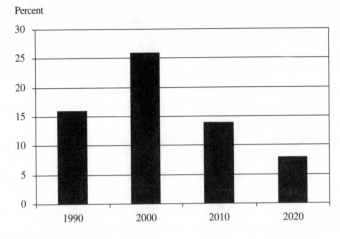

Percent

*Source:* Statoil, 2003.

of the country's gross domestic product (GDP). Although it is projected that oil's share of total GDP will decline in the future, it will continue to dominate the country's economic activity (figure 16.9).

The Norwegian oil and gas industry has had a brief but successful history. In 1972, hydrocarbons resources were discovered in the North Sea, and Statoil was created as a state-owned enterprise charged with the exploration, production, processing, storage, and distribution of oil, natural gas, and any other petroleum derivatives. The company became the principal commercial instrument in all exploitation activities. In 1990, Statoil started activities abroad and formed an alliance with British Petroleum (now BP) for international operations.[26]

Statoil's role in formulating Norwegian oil and gas policy has changed fundamentally during the past ten to fifteen years. The company operates today under the same commercial terms as other participants on the Norwegian continental shelf, and it is no longer responsible for oil policy. In other words, it competes with other participants in the industry. In 1999, as a result of strong competition in the oil and gas industry and the mergers of large multinational corporations, Statoil launched a program aimed at increasing its efficiency by introducing corporate practices, such as a policy of cost and staff reduction plus an organizational redesign.[27] One of the most important elements in the plan that contributed to its success was the institutional division of the activities carried out by the state in the industry.

As a result, Norway became one of the few countries that had one authority to conduct an energy policy (the Ministry of Petroleum and Energy), another to implement efficient and appropriate regulation (the Norwegian Petroleum Directorate), and another to represent the nation's property rights (a Shareholders' Assembly presided over by the Ministry of Petroleum and Energy). In addition, Norway's fiscal scheme is aimed at maximizing revenues from net income and from excesses over net gains on oil activities carried out in the continental platform, either by Statoil or by other companies.

Moreover, in 2003, Statoil was partly privatized and listed on the New York and Oslo stock exchanges to raise capital. The state remains the dominant shareholder, owning about 80 percent of the company. Shares have been very well accepted on the stock exchanges. In fact, during its first eighteen months of participation in the New York Stock Exchange, Statoil's shares (company symbol: STO) increased more than 25 percent.

In addition to being the major shareholder of Statoil, the state participates directly in petroleum activities in Norway through special ownership arrangement through the distribution of production licenses. The state pays its equal share of all costs and gets a profit in return.

The benefits of the entire process have been substantial. Norway, for example, has the most advanced oil exploration and production technology, particularly offshore facilities, something that has allowed the country to have a production platform of more than 3.1 mmbpd. It is expected that with its new competitive structure, Statoil will continue to be a major contributor to government revenues. Under the competition regime, Statoil will be able to perform more efficiently, increase its exports, and participate in markets abroad. Therefore, energy resources, particularly oil, will be more efficiently exploited, allowing the government and thus the Norwegian people to better benefit from the country's resources.

In this new scenario, Statoil is foreseen to perform a new role in the global economy and in the oil and natural resources regional markets. At the same time, it will continue to be a major player in the Norwegian economy and society by enriching the state's coffers and by creating jobs.

Although the Statoil example cannot be considered as the sole recipe to improve efficiency in Latin American state-owned companies, such as Pemex or Petróleos de Venezuela, it might provide important guidelines. Private coparticipation as in the Statoil ownership structure, and a competitive participation of private firms as in the Norwegian oil industry, should be considered for Latin American countries. Institutional change might allow state-owned companies in these countries to pass from controlling exploration and production on a nearly exclusive basis to a more limited joint ownership of the national energy enterprise.

## Mexico Should Make Strong Efforts to Free Natural Gas Markets

Mexico is the eighth largest oil-producing and the ninth largest natural gas-producing country in the world. As such, and to meet an increasing demand of natural gas in the foreseeable future, the country could implement four nonexclusive policy alternatives: (1) increase domestic production, (2) increase the number of interconnections with the United States, (3) foster the construction of LNG receiving terminals, and (4) promote demand-side measures to reduce natural gas consumption.

As has been discussed, Mexico has great potential to increase its production of natural gas. However, due to the discussed limitations, investment in exploration and production has been insufficient to increase domestic production and thus the country is, and is foreseen to continue to be—at least in this decade—a net importer.

In 1945, a new basin of nonassociated gas was discovered in the northwestern states of Tamaulipas, Nuevo León, and Coahuila. The Burgos Basin, as it is called, is the biggest producer of nonassociated natural gas in the country, and it accounts for more than 20 percent of current domestic production.[28] It also has important dry natural gas reserves; on January 1, 2003, the Burgos Basin was estimated to contain 1.8 tcf of proven reserves, 2.9 tcf of probable reserves, and 4.5 tcf of possible reserves.[29]

To double the current production in the Burgos Basin by 2006, the Mexican government has already announced its intentions to allow the participation of private firms through the Multiple Service Contract (MSC) program. This program is expected to be a key element in the future development of exploration and production projects in Mexico, because it represents a new contractual arrangement that opens up a broader range of services to private firms, without permitting the companies' investments or profits to establish ownership of the reserves, which is prohibited by the Mexican Constitution. The companies would enter into a service contract agreement with Pemex, and they would be paid a predefined fee for their services.

Although Pemex will maintain strict control over these activities, MSCs have been designed to complement Pemex's work with private participants. The main disadvantages of MSCs for potential participants are that Pemex will retain ownership of all resources and of all works performed, and international companies will not be allowed to participate in profit-sharing schemes. This of course reduces economic incentives for the participants. Despite the fact that political opposition to opening up the gas sector continues, Pemex anticipates that at least three to five bidding rounds for non-associated gas development will be held under the Law of Public Works and Related Services to implement this strategy. Concerns about the profitability of the contracts on offer reduced the interest of potential investors during the first bidding round, held at the end of 2003. A second round was launched in July 2004 with the expectation of increasing production under the MSC scheme to about 800 million cubic feet per day.

By increasing domestic production in Mexico, natural gas imports from the United States can be substantially reduced. Furthermore, it is likely that an increase in natural gas production would lower gas prices throughout North America, which could result in a savings of nearly $1.3 billion in imports.[30]

Should Pemex be successful with the MSC program, and if it is able to adopt a different fiscal regime that allows it to channel large amounts of investment to exploration and production of dry natural gas, the country could become a net exporter sooner than expected. This could have a double effect on natural gas prices: (1) the price of natural gas in Mexico would tend to decrease, due to the "netback effect" on transportation costs; and (2) a larger supply of gas to the South Texas markets might, at the margin, have a positive effect on prices in these markets. Moreover, besides securing the supply of the natural gas needed for the economic development of Mexico, the MSC project will contribute to creating thousands of new jobs in the region.[31]

Together with the MSC, the Mexican government implemented the Strategic Gas Program (PEG) to increase investments and foster production of natural gas in the Cantarell field and incorporate the newly discovered offshore gas fields located in the state of Veracruz.[32] With these two programs alone, Pemex could produce as much as 5.7 billion cubic feet per day (bcfpd) by 2006, representing an increase of nearly 1.5 bcfpd in three years.

Furthermore, the development of LNG receiving terminals in Mexico will also play an important role in transforming Mexico into a net exporter of natural gas to the United States. As of October 2004, Mexico's Energy Regulation Commission (CRE) has granted four storage permits to develop and operate LNG terminals in Mexican territory, three permits were granted for projects in the Baja California region, and one more was authorized for a terminal in the Port of Altamira. The Shell-Total project in Altamira is under construction, and it is expected that Sempra will start the construction on an LNG terminal in Ensenada, Baja California, in early 2005.

The peak throughput capacity of the two terminals will be more than 2.1 bcfpd and will begin operations in late 2006 (Altamira) and mid-2008 (Ensenada). The estimated investment in both projects will reach $1 billion.

In addition, as of October 2004, the CRE is in the final phase of the evaluation of an offshore LNG terminal application submitted by Chevron-Texaco. The project consists of a gravity-based structure to be located approximately 13 kilometers off the coast of Tijuana and south of the U.S. border. The project will have an estimated throughput of 1 bcfpd and investment of up to $700 million. If at least two of these projects become a reality, Mexico could reverse the flow of natural gas with the United States by 2007–8.

In the long term, it would be beneficial for Mexico to consider the possibility of promoting legal reforms to allow private firms to participate in the exploration and production of nonassociated natural gas without the restrictions present today under the MSC scheme. Through an intelligent scheme, such as the Norwegian one, Mexico could promote competition in this activity and benefit from the increased efficiency and associated fiscal revenues.

To lift restrictions on private foreign investment, promote competition, and foster investment in the energy sector, there is an urgent need to find a consensus among all three of Mexico's most important political parties. Some political analysts, myself included, consider that there are reasons to be skeptical, given the lack of consensus that has characterized the Mexican political environment for the past six years.

## The Importance of U.S. Foreign and Energy Policies in the Region

To address the importance of U.S. foreign and energy policies in Latin America could take an entire book. However, to consolidate an energy security plan that is beneficial for both the United States and Latin America, two elements should be taken into consideration.

First, some countries' fiscal budgets are still highly dependent on oil

Figure 16.10. Percentage Share of Oil in Fiscal Revenues, 2002

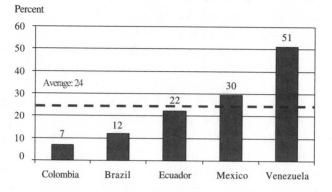

*Source:* Morgan Stanley, 2003.

revenues, as can be seen in figure 16.10. Despite government efforts to diversify the economy, Mexico is still heavily dependent on oil revenues to finance governmental expenditures; nearly a third of all fiscal revenues still come from oil proceeds.[33] This situation is even more pronounced in Venezuela, where oil revenues represent more than half of total fiscal revenues. As long as oil prices remain high, there are no incentives for the political establishment in either country to take the leadership, pay the short run political cost, and change this pattern.

Second, as has been said above, the United States is heavily dependent on oil imports from politically and socially unstable regions of the Middle East and, to a lesser degree, Africa. Should any disturbance cause a disruption in the supply of oil, as was seen during the social unrest in Nigeria in March 2003, oil prices would tend to increase, as they did, thus reducing the likelihood of a sound global economic recovery.[34]

Given that the Latin American region has the potential to become an important player in the international oil markets and that its fiscal revenues are highly "oil dependent," this region must take the necessary steps to reduce the uncertainties surrounding its energy-producing sectors, particularly those related to social unrest, legal restrictions, and a monolithic unionism.[35] From this standpoint, the United States could play an important role in helping Latin American countries to achieve these goals as a strategy toward the consolidation of an energy security plan for the hemisphere. To become a major player in the energy markets, and potentially supplant the Middle

East and Africa as main oil suppliers to the United States, the region must create more stable conditions. Although it is not universally accepted that the creation of commercial regional blocs would be beneficial to all parties involved, in general terms it can be said that the creation of a Free Trade Area of the Americas (FTAA) could help investors allocate more funds to the region, and thus collaborate in the creation of more jobs and reduce social unrest.

Because remittances from the United States to Latin America are considered an important source of funds for the region (in Mexico, they account for close to all foreign direct investment in the country), the establishment of some migration agreement might be used as a powerful bargaining element in exchange for more ample opportunities for private (foreign or local) investment, and might be also considered as a step toward the consolidation of more stable conditions in the region.

In countries such as Mexico and Venezuela, where economic and budgetary conditions do not permit or attract adequate private (foreign or local) investment, governments will need additional time to create the necessary political consensus to allow capital flows into the energy sector. At present, there is little the United States can do to induce this change. A policy of "wait and see" is the most recommended, because, as discussed above, it will require major efforts by the political actors to alter the domestic conception of sovereignty.

## Conclusion

The energy resources of Latin America should be considered an important element of global, regional, and U.S. energy security. Latin America can be a stable and reliable supplier, particularly when compared with the volatile and unreliable countries in the Middle East. I believe it is in the United States' best interest to promote the region's economic development by facilitating, through commercial and economic incentives, the exploitation of the large energy reserves present in the region.

Promoting stability throughout Latin America should be the cornerstone of U.S. foreign and energy policy in the Western Hemisphere. The United States could endorse the creation of the FTAA and support a migration agreement to give Latin American governments the political capital that will allow them to adopt a more flexible position toward private investment in the energy sector.

Mexico and Venezuela have enormous oil and natural gas reserves that are waiting to be exploited. Along with the potential growth found in other countries such as Argentina and Bolivia, these countries will have to remove restrictions on private investment to be able to benefit from these resources.

Any solution adopted by these countries has to take into consideration the complex political, social, and economic realities. In this sense, the Norwegian experience can shed some light on how to modernize and increase the efficiency of the energy sectors in Latin America.

## Notes

1. *BP Statistical Review of World Energy,* June 2004, 4, 22; available at http://www.bp.com.

2. U.S. Energy Information Administration (EIA), *International Energy Outlook 2003* (Washington, D.C.: EIA, 2003), 235.

3. See Adam Sieminski's projections for reserves and production of natural gas in chapter 1.

4. EIA, *Annual Energy Outlook 2003* (Washington, D.C.: EIA, 2003), 147.

5. EIA, *International Energy Outlook 2003,* 38–40.

6. An analysis of the MSC program can be found in the section below titled "Mexico Should Make Strong Efforts to Free Natural Gas Markets."

7. Morgan Stanley, *Mexican Energy Industry: Barriers to Growth,* Industry Series: Oil & Gas (New York: Morgan Stanley, 2003), 5–6.

8. Pemex, *Producción de hidrocarburos líquidos,* September 2003.

9. EIA, *International Energy Outlook 2003,* 47.

10. EIA, *International Energy Outlook 2003,* 47.

11. EIA, *International Energy Outlook 2003,* 47–48.

12. Sener, *Prospectiva del Mercado de gas natural,* 2002, 92.

13. EIA, *International Energy Outlook 2003,* 42.

14. EIA, *International Energy Annual 2001* (Washington, D.C.: EIA, 2001), 5.

15. EIA, *Annual Energy Review 2001* (Washington, D.C.: EIA, 2001), 133.

16. EIA, *Annual Energy Outlook 2003,* 136.

17. EIA, *Annual Energy Outlook 2003,* 54.

18. J. Shore and J. Hackworth, *Impacts of the Venezuelan Crude Oil Production Loss* (Washington, D.C.: EIA, 2003), 2.

19. EIA, *Annual Energy Outlook 2003,* 83.

20. EIA, *Annual Energy Outlook 2003,* 76.

21. Almost a third of all fiscal revenues comes from Pemex through a highly complicated scheme. The Mexican government provide the state-owned company with enough resources to continue operating so it hardly reinvests on exploration or exploitation.

22. C. Schmidt, *Teoría de la constitución,* Francisco Ayala, translator and ed. (Madrid: Revista de Derecho Privado, 1934).

23. D. North, *Institutions, Institutional Change and Economic Performance* (Cambridge: Cambridge University Press, 1990).

24. For a clear review of the context in the region, cf. O. Dabené, *América Latina en el siglo XX* (Madrid: Síntesis, 1999).

25. See Willy Olsen's description of Norway's model in chapter 14.

26. These data are from Statoil, 2003.

27. This information is from the author's conversation with O. Fjell, president and chief executive of Statoil, 2001.

28. It currently produces 1 billion cubic feet per day of natural gas.

29. Pemex Exploración y Producción, *Estimate Burgos* and *Sabinas Basins* (Mexico City: Pemex, 2001).

30. The estimated cost of producing natural gas in the Burgos basin is $2.5 per thousand cubic feet.

31. At least 10,000 new jobs are expected to be created. The spillover effects in the region are expected to be close to $140 million every year.

32. The field of Lankahuasa might hold up to 1 tcf of natural gas and, combined with the other two fields, Playuela and Hap, these new discoveries could account for one quarter of total Mexican natural gas reserves.

33. At the beginning of the 1980s, nearly three-quarters of all exports were oil. In 2002, the diversification of the economy and its degree of openness led to a reversal of this situation, leaving oil exports to represent a tenth of total exports, while manufacturing exports accounted for the vast majority.

34. As a rule of thumb, it is estimated that for every 1.0 mmbpd disrupted and not made up by any other supplier, world oil prices could increase up to $3.00 to $5.00 per barrel. The GDP rule of thumb suggests that if these price increases were sustained, the United States' GDP growth rate could be reduced by 0.05 to 0.08 percent a year. The source for this is "Rules-of-Thumb for Oil Supply Disruptions," http://www.eia.doe.gov/-emeu/security/rule.html.

35. This is particularly true for Colombia, Ecuador, and Venezuela, where it has become urgent to create more stable conditions through the creation of a democratic consensus among political actors.

# Commentary on Part V

## Michelle Michot Foss

By now, the reader of this book may have reached a conclusion: Nations have access to abundant energy resources and options. Yes, there are quibbles here and there as to the ultimate economic limit of the world's natural resource endowments, ongoing arguments about when it might "reach the peak" of its hydrocarbons production, and varying degrees of faith in technology and markets to sort it all out. But this section on the North Atlantic and the Americas resonates on a key point: *"It ain't the resource, it's the framework."*

We have the case of the North Atlantic, as presented by Willy Olsen, and the observation that Norway has produced only one-fourth of its ultimate, attainable known resource base in a region that has benefited hugely from technology gains in exploration and production (E&P) applications. The key consideration going forward for Norway and the North Atlantic is how best to provide frameworks for continued investment and renewal of industry activity, especially to shepherd production from maturing fields and stretch out into more demanding frontier plays. We hear from Shirley Neff that natural gas is the future, and learn the possibilities for energy efficiency gains to extend the life of this resource beyond even the knowable limits. That is, technology matters on both sides of the energy supply/demand balance, and the question is how best to design frameworks to facilitate innovation and adaptation. And from Luis Tellez, we have the bottom line, that the optimal discovery and recovery of hydrocarbon resources are best done with a more constructive role for the state than the Latin American region has experienced. The challenge is how to design frameworks needed to engineer transitions in a region marked by a special relationship between oil and sovereignty. Moreover, for all three chapters—indeed throughout this

399

book and our modern human experience to date—the fundamental dilemma is finding the political will to implement frameworks once they are designed. Disengaging the state, enabling the flow of price information to facilitate demand-side response (however uncomfortable those price signals may be), and making firm commitments to market liberalization even when doubts persist about the reliability of suppliers—these are themes that run through all these chapters and that share a common heritage at the intersection of energy economics and politics.

The concepts of energy security can be simply stated.[1] *Supply diversification is essential to reduce geopolitical risk.* Tellez makes this point elegantly, emphasizing the role Latin America should be playing as a major supply region, and Olsen alludes to diversification as an element of European energy (i.e., import) security. *Demand-side response should not be isolated, but rather made an integral part of the supply portfolio.* The gains to which Neff points clearly enhance inventories of natural gas and should be thought of that way. *Flexible, transparent frameworks provide for price discovery and the consequent adjustments in technology.* The North Atlantic and Americas are poster children for the power of technology, and not just for improvements that extend the lives of marginal fields or enable dreams of ultra-deepwater production to come true (a point not addressed specifically in these chapters, but one that is implicit, given the dominance of offshore regimes throughout Europe and the Americas).

The emergence of liquefied natural gas (LNG) and the depth of LNG trade and commercial activity that can be achieved for the Atlantic basin, as well as the potential for gas-to-liquids technology to integrate natural gas more deeply into crude oil applications especially for transportation, mean that "barrels" are no longer relevant. We are moving into an era in which it is "barrel equivalents" that are important and in which we can put aside the tired debate about whether and when we will run out of oil. *Flexible, transparent frameworks also help to facilitate trade flows.* Energy trade is an essential component in both Europe and the Americas as well as globally. Imagine a world in which international comparative advantages could not be exercised and markets not cleared! Well, perhaps some can, but I cannot.

Apart from higher-altitude principles, specific framework considerations can be teased out and tested against these chapters. Perhaps foremost is the role of government, a hallmark of the energy security arena. Three models are most in evidence in this part of the book: (1) what I call Norway's "beneficent overseer" model, with the state as a "commercial shareholder";

(2) the private-sector model so strongly represented by the United States and Canada; and (3) the Latin American system of patrimony and state monopoly control (spiked with various experiments, e.g., those in Argentina and Brazil, to rely on private markets and enterprise). In the United States and Canada (and Canada more so in recent years), decisions about the timing of hydrocarbon production are largely left to private-sector interests and market drivers. Latin America and Mexico in particular encapsulate the nuanced government and social debate about whether resources should be produced now or held for future generations. Here, Tellez's argument is telling for the entire Latin American region—in a part of the world dominated by youthful populations, the most critical factors for its future will be the health, education, and attainment of opportunities by the children of today. This places a burden on Latin American governments to rejig energy policies and provide the necessary resources for their younger citizens, and quickly.

How well institutions are designed and function dictates both the quality of government performance and the soundness of free markets and, hence, successful implementation of frameworks. Here, Tellez rightly points out, Latin American institutions are subject to the social and political histories of each country. Of course, this is true for every nation-state. The history of oil as an expression of national sovereignty for countries like Mexico and Venezuela (and elsewhere, Central Asia being a prime example) creates an especially complicated context for institutional development. Labor and labor unions are also critical factors (indeed, for Mexico, it could be argued that it is the unions that are the national symbol, rather than the national oil company). I would add to the list civil societies, representing in many cases the "humaneness" that has been missing from Latin American governments, as well as the demands of democratization and the extent to which so many of the institutions needed by Latin American countries are either new or underdeveloped. Of all the chapter authors, Tellez is bluntest in his assessment of the role of government in energy, and it is worth repeating his words, which have relevance for broad swaths of the world:

> If Latin American countries are not capable of understanding that being the monopolistic providers of energy does not intrinsically lead to the maximization of natural resources wealth, and if they do not integrate a "modern" concept of sovereignty to their basic institutions, they are running the risk of letting opportunities pass, having done nothing but leaving their "sovereignty"—whatever it means—intact.

But how to change the role of state where it is too overpowering? The Norwegian model is one alternative, yet it has been studied and examined perhaps more closely than any other for its potential application to other countries. Some of us would argue that the "beneficent overseer" continues to have too much, and perhaps undue, influence. Many of us were disappointed that more of Statoil was not offered to the private markets in 2002. Norway has indeed achieved an admirable level of public transparency and public benefits through its petroleum fund. Yet in the United States, we can look to a similar case in Alaska and detect a welfare state with few economic prospects except for its natural resource endowment. Dependence on a petroleum fund can lead to distortions in energy policy— the current debate on Alaska natural gas pipelines being a case in point— that affect not only Alaska but all of the United States and North America. Clearly, there is a delicate balance to be achieved.

Upstream frameworks must reflect the risk and uncertainty of discovery and the process of replenishment that must occur to replace reserves. The U.K. experience and Norway's story offer differing results with regard to expanding the universe of industry players, with greater apparent success in the United Kingdom. Both sectors of the North Sea have been adversely affected from time to time by their fiscal regimes (tax and royalty provisions); in Norway, it took the exit of international companies in 1986 to impress upon the government that the fiscal regime needed to better reflect the maturity of the Norwegian continental shelf.

In similar fashion, U.S. and Canadian fiscal regimes are continually tested by industry, and adjustments are quickly made if the regimes do not provide competitive returns relative to the risks and costs associated with resources that lie in the public domain.[2] Canada has been of particular interest in recent years. The emerging Atlantic Canada offshore, which offers demanding physical operating conditions akin to the North Sea, has been marked by efforts to build competitive fiscal regimes that can attract and retain a diverse fleet of operating companies. For both Canada and the United States, building successful frameworks for exploration and production involves balancing interests at the national and state or provincial levels. The answer for Atlantic Canada was the creation of provincial petroleum boards, which administer the regimes and the portion of revenue that flows to federal coffers. Besides tax and royalty schemes, a number of issues revolve around "local content"—the employment of indigenous workers and the use of indigenous goods and services. Local content has proved to be a hurdle to expanding investment in the Atlantic Canada offshore, given the uncertainty about reserves and returns. Olsen offers Norway as an example of a successful approach to local content, and the United Kingdom is mentioned for its attention to economic development benefits. Altogether, the Aberdeen–Stavanger axis of the North Sea represents the second largest collection of private companies in engineering and support services for oil and gas development, with the U.S. Gulf Coast being the largest. These dynamic clusters are often looked to by other countries seeking to extract enhanced benefits from upstream activities, from Mexico's upper Yucatán, to China's enormous production "cities," to West Africa's evolving corner of the "Golden Triangle" for deepwater exploration (the other two anchors being the U.S. Gulf of Mexico and Brazil, with the latter being an international leader in expanding local content requirements).

A particular problem in establishing upstream fiscal regimes is accommodating the state in those countries where state control is prevalent. Sadly, Latin America shows how not to do things. As Tellez shows, Petróleos Mexicanos (Pemex) exceeds other major, sovereign national oil companies (NOCs) with regard to taxation. The tendency to skim from NOCs creates capital budget constraints for these organizations; the lack of alternative revenue for government treasuries means little relief when it comes to the inadequate funding of NOC reinvestment. The dire situation for Venezuela's Petróleos de Venezuela (PdVSA), not fully addressed in Tellez's chapter, could set back progress for the entire country for the foreseeable future, as well as add to supply security risk for PdVSA's customers. Even though PdVSA seems to have stabilized production, the strike begun in December 2002 and the dismissal of 18,000 workers cut deeply into the company's capabilities and is affecting forward outlooks.

Again, the key question is how to engineer transitions. The example of Mexico's Multi-Service Contract experiment represents only a tiny step in supplanting public with private investment, albeit one burdened with controversy as to both legality and financial net benefits for Pemex. In re-engineering upstream fiscal regimes for countries like Mexico and Venezuela, the trick is to ensure comparable revenue streams to government treasuries through other means. Endless demonstrations of how to do this have been provided, and in all cases the analysis leads to conclusions that revenues to treasuries would actually increase because of the overall boost to the producing nation's economy and because these steps would represent a move to unlock market forces and entrepreneurship. Once more, the issue is one of political will and commitment.

Dealing with maturing resource fields is a growing challenge as well as opportunity. None of the authors suggests—but I know they have all given thought to—tiered tax collections to reflect production declines and increasing costs with maturity. There have also been quite clever incentives for risk taking in deeper-water frontiers, the U.S. deepwater relief program being one (with acknowledgment to both former senator Bennett Johnston and Shirley Neff for their roles in designing this policy). Without careful thought and policymaking, the course of industry maturity and consolidation can lead to a "death spiral" in basins and countries with mature fields and diminishing prospects. Such a trend would hasten the economic end to what might otherwise be abundant and long-lasting resource endowments. Considerable effort also is being made to attract and retain smaller producers. Norway's white paper, as recounted by Olsen, and efforts within the U.S. Congress to develop neutral (as much as possible) and targeted fiscal incentives are two such examples. Others include Brazil's learning curve in offering onshore fields and recent efforts by individual U.S. states, like Mississippi, to rebuild their petroleum sectors. Along with fiscal incentives, policymakers need to consider how best to provide oversight and regulation for small operators, especially for compliance with environmental protection rules.

But who are the players, and what role do they play? Small producers often do not have access to cash-flow wealth to launch production development programs, much less for risky exploration ventures. The upstream sectors of the United States, Canada, and Europe all benefited from the ready funding provided by energy merchant businesses, which supplemented their trading and marketing operations with mezzanine and, in some cases, equity financing. The energy merchant sector collapse left a looming gap in critical, incremental funding for E&P activities, making it more difficult for smaller companies to move into the gaps created as large companies lose interest in maturing and less prospective basins. In addition to reducing the global capital supply base for E&P, the energy merchant collapse also directly removed potential new players. In 2000, I participated in a workshop in Oslo hosted by the Norwegian School of Management. At that time, speculation was rife as to whether Norway could extend the development of its continental shelf with new companies attracted from the energy merchant sector. These companies not only would participate in production but also in innovative, market-making natural gas midstream businesses (pipeline transportation, storage, etc.). That conversation would be very different today.

Finally, there is the matter of the environment and access, and here there is a chasm between experience and hype. Little difference exists between arguments for "petroleum-free zones" along Norway's coast and the U.S. offshore moratoriums that are contributing directly, in my opinion, to uncertainty about the deliverability of natural gas supply in America, with commensurate economic dislocation. And in neither case does the performance of industry, or government, merit such extreme reactions.

When it comes to the role of oil and gas in energy security, especially with regard to the rapidly developing linkages between natural gas and electric power, frameworks to facilitate markets are unlikely to succeed without competitive supply, including E&P activities. This is true no matter how much time, energy, and creativity are poured into the endeavor. Mexico should know. When Tellez refers to creating free markets for gas, in large part his prescriptions would solve shortcomings of the "partial" or "virtual" markets Mexico currently has in place. For there can be no downstream competition—no competition among suppliers to the benefit of customers—if only one producer exists! Over the years, we have seen a number of new regimes emerge to connect production with markets, such as producer-led pipeline development in North America (e.g., Canada's Alliance pipeline). Norway's agreement with the United Kingdom on Stratfjord seems to represent another such illustration. But more are needed, because the impact of the energy merchant decline is being felt in the midstream as well. The challenge for market-facilitating frameworks is exactly how best to introduce and sustain competition. This is most problematic for natural gas transportation and distribution, which tends to have monopoly characteristics no matter what the overall government and market regimes, and for the affiliate relationship between natural gas marketers and infrastructure operators.

Last, there are inherent geopolitical considerations, as there are in every other part of this book. Of note is the debate about the relationship between OPEC and Norway, as well as OPEC and Mexico. Is it good or bad? Do these key, non-OPEC producers tend to "go along," or are they independent? There is the matter of regional integration and trade. As stated at the outset, these are vital, pervasive, and unstoppable; and they require flexible, transparent frameworks as well. But what if the frameworks of one partner are an imposition of the other? Norway and the need to bend to E.U. liberalization and regime change is an interesting example. The hope with the North American Free Trade Agreement was that energy liberalization would get a boost and that North American energy policies would become more harmonious. Instead, state-owned monopolies remain firmly in place (e.g., the Crown corporations in Canada, federal power authorities in the United

States, and Mexico's national energy companies). Mexico, with abundant resource endowments (by all accounts), is a net importer of natural gas from the United States, and will soon be an importer of LNG. The stymied World Trade Organization negotiations have also interrupted negotiations on energy services, which are viewed as essential to resolving such problems as access for investment and to equalize rules with regard to how facilities like pipelines are used for shipping.

Not mentioned in these chapters is the European Energy Charter Treaty, which at least has provided signatories some options for reciprocity in Russia. Are there potential frameworks to deal with the risks and unknowns of a globalizing natural gas industry? And are there frameworks that can be devised to solve the pervasive problem of socioeconomic development in key producing regions? On this last question, Tellez is right—it is in the best interest of the United States that shared solutions be found to achieve both U.S. energy security and sustainable development of energy in Latin America. More broadly, it is in America's best interests to engage in shared solutions worldwide, and to ensure that sustainable energy development and sustainable economic development go hand in hand.

## Notes

1. See also Michelle Michot Foss, "Global Natural Gas: Issues and Challenges," forthcoming in *Energy Journal,* 2005.

2. All too often, however, companies accept terms from governments, as a result of competitive pressure, that do not enhance shareholder value. The "herd effect" is a powerful phenomenon in the cutthroat international oil and gas business.

# Part VI

# A New Energy Security Strategy

This concluding part advances a new energy security strategy for the United States and its partners in the new century. Underlying all the chapters is the recognition that, especially after September 11, 2001, U.S. energy lifelines are exposed to a multiplicity of threats that represent a quantum leap from the 1972–73 oil embargo, which preoccupied energy strategists in the past quarter-century. Now the threats include terrorism and religious extremism at the subnational level; corruption and instability at the national level; conflict at the international level; and disease, poverty, and environmental degradation at the global level—in addition to only modestly lessened dependence on OPEC producers. The requirement, then, is for a multifaceted strategy to deal with these multiple threats, which will be the principal subject of this book's concluding chapter.

To address these questions, Leon Fuerth considers threats and their dilemmas from homeland security to the energy–nuclear weapons nexus. Melanie Kenderdine and Ernest Moniz discuss how America can maximize the use of technology. Charles McPherson analyzes transparency, governance, and sustainable development. Kevin Baumert looks at how to balance energy and the environment. David Goldwyn and Michelle Billig discuss the building of strategic reserves. And Donald Juckett and Michelle Foss consider whether a global natural gas market can be achieved.

In chapter 17, Fuerth considers the national security dimension of oil and gas development in its broadest political and economic sense, arguing that United States grand strategy requires that it never lose the ability to respond to any serious threat to the stability of the energy marketplace. He assesses the terrorist threat to critical nodes of the U.S. energy infrastructure as well as the political relationships that enable the country to influence the decisions that make or break the stability of energy markets. He points out the growing threat of nuclear weapons proliferation from ostensibly peaceful uses of nuclear energy, and he warns of the mounting threat of environmental disaster from failure to confront global warming now. He concludes by considering those foreign policy strategies that can best enhance energy and national security.

In chapter 18, Kenderdine and Moniz present a comprehensive assessment of technology and energy security. They discuss the requirement for goal-driven technology programs to increase U.S. energy security. After reviewing key energy-related security challenges and objectives, they analyze available technology pathways that can address these objectives through further research, development and demonstration, and/or technology-enabled policy initiatives. They home in on technology solutions that can have the greatest impact on energy supply: higher efficiency vehicles and alternative fuels including biofuels, Fischer Tropsch diesel, and hydrogen. They consider how technology can boost the use of natural gas, and the impact of technology on a range of other energy sources, including coal, renewables, and nuclear power. They make technology proposals for dealing with climate change, nuclear proliferation, and terrorist threats to energy infrastructure, as well as organizational proposals for ensuring that technology and policy can be properly integrated.

In chapter 19, McPherson argues that transparency and good governance are essential for energy security and sustainable development. He analyzes the principal challenges to good governance presented by oil, including Dutch disease, market volatility, weak institutional capacity, corruption, and uneven distribution of wealth. He considers models for petroleum revenue management and transparency, reviews lessons from initiatives in Chad and other countries, and advances proposals based on active roles for international, governmental, and nongovernmental stakeholders.

In chapter 20, Baumert addresses the challenge of climate protection in balancing energy and environment. After he reviews the experience with the Kyoto Protocol as well as the sources of current U.S. opposition to the treaty, he concludes that the core features of the agreement are fundamentally sound but that it can be improved by reframing engagement with the developing countries and improving cost predictability. He then offers a set of Kyoto and post-Kyoto options, and next steps to promote climate protection in the context of increased energy security.

In chapter 21, Goldwyn and Billig analyze how strategic reserves can become a more robust component of a new energy security policy. They describe the origins of U.S. strategic reserve policy and how new threats and economic realities have outpaced the policy. They then consider how U.S. policy itself has handicapped the effective use of the U.S. Strategic Petroleum Reserve, and they propose a new policy for the management of U.S. and global strategic stocks, including mandatory stock requirements, improved decision making, modernized national reserves, and the creation of a global strategic reserve.

In chapter 22, Juckett and Foss ask whether and how a global gas market can be achieved, to address vast increases in demand for natural gas, provide price stability, and ensure security of supply. They describe major challenges to developing such a market: the need for major investment in exploration and transport infrastructure, the lack of gas receiving capacity and the associated regulatory and political hurdles, and the need for government leadership and support to bring about a responsive and efficient global market. They conclude that such a market can and should be achieved with major economic and security benefits for the United States and its partners.

In his commentary on part VI, John Holdren agrees with the thesis of this volume—that a new foreign policy strategy integrating energy interests into the U.S. calculus can vastly improve U.S. energy, economic, and national security interests. He highlights the threats posed by energy consumption, access to nuclear energy, and the use of centralized electric power systems, and he concurs with proposals advanced by the authors, including enhanced physical security, stepped-up nonproliferation measures, and moves to decentralize U.S. power systems. He underlines the importance of frontally addressing the threat of global climate change and the need to take the energy–environment–security connection much more seriously.

# 17

# Energy, Homeland, and National Security

## Leon Fuerth

It is hard to imagine any combination of forces that might seriously challenge the preeminence of the United States. But the same might have been said—the same *was* said—in city-states, republics, and empires at the zenith of their power and influence. Permanence is an illusion, and the single most important lesson of history is that nothing is forever. Even the mightiest human accomplishments have their hidden weaknesses. Great nations that recognize their vulnerabilities and move in time to deal with them will keep their primacy. Others that are less farsighted will not.

The economic strength of the United States is the foundation upon which all else depends, including ultimately even the survival of this country as a democracy, and as a unified state. Visualize an America that has lost faith in itself—for example, the America of the Depression, *without* a Franklin Roosevelt—and you get a glimpse of the possible.

Access to energy at stable prices is a fundamental requirement for the stability and success of the economy of the United States. Any external threat to supplies of energy involves the vital interests of the United States, and it could bring on a direct military response from this country. Because the United States draws energy resources from a worldwide marketplace, within the context of global trading and financial systems, any serious threat to the stability of the energy marketplace is a threat to the United States.

The grand strategy of the United States requires that it never lose the ability to respond effectively to any such threat. The elements of an effective response include military power; but military power—even dominance—must be complemented by a strong international diplomatic position, by the financial strength of the United States, and by the presence of effective policies for shaping U.S. patterns of consumption and for assuring the adequacy of internal systems of regulation and of distribution of energy.

International terrorists realize that the energy security of the United States is a strategic target, and they have the capacity to attack it at several levels. Because one of the fundamental objectives of a group such as al Qaeda is to destroy American influence in the Middle East, by definition it aims to destroy political relationships that enable the United States to influence decisions that make or break the stability of world energy markets. By attacking vulnerabilities in the U.S. domestic energy supply system, international terrorism could cause great economic damage to the United States and possibly even major loss of life. Even the mere threat of hypothetical terrorist strikes against critical nodes in the nation's energy infrastructure can deeply exacerbate difficulties that already afflict decision making about domestic energy policy, and thereby delay and distort economically vital decisions.

With or without a terrorist threat, the proliferation of nuclear weapons is a threat to the vital security interests of the United States. The scientific knowledge and computational capacity for making nuclear weapons have already been widely disseminated. Access to highly enriched fissionable materials in quantities sufficient for bomb making is now the single most important threshold for proliferators to cross. Fear that reactors constructed for peaceful purposes *can* be used to supply such materials has become a major constraint on the development of nuclear energy, parallel to and independent of environmental and safety concerns.

Energy and the global environment are intimately related, although that factor is not adequately reflected in the grand strategy of the United States. At some point, it may become painfully clear that an energy policy based on unfettered consumption is increasing U.S. vulnerability to the environmental, as well as to the economic and security, threats the country faces. One may hope that advances in science and technology will restore flexibility and room to maneuver. But as time passes, America is accumulating an ever greater challenge by shirking present responsibilities and leaving the consequences to future generations.

It is an error to think that this problem stands in isolation from all others, and that it can be deferred until all others are resolved. On the contrary, the resolution of the conflict between America's current approach to energy and the environment is one of the most effective ways to bring the country back toward a more constructive general relationship with the rest of the world than it now has, or that now seems in prospect.

## Oil, Gas, and National Security

The most serious foreseeable threat to national security related to oil and gas is not the physical availability of these resources but the political stability of the regions of the world where they are located. Fundamentally, the problem is that with few exceptions, possession of these resources is associated with corruption and authoritarian rule. In the presence of well-established democratic governance, this problem can be controlled—though not without constant vigilance. But the largest part of the world's reserves are located in regions where democratic governance does not exist at all, exists in name only, or exists in patterns that are not yet reliable. Consequently, the world market for these two resources is subject to severe distortions that are political rather than economic in nature.

The security of the United States also depends upon the economic vitality of its friends, allies, and trading partners. Serious instability in the global energy market simultaneously affects all of them, and what damages them reflexively damages America one way or another. Even the possibility of instability can strongly influence the willingness, even of the closest U.S. allies, to collaborate with America in any enterprise that might lead to such consequences.

The United States has become accustomed to the Organization of Petroleum Exporting Countries (OPEC) and even views it as part of the machinery by which the world supply of energy is regulated. OPEC, however, is actually a cartel—the goal of which is restraint of trade through manipulation of supply, by means of monopoly control of the market. Fortunately for America, there are divergent interests operating among cartel members, which frequently prevent them from achieving the level of cohesion needed for truly dangerous behavior. But growing world energy consumption works to overcome these divisions, and to diminish consumers' economic leverage on the decision making of the exporting countries. The deepening need for imported energy hastens the time when the West may face the choice of paying extortionate prices or having to use military pressure to influence suppliers. Either course presents severe risks to the economic security and political stability of the United States.

America also faces the problem that inbred and corrupt governance in the oil-producing regions stimulates domestic forces that can challenge the stability of the major suppliers. All governance depends upon a combination of moral legitimacy and an effective monopoly on the use of force. As legitimacy erodes, the need for force increases. However, a regime that increasingly depends upon force is mortgaged to those who directly control it, whether in the police or the military. Such regimes are therefore increasingly at risk of being overthrown by intrigue or by putsch. However, beyond a certain level of violence, even those who are in charge of the use of force begin to lose their will to employ it, which is when systems of government are washed away by revolution.

It is now both fashionable and official to advocate democracy as the way to arrest this cycle. The president of the United States has directly criticized "ruling elites" in the Middle East, he has blamed his predecessors for policies that fastened repressive governments on the peoples of the region, and he has predicted that an age of rapid democratic reform is about to begin.[1] Most Americans, including this writer, agree that democratic transitions may be the only way to break through patterns of thought that trap the Middle East in its history, while denying it a better future.

But democracy is a Promethean force, capable of great destructive power. There is no guarantee that democratic reform will not slide into revolutionary violence. Anyone who thinks differently needs to explain how to interpret Iran's slide from the shah's tyranny to the ayatollah's. It would be useful also to explain how democracy helped the people of Algeria, when a free and fair election there that pointed toward the victory of an Islamic party caused the military to insist on voiding the results, resulting in a civil war costing the lives of an estimated 100,000 people. Advocates of democratic transition in the Middle East should also present a theory of the case whereby the Saudi Royal Family somehow is able to transcend itself and yield power. It would also be good to know what plan B would look like if a democratic transition in Saudi Arabia were to spin out of control and lead to a fundamentalist regime.

Egypt is not a major factor in energy production, but it is certainly a major player in every other way in the Middle East. Here, too, official American opinion seems to be shifting toward the idea of a democratic transition, although it is unclear whether the administration is thinking of encouraging President Hosni Mubarak's departure from the scene or just musing about the consequences. In any event, anyone looking at Egyptian demographics must wonder what will follow him. The tens of millions of young persons who are coming of age are underemployed and not well educated for life in a globalized world economy. They may well desire greater freedom of expression. But America ought to be concerned about the kind of politics

Egypt's successor generation will support, and what that may portend for the region as a whole, and therefore, for America.

In short, talking up democratic transformation in parts of the world that are vital to U.S. interests, where democracy is not part of the culture, and where even those who use the term do not necessarily understand its implications, is not risk free. The current U.S. experiment with democracy as panacea begins with an effort to install it by diktat in Iraq as a by-product of military occupation, and it faces an uncertain future in the hands of a besieged "sovereign" government. That does not bode well for happy sequels elsewhere in the Middle East.[2]


## Oil and Gas and the Economic Challenge to American Security

Our constantly growing need for external sources of oil and gas exposes another American vulnerability: economic. Even if there were no threat to adequate physical reserves of energy, it must nevertheless be paid for. As long as the medium for settling energy accounts is the dollar, the United States can more or less hold its own. But when the dollar loses a substantial portion of its value against other major trading currencies, as it did significantly in 2003–4, then energy suppliers that are holding dollars take a loss. It is natural for them to look for ways to buffer themselves against the consequences of American economic mismanagement.

In the past, the dollar had no effective competitor as a store of value, and the United States was without peer as a refuge for capital. The advent of the euro and the ongoing expansion and consolidation of the European Union have changed that equation.[3] Countries holding large amounts of dollars as payment for energy can now look for ways to spread risk, by cutting back on their purchases of U.S. debt. True, Saudi Arabia has resisted calls to reduce its reliance on the dollar. Given the size of the U.S. economy, and the scale of Saudi investment in the United States, it is hard to imagine a Saudi collapse of faith in the dollar, but it is certainly not impossible to think of a serious erosion.[4] Presidential attacks on "privileged" groups responsible for misrule in the Middle East are not likely to reassure the Saudi Royal Family that it is prudent to manage its economic relationship with the United States, as if it could still take U.S. support to the bank.

There are already rumbles from major international lending authorities, and also from globally influential debt-rating services, that the United States must get a grip on its fiscal situation and also on its current account deficits.[5] But there is no sign that the United States is likely to do this any time soon. The recent surge in U.S. economic growth may do little if anything to help because of the way in which the tax base of the United States has been transformed under the George W. Bush administration. There are also some potentially major problems for the dollar in China, which now holds the largest share of U.S. debt. The United States and China are now locked in an unhealthy relationship, within which soaring U.S. imports from China are paid for by soaring U.S. debts held by China.[6] How long that process can go on before upward spiral tips into downward plunge, no one can say. But not forever.

China faces major economic challenges of its own, notably in the weakness of its banking system and in the role of the People's Liberation Army as an actor in the civilian economy. However, if China manages to navigate past its own major economic hazards, the continuation of its rapid growth must eventually present a challenge to the United States at many different levels, including access to energy. Not only has China become a competitor for access to oil and gas, but it is a competitor with extremely deep pockets—aiming to buy itself a major stake in the ownership and management of world energy resources. It would be ironic if Taiwan eventually fades as a source of instability in the United States–China relationship, only to be replaced by a protracted competition focused on access to energy.

There is no precedent for this kind of economic relationship between the United States and China. The Chinese, certainly, understand that for the time being their prosperity is closely tied to America's, and America may not have really come close to the limits of what China is prepared to do to make sure that relationship is undisturbed. So one should not rule out both explicit and tacit forms of economic cooperation in relation to energy.

However, it takes two to make this kind of cooperation work. China, for example, has become environmentally aware, and it is attempting to make sure that the dramatic expansion of its economy is not accompanied by an equally dramatic decline in its environmental resources. China is insisting, for example, that its burgeoning capacity to manufacture automobiles be tempered by mandated mileage and emissions standards.[7] Nothing could be further from the policies of the U.S. government, as this is written. It should be a matter of concern that because of this mismatch, America will miss a huge economic opportunity to meet China's needs for a second-generation industrial economy that is energy efficient and environmentally moderated.

## Energy and the Terrorist Threat to National Security

Energy distribution systems located in the United States, from port and storage facilities to pipelines, are vulnerable to sabotage and difficult to protect. Attacks on oil refineries could produce not only local but also national consequences, given the shortage of refinery capacity relative to demand. Attacks on liquefied natural gas facilities could produce mass casualties. Attacks on nuclear power plants and/or waste storage facilities could produce regional damages on an immense scale, with long-term national environmental consequences.[8]

The electric energy system is a particularly strategic and vulnerable part of the U.S. energy infrastructure. The power grid is a patchwork both technologically and in terms of ownership and regulatory jurisdiction. The system, if it deserves to be so called, has a well-demonstrated potential for catastrophic failure as the result of natural or accidental human causes. These same weaknesses also make the system an obvious and lucrative target for exploitation by terrorists. It should be noted that physical attack on critical nodes of the system might not be needed if a cyberattack on control systems were attempted and proved to be effective.[9]

Public fears about the safety of different elements of the U.S. energy system are already a major factor in decision making. Health concerns, fear of operating accidents, fear of local environmental damage, and the like have all played a role in influencing public policies and investments. These fears are intensified because of widespread public distrust of the motives and managements of energy corporations, and by well-founded pessimism concerning the effectiveness of government oversight and regulatory mechanisms. Any terrorist attack against an energy target capable of producing massive loss of life, even if unsuccessful, would exacerbate public fears to the point of psychosis—trapping all major decisions, even the most vital, in political struggle and litigation.

To date, the accomplishments of the Department of Homeland Security are not a source of reassurance. At the macro level, it appears that the agency's budget is well below requirements, and that shortage shows in the halting progress reported in moving resources out of Washington and into the hands of those who are locally responsible for boosting physical security of critical installations, and for damage control.[10]

Ironically, deep modernization of parts of the energy system, such as the electrical distribution network, could simultaneously reduce vulnerabilities to attack. But the United States is hundreds of billions of dollars short of meeting the requirements for sensible renovation of infrastructure; nor is there a way to finance requirements of that magnitude, given the new fiscal realities.[11]

The nuclear industry of the United States is precisely at the confluence of public concerns about the environment and fears about terrorist threats to national security. There is virtually no place in the country where nuclear power plants are welcomed, and domestic construction has basically flat-lined. U.S. policy as regards the export of nuclear energy gives far more weight to security considerations than to trade promotion. For these reasons, nuclear energy is not an option for reducing U.S. dependence on energy imports. Its fate was written at Three Mile Island and sealed at the World Trade Center.

## How Do Nuclear Proliferation and Other Threats Add to the Security Dilemma?

As the 1990s began, the United States was mainly concerned about the proliferation of nuclear weapons and delivery systems to states such as India, Pakistan, North Korea, and Iran. Since the turn of the century, the problem has intensified, and there is a sense that the nonproliferation regime is beginning to unravel. Pakistan has been given virtually a pass on its nuclear weapons, and although Pakistan and India have agreed to establish a crisis-control hotline, the underlying reality is volatile and dangerous. North Korea is actually a declared, if not yet a demonstrated, nuclear weapons state. No one can say whether, at the end of the day, any kind of deal is possible with North Korea, and it is entirely possible that negotiations with it are—from its perspective—no more than stalling tactics. Iran finally has been caught in the act of pursuing the elements of a nuclear weapons program. Pressures from the European Union are welcome, but nowhere near a threshold that could change the Iranian perspective.

For thirty years, the core of the U.S. nonproliferation strategy was the Nuclear Non-Proliferation Treaty (NPT), under which nations agreed to forswear nuclear weapons in return for access to peaceful nuclear technology. That core may now be broken beyond repair, because it has been repeatedly demonstrated that nations will use peaceful nuclear energy as a path toward the acquisition of nuclear weapons. The European Union hopes that the damage can be mended by adherence to strengthened International Atomic Energy Agency inspection standards, and by efforts to assure that countries such as Iran, whose nuclear programs are the source of concern about proliferation, do not acquire full nuclear fuel cycles. The attitude of the United States towards this approach is dubious at best. Conversely, the Bush administration appears ready to believe that enhanced international inspection of Libya's facilities for weapons of mass destruction may be adequate assurance. Even in the case of Libya, however, the administration wants to see political reform as a guarantee against backsliding.

It would clearly be in the U.S. interest to bolster the NPT, but U.S. policies have done the reverse. By destroying the Comprehensive Test Ban (CTB) Treaty, the Bush administration has broken faith with a fundamental premise of the NPT: that the nuclear weapons states that had joined the treaty would work to eliminate their arsenals. The CTB was universally understood to be a major step toward fulfillment of that pledge. Meanwhile, the United States appears to be moving toward the development of new designs for nuclear weapons.[12] By so doing, America makes it clear that U.S. exceptionalism applies to nuclear weapons: that even in principle, what is good for America is not good for anyone else. This is not a premise that the United States should expect other countries to accept.

If this trend continues, certain governments that are members of the NPT may eventually reconsider their positions. Saudi Arabia is a prime candidate, in the event that Iran ultimately acquires nuclear weapons to go along with the medium-range ballistic missiles it has already developed. Israel is universally believed to have an inventory of deliverable nuclear weapons. Nations such as Libya and Syria are not under trustworthy leadership, and they could on any given day decide that the only way to deal with the threat of American preemption is to somehow acquire a nuclear capability, perhaps by direct purchase. In this worst case, nuclear weapons will not only surround but be located at various points in the Middle East, effectively creating the equivalent of a doomsday machine strapped to the global economy —including that of the United States.[13]

In the new century, old fears about nuclear weapons in the hands of governments are blending into new fears about nuclear weapons in the hands of terrorists. The inevitable consequence of this fear must be an even greater delegitimization of peaceful nuclear energy, unless there can be not only technical but political agreement on the effectiveness of strongly upgraded safety and security measures applied at practically every point in the nuclear fuel cycle.

## The Environment and National Security

Especially under the Bush administration, the relationship between energy and national security has been visualized primarily in terms of the supply side. Consumption is left to the marketplace, and so too are the consequences. Global warming is the largest of those consequences, and here the administration's legacy is its repudiation of the Kyoto Protocol and its failure to introduce any credible substitute.

In time, the administration hopes that radical improvements in automotive efficiency will contribute to diminish U.S. emissions of carbon dioxide. But the time horizon for the transition to such technologies is long range and indistinct. Meanwhile, worldwide emissions of greenhouse gases, including principally carbon dioxide, continue to accelerate, while the potential for severe environmental disturbance grows.[14] If America is lucky, the costs of coming to terms with these consequences will be merely heavy. If it is not lucky, the consequences may arrive so fast and be so severe as to be insupportable, in the sense of exceeding the adaptive capacities of existing political and economic systems.

From 1945 onward, the United States lived with the knowledge that nuclear weapons could destroy civilization. In the 1980s, calculations about the atmospheric effects of a general nuclear war showed that such weapons might destroy not just civilization but also our species. In the 1990s, Americans began to realize that even peaceful industrial technologies can have similar consequences: the destruction of the environment not in half a day, but certainly within the lifetimes of persons presently alive, or their children.[15] After World War I, the League of Nations was to have been the means to prevent another global war. Its failure owed a great deal to narrow-minded opposition in the U.S. Senate. The Kyoto Protocol was to have been the environmental analogue to the league. It is possible that future generations will deplore its repudiation by the United States as one of the capital blunders of our era.

For all its faults, the Kyoto treaty represented the possibility that the world would invoke marketplace forces to save the environment. To do this required, of course, the creation of a market by way of monetizing emissions and making them the basis of a tradable value. There will be no such market in the absence of the Kyoto agreement. It is also very hard to see how market forces will encourage the development of new super-efficient technologies. Absent the intervention of government on a global scale, energy will remain relatively cheap—or at least, cheap enough to prevent the spontaneous development of powerful inducements to efficiency and conservation.

It is a sad thing that the fate of the Kyoto agreement rests not in the hands of an American president but in those of Vladimir Putin, who has acquired a power over the future of humankind because of the default by American leadership. His agreement to ratify the treaty, as part of a still-private deal for World Trade Organization entry worked out with the European Union, will take another five years to execute, and may—according to some reports—have been poorly negotiated by the Europeans.

## What Foreign Policy Strategies Can Best Enhance Energy and National Security?

Growing dependence on imported oil and gas increases the vulnerability of the United States to extortionate behavior on the part of suppliers; political instability affecting the suppliers; financial instability owing to excessive levels of debt; the risk of a strategically successful terrorist strike against an energy-related domestic target; and environmental dislocations severe enough to disturb the stability of the international system.

There is no way to design an effective foreign policy strategy to enhance U.S. national security as it relates to energy, in the absence of effective, complementary initiatives in domestic policy. On the domestic side, there are two categories of action the United States ought to take: measures to constrain the rate of increase of demand for imported energy; and measures to rebalance the fiscal policies of the country.

With respect to foreign policy, U.S. strategy should be to encourage diversity of sources, political stability among suppliers, security against terrorist attacks on critical nodes in energy systems from wellhead to delivery points in the United States, a maximalist effort to prevent further nuclear proliferation, and the resumption of American leadership—or at least, responsible participation—in the cause of safeguarding the environment.

The missing environmental component is actually the most important part of an effective worldwide energy strategy. The rise of China, followed by India, as major economic powers means that demand for energy resources is going to increase rapidly in coming years. Should a deep Russian economic recovery get under way, that country will use more of its oil and gas output to support internal growth. It appears that Iraqi oil, if exports can indeed be brought closer to potential, will be needed for a long time to cover the costs of general economic reconstruction in that country.[16] Notions that Iraq would rapidly enter world markets at levels sufficient to create price leverage against the Saudis have proven to be illusory. Although supplies of energy are increasing, it is not in the best interests of the United States to risk entering a period of long-term tightness of supply. Efficiency and conservation will help sustain rapid economic growth while moderating pressures on supplies of energy, and hence on prices. To accomplish this requires leadership by example, which America is not practicing at present.

As important as energy is to the security of the United States, it is not truly at the heart of the challenge it faces. The fight against terrorism is also vital and, for that matter, related to energy because the struggle originates out of, and is organized around the control of, the Middle East. But terrorism is also not at the heart of the challenge to America. In the end, U.S. foreign policy is about the broader hopes of humankind—in which case, the country is surrounded and upheld by people who see their hopes invested in U.S. success; or it is about American privilege and advantage—in which case, America is alone.

At the technical level, America requires greater integration of domestic and international policy. Fiscal policy shapes its position among nations. Educational policy does the same. The country requires integrative vision and better machinery for planning: particularly, for planning in the longer term.

Even with these accomplishments, the United States would still need a sense of purpose that unites it with rather than sets it apart from the rest of the planet. One can dominate by force of arms and still not be the victor. One can preempt to destroy a feared enemy, only to become an object of fear to others. America must display less arrogance, not by hiding it, but by dispensing with it. The country needs to stop glorifying the power and independence of its actions, and instead make it clear that it aims to work with others to build global consciousness in hopes of securing global action.

Nothing could more powerfully signify American support for such values than would a resumption of U.S. leadership for purposeful management of the global environment. Nothing isolates the United States more effectively than its refusal to do so. Ironically, this is the course more likely than any other to bring U.S. national security and energy requirements into balance.

## Notes

1. "President Bush Discusses Freedom in Iraq and Middle East: Remarks by the President at the 20th Anniversary of the National Endowment for Democracy," U.S. Chamber of Commerce, Washington, November 6, 2003, available at http://www.whitehouse.gov/news/releases/2003/11/print/20031106-2.html. Also, "President Dis-

cusses the Future of Iraq," Washington Hilton Hotel, Washington, February 26, 2003, available at http://www.whitehouse.gov/news/releases/2003/02/print/20030226-11.html.

2. It may be that the president simply believes that democratic transformation will occur as an automatic by-product of the invasion of Iraq. History does not reward teleological assumptions of that sort. Shaping the future requires the persistent application of effort, applied in accordance with subtle and flexible planning. What we have seen of administration planning does not encourage confidence about its attention to detail when it comes to a vastly larger effort, affecting the destinies of hundreds of millions of persons.

Moreover, even the best effort on the part of the United States will prove inadequate, unless it is backed up eventually by parallel efforts from other democracies that have significant influence in the Middle East. We would need to make it clear simultaneously that there was universal accord as to the need for a democratic transition, and that governments were prepared not only to use suasion but leverage. Such support, however, is unlikely. It runs contrary to the perceived interests of most of our allies, and even if it did not, there is little likelihood that other governments will take actual risks to follow our lead on democratization, given the climate of distrust and disrespect for U.S. purposes and policies that now exists.

No one would take fundamental issue with the president's espousal of democracy. But there is a thin line between optimistic rhetoric and dangerous incitement, as was the case in 1991, when the administration of the day encouraged the people of Iraq to undertake a rebellion against Saddam Hussein which it then declined to support. It remains to be seen whether the Bush administration's rhetoric about democracy will be converted into a systematic, painstaking diplomatic effort that takes fully into account the hazards of transition, and the attendant risks to the interests of the United States in the internal stability among the nations of the Middle East: interests that inevitably relate to the region's resources.

3. Mark Landler, "Euro Beginning to Flex Its Economic Muscles," *New York Times,* May 18, 2003, 17.

4. Michelle DaCruz, "OPEC Hints at Output Cut in 2004: Cartel Revenue Slips—Falling US$ May Lead to Oil Being Priced in Euros," *Financial Post* (Canada), December 4, 2003; Peter Kemp and Karen Matusic, "Naimi: Soft Dollar Tempers Oil Price Rise; Saudi Arabia's Oil Minister Ali Naimi," *Oil Daily,* December 4, 2003.

5. Christopher Swann, "IMF Concern at US Budget Deficit," *Financial Times* (London), August 7, 2003, 8. Also, *IMF Survey,* August 18, 2003, 233, available at http://www.imf.org/external/pubs/ft/survey/2003/081803.pdf.

6. John Schmid, "Same Bed, Different Dreams; With US Reliant on Chinese Lending, Two Economies Deeply Linked," *Milwaukee Journal Sentinel,* December 29, 2003, 1A.

7. Keith Bradsher, "With an Eye on Its Oil Bill, China Drafts Fuel-Economy Rules," *New York Times,* November 20, 2003, 1; Katharine Mieszkowski, "Green China?" *Salon.com,* http://www.salon.com.

8. Paul Merolli, "Big Oil Beefs Up Protection against Possible Terrorist Strike." *International Oil Daily,* February 13, 2003; Jeff Gosmano, "Energy Industry Pleased with Security Steps Taken since 9/11," *Oil Daily,* September 10, 2003.

9. David Jones, "Homeland Security Department to Plan Shields Against Cyber Assaults on Energy Sites," *Inside Energy,* May 26, 2003, 9.

10. "Emergency Responders: Drastically Underfunded, Dangerously Unprepared,"

Report of an Independent Task Force Sponsored by the Council on Foreign Relations, July 29, 2003, available at http://www3.cfr.org/pdf/Responders_TF.pdf. Also, "Nation's Mayors Call for Better Distribution of Homeland Security Funding to Cities," Associated Press, September 18, 2003, and "White House Issues New Homeland Security Policies," *Intellibridge Homeland Security Monitor,* December 2003.

    11.  John Mintz and Christopher Lee, "Homeland Security Dept. Faces a Funding Gap for Years," *Washington Post,* January 24, 2003, A10; "Border Security, Infrastructure, Communications among Top Homeland Security Concerns for Nation's City Leaders," US Newswire, December 12, 2003.

    12.  "Special Briefing on the Nuclear Posture Review," U.S. Department of Defense Briefing, January 9, 2002, available at http://www.defenselink.mil/news/Jan2002; Michael R. Gordon, "U.S. Nuclear Plan Sees New Weapons and New Targets," *New York Times,* March 10, 2002, 1.

    13.  Cf. Kurt M. Campbell, Robert Einhorn, and Mitchell Reiss, eds., *The Nuclear Tipping Point: Why States Reconsider Their Nuclear Choices* (Washington, D.C.: Brookings Institution Press, 2004).

    14.  Michael Burke, "Going Green: A Global Warning; Cut $CO_2$ or Face Extinction," *The Mirror,* March 29, 2002, 53; Tom Athanasiou and Paul Baer, "Dead Heat: The Science Is In on Global Climate Change, and the Picture Isn't Pretty," *Earth Island Journal,* June 22, 2003, 26; "Climate Change: Emissions Responsible for Warming of North America–Study," *Greenwire,* November 17, 2003.

    15.  "Climate Change 2001: Impacts, Adaptation and Vulnerability," Report of Working Group II, Intergovernmental Panel on Climate Change, available at http://yosemite.epa.gov/oar/globalwarming.nsf/content/ResourceCenterPublicationsReference.html; "Emissions of Greenhouse Gases in the United States 2002," U.S. Department of Energy, October 2003, available at http://tonto.eia.doe.gov/FTPROOT/environment/057302.pdf.

    16.  Edward Alden and Guy Dinmore, "Call for Mortgaging of Future Iraq Oil Revenues," *Financial Times,* September 26, 2003, 14; Jeff Gerth, "The Struggle for Iraq: Reconstruction; Report Offered Bleak Outlook About Iraq Oil," *New York Times,* October 5, 2003, 1.

# 18

# Technology Development and Energy Security

*Melanie A. Kenderdine and Ernest J. Moniz*

Technology is generally viewed as the answer to many energy challenges—supply, security, environmental stewardship. Both the public and private sectors have extensive energy technology research and development efforts, typically with different objectives and time horizons. The private sector often supports technology that is focused on relatively near-term return on investment, while the public sector can take a longer view, supporting technologies to advance public goods that are not easily or appropriately valued in the marketplace. Both sectors do, however, share the objective of actually deploying those technologies to serve societal needs—trying to ensure that they do not just "sit on the shelf," without contributing to commerce or to public benefits such as increased security or cleaner environment.

The deployment of energy technologies is often deeply influenced by public policy, which through its shaping of the marketplace, can help open markets or raise barriers to their formation or expansion. This puts a responsibility on government to have focused and informed strategic goals and policy objectives that address important public goods; policies and an energy research, development, and demonstration (RD&D) portfolio aligned with the goals and objectives; and appropriate management and support.

Security is near or at the top of the list of public goods addressed by government. The oil embargo of 1973 seared into the public consciousness the somewhat singular energy security objective of "decreasing reliance on imported oil." This provided the basic impetus for significant action: Corporate Average Fuel Economy (CAFE) standards were passed into law in 1975 with a commitment to essentially double new car fuel economy in a decade; and the reorganization of the U.S. government, which then dramatically increased and broadened its investments in energy technology RD&D, largely through programs at the Department of Energy (DOE).

The work of these RD&D programs has met with some significant successes. A recent National Academy study, having reviewed energy efficiency and fossil energy programs since the DOE's inception, found that they provided substantial economic, environmental, and national security benefits, developed technology options, and made additions to scientific and engineering knowledge.[1]

Conversely, when the simple metric of oil imports is paired with the motivation to "decrease reliance on foreign oil," these programs and the policies they seek to implement appear to have failed. Oil imports have, in fact, increased dramatically in the past three decades. Also, some very large energy research and development (R&D) projects designed to address energy security or related objectives—the Synfuels Corporation and the Clinch River breeder reactor, for example—were deemed "white elephants" and abandoned only after significant expenditures of tax dollars.

These "failures" have damaged both the public and private perceptions of federal energy research. But their history and design did not adhere to key conditions for success: informed and focused policy objectives and strategic goals, and research models and programs that make those goals feasible. The simplistic framing of the oil security objective and its metric—reduced imports—simply does not square with the global oil marketplace, the geological realities of U.S. oil reservoirs, and an ever-growing appetite for energy. This misalignment—and some of the programs that followed—has served to frustrate policymakers and research performers alike, and divorced some U.S. energy policies and technology investments from the realities of the twenty-first-century global energy marketplace.

Future successes will hinge on informing, updating, and expanding the integration of security objectives into today's complex energy marketplace. With thirty years of public energy R&D experience—both good and bad—and some new and serious security imperatives, the United States must reexamine the federal government's approach to setting strategic energy objectives, revise those objectives where appropriate, and more closely align its energy R&D programs with its energy security objectives. This can guide more coherent regulatory and statutory initiatives, as well as help set a sound agenda to do and manage research. In this chapter, we discuss energy security challenges, key objectives, and some of the important associated technology pathways that can address these objectives with further RD&D and/or technology-enabled policy evolution. We conclude with priorities for action toward meeting twenty-first-century energy security challenges.

## Energy Security Challenges and Objectives

Today's preeminent energy security challenges are broader, more diverse, and significantly more complex than those suggested by the tired rhetoric about foreign oil dependence:

- the uneven distribution of oil (and, of increasing concern, natural gas) supplies and production capacity, nonassured access to those supplies, and volatile energy prices threaten national, regional, and world stability and economies;
- environmental stress increases the potential for regional political instability and tensions;
- the technologies and fissionable material associated with the nuclear power fuel cycle raise the specter of nuclear weapons proliferation; and
- the key—and expanding—infrastructures required to move energy to demand centers are vulnerable to malevolent threats.

These challenges share a common feature: They are all global or regional in scope and impact. Pathways—technology or otherwise—must reflect the essential international nature of these problems and contemplate solutions that acknowledge the growing global interdependencies of energy security.

There is also a new urgency to meeting these energy security challenges, driven by global development and demographics. Emerging economic giants and regional population growth during the next twenty years, particularly in developing Asia and Latin America, will mean greater competition for energy resources. This is already a reality in Eastern Asia where Japan, with the world's second largest economy but virtually no domestic energy resources, is vying for energy resources with China, which is experiencing enormous growth in oil and gas demand. This competition for energy could have security ramifications from far-eastern Russia, to Southeast Asia, to the Middle East.

Increased energy consumption will further exacerbate its effects on the environment. The environmental risks posed by global warming and climate change raise security risks by their capacity to change agricultural or disease patterns that stress particular populations; and, as the world struggles with mitigation costs and strategies, by increasing tensions between adversaries as well as allies, between industrial and developing economies, and between coastal and inland regions.

In addition, the terrorist attacks of September 11, 2001, crystallized public fear of the ultimate energy security nightmare: less-than-secure nuclear materials, by-products of nuclear weapons programs or of the nuclear power fuel cycle, falling into the hands of terrorist organizations. Such organizations can also carry out malevolent attacks on critical energy infrastructures, as energy resources, remote from demand centers, are moved over greater and greater distances. Complex energy delivery networks can provide tempting targets for those bent on societal disruption.

Each of these challenges can be addressed through the large-scale deployment of new energy technologies. However, the long lead times required for energy capital stock turnover and investments underscore the need for informed, focused, and timely action.

Each of the energy-related security challenges is listed in figure 18.1, together with key policy objectives and some associated technology pathways for advancing toward these objectives. The next sections address each of these challenges and objectives, together with current issues concerning

Figure 18.1.  Energy-Related Security Challenges, Key Related Policy Objectives, and Representative Associated Technology Pathways (*from left to right*)

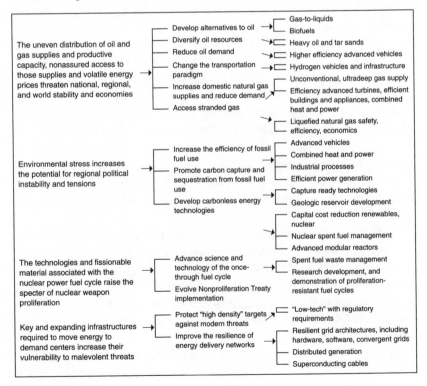

technology status, development, and/or deployment. The discussions are not intended to provide in-depth discussion of any of the specific technology examples, but rather an overview and map between potentially important technology pathways and the energy security challenges. Various economic, political, and policy limitations on the application of technology to meeting the energy security challenges will be discussed for context. These discussions provide the framework for a list of possible priorities for action.

As is evident from figure 18.1, many of the technology pathways serve multiple objectives: Improved transportation fuel economy and alternative fuels address both oil dependence and environment; improved nuclear technology and oversight institutions can address nonproliferation concerns and thus enable broader acceptance of this "carbon-free" source of electricity; and resolving issues of electricity grid architecture can both provide greater resilience against disruption and enable highly efficient distributed generation. These technology pathways also create the possibility of increasing the fungibility of primary fuels for different end uses. The successful development of carbon sequestration, for example, may enable widespread deployment of coal gasification for both electricity and transportation fuel supply. Multiple benefits and applications can be crucial for stimulating policy initiatives and timely technology deployment.

## Oil and Gas: Uneven Distribution of Supply and Demand

Oil is the most pervasive energy-related security issue, largely because of four factors: the distribution of conventional oil reserves, 56 percent of which are in the Middle East (66 percent in nations belonging to the Organization of Petroleum Exporting Countries, or OPEC);[2] the concentration of the world's excess production capacity exclusively in OPEC nations; growth in oil demand, particularly in areas with few domestic resources; and the near total dependence of the world's transportation systems on oil-based fuels.

The security implications of these factors are already apparent and will intensify during the next two decades as world oil demand increases and regional economies develop. By 2025, oil consumption is forecast to exceed 119 million barrels per day (mmbpd), a 54 percent increase over 77 mmbpd in 2001.[3] Also, growth in oil consumption will not be evenly distributed. Between 2005 and 2025, North America and developing Asia alone will represent approximately 65 percent of incremental demand, with increases of 11 and 14 mmbpd, respectively.[4]

In addition, current excess production capacity (the capacity to produce additional oil or leave production idle depending on market conditions) typically has been only about 3 mmbpd, with 80 percent of that in Saudi Arabia. Through OPEC, Saudi Arabia and the Persian Gulf nations control essentially all the world's excess production capacity, giving them tremendous ability to manipulate the near-term price of oil and to greatly influence the longer-term geopolitical equation.

U.S. demand for oil is expected to increase by 8.7 million barrels per day (42 percent) between 2005 and 2025, totaling almost a quarter of the world's consumption.[5] The United States has less than 1 percent of the world's oil reserves, and its production has been declining since the late 1970s. There is simply no way for the United States to produce its way out of oil dependence. It will not be able to isolate its economy from global oil prices or price volatility by supply side action.

In the next quarter-century or so, the world will have 1.3 billion automobiles, roughly double the 700 million vehicles now on the road, with about 20 percent of that increase in China alone.[6] More broadly, per capita motorization is expected to double in the developing world by 2020. Three realities must be considered in the context of this enormous growth in demand: the great convenience and opportunities offered to individuals, families, and commerce by automobiles and light trucks; the cost-effectiveness of internal combustion engines and of petroleum-based fuels; and the existing large and costly infrastructure that safely and conveniently produces, refines, and distributes these fuels.

Petroleum-based fuels are close to ideal for transportation applications. They have the highest volume energy density of known fuels and are distributed as liquids at standard temperature and pressure. Putting aside taxes, which are higher than the cost of the product in some countries, gasoline and diesel fuels are quite inexpensive if measured on the basis of dollars per unit of energy. This inherent attractiveness makes proposals for new fuels and the infrastructures to use them difficult to advance in the political and business communities.

## Technology Options for Oil Security

There are four general technology pathways that could, at a minimum, put the United States on a trajectory to reduce the stranglehold oil holds over its overall strategic, economic, and energy security objectives:

- Alternative fuels could alter OPEC's calculus.
- Unconventional oil resources could alter the geopolitics of oil.
- Transportation efficiency could reduce oil demand.
- There could be a change in the transportation paradigm.

These pathways are not necessarily mutually exclusive; they could—and should—be pursued concurrently, with a clear understanding of the associated time scales, an appreciation for investment requirements, the potential for stranding private assets, and the willingness to commit the necessary financial and intellectual resources and political capital for their advancement.

## Alternative Fuels Could Alter OPEC's Calculus

It is very difficult to alter the economics of oil, given the location of the world's oil reserves, the very different lifting costs in different locations, and the vast infrastructure that produces and moves it to demand centers. It is possible, however, to devise ways to somewhat restrain OPEC's cartel behavior by investing in a suite of alternatives that could, if oil prices rise too high, threaten OPEC's market share, specifically through development of unconventional oil and alternative fuels derived from feedstocks other than oil.

### Gas to Liquids

Fischer Tropsch diesel fuel is derived from the conversion of natural gas (or, potentially, other feedstocks such as coal or biomass) to syngas to diesel fuels and other high-value products. Transforming natural gas to liquids—GTL—is attractive for many reasons. Currently, as much as 60 percent of the world's proved reserves of natural gas are believed to be stranded due to transportation limitations. GTL could serve to help monetize tremendous reserves of stranded gas, greatly diversifying and increasing U.S. and global sources of supply.

GTL could also fill a market space not traditionally held by natural gas, providing a cleaner alternative to current oil-based diesel products. The market for low sulfur and low-aromatic transportation fuels (diesel and gasoline) and engines will grow dramatically in the 2008–10 time frame, driven by stricter environmental requirements in Japan, the United States, and Europe, the three global leaders of engine and vehicle manufacturing. During the next twelve years, global demand for middle distillates is expected to increase from about 27 to 35 mmbpd, an amount equal to more than 10 percent of current oil consumption.[7]

However, GTL remains expensive. GTL economics favor large facilities (capable of consuming at least 2 tcf of gas over a twenty-five-year period) to take advantage of economies of scale. The economics of GTL production are also improved by the monetization of relatively small stranded gas fields and associated flared gas, which are of insufficient size to support the more mature and capital-intensive liquefied natural gas (LNG) market. The capital costs of GTL have been reduced by 50 percent in the past decade.[8] Still, the syngas step in the process accounts for about 60 percent of the production costs. Research to address this cost component in the GTL production chain includes direct conversion, catalysis improvements for indirect conversion, and ceramic membrane technology. Additional research to reduce general capital costs is also needed. With a capital cost of about $20,000 per barrel per day, GTL is attractive with sustained oil prices in the range of $25 per barrel, assuming that stranded gas remains very inexpensive. The mid- to long-term potential for GTL to help affordably meet low-sulfur middle distillate and general fuel demand—particularly with a breakthrough in chemical conversion—could alter the world energy equation, enabling the movement of large reserves of stranded gas to growing markets, helping to satisfy new environmental requirements, and potentially easing political tensions.

## Biofuels

Biofuels have been used in automobiles since early in the twentieth century —the Model T Ford was capable of operating on gasoline or pure alcohols. Today, the United States produces 50 million barrels of ethanol a year (about 1.6 percent of gasoline consumption), which is used primarily as a blend with gasoline. Realistically, any substantial growth in biofuel consumption during the next ten to twenty years will be from increased ethanol production.

Currently, the principal U.S. feedstock for ethanol production is corn, which is a food product rich in carbohydrates that can be easily converted to fermentable sugar, in particular, glucose. This is not economic, but a large ethanol subsidy has led to significant market growth. The cost of corn-derived ethanol, driven by corn prices (which can be quite volatile), is unlikely to become competitive with gasoline unless oil prices are much higher, above $50 per barrel.

Cellulosic feedstocks are, however, much less expensive than corn and have the potential for a much larger biofuel industry. There are estimates of a 100 exajoules a year global potential for bioenergy from biomass residues, which equates to about a quarter of today's total world energy consumption.[9] Cellulosic ethanol is, however, much more difficult to break down into fermentable sugars. Enzymatic hydrolysis is probably the most promising conversion process, with significant potential for process cost reductions. Genetic engineering could lead to a process within a decade or so that would produce ethanol at costs that are competitive with gasoline (assuming today's oil prices). Thermal processes, such as biomass gasification, may also lead to practical liquid fuels. A reduction in the cost of producing cellulosic ethanol could have a substantial impact on oil use within the next two decades.

## Unconventional Oil Resources Could Alter the Geopolitics of Oil

Over the medium to long terms, both GTL and biofuels could theoretically displace oil-based fuels. Technologies to develop heavy oil and tar sands, conversely, have the potential to alter the geopolitics of oil without necessarily reducing oil consumption.

The technically recoverable heavy oil in Venezuela and tar sands (bitumen) mostly in Canada and Russia are roughly equal to the remaining conventional (light) oil reserves: 1.1 trillion barrels of heavy oil or bitumen, compared with 1 trillion barrels of conventional oil.[10] About 600 billion barrels of that oil is in the Western Hemisphere (Saudi Arabia has about 260 billion barrels of conventional oil reserves).

Producing, transporting, and refining heavy oil requires technologies to reduce viscosity, additives to enable transport, and the removal of significant contaminants in the refining process. There are significant research challenges associated with producing heavy oil and bitumen, including formation evaluation; more hydraulic fracturing; horizontal and multibranched well bores; advanced drilling technologies; new completion methods; removal of sulfur oxides and nitrous oxides and heavy metals; new downhole sensors; fluid injection management; and specialized pumps.[11] In addition, there is a lack of upgrading capacity in North America to refine heavy oil.

Research investments to improve the economics of these resources could help counter the influence of the Persian Gulf and more closely align the geopolitical interests of countries in the Western Hemisphere. The heavy oil in Venezuela holds great midterm potential for development; Venezuela is, however, a member of OPEC. Canada is investing heavily in developing its tar sand resources and is diverting natural gas supplies to enable their production, but tar sand production still faces economic challenges. Nevertheless, the United States should make significant efforts to advance the development of these resources, through research and investments that will enable their affordable production.

Each of these options is expensive and the strategic objective—diminishing OPEC's market power—would be enhanced if technology investments were made in conjunction with policies to increase global strategic oil reserves and heavy oil refining capacity. Mitigating the environmental impacts of heavy oil production is also a necessity.

## Transportation Efficiency Reduces Oil Demand

Since the oil shocks of the 1970s, policymakers have recognized that the United States can reduce its oil dependence by improving vehicle fuel efficiency. CAFE standards for automobile and light truck fuel efficiency were introduced in the United States in 1975. These standards, or alternative approaches to mandating better fuel economy, have always faced stiff political opposition from the automobile industry, labor, and others. Consequently, the impact of CAFE standards has lost ground relative to increased miles traveled and consumer preference for light trucks (which come under a lower standard than do automobiles).

Politically attractive approaches such as hybrid car tax incentives have been introduced but, at this early stage of hybrid introduction, have not curbed the U.S. appetite for oil. In fact, the average fuel efficiency of the new light-duty vehicle fleet has actually decreased in the United States during the past few years as sport utility vehicles and light trucks have captured a larger share of the passenger vehicle market—although there are signs that prices in excess of $2 a gallon may be altering that trend.

Technologies to dramatically reduce oil consumption without the need for new infrastructure are available and will likely improve still more through evolutionary advances. Commercially available automobiles already achieve more than 50 miles per gallon (mpg). A partnership between the federal government and U.S. automakers during the 1990s, the Partnership for a New Generation of Vehicles (PNGV), met its milestone of a prototype 80 mpg family size car in 2000.[12] The 2004 PNGV goal of turning this prototype into production models was abandoned, along with the entire program, when the new George W. Bush administration took office and changed priorities. This demonstrates the precariousness of large goal-oriented time-driven federal programs subject to political vagaries and annual appropriations.

Nevertheless, it is expected that commercially viable midsize hybrid automobiles that achieve 70 to 80 mpg will be available by 2020.[13] Though some technical challenges remain, such as exhaust cleanup for diesel hybrids, the principal need is for large-scale systems engineering and significant capital commitments for retooling by the major U.S. automakers. Accomplishing widespread deployment of advanced automobile technologies in a timely fashion may require, however, both consumer and producer incentives, such as investment tax credits for the retooling of manufacturing capability, and/or higher fuel economy standards.

A life-cycle analysis of the various credible 2020 technologies provides an interesting perspective on future technology pathways. Figure 18.2 reproduces the relative consumption of life-cycle energy for various technologies from Weiss and others.[14] It is noteworthy that the hybrid technologies, which employ existing infrastructure for petroleum-based fuels are comparable to hydrogen-fuel-cell vehicles; this conclusion also holds for green-

Figure 18.2. Life-Cycle Energy Use for a Variety of Projected 2020 Automotive Technologies, Including Internal Combustion Engines (ICE), Hybrids, and Fuel-Cell (FC) Vehicles

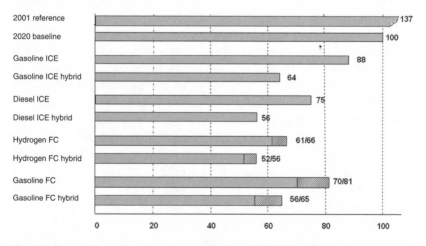

*Note:* Total energy from all sources consumed during vehicle lifetime; shown as percentage of baseline vehicle energy consumption; total energy includes vehicle operation and production of both vehicle and fuel. The 2020 baseline vehicle represents evolutionary development of today's 2001 reference vehicle.

*Source:* M. A. Weiss, J. B. Heywood, A. Schafer, and V. K. Natarajan, *Comparative Assessment of Fuel Cell Cars* (Cambridge, Mass.: Massachusetts Institute of Technology, 2003).

house gas emissions, assuming the hydrogen is produced from natural gas steam reforming and the carbon dioxide is not captured and sequestered. The hydrogen-fueled car is not necessarily the obvious long-term "winner," even discounting the need for a new infrastructure. The fuel-cell vehicle will be quieter and have lower conventional pollutant tailpipe emissions, but it will probably be considerably more expensive. Further, the hybrid technology is largely at hand; this provides a technological foundation, if the political will can be marshaled, for a government incentive or regulatory program that aims to reduce oil use significantly—or at least to temper any increases—during the next few decades, consistent with security policies.

## Changing the Transportation Paradigm

For the long term, one can certainly entertain more radical transformation of the transportation paradigm. The "holy grail" of such transformations is the hydrogen-fuel-cell vehicle, although the eventual dominance of the so-called hydrogen-based economy is far from a sure thing.

Hydrogen is attractive because it can be extracted by chemical or electrochemical means from numerous common hydrogen-bearing substances—fossil fuels such as natural gas and coal, and renewable sources such as biomass and water—and its end use is free of pollution and greenhouse gases. Also, using renewable energy as a source of hydrogen could mean long-term sustainability for the entire production process.

Conversely, the challenges are formidable with respect to both technology and economics. The Bush administration, in announcing its "Freedom Car" R&D program as a centerpiece of its energy security strategy, acknowledged that it would be decades before widespread commercial deployment of hydrogen-powered vehicles. The central challenges that must be met for this to occur include the development of the fuel-cell vehicle, the economic production of hydrogen at a meaningful scale, and the design and development of the new "fuels" infrastructure.

Fuel-cell development has probably benefited most from R&D to date, but even here there is much to be done, particularly as the evolutionary improvement of internal combustion engines continues to provide a "moving target" with regard to cost and performance; a few tens of dollars per kilowatt is one to two orders of magnitude below current fuel-cell economics.[15]

Onboard storage of hydrogen is another major technical challenge. Even liquid hydrogen—an impractical approach—has a volume energy density about one quarter that of gasoline or diesel fuel. Gaseous hydrogen needs to be compressed to very high pressure to be practical, over 5,000 pounds per square inch. Even putting the engineering issues of storage aside, a "refill" is likely to present a much greater system challenge than is the case for petroleum-based fuels. Other approaches are being explored, such as storage in nano-engineered structures or onboard reforming of a fossil fuel. The latter can minimize the need for new fuels infrastructure, but it significantly complicates the fuel-cell challenge.

The design of the hydrogen supply infrastructure is also far from clear. A recent study by Simbeck and Chang examined the costs of centralized and distributed hydrogen production for supplying vehicles.[16] Figure 18.3 shows a summary, indicating the relative economic advantage of production from natural gas in centralized facilities and distribution to vehicle filling stations by cryogenic truck transport. Further, the costs of all options are substantially higher than those for gasoline on an energy equivalent basis.

Finally, the scale of the hydrogen supply that will be required to displace a substantial part of oil use is daunting. DOE's Energy Information Administration (EIA) projects an increase in world oil consumption, assuming business as usual, of about 40 mmbpd by 2025 (about a 50 percent increase), driven mostly by transportation demand. This is the equivalent of about 80 exajoules a year. On an energy equivalent basis (i.e., not accounting for net efficiency in producing or using the hydrogen), this corresponds to about 600 billion kilograms of hydrogen a year (one kilogram has approximately the energy content of a gallon of gasoline). Supplying this from natural gas would require about 75 tcf a year, approximately equal to today's total world demand. The implications for natural gas prices would presumably be very significant. Supplying hydrogen by conventional electrolysis of water, at 50 kilowatt-hours per kilogram (kWh/kg),[17] would require about 30 trillion kWh of electricity, more than double today's total world supply of electricity. About 3.5 terawatts (TW, or billion kilowatts) in electric capacity would be needed to produce this quantity of hydrogen, all of it operating at full capacity factor. This would still displace only about a third of total oil use projected for 2025. Even with relative efficiency benefits, large-scale hydrogen supply is a major challenge.

Although these requirements are impressive, they do not preclude a "hydrogen-based economy." Indeed, a strong R&D program is both essential and warranted to address the key technological and economic issues. However, it is the other pathways discussed above to increase energy security— alternative fuels, heavy oil, efficiency in oil use—that provide the basis for effective policy during the next two to three decades, at least.

Figure 18.3.  Hydrogen Cost for Production (from water, biomass, coal, natural gas) and Distribution (from central plant production with distribution by pipeline, gas trailer, or liquid tanker or from forecourt production)

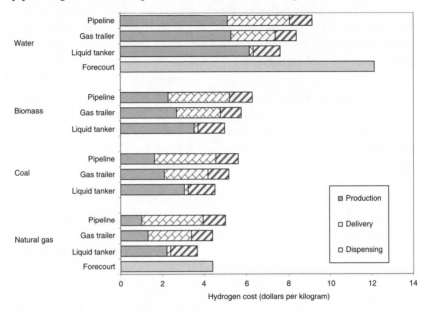

*Note:* A kilogram of hydrogen is roughly energy equivalent to a gallon of gasoline.
*Source:* D. R. Simbeck and E. Chang, *Hydrogen Supply: Cost Estimate for Hydrogen Pathways: Scoping Analysis* (Golden, Colo.: National Renewable Energy Laboratory, 2003).

## Changes in Natural Gas Markets: The Technology Dimension

Global gas consumption is the fastest growing component of world fossil energy demand, expected to increase by 95 percent between 2001 and 2025.[18] Strong drivers are price (at least until recently), environmental performance, and relatively low capital requirements for electricity production. This is based on arguably the most important energy technology development of the past twenty years: natural gas combined-cycle turbines.

In chapter 22 of this book, Foss and Juckett describe both the opportunities and the challenges of the developing natural gas marketplace. Some salient points for our discussion are:

• Worldwide, natural gas is abundant. Proved reserves could get the world through the next 50 years and unproved reserves could take us through the next 200. More than 70 percent of the world's gas reserves are found in just two regions, the former Soviet Union (36 percent), and the Middle East (36 percent).[19]

- Natural gas is transportation constrained and much more expensive to transport than oil on an energy equivalency basis (at least three times). As such, much of the world's gas is "stranded," without monetary value.
- Natural gas demand is growing as unevenly as it is dramatically, with the most rapid increases in those regions of the world with the fewest indigenous resources.
- The United States will represent about 20 percent of the world's total gas consumption in 2020, but its reserves are under various production moratoriums or are increasingly "unconventional" and are therefore constrained by technology limitations.

Viewed against this background, natural gas has become a critical component of U.S. economic and energy security. U.S. natural gas security policy—and the technologies that support it—should be guided by these objectives:

- fostering competitive global and regional gas markets that are guided by free market principles;
- developing U.S. gas resources sufficient to ensure affordable domestic gas supplies;
- maximizing the value of natural gas resources through efficient end use; and
- reducing potential geopolitical tensions arising from competition for gas supplies by promoting the global development of gas resources and infrastructure.

## Technologies to Increase Domestic Gas Supplies

The United States is today at a technology crossroads in natural gas supply. To meet its natural gas needs, it will have to continue to push the R&D envelope and support a suite of technologies in several areas.

One such area is ultra-deepwater production and unconventional gas. The U.S. National Petroleum Council's (NPC) 1999 report, *Natural Gas: Meeting the Challenges of the Nation's Growing Natural Gas Demand,* concluded that U.S. reserves of natural gas were sufficient to meet demand during the next two decades.[20] It also noted that major increases in U.S. gas supply—as much as 50 percent of current consumption—would be, in part, attributable to successful and accelerated R&D investments in technologically difficult production areas such as ultra-deepwater and unconventional formations.

After the modeling of the ultra-deepwater Central and Western Gulf of Mexico indicated significant reserves of natural gas, DOE developed an ultra-deepwater technology road map in 2000.[21] This exercise concluded that costs of production in the region would have to be lowered by 30 to 50 percent for commercial viability and that cost reductions of this magnitude would most likely involve the development of a new architecture that moved production platforms from the ocean surface to the ocean floor. This road map envisioned a substantial R&D effort in five focus areas: high intensity design; accelerated reservoir exploration; rigs and reach; energy to market; and environmental management.

The NPC also recommended further R&D investments in developing unconventional onshore gas resources. The research collaboration to develop U.S. coal-bed methane resources, led by the Gas Research Institute,[22] enabled substantial increases in gas supply in the recent past and suggests a path forward for meeting U.S. midterm gas supply. A relatively small investment of about $70 million, matched by industry and managed as an industry-led R&D collaboration, with synergistic tax incentives from government, took the United States from zero production of coal-bed methane in 1985 to more than 8 percent of its current domestic production. Similar results were seen in other unconventional gas resources, including shales and tight gas sands. The NPC estimates that expanded R&D investments in other unconventional gas sources—tight gas sands, gas shales, and advanced coal-bed methane production—would likely result in an additional 4 tcf per year of natural gas production by 2015, more than 20 percent of current domestic production.

## End-Use Efficiency Can Substantially Reduce Gas Demand

Using natural gas more efficiently will enhance both economic performance and energy security. The American Council for an Energy Efficient Economy (ACEEE) estimates that every dollar invested in gas efficiency technologies and best practices will mean as much as $100 saved in natural gas expenditures.[23]

Efficiency in gas-fired power generation can be achieved through advances in baseload generation, as well as distributed technologies that would address the energy inefficiencies inherent in long-distance electricity transport. DOE's Advanced Turbine System program has already resulted in the development and testing of utility-scale advanced turbine systems that are 60 percent efficient, provide power at 10 percent lower cost, and produce very low emissions.[24]

The increased use of natural gas for power generation is also causing a fundamental shift in patterns of gas usage, with a dramatic increase in gas consumption during the summer months. This indicates the need for other types of end-use—as opposed to power-generation—efficiency technologies, ranging from more efficient air conditioners, to smart buildings, to smart metering.

Industrial technologies are critical to arresting the possible loss of manufacturing jobs to overseas locations where natural gas is significantly cheaper. ACEEE modeling and analysis indicates a five-year savings (2004–8) in natural gas ranging from 4.3 to 5.2 percent, depending on the regional industrial mix if the industrial sector deployed efficiency technologies including more efficient motors, heating, boilers, and lighting.[25]

Residential and commercial efficiency technologies could save more than 2 tcf of natural gas by 2008,[26] assuming wide-scale penetration of the following technologies: improved windows; duct sealing and infiltration reductions; more efficient space- and water-heating units; more efficient commercial boilers; integration of efficiency technologies into new commercial and residential construction; more efficient commercial cooking; and increased appliance efficiencies.

## Moving Resources to Demand Centers: Liquefied Natural Gas

LNG is one of the most rapidly growing sources of gas supply. Exports and imports of LNG have grown globally nearly 8 percent a year since 1980,[27] and they now account for 26 percent of all natural gas traded internationally.[28] LNG is a relatively mature technology, and many of the near-term issues associated with LNG are more oriented toward economics and policy than research: the development of a viable global and U.S. market from an investment and finance perspective, contract structure, supply diversification, and so on.

LNG costs have been cut in half in the past two decades, attributed in part to technology improvements in value engineering. Current research needs include air dispersion to address some of the security, safety, and not-in-my-backyard concerns of the U.S. public; LNG interchangeability to ensure that imported gas from different locations is compatible with the wide range of end uses in the United States; increased tanker efficiency to reduce transportation costs; improved economics for offshore terminals; subsea cryogenic pipelines for offloading product to onshore gasification and storage facilities; and micro-LNG facilities to improve LNG economics for smaller stranded gas fields.

More pressing issues for LNG are associated with demands for infrastructure expansion, along with a market structure to support it. Significant capital is needed to build new trains and other components of the supply chain, at a time when there is enormous competition for capital for a variety of energy projects. U.S. policymakers need to establish conditions that enable investment, ensure the continued benefits of deregulated gas markets, promote competition, and protect against monopoly behaviors.

Also, more legal and regulatory guidance is needed to adapt the historical LNG market structure, which has been governed by long-term contracts, to the deregulated natural gas market structure in the United States. Historically, long-term contracts have been essential for financing the capital-intensive LNG infrastructure; this contract structure is not, however, conducive to the formation of an LNG spot market that could provide risk management tools for those who want to invest in the deregulated gas markets of the United States and Europe. Further, U.S. policymakers need to clearly understand the dynamics of an Atlantic Basin LNG market and the potential for LNG arbitrage with Europe, especially concurrent with the same conditions in fuel oil markets.

## Climate Change and International Security Threats

As Kevin Baumert makes clear in chapter 20 of this book, climate change presents an environmental challenge of truly global dimensions, one that can have a profound impact on energy security. Its precise implications are the subject of ongoing research. Nevertheless, three factors combine to recommend immediate action. First, the scale of potential effects—shifts of water resources, agricultural losses, or disease vector modification, for example—is large and could cause regional instability. Second, dramatic increases in global energy demand by midcentury could mean corresponding increases in greenhouse gas emissions. Finally, the time scales for capital stock turnover in the energy sector are very long, adding to the scale of the challenge with each passing year.

The prevailing scientific opinion is that atmospheric carbon dioxide should be restricted to about double preindustrial levels (preferably less) to avoid highly disruptive impacts.[29] Carbon dioxide concentrations in the atmosphere are already about a third above preindustrial levels, with a total atmospheric "load" of about 750 billion metric tons of carbon (about 2,750 billion metric tons of carbon dioxide). This equates to a "budget" of an additional 200 to 400 billion metric tons of carbon.

Anthropogenic sources release about 6.5 billion metric tons of carbon equivalent per year and, under a "business-as-usual" scenario, the doubling of the rate of emissions by midcentury is a common expectation. At this rate (assuming about half of the emitted carbon is absorbed by oceans and plants), the "budget" for carbon emissions will be used up in the second half of this century. At that point, we cannot rule out major disruptions and instability, unless action is taken to alter the emissions trajectory.

The difficulty inherent in addressing this challenge is rooted in global primary energy use patterns; about 85 percent is fossil fuel combustion, the primary source of anthropogenic emissions. The doubling of energy demand while keeping carbon emissions at or below today's levels will require an increase in non-carbon-emitting energy sources of an order of magnitude.[30] Today, the bulk of nonfossil energy is supplied by hydroelectric and nuclear power. There are, however, substantial challenges to the large-scale expansion of these energy sources. Also, the nonhydropower renewables—biomass, wind, geothermal, solar—are a very small part of today's primary energy use and face major hurdles (competition for land, intermittency, high cost) for expanded use on the scale needed to meaningfully address climate change.

In addition, the developing world will represent a significant portion of energy demand growth, where consumption is expected to exceed that of the industrial world in about two decades and to climb even more rapidly thereafter. Global warming is affected by total emissions, not by their geographic source; there is simply no credible long-term solution without the participation of developing nations. Until there is an international agreement to limit emissions, there will always be a "free-rider" problem and, at best, mixed results. Also, the impact of any kind of carbon "tax" on the fragile economies of developing nations could impede their economic and social progress, creating security challenges of a different nature.

## Technology Options to Mitigate Climate Change

These difficulties have served to severely limit the international response to the climate change challenge. Technology could help reduce some of the international tensions posed by these challenges, and also reduce the overall threat of global warming to human health and political stability. A more energetic response would involve all of the following technology pathways:

- greatly increased efficiency in the use of fossil fuels, so that total use is reduced substantially for the same amount of activity;
- rapid expansion of non-carbon-emitting technologies; and
- carbon dioxide capture and sequestration from fossil fuel use.

The first two technology pathways satisfy multiple objectives—for example, mitigating a range of environmental effects, enhancing energy security, reducing energy intensity, and increasing energy supplies—and are obvious choices for policymakers seeking to maximize options and resources. Carbon sequestration, however, is motivated uniquely by global climate change concerns, because it is always less expensive to vent carbon dioxide directly to the atmosphere.

## Slowing the Rate of Growth in Emissions in the Midterm

Near-commercial efficiency technologies in the transportation, industrial, residential and commercial sectors are one of the few meaningful alternatives for substantially reducing greenhouse gas emissions in the medium term—before the introduction of an entirely new fuels infrastructure. Policy tools for doing so include market-based incentives to push available technologies into the market, funding the last stages of R&D demonstrations, supportive regulatory regimes, education on best practices, tax incentives, and aggressive funding of and support for these options in the international arena.

Increasing the use of natural gas in lieu of coal or oil would also provide substantial midterm benefits for reducing greenhouse gas emissions. As has been noted, however, gas consumption sufficient to have an impact on greenhouse gas emission targets must be accompanied by an aggressive program to develop stranded and unconventional gas reserves.

## Aggressive Promotion of Non-Carbon-Emitting Energy Sources

Over time, even with significantly greater energy efficiency, climate change imperatives will be met only through a much broader deployment of non-carbon-emitting energy sources, namely, renewables and nuclear power. Nuclear power now generates about one sixth of the world's electricity, but its growth as an energy source has been stalled for decades. The accidents at Three Mile Island and Chernobyl and unresolved questions about nuclear waste have left much of the public with serious doubts about nuclear power. As a result, no new nuclear plants have been ordered in the United States for a quarter-century.

Climate change has, however, reopened the discussion of nuclear power. A recent interdisciplinary study at the Massachusetts Institute of Technology (MIT), *The Future of Nuclear Power,* identifies the "first mover issue" as key to the viability of nuclear power as an option for greenhouse gas mitigation.[31] There are significant risks and costs for the early builder—the "first mover"—of a new generation of evolutionary light-water reactors that incorporate passive safety systems. Past experience with nuclear plant capital costs has generally not been good ($2,000 per kilowatt of electricity or higher), although new designs and construction techniques may lead to a significant reduction (perhaps 25 percent or so). Until this is demonstrated, and streamlined licensing procedures are utilized successfully, the risk premium for financing new nuclear plants in a deregulated environment will be high.

To encourage first movers, the MIT study group recommended a production tax credit similar in structure to the current credit for wind power.[32] This credit offers a technology-neutral way to incentivize the deployment of existing state-of-the-art technology, leaving primary financial risk with the private sector, and providing a timely, market-based means for determining the viability of a new generation of nuclear power plants. But this approach will not address other challenges to nuclear power such as waste management and proliferation.

Nonhydropower renewables, including wind and photovoltaics (PV), are thought by many to be the ultimate solution to environmentally responsible energy supply. Wind power has made considerable strides in several countries in recent years (including the United States) through technology development coupled with financial incentives. About 15 gigawatts of capacity has been deployed globally, about 40 percent of which is in Germany and nearly one-third in the United States. Capital costs are now below $1,000 per kilowatt and in the range of 4 to 5 cents per kilowatt-hour at good wind sites, without a subsidy.

Windmills come under severe structural stress, as wind speed fluctuates dramatically. Key areas for further development are advanced blade materials, less expensive power electronics, and designs for higher efficiency at lower wind speeds.

Photovoltaics offer a contrast to wind in that both the potential contribution to energy supply and its costs are much greater. Technically feasible energy from solar technology is two orders of magnitude greater than for all other renewables—perhaps as high as 600 TW of capacity.[33] However, a representative capital cost for solar modules today is in the range of $3,000 to $5,000 per peak kilowatt, with another $1,000 to $2,000 needed for other components, such as invertors.

Capacity factors in the United States are in the 20 to 25 percent range, depending on the region. Efficiencies of most commercial units are in the 10 to 15 percent range. The net effect is a representative levelized electricity cost of 35 cents per kilowatt-hour in countries like Japan. Consequently, there are only two to three gigawatts of peak capacity worldwide.

In the United States, PV account for about 1 billion kilowatt-hours per year, about 0.02 percent of the total. Nevertheless, PV deployment is growing at a rapid pace, helped by large government subsidies in countries such as Japan and Germany and by internationally subsidized installations that serve rural needs in developing countries. Japan (where consumer electricity prices are very high) has nearly half a gigawatt of installed peak capacity, growing at 30 percent a year. The target of $1,000 per peak kilowatt, or less, for PV modules may be achievable in ten to twenty years. Accelerated research is needed on higher conversion efficiency, lower-cost materials, along with ongoing incentives for high-value applications.

Both wind and solar power have the immense challenge of intermittency. They suffer extreme day/night, seasonal, locational, and weather-related variability. This problem will be a fundamental limitation to the deployment of these technologies, perhaps 10 to 15 percent of grid-connected capacity, unless inexpensive energy "storage" options are developed. Intermittency causes several problems. It affects the economics of the transmission infrastructure for remote energy "farms" and seriously complicates grid management, unless considerable redundant dispatchable fossil fuel plants are also available. Storage is a critical-path technology for a robust renewables future and should be elevated as a research priority. It can take many forms—mechanical (flywheels, pumped water, compressed air), electrical (advanced batteries), and chemical (transportation fuels, hydrogen)—but none have yet met the test of favorable system economics for widespread application.

## Carbon Capture and Sequestration

The third technology pathway is carbon capture followed by sequestration, with capture occurring either postcombustion for stationary sources or by "decarbonizing" fuel before use. The technical and economic viability of this approach is especially important for the future of coal. Coal currently supplies about a quarter of the world's primary energy (almost a hundred exajoules) and is the most carbon intensive of the fossil fuels. In the near term, higher efficiency in coal combustion, achieved with supercritical boilers, for example, offers the greatest opportunity to both burn coal and mitigate its environmental impacts.

The expanded use of coal in a world constrained by greenhouse gases, however, calls for "new" technology. The most promising direction is the gasification of coal into syngas (hydrogen and carbon monoxide, which is then shifted to carbon dioxide). Coal gasification is attractive because it satisfies multiple objectives:

- cleaner power generation, which, by utilizing integrated-gasification combined-cycle (IGCC) technology, removes traditional pollutants and captures carbon at considerable cost reductions compared with traditional pulverized coal plants;
- the potential to alter the geopolitics of oil by producing a substitute for petroleum based fuels;
- a method for hydrogen production to serve a new transportation paradigm; and
- a means by which many of the world's energy-consuming giants—the United States, China, and India—can utilize abundant indigenous coal reserves, thereby diminishing tensions arising from competition for other energy resources.

There are already nearly 50 gigawatts (thermal) of installed commercial gasification worldwide, mostly for chemicals and liquid fuels, using various low-value feedstocks. Gasification, however, confronts significant challenges. For power production, IGCC plant capital cost estimates range from

$1,100 to $2,000 per kilowatt of electricity. The plant's complexity (fuel handling, gasifier, oxygen plant, power plant, carbon sequestration) leads inevitably to higher operating and maintenance costs and to uncertainty about reliability of operations.

In addition, financial markets will place a high-risk premium on development until large scale plants are demonstrated as economically competitive. Also, while IGCC encourages multiple technology participants, investors will demand a single, responsible creditworthy entity.[34]

Finally, competitiveness of gasification for any product mix rests in part on the greatly reduced carbon capture costs. This comparative advantage will only be relevant if long-term, large-scale carbon sequestration in geologic reservoirs is shown to be scientifically sound, achievable, and deployable. This has not yet been shown. A significant amount of experience has been accumulated on carbon dioxide reinjection to oil wells for enhanced oil recovery, and a variety of pilot programs have been launched internationally.[35] However, a long-term program of sequestration of carbon at the level of metric gigatons per year will require higher capacity, geographically well-distributed reservoirs (e.g., deep saline aquifers). In addition, critical policy issues need to be resolved, such as liability for carbon dioxide leaks from a sequestration site. It will take decades to answer these questions, leaving the sequestration route to greenhouse gas stabilization uncertain.

## Nuclear Proliferation and Nuclear Power

A unique security concern raised in the energy sector is that of possible nuclear weapons proliferation facilitated by the introduction and expansion of nuclear power. The Nuclear Non-Proliferation Treaty (NPT) requires signatories, except for the P-5 weapons states (China, France, Russia, the United Kingdom, and the United States), to forgo nuclear weapons development in exchange for assistance in developing peaceful uses of nuclear technology, especially nuclear power and nuclear medicine. Some states—India, Israel, Pakistan, and now North Korea—remain outside the treaty framework and its benefits and constraints. Despite the fact that some signatories have taken steps toward a nuclear weapons capability that went undetected for some time, the NPT regime is generally viewed as successful in restraining the spread of nuclear weapons over the last decades.

Several developments have combined to raise questions about the robustness of the NPT regime going forward:

- The end of the Cold War changed regional security relationships, leading some states to reevaluate the uses (e.g., the United States) and the value (e.g., North Korea) of nuclear weapons.
- With the dramatic spread of advanced manufacturing and technical capabilities (project management, advanced materials, design tools, machine tools), the NPT regime could actually be viewed as a pathway to nuclear weapons capability since knowledge about dual use technologies can be gained (e.g., Iran may fall into this category).
- The terrorist attacks of September 11, 2001, have refocused attention on the importance of controlling nuclear-weapons-usable material, such as plutonium produced in the nuclear power fuel cycle.

These developments and concerns present an energy security conundrum: How does the global community protect against increased traffic in nuclear materials and technologies (and the proliferation threat this poses in the hands of terrorists or rogue nations), when we may need nuclear power to mitigate global climate change?

Ultimately, the solution to this dilemma requires the control and elimination of weapons-usable fissionable material (highly enriched uranium, HEU; or plutonium), because the knowledge and skills needed to make at least crude (but still potent) devices are rather widespread. For the nuclear power fuel cycle, this focuses attention on two technologies: uranium enrichment technology, the path to HEU; and disposition of irradiated reactor fuel, the path to plutonium.

Centrifuge enrichment is the increasingly dominant technology for commercial nuclear fuel enrichment and has spread to countries that have an interest in nuclear weapons. This calls for strengthening the international coordination of export-control restrictions on specialized materials and components, together with new institutional and diplomatic arrangements to mitigate proliferation potential.

However, a new technology-driven concern has arisen. The strong interest in isotope separation for a variety of medical, industrial, and scientific applications has provided impetus for pursuit of a multiplicity of additional technology pathways for enrichment, such as several laser and chemical separation processes. These technologies are not yet in, and may never reach, the marketplace. Nevertheless, when unconstrained by economic performance, they may prove to be dangerous because of the small material quantities needed for an explosive and because they may be difficult to track. International attention and coordination needs to be devoted to establishing strong detection and control regimes for such technologies.

The disposition of irradiated fuel is a particularly contentious international issue. Out of concern that a "plutonium economy" would aid nuclear proliferation, the United States maintained a policy of "no reprocessing"— the extraction of plutonium from commercial spent fuel to recycle. However, countries such as France and Japan, which are nearly devoid of fossil energy resources, are recycling plutonium with the intent of minimizing uranium needs, using the energy value of the produced plutonium, and simplifying long term geological isolation of high-level nuclear waste (that is for the millennium time scale and beyond). This approach, however, creates a near term proliferation risk by separating weapons-usable plutonium from the radiation barrier created by fission products. In a sense, the trade-off is between some benefits (possibly modest) for very long term waste isolation versus increased proliferation risk in this century. Currently, the plutonium recycle approach has resulted in accumulated storage of about 200 metric tons of separated plutonium, enough to make tens of thousands of weapons.

This concern has generated considerable interest in developing more advanced reactors and reprocessing-based fuel cycles that do not isolate plutonium and therefore lower the proliferation risks inherent in plutonium recycle. The United States and other interested nations should focus their work in three general areas: advancing the once-through (i.e., "direct" disposal of spent fuel in geological repositories) fuel cycle; for the long term, R&D on closed fuel cycles that do not isolate plutonium and on "lifetime" reactors; and a new implementation framework for the NPT.[36]

The once-through fuel cycle is currently favored by both economic and nonproliferation considerations and will remain so for at least several decades. Though very-long-term waste management is somewhat simplified by plutonium removal, there is no significant benefit for the century time scale. Even the very-long-term benefits are arguable because the fundamentals of long-term geologic isolation appear quite sound. In addition, substantially enhanced isolation may be achieved through other technologies, such as advanced engineered barriers for containment and alternative geological isolation schemes such as very deep bore holes (holes in solid crystalline formations that are 4 to 5 kilometers deep).

Advanced closed fuel cycles must overcome major economic and technical challenges, placing its commercialization many decades away. The United States could lay the foundation, in cooperation with international partners, to possibly deploy such advanced closed fuel cycles in the second half of this century and thereby help to properly shape the R&D. U.S. leadership and support, however, must be contingent on an understanding that plutonium recycling would not be advanced, even as demand for nuclear power grows. Further, the R&D program itself must be carefully structured and managed so as not to exacerbate proliferation concerns.

A new implementation framework for an NPT that more effectively addresses current security concerns might involve an arrangement between "fuel-cycle" and "privileged" states, operating under internationally secure arrangements.[37] Privileged states would have access to reactor technology and operational assistance, but not to those fuel-cycle technologies (e.g., enrichment, reprocessing) that raise proliferation concerns. In return, fresh fuel supply and spent fuel removal would be provided by a small number of "fuel-cycle states" or by internationally operated fuel-cycle centers. Privileged states would avoid the cost of fuel-cycle infrastructure development, more intrusive safeguards regimes, and, most important, waste disposal challenges. The fuel-cycle states and/or international fuel-cycle centers would accept spent fuel in order to provide a secure international nonproliferation regime as nuclear power expands.

The establishment and location of international spent fuel storage and disposal facilities, however, is an especially difficult issue for this approach. It can be resolved only by addressing nuclear waste management to the public's satisfaction. So far, only the Russian government has expressed a willingness to accept spent fuel from other countries, outside some reprocessing services provided in Europe. Other technology developments can facilitate such an approach. In particular, successful development of "nuclear batteries"—long-lived cores placed in sealed transportable reactor vessels that are returned to the supplier—would be especially attractive. However, these approaches are not imminently deployable and must demonstrate economic viability.

## Energy Infrastructure Security

The terrorist attacks of 9/11 have raised concerns about possible high-value targets in the energy infrastructure that must move significant volumes of primary energy from many locations to a broadly distributed set of customers. This is the case both on a national and international scale, where supply and demand centers are often geographically dispersed.

First, there are "high energy density" targets, such as nuclear reactors, large dams, or major concentrations of fuels (refineries, oil storage farms, LNG tankers or terminal). A sophisticated large-scale attack on these targets could lead to substantial regional damage. A major disruption in one part of the world, especially a significant disruption of the Middle Eastern oil infrastructure, can ripple throughout the world economy.

Second, the oil and oil products, natural gas, and electricity networks are highly distributed and often in isolated areas, providing "soft targets" for disruption. Increasingly, these networks cross over national borders, further complicating security. A coordinated network attack—physical or cyber—could conceivably disrupt energy delivery, the economy, and social systems and services for an extended period. Though not associated with terrorism, the major blackouts in the United States and Europe in 2003 highlighted the fragility of the networks and the societal impact of disruption. Another example directly associated with terrorism: In 2001, guerrilla activity temporarily shut down an LNG facility in Indonesia at the same time Japan's gas demand had increased due to maintenance of several nuclear plants. The economic effects of these concurrent events were felt throughout Asia.[38]

Technological response to these concerns varies from relatively low-technology conventional security measures (especially important for high energy density localized targets) to sophisticated strategies for increasing the resilience of energy networks. There have been numerous barriers, however, to the timely, large-scale introduction of these technology solutions. Much of the energy infrastructure is privately owned and operated, where the calculus that balances private return on investment with public goods such as security is quite different from that of the government. Also, the energy infrastructure that is owned or controlled by the private sector is generally designed for operational simplicity, which can lead to higher security vulnerability.

Increasing the resilience of energy networks is strongly technology dependent. Much of the technology exists, but implementation often requires regulatory clarity, which is lacking in the United States, where there remains ongoing confusion and regional disagreement about the restructuring of the power sector. This has impeded investment in the infrastructure, created fissures in grid management across regions, and slowed distributed generation deployment, all of which affect the resilience of the grid to major disruption. Nevertheless, there are significant technology opportunities for improving security, lowering system vulnerability, and increasing resilience, often simultaneously addressing economic, reliability, and environmental criteria. Focusing only on electricity, some of the technologies that can yield improvements include:

- *Compact underground super-conducting cable installations,* which can incorporate greater redundancy and interconnection, which in turn increase reliability and resilience to disruption.
- *Distributed generation,* which can provide security against major disruptions by placing smaller energy sources close to the consumer.[39]
- *The "self-healing" grid architecture,* which would integrate sensing, communications, control, and response capabilities to dynamically optimize system operation, anticipate problems, and react to eliminate or minimize impact, reduce recovery time, and restore the system to stable operation.[40]

## Integrating Technology Development and Energy Security

Energy security is not easily achieved. As a "public good," it is a government responsibility. In addressing it, the government needs to bridge the gap between its policy imperatives and the needs of the private-sector energy industry and consumers. Available tools include regulation, incentives, and technology development, all of which face politically difficult paths. Regulation and incentives directly affect the economics of a huge, dispersed industry, which accounts for the better part of a trillion dollars of annual economic activity in the United States. Applied research and technology development and demonstration often face criticism as "picking winners," particularly as the activity moves closer to marketplace deployment. Yet such programs are exactly those most likely to be needed if the government is to follow through on its stated commitments to achieve security goals in the near to intermediate term.

Adding to this difficulty is the "derivative" nature of energy policy: The value of energy is primarily measured by the infrastructure it provides to enable other important goals of society—such as environmental stewardship or security. As such, measures of a successful energy policy run the risk of being somewhat disconnected from energy fundamentals and the realities of the energy marketplace. This heightens the need for clearly defined and articulated goals as necessary conditions for success, as well as an institutionalized, more formal energy R&D portfolio management process.

This portfolio approach will lower the risk of unintended consequences, an outcome that is illustrated by the deployment of combined-cycle gas turbine technology. The development of highly efficient turbines dramatically accelerated natural gas consumption for power production. Though this development was desirable from the perspective of power generation and the environment, it placed considerable strain on natural gas supply, leading the National Petroleum Council in 1999 to call for an aggressive technology development government–industry partnership to enable production from technically and economically challenging reservoirs.[41]

When examined at the next level, the National Petroleum Council's recommendation provides an instructive example of new research management approaches needed to meet time-driven security goals. The NPC study notes that the resources to meet intermediate-term gas demand will, in part, be found in deeper and deeper water and that accelerated technology development will be required to develop these and other regions.

A follow-up DOE document, the *Ultra-Deepwater Technology Roadmap,*[42] concludes that the development of these resources will likely require new production architectures, a very expensive proposition. Industry will likely develop these regions eventually, but it has more profitable options to pursue overseas for the moment. Rational business decisions on the part of industry in this case would not align with national energy security objectives that place a premium on time horizons and domestic production.

Federal program managers and national laboratories have been creative and often successful in structuring consortiums of, or partnerships with, industry to pursue applied R&D. However, achieving security objectives through goal-oriented time-driven programs will likely require new and varied research models and mechanisms. Specifically, the development of new architectures to exploit ultra-deepwater resources will require major industry participation and cost-sharing, highly intricate multiyear management of complex program elements and multiple performers toward a production goal, and stability of support spanning different administrations. For such programs (presumably few in number), the standard management approach to applied energy R&D—incremental and uncertain funding, inadequate experience base, rigid contracting requirements—is ill suited for the ruthless execution that will be needed to meet the natural gas production objectives in the defined time frame.

Energy security will be advanced, in part, by policy, political, and financial support for a set of technology-driven priorities. We conclude with a set of priority areas that would integrate technology development with energy security:

- *The Department of Energy should institutionalize an energy research and development portfolio process,* organized around security and other strategic objectives set by administration policy. This portfolio could, in turn, serve as a means of engaging other agencies and enhancing the appropriateness and effectiveness of energy regulations and deployment incentives. It would also provide a basis for tailoring technology development program management approaches to strategic objectives, as well as to the specific requirements of private-sector partnerships.
- *Efficiency in fuel combustion, energy conversion, and end use* offers the shortest path to relieving numerous energy security challenges. Most important, a serious commitment to reducing oil dependency will require that the government—administration and Congress—jointly map out a long-term plan that engenders broad political support for deploying large numbers of dramatically more efficient vehicles over the next twenty years. The "net present value"—both literally in an economic sense and figuratively in terms of security benefits—of realizing such a deployment earlier is highly leveraged.
- *Efficiency in other sectors, such as combined heat and power or appliances, is also important.* The administration and Congress should endorse and act on the general principle of aligning technology and regulation so that standards regularly advance high-efficiency technology development and market penetration in the private sector.
- *The U.S. government should reestablish and accelerate oil and natural gas exploration and production R&D* particularly appropriate to large resources in the Western Hemisphere that are not currently economic to produce. Preeminent among these are heavy oil and natural gas from low-permeability reservoirs, both on and off shore. The ultra-deepwater component in particular calls for a new program management, oversight, and funding approach.
- *Alternative fuels from biomass, coal, and stranded natural gas feedstocks* are attractive for displacing oil and creating a more competitive environment for oil. Congress and the administration must decide if energy security warrants a major expensive federal investment to create markets for alternative fuels (government fleets, price supports, etc.).

- *Hydrogen offers an attractive long-term vision* for reducing and then eliminating the economy's reliance on oil, eventually in a way that is truly sustainable. Significant R&D is focused on hydrogen. This should continue and expand but should not do so at the expense of other critical research programs with an earlier payoff, such as efficiency. The merits of large-scale demonstration plants at this time are less clear, and such projects need very careful design if they are to prove important (the synfuels history suggests caution). The possible energy security benefits will not materialize for decades.

- *The United States should join with other industrial and major developing economies to implement programs that meaningfully begin the job of controlling greenhouse gas emissions.* The risks, including security risks, are sufficiently great that prudent government action is called for now, especially because many steps to address climate change (e.g., greatly accelerated efficiency gains) help to meet other public policy objectives. Immediate and significant actions should be taken by the leading emitters to reduce greenhouse gas emissions in roughly a ten-year time scale if the goal of limiting them to twice preindustrial levels is to be realized. Actions by developing economies must follow closely on those of industrial countries. For the United States, a greenhouse gas cap-and-trade system is the most realistic option. In addition, the United States should expand and strengthen programs, working with international financial institutions, to deploy high-efficiency and/or renewable technologies in developing economies to curb greenhouse gas emissions, to engage these nations in climate change mitigation, and to stimulate American clean energy technology deployment. The 1999 report of the President's Committee of Advisors on Science and Technology, *Powerful Partnerships,*[43] provides a good starting point.

- *The United States should broaden its current production tax credit offered for wind power to include all carbon-free technologies.* This credit should include "first-mover" nuclear power plants to demonstrate both their economic viability and their potential as a pathway for limiting carbon emissions. Research that can advance the large-scale deployment of affordable storage is very important for renewables and should be strengthened.

- *A strong program on large-scale carbon sequestration science and technology research, development, and demonstration* should be continued and expanded. It will take decades to resolve the scientific issues associated with large-scale sequestration.

- *Efforts to reduce and eliminate the proliferation threat* posed by global nuclear power growth should be addressed aggressively, particularly in view of the role nuclear power might play in mitigating climate change. Evolution of the NPT implementation framework is called for to further confine full fuel-cycle services (especially enrichment and irradiated fuel separation) to a small number of states with advanced infrastructures and/or international fuel-cycle centers. In addition, the United States should engage its partners in an advanced fuel-cycle technology R&D program that focuses work on fuel cycles with superior proliferation resistance.

- *The protection of the energy infrastructure* must be advanced, with the reality that most of it is owned and operated by the private sector. The government should work with industry to develop mandatory enforceable security standards for "high-energy-density" targets, because a failure here could have tragic consequences for the public.
- *With regard to the electricity infrastructure,* the government must finally complete the job of determining the "rules of the road" that will enable accelerated grid investment, create a level playing field for distributed generation, and improve resilience.

Placing the United States on a trajectory to pursue these technology pathways for the next two decades will entail a serious national dialogue, involving the administration, Congress, industry, and the public. Without the unwavering, sustained, and nonpartisan commitment and involvement of these institutions and individuals, the country will again find itself looking back over twenty-five years of investment in technology—wondering why its policies have not "reduced our reliance on oil," moved the world's abundant natural gas resources to demand centers, diminished geopolitical tensions, mitigated energy's impact on the environment, protected the country's energy infrastructures, and lessened the threat of nuclear proliferation. In short, the United States must take these steps to avoid being in the same position today as it was relative to the oil shocks of the 1970s—with an abundance of exhortations framed by ill-considered goals, but without a coherent energy security policy.

## Notes

1. National Academy of Sciences—National Research Council, *Energy Research at DOE: Was It Worth It? Energy Efficiency and Fossil Energy Research 1978 to 2000* (Washington, D.C.: National Academy of Sciences—National Research Council, 2001).

2. U.S. Energy Information Administration (EIA), *Energy Outlook 2003* (Washington, D.C.: U.S. Department of Energy, 2003).

3. EIA, *Energy Outlook 2003.*

4. EIA, *Energy Outlook 2003.*

5. EIA, *Energy Outlook 2003.*

6. Daniel Sperling and Eileen Claussen, "The Developing World's Motorization Challenge," *Issues in Science and Technology,* Fall 2002.

7. Robert Leidich, *Progress in Complying with Diesel Regulatory Programs* (Chattanooga: North American Motor Vehicle Emissions Control Conference, 2003).

8. David Griffiths, *Bringing Gas to the Markets: Gas to Liquids* (Middlesex, England: British Petroleum, 2002).

9. H. Yamamoto, J. Fujino, and K. Yamaji, "Evaluation of Bioenergy Potential with a Multi-Regional Global-Land-Use-and-Energy Model," *Biomass & Bioenergy* 21 (2001): 185–203.

10. S. A. Holditch, "The Increasing Role of Unconventional Reservoirs in the Future of the Oil and Gas Business," *Journal of Petroleum Technology,* http://www.spe.org/spe/jpt/jsp/jpttoc.

11. Holditch, "Increasing Role of Unconventional Reservoirs."

12. Partnership for a New Generation of Vehicles, *Review of the Research Program,* Sixth Report (Washington, D.C.: National Academy of Sciences—National Research Council, 2000).

13. M. A. Weiss, J. B. Heywood, A. Schafer, and V. K. Natarajan, *Comparative Assessment of Fuel Cell Cars* (Cambridge, Mass.: Massachusetts Institute of Technology, 2003).

14. Weiss et al., *Comparative Assessment of Fuel Cell Cars.*

15. Weiss et al., *Comparative Assessment of Fuel Cell Cars.*

16. D. R. Simbeck and E. Chang, *Hydrogen Supply: Cost Estimate for Hydrogen Pathways: Scoping Analysis* (Golden, Colo.: National Renewable Energy Laboratory, 2003).

17. Simbeck and Chang, *Hydrogen Supply.*

18. EIA, *Energy Outlook 2003.*

19. EIA, *Energy Outlook 2003.*

20. National Petroleum Council, *Natural Gas: Meeting the Challenges of the Nation's Growing Natural Gas Demand* (Washington, D.C.: National Petroleum Council, 1999).

21. Office of Fossil Energy, U.S. Department of Energy, *Offshore Technology Roadmap for the Ultra Deepwater Gulf of Mexico* (Washington, D.C.: U.S. Department of Energy, 2000).

22. K. F. Perry, *The Future of Natural Gas: Managing Interdisciplinary Programs* (Laramie, Wyo.: Institute for energy Research and National Science Foundation Proceedings, 1995); E. M. Kim and S. W. Tinker, *Economic Analysis for a National Ulterdeepwater and Unconventional Oil and Gas Supply Research Fund* (Austin, Tex.: Bureau of Economic Geology, University of Texas), 2003; EIA, *The Global Liquefied Natural Gas Market: Status and Outlook* (Washington, D.C.: U.S. Department of Energy, 2003).

23. R. Neal Elliott, Anna Monis Shipley, Steven Nadel, and Elizabeth Brown, *Natural Gas Price Effects of Energy Efficiency and Renewable Energy Practices and Policies,* Report E032 (Washington, D.C.: American Council for an Energy-Efficient Economy, 2003).

24. U.S. Department of Energy, *Powering the New Economy: Energy Accomplishments, Investments, Challenges* (Washington, D.C.: U.S. Department of Energy, 2000).

25. Elliott et al., *Natural Gas Price Effects.*

26. Elliott et al., *Natural Gas Price Effects.*

27. Gas Technology Institute, *LNG Source Book* (Des Plaines, Ill.: Gas Technology Institute, 2000).

28. EIA, *The Global Liquefied Natural Gas Market: Status and Outlook* (Washington, D.C.: U.S. Department of Energy, 2003).

29. J. T. Houghton, Y. Ding, D. J. Griggs, M. Noguer, P. J. vanderLinden, and D. Xiaosu, *Climate Change 2001: The Scientific Basis,* Contribution of Working Group 1 to the Third Assessment Report of the Intergovernmental Panel on Climate Change (Cambridge: Intergovernmental Panel on Climate Change, 2001).

30. E. J. Moniz and M. A. Kenderdine, "Meeting Energy Challenges: Technology and Policy," *Physics Today,* April 2002.

31. Massachusetts Institute of Technology, *The Future of Nuclear Power: An Interdisciplinary MIT Study* (Cambridge, Mass.: MIT Press).

32. Massachusetts Institute of Technology, *Future of Nuclear Power.*

33. N. Lewis, "Scaleable Solar Energy Technology," paper presented at Conference on Energy and Nanotechnology, Rice University, Houston, 2003.

34. P. J. Miller, private communication.

35. J. J. Heinrich, H. J. Herzog, and D. M. Reiner, "Environmental Assessment of Geologic Storage of CO2, Report MIT LFEE 2003-002," in *Proceedings of the Sixth International Conference on Greenhouse Gas Control Technologies, Kyoto, 2002* (Cambridge, Mass.: Pergamon Press, 2002).

36. Massachusetts Institute of Technology, *Future of Nuclear Power.*

37. Massachusetts Institute of Technology, *Future of Nuclear Power.*

38. James Jensen, "The LNG Revolution," *Energy Journal* 24, no. 2 (International Association for Energy Economics, 2003).

39. Consumer Energy Council of America, *Distributed Energy: Towards a 21st-Century Infrastructure* (Washington, D.C.: Consumer Energy Council of America, 2001).

40. Consumer Energy Council of America, *Positioning the Consumer for the Future: A Roadmap to an Optimal Electric Power System* (Washington, D.C.: American Electric Industry Restructuring Forum, 2003). Electric Power Research Institute, *Electricity Sector Framework for the Future* (Palo Alto, Calif.: Electric Power Research Institute, 2003).

41. National Petroleum Council, *Natural Gas.*

42. Office of Fossil Energy, *Offshore Technology Roadmap.*

43. President's Committee of Advisors on Science and Technology, *Powerful Partnerships: The Federal Role in International Cooperation on Energy Innovation* (Washington, D.C.: President's Committee of Advisors on Science and Technology, 1999).

# 19

# Governance, Transparency, and Sustainable Development

*Charles McPherson*

Developing countries and economies in transition hold 94 percent of world oil reserves and account for 88 percent of the world's exports of oil. The same countries also account for 96 percent of world reserves of natural gas and, excluding Canada–United States trade, close to 70 percent of the increasingly important international export trade in gas, either in the form of pipeline gas or liquefied natural gas (LNG).[1]

Dependable access to these oil and gas supplies is critical to the energy, and indeed economic, security of the major oil- and gas-importing countries, the United States foremost among them. Dependable access, in turn, is inextricably linked with the stability of the exporting countries and in particular with their ability to put themselves on paths of sustainable development. Unfortunately, these goals have proved elusive. Most oil-rich developing countries have records of serious economic underperformance and have experienced significant social and political unrest and often violent conflict. The sought-after stability and sustainable development simply have not materialized.

The roots of this "paradox of plenty"[2] lie in weak governance—bad policies, corruption, economic mismanagement, and limits on public participation and access to information. Weak governance can, in good part, be traced to the resource endowment itself.

Successfully addressing this problem will depend fundamentally on better petroleum revenue management, which covers a range of initiatives,

The views expressed in this chapter are those of the author and do not necessarily reflect the opinions of the World Bank Group.

from petroleum-specific measures to macroeconomic policies and improved strategies for poverty alleviation.

Ensuring better petroleum revenue management in practice is not so much a technical or economic issue. Rather, it is essentially an issue of political will. Though exercising that will is primarily the responsibility of the government of the petroleum-producing developing country, responsibility must be shared among all stakeholders—industry, civil society, international financial institutions and organizations, and the governments of petroleum-importing donor countries, like the United States. That responsibility may take a variety of forms, including but not limited to financial and technical support, contributions to capacity building, public information campaigns, and political and economic leverage. Given its relevance to energy security, it seems entirely appropriate that developing-country performance on petroleum revenue management be prominently featured in the foreign policies of major petroleum-importing countries. This chapter looks in more detail at these issues and possible remedies, with particular emphasis on the challenge and role of good governance and of one of its key components, transparency.

## Are Petroleum and Sustainable Development Compatible?

Whether or not petroleum resources are translated into sustainable development depends on the management or mismanagement of sums of money that can be enormous, both in absolute and relative terms. Figures for a selection of non–Middle Eastern countries suggest the potential for good and the room for abuse. At $30 per barrel of crude oil, oil rents accruing to Mexico are estimated at $35 billion; to Venezuela, $30 billion; and to Nigeria, $22 billion.[3]

Given sums like these, it is not surprising to find that dependence on oil and gas in many petroleum-producing states, particularly in the developing world, is high. For example, oil accounts for 40 percent of Nigeria's gross domestic product (GDP), 70 percent of its government revenues, and 95 percent of its foreign exchange earnings. The respective numbers for Venezuela are similar: 30, 55, and 70 percent. Even a country like Mexico, which in recent years has succeeded in diluting its dependence on oil in GDP and export terms, still depends on oil for more than 30 percent of government revenues.[4]

Given their scale and relative significance, it seems reasonable to expect oil and gas revenues to be major drivers of development in the countries concerned. Unfortunately, as suggested at the outset, such results are hard to find.

That something has clearly gone wrong in the connection between oil and development is evidenced in a growing volume titles from books, journals, and the press. A sampling of these is listed here:[5]

Oil Windfalls: Blessing or Curse?

Angola's Oil Wealth Fuels War and Corruption

The Natural Resource Curse: How Wealth Can Make You Poor

Sudan Tops List Causing Agony from Oil

Caspian Oil Windfalls: Who Will Benefit?

Does Mother Nature Corrupt?

As Oil Riches Flow, Poor Village Cries Out

During the past decade, a growing body of research has documented the underperformance of resource-abundant developing countries relative to resource-deficient developing countries. One of these studies shows that between 1960 and 1990 countries that were resource poor, whether large or small, significantly outperformed resource-rich countries, performance being measured in terms of per capita GDP growth.[6] The comparison is especially startling when performance is measured against the experience of small oil-exporting countries, whose oil dependence is likely to be high. Over the 1970–90 period, GDP per capita grew in these countries at 0.8 percent, versus 2.1 to 3.7 percent growth in resource-poor countries.

GDP growth per capita is just one dimension of a country's well-being, albeit a very important one. However, the evidence to date with respect to other developmental indicators is equally disturbing. The development outcomes in one high-profile oil-exporting country, Nigeria, corroborate the cross-country evidence on relative underperformance with respect to GDP growth and illustrate the more pervasive negative outcomes often associated with oil-dependent developing countries. Its oil wealth notwithstanding, Nigeria is far behind United Nations targets for a variety of developmental indicators. For example, GDP per capita is $400, not the target $895; 60 percent of the population lives on less than $2 per day, while zero percent is considered an attainable target; and so on. The record is dismal, yet over the past twenty-five years, oil rents accruing to Nigeria have amounted to an estimated $300 billion.

Another discouraging finding, noted above, is that oil-dependent states disproportionately experience social and political unrest and often violence. Research at the World Bank and elsewhere points to resource dependence, and especially oil dependence, as one of the most important causes of civil war.[7] Violent secessionist movements can often be traced to oil—examples include Aceh (Indonesia), Biafra (Nigeria), and Cabinda (Angola).

## Governance and Oil: An Uneasy Mixture

These outcomes—all of which work against stability and, where petroleum exporters are involved, against the international security of energy supplies—are generally attributed to weak governance in the countries where they are experienced. We have seen that oil wealth is often inversely correlated with growth and other measures of development. The available evidence suggests strongly that oil wealth is also inversely correlated with governance. Oil-exporting countries come out poorly in rankings of countries against a broad range of governance indicators (e.g., the rule of law, quality of public service, political stability, transparency, and perceptions of corruption). Typically, oil-exporting developing countries are heavily clustered in the bottom one-third of such rankings.[8] Weak governance in many of these countries may have predated oil development. However, a range of arguments and evidence exists that suggests that the arrival of significant oil wealth can itself undermine governance, creating a vicious cycle.

A recent World Bank study of the Middle East and North Africa traced the region's poor growth performance directly to weak governance and especially highlighted the strong correlation between underperformance in governance and the presence of oil. "Riches from hydrocarbons have undermined the emergence of institutions of good governance," according to the authors of the report.[9]

Transparency International's widely referenced Corruption Perceptions Index spotlights one key aspect of governance: corruption. In the index's most recent survey, petroleum-exporting developing countries and economies in transition once again find themselves in the bottom one-third of country rankings.[10] This is a particularly serious finding because corruption is regarded as one of the largest single inhibiting factors to private-sector investment and growth.

Why does petroleum wealth cause problems? In answering this question, it is helpful to briefly consider the principal economic, political, and social challenges that oil and gas present to good governance: Dutch disease, volatility and asymmetry, the expansion of the public sector, insufficient investment, excessive credit expansion, weak institutional capacity, diminished accountability, political sensitivity, revenue sharing, and corruption.

*Dutch disease.* This "disease" was named for the problems experienced by the Netherlands following the discovery and initial exploration of vast reserves of natural gas. The rapid growth in petroleum exports led to an appreciation of the exchange rate, resulting in an increased price of non-petroleum exports, and put upward pressure on the costs and prices of non-traded domestic goods and services, diminishing their competitiveness and eroding the diversity and balance of the domestic economy. Evidence of the disease has been subsequently identified in almost all countries where petroleum exports play a major economic role. Nigeria again provides an example. The arrival of oil devastated Nigeria's traditional agricultural export industries, with negative consequences for diversity, employment, and even political stability. Angola's experience has been similar, with coffee declining from close to 50 percent of exports in 1966 to zero in 1991 and oil increasing from zero to 90 percent over the same period.[11]

*Volatility and asymmetry.* The oil industry is notorious for its often violent cyclical behavior. Volatility makes life difficult in itself, especially if cyclical swings are not predictable. It is particularly hard on poor people, who have fewer options to protect themselves against downswings in the economy and public expenditure. The difficulties created by cyclical volatility are compounded by the frequent asymmetry of policies and decisions associated with these swings. Bad decisions or investments made in boom years are very difficult to undo in bust years.

*Expansion of the public sector.* The popular perception of oil as being of strategic importance has led governments to take a prominent role in the sector, typically through a national oil company.[12] Significant sector revenues have masked the inefficiencies that commonly result and have often encouraged governments to move into other sectors they see as strategic, spreading inefficiency and crowding out private-sector participation, which many would argue offers the best chance for economic growth and diversification.

*Inefficient investment.* Oil wealth often comes suddenly, with new discoveries or an upward spike in prices. In developing countries, the new wealth typically exceeds the absorptive capacity of the domestic economy and the institutional capacity of government agencies to ensure its efficient investment. Investments in reaction to the run-up in wealth are often wasteful white elephants. Examples within the petroleum sector may include noneconomic domestic refineries, or ill-advised flagship LNG facilities. Examples other than petroleum are likely to be found in other "strategic sectors" and might include major steel or aluminum complexes.

*Excessive credit expansion.* When oil revenues get into the domestic banking system, they are very likely to result in excessive credit expansion, fueling inflation and threatening financial stability. Unfortunately, the impact of inflation is regressive. Like volatility, its hardest impact will be on the poor.

*Weak institutional capacity.* As already noted, oil revenues often exceed a host country's institutional capacity to manage them effectively. Oil itself is likely to erode incentives to create a more efficient civil service because, on the collection side, revenues are typically concentrated and require relatively small staffs to administer and, on the disbursement side, accountability is limited. Within the petroleum sector, the challenge of building effective administrative capacity may be considerably increased by the often one-sided competition with international oil company investors for qualified local staff.

*Diminished accountability.* Oil revenues provide government with a source of income independent of its citizens. Where oil revenues are significant, this independence diminishes the need for accountability, and at the same time increases government's ability to buy off or intimidate opposition. This point is repeatedly underscored in the World Bank study of the Middle East referred to above: "Exceptionally high oil and gas revenues have accrued directly to government coffers, thereby reducing the incentives of incumbent regimes to strengthen mechanisms of external accountability."[13] Significant petroleum revenues make it much easier for governments to postpone much-needed economic reforms, and indeed may encourage initiatives in the opposite direction to reform, as noted below.[14]

*Political sensitivity.* Oil wealth provokes strong emotional responses related to its "national heritage" or "national patrimony" qualities. As a result, there is a strong temptation to use oil wealth and oil policy to score political points and achieve political outcomes that may be, but are more likely not, consistent with sound development policy. Common examples include use of "the nation's oil" to fund food subsidies in urban areas, or petroleum product price subsidies, resulting in the case of the former in population shifts from rural areas and urban overcrowding, and in the case of the latter in product shortages and black market activities.

*Revenue sharing.* Sharing public revenues among different societal and geographical groups is a difficult challenge under any circumstances. Difficulties intensify in the case of oil revenues, not only because of their scale but also because of the fact that their sources are virtually never evenly distributed within a country. In Russia, competition over oil revenues has been a source of severe political strains between Moscow and the oil-producing provinces or *oblasts*. In Nigeria, it contributed to the Biafran war, and it is currently behind intense struggles between the federal government and regional, state, and local authorities. In Sudan, it has fed a long-standing civil war between the national government based in the north and a separatist movement in the oil-producing south.[15]

*Corruption.* Last, but far from least, is the corrosive influence of corruption. Petroleum wealth is a lightning rod for corruption at every stage in the revenue chain from taxation and collection through expenditures. Where corruption is deeply rooted, little attention will be paid to meeting any of the challenges listed above. Improvements in the areas of macroeconomic management or institutional capacity in the medium to longer terms are of little interest when the focus is on near-term theft for the benefit of a few; and the enhancement of accountability runs directly counter to the objectives of corruption. Corruption is greatly facilitated by the all-too-common lack of transparency when it comes to oil revenues. Those with ulterior motives for political or personal gain can be very successful at making the petroleum industry and its revenues opaque.

As must be readily apparent, many of these challenges are overlapping. It nevertheless is a daunting list, and it is not surprising that the governance record of so many oil-dependent exporting states has been poor.

## Addressing the Issues: Petroleum Revenue Management

Successfully addressing the issues and challenges noted above depends fundamentally on carefully designed and implemented strategies for petroleum revenue management, which includes revenue collection, revenue management per se, and revenue utilization or expenditures. A fourth critical component of any petroleum-revenue management strategy is the efficient and equitable sharing of revenues among levels of government and across regions and societal groups.

## Revenue Collection

Revenue collection encompasses issues of tax design (a number of these being peculiar to petroleum because of the significant investments and rents involved, the volatility of revenue, and the variability of cost conditions), tax administration, and the institutional capacity to monitor and control the flow of funds in the sector. Efficient revenue collection, whether through taxes or the fiscal provisions of contracts, is the starting point for good revenue management. The design of the fiscal system is important to ensuring that resources are efficiently exploited, investor interest is maintained, and revenue flows to the host government are timely, dependable, and adequate.

Although there is a growing understanding of what constitutes good petroleum tax design, a number of difficulties are still encountered in practice. These include finding the appropriate "competitive" level of tax take, assuring governments of a progressive share of project rents (i.e., a share that increases as profitability increases), and creating incentives for cost containment.[16]

Good tax design can help tax administration by limiting opportunities for investor tax evasion or tax "management" and by reducing the number of disputes arising and the need for special exceptions. It is, however, no substitute for good administration. Good administration requires adequate skills, salaries, and resources in terms of both labor power and technology. Monitoring and controlling revenue flows in the petroleum sector will require clear definitions of the roles of the different agencies involved—typically including a regulatory agency, perhaps the national oil company, the central bank, and the ministry of finance—and clear procedures for the interagency reconciliation of reported revenues. Regular and public reporting and audits are an essential part of the process, and these are too often lacking in developing countries. Weak capacity and underfunding of the tax administration function opens the door to corruption and revenue loss, especially when revenue flows are nontransparent. Effective administration, monitoring, and control will provide a basis for responsible revenue management and utilization policies and practice.

## Revenue Management

Once revenues are anticipated or collected, a well-articulated plan for their management per se is essential. Management objectives may include stabilization of the economy and budget revenues and expenditures in the face of price shocks; saving of funds for future generations; saving until there is a better match between revenues received and needs; and/or the local economy's absorptive and institutional capacity. A variety of instruments is available to pursue these objectives: regulation of the pace of exploration and production, special petroleum revenue funds, overall asset and budget management, and petroleum price-hedging instruments.

Although not infrequently referenced as a policy concern, regulation of the pace of petroleum exploitation is not commonly applied as a means of revenue management, at least in developing countries.[17] Pressure to access the revenues is usually too great. Further, government's ability to defer the development of oil and gas discoveries once made is often contractually limited.

A much more likely focus of debate on petroleum revenue management turns on whether its objectives are better met through special petroleum funds independent of central government asset management and budget functions, or through fully integrating the management of oil revenues with central asset management and budget decision making. Skeptics of independent fund management argue that it creates confusion in overall economic management by creating parallel and probably uncoordinated systems.[18] Those in favor of continuing the experiment with funds believe that, if carefully designed and properly administered, petroleum funds can play a very useful role in enhancing economic management and accountability. They would argue that independent management of oil revenues need not—and indeed should not—preclude close coordination with central economic management functions.[19]

A number of oil-producing countries or regional units have established oil funds. The list includes Norway, Alaska, Alberta, Kuwait, Oman, Venezuela, and Colombia. The results to date have been mixed, although not especially encouraging. These funds seem to work best where oil does not dominate the local economy and where a long tradition of good governance exists, as in Norway. The jury on oil funds is still out, however. Chad's recently developed model for oil revenue management, discussed further below, is just entering its implementation phase. It includes oil funds and special accounts designed with all the reservations of the skeptics in mind.

Azerbaijan, a newcomer to both independence and major oil wealth, recognized the risks that attend oil wealth and acted relatively quickly to establish special petroleum funds. Its funds have acted to delink surging petroleum revenues from pressures to spend, thus maintaining fiscal discipline, and to safeguard financial and exchange rate stability through rules requiring surplus fund assets to be invested abroad. These funds are still works in progress, and a number of technical drawbacks have already been identified. But like their Chadian model, they appear promising and bear watching.

As an alternative to setting up a fund to pursue stabilization objectives, governments might consider the use of market hedging to protect themselves against the social, political, and economic costs of price and revenue volatility. Developing countries, however, have been reluctant to take up the hedging option. This may be attributable to lack of information and/or capacity. A perhaps more powerful explanation is political. When oil prices fall sharply, ministers or other officials with sector responsibilities, having chosen not to hedge, are unlikely to be blamed for global market forces that are beyond their control; conversely, they are likely to be severely criticized if, as a result of hedging, the country fails to cash in on dramatic increases in prices.

## Revenue Utilization

Revenue utilization is concerned with the mechanisms applied to ensure the appropriate developmental use of oil revenues. This process starts with the identification of priority uses of resources, whether directly from special funds or from the budget. The front end of the revenue utilization process can be greatly helped by a Poverty Reduction Strategy (PRS). Now a requirement of World Bank and International Monetary Fund country programs, the PRS is prepared by government on the basis of extensive stakeholder consultation on poverty reduction priorities and on the articulation of a poverty reduction implementation program. Typical priorities include health, education, infrastructure, and the environment.

The back end of the process—making sure that revenues go where they are intended to go—is the province of budget screening and Public Expenditure Reviews (PERs), a standard World Bank product, although by no means exclusive to it. PERs identify lapses in implementation, areas in need of improvement, and recommendations for future practice. In addition to increasing the effectiveness of expenditures, PERs can assist in the detection and deterrence of corruption.

Although the main vehicle for transferring growth in the petroleum sector to the nonpetroleum sectors and to the poor will be the pattern of spending the increased revenues, institutional factors will also play a critical role. There is strong evidence, some would argue, that passing revenues down to local communities, empowering them and enforcing a governance structure, produces a pattern of spending much more likely to answer the needs of the poor than a hierarchical, centralized structure.[20] Finally, the overall policy context will be important. Decisions on the composition of spending should be complemented by policy reforms and initiatives supportive of economic diversification and poverty reduction. Beyond policies directed at macroeconomic stabilization, these would include the removal of legal and institutional barriers to private-sector development, and agriculture-related reforms such as the clarification of property rights and land-titling procedures.

These comments on the design and implementation of revenue utilization or expenditure programs should apply regardless of the revenue source. Why single out petroleum revenues? Why not simply reference the consolidated budget? In oil-dependent countries, the high-profiling of oil revenues is understandable because of the dominance of those revenues, and the "hot-button" character of oil issues. Often, an insistence on independent accounting for the disposition of petroleum revenues can be attributed to a profound skepticism with respect to the overall budgeting/expenditure process, especially where oil is concerned.

The largest losses in the whole petroleum revenue management chain probably occur at the revenue utilization or expenditure stage, through wasteful or premature investment or expenditure, nontransparency, political favors, and especially corruption. In its more extreme forms, this skepticism has led to recommendations that all or at least a large part of petroleum revenues should be distributed directly to the general population, which in many countries, it is argued, may be better placed than government or the legislature, at whatever level, to make the right decisions on expenditure and savings.[21]

## Revenue Sharing

Coming to closure on the contentious issue of petroleum revenue sharing among different regions and levels of government can be fundamental to effective overall petroleum revenue management.[22] One of the strongest arguments in favor of allocating oil and gas revenues to regional or local levels is based on the fact that many of the social costs of exploiting these resources are localized. These include environmental degradation and special infrastructure requirements, for example, roads, airports, school, and heath facilities. This argument accounts for the frequent allocation of a high share of royalties to regional or local levels, royalties being activity-based charges.

The appropriate allocation of rent- or profit-based taxes is more complex. How these revenues are finally shared will depend heavily on politics, and in particular on the nature of federalism in the country involved, that is, the relative importance of federal and regional views. As noted above, many believe that shifting revenues to the regional or local level will result in expenditure patterns that are more responsive to the needs of the poor. There is also a feeling that sharing is good for nation building. Where both oil and nonoil regions feel they are receiving a fair share, revenue sharing becomes an instrument of conflict prevention or conflict resolution.

If there are arguments for revenue sharing, there are also arguments against it. There is no doubt that the automatic allocation of a high share of rents to subnational levels of government will seriously complicate attempts to pursue national policies of revenue and expenditure stabilization. In Nigeria, for example, automatic sharing formulas transfer more than 50 percent of oil revenues to state and local governments and there is no mechanism as yet to assure fiscal discipline among lower levels of government. The entire burden of macroeconomic adjustment falls upon the federal government, which controls less than half of national revenues.

In general terms, local governments, because of their narrower revenue base, are not as well equipped as national governments to deal with the instability that is characteristic of oil revenues. A number of the other arguments against revenue sharing are simply the reverse of those in its support; these include arguments that issues of lack of capacity, incompetence, and corruption are actually more rather than less serious at the local than at the national level, and that a failure to get revenue-sharing formulas right, whether horizontal or vertical, will work against rather than in favor of national unity. The latter argument appears to be supported in Indonesia, where petroleum revenue-sharing schemes, on top of a recently introduced program favoring the decentralization of all revenues and expenditures, have left some local governments with relatively little and others with three times their annual budgets in one year, creating considerable interregional tension. Bolivia is going through a similar experience.

Given the importance of individual country circumstances, and the many pitfalls that are likely to attend uninformed policies, public debate and broad participation in the decision-making process would seem to be minimum conditions for the acceptance and success of any petroleum revenue-sharing scheme.

## Petroleum Revenue Transparency and Other Core Elements of Good Governance

At each stage of the petroleum revenue cycle—revenue collection, management per se, utilization, and sharing—the core elements of good governance —transparency, along with the related elements of accountability, inclusion, and adequate institutional capacity—are essential to success. Transparency is fundamental to all aspects of governance, and as such it has received growing attention from stakeholders at both international and regional levels. A number of arguments can be made in favor of greater revenue transparency in the petroleum sector, which pertain to the related elements of inclusion, accountability, institutional capacity, and access to finance and investment.

*Inclusion.* Transparency is needed to allow democratic debate on fiscal policy and spending priorities. Accurate information on revenues received is the starting point for such debate. An argument sometimes advanced against transparency in petroleum sector operations is that unwarranted pressure to increase spending will build up once the availability of fiscal resources from that sector is made known. However, it would seem better to inform the public and foster constructive debate. The existence of oil resources cannot be kept secret, and a lack of information on resulting revenues can be a source of debilitating social and political tensions. For example, rebel leaders in the petroleum-rich Aceh Province of Indonesia, in the absence of information to the contrary and in order to build support for their movement, propagated the notion that secession would turn their province into another Brunei—a tenfold exaggeration.[23]

*Accountability.* Revenue transparency will act to increase accountability in both the executive and legislative branches of government at all levels (federal, state, and local), reducing opportunities for corruption and the potential waste of funds, and defusing the potential for social and political unrest.

*Institutional capacity.* For economic management, budget decisions, and forward planning, government needs to be able to accurately monitor its current financial position and make adequately robust forecasts of future revenues. Enhanced macroeconomic management, in turn, improves growth prospects and fosters stability.

*Access to finance and investment.* Enhancements in transparency are increasingly demanded not only by citizens within the country but also by international financial institutions (both public and private), donor organizations, and international civil society. Because of transparency's importance to good governance, a lack of transparency is seen as a major obstacle to the creation of a favorable investment climate, better management of public resources, and poverty reduction. Progress on the transparency front can be expected to attract increased finance and investment, and the resulting international linkages can be expected to promote global energy security.

The focus on transparency in oil and gas, and in other extractive industries, notably mining, has led to two influential international campaigns with revenue transparency as an objective: Publish What You Pay (PWYP) and the Extractive Industries Transparency Initiative (EITI). The PWYP campaign is a coalition of about 150 nongovernmental organizations (NGOs), led by George Soros's Open Society Foundation and the NGO named Global Witness. Because PWYP is skeptical of getting numbers from governments of countries where transparency has been an issue, it has lobbied to have oil, gas, and mining companies individually publish the payments they have made to governments. PWYP hoped to have leverage exerted on such companies by the stock exchanges listing them in their home countries, such as the London and New York stock exchanges. The idea was to have the exchanges make publication of payments a condition or requirement of listing.

The PWYP campaign ran into a number of practical obstacles: (1) the companies' contracts with host governments typically contain confidentiality clauses that prohibit the unilateral release of information; (2) coverage would not extend to those companies that were not listed on major stock exchanges; (3) the exchanges themselves have not been prepared to make publication a condition of listing fearing, not unreasonably, a flood of demands from other interest groups for similar linkages (e.g., linkage of listing to environmental or human rights records); and (4) coverage would not include the revenues of state-owned oil companies, which are a major source of revenue to the state. Though these obstacles have caused interest to shift to EITI, PWYP has had, and continues to have, a major catalytic impact on the transparency movement.[24]

EITI was inspired by PWYP and was launched by British prime minister Tony Blair at the 2002 Johannesburg Summit on Sustainable Development. In contrast to PWYP, EITI relies on the countries that are hosts to oil and gas and mining companies to step forward and commit to revenue transparency, at least at the aggregate sector level.[25] Under EITI, a country would commit to the audit and publication of payments made by industry, and to the publication of the not always consistent revenues recorded as received by government. Audit and publication functions would be assigned to an independent qualified auditor. Other criteria judged central to achieving EITI's objectives include the application of transparency requirements to all sector participants, national oil companies among them; the engagement of civil society; and a concrete, time-bound, action plan for implementing a transparency agenda. Contrary to PWYP's expectations, a number of countries, several among them troubled by revenue management issues, have stepped forward as early participants in EITI. A June 2003 EITI summit in London recorded significant stakeholder buy-in, with about seventy government, industry, and NGO participants registering support.[26]

EITI is now moving toward the practical application of its principles. A multidonor trust fund, to provide technical assistance to those governments committing to the campaign's implementation, is to be established under World Bank management. The bank itself has enhanced its support of the extractive industry revenue transparency agenda. Among developing countries, Nigeria is quickly assuming a leadership position on the issue, as evidenced by public commitment at the highest political levels; monthly publication of revenue figures at all levels of government; establishment of a regularly meeting multistakeholder working group to guide the process; draft terms of reference for independent audits; and a detailed action plan for institutional capacity building in petroleum revenue management.[27]

Other countries with planned or active programs include Azerbaijan; Equatorial Guinea; São Tomé and Príncipe; and Timor-Leste, which is just entering the ranks of petroleum producers but was one of the first to endorse transparency along EITI lines. Angola, which has had serious credibility problems with respect to its management of petroleum revenues, has shown a significant shift in the direction of transparency and accountability. Chad's revenue transparency measures, which are very thorough, actually predated both PWYP and the EITI.

A commonly expressed reservation with respect to EITI and other transparency programs is that they do not go far enough; if there is to be real accountability, it has to go beyond revenues to how they have been spent. This point has been made by the U.S. government and by the Group of Eight (G-8), both of which have endorsed the transparency movement but want to see its reach extended. Though this is very clearly desirable, three main points should be kept in mind. The first is that effective expenditure tracking must have credible revenue numbers as its starting point.

Second, expenditure accountability is not an agenda item that is waiting on transparency to be fully implemented. There is already, and has been for some time (certainly among development agencies such as the World Bank and International Monetary Fund), a considerable commitment of resources to expenditure oversight. The PRSs and PERs discussed above are just one manifestation of this. If there is something missing at the moment, it may be closer coordination between the two programs—transparent revenue reporting and expenditure tracking. This is likely to be remedied very quickly. Third, for initiatives like PWYP and EITI to succeed as well as they have, it was important that they stay focused on a manageable agenda, which would have been jeopardized by reaching as far as expenditure tracking.

## Stakeholder Roles

Getting positive results from petroleum wealth will depend on the active commitment of all stakeholders. These include host governments; the private sector; NGOs, civil society, and the media; and international financial institutions and bilateral and multilateral development agencies. This section examines each of these.

### Host Governments

The governments of petroleum-producing developing countries are the recipients of the lion's share of petroleum revenues and must play the central roles in developing, legislating, and administering the policies and programs required to deliver beneficial developmental effects. Though the issues to be addressed are admittedly difficult, as suggested above, they have much more to do with political will than with economic or technical complexity.

Governments seem to be increasingly aware of their responsibilities in this area. Meeting the challenges involved will depend not only on their initiative but also on the support provided and pressure brought to bear by other stakeholders.

## The Private Sector

The historical role of the private sector has been to create petroleum wealth through investment and the application of its operational, technical, commercial, and managerial expertise. This will, and should, remain its core role. Increasingly, however, the private sector is paying serious attention to ethical, social, and environmental issues, which are closely linked to governance and revenue management. The performance of investors in this regard is beginning to affect not only their "license to operate" in many countries but also their ability to raise capital as social awareness slowly but surely increases in importance among the investment criteria of professional fund managers.

Indices are now regularly published measuring the performance of shares on New York and London stock exchanges against a variety of socially responsible criteria. ISIS, a London-based organization of major fund managers, was endorsed by EITI at its 2003 London conference and has been active in its follow-up. Major private-sector players are beginning to adopt internal codes of conduct and put in place corporate social responsibility programs designed to address the risks or ills perceived to be associated with petroleum wealth. Some of these are directed at the symptoms of government failure, for example, in the provision of public health, education, or other social infrastructure. Others focus on improving government performance through technical assistance in capacity building. The private sector's commitment to transparency principles, whether at the individual company or aggregate sector level, will be critical to advancing the governance agenda.

In the end, it is extremely important to recognize that (1) what the private sector can afford to fund in these areas is orders of magnitude less than the what the government can finance out of the revenues it receives from the private sector; (2) the private-sector oil and gas companies do not have a comparative advantage in delivering social goods; and (3) private-sector expenditures in this area are often deductible against tax at favorable rates and as such may constitute a very expensive source of development finance. In other words, where the delivery of benefits from oil and gas is concerned, the primary focal point should be government rather than industry, industry's important contributions and goodwill notwithstanding.

## NGOs, Civil Society, and the Media

NGOs, civil society, and the media play critical roles informing the public —both local and international—and in keeping other players' feet to the fire.[28] International NGOs and civil society can also play an important role in advising governments and local counterparts on emerging global best practices. Local NGOs and civil society, leveraging their grassroots connections, have the potential to be particularly effective in promoting good petroleum revenue management, especially on the revenue utilization or expenditure side.

## International Financial Institutions and Bilateral and Multilateral Development Agencies

International financial institutions and bilateral and multilateral development agencies can use their political and financial leverage to press for favorable revenue management policies. They are also leading providers of related technical assistance.

Certainly the World Bank and the International Monetary Fund are increasingly preoccupied with using their policy and lending instruments and related conditionality to address issues of oil revenue management. These institutions currently have active dialogues on, and programs of technical assistance related to, petroleum revenue management in Angola, Azerbaijan, Bolivia, Chad, Congo (Brazzaville), Equatorial Guinea, Kazakhstan, Timor-Leste, and Nigeria. The World Bank Group in particular has completed an intensive review of its appropriate role in the oil, gas, and mining industries. Among other things, the review points to governance as a key requirement for translating resource revenues to sustainable benefits, and to transparency as a fundamental building block, at both governmental and corporate levels.

Good examples of bilateral initiatives in this area include the United Kingdom's EITI and the U.S. government's Millennium Challenge Account. Transparency in the reporting of resource revenues and expenditures will be one of the conditions of access to the latter. In the longer run, this should have a direct positive influence on the security of energy supplies to the United States. As noted, the G-8 have also shown a serious interest in the proper management of resource revenues.

More recently, the New Economic Program for African Development (NEPAD) has added resource revenue management and transparency to its regional agenda. This step, together with individual country initiatives such as Nigeria's, should encourage an number of the regional oil producers to "come to the table."

Finally, by working together in alliances, responsible stakeholders should be able to multiply their effectiveness in addressing revenue management issues. The modalities of such alliances are now being actively explored in a number of different global and country contexts.

## Getting It Right? Chad and Other Country Initiatives

Chad has attracted considerable attention as a country in the early stages of exposure to oil wealth that has taken careful steps to avoid the resource curse or "paradox of plenty" and translate expected oil revenues into positive developmental effects. The project that will generate these benefits involves the multi-million-dollar development of the billion-barrel Doba oil field in southern Chad and its connection to an export terminal on the Atlantic coast of Cameroon via a 1,000-kilometer pipeline. The impact of the project on Chad will be significant—in excess of $2 billion in revenue over twenty-five years, or approximately $100 million a year. Production revenues have just begun. Though sizable in absolute terms, the implication of these revenues in relative terms is enormous. Chad is one of the world's poorest countries, with an annual GDP per capita of $230. On a human development scale prepared by the United Nations, Chad ranks 164th out of 175 countries. It is also a country that has been plagued with regional tensions and violent conflict.

Working closely with the World Bank, the International Monetary Fund, local and international civil society, and the project sponsors (and of particular importance, two major U.S. international firms, ExxonMobil and ChevronTexaco), the Chadian government has been carefully preparing for the arrival of its oil revenues. Key steps include:[29]

- *Economic and political reforms:* Measures taken with respect to the oil sector were preceded by wide-ranging reforms that improved overall economic management and performance, established democratic institutions, and expanded the role of the private sector. Though there is still a large unfinished agenda, these steps were critical to creating a favorable environment for good oil revenue management.
- *Public opinion surveys:* A series of information seminars, opinion polls,

and consultations with a wide range of stakeholders began with the signature of the oil concession in 1996 and is continuing. The results of the polls are published and openly debated.

- *Legislation:* As a first step toward petroleum management, a law was passed by Parliament covering revenue disposition and the creation of special accounts; linkages to overall budget and public expenditure management; priority areas for expenditure; oversight monitoring and control; disbursement authorization and audit; and reporting and extensive public access to all documentation.
- *Management plan:* The law was followed by publication of a strategy for "management of the petroleum economy" that provides background to and fills in the details of the law.
- *Oversight:* Both the law and the management plan call for an independent Petroleum Revenue Oversight Committee staffed by representatives from government, parliament, and civil society to ensure that established procedures are adhered to.
- *Poverty Reduction Strategy:* Chad's PRS, which is being prepared by the government with the participation of civil society groups, will guide the allocation of resources to five priority areas: education, health, rural development, environmental protection, and basic infrastructure.
- *Loans and technical assistance:* International financial institution funding, mostly from the World Bank Group, was arranged to strengthen the national capacities of each agency responsible for revenue collection and management, as well as the key ministries charged with overall economic management.

The World Bank Group was also involved in funding the oil development project itself. The Bank Group's financial participation is very small relative to total project costs, but it has enabled the Bank Group to play an important role in structuring revenue management and other safeguards. Indeed, this was the basis on which the group was invited to become involved. The World Bank has set up an Independent Advisory Group (IAG) to monitor the environmental and social performance of the project, a brief which extends to revenue management issues. The IAG visits Chad regularly, consults with all stakeholders, and publicly reports its findings.

The real test of Chad's oil revenue management program will come over the next two or three years as revenues from the Doba field grow rapidly.[30] That said, it is an extraordinary, and was at the time virtually unique, start among oil dependent developing or transition countries. It will be watched closely by all countries and institutions concerned with the management of petroleum revenues.

A number of countries have attempted in the past to better manage their oil revenues, focusing primarily on stabilization aspects and on petroleum funds. These attempts have met with very mixed results at best. The issues involved are perhaps now better understood, particularly the comprehensive approach to governance that is required. There is now a new wave of interest in the issues taking root in a wide range of countries, ranging from small, new petroleum producers such as Timor-Leste and São Tomé and Príncipe, to much larger newcomers such as Azerbaijan and Kazakhstan, to major, long-established producers such as Nigeria and Angola. Nigeria and Angola will be bellwether cases, testing the ability of a country to make profound changes where practices of petroleum revenue mismanagement and corruption are well established.

## Conclusions and Recommendations

Poverty and instability are all too often associated with petroleum wealth in developing countries and economies in transition. The international community depends on these countries for an important share of its oil and gas supplies, yet the conditions that exist in many of them, whether located in the Middle East or in more recent major producing provinces such as Central Asia and West Africa, represent a direct present or future threat to supply security.

It will take a concerted effort by all stakeholders in industrial and developing countries alike to ensure that this threat does not materialize. The producing countries must take the lead in that effort, showing the political will to deliver the good governance and petroleum revenue management required to reverse these findings.

That still leaves a major role for other stakeholders, supporting producing governments with required funding, technical assistance, and corporate social responsibility activities. These stakeholders can also exert healthy leverage on producing governments through the possible conditioning of broader development funding on revenue management performance, through political forums such as the G-8 and NEPAD, and through global and local public information campaigns. Given their clear relevance to global and regional stability and to energy security, good governance and transparency in the petroleum sectors of the major oil- and gas-exporting developing countries deserve an important place in the foreign policy agendas of donor countries, including the United States.

## Notes

1. These data are for 2002.

2. The phrase was coined by Terry Lynn Karl in her path-breaking book of the same title, which examined the social and economic troubles experienced in major petroleum-producing developing countries, *The Paradox of Plenty: Oil Booms and Petro-States* (Berkeley: University of California Press, 1997).

3. Author's estimates.

4. Author's estimates.

5. Alan Gelb and Associates, *Oil Windfalls: Blessing or Curse?* (New York: Oxford University Press for the World Bank, 1988). This influential book is the starting point for much of the literature on petroleum governance and revenue management issues, which includes M. Ross, "The Natural Resource Curse: How Wealth Can Make You Poor," in *Natural Resources and Violent Conflict*, ed. Ian Bannon and Paul Collier (Washington, D.C.: World Bank, 2003); Svetlana Tsalik, *Caspian Oil Windfalls: Who Will Benefit?* (New York: Open Society Institute, 2003); and Carlos Leite and Jens Weidmann, *Does Mother Nature Corrupt?* IMF Working Paper WP/99/85 (Washington, D.C.: International Monetary Fund, 1999). Other titles are a sampling of a growing volume of press stories. Those shown are from the *Washington Post, New York Times,* and *Economist.*

6. R. M. Auty, ed., *Resource Abundance and Economic Development* (Oxford: Oxford University Press, 2001).

7. See Bannon and Collier, *Natural Resources and Violent Conflict.* Also see Paul Collier, "Economic Consequences of Civil Conflict and their Implications for Policy," in *Turbulent Peace: The Challenge of Managing International Conflict,* ed. Chester A. Crocker, Fen Osler Hamson, and Pamela Aall (Washington, D.C.: U.S. Institute of Peace Press, 2001).

8. See Charles McPherson, " Petroleum Revenue Management in Developing Countries," in *Paradox of Plenty: The Management of Oil Wealth,* Econ Report 12/02 (Oslo: Econ Centre for Economic Analysis, 2002).

9. World Bank, *Better Governance for Development in the Middle East and North Africa* (Washington, D.C.: World Bank, 2003).

10. The survey does not include a number of countries which, on the basis of other evidence, could well be expected in the bottom third of the ranking.

11. Clearly, Angola's civil war also played a part, but the negative influence of oil wealth would be hard to dispute.

12. See Charles McPherson, "National Oil Companies: Evolution, Issues, Outlook," in *Fiscal Policy Formulation and Implementation in Oil Producing Countries,* ed. J. M. Davis, R. Ossowski, and A. Fedelino (Washington, D.C.: International Monetary Fund, 2003). The chapter outlines the mostly negative contribution of national oil companies to date in sector governance in most developing countries, together with examples of reform. The book provides an excellent collection of up-to-date essays on different aspects of petroleum revenue management.

13. World Bank, *Better Governance;* see footnote 8.

14. A title from the *Washington Post* makes the point: "Russian Oil Boom Washed Away Economic Reform Impetus," *Washington Post,* January 8, 2001.

15. Revenue-sharing arrangements are now at the core of the long-awaited peace agreement.

16. Thomas Baunsgaard, *A Primer on Mineral Taxation,* IMF Working Paper WP/01/139 (Washington, D.C.: International Monetary Fund, 2001) gives a good introduction to petroleum taxation objectives and instruments.

17. Norway and the United Kingdom have paced licensing rounds with revenue management in mind. Angola has also pointed to the need for revenue management in slowing the pace of its development approvals, although some skepticism has been expressed as to the weight this argument actually has in Angola's strategy. For a number of countries, of course, the pace of development is regulated by their commitments to the OPEC cartel.

18. This argument is very persuasively made in J. M. Davis, R. Ossowski, J. Daniel, and S. Barnett, *Stabilization and Savings Funds for Nonrenewable Resources* (Washington, D.C.: International Monetary Fund, 2001).

19. John Wakeman-Linn, Paul Mathieu, and Bert van Selm, "Azerbaijan and Kazakhstan: Oil Funds and Revenue Management in Transition Economies," paper presented to workshop on petroleum revenue management, World Bank, Washington, October 23–24, 2002.

20. Some might argue against this. See the next section on revenue sharing.

21. X. Sala-i-Martin and A. Subramanian, *Addressing the Natural Resource Curse: An Illustration from Nigeria,* IMF Working Paper WP/03/139 (Washington, D.C.: International Monetary Fund, 2003).

22. A good discussion of revenue-sharing issues and options is contained in Roy Bahl, "Revenue Sharing in Petroleum States," paper presented to petroleum revenue management workshop, World Bank, Washington, October 23–24, 2002.

23. Ross, "Natural Resource Curse."

24. See the Web site http://www.publishwhatpay.org.

25. EITI is in no way opposed to publishing payments at the individual company level, which may represent the ultimate evolution of the process. Publication at the aggregate level is expedient in that it avoids confidentiality issues. Further aggregate numbers in any event go a very long way towards meeting the accountability objectives of both PWYP and EITI.

26. See the Web site http://www.dfid.gov.uk, under EITI.

27. E.g., see President Olusegun Obasanjo, "Nigeria: From Pond of Corruption to Island of Integrity," speech to Transparency International, Berlin, November 7, 2003.

28. Examples of high-profile, often controversial NGO campaigns include Global Witness, *A Crude Awakening,* 1999, and *All the President's Men: The Devastating Story of Oil and Banking in Angola's Privatised War,* 2002. Both publications address oil revenue management issues in Angola and are available at http://www.globalwitness.org/campaigns/oil/index.htlm. Also see Catholic Relief Services, *The Bottom of the Barrel* (New York: Catholic Relief Services, 2003). And see Human Rights Watch, *Angola Unravels* (London: Human Rights Watch, 1999), and *Angola: Account for Missing Oil Revenues* (London: Human Rights Watch, 2004), available at http://www.hrw.org.

29. A more detailed description of the Chad project's revenue management components can be found in World Bank, *Chad: Management of the Petroleum Economy*

*Project,* PAD Report 19427-CD (Washington, D.C.: World Bank, 1999), available at http://www.worldbank.org/afr/ccproj/project/rdpadmpe.pdf.

30. An equal challenge relates to whether or not the government will apply Doba revenue management procedures to expected new field developments, which do not automatically come under the Doba arrangements.

# 20

# The Challenge of Climate Protection: Balancing Energy and Environment

*Kevin A. Baumert*

Energy use has a greater impact on the environment than any other human activity. Energy is associated with a wide range of social and environmental issues, beginning with local air pollution and waste, and extending to transboundary problems like acid rain. Foremost among these issues is global climate change. Climate change differs from most environmental issues— it is long term, global in scope, and linked to a broad range of activities, including electric power generation, transportation, and industry. Most worrisome, due to large projected increases in global energy use, climate change solutions appear to be especially elusive.

This chapter addresses the links between energy and climate change and explores ways that the international community can address climate change against the backdrop of rapid growth in worldwide energy use. With the adoption of the 1992 UN Climate Convention and the 1997 Kyoto Protocol, the international community has already begun to tackle climate change.

But even the modest efforts to date are in danger of failing. Considering that the United States has withdrawn from the Kyoto Protocol, the Kyoto commitments cover fewer than 30 percent of the world's heat-trapping emissions, although Russian ratification has made it possible to enter into force. After reviewing the experience with the Kyoto Protocol, as well as the sources of U.S. reluctance about the protocol, this chapter concludes that some core features of this agreement are fundamentally sound. Despite the setbacks and the protocol's shortcomings, the reliance on cost-saving international emissions trading remains the most promising path to climate protection. Yet the protocol can also be improved in several respects, especially by reframing engagement with developing countries and improving cost-predictability. Such improvements offer the potential to address climate protection in the context of improving global energy security. The diversification of energy supply (especially toward natural gas and renewables), coupled with improved energy efficiency and conservation measures, can help reduce the demand for high-carbon fuels like oil and coal while maintaining access to energy services.

The first section of this chapter describes the challenge of climate protection and the linkages between climate change and energy. The second section outlines how the international community has responded to climate change through the adoption of the UN Climate Convention and Kyoto Protocol. This section examines the Kyoto Protocol and gleans lessons from the many critiques of the accord. Recognizing which criticisms warrant attention, and which are specious, can help lead to crafting a better agreement— one that includes the United States and also engages major developing countries. In light of the analysis in the preceding section, the third section offers a set of options for restoring the protocol or replacing it with a more robust instrument. The fourth and final section offers next steps to help hasten the adoption of such an agreement, concluding that the United States must lead by example.

## Climate Change and Energy

Addressing global climate change is a paramount challenge of the twenty-first century.[1] Since the beginning of the Industrial Revolution, atmospheric concentrations of carbon dioxide, the chief heat-trapping greenhouse gas, have risen 35 percent—from about 275 parts per million by volume (ppmv) then to 375 ppmv today. This increase is mainly due to human activities, primarily from the burning of fossil fuels and from deforestation. Carbon that has been sequestered in the Earth's crust (in the form of oil, coal, and other fossil fuels) for millions of years has been extracted, burned, and released into the atmosphere in large quantities over the past 200 years. Changes in the composition of the Earth's atmosphere have increased the average global surface temperature by about 0.6° C (1° F) over the past 100 years. Regional climate changes due to temperature increases have already affected many physical and biological systems, and emerging evidence suggests effects on human settlements from recent increases in floods and droughts.

If the trends in greenhouse gas emissions growth are not altered, global temperatures are expected to rise between 1.4 and 5.8° C (2.5 to 10.4° F) by 2100, according to the Intergovernmental Panel on Climate Change (IPCC). The effects of such temperature changes on agricultural production, water supply, forests, and overall human development are unknown but will likely be detrimental to a large portion of the world's population. Box 20.1 describes the characteristics that make climate change a unique and especially challenging issue.

To prevent atmospheric carbon dioxide concentrations from exceeding a level of 450 ppmv—which still represents a 60 percent increase in atmospheric concentrations—global emissions would need to decrease dramatically during this century, perhaps on the order of 60 to 80 percent below 1990 levels. Yet, over the next hundred years, the global population is expected to increase by 40 to 100 percent (from today's population of 6 billion), and economic growth is projected to climb tenfold to twentyfold. In the absence of action, atmospheric concentrations could exceed 1,000 ppmv—nearly four times preindustrial levels—by the end of the century. Even limiting atmospheric carbon dioxide concentrations to a level near 550 ppmv (a *doubling* of the concentration), would entail major emission reductions from projected levels and eventual reductions far below today's emission levels.

Climate change is primarily an energy problem. Eighty-five percent of all greenhouse gas emissions in the United States come from energy-related activities, including from fossil fuel combustion, waste combustion, coal mining, and transmission and distribution of natural gas. Globally, about 75 percent of all emissions are energy related. Of these emissions, fossil fuel combustion is far and away the largest source, constituting about 70 percent of global greenhouse gas output. The largest shares of these emissions come from electricity and heat production (42 percent) and transportation (23 percent). Smaller shares come from manufacturing and industry (about 20 percent) and residential fossil fuels use (9 percent).

Global trends suggest massive future increases in energy use that, in turn, drive carbon dioxide emissions. According to the International Energy Agency, primary energy use worldwide is expected to grow 67 percent by 2030, resulting in a 69 percent increase in carbon dioxide emissions. The U.S. Energy Information Administration has developed three global economic scenarios—high growth, reference, and low growth—which imply worldwide emission increases of 31, 59, and 90 percent respectively by 2025. A scenario development exercise led by the IPCC likewise suggests tremendous future growth in energy use and emissions, largely dominated by fossil fuels.

*Box 20.1. Key Characteristics of the Global Climate Change Problem*

*The problem is global.* Climate change is related to the concentration of greenhouse gases (GHGs) in the Earth's atmosphere. Emissions from all sources from all countries determine the concentration of these gases. Acting alone, most countries that reduce emissions will have a small overall effect.

*The problem is long term.* Emissions of carbon dioxide, on average, remain in the atmosphere for about 100 years (some other gases persist for thousands of years). Thus, GHG concentrations are related to the net accumulation of gases over long periods of time, not to a single year's emissions. This raises complicated ethical questions because the future generations that will be most affected by climate change are not present to participate in today's decisions.

*Associated human activities are pervasive.* GHG emissions are linked to a broad array of human activities, including transportation, industry, and electric power usage.

*Uncertainty is pervasive.* Many uncertainties exist regarding the magnitude of future climate change and its consequences, as well as the costs, benefits, and barriers to implementation of possible solutions.

*The consequences are potentially irreversible and are distributed unevenly.* Rising sea levels and other potential consequences of a global temperature increase can take more than a thousand years to play out. Likewise, societies differ in their vulnerability to the effects of climate change, with poorer societies less able to adapt to these consequences.

*The global institutions needed to address the issue are only partially formed.* The 1992 UN Climate Convention has nearly universal membership (including the United States), but it has not spurred global reductions in emissions. The 1997 Kyoto Protocol has expanded the decision-making process for climate change policy, but it has yet to take full effect.

*Source:* Adapted from Intergovernmental Panel on Climate Change, *Climate Change 2001: Mitigation,* ed. B. Metz and O. Davidson, Contribution of Working Group III to Intergovernmental Panel on Climate Change Third Assessment Report (Cambridge: Cambridge University Press, 2001), 606–9.

In all scenarios, the largest increases in energy use and emissions come from developing countries. This is not surprising, given that one-third of the world's population—mainly in developing countries—does not yet have access to electric power services. Accordingly, many energy-using technologies have not yet widely penetrated developing-country economies. As incomes rise and poorer populations increase their access to electric power, the attendant use of energy-intensive goods—like refrigerators, air conditioners, and computers—will put strong upward pressures on greenhouse gas emissions for many decades. This is particularly true in the transportation sector, where rates of motor vehicle ownership are about 100 times higher in the United States than in China, India, and many other developing countries.

It is simply not possible to protect the climate without changing the way energy is produced and consumed worldwide. Arresting and reversing the above trends is a challenge of the highest order; meeting it will require technological, institutional, and behavioral change. Some opportunities are apparent already. For example, switching energy sources from coal (the highest carbon-content fuel) to natural gas can cut emissions by about 50 percent, illustrating a major near-term emission reduction opportunity. Increasing the (already rapid) market penetration of renewable energy sources like wind, biomass, geothermal, and solar is likewise an attractive option. Other existing opportunities include the adoption of more energy-efficient technologies and practices, growth in the use of efficient gas turbines and combined heat and power systems, energy conservation measures, and improved vehicle efficiency, perhaps with gasoline-electric hybrid vehicles. According to the IPCC, if existing technological and economic potential can be harnessed, the worrisome emissions trends described above could be overcome, resulting in *global emission levels in 2020 that are below current levels.*[2] Over the longer term, carbon sequestration and hydrogen-fuel-cell technologies hold enormous potential, although the commercialization of these technologies may be several decades away.

The kinds of changes described above, though challenging, are consistent with maintaining or improving U.S. energy security and economic growth. Driving these changes will require the adoption of new policies—such as carbon taxes, tradable permits, or technology standards—covering sectors that are important to national security and economic growth, such as power generation, transportation, industry, and agriculture. Entrenched interests in these sectors, as well as the high costs (real or perceived) of adjusting to a new policy environment make the transition to a low-carbon future an uphill climb. This climb becomes even steeper considering the foreign policy and international cooperation challenges. Governments tend to resist acting alone to rein in their emissions, given that the rising greenhouse gas output in other countries could undermine their own potentially costly actions. These efforts at cooperation are discussed in the next section, beginning with the UN Climate Convention.

## The Climate Convention and Kyoto Protocol: Lessons and Criticisms

Governments adopted the UN Framework Convention on Climate Change (UNFCCC, or "Climate Convention") in 1992. This agreement has nearly universal membership—including the United States—and establishes the basic principles and preliminary steps for addressing climate change at a global level. Most important, the Climate Convention establishes an ultimate objective of stabilizing atmospheric concentrations of greenhouse gases at a level that avoids dangerous human interference with the climate system. Yet the Climate Convention established little in the area of firm governmental commitments. Recognizing this shortcoming, and responding to firmer scientific findings, governments agreed in 1997 to the Kyoto Protocol.

The Kyoto Protocol has several basic design features. First, under the agreement, industrial countries and economies in transition assume legally binding emission caps to be achieved during the five-year period from 2008 to 2012 (see table 20.1).[3] For their part, developing countries like China and India have no emission limits under the protocol.

*Table 20.1. Kyoto Protocol Targets for Selected Countries and Group (percent change relative to 1990 levels)*

| Country or Group | Percent Change |
| --- | --- |
| Australia | +8 |
| Canada | −6 |
| European Union | −8 |
| Japan | −6 |
| Russia | 0 |
| United States | −7 |

*Source:* UN Framework Convention on Climate Change.

Second, the Kyoto Protocol contains so-called market mechanisms designed to reduce the costs of meeting emission limitation targets. Under international emissions trading, for example, industrial-country governments—or their private entities—can buy and sell emission allowances as needed to minimize compliance costs. In addition, under the protocol's Clean Development Mechanism, industrial countries may credit against their targets emission reductions that result from climate-friendly investments in developing countries. Third, the protocol includes a set of accountability mechanisms to promote fair trading and adherence to targets. These provisions include greenhouse gas measurement, reporting, and independent review procedures, as well as mandatory consequences for countries found to be in violation of certain commitments.

The standing of the protocol has waxed and waned since its adoption in 1997, largely due to shifts in U.S. foreign policy. After more than three years of work refining the agreement, the protocol was dealt a major blow when, in March 2001, newly elected U.S. president George W. Bush declared that the United States did not intend to become a party to the protocol. After declaring the protocol "fatally flawed in fundamental ways," the Bush administration did not offer an acceptable alternative to the world community.[4] The effect was to energize the Japanese, European, and other governments, leading them to resurrect the protocol and finalize details for its implementation later in 2001. At that point, the agreement was essentially in the hands of Russia, whose ratification was required for the agreement to come to life.[5]

In deciding the fate of the Kyoto Protocol, Russia faced a major foreign policy decision, embodying a complex of trade-offs. Though the United States was officially indifferent on Russian ratification, a repudiation of the protocol might have brought Russia closer to the United States in the realm of domestic and international security, including in important hot spots like Chechnya. Yet Russian president Vladimir Putin received dozens of appeals from European and other leaders strongly urging ratification. Indeed, after a May 2004 deal with the European Union involving World Trade Organization accession, climate change, and the oil and gas sector, Putin announced that Russia "will rapidly move towards ratification of [the Kyoto] protocol."[6] In September 2004, the Russian cabinet officially approved the protocol and forwarded the ratification instruments to Parliament, whose ratification in October helped to boost Putin's standing in the eyes of European leaders and bring Russia closer to the European Union, already its largest trade and investment partner.[7]

As the Kyoto Protocol enters into force, the international community will quickly turn its attention to a successor agreement that builds on it but seeks to engage the United States and key developing countries. The United States will face a major decision on how (or whether) to reengage in international efforts to protect the climate system. Despite obstacles, as discussed below, international engagement on climate change could help rebuild U.S. credibility and trust with important allies. In the eyes of many governments, the United States is not responding to a major global problem that it has contributed the most to creating and has the greatest resources to correct. Accordingly, a policy shift could deliver direct and indirect foreign policy benefits across a range of areas of U.S. interest.

In any event, the protocol's merits and flaws provide lessons for crafting future agreements that engage a larger portion of the global community, including the United States. The remainder of this section discusses several persistent criticisms of the protocol, primarily made by the United States. Understanding the merits and flaws of these criticisms (and of the protocol itself) is essential if the international community wishes to build a better agreement to either replace or supplement the protocol.

## "Kyoto Is Not Global"

As noted, the Kyoto Protocol includes only commitments from industrial countries and economies in transition.[8] Accordingly, a major concern with such a regime is what is known as *leakage,* whereby industries shift their production to countries that do not have emission limits. Leakage may represent two problems: the environmental benefits of the treaty would be undercut, and the economic competitiveness of key industries would likewise suffer.

In its review of this issue, the IPCC concluded that the worst case scenario is 20 percent leakage. In other words, a *5 percent reduction* in greenhouse gas output in the industrial world (roughly what the Kyoto Protocol calls for) leads to a *1 percent increase* in the developing world. This would be significant, although not highly damaging environmentally. Potential leakage can also be further minimized through emissions trading and other prudently designed domestic regulations. If history is any guide (e.g., the 1990 U.S. Clean Air Act Amendments and the E.U. emissions-trading system), governments can adopt special provisions in domestic legislation for industries that will be significantly affected.

From an investment point of view, it is unlikely that energy-intensive industries will summarily flee to developing countries in response to carbon constraints. Many factors shape competitiveness and decisions on foreign direct investment. Labor costs and skills, market size, political stability, income levels, physical infrastructure, and a wide range of government policies (e.g., tax, financial, and investment policies) are typically the main considerations.

Another factor is energy prices, which could rise due to the adoption of domestic climate policies. However, there is a relatively narrow class of industries—constituting a small share of U.S. emissions—whose energy prices would be sufficient to tip the scales of investment and relocation decisions. Even in energy-intensive sectors, energy costs account for between 10 and 20 percent of the value of sales—not trivial, but hardly dominant either. And where there is substantial foreign direct investment in energy-intensive industries, such investments are better explained by other factors, like market opportunities and tax policy.

Although competitiveness and leakage will remain noteworthy political issues, there is less substance to back them up. Leakage is likely to be sporadic, not pervasive. A more relevant concern regarding the Kyoto Protocol's geographic coverage is that the lack of developing-country commitments, on its face, is tantamount to a lack of environmental effectiveness. The largest future energy and emissions growth will be in China, India, and other developing countries and regions (figure 20.1). Leaving these emissions unconstrained, many argue, is more than an imperfection of the protocol; it is a fatal flaw.

The severity of this problem depends partially on whether one views an international agreement like the Kyoto Protocol as an *outcome* or a *process*. Viewed as an outcome, the protocol is undoubtedly a failure in this and other respects. Viewed as a process, it is merely a first step that reflects a shared understanding in the 1990s that industrial countries would "take the lead" in addressing climate change (UNFCCC, article 3.1). Typically, international agreements, including those covering trade, arms control, and other issues, develop sequentially over time. Whether sequential decision making can eventually improve the protocol by bringing in developing countries is unknown. Experience to date, however, suggests that it will be difficult. Though the outright exclusion of developing countries cannot persist forever, it is not apparent that the developing-country issue can be remedied by simply imposing emission caps on poor countries. Crafting modalities for developing-country participation may require creativity and innovative new approaches. This topic is returned to in the next section.

Figure 20.1. Carbon Emissions, 2001, and Projected Emissions, 2025

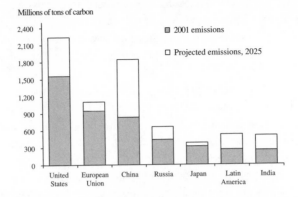

Millions of tons of carbon

□ 2001 emissions

□ Projected emissions, 2025

*Source:* U.S. Energy Information Administration, *International Energy Outlook* 2003 (Washington, D.C.: U.S. Energy Information Administration, 2003), n. 6 and reference case scenarios.

### *"Kyoto Costs Too Much"*

Cost is the staple of U.S. opposition to the Kyoto Protocol. Whether implementing the protocol will cause a serious economic burden is indeed an important question for governments to face. Cost issues are far from settled, as dozens of economic studies offer disparate forecasts of the costs and benefits. Some studies project high economic costs for implementing the protocol—about 2 percent of U.S. gross domestic product (GDP) in 2010.[9] Other studies have shown that emission reductions may have net benefits due to energy savings and secondary effects like cleaner air and water. The model results depend on widely varying underlying assumptions, including the capability of the U.S. economy to adapt, innovate, and develop new technologies in response to climate policies.

A comparison of models also reveals certain policy choices that can minimize the cost of controlling carbon. There is a broad consensus that the costs will be lower if the policy framework includes an economy-wide price signal (e.g., through a trading system or carbon tax), a broad range of gases (i.e., not just carbon dioxide but also methane and other gases); carbon sequestration provisions (e.g., in the forestry sector), and flexibility in the timing of emissions reductions (e.g., five-year commitment periods) to reflect inevitable fluctuations in economic growth, weather, and the like. Against enormous odds, the U.S. government successfully negotiated for the accommodation of each of the above provisions in the Kyoto Protocol. The agreement further opens the door to the direct engagement of private companies in international permit-trading transactions. These innovative provisions are designed expressly to enable emission reductions to take place where they are least costly and to unleash market forces to generate solutions to the climate problem.

Yet despite these features of the Kyoto Protocol, the cost arguments maintained by its opponents have ultimately proven persuasive. Though the protocol is replete with cost-effectiveness provisions, that does not make it cheap to comply with; *cost-effectiveness* and *cost* are distinct (though related) concepts. Having done little since 1997 to stem the increases in U.S. emissions, no amount of "flexibility" can now make the Kyoto targets achievable. For every day that passes without a domestic climate policy in place, compliance with the protocol becomes increasingly expensive.

Overall, the issue of costs will not be settled by theory or models, where disagreements will continue to abound. Until theory is tested in practice, *uncertainty* prevails. Yet uncertainty over cost itself militates against establishing a climate policy to begin with. With uncertainty on their side, categorical opponents of climate protection can continue to skillfully brand "energy rationing" and skyrocketing gas prices as inherent in almost any kind of climate policy, with the Kyoto Protocol being the epitome of an economy-wrecking international agreement. Accordingly, future actions should be oriented, as least in part, toward improving *cost predictability,* as discussed in the next section.

## *"Kyoto's Targets Are Scientifically Arbitrary and Unfair"*

A final concern is whether the science justifies the imposition of the Kyoto Protocol's emission limitations. The Bush administration points out that Kyoto targets were "arrived at arbitrarily as a result of political negotiations, and are not related to any specific scientific information or long-term objective."[10] These concerns are shared by many who are generally in favor of climate protection. In arguing for less stringent targets, for example, Stewart and Wiener observe that the Kyoto accord does not "address the degree or rate of climate change worth preventing; nor the optimal overall concentration of greenhouse gases in the atmosphere needed to avoid such climate change."[11]

It is appealing from a policy perspective to try to shape emission limitation targets that are socially optimal; that is, those that achieve benefits (in avoided climate change) that are commensurate with costs (in emissions abatement). However, determining such targets leads to analytical dead ends and potentially interminable delay. Finding the socially optimal emission requirements requires a more complete understanding of the damages expected from climate change than currently exists. Moreover, even if we had such an understanding of damages, those damages will be unevenly distributed across the globe, meaning that the socially optimum amount of climate protection will be different for each country. Thus, a conceptual basis does not even exist for achieving an international agreement on this issue. In the future, governments can perhaps do better than the Kyoto Protocol; but a global consensus on this issue is unreachable. A certain degree of "arbitrariness" should be accepted as an inevitable feature of political decisions shaped in the context of scientific and economic uncertainty.

A related concern about the Kyoto Protocol is the unfair distribution of emission reduction burdens (implicit in the targets) among the industrial countries. Though seemingly similar in percentage terms (e.g., 8 versus 7 percent reductions below 1990 levels for the European Union and United States, respectively), the targets ultimately adopted are not remotely equal with respect to the level of effort required by countries. After 1990, emissions drastically declined in some countries for reasons having nothing to do with climate change. Most significantly, economic dislocation in economies in transition like Russia and Ukraine caused emissions to drop on the order of 35 percent by 1997. Emissions likewise declined precipitously in Germany (–10 percent) and the United Kingdom (–6 percent), largely as a result of political reunification and coal-to-gas fuel switching in the power sector, respectively.

Meanwhile, U.S. emissions grew by about 12 percent from 1990 to 1997, partially fueled by higher than expected population growth. Thus, while the choice of a 1990 base year was a vestige of the Climate Convention, it disadvantaged the United States, at least at the level of perception. The U.S. target represented roughly a 30 percent reduction relative to "business-as-usual" trends, which was more ambitious than those of most other countries. While Europeans and others might insist that a higher burden for the United States is "fair" (due to much higher energy consumption levels), the steepness of the U.S. target made domestic political support hard to muster.

Regarding the overall concerns about the Kyoto Protocol, two points warrant further attention. First, some of these criticisms have merit. Upon digesting the lessons of nearly fifteen years of climate negotiations, it may be that the international community can improve significantly upon the protocol; but this will likely require U.S. leadership and an injection of new approaches (and the retention of some enduring ones), such as those discussed in the next section. Second, from the standpoint of the international community, the pathway to U.S. reengagement remains open. It is worth noting that, after the U.S. repudiation of the protocol, the international community was willing to make significant concessions to win back U.S. participation, which was perhaps naively taken for granted only months earlier. If the United States can muster the political will to reengage internationally, it will find willing negotiating partners. However, as discussed below, to rebuild trust and gain credibility, international reengagement must be accompanied by meaningful domestic action.

## Next Steps: Improving the Climate Regime

This section offers several recommendations for strengthening the international climate regime. First, the market-based systems policy approaches need to be maintained and also strengthened by improving predictability of compliance costs. Second, a suite of new approaches is needed to engage developing countries. Third, negotiators should consider employing bilateral or other subglobal cooperation strategies to strengthen what must ultimately be a global regime. Finally, greater attention is needed on the development of "transformative" technologies needed to move toward a carbon-neutral economy over the longer term. Each of these is now elaborated upon.

### Creating Markets and Addressing Costs

As discussed above in the second section, given economic expansion and massive future increases in energy use, preventing atmospheric concentrations of greenhouse gases even from *doubling* will require dramatic reductions in emissions of these gases during this century. If climate protection is expensive, then reductions will be fewer, and adverse climate effects will be greater. Thus, devising cost-effective ways to achieve emission reductions is essential from not just a business perspective but also an environmental one.

As discussed above, the basic architecture of the Kyoto Protocol—emission limitations underpinned by market-based trading instruments—is designed to promote cost-effectiveness and capitalize on the particular characteristics of the climate problem (e.g., that the location of emissions is irrelevant to the problem). Greenhouse gas trading systems—borne in the protocol's wake—are already being implemented across international borders in Europe, in U.S. states, and among U.S. companies through private exchanges like the Chicago Climate Exchange. These systems are partially modeled on the successful U.S. Acid Rain program, which has delivered sulfur dioxide emission reductions at costs per ton (about $200) dramatically lower than initial industry estimates ($1,300 per ton) or official government predictions ($600–800 per ton). Though hardly perfected for greenhouse gases, this approach of creating markets for emission reductions is fundamentally sound and—due to past U.S. insistence—already has the support of most of the world. Perhaps most important, this approach has the strongest backing from the those in the private sector, which has been telling government regulators for decades that they prefer market-based regulatory approaches to command and control. Ditching market mechanisms now, in favor of untested or previously failed alternatives, is premature.

Those supporting "radical" shifts away from the Kyoto Protocol's architecture tend to support instead agreements establishing common policies and measures, technology standards, or global carbon taxes. The hallmark of many of these options is policy *harmonization* across countries. Yet the prevailing principle of the Climate Convention that has facilitated cooperation is *differentiation,* not harmonization. A decade of experience with the Climate Convention suggests that policy harmonization strategies (e.g., global standards for power plants) intrude too much on sensitive domestic policy terrain. This differs from the protocol, whereby governments are free to achieve their targets in any way they deem appropriate, including by using trading and other regulatory approaches consistent with their unique national circumstances.

Accordingly, not everything about the protocol needs fixing. A reformed international agreement on climate change should include a broad range of trading and other cost-effectiveness features. But a future agreement can improve on the protocol with respect to cost issues. One obvious approach is to ensure that initial emission limitations are not too overwhelming. Clearly, the prospect of a long-term carbon-neutral economy is daunting; but if the first step is too intimidating, it might prevent the train from even leaving the station. A more modest first step—as envisaged by the Climate Stewardship Act advanced by U.S. senators John McCain and Joseph Lieberman in 2003—would improve the prospects of eventual Senate ratification of a treaty.[12]

A second possible improvement on the cost front is to employ a *cost cap,* sometimes referred to as a "safety valve" or "price cap." A cost cap places an upward limit on the costs of emission reductions, thereby providing some up-front certainty about the worst-case cost scenario for a given target. If abatement costs exceed the cap (e.g., $50 per ton), the government may issue additional emission allowances (or purchase them from a central authority), rather than require more costly emission reductions.

To be sure, using the cost cap would allow greenhouse gases to exceed the target level, thereby reducing environmental certainty. This should not be too troubling, however, even from an environmental perspective. The knowledge that costs cannot skyrocket might even enable governments to agree on more substantial environmental targets over the longer term. Indeed the mere possibility, however remote, of "out-of-control" costs puts a strong incentive on negotiating weaker environmental goals. And given the long-term nature of the climate problem, achieving precise near-term environmental outcomes is not essential.

## Engaging Developing Countries

According to some analysts, fixing the Kyoto Protocol is relatively simple: Extend emission limitations to cover developing countries. Some even go further by advocating negotiations on the global allocation of emission rights (i.e., caps for *all* countries) according to various criteria, such as equal per capita rights. Though appealing in some respects, these approaches are fraught with technical and political problems, and they are likely to fail at least in the near term.

Technically, many developing countries do not have the institutional capacity to meet the necessary monitoring, reporting, and other requirements embedded in a legally binding obligation. Likewise, the successful operation of market mechanisms may be possible in some countries, but these instruments require a high degree of regulatory capacity and a culture of compliance enforcement that is lacking in many developing countries. An even more potent technical obstacle is how developing-country emission targets might be set, given the large uncertainties over future emission levels in rapidly growing developing countries.[13] Translating shaky emissions figures into firm legal commitments presents serious environmental risks (globally, if the target is too loose) and economic risks (nationally, if the target is too stringent). Overall, the materials for Kyoto-style targets may not yet exist in many developing countries.

Politically, major developing countries have shown little willingness to follow a path of legally binding emission caps, at least in the foreseeable future. The political costs are high for addressing greenhouse gas emissions in the face of more compelling and urgent domestic priorities. The income level of the average Indian or Chinese citizen is a factor of ten or more below American levels. Broader social and economic data reveal similar patterns, with more than 1.3 billion people living on less than $1 a day and an equal number lacking access to safe drinking water. Efforts to control greenhouse gases are simply not a major domestic or foreign policy issue for most developing countries. Accordingly, successful engaging developing countries may require reframing climate protection in a way that is consistent with energy security and development agendas. Three approaches focus less on greenhouse gas emissions and more on energy and economic interests that are paramount in developing countries: undertaking clean development initiatives, expanding the Clean Development Mechanism, and setting alternative emission targets.

*Undertaking clean development initiatives.* One promising approach is to focus the debate over developing-country participation on something the governments actually care about—sustainable economic development—rather than a distant priority like climate change. For example, Winkler and colleagues outline the concept of "sustainable development policies and measures," under which countries would pursue a basket of policies and measures that are primarily geared toward their own national sustainable development needs.[14] From a climate point of view, the expectation is that, by moving toward greater sustainability in their development paths, developing countries will begin bending the curve of their greenhouse gas emissions trajectory downward.

In South Africa's context, for example, Winkler and colleagues suggest policies for diversifying electric power generation, restructuring the electricity market, and improving the energy efficiency of housing. India has already converted New Delhi's public transport system (buses and autorickshaws) to natural gas. Other initiatives could focus on replacing coal-fired electric power generation with new investments in natural gas infrastructure. These and many other initiatives in developing countries could promote public health and energy security as well as deliver significant emission reductions.

*Expanding the Clean Development Mechanism.* As noted above, the Clean Development Mechanism (CDM) allows companies headquartered in industrial countries to invest in and receive emission reduction credits from projects based in developing countries. CDM rules and institutions are designed primarily to encompass projects that are relatively narrow in scope, such a single electric power plant. However, among other problems with the CDM, it is not clear that a *project-by-project* approach is sufficient to induce the larger transformative shifts needed to change emission trajectories in developing countries, particularly in the energy sector. In recognition of this problem, governments should consider expanding the scope of the CDM to encompass entire sectors (e.g., cement or power production) or geographic regions (e.g., a municipality). Consortiums of the host government (local and/or national), private actors, development banks, and other stakeholders might come together to forge large, transformative strategies, particularly in advanced developing countries. Such initiatives could both improve the cost-effectiveness of the regime (through CDM crediting) as well as promote durable and broad-based development benefits in host countries.

*Setting alternative emission targets.* Emission limitations need not be of the Kyoto variety (i.e., fixed and binding). One alternative is a so-called *intensity* target. Here, the target itself is expressed in terms not of absolute emission levels but of emissions intensity—a ratio between greenhouse gas emissions and economic output (greenhouse gases per unit of GDP, or *tons per dollar*). Intensity targets help address the technical challenges associated with setting an emission limit under extreme uncertainty (which is characteristic of most developing countries). Perhaps more compelling, intensity targets are likely to be viewed as compatible with economic development because they are geared toward achieving emission reductions *relative* to economic growth. Intensity indicators might better reflect the real climate challenge in developing countries—decoupling economic growth and emissions growth (rather than "reducing" emissions).

None of these suggestions is a silver bullet. It is not clear that climate-friendly policies and measures, even if pledged, would be financed and implemented. An expanded CDM will entail significant technical challenges and be hard to negotiate. Alternative targets can encounter technical problems and are not supported by some developing countries. Though these options present challenges, they open up a dialogue where win–win opportunities can be identified and pursued across North–South lines. Their common thread is a recognition and acceptance of the need for developing countries to increase their use of energy and resulting emissions. Yet these alternatives also tame and mitigate the inevitable greenhouse gas increases that stem from economic development. They are also relatively modest first steps that can be upgraded in the future.

Given the diversity of developing-country circumstances, it might be that the best strategy is a menu that includes several of the approaches outlined above and perhaps others. Having no items on the menu is unlikely to be a viable option, either in the short term politically (in terms of U.S. engagement) or the long term environmentally. If it turns out that developing countries completely reject *all* options, even in the presence of demonstrated action by the United States and other industrial countries, then governments can investigate trade sanctions, aid conditionality, or other coercive measures. However, such approaches are likely to be counterproductive unless industrial countries themselves (especially the United States) adopt serious domestic commitments to climate protection. As with any negotiation on a matter of global importance, discourse and persuasion will be needed. And talks are more likely to bear fruit if industrial countries reframe their demands in terms more appealing to developing-country interests, along the lines discussed above. Another strategy, described below, is to advance progress in smaller groups of willing governments.

## Negotiating Nonglobal Pacts

Although the Climate Convention is an instrument for global cooperation, it can also be an instrument for obstruction and delay. Any agreement on climate is burdened by consensus requirements. Nonglobal pacts address this reality by reducing the number of players in the game, and they present a possible alternative in the event that particular countries are unwilling to cooperate in a multilateral setting. Stewart and Wiener, for example, suggest that the United States seek an agreement with China and possibly other major developing countries, outside the Kyoto framework.[15] Here, countries would adopt modest emission targets and make use of emissions trading. This agreement could operate in parallel with a Kyoto trading system, and it might eventually merge with Kyoto.

Such an arrangement is clearly an improvement relative to the status quo, but there are some drawbacks of adopting extra-UNFCCC agreements. Namely, developing countries favor negotiations in multilateral settings, where they can improve their leverage by operating in blocs. Likewise, the Bush administration has opposed *any* kind of mandatory emission targets with trading, whether bilateral, multilateral, or unilateral.

In any case, as the politics evolve in the United States, such approaches should be given serious consideration and perhaps pursued with vigor. It might be the case that, ultimately, neither the United States nor China is willing to join a multilateral agreement without the other. Progress toward such an outcome could begin bilaterally or trilaterally and gradually expand. Indeed, the United Nations Charter itself—the paragon of multilateralism—was shaped primarily by only three countries, with others engaging meaningfully only after the initial structure was hammered out by the great powers. Being open to this kind of starting point (e.g., perhaps involving Europe, the United States, and China and/or India) might help overcome the well-known problems of achieving global consensus. If a new climate agreement were pursued in this fashion, it could still build on and borrow from previous achievements under the UNFCCC and the Kyoto Protocol.

## Pushing Technological Development

Addressing climate change will require a technological revolution, one that ultimately leads to a global society producing *zero* net emissions of greenhouse gases. Accordingly, governments and the private sector need to focus on technological development and deployment of low or carbon-free technologies.

The Bush administration's focus on a "technology push" illustrates such an approach, with domestic and international research and development (R&D) initiatives aimed at developing carbon sequestration, nuclear power, and hydrogen technologies. This combination of technologies represents a viable long-term path to climate protection. First, hydrogen would replace many existing (and dirtier) forms of primary energy consumption, including in the transportation sector. Second, using improved nuclear and carbon sequestration technologies, hydrogen and electricity could be produced without emitting greenhouse gases, including via coal-fired power plants.

This *technology-push* approach departs from the *market-pull* strategy implicit in emissions trading systems described above. The end goal is the same—a technological revolution—but the catalyst differs. The logic of a market-pull strategy is that the government sets emission limits (with resulting price signals) and private firms respond to economic incentives by developing technologies to meet those limits at the lowest possible costs. In this way, the government avoids having to "pick winners," a costly venture with a poor track record of success. Further, the prospect of picking the wrong technologies makes this strategy a particularly risky one. Given these differences, technology-push and market-pull advocates naturally have different policy prescriptions. The former focus on R&D and technology standards, the latter on creating economic incentives through regulation, which in turn spurs technology improvement.

Figure 20.2.  The Technology Innovation Chain

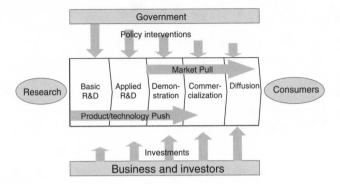

*Note:* R&D = research and development.
*Source:* M. Grubb and R. Stewart, "Promoting Climate-Friendly Technologies: International Perspectives and Issues," introductory paper presented at the INTACT High-Level Transatlantic Dialogue on Climate Change, Villa Vigoni, Italy, October 2003, n. 42.

    This choice of rival strategies—technology push versus market pull—
represents a false dichotomy. Grubb and Stewart show this by analyzing five
distinct phases in the chain of technological transformation: basic R&D, applied R&D, demonstration, commercialization, and diffusion (figure 20.2).
They note that "each stage involves technology improvement and cost reduction, but the principal barriers and driving forces change across the different stages: 'technology push' elements dominate early stage research,
whilst 'market pull' is increasingly important as technologies evolve along
the chain." Government and the private sector both play a role in each stage,
but with government investment more prominent initially and private sector investment (coupled with government regulation) playing a stronger
role in the later stages.[16]
    Thus, this issue is not whether to choose between a technology-centered
and market-centered approach but how to balance the two. Either, operating
alone, is probably insufficient. The Bush administration has brought needed
attention to technology-push strategies—which ought to be strengthened—
but has deserted the market-pull strategy that the United States successfully
pioneered in the 1990s. This is a risky and expensive path to climate protection. It also abandons much of the technological progress achieved over
the past few decades. Some of the most promising climate-friendly energy
technologies—including solar photovoltaic, wind, geothermal, and others—

are already in the latter stages of the chain of transformation shown in figure 20.2. Here, R&D will be less effective in increasing market penetration rates than a market-pull strategy, where the government promotes diffusion through fiscal and regulatory mechanisms.

## Conclusion: A Path Ahead

Ultimately, a mix of the approaches considered above will likely be needed to protect the climate system. A greater focus on development is needed—especially poverty alleviation and access to energy services. These goals have not yet been aligned with the longer-term interests in a stable climate system, nor have capacities of most developing countries improved to the point where they can take legally binding emission caps. Likewise, a stronger effort is needed to promote long-term technology solutions—that is, "gigaton" technologies in the areas of carbon sequestration or hydrogen production. The price signal from a trading regime may indeed be insufficient to incentivize the private sector to develop these technologies in its own. Finally, though a global regime is ultimately needed to protect the climate system, cooperation among smaller groupings may offer prospects for more aggressive near-term action.

Overall, the Kyoto Protocol's structure—though fundamentally sound—will need modification along the lines suggested above to gain wider future support. This includes possible provisions such as a cost cap. The use of international emissions trading, however, remains essential. Such a trading system—which was promoted by the United States in the 1990s and endorsed in the protocol—holds the promise of providing an accurate price signal, thereby instilling carbon considerations into the trillions of dollars that continue to be sunk into the physical infrastructure of a world economy dependent on fossil fuels. Trading also meshes well with corporate strategies in a globalizing world, characterized by intense cross-border movements of primary energy as well as goods and services that embody energy and carbon. Although there are formidable hurdles to an international emissions trading system, the incipient markets already in place in Europe and even in the United States are cause for optimism and warrant further expansion.

A successor agreement to the Kyoto Protocol that embodies such cost-taming market mechanisms, new technology, and clean development initiatives offers the best prospect of bringing climate protection in line with energy security objectives. Such an approach would promote the diversification of supply in the industrial world, especially in the direction of lower carbon natural gas and renewable sources, as well as an overall curbing of energy demand. In developing countries, such an approach will help avoid a further lock-in of high-carbon energy sources, while improving overall access to energy services.

Having identified the key elements of a successful international climate regime, how does the United States get there? A successful strategy begins with U.S. domestic action and leadership. Though state-level action is already flourishing, an overarching federal program is needed, both to provide a coherent national strategy and to avoid subjecting private actors to potentially incongruous state regulatory regimes. Modest mandatory greenhouse gas limits with a domestic trading system—modeled along the lines of the 2003 McCain-Lieberman Climate Stewardship Act—would be the critical step in the right direction. Though the McCain-Lieberman bill did not pass the Senate in 2003, its defeat by a surprisingly narrow margin of 43 to 55 votes suggests that congressional passage is eventually feasible.

Eventually, however, passing this kind of domestic climate legislation will require presidential support. The Bush administration has steadfastly opposed mandatory emission limits, and it has only advanced voluntary initiatives requiring little effort. In his second term, there remains a possibility that President Bush could change course and support a cap-and-trade program. Indeed, some moderate Republicans and even elements of the conservative establishment believe that Bush has erred on an issue of planetary importance. A modest domestic cap-and-trade system is consistent with conservative principles and merits reconsideration by the president.

In any event, it is important to begin climate protection at home, not as a matter of principle but because of domestic and foreign policy dynamics. By mustering a reasonable domestic climate policy, the United States can transform the political dynamics to favor global cooperation that furthers U.S. interests, including in areas of cost saving and technology exports. First, the logic of the United States remaining outside an international trading system will be turned on its head. With a domestic system in place, companies would increasingly lobby for access to international trading markets to further reduce their own costs, while ensuring that competitors abroad face compliance requirements commensurate with their own. Thus, support for Senate ratification of a climate treaty that governs international emissions trading would be significantly enhanced. Indeed, one of the reasons for U.S. support and leadership in the 1987 Montreal Protocol on ozone-depleting substances was that the United States was already regulating some of the relevant gases *before* the treaty's adoption.

Second, a respectable domestic climate policy will strengthen the hand of U.S. negotiators in the international arena. After the Kyoto Protocol, calls by the United States for "developing-country commitments" only angered Europeans and energized developing countries to avoid such commitments. If the United States relaunches a diplomatic "full court press" on developing countries without itself taking meaningful domestic steps, the stalemate will persist. Poor countries, home to 2 billion people that still lack access to basic energy services, will continue to react indignantly to suggestions that *they* do more as a condition of U.S. participation.

Yet if the United States leads by putting firm domestic commitments in place, it will have the standing not only to ask others to do more but also to shape bilateral or multilateral accords in ways that favor cost-effectiveness, flexibility, and robust market development—the factors needed to ensure a smooth transition to a low-carbon energy future. Such an approach likewise offers broader foreign policy and economic benefits. The United States' leaders, beginning at home, can rebuild credibility and replace the lost trust in a domain of foreign policy important to its European and other allies. By meaningfully engaging on climate change, the United States can improve the prospects for international cooperation in other areas of strategic interest. And by fashioning a successor agreement to the Kyoto Protocol that helps slow coal and oil demand in developing countries, the United States can open up new areas of strategic cooperation and private investment opportunity.

## Notes

1. The first three paragraphs of this section draw on *Climate Change 2001: The Scientific Basis,* ed. J. Houghton et al., Contribution of Working Group I to the Third Assessment Report of the Intergovernmental Panel on Climate Change (IPCC) (Cambridge: Cambridge University Press, 2001), and *Climate Change 2001: Impacts, Adaptation and Vulnerability,* ed. J. McCarthy et al., Contribution of Working Group II to the Third Assessment Report of the IPCC (Cambridge: Cambridge University Press, 2001).

2. B. Metz and O. Davidson, eds., *Climate Change 2001: Mitigation,* Contribution of Working Group III to the Third Assessment Report of the IPCC (Cambridge: Cambridge University Press, 2001).

3. Although energy is critical to climate protection, Kyoto is not an "energy treaty" per se—the targets cover six major greenhouse gases (including carbon dioxide), as well as absorptions of carbon dioxide from certain land-use change and forestry activities.

4. In place of the Kyoto Protocol, the Bush administration formulated a voluntary greenhouse gas intensity reduction target. This target will, according to the government's

own economic forecasts, result in a 14 percent increase in emissions over the next decade, approximately the level of increase in the 1990s. The Bush administration has also offered potentially fruitful technology development initiatives, discussed in the final section of the chapter.

5. To enter into force, the protocol must be ratified by no fewer than 55 countries, accounting for at least 55 percent of industrialized (Annex I) country emissions in 1990. Although more than 120 countries have ratified the agreement, these countries account for less than 55 percent of industrialized-country emissions. Without ratification from the United States (36.1 percent) or Russia (17.4 percent), entry into force is impossible.

6. "Putin Says Moscow Moving Towards Backing Kyoto," Reuters, May 21, 2004.

7. "Russian Government Approves Kyoto, Sends to Parliament," Reuters, September 30, 2004.

8. The Kyoto Protocol is, literally speaking, a global accord. It is open to all countries, including developing countries (most of which have ratified the pact). It is with respect to emission limitations and other obligations that the protocol is understood to be "not global."

9. According to the range of models included in the IPCC Third Assessment Report, estimates of U.S. costs for complying with its Kyoto target (7 percent reduction below 1990 levels) range from 0 to 2 percent of GDP in 2010. With emissions trading among Annex I countries, the maximum compliance cost estimate is 1 percent of GDP.

10. White House Initial Climate Change Review, February 2002, available at http://www.whitehouse.gov/news/releases/2001/06/climatechange.pdf.

11. R. B. Stewart and J. B. Wiener, *Reconstructing Climate Policy: Beyond Kyoto (Summary)* (Washington, D.C.: AEI Press, 2003), 2.

12. A useful summary by the Pew Center on Global Climate Change, as well as fact sheets discussing various economic analyses of the bill, can be found at http://www.pewclimate.org/policy_center/analyses/.

13. E.g., according to the U.S. Energy Information Administration (EIA), emissions in China in 2020 are projected to be between 38 and 131 percent above 2000 levels, depending on economic growth and other assumptions. EIA, *International Energy Outlook 2003* (Washington, D.C.: EIA, 2003). Forecasting problems are less acute for mature, industrial economies.

14. H. Winkler et al., "Sustainable Development Policies and Measures," in *Building on the Kyoto Protocol: Options for Protecting the Climate,* ed. Kevin Baumert (Washington, D.C.: World Resources Institute, 2002), 62–67.

15. Stewart and Wiener, *Reconstructing Climate Policy.*

16. M. Grubb and R. Stewart, "Promoting Climate-Friendly Technologies: International Perspectives and Issues," introductory paper presented at the INTACT High-Level Transatlantic Dialogue on Climate Change, Villa Vigoni, Italy, October 2003.

# 21

# Building Strategic Reserves

## David L. Goldwyn and Michelle Billig

Since the United States created the Strategic Petroleum Reserve (SPR) in 1975, the oil market has become more globalized, the threats to U.S. energy supplies have changed, the level of U.S. and world demand has grown, and the adequacy of government and commercial oil reserves has diminished. U.S. strategy has not evolved to meet these challenges. The size of the SPR and the ad hoc policy for utilizing it have remained unchanged. The SPR can be a powerful tool to ensure U.S. energy security, but only if there are the will and the means to modernize and wield it effectively. In this chapter, we describe the origins of U.S. strategic reserve policy, how new threats and new economic realities have outpaced U.S. energy policy, and how U.S. policy has handicapped effective use of the SPR. In concluding, we propose a new policy for the management of U.S. and global strategic stocks.

### The Evolution of U.S. Strategic Reserve Policy

The 1973–74 Arab oil embargo targeted at the United States and the Netherlands created a physical shortage of crude oil that could not be replaced from other sources.[1] The United States acted to secure itself against another embargo by creating its own stockpile of crude oil and forging a multilateral coalition of consuming countries to maintain and share additional strategic stocks.

In 1975, Congress passed the Energy Policy and Conservation Act,[2] which created the SPR. The SPR was designed to equip the United States with enough oil to temporarily replace oil imports for ninety days in the event of a major disruption, particularly in the Middle East. The rules for

509

tapping the SPR were restrictive.[3] To create a defensive coalition that could share the burden of overcoming an embargo, U.S. secretary of state Henry Kissinger led the formation of the International Energy Agency (IEA).[4] Upon its inception, the IEA agreed to an emergency response policy. Each member committed to hold ninety days of import cover in stock, either in government stocks or government mandated, but privately held stocks. Members agreed only to draw on these stocks by consensus and committed to an oil-sharing policy. If one member suffered a shortage of more than 7 percent of its prior year's oil imports (as both the United States and the Netherlands had during the 1973–74 embargo), other countries would share their oil with the ally in need.[5]

Economic reality quickly overwhelmed this system. By 1979, it was apparent that a physical shortage of less than 7 percent could cause severe economic damage. The sharing mechanism was too complicated. The supply interruptions that resulted from the Iranian revolution in 1979 and then the start of the Iran-Iraq war drove prices to $39 a barrel in the early 1980s. Global consumption exceeded production by almost 2 million barrels per day (mmbpd). The IEA made a fleeting attempt at using collective demand restraint to provide liquidity. The IEA's Governing Board adopted a policy whereby each member would agree to restrict its oil imports to 5 percent less than its prior year's imports to create a cushion of supply. However, countries proved unwilling to suffer economic pain for the collective good. When the U.S. East Coast endured a heating oil shortage in the winter of 1979, the United States used federal subsidy programs to outbid Europe for heating oil supply. [6]

The price shocks of 1979 persuaded U.S. energy and IEA officials that a system of stock sharing was politically insupportable. A new policy of coordinated drawdown of oil stocks by individual countries was devised, to address price and supply shocks. From 1979 on, IEA members agreed to consult in the event of an oil disruption and to coordinate the release of their strategic stocks.

With respect to the SPR itself, U.S. congressional politics and the high cost of oil complicated efforts to fill the reserve. When the Energy Policy and Conservation Act was first enacted, the legislation set a policy goal of 1 billion barrels of oil. In the early 1980s, a government report concluded that storage of more than 750 million barrels would be economically inefficient.[7] In 1975, ninety days of import replacement would have equaled close to 500 million barrels in storage. The SPR did not reach the level of 500 million barrels until 1986.

Today, the SPR contains more than 670 million barrels, barely enough for sixty days of import cover if the United States relied exclusively on strategic stocks.[8] In the wake of the terrorist attacks on September 11, 2001, the George W. Bush administration committed to fill the SPR to the maximum level of 700 million barrels. At the current delivery rate, the reserve will be filled by 2005. But at the current level of oil demand, even a reserve of 700 million barrels will provide the United States with only two months of import cover from strategic stocks.[9] The United States can rely on commercial stocks to meet its commitments on minimum reserves to the IEA. But with no legal minimum for maintenance of commercial stocks, U.S. energy security rests on an uncertain platform.

## Historical Uses of the SPR

The SPR has only been drawn down once in its history, to avert a potential oil shortage on the eve of the first Gulf War. However SPR oil has been sold and exchanged several times for a variety of reasons, including test sales to check SPR facilities and sales to generate revenue for the federal budget.[10] Over time, U.S. officials have been willing, on occasion, to manage the SPR to moderate short-term supply disruptions. Many of these steps have been time exchanges, or swaps, where the SPR puts crude oil on the market in exchange for repayment of the oil (usually of a greater quantity) at a later time. A brief survey of historical practices reveals that while the authority and ability to use the SPR has grown, the U.S. government's willingness to use the reserves has varied broadly from administration to administration.

### Responses to War

The 1990 Iraqi invasion of Kuwait illustrated the challenge of using the SPR effectively. The global economy suffered a major price shock when Iraq first invaded Kuwait in August 1990. Prices jumped from $15 to $33 West Texas Intermediate (WTI) with the loss of Kuwaiti oil and, due to the UN embargo, the subsequent loss of Iraqi supply as well. Saudi Arabia scrambled to tap its excess capacity and replace the lost oil, but the time lag to ramp up production and deliver oil to Western markets was significant. U.S. policymakers debated whether to tap the reserve for almost a year, with no one driving the process to a decision. Treasury and State Department officials, attuned to Saudi sensibilities about a drop in oil prices, opposed the market interference while National Security Council and Energy Department officials lobbied to provide the U.S. market with security and liquidity. Policymakers finally agreed to a drawdown of 33.75 million barrels to be announced on the eve of Operation Desert Storm. Although White House officials feared that prices would spike drastically over concerns that Iraq might retaliate against Saudi Arabia and an extended war, only 17.2 million barrels were drawn as markets quickly perceived that the war would be brief and that Saudi oil supplies were not in danger. The Gulf War drawdown was a case of too little, too late. By the time of the emergency drawdown, the United States was mired in a deep recession.

The 1991 drawdown created the expectation that the United States would authorize a similar draw down when faced with a comparable supply threat. That did not turn out to be the case. In March 2003, with oil prices near $34 WTI, global excess capacity at 1.5 to 2 mmbpd, and U.S. crude oil and product inventories at record lows, the United States faced a decision on whether to release oil from the SPR. Global oil supplies were already tight because of the political crisis and strike in Venezuela that took almost 3 mmbpd of oil off the market. A U.S. invasion of Iraq was imminent, and possible missile attacks were feared against Saudi Arabia or Kuwait as in 1991. Oil traders expected a repeat of the 1991 decision and declined to buy inventories for fear of being caught short if SPR oil was released. Unlike National Security Council decisions, there was no regularized or transparent process for decision making. In the end, the George H. W. Bush administration declined to tap the reserve. The administration believed it was more prudent to save all available reserves in case the United States faced a catastrophic terrorist attack on itself or on Saudi Arabia. Yet its decision confused the market, which had anticipated an SPR release, and delayed commercial transactions to replace disrupted supply, ultimately pushing up prices.

### Temporary Disruptions

Congress approved additional drawdown authority in 1990, which increased the president's flexibility to use the SPR for more limited supply interruptions following West Coast supply interruptions associated with the Exxon Valdez Alaskan oil spill in 1989.[11] The provisions authorize a limited drawdown without a declaration of a severe energy shortage or the need to meet IEA obligations.[12]

After ice blockages prevented deliveries of heating oil to New York and Connecticut by barge or truck in the winter of 1999, President Bill Clinton authorized a swap in February 2000 to create a Northeast Heating Oil Reserve. He authorized another swap in September 2000 to address another anticipated shortage in heating oil supplies. In early 2000, oil and product prices skyrocketed and refiners drew down low-cost inventories rather than purchase new supplies at higher prices. In September 2000, the low inventories combined with a severe winter forecast and scheduled refinery maintenance to keep oil prices high. Marginal supply increases by the Organization of Petroleum Exporting Countries (OPEC) were insufficient to reassure the market. On September 22, 2000, Clinton directed Energy Secretary Bill Richardson to conduct an SPR swap of 30 million barrels, to provide the liquidity that would allow refiners to build stocks to refine heating oil. The decision triggered mixed reaction. Within two weeks of the swap award, crude prices dropped from $37 to $31 a barrel. At the same time, critics argued that using the SPR to address the U.S. heating oil market would be ineffective and that the arbitrage window would pull crude to Europe where product prices were higher.[13] Furthermore, the initial award had difficulties when two of the offers could not provide financial guarantees. Tight market conditions prompted the Department of Energy to delay deliveries into 2002 and 2003 in exchange for more oil.[14] The unconventional nature of the swap and subsequent price drop triggered partisan speculation that the swap was a political move to bolster the Democrats before the 2000 presidential elections.

Most recently, President George W. Bush used the SPR in 2002 and 2004 to address logistical issues associated with Gulf Coast hurricanes.[15] All these cases would have suggested a willingness to provide short-term liquidity to the market during a significant, but temporary, disruption. Yet in the winter of 2002–3, when a strike in Venezuela left U.S. refiners geared to accepting Venezuelan crudes short of supply, the Bush administration declined to use the reserve. Refiners petitioned for short-term releases of comparable grades of crude oil to replace Venezuelan crude. The administration refused, and the U.S. wholesale price of gasoline and heating oil spiked to more than double their 2002 levels. U.S. policy for using the SPR to address temporary disruptions therefore remains uncertain.

## New Realities, New Threats

In the three decades since the SPR was first created, the nature of the oil markets and the threats to U.S. energy security have changed dramatically.

Though less reliant on OPEC (which supplied 55 percent of global oil production in 1973, vs. 38 percent today), the United States is increasingly reliant on a larger, far less stable set of countries, where economic and social instability is on the rise.[16] The unpredictable nature of these suppliers creates uncertainty in the oil market and increases the volatility of oil prices. Oil supplies are global not regional; a supply disruption anywhere is a price increase everywhere.

*Price volatility.* Price swings rather than supply shortages characterize the current market. Prices fluctuated from $10 to $30 WTI in 1998-2000, and from $20 to $55 WTI in 2002–5. Volatility creates price shocks across the U.S. economy through high gasoline, heating oil, jet fuel, or natural gas prices. Price volatility works in both directions, but the current market climate encourages bias toward higher prices. The impact on developing-world economies that subsidize energy prices—and on those nations that rely on the United States as an export market—can be more severe. When oil supply is interrupted, wealthy nations can usually find supplies by outbidding less wealthy nations. In the winter of 2003 when Venezuela, a top supplier to the United States, nearly ceased all oil production due to a crippling strike, the United States was able to locate replacement supply within a few days. But the supply it mustered came at a higher price. Though the United States has insulated itself from price shocks, its economy is not yet immune. For the United States, price shocks are the modern threat to energy and economic security.

*Market speculation.* The growth of futures trading has increased price volatility and added a powerful, nonsovereign factor into oil disruption response. Market psychology plays a powerful role, because most trades are speculative and do not result in physical delivery of oil. Close to 240 mmbpd in paper are now traded on the International Petroleum Exchange in London alone,[17] three times the amount consumed globally. The volume of trade magnifies the impact of supply and price changes. It can drive prices higher, when fear leads speculators to bid up contracts for future delivery to hedge against high prices. This volume also makes the SPR a force multiplier, making an impact on the market with a power greater than the amount of barrels released by signaling that replacement volumes will limit the impact of a particular disruption.

*Spare capacity.* The most important and destabilizing new threat to energy security today is that spare production capacity by energy-producing nations has not kept pace with the growth in demand. By October 2004, with oil prices over $55 WTI (in 2004 dollars), OPEC excess capacity was barely

1 mmbpd, just 1 percent of global supply.[18] As a result, there has been little additional supply commercially available to respond to supply disruptions. Maintaining excess capacity is costly; a country must spend billions of dollars to keep oil in the ground but have it ready to be brought swiftly to market. Most developing nations, indeed all non-OPEC nations, sell all they produce internally or for export. U.S. companies do the same, to maximize shareholder value. The burden of maintaining excess capacity has long been borne by OPEC, but OPEC has not made the investment in capacity to meet rising demand or provide adequate excess capacity.[19]

*Commercial inventories.* Due to industry restructuring and cost cutting measures, oil inventories held by private companies have also not kept pace with the increase in oil demand. Today's privately held inventories make up less than half of total U.S. crude oil reserves and account for less than two months of import protection,[20] which is significantly lower than the four months of protection they provided in 1975. U.S. oil companies are not required to maintain inventories and do not have the independent ability to provide emergency oil and product supplies to the United States in the event of an oil disruption.

The size of privately held stocks also has an impact on price volatility. The price of oil is inversely related to the size of global oil stocks. Low inventories scare traders when political uncertainty arises. If demand and supply are in balance, and private inventories are low, oil traders worry that there will be no commercial reserve capacity to replace the potentially missing supply if the threat of a strike or regime collapse looms. To hedge against a potential shortage, traders buy spot supplies, driving up prices. If privately held stocks are high or if the United States indicates that it will use the SPR to address an emergency, traders and consumers can transparently see where replacement supply will come from. They will not hoard existing supplies or drive up prices out of panic.

*War, internal unrest, and terror.* The greatest disruptions in the oil markets in the past thirty years have come from war, internal unrest, and terror. The largest disruptions on record since the 1973–74 embargo resulted from the Iran–Iraq war, the Iraqi invasion of Kuwait and the first Persian Gulf War, and the Venezuelan strike of 2002–3. In October 2004, commentators widely cited a discrepancy of more than $10 between actual prices and the prices that strict supply and demand fundamentals would suggest as concerns about disruptions in oil-producing countries combined with a shortage of high-quality crude and rising demand for light petroleum products to push oil prices to a postwar high over $55 WTI.[21]

The greatest decreases in oil production have followed revolutions. Libyan and Iranian oil production dropped dramatically after each of their national revolts. In 2003, political and social instability in Venezuela and Nigeria disrupted nearly 4 mmbpd of supply, equivalent to 20 percent of total U.S. oil supply. Though isolated incidents may not cause a severe shortage, a combination of disruptions, as experienced in 2002–3 with Venezuela, Iraq, and Nigeria, has the potential to cause a significant rise in the price of oil and products.

The newest threat, likely to remain for the foreseeable future, is terrorism. Terrorist organizations, such as al Qaeda, have begun targeting key oil installations around the world. There have been early indicators of terrorists' desire and ability to disrupt oil supply in Iraq, Yemen, and Saudi Arabia. The attacks on the *USS Cole* signaled the willingness of al Qaeda to target ships at sea. The May 2004 attacks on the Yanbu petrochemical complex and the Khobar residential compound in Saudi Arabia raised market concern that the potential for terrorists to attack Saudi facilities from inside their robust security perimeter was more serious than most experts believed. Terrorism poses a unique challenge to U.S. stockpile management, which historically has focused on the impact of a supply disruption outside the United States. Strategic stocks need to respond to a disruption to energy delivery within the United States as well as abroad. Moreover, U.S. policymakers must evaluate whether it make sense to concentrate the nation's stockpile in one part of the United States, with no significant stockpiles of oil products closer to consumption centers, in an age when pipelines or refineries can be a target of terrorist attack.

## The Power of Strategic Stocks

The existence of strategic stocks has been a powerful deterrent to politically motivated embargoes, an intermittent check on high oil prices, and a counterweight to OPEC's control of the market. The ability of a nation to release oil gives it the power to deflate prices and have a negative impact on the revenues of oil-producing nations. It has also created a ceiling for market speculation, when governments show a willingness to use them. Though the size of existing reserve stocks cannot replace the vast reserves of the oil-producing nations, the global nature of the oil market empowers the seller of the marginal barrels of oil to affect the price. Strategic stocks can be a deterrent to price manipulation, but only if the use of these stocks is a credible threat.

The threat of an SPR draw can help elicit production increases from OPEC, which stands to lose revenue if an SPR draw collapses artificially high prices. In September 2000, low oil inventories, a severe winter forecast, and scheduled refinery maintenance boosted oil prices to $37 WTI (in 2000 dollars). Energy diplomacy by Secretary of Energy Bill Richardson to encourage increased production was backed by the implicit threat of an SPR release. Diplomacy may have helped motivate OPEC producers to modestly increase production several times during the year. The expectation of an SPR release in March 2003 before the U.S. invasion of Iraq (mirroring the SPR release just before Operation Desert Storm), together with self-interest in revenue maximization, helped prompt Saudi Arabia to increase oil production by close to 1 mmbpd. The extra oil helped moderate the nearly $38 price spike that resulted from prewar speculation.

The power of strategic stocks is the power to self-insure against an oil disruption, or the abuse of monopoly power by OPEC, rather than rely solely on the ability of others to maintain and use spare production capacity. U.S. analysts must look carefully at the adequacy of strategic stocks when the other two legs of the country's security triad—commercial stocks and commercial excess capacity—are so weak. Private spare capacity has not kept pace with the growth in demand, and nearly 100 percent of the world's excess capacity, which is itself at modest levels, rests in Saudi Arabia, Kuwait, and the United Arab Emirates.[22] If Nigeria, Venezuela, or in the worst case, Saudi Arabia ceases production, the market faces three options: (1) suffer higher prices, (2) seek relief from countries that have excess capacity, or (3) draw down strategic stocks.

Some analysts argue that OPEC's modest levels of excess capacity are a temporary phenomenon because it has invested in spare capacity in the past and demonstrated a willingness to use it to try to calm markets. Other analysts question OPEC's willingness and ability to maintain adequate capacity in the future. Edward Morse and Amy Jaffe touch upon this in chapter 3 of this volume when they discuss whether Saudi Arabia has shifted from a policy of price moderation to revenue maximization. Press reports suggest that the elevated security threat in Saudi Arabia and the potential for disruption of Saudi supplies may also limit its ability to significantly increase capacity.[23] In addition, the failure of OPEC suppliers to adequately invest in excess capacity sufficient to meet global demand could become an ongoing problem. In chapter 1, Adam Sieminski notes the historic decline in investment and productive capacity by OPEC nations.

For the United States to insure itself adequately, it must examine how large a strategic reserve it needs, whether global strategic reserves are enough to satisfy global demand, and whether it is willing to use the reserve in a way that will adequately protect its economy against a major price shock.

## A New Policy Is Needed

The strategy of the 1970s can no longer adequately protect the United States. The size of U.S. and global reserves is insufficient, and its policy for utilizing the stocks has not kept pace with market changes. Strategic stockpiles cannot deter today's supply threats, only mitigate their ability to increase oil price volatility.

At its current size, the SPR will soon be too small (figure 21.1). When the SPR was created in 1975, the reserve target was set at 500 million barrels, the United States imported less than one-third of its total supply, and the reserve provided the United States with enough oil to cover close to ninety days worth of oil imports.[24] Today, when the United States imports nearly 12 million barrels of total petroleum products, more than 60 percent of its total supply and the SPR can barely provide sixty days of import replacement and thirty days of supply protection.[25] The amount of product import protection will become increasingly important as U.S. demand for gasoline and heating oil continues to outpace domestic refining capacity and as future supply disruptions increasingly threaten product imports. For example, the December 2002 general strike in Venezuela disrupted both crude and product exports to the United States—1.2 mmbpd of crude imports and 400,000 barrels per day of product imports.[26] It is likely that in the future the SPR will be needed to respond to a disruption of both oil and product imports.

The criteria and policy mechanism for deciding whether to draw down the SPR are also ineffective. SPR policy does not take into account the psychological dimensions of an oil disruption. In a globalized market, the United States will never see a physical shortage. It has seen and will continue to see major price shocks. The expectation of an SPR decision can have as much of an impact as the actual SPR decision. If producers anticipate that an SPR release will occur, they will postpone taking actions to add more supply to the market and exacerbate the existing supply shortage, push-

Figure 21.1. U.S. Strategic Protection Reserve (SPR) and Import Coverage, 1975–2010 (millions of barrels)

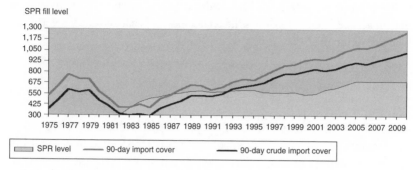

*Note:* Data for 2005–10 are estimates.
*Source:* U.S. Energy Information Administration.

ing prices even higher. Conversely, the expectation that the SPR will not be released can escalate fear of a shortage, resulting in rampant speculation and severe price spikes.

SPR policy does not consider the possibility of short-term geographical disruptions. Though oil is a globally traded commodity, regional markets have emerged to take advantage of geographical synergies. The importance of regional markets was apparent during the Venezuela disruption in December 2002, which had a disproportionate impact on the U.S. market. If the United States suffers a disruption from one of its short-haul suppliers— such as Canada, Mexico, and Venezuela, which are located in the Western Hemisphere—replacement supplies can take up to forty-five days to arrive. It can take several weeks for the market to adjust and bid supplies away from other consumers in Europe and Asia. In the interim, the world economy is forced to absorb the loss of supply through higher prices. The SPR could be used as a transitional measure to bridge supply until additional supplies can reach the market.

Finally, there is no formal process for making SPR decisions, and no clear guidelines or indicators govern the use of the SPR. Precedents carry little weight. The lack of transparency adds to market speculation and exacerbates the supply and price volatility during a crisis. There needs to be a more coordinated and transparent process.

History has shown that the United States has largely failed to tap the SPR to protect American consumers from price shocks, despite its power to do so. The greatest source of this failure is that U.S. policymakers have failed to interpret the Energy Policy and Conservation Act to account for the modern oil market or, if need be, update the law to provide the discretion they need. A collateral reason is the ad hoc process that currently determines whether to tap the SPR.

## A New Policy for Managing Strategic Reserves

The United States and its allies are facing a uniquely vulnerable period. Without a major shift in transportation policy, by 2020 the United States will still use oil for 40 percent of its energy consumption. By that time, the United States is projected to import 65 percent of its crude oil needs and OPEC is expected to control 45 percent of world oil production.[27] At a projected consumption of 27 mmbpd in 2020, and crude oil imports of 17.6 mmbpd, even a billion-barrel SPR will provide only fifty-seven days of crude import cover.

Unless the United States and other nations expand their reserves, and demonstrate a willingness to deploy strategic reserves to combat an intentional or inadvertent price shock, they will continue to buy their economic life insurance policy from OPEC. Five steps are required.

First, the United States must fill the SPR to capacity, evaluate the optimal size for additional reserves, and, in the interim, return to the idea of maintaining ninety days of import cover.

Second, the United States must motivate companies operating in the country to maintain above minimum stocks of crude oil and products to create a distributed network of energy reserves.

Third, the United States must empower the secretary of energy to recommend SPR decisions directly to the president, which the president may accept or refuse, but which proceeds through a coordinated and transparent process that cannot be stalled by staff resistance.

Fourth, the U.S. secretary of energy must be empowered to manage the SPR, on his or her own authority, to address short-term disruptions with significant price effects.

Fifth, the United States and its allies must help modernize global oil reserves by promoting the development of strategic stocks in non-IEA consuming countries, and by creating a self-financing global oil reserve to address the consumption demands of nations with no access to strategic stocks.

## Filling the SPR

The United States needs a two-tiered approach—filling the existing SPR to its capacity of 700 million barrels and constructing additional facilities. Policymakers should evaluate the optimal size of additional reserve capacity and in the interim return to the original policy goal of ninety days of import cover. Supplying the SPR with ninety days of import cover by 2010 will require increasing the SPR to at least 1 billion barrels, and the United States must therefore initially develop plans for an additional 300-million-barrel reserve. The plans should consider the need for reserve capacity outside the Gulf Coast (in California or the East Coast) to ensure access to emergency supplies should the Gulf Coast be cut off by a terrorist attack or other catastrophic event. An interim plan could be to use the unused existing storage at private facilities.

The cost of building and filling a supplemental reserve is considerable. Experts project construction costs at $1.5 billion,[28] and financing would need to come from Congress. The House of Representatives authorized such an appropriation in the 2003 Energy Bill, which stalled in the Senate in November 2003. At an average price of $30 WTI, filling an additional reserve of 300 million barrels would cost $9 billion. If global oil prices are sustained at the $40 mark, the costs would be even higher. However, the oil acquisition could be financed through the current royalty-in-kind program, whereby producers pay a portion of government royalties in oil rather than cash. Though the royalty oil results in lost revenue, it eliminates the need for congressional appropriations.

When filling the SPR, the government must avoid pushing up prices when supplies are tight. It needs to develop a flexible fill policy that does not put upward pressure on prices in a tight market. Companies should be offered the opportunity to suspend deliveries when there is steep backwardation (i.e., when prices for future deliveries are progressively lower) for a prolonged period of time or when prices hover over a determined level and encouraged to fill when prices are in contango (i.e., when prices for future deliveries are progressively higher). This will extend the length of time required to reach the 700-million-barrel mark, but it will avoid driving current prices higher.

The costs implied here are considerable. The alternative is reliance on pure market responses, which are not always immediate or forthcoming. The benefits of enhanced energy security are high. An expanded reserve and rational fill policy will demonstrate U.S. willingness and ability to address oil shocks, creating a notional ceiling for oil speculation. Without this policy, price spikes will become even more extreme, as demonstrated by the $20 oil price rise between November 2003 and October 2004. A sustained $10 increase in oil price cuts global gross domestic product by at least half a percent, equivalent to a net loss of $255 billion worldwide.[29]

### Motivate Companies to Hold Above-Minimum Stock Levels

During the past thirty years, companies have reduced the amount of oil they keep in storage, relative to demand. There is little market incentive for oil refiners and marketers to maintain high levels of inventory, especially in a high-price environment when it is profitable to sell oil but not cost-effective to stockpile it. Low inventories pose a serious challenge to maintaining a supply cushion in the event of a severe oil disruption and put added pressure on prices when oil traders perceive a shortage in replacement supplies.

Under these circumstances, we should encourage companies to maintain a sufficient level of crude oil and products to respond to disruptions. The incentives should be flexible and designed to prevent a dangerous decline in U.S. oil inventories, while minimizing the economic burden on private companies. Tax credits could be offered to offset part of the cost of additional stocks and capacity. Maintaining inventory is expensive. The U.S. Energy Information Administration (EIA) estimates the cost of oil storage at between $1.50 and $4 per barrel.[30] Using these estimates, the maintenance cost for U.S. commercial oil stocks in 2003 totaled between $400 million and $1 billion.[31]

Responding to a terrorist attack poses a unique challenge to U.S. stockpile management, which historically has focused on the impact of a supply disruption outside the United States. Because a majority of the U.S. reserves are located on the Gulf Coast (including the SPR), policymakers could use private inventories to create a distributed network of oil products to supply consumers across the country in the event of a terrorist attack on pipelines and refineries. Additional tax credits or other incentives could be offered to companies that keep inventories in sales markets outside the Gulf Coast.

### Improving the Decision-Making Process

The SPR decision-making process is opaque, complex, and ad hoc. The lack of oversight and structure encourages interference from political and bureaucratic interests within the White House and subordinates the technical merits of a decision. There is no schedule or automatic trigger to launch an SPR debate or decision. The market is left to speculate as to when and how an SPR decision will be taken. The situation confuses the market and increases price volatility. We must establish a direct and transparent process for SPR decisions that empowers the secretary of energy to make direct recommendations to the president.

We must clearly identify the decision makers and the decision points. We should create an SPR committee chaired by the secretary of energy with participation from Treasury, Interior, and the National Economic Council to create both responsibility and accountability for SPR decisions. This committee would be tasked with evaluating the need for a drawdown in response to a supply emergency or in anticipation of a supply disruption. If needed, the SPR committee would provide a single recommendation to the president. The secretary of energy would have the authority to convene the SPR committee whenever domestic or international events threatened oil supplies. The SPR committee would not have regular scheduled meetings. However, the Department of Energy would advise the public when a meeting was scheduled. Convening an SPR committee meeting would act as an indicator that an SPR decision was imminent and minimize market speculation.

The SPR committee meetings would function in a manner similar to the Federal Reserve's Open Market Committee Meetings. They would be closed to the public but set clear parameters. In certain cases, SPR committee decisions would require presidential approval. In those situations, the public would be informed that a recommendation has been forwarded to the president for action, and the president would commit to accept or reject the recommendation immediately. The committee's recommendation would be kept under wraps, but the presidential decision would be made public.

## Addressing Short-Term Disruptions with Significant Price Effects

With increased liquidity in the oil market, price swings have replaced physical shortages and psychological reactions have magnified supply imbalances. This "wait and see" approach unnecessarily damages U.S. refiners and consumers. The country needs a flexible SPR policy, which allows the secretary of energy to use the SPR to respond to a short-term disruption and prevent major price spikes from subsequent speculation.

U.S. policymakers should use the limited drawdown authority as the basis for a new policy approach. In 1991, Congress authorized the president to use the SPR for a short period of time without having to declare a severe oil interruption or meet international obligations. The president can draw down up to 30 million barrels over a two-month period.[32] However, the authority has never been formally used. Policymakers should expand the limited drawdown authority to the secretary of energy and create specific guidelines for its use.

The secretary of energy should be permitted to use the SPR to prevent or redress a short-term disruption in U.S. or global oil supplies, which could result from a set of circumstances including war, internal unrest, and terrorism, or from related market speculation. The decision would take into account the projected shortage as well as current and future price curves. There would be no automatic price trigger, but the decision would be based on specific indicators such as price spreads, arbitrage windows, and inventory numbers. Special consideration should be given to regional disruptions when interim supply is needed to balance the market until long-haul supplies can replace the missing short-haul supplies.[33]

In determining whether a limited drawdown is appropriated, the secretary of energy would convene an SPR committee meeting, but his decision should not require presidential approval.[34] Some will argue that the use of the SPR for such disruptions will increase volatility as futures traders anticipate and hedge against SPR decisions. But restricting swaps to relief for real disruptions will moderate price escalations from panic buying and ameliorate economic dislocations rather than enduring them. Use of the SPR to counter disruptions will also introduce some downside risk to the market when a disruption occurs. Renouncing use of the SPR for anything less than a catastrophic attack on the United States signals that there is no ceiling to the prices the United States will suffer if a supply disruption occurs, or if OPEC refuses to use its spare capacity.

### Modernizing Global Reserves

The United States and its allies cannot protect themselves from the economic impact of supply disruptions if the countries that belong to the Organization for Economic Cooperation and Development are the only consuming nations with strategic reserves. Oil consumption in the developing world, led by China and India, is already growing faster than in the industrial world. In recent months, China has stepped up its efforts to develop government reserves. According to press reports, the Chinese government has identified four to six coastal storage facilities that will hold up to 50 million tons (350 million barrels) of oil. A recent Deutsche Bank report estimates that China will need to stockpile at a 100,000-barrels-per-day rate to reach thirty days of import cover (75 million barrels) by 2005 and fifty days of import cover (165 million barrels) by 2010.[35] Similarly, in January 2004, India's cabinet approved the construction of strategic oil reserves at three coastal locations. Once constructed, the emergency reserves will hold 5 million metric tons of crude oil (37 million barrels), equivalent to fifteen days worth of oil demand.[36] Though recent developments demonstrate good faith efforts, few other developing nations have started holding significant strategic reserves to date. To complicate matters, political uncertainty and market obstacles have delayed Russia's plans to increase its proven reserves. This leaves Saudi Arabia as the only oil producer with significant spare capacity.

## A Global Strategic Petroleum Reserve

We recommend that the IEA encourage an effort to create a global strategic petroleum reserve (GSPR) adequate to supply developing Asia with sixty days of supply. Estimating regional demand at 12.5 mmbpd, a GSPR of 750 million barrels would be needed—equal to another U.S. SPR at full capacity. At $35 per barrel, this would require financing of $26.25 billion.

The IEA, the United States, and other Group of Seven nations could finance the construction of a GSPR, with contributions of cash or oil. It should be run under IEA rules—tapping the reserve only when a significant supply emergency occurs—and managed by an independent organization. The reserve should be self-financed. The organization should sell drawing rights to nations, allowing them to finance the cost of the oil, but avoiding the need for many nations to build expensive tankage.

As a purely economic matter, the reserve could be located close to consumption centers. In a global market, a release of crude in the Gulf Coast in the event of a crisis could facilitate swaps on the market that would deliver the needed crude to Asia from shipments on the high seas. The United States could double its current, relatively inexpensive, salt cavern storage and house the SPR in the United States, much as it provides land for the United Nations. As a political matter, nations may want to see a reserve closer to Asia. The Department of Energy's efforts to lease space in the SPR to other nations have failed to draw interest for more than two decades. One or more reserves could be built on abandoned military bases, such as in the Philippines, or in salt caverns in other countries.

A GSPR would have six main benefits. First, it would allow consuming nations to provide their own economic insurance in the event of a crisis. Second, it would provide a powerful long-term counterweight to OPEC's power. If OPEC failed to provide enough supply to the market in the event of a war or crisis, nations would have the option of self-help. Third, it would ensure respect for market principles. There is no guarantee that other nations, particularly China, would not build reserves and use them to intervene in the markets purely to manipulate prices.

Fourth, a GSPR would provide a real near-term remedy. China is at the beginning of a long-term process of building strategic reserves. Other countries have failed to build significant storage because it is very expensive. By leading the construction of a reserve, the United States would assert global leadership in providing others with economic security. China and India need an incentive to respect market principles and make common cause with the United States to seek stability in the Middle East and elsewhere. Offering these nations an energy security umbrella could be a powerful incentive to collaborate with the United States and resist the urge to compete or pursue bilateral policies. Through this mechanism, the United States could "sponsor" China or India's membership in the IEA.[37] Fifth, the reserve could be filled over time, and used as an incentive to promote transparency in oil producing nations. While it would be economic to fill the reserve with oil from the lowest cost provider, there are other choices. GSPR oil providers could be restricted to nations that agreed to publish their aggregate oil revenues and public expenditures, nations that welcomed foreign investment, or both.

Sixth and finally, a GSPR need not be offensive to OPEC. An offer to buy supply for a new reserve would be an incentive for nations belonging to OPEC such as Nigeria and Algeria to increase their investment above existing quotas and for nations such as Mexico, Angola, and Russia to seek to ramp up production. A GSPR could provide a haven for new production without raising fears of a major drop in price levels. Another option would be to fill a GSPR with nonconventional oil. A global pact to invest in oil sands in Canada and heavy oil in Venezuela, with all production committed to the GSPR, could spur new production and commercialize nonconventional oils.

## Conclusion

Strategic reserves are a powerful weapon for ensuring price stability, countering OPEC's power, and extending the reach of American political influence by providing security to other cooperating nations. To wield this powerful tool effectively, the United States must ensure that the reserves are large enough to be effective and that the country's leaders and policymakers have the skill and the will to use them when needed. We believe the recommendations offered here provide a path to strengthening and projecting that economic power.

## Notes

1. The Netherlands was targeted because of its support for Israel in the 1973 Arab-Israeli War and Rotterdam's role as a primary transit point for crude imports into Northern Europe.

2. Public Law 94-163, S 622 (Jackson), introduced February 7, 1975, reported from the Senate Committee on Interior and Insular Affairs with Amendment, S Rept. 94-26, and passed the Senate and House on December 18, 1975. Signed into law on December 22, 1975.

3. Only the president can authorize the drawdown of the SPR. The Energy Policy and Conservation Act specifies that the SPR could be tapped to counter "severe energy supply interruption," honor energy-sharing agreements with other International Energy Agency members, and respond to price hikes that can have "a major adverse impact" on the U.S. economy.

4. William Martin and Evan Haarje provide a colorful and detailed history of this evolution in chapter 4 of this volume.

5. Terrence Fehner and Jack M. Hall, "Department of Energy 1977–1994: A Summary History," and Alice Buck and Roger Anders, "Institutional Origins of the Department of Energy" in *The Department of Energy: 25 Years of Service*, ed. Charles Oldham (Tampa: Faircount, Government Services Group, 2002), 24–49.

6. In a meeting at the IEA in Paris, the Japanese ambassador to the Organization for Economic Cooperation and Development (OECD) advised U.S. assistant secretary of energy Les Goldman and Belgium's OECD ambassador Stevie Davignon that Japan planned to make a large purchase, above its prior-year quota, to build its reserves. Davignon cautioned him that if Japan proceeded they could forget about selling their cars in Europe.

7. Robert Bamberger, *Issue Brief for Congress: Strategic Petroleum Reserve* (Washington, D.C.: Congressional Research Service, 2003), 16.

8. U.S. Department of Energy, Office of Fossil Energy home page, http://fossil .energy.gov:7778/programs/reserves/spr/spr-facts.shtml.

9. According to the Energy Information Administration (EIA), imports of crude oil in 2005 will equal 10.29 million barrels per day; http://www.eia.doe.gov/oiaf/aeo/pdf/appd.pdf.

10. President Clinton authorized three SPR sales in 1996 to finance the fiscal budget.

11. Bamberger, *Issue Brief for Congress*, 3.

12. Public Law 101-383, S.2088 (Johnston). Introduced February 7, 1990. referred to the Committee on Energy and Natural Resources March 6, 1990. Passed by the Senate and House September 14, 1990. Signed into law September 15, 1990.

13. Bamberger, *Issue Brief for Congress*, 8–9.

14. Office of Fossil Energy, *Strategic Petroleum Reserves: Releasing Oil from the SPR*, available at http://www.energy.gov.

15. Office of Fossil Energy, *Strategic Petroleum Reserves: Frequently Asked Questions*, available at http://www.energy.gov.

16. According to the IEA, non-OECD countries accounted for 60 percent of production growth from 1971 to 2000 and are expected to account for almost all production growth from 2000 to 2030.

17. *Oil Daily*, October 10, 2003.

18. According to the EIA, surplus capacity in September 2004 was between 0.5 and 1.0 million barrels per day. EIA, *Short-Term Energy Outlook: October 2004*, available at http://www.eia.doe.gov.

19. See Adam Sieminski's projections of OPEC capacity in chapter 1 of this volume and Morse and Jaffe's analysis in chapter 3.

20. According to the EIA, 2003 ending stocks of private crude oil and gasoline equaled 478 million barrels. In 1975, private crude oil and gasoline stocks totaled 506 million barrels. U.S. Department of Energy, *US Monthly Stocks of Crude Oil and Petroleum Products*, available at http://www.eia.doe.gov.

21. Fiona O'Brien and Andrew Mitchell, "OPEC Battles for Control of Oil Price," Reuters, June 2, 2004.

22. The EIA defines excess capacity as the maximum amount of production that could be (1) brought online within a period of thirty days, and (2) sustained for at least ninety days.

23. Supply concerns have led to a premium for sweet crude of as much as $12.50 per barrel over the heavier, sour grades that are more plentiful" from Tim Ahmann. "Greenspan says economy can weather record oil," Reuters, October 16, 2004. Also see coverage of the attacks on Yanbu and Khobar residential complex in Simon Romero, "Attacks Increase Doubts about Saudi Ability to Pump More Oil," *New York Times*, May 31, 2004; Megan K. Stacks, "Fear Enters the Pipeline of Saudi Oil Industry," *Los Angeles Times*, June 5, 2004; and Richard Allen Greene, "Is the Saudi Oil Industry Safe?" BBC News Online, London, May 29–30, 2004.

24. EIA, *Crude Oil Imports (1973–Present)*, http://www.eia.doe.gov.

25. EIA, *Crude Oil Imports (1973–Present)*.

26. EIA, *Crude Oil Imports (1988–Present)*, http://www.eia.doe.gov. The figures are based on imports from Venezuela, the Virgin Islands, and the Netherlands Antilles and calculated using the share of Venezuelan crude used in those countries' refineries.

27. See http://www.eia.doe.gov/oiaf/aeo/aeotab_11.htm.

28. As part of the Energy Policy Act of 2003, the House of Representatives appropriated $1.5 billion for the expansion of the SPR to 1 million barrels. HR 6 (as passed by the House), Sec. 12102, introduced April 7, 2003, and passed by the House on April 11, 2003.

29. International Energy Agency, *Analysis of the Impact of High Oil Prices on the Global Economy* (Paris: International Energy Agency, 2004).

30. EIA, *Why Stocks Are Important*, http://www.eia.doe.gov.

31. At the end of 2003, commercial stocks equaled 268 million barrels. EIA, *Monthly Crude Oil Stocks, 1973–Present (Million Barrels)*, http://www.eia.doe.gov.

32. Bamberger, *Issue Brief for Congress*, 3.

33. E.g., if Saudi Arabia were to increase supplies by 1 mmbpd to replace an oil supply disruption in Latin America, the United States could use the SPR to provide real

supplies in two weeks, and replace that supply in ninety days when Saudi replacement arrived from the Gulf.

34. The Petroleum Industry Research Foundation, Inc. (PRINC), has proposed a similar entity with representatives from the Energy Department, Treasury Department, and the Environmental Protection Agency with authority to approve drawdowns of up to 30 million barrels for no more than sixty days without presidential approval.

35. Deutsche Bank, *Global Energy Wire: Taking Stock of China's Energy Challenges,* December 9, 2003.

36. "India to Build Strategic Oil Reserves This Year," *Asia Business Times,* June 4, 2004.

37. The concept of sponsoring Chinese and Indian membership in the IEA is also suggested by Morse and Jaffe in chapter 3 and by Martin and Haarje in chapter 4.

# 22

# Can a "Global" Natural Gas Market Be Achieved?

## Donald A. Juckett and Michelle Michot Foss

Like it or not, crude oil is an alluring fuel. Crude oil and petroleum products can be moved from the location of supply to that of demand by pipeline, truck, rail, barge, or tanker with great interchangeability. A barrel of crude oil can be disassembled into an array of products that provide both fuel (for everything from heating homes and running factories to powering planes, trains, automobiles, and electricity generation plants) and materials (to create the stuff of everyday life—plastics, fibers, chemicals, etc.). In spite of the presence of the Organization of Petroleum Exporting Countries (OPEC), crude oil is bought and sold in a vast, "liquid" global marketplace.[1]

Given the relative ease of finding new sources of oil (at least to date), the options available for transportation, and the vast global refining and petrochemicals infrastructure used to convert crude oil to usable products, it is no wonder that the United States has come to depend upon this hydrocarbon for so much of its national and international energy security. What will it take for natural gas to achieve something akin to oil's status as a global, fungible energy source?

Natural gas, until recently, has been a poor stepchild to oil. Also a hydrocarbon, often found in association with crude oil and thus historically treated as a by-product of oil production, natural gas—mainly methane, the most stable of hydrocarbons—is poised for much greater penetration of the global energy portfolio. However, fundamental differences exist between these two vital fossil fuels of oil and natural gas and in the style and history of how they have been developed and used. These differences imbue both industry activity and public policymaking, and they are fundamental to any energy security discussion of natural gas as a "global" commodity.

531

*Table 22.1.  Global Energy Investment Requirements (trillions of dollars)*

| Type of Investment | Oil | Natural Gas | Compared with Electric Power |
|---|---|---|---|
| Exploration and production | 2.25 | ˙1.73 | |
| Refining | 0.33 | | |
| Liquefied natural gas | | 0.25 | |
| Pipelines | 0.22 | 0.71 | |
| Power generation | | | 4.20 |
| Power transmission | | | 1.60 |
| Less developed countries | | 0.63 | 4.20 |
| | | (includes storage) | |
| World total | 2.80 | 3.32 | 10.00 |

*Source:* International Energy Agency, *2003 Global Investment Outlook* (Paris, International Energy Agency, 2003).

First, oil and natural gas face common problems worldwide in the distribution of ownership (dominance of sovereign governments), need for investment (see table 22.1), and access for investment (in particular, to facilitate private capital inflows). These constraints have an impact on both resources and related infrastructure so that these fuels can be delivered and used (including electric power generation).

Oil and natural gas resources lie predominantly in the hands of sovereign governments. Sovereign fiscal management and capital deployment related to oil and natural gas resource development have been weak, often politically compromised, and rarely adequate to ensure the long-term sustainability of both sovereign entities and resource production. Though available in many countries, frameworks for foreign direct investment in upstream exploration and production (E&P) often do a poor job of balancing and protecting public and private interests, providing for environmental integrity, and ensuring transparency.

## Gas Challenges and Opportunities

The *first problem* in building a global natural gas scenario lies in the nature of the resource base. Generally, oil and natural gas occur in comparable geologic environments—the same factors conducive to the generation and entrapment of oil resources tend to work for natural gas as well. Some natural gas always exists in solution with oil; if enough "free gas" occurs to form separate pools, then "dry" nonassociated natural gas can be produced. Of particular importance, if substantial associated gas occurs in oil pools and fields and must be produced for oil to be obtained, then natural gas becomes a crucial variable in converting the oil resource to reserves.

If no markets for the natural gas exist or can be developed, then the natural gas is disposed of by flaring or reinjection. The negative environmental and economic consequences of flaring prompted the Global Gas Flaring Reduction initiative,[2] a public–private effort under the auspices of the World Bank. Pressure to reduce flaring means that markets for natural gas must be developed. The lack of commercial opportunities for natural gas production means constraints in converting both natural gas and crude oil resources into reserves, with far-reaching implications for companies and governments. A strong link exists between the commercialization of associated natural gas resources and the notion of global gas markets.

Like crude oil, natural gas is valued for its properties as both a source of energy and a feedstock for critical materials. But again like oil, the opportunities to use natural gas at or near the source of production are relatively rare. The *second problem* with a global natural gas scenario is, consequently, transport. Transporting natural gas via pipeline has, over time and worldwide, proven to be the most cost effective mode of delivery. The result is that natural gas use has evolved largely in local, national, or regional markets that can be connected via pipeline grids.

Natural gas pipeline grids, like other kinds of grids in heavily networked industries, present a number of public policy challenges. Issues of monopoly or other forms of market power quickly arise and with them questions about the extent of public interest, the proper role of government, and government/market trade-offs. The construction of local grids and associated challenges in meeting investment returns were key underlying factors contributing to the emergence of public utilities and state public utility regulation in the United States.

The dilemma of pricing natural gas for transportation to local markets, especially in a country where the ownership and operation of production and transportation assets are fragmented and where multiple jurisdictions are involved, along with public interest concerns regarding location and operation of major pipelines, led to federal government involvement in the U.S. natural gas industry. In most other countries, the sovereign government assumed direct responsibility for natural gas service, extending to the sovereign ownership of natural gas assets and operations. It has only been in recent years that experiments have taken hold to create discrete commodity markets for natural gas molecules that can be moved by a variety of shippers through pipelines that operate as common carriers. Canada, the United

States, Argentina, and the United Kingdom have been some of the most aggressive countries in this regard, with continental Europe, Mexico, Brazil, and others dipping into the liberalization process. The results have been mixed, leaving as uncertain the prospects for continued experimentation with liberalization and third-party or open access to natural gas pipeline grids and local distribution networks. Developing frameworks that enable workable competition in the development and pipeline delivery of natural gas resources, the compatibility of these frameworks with private investment, and the balance between private and public interests constitute important policy problems going forward. When frameworks for workable competition in electric power generation, transmission, and distribution, including natural-gas-fired power generation, are added to the mix, the public policy and related energy security considerations for natural gas come into even sharper relief.

## Liquefied and Compressed Natural Gas

Over longer distances, and across oceans, the shipment of natural gas via pipelines has less appeal or is simply impossible. But whereas oil and petroleum products can be loaded onto tankers and barges with minimal alteration, natural gas is typically converted to liquid form (liquefied natural gas, or LNG). Refrigeration, in effect, enables natural gas molecules to be more densely packed (roughly 600 times by volume) into available storage space on LNG carriers so that long-distance, transoceanic carriage is economic. The *third problem* in building a more global profile for natural gas, therefore, is achieving the affordable expansion of the LNG supply chain or the substitution of a viable alternative.

The shipment and use of natural gas as LNG have grown rapidly since the 1960s when international LNG trade was launched. LNG cargoes today still constitute less than one-third of natural gas movements worldwide, with pipeline transport making up the balance. At the same time, as demand for natural gas exports increases, the demand for natural gas as a domestic fuel in the countries and regions where it is produced is likely to increase as well. LNG is also subject to both domestic gas pricing in receiving countries and global oil price trends. Though a great deal has happened on the commercial front to make LNG supply contracts more flexible, the industry will remain dominated by longer-term, oil-linked transactions for some time to come.

The LNG supply chain is expensive, requiring billions of dollars to put all the pieces together, with liquefaction and shipping dominating costs downstream from the wellhead. Though gains have been made to reduce costs—largely by increasing economies of scale with bigger liquefaction trains and larger LNG ships—the delivered cost of LNG and its competitiveness very much hinge on relative prices for competing fuels (including domestic natural gas production) and willingness and ability to pay in receiving markets.

Last, LNG involves access to harbors and ports with deep water entry, well positioned for either colocated electric power generation (the Japanese model) or entry into pipeline grids for shipment to local markets (the U.S. model). Crowded coastlines, the intensive use of coastal waters for recreational and commercial purposes, coastal urban sprawl, concern about the protection of delicate coastal ecosystems, and, in the post–September 11, 2001, world, concern about safety and security of LNG facilities and operations—all conspire to present barriers to LNG expansion, notably in the United States but elsewhere as well.

LNG is not the only option for the "globalization" of natural gas. In fact, the notion of "global LNG" is something of a misnomer: The international LNG trade is bifurcated into Atlantic- and Pacific-basin shipments. The Panama Canal is a notable bottleneck, at least until a larger facility is constructed. For shorter distances water transportation might be achieved by compressing natural gas. Compressed natural gas tankers are under development that can serve regional markets, such as the Caribbean. The conversion of natural gas to middle distillates that can be shipped in conventional oil tankers or in any of the other modes available to crude oil and petroleum products, and serve as refining feedstock, offers perhaps an even more intriguing set of possibilities. In this scenario, not only would transportation options for natural gas be greatly facilitated but natural gas also would be able to compete in transportation fuels markets, offering a new panorama of energy security options to crude oil. Gas-to-liquids conversion is a target of much industry interest, and research and development, but large-scale commercial projects are not yet being launched.

## Evolution in Natural Gas Use

The *fourth problem* for any global natural gas scenario is the evolution in how natural gas is used, and the policy and energy security dimensions associated with natural gas supply–demand interactions. Growth in natural gas demand has largely come about because of the increased use of natural gas for electric power generation and the expanding industrial use in petrochemical applications, particularly in the gas-rich producing regions of Asia and the Middle East. The changes for electric power reflect long-term transitions associated with crude oil supply and pricing. In the United States, Japan, and Europe, crude oil for electric power generation declined rapidly as a consequence of the 1970s price shocks. Nuclear power and coal, and LNG in Japan, were the primary substitutes. The environmental attributes of natural gas as a cleaner-burning fossil fuel spurred both policy and industry emphasis on natural-gas-fired power generation in the United States and elsewhere. Environmental preferences for natural gas were augmented by relatively cheap supplies from the mid-1980s through the 1990s, improvements in natural gas turbine technologies, and much cheaper construction and maintenance costs for natural-gas-fired power plants.

Developing countries followed suit, resulting in a general surge of interest worldwide in natural gas as a priority fuel for electric power generation. The problem lies in whether natural gas resource development and the infrastructure for delivery can and will keep pace with demand. In the United States, this means a serious look at the misalignment between policies that encourage natural gas use for power generation and those that inhibit resource development or options for expanding imports. In a country in which feedstock for materials is also important, the debate has quickly converged on whether natural gas is too valuable a feedstock to simply be burned for electric power. This suggests a future for the United States, where *supply security for critical materials* might be at least as important as *supply security for energy,* and it pits different classes of customers against each other —industrial users that hope for major resource and infrastructure investments and individual consumers who oppose or are concerned about having these new investments in their backyards.

Because of its relative abundance, versatility, and environmental benefits compared with other fossil fuels, natural gas is widely viewed as *the* "bridge fuel" to the next energy future (whatever that may be). Whether the global demand for natural gas will grow during the next two decades and whether natural gas will graduate to the full status of a global energy source like oil will hinge on how these four challenges—supply development, frameworks for delivery and use, the expansion of international trade through LNG or other options, and balancing supply availability and use—are met.

## Prospects for Increased Global Gas Supplies and Usage

Because extensive investment in transportation infrastructure is required, natural gas has not been exploited on a global scale to the same extent as crude oil. Estimates of natural gas abundance in the Earth's crust are the same order of magnitude as crude oil; however, of the more than 690 billion barrels equivalent of crude oil and natural gas extracted in the history of industrial utilization of fossil energy, only about 22 percent has been natural gas. This low level of historical use, coupled with its relative abundance, makes natural gas an attractive growth fuel option for all the world's economies. Natural gas could grow proportionately faster in the global fuel mix than other primary fuels (oil, coal, nuclear power, and renewables) because the global abundance of natural gas is equal to that of crude oil and historical use is a fraction of that of crude oil.

The natural gas supply potential is equal to the ability of the industry to extract remaining reserves and convert resources to reserves for delivery to customers in the current and anticipated future global energy policy environment. For the purpose of this discussion, future supply potential is defined as the sum of current total remaining reserves and undiscovered conventional resources as defined by the U.S. Energy Information Administration (EIA)[3] and the U.S. Geological Survey (USGS).[4]

Global natural gas supplies, as measured by published values for reserves, grew each year from the mid-1970s to 2003. Data from the EIA's *International Energy Outlook 2004* show gas reserves in 2004 measured at 6,076 trillion cubic feet, having grown regularly from approximately 2,600 trillion cubic feet in 1975. Natural gas reserve estimates are volumes of natural gas that can be brought to market at current natural gas prices and technologies.[5] Reserves in five countries—Russia, Iran, Qatar, Saudi Arabia, and the United Arab Emirates—account for more than 60 percent of the world's known gas reserves.[6] Russia's position as the holder of the world's largest volumes of natural gas reserves has significance for the discussion of global energy security.

The distribution of natural gas in the world's sedimentary basins has been the subject of several studies, including those from the Potential Gas Committee[7] and USGS. The global resource distribution of natural gas from the USGS is shown in figure 22.1. Reserves are inferred from actual exploration and/or production of natural gas in a petroliferous basin. Resources are inferred by analogue in sedimentary basins or subunits of basins where limited exploratory confirmation exists.

Figure 22.1.  Gas Endowment for the Eight U.S. Geological Survey Regions of the World (billion cubic feet of gas)

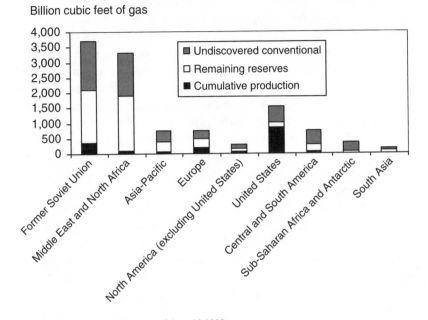

*Note:* Cumulative production is as of the mid-1990s.
*Source:* U.S. Geological Survey.

Undiscovered natural gas resources in those regions assessed by the USGS, including the United States, measure 5,196 trillion cubic feet. The potential future supply for the world's markets, the sum of reserves and resources, is well in excess of 10,000 trillion cubic feet, or nearly seventy years of natural gas supply at the EIA's 2025 projected gas utilization. An important caveat must be recognized: USGS, and other agencies, focus on technically recoverable reserves and resources. At any point in time, technical recovery is subject to price and technology, among other things. To actually discover, extract, and utilize the natural gas supply that is believed to be ultimately available will require favorable commercial and industry conditions, at least.

Technical demonstration of adequate global supply is necessary but not sufficient to translate into a global market for natural gas. Historically, the replacement of consumed reserves with fresh supplies has been relatively easy. Going forward, reserve replacement in mature provinces like the United States, Canada (on which the United States depends for about 16 percent of annual gas supplies), the North Sea, and elsewhere will be more challenging as the productivity of natural gas wells continues to diminish and resource development moves into frontiers that are ever more remote from key markets. The resource policies and fiscal regimes of individual sovereign nations, the regulatory frameworks for E&P as well as for transportation and end use, the infrastructure and commercial arrangements for regional and global trade, capital availability for investment given competing opportunities, and many other uncertainties are likely to yield only with time and persistence. Creating a global natural gas market with the same robustness of the global crude oil and products marketplace, while bolstered by resource potential and determination, will take work and a great deal of cooperation.

As figure 22.1 illustrates, the most prospective regions for natural gas production for export are those where domestic demand, even with growth, is far below what might be achieved in resource development. The bulk of estimated natural gas resources lie in the "petroleum heartland" extending from West Africa through North Africa into the Middle East and ultimately the former Soviet Union. This raises a distinct prospect that, at some point in the future, natural gas supplies will be concentrated in geographic locations where most of the world's oil supplies are also located and thus in regions that have presented, and continue to present, numerous energy security and foreign policy dilemmas.

## A New Gas Cartel?

A new parlor game is speculating on the potential for natural gas producers to associate and coordinate in the same way that the OPEC cartel has operated.[8] The "rules" of cartel formation and operation are specific, among them that the target of interest must be homogenous and closely held with respect to supply (i.e., few producers), and that the mutual interests of cartel members should be quite compatible. In contrast to oil, whereas global supplies of natural gas are clearly dominated by certain geographic locations, natural gas resources are much more widely dispersed (largely as a result of natural gas not having been a priority for development). Attempts to form a successful producer association or cartel for natural gas would be burdened with the requirement of co-opting and monitoring the activity and interests of a wide assortment of suppliers.

At some point in the future, a natural gas cartel could perhaps become more viable, but only if new resources like methane hydrates never become economically recoverable. Likewise, breakthroughs in gas-to-liquids applications would render global energy markets even more intensely competitive and much more difficult to influence and control.

Notwithstanding the weak arguments for cartel formation, natural-gas-producing countries are certainly in communication. The fifteen-nation Gas Exporting Countries Forum (GECF) is developing a permanent executive bureau and headquarters.[9] A clear incentive exists for natural-gas-exporting nations to form an alliance. Natural gas market information is sparse, and the pace and style of natural gas market development uncertain. The GECF thus presents a means for major natural-gas-producing and -exporting countries to cure or reduce information asymmetries with natural-gas-consuming and -importing countries.

The accelerated development of natural gas resources could create the same problems with respect to transparency and ethical governance that have plagued oil production in developing economies and those in transition. There also is a clear incentive for governments of natural-gas-exporting countries to want a greater share of both economic rents from their natural resource endowments and the value that is created throughout the natural gas supply chain. This last objective is most clearly evident when it comes to LNG as the main option for international trade and bears implications for the economics of LNG investment and delivery. LNG projects are sensitive to the fiscal terms offered by resource-rich producing countries; the less favorable those terms relative to other factors (e.g., transportation distance), the more difficult it will be to achieve a commercially sustainable, more global natural gas industry.

## Major Natural Gas Pipeline Projects

Even when countries successfully implement frameworks for investment in natural gas pipeline grids for transportation and distribution, there is the matter of coordinating policies for cross-border pipeline development. Canada and the United States stand out for the unique emergence of a "common market" for natural gas, bolstered by parallel interests in both the commercial and government domains. Regulatory approaches used by both the national governments and their respective provincial and state jurisdictions are notable for common practices and philosophies with regard to the role of competition and market-based approaches.[10] Open, competitive pricing of natural gas production and pipeline capacity have not inhibited major new projects from being certified; those projects that face controversy are generally in locations where local politics and support are weak. Pipelines are not cheap to build. The United States—which, in spite of the density of its pipeline network, needs additional investment—is a case in point. A typical, onshore natural gas pipeline can cost roughly $1 million per mile, but costs can jump to $6 to $8 million per mile in urban areas where rights of way are difficult to obtain and opposition is strong. Worldwide, pipeline construction costs range from about $750,000 per kilometer onshore to about $1 million per kilometer offshore.[11]

Elsewhere in the world, the situation of harmonizing natural gas transportation frameworks is not so hopeful. Countries struggle to resolve sovereign differences in order to establish major new natural gas cross-border pipelines. The Caspian Sea region, West Africa, and the Southern Cone of Latin America are good examples, with disputes surrounding Bolivia's desire for Pacific Coast access serving as an ongoing and provocative illustration. The desire to benefit from natural gas transportation leads governments to impose transit fees and tariffs that are often "deal breakers" relative to the overall costs and risks of the pipeline project. Disagreements persist about how to price gas for delivery in different locations and about whether or how to provide competitive access to natural gas supplies and pipeline transportation.

There is also the reality that, beyond a certain distance, natural gas (or oil) pipelines simply may not make much sense unless "special frameworks" can be devised, and these may be hotly debated for the long-lasting distortions they create in natural gas markets. LNG begins to make sense as a transportation option for pipeline distances of roughly 600 miles for offshore costs and 2,000 miles for onshore costs, as shown in figure 22.2. Further, extraordinary pipeline costs to move natural gas to coastal liquefaction facilities can sharply constrain the economics of LNG projects.

## The LNG Future

The recent resurgence of interest in LNG, especially in the United States and the rest of North America, as a means of linking distant natural gas supplies to growing natural gas markets is driven by a number of factors. In 2003, LNG imports represented 6.5 percent of the natural gas marketed

Figure 22.2.  Costs for Natural Gas Transportation, Pipelines versus Liquefied
Natural Gas (LNG)

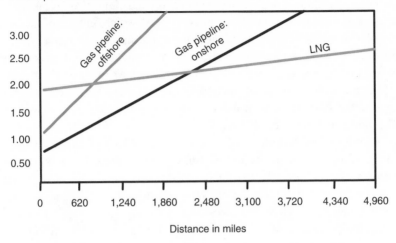

Dollars per million British thermal units

*Source:* Institute of Gas Technology.

globally and 37 percent of total world cross-border trade in natural gas.[12]
In Asia, South Korea, Taiwan, and Japan have no significant natural gas resources, and as a result must import the natural gas they need as LNG. Together, these economies represented 67 percent of global LNG demand in
2003. Europe, including France, Spain, Belgium, Italy, Greece, and Turkey,
represented 24 percent of the LNG trade in 2003. In contrast to East Asia
and Europe, demand for LNG during 2003 in North America, the world's
largest integrated natural gas market, represented 8 percent of global trade
and 1.9 percent of total global supply. The remainder of demand was met
by indigenous production and pipeline exports from Canada to the United
States and from the United States to Mexico. Growth prospects for LNG
markets are assessed in detail in recent publications by Jensen Associates,
Deutsche Bank, the University of Houston, and the U.S. National Petroleum
Council.[13]

The projected growth in demand, or "demand pull," for natural gas in the
highly industrialized nations of Western Europe, North America, and Asia
underlies the renewed interest in developing global LNG markets. On the
supply side of the natural gas value chain, new discoveries of associated and

nonassociated natural gas and the need to commercialize large natural gas reserves in the Middle East, Russia, Latin America, West Africa, and other regions of the world provide a "supply push" to expand the global LNG trade. As noted above, in many areas, the presence of large volumes of associated natural gas is creating additional emphasis on LNG development to establish a commercial outlet for the coproduced natural gas that would limit production of the associated crude oil.

The LNG marketplace is lively, with new world-class project proposals for supply, expansions of existing supply facilities, and cost reductions throughout the LNG supply chain. In the Americas, new LNG liquefaction facilities are being contemplated in Bolivia, Peru, Venezuela, Brazil, and the United States (in Alaska, which serves as the single export point for United States–derived LNG from natural gas production in the Cook Inlet). Expansions of existing liquefaction capacity in Trinidad and Tobago are under way, with recent approvals and proposals for additional LNG trains. Angola, Nigeria, and Equatorial Guinea in West Africa and Egypt in North Africa are building or have proposals for new facilities or expansions of existing LNG supply facilities. Liquefaction capacity is under construction in Norway (in spite of ongoing questions about economics) that will commercialize large deposits of natural gas in the northern Norwegian territorial waters. In the Middle East, new capacity and expansions are contemplated in Egypt, Yemen, Qatar, Oman, and Iran. In Russia, plans to construct LNG supply facilities on Sakhalin Island are well into the approval process (as of this writing, Sakhalin LNG is now slated for delivery to Mexico's northern Baja California). More recently, the potential for LNG facilities at the terminus of a proposed pipeline transporting natural gas from Western Siberia to an all-weather shipping port on the Baltic Ocean have been discussed. In South Asia, new facilities and expansions are contemplated in Indonesia, Australia, Brunei, East Timor, and Malaysia.

In the LNG world, timing is everything. Much new supply capacity is aimed at the North American marketplace. In North America, recent surges in natural gas prices are attributable partly to crude oil price strength but mostly to imbalances between domestic supply and demand. Signs of aging in domestic natural gas fields, more conservative estimates for new domestic production, and growth in demand all combine to sustain aggressive outlooks for LNG. However, natural gas demand in North America is clearly elastic with respect to price—the issue is to what degree. The United States, specifically, has experienced sharp reductions in natural gas demand during periods of historically high natural gas prices. The young, emerging economy of Mexico is also sensitive to natural gas prices. The constant question is what floor in market prices for natural gas will support long-term, sustainable growth in LNG imports and new receiving capacity, and under what conditions when it comes to interfuel competition and the entry of new domestic natural gas supplies such as pipeline deliveries from Alaska, ultra-deepwater discoveries in the offshore Gulf of Mexico, or—with the right upstream policy approach—a significant push to establish new oil and natural gas production from Mexico's rich basins.[14]

Timing for LNG also means connecting supply development, and supply contracts, with receiving capacity in importing countries, and here also lies a rub. As noted above, the public acceptance of new LNG import terminals in the United States, and other countries, is thin. In spite of demonstrated success in the most intensively developed LNG market in the world, Japan, achieving approvals for new import terminals in key locations has been difficult at best. Public concerns range from safety and security associated with local populations and property proximal to LNG import facilities to security fears associated with LNG shipments and shipping operations derived from countries with histories of insurgencies. And yet, the United States operates a large number of LNG facilities—more than 100 onshore peak shaving and satellite storage locations where domestic natural gas production has been liquefied and stored for decades. Indeed, the most notable safety event in the history of U.S. LNG operations occurred at a satellite storage facility in Cleveland during World War II, which was the result of a lack of knowledge regarding proper materials to use when dealing with a cryogenic material.[15]

Overall, LNG development in the United States encapsulates the full extent of public debate and emotion regarding energy supply, energy security, and energy infrastructure needs (including siting new infrastructure), and points to the deficit of public policy and consensus-building processes to support critical decision making. Presently, for instance, nearly 50 percent of the natural gas dispatched to the New England market during peak winter demand is supplied by imported LNG. As demand in that region increases, the options for supplying natural gas are the construction of new pipelines (some of which could carry natural gas from LNG imported into eastern Canada) through heavily populated and difficult to access areas, or the continued expansion of LNG import capacity based in the region. Public resistance to pipeline construction in the Northeast has resulted in significant delays in projects in recent years. In turn, these delays threaten to increase the costs and risks associated with gas supply projects in that region, while public resistance to new LNG import capacity suggests a complicated trade-off, at best.

## "Going Global": Summary and Conclusions

Broadly stated, the challenge to natural gas utilization is whether investment can mobilize quickly enough to link natural gas supplies with demand once market signals are detected. The more distant natural gas supplies are relative to demand, the trickier is the match making. The trickier the match making, the more uncertainty there is in forward-looking price trends (e.g., a considerable portion of natural gas price volatility experienced in the United States since 1999 has been derived from uncertainty about the timing and deliverability of supplies). Private-sector incentives to natural gas supply chain investment clearly exist at present. Whether these incentives remain in the future will hinge on both supply and demand adjustments. At stake in the public-private, government-market nexus is the extent to which governments should engage themselves, and in what manner.

A scenario for natural gas globalization might go something like this: Natural gas is an abundant but relatively underused energy source on a worldwide basis. North America, Western Europe, and Japan—the global economic leaders—have the highest utilization of natural gas. The development of natural gas resources and infrastructure in emerging economies will supply both energy and the raw material for economic development.

The expansion of existing networks and development of new pipelines and LNG supply routes and new markets will increase global and regional trade opportunities. Large, fast-growing economies like China and India are experiencing rapid increases in electricity demand to power their expanding economies as well as surging demand for feedstock for materials. Natural gas resources exist in both countries, but natural gas resource development is not keeping pace with demand increases. Neighboring countries, Bangladesh and Myanmar for example, have abundant resources, and are close enough to supply natural gas via pipeline into an expanding Asian market. The resource-rich Middle Eastern countries, Qatar in particular, have the capability to expand LNG facilities to supply the burgeoning demand centers as well. Much of the Asian region depends on coal-fired electricity generation and could reap significant benefit in a reduction of air pollution by using efficient and clean natural gas, adding the dimension of a commercial route to carbon emission mitigation as well as reducing other pollutants.

Pipeline transport of natural gas can and will compete effectively with LNG supply in countries and regions with strong resource fundamentals. Within distances represented by the borders of most nations, pipeline delivery of natural gas is competitive with LNG on a delivered cost of natural gas basis, as illustrated in figure 22.2. In other areas, pipelines will compete with LNG because there is strategic advantage in developing indigenous resources or trade with neighboring-country suppliers. The construction of the west–east pipeline in China is seen as a project where strategic interests predominate in the decision to bring indigenous resources to demand centers. Recent discussions between Trinidad and Tobago and several neighboring Caribbean island nations, focused on the construction of undersea natural gas pipelines, highlights the growth in strategic interest in the development of regional pipeline networks. And, as mentioned at the outset, pipelines and LNG do not represent the only options for globalizing natural gas. The devil is always in the details.

## Natural Gas Resource Development

Significant amounts of the remaining U.S. domestic resource base are unavailable to the market, either because of access issues (moratoriums and permitting) or because of a lack of infrastructure (Alaska) or adequate takeaway capacity (Rocky Mountains) to transport natural gas to markets. By and large, these are problems that, for the most part, will benefit from market-based solutions, with ideas already under discussion. In any case, many of these options face commercial tests; for example, no pipeline capacity from the Rocky Mountains will get built unless that investment is supported by the marketplace. In spite of restrictions to new areas for drilling, the United States stands out as a province that has exhibited, and hopefully will continue to exhibit, amazing flexibility with regard to E&P industry responsiveness to price signals, supported by one of the most creative capital markets for upstream development in the world.

In the international arena, other issues, often politically motivated, preclude the development of indigenous resources for the world market. In Bangladesh, for example, even very conservative resource estimates put the natural gas potential at large multiples of projected future use. Patrimony and nationalistic sentiments within Bangladesh, as well as among countries that could benefit from importing Bangladeshi production, have created an unattractive investment climate through protracted indecision on whether to export natural gas to regional markets, although this is beginning to be overcome.[16]

Implicit in the expansion of the number of global suppliers and markets is the potential for increased diversity and more robust competition. The intense competition that is the hallmark of the global E&P industry has important implications for energy security, supply costs, and the availability of crude oil in the global market as well. The development of a global natural gas market that fosters competition among suppliers could ensure that there are market-based options for the acquisition of incremental supplies, reducing the potential for both supply and price volatility everywhere. Moreover, for those countries like Nigeria and Angola, where extensive petroleum resources exist as associated oil and natural gas in a single reservoir environment, the development of a global natural gas market coincidentally provides an opportunity to develop the value of the associated oil resource.

For these things to happen on the resource development front, however, governments need to be convinced of the value associated with competitive investment and the exploitation of natural gas resources, to be willing to accept the greater transparency that accompanies a more competitive global natural gas E&P industry, and to have the political will to relinquish control of their sovereign interests and find new and better ways of reaping the benefits from their natural gas resource assets.

## Pipeline Transportation

The state of Alaska has large proven reserves of natural gas. Though the concept of building a pipeline to transport gas from the North Slope of Alaska has been in play since the early 1970s, the costs, engineering requirements, and concerns about the environmental impact have kept plans in the study and prefeasibility mode for three decades. The resource owners of North Slope natural gas estimate that the construction of an onshore pipeline from the North Slope to U.S. Midwest markets would cost approximately $20 billion. The supply potential of an Alaska natural gas pipeline would be less than 25 percent of the projected U.S. demand growth in 2025, but it could constitute a critical increment of energy security for North America.

## LNG

LNG could play an increasing role in the global natural gas trade. The industry is well established, with global trade extending in excess of forty years. With projections of aggressive natural gas demand growth, the industry is poised for significant expansion. Improvements in processes, economies of scale, and increased competition in LNG tanker construction have reduced project costs by 30 percent or more in the past decade. However, even with improved efficiencies, typical full-cycle investment costs for any given field project are estimated at $5 billion to $7 billion or more. LNG supply chain costs include field development, processing, liquefaction, tankers, and receiving terminals. Historically, investments in LNG projects have been possible only after long-term commitments have been finalized for off-take anchored by (typically) twenty-year contracts.

This is changing slowly. As more projects are developed along with regulatory flexibility for terminal construction, and as pressure increases to commercialize resources that would otherwise be "stranded" (e.g., natural gas supplies for which no current market exists), incremental surplus LNG capacity will develop. When coupled with the already achieved cost-efficiencies and increased demand, the limited arbitrage that exists will grow toward a true market-driven environment.

Given the demonstrated abundance of natural gas available to the global market, LNG is an attractive alternative to augment future domestic supply. Because no new greenfield LNG receiving terminal has been permitted and built in the United States in more than thirty years, both the public at large and public officials need to be educated on the benefits and on the safety and security issues associated with large-scale receiving terminals.

## The Evolution of Market Frameworks

In light of existing LNG trade and cross-border pipeline transfers of natural gas, it is safe to say that movement toward some form of a global natural gas market has begun. To develop more fully, broad regional and global natural gas trading will have to assume more of the characteristics of natural gas commoditization. Globally, where pipeline systems exist, market power issues and the feasibility of common carriage must be addressed. Transportation of natural gas in those pipelines needs to become simply a service offered to sellers and buyers that have greater ability to bid for pipeline capacity. To meet expanded demand in regions where pipelines provide the most cost-effective delivery service, new pipeline capacity will need to be built, for which clear market signals will be vital. The regulatory environment developed by the governments of the nations that these new pipelines cross will have to be designed with the common carrier function as the goal of operation.

## Implications for U.S. Energy Security and Foreign Policy

The United States can clearly benefit from greater efficiency and conservation with respect to the use of such a valuable resource as natural gas, and this is widely acknowledged. It is also widely acknowledged that efficiency and conservation alone are not sufficient, unless Americans are prepared to make even more dramatic trade-offs in lifestyle than what has been discussed thus far in the modern debate. Natural gas is an exhaustible resource; even if long-term demand was to remain essentially flat (and in many outlooks, this is the case), new supplies would need to be developed to offset reductions in current reserves, including in Canada.

Gas customers and consumers in many locations around the United States would clearly benefit from new exploration and production in regions where access is limited or prohibited. But public opposition to access for new drilling as well as to new pipelines and to new LNG import terminals creates a situation of "energy poverty" for those customers and consumers least able to afford their energy costs as a proportion of disposable income.

In contrast, if natural gas demand growth of as much as 50 percent in the next two decades is considered a reasonable prospect by conservative standards, U.S. energy policy will need to become more strongly focused on the role of natural gas to sustain the availability of abundant supplies of natural gas from both domestic and international sources. Natural gas could be important enough in the U.S. energy picture to warrant a separate legislative initiative that recognizes the dramatically increasing role of this fuel and feedstock. In many instances, existing policies and regulations are sufficient to permit the expansion of natural gas availability to users, and new and more creative approaches are required only for effective implementation.

Natural gas has the potential to serve as a major source of clean and efficient primary energy to move the global economy into and beyond the first half of the twenty-first century. To realize that vision, governments, industry, the investment community, and the public need to move consciously toward a global market that ensures the greatest efficiency from the massive investments required to both develop resources and build transportation and end-use infrastructure in a timely fashion. A global market encourages competitive supply that provides natural gas consumers with the most cost-effective access to energy. The key to moving development forward is increased legal and regulatory transparency in the marketplace.

## Bilateral and Multilateral Cooperation

Energy issues increasingly are recognized as a major factor in U.S. foreign policy. The United States, with the largest and most mature natural gas market in the world, is well positioned to take a significant lead in encouraging allies and trading partners to recognize the strategic importance of natural gas to their national interests and the global economy. In a consistent fashion, the United States needs to offer to the international community the lessons learned from its experience, both good and bad; help to coordinate producing and consuming nation-states; and encourage regional trade agreements that facilitate markets and trade.

The United States should help to lead efforts to define and implement mechanisms that encourage multilateral banks, nongovernmental organizations (NGOs), governments, and industry investors to identify less confrontational approaches to resolving the traditional issues associated with infrastructure. Most confrontations involving NGOs, governments, and industry typically occur well after significant investment commitments have been made. This pattern, both in the United States and the international arena, adds significantly to project costs and to the level of uncertainty associated with project execution. The United States can encourage early and effective consultation with local citizen groups for projects that seek trade financing or multilateral funding to push investors to take these consultations seriously, and also to complete consultations in a timely fashion.

In the United States, new natural gas infrastructure and LNG facilities require special attention. Because LNG is poised to play a growing role in the U.S. energy mix, special attention should be focused on engaging regulatory leads, state officials, industry leaders, and consumer and environmental interests. For the United States, a renewed consensus approach should be a priority that brings together a broad coalition, beginning with federal agencies with policy and regulatory responsibilities. Particular focus is needed to address issues of public education related to siting, safety, and security in a post-9/11 environment where information is scarce and often dated. The Departments of Energy and Commerce, as well as the Federal Energy Regulatory Commission, should launch a new, coordinated public diplomacy program to address the energy and the public safety concerns about LNG facilities.

Similarly, new infrastructure projects, particularly pipeline construction and gas storage facilities to supply natural gas to growing-demand markets, will need to be advanced efficiently. Regulatory streamlining at the federal and state levels—though maintaining environmental and public interest integrity, and including policies like the National Environmental Policy Act and Coastal Zone Management Act—could be considered.

Outside the United States, creative energy diplomacy to support natural gas development with current suppliers (e.g., Russia, Nigeria, Trinidad and Tobago, Algeria, Norway, and Qatar) and future suppliers (e.g., Venezuela, Mexico, Bolivia, and the nations of Central and West Africa) will be an essential part of crafting an effective global gas strategy and enhancing U.S. energy security.

Both U.S. and international energy security—and, more specifically, global natural gas supply security—will depend upon emerging new bilateral and multilateral relationships and arrangements, especially on two fronts. First, as with oil, non-OPEC natural gas supply and pricing will hinge on the congruence of interests between the largest non-OPEC supplier, Russia, and its major customers. The security of supply from Russia remains a concern in continental Europe and an influence on thinking about, and the implementation of, natural gas market liberalization, albeit less so than in the early days of experimentation with the E.U. directives.[17] With its huge potential customer to the east—China—Russia's trade relationships for both oil and natural gas are more tenuous. These nations are testing their common ground as economies in transition struggling to adjust to new political freedoms and a changed world status.

The second major front for U.S. and international energy security is clearly China. Together, China and India present the most significant reordering of the energy supply pie going forward. Both are expected to be huge natural gas consumers; attention to efficiency and conservation can help to balance their needs somewhat but will not eliminate the sheer impact of size and requirements for energy fuels, or the right to gain access. This last realization places serious foreign policy questions at the U.S. doorstep—questions that cut across a multitude of dimensions, such as trade and investment flows, knowledge sharing, relationships with key oil and natural gas supplier countries, and the definition of acceptable trade-offs to keep the peace.

## Notes

1. The terms "liquid" and "liquidity" are used in a financial, not physical, sense. "Liquidity" in commodity markets is a function of the number of market participants and associated financial commercial contracts and transactions. Typically, the more liquid

a commodity market is, the more efficiently that market works with respect to price discovery and transparency.

2. See http://www2.ifc.org/ogmc/global_gas.htm for information.

3. U.S. Energy Information Administration, *International Energy Outlook 2004,* available at http://www.eia.doe.gov/oiaf/ieo/index.html.

4. U.S. Geological Survey, *World Petroleum Assessment 2000,* available at http://greenwood.cr.usgs.gov/energy/WorldEnergy/DDS-60.

5. It is particularly important that the production of natural gas must be achieved for estimates of reserves to be valid. This means that commercial arrangements must exist for the disposition of natural gas production.

6. "Worldwide Look at Reserves and Production," *Oil and Gas Journal* 100, no. 52 (December 23, 2002): 114–15. See also chapter 1 in this volume by Adam Sieminski.

7. "Potential Supply of Natural Gas in the United States," Report of the Potential Gas Committee (Golden, Colo.: Colorado School of Mines, Potential Gas Agency, 2002).

8. See chapter 2 in this volume by Daniel Yergin.

9. This account is based on news media reports and communication with the government of Trinidad and Tobago during June 2004, as well as proprietary reports by the Institute for Energy, Law & Enterprise at the University of Houston (UH IELE).

10. See UH IELE, *North American Energy Integration* (Houston: UH IELE, 1999).

11. Pipeline cost information is from industry sources for the United States and from the International Energy Agency's *Global Investment Outlook* for the world. Worldwide data are as of 2000.

12. *BP Statistical Review of World Energy,* 2004, available at http://www.bp.com.

13. See James T. Jensen, "The LNG Revolution," *Energy Journal of the International Association for Energy Economics* 24, no. 2 (2003); Paul Sankey, C. Cook, and J. J. Treynor, *LNG: Going . . . Going . . . Gone Global. Picking the Winners from the Liquid Gas Boom* (London: Deutsche Bank, 2003); UH IELE, *Introduction to LNG* (Houston: UH IELE, 2003); and UH IELE, *The Role of LNG in North American Natural Gas Supply-Demand Balances* (Houston: UH IELE, 2004). Also see the UH IELE Web site on LNG, http://www.energy.uh.edu/lng; and National Petroleum Council, *Balancing Natural Gas Policy—Fueling Demands of a Growing Economy* 1 (2003), available at http://www.npc.org.

14. See chapter 16 in this volume by Luis Tellez Kuenzler and the related commentary on part V by Michelle Michot Foss.

15. See UH IELE, *LNG Safety and Security* (Houston: UH IELE, 2003), http://www.energy.uh.edu/lng.

16. Bangladesh provisionally agreed in 2005 to participate in a gas pipeline from Myangmar through its territory to India.

17. See chapter 7 in this volume by Loyola de Palacio.

# Commentary on Part VI

## John P. Holdren

The two-part thesis of this volume is that (1) the national security interests of the United States are being negatively affected by the choices it has made and continues to make about energy; and (2) fundamental changes in thinking about energy strategy, foreign policy, and the interaction of the two will be needed to effectively address the interlocking technical, economic, environmental, and national security dimensions of this predicament. As someone who has been grappling with "energy and society" issues for more than thirty years, not only as a full-time academic but also as a part-time energy adviser to decision makers in the United States and abroad, I agree wholeheartedly with both propositions.

The security of the United States depends not only on the capabilities and morale of the country's armed forces and on the judgment and resolve of its leaders but also on the strength of its economy; the health, confidence, and optimism of its people; the integrity of the environmental conditions and processes that, no less than economic ones, underpin its prosperity; and the robustness of its infrastructure—pipelines, power grids, communications networks, information processing, highway, and rail systems—against attack from without or within. The security of the United States also depends on a wide range of conditions and attitudes prevailing outside its borders—conditions and attitudes that are affected by U.S. actions and policies, but often in ways more complicated and more threatening than the architects of these actions and policies suppose.

As the diverse and distinguished authors in this part of the book establish in great detail, the choices America makes about how it obtains, converts, and uses energy affect all these aspects of U.S. national security, often very directly. Their chapters show, moreover, that—viewed through the prism of national security concerns—we have mostly have not been choosing well. For example:

- The risk to the U.S. economy from dependence on oil is proportional to the country's *total* oil use (because, in a global oil market, price spikes equally affect the domestically produced and imported portions of oil used in the United States). The large share of U.S. energy supply contributed by oil therefore constitutes a major risk to the country's economy —and indirectly to its national security—because factors outside U.S. control can cause the world oil price to sharply increase. The probability of such price spikes is, of course, heightened by the concentration of two-thirds of the world's oil reserves—and an even larger fraction of the estimated ultimately recoverable resources—in the politically volatile Middle East. America's dependence on imports for more than 50 percent of its oil creates additional economic-security risks: Oil imports severely undermine the U.S. balance of payments; and, closely related, foreign earnings from oil are invested heavily in U.S. economic assets, sometimes bringing them under significant de facto foreign control.
- Oil imports have more direct security implications through increasing the probability of going to war to protect access to foreign oil supplies; using oil revenues to fund the buildup of military forces and the acquisition of weapons of mass destruction by potential adversaries of the United States and its allies; and providing oil revenues to countries that foment hatred for the United States and train and support terrorists to attack it.
- Building and maintaining the military capability needed to protect oil supplies has very significant economic and political costs, even if the capability is not used. Should military forces actually be needed to protect oil, moreover, there may be military opportunity costs that prevent the United States from adequately dealing with other security threats that may arise at the same time.
- The promotion of nuclear energy as an electricity source around the globe, by the United States and others, has been accompanied by a failure to face up to the need for more stringent measures to prevent the proliferation of uranium-enrichment and plutonium-separation capabilities. This failure has not only greatly complicated the problem of constraining the proliferation of nuclear weapon programs among nations, but it has also multiplied the opportunities for terrorists to acquire the wherewithal to make nuclear explosives.
- Although there have been warnings from individual analysts and research

groups for decades, until the terrorist attacks of September 11, 2001, there was no systematic attention from the U.S. energy industry or the government to the vulnerabilities to terrorist attacks on U.S. energy facilities—for example, oil refineries, liquefied natural gas (LNG) terminals, nuclear power plants, hydroelectric dams—and energy-distribution infrastructure. The long neglect of this issue and the correspondingly deep embedding of the vulnerabilities in the structure of an energy system that is much too costly to replace quickly mean that the associated security risks will not be easy to abate.

- The failure of the United States to ratify the Kyoto Protocol or take other significant action to reduce its own emissions of carbon dioxide from fossil fuel burning has reduced substantially the chances of avoiding global climatic disruption serious enough to damage economies, destabilize governments, and increase international tensions all over the world.
- The U.S. failure to provide significant resources to cooperative efforts with developing countries to put in place energy technology for environmentally sustainable economic development has contributed to arguably the most fundamental security risk of all. This risk arises from enduring poverty and associated despair, which breed political instability, interstate conflict, and terrorism (although, of course, economic deprivation, including underdeveloped energy technology and resources, are far from the only causes of these security threats to the United States).

But the authors of the chapters in part VI do not stop with elaborating and clarifying the character of the security risks that arise from the energy choices (and nonchoices) that the United States has made. They go on to offer a variety of thoughtful, practical approaches for reducing those risks in the short, medium, and long terms.

In the most sweeping of these essays, Leon Fuerth illuminates the many ways in which the global character of both energy problems and the security issues with which these are entangled make it essential that the United States pursue a collaborative, multilateral approach to both. He treats the dangerous dimensions of U.S. oil dependence with sophistication and subtlety, and he focuses perceptively, as well, on the vulnerabilities of the U.S. energy system to terrorist attack and how these might begin to be abated.

I strongly agree with Fuerth that the energy-environment relationship has not been emphasized nearly enough in the formulation of U.S. energy policy. He states that by refocusing energy policy on the environment, the United States could restore "a sense of its purpose that unites it with rather

than sets it apart from the rest of the planet." As Fuerth himself notes earlier in his chapter, the benefits of such a refocusing would not only be pro-
cedural and symbolic. Climate change poses a real, long-term security threat
to the United States—one that can only be effectively addressed through
international cooperation.

As indicated above, a very substantial part of the world's energy-security
predicament in the short and medium terms revolves around oil. Two approaches for ameliorating these risks are (1) to expand—and make better
use of—strategic petroleum reserves for consuming countries and (2) to
increase the role of natural gas in applications that can displace oil, as one
way of reducing the overall dependence of the world's economies on oil.
(Natural gas is also attractive, of course, for its lower emissions per unit of
energy—compared with those from oil and coal—not only of conventional
air pollutants but also of climate-altering carbon dioxide.)

The possibilities for strategic petroleum reserves are admirably set out
in the chapter by David Goldwyn and Michelle Billig, and I can add little
to their analysis or their sensible suggestions. Both the opportunities and
the obstacles related to the expanded use of natural gas are treated in the
chapter by Donald Juckett and Michelle Foss. Their suggestions also are
very sensible, although I would add that I think the problem of siting new
LNG facilities will require more than a campaign of public diplomacy. This
could ultimately prove to be a not-in-my-backyard problem comparable to
those that nuclear energy facilities (and now offshore wind farms) have
encountered in the past.

Many of the keys to addressing the energy security problems faced by
the United States effectively and affordably lie in improving technologies
for energy supply and use. In their chapter, Melanie Kenderdine and Ernest
Moniz identify the essential preconditions for managing the U.S. energy
innovation effort in a more coordinated, focused, and efficient way—in part
through a "portfolio process" that would "tailor" choices of research and
development (R&D) programs and projects to strategic priorities, including
those related to national security. The authors pointedly note that the past
twenty-five years of energy R&D have *not* reduced dependency on oil,
which is—or should be—one such security priority.

Today, the U.S. government spends too much R&D money on badly
managed projects or on technologies that would more appropriately be pursued by the private sector. It spends too little money on many technological
opportunities for which long time horizons, lack of appropriability of re-

search results, and other factors involving externalities and public goods combine to ensure that the private sector by itself will not do enough.

Among the several valuable priorities for energy technology R&D stated at the conclusion of Kenderdine and Moniz's chapter, I would underscore the need for sharply increasing vehicle efficiency in the short and medium terms, primarily through incentives for hybrid technology, as well as for longer-term solutions, including hydrogen technology. By including among America's energy policy priorities what it can do *now* (or in the relatively near future) to increase vehicle efficiency, it will simultaneously reduce dependence on foreign oil and alleviate greenhouse gas emissions, both crucial national security goals.

The Kenderdine-Moniz proposals on nuclear energy closely parallel those of the recent Massachusetts Institute of Technology nuclear energy study,[1] of which Moniz was one of the cochairs and I (as truth in advertising requires that I admit) was one of the coauthors. A large expansion of nuclear energy in the United States and around the world could make a significant contribution to the transition to a climate-friendly energy system. But for this to be possible, it will be necessary to achieve—through a combination of technological and institutional innovation—improvements in nuclear energy's cost, safety, resistance to terrorist attack, radioactive waste management, and proliferation resistance.

In the studies of the U.S. federal energy—technology—innovation strategy by President Bill Clinton's Committee of Advisors on Science and Technology (which I had the privilege of leading), we started to describe a more coherent, comprehensive, and appropriately multisectoral and international approach to this issue.[2] I am happy to see the Kenderdine-Moniz suggestions advancing our thinking about energy technology innovation another notch. I would only add to their proposals the suggestion that, in promoting increased international cooperation on energy technology innovation, the U.S. federal government could more effectively utilize existing international collaborations on energy and the environment among U.S. universities and cooperating foreign institutions, and among academies of science and engineering around the world.

I noted above that underdevelopment abroad, including its important energy-related components, is perhaps the most significant security threat to the United States. An energy-related aspect of the underdevelopment problem, besides the lack of clean and affordable energy for development needs, is addressed in the chapter by Charles McPherson: the almost universal mismanagement of oil export revenues by developing-country governments. He rightly points to the need to help oil-exporting nations manage their wealth and improve governance through enhanced transparency, thus making much of this wealth available for development that benefits a broader range of society. The result will be greater social stability, which will certainly tend to enhance U.S. national security.

Although several authors emphasize the importance of climate change as an environmental and security threat, Kevin Baumert makes this topic the main focus of his chapter. He ably revisits the sins of both commission and omission in U.S. performance on climate change policy. He is absolutely right that the United States must both put its own house in order (with serious measures to reduce this country's emissions) and reengage in the fashioning of a cooperative, equitable, and adequate global effort to limit climate change risks. Alas, the needed steps are impeded in America by a widespread underestimation of the magnitude of the risks—an underestimation that has been perpetuated through the efforts of a vocal but well-funded handful of climate change "contrarians" who have exploited the appetite of the mass media for controversy and "balance."

These contrarians tout "science" in support of their contention that too little is known about the climate change threat to warrant taking significant action against it. But the "science" they are offering consists mainly of propositions that either have been discredited in the peer-reviewed literature or have not yet been examined there. The overwhelming consensus among credentialed scientists in fields relevant to climate change is that it is caused in substantial part by greenhouse gases emitted by human activity. Furthermore, there is a consensus that greenhouse-gas-induced climate change will entail not only higher average and extreme temperatures but also an increasing disruption of weather patterns, increases in both floods and droughts, rising sea level, and more, with adverse effects on agriculture, forestry, fisheries, patterns of disease, the livability of cities in summer, and many other aspects of human well-being. It is time for public policy to begin to take this reality into account, and Baumert offers a variety of good suggestions as to how.

The United States needs a strategy to advance its interests in the world as it is, and as it will be. Increasingly, the energy world will be dominated by issues of resource availability and scarcity, facility siting and vulnerability, and environmental opportunities and constraints—all interacting with the economic imperatives of energy for development and sustainable prosperity. These issues will inevitably rise to the very top of the U.S. political, economic, and security agenda. The very important question that the editors and authors of this book ask is, "How—and in what form—can we increase the salience of these issues in U.S. policymaking now, when we can still do a great deal to determine the nation's energy and environmental future?" In addressing that question with clarity and insight, the authors make an important contribution to America's capacity to achieve its energy and national security goals in this new century.

## Notes

1. John Deutsch (cochair), Ernest Moniz (cochair), Stephen Ansolabehere, Eric Beckjord, Michael Driscoll, Paul Gray, John Holdren, Paul Joskow, Richard Lester, and Neal Todreas, *The Future of Nuclear Power* (Cambridge, Mass.: Massachusetts Institute of Technology, 2003).

2. Panel on Federal Energy R&D (J. P. Holdren, chair), President's Committee of Advisors on Science and Technology, *Federal Energy R&D for the Challenges of the 21st Century* (Washington, D.C.: Office of Science and Technology Policy, 1997); Panel on International Cooperation in Energy Research, Development, Demonstration, and Deployment (J. P. Holdren, chair), President's Committee of Advisors on Science and Technology, *Powerful Partnerships: The Federal Role in International Cooperation on Energy Innovation* (Washington, D.C.: Office of Science and Technology Policy, 1999).

# Conclusion:
# Energy, Security, and Foreign Policy

*Jan H. Kalicki and David L. Goldwyn*

The need for energy security—primarily, access to stable and affordable supplies of fuel for transportation and electrification—colors the foreign policy of every industrial and industrializing nation. The great powers of the twentieth century—the United States, the United Kingdom, France, Italy, Germany, and Japan—all moved to secure access to energy, and their bilateral and multilateral relationships, security alliances, international institutions, and a lucrative and transparent free market trading system all served to promote the security of energy supplies. The extensive natural resources of the remaining great power—the Soviet Union, now the Russian Federation—gave it the unique ability to achieve energy self-sufficiency by the end of the twentieth century.

During the Cold War, the hierarchy of interests was, first and foremost, the confrontation with Soviet power, followed by assuring that the economic and energy lifelines of the United States and the West would prevail. The non-Soviet oil producers—preeminently the states of the Gulf—aligned with the United States in these two overriding sets of interests in return for Western, primarily U.S. and British, defense and protection. Other political and economic interests simply took a back seat—and good governance, not to mention democracy and human rights, were given short shrift.

As the Cold War confrontation receded, a new opportunity presented itself to refocus U.S. policy on the impact of its demand for energy on the governance of the oil-exporting nations and, in turn, the implications of that poor governance on its security and values. But, as in the previous period, "energy" and "high diplomacy" were two separate worlds. "Energy"—the world of the oil companies, oil producers, and energy, commerce, and trade ministries—continued to ratify the compact of protecting regimes in return for assuring supply. "High diplomacy"—the world of the foreign ministries and national security advisers—remained preoccupied with conflict prevention, crisis management, and great-power relations after the Cold War. Foreign policy deferred to the energy world in the oil-producing Arab states of the Gulf and Africa; energy policy deferred to the world of high diplomacy, where countries were separating from Soviet power (as in the Caspian Sea region) or were hostile to the United States (as in Iran and Iraq).

But at no time, during or after the Cold War, did energy policy and foreign policy become properly integrated. As a result, over the past half-century, the United States and the other OECD nations made a major strategic oversight. They missed the long-term consequences of their actions as they developed an unprecedented system of wealth, power, and modernization that depends excessively on undemocratic, unstable, and repressive governments. They failed to redress the environmental consequences of their consumption for the globe, and the costs of remediation have escalated. They failed, over and over, to invest adequately in the technology or to adopt the policies that would have sufficiently reduced this strategic vulnerability and saved them from facing its consequences in coming generations.

The results of this policy myopia are far graver in the twenty-first century than they were in the twentieth. In the twentieth century, the OECD countries' energy security was at risk from an oil embargo. Today, it is at risk from the internal instability of their suppliers; the lack of redundancy in their critical infrastructure, and its vulnerability to terrorist attacks; the lack of adequate refining and transportation capacity, as well as of energy supplies; the resulting volatility in the price of energy and its impact on the global economy; and an unchecked rate of growth of carbon emissions that would take a century to redress, even if emissions stopped today. Poor governance is an underlying challenge that, when combined with oil wealth, may fuel crime syndicates or terrorist cells.

These risks are far more difficult to reduce or rectify than the risks of the past. Moreover, the rising powers of the twenty-first century—China, India, and Brazil—and most of the developing world are embarked on an identical pattern of consumption and dependency. These new consuming nations are growing to rely on the same unstable, undemocratic governments that have used recycled petrodollars to escape the hard task of fundamental reform. The foreign policies of these new powers are already being shaped by their dependency. This, too, is a vulnerability for the United States, its allies, and its partners. There is also a fraying of the U.S. compact with Saudi

Arabia—exchanging moderate oil prices for military security—at the same time as it becomes more difficult in both countries to update that compact with popular support. As Edward Morse and Amy Jaffe note, "the rise in democratization, freedom of the press, and political debate and a growing tide of anti-Americanism are bringing a greater concern for popular opinion inside OPEC countries, especially in the Arabian Gulf. This new concern for popular sentiment is restricting the options of regional leaders to accommodate Western interests."

These vulnerabilities will not be reduced unless the United States moves now to integrate energy policy into its foreign policy. As Leon Fuerth points out, U.S. grand strategy requires that it never lose the ability to respond to any serious threat to the stability of the energy marketplace. An enlightened U.S. foreign policy, in addition, must address the impact of its demand on the governance of the exporting nations, build a stronger collective energy security system to enable it to overcome today's risks of disruption, and use the need of developing nations for energy and modern technology as a tool for promoting positive political and environmental change.

In this concluding chapter, we explain why the need to adopt a new integrated approach is urgent, how a new energy security strategy should be implemented, and how integrating energy policy into the United States' foreign policy will advance its national security interests.

## The Time to Act Is Now

The United States is at a unique moment in history that presents both dangers and opportunities with regard to its energy security. As a nation, America is wealthier and more powerful militarily than at any time in its history. Yet its "soft power"—the degree to which other nations emulate its values, seek its alliance, and respect rather than fear it—is at low ebb. New powers are emerging, and they may seek to align against the United States to balance its enormous military strength. As a prime example, America faces a hidden and formidable enemy in al Qaeda, which uses the vast poverty and ignorance around the globe as a recruiting device to attack the American way of life, its values, and the infrastructure that undergirds its economy.

In truth, both industrial and developing nations have far more to gain by making common cause with the United States than in combating it. America has far more to gain in persuading them of this reality than in trying to subjugate them or to simply defend itself against their fear or hatred. The

United States and these other nations have the desire for development and freedom in common. They share the need for access to the feedstocks of development, basic energy being key among them (as well as education and access to capital).

The United States can expect to live in one of two worlds in the coming generation. Either it will forge a greater coalition of nations based on common needs and promote development and cooperation, or it will see continued instability and unrest—and endure cyclical shocks to the global economy and sustained attacks on its people and property. In his commentary, the deputy prime minister of Qatar, Abdullah bin Hamad Al-Attiyah, whose nation outpaces the entire Gulf in foreign investment, reminds America that opportunities for cooperation should extend to both producers and consumers of gas as well as oil, in a balance of economic and security benefits for all parties—in short, collective energy security.

The contributing authors in this book make clear that for the United States and its allies to sustain its current course of energy demand and consumption without reform is a strategic liability. Adam Sieminski demonstrates that without a change in policies affecting energy demand, America as a nation and the entire Earth will be as dependent on oil and gas twenty years from now as they are today. The future growth of oil supply will be almost entirely outside the OECD nations. The nations America relies on will be more unstable, and the volatility of the price of oil and gas will increase.

Renewable technologies will not grow fast enough. Carbon emissions are rising largely unchecked. A commercially viable hydrogen-powered car is decades away. China, India, and other rising countries will build their infrastructure for electricity and their fleets of cars now and thus will not turn over this capital stock for decades. Most of the world is largely locked into its patterns of dependence and consumption for decades to come. Though new vehicle technologies, such as electric-gasoline hybrids or fuel cells, are expected to make progress over the next few decades, momentum still favors the traditional gasoline combustion engine. The U.S. market does not properly reflect the external costs of this gasoline use—from pollution all the way to security commitments to petroleum producers—making gas at the pump appear far cheaper than in Europe or Japan, where as a result of taxation gasoline costs are far higher, and per capita consumption and the rate of demand growth far lower than the United States. Unless America changes these patterns, its vulnerabilities will only grow.

The United States does have the power to change course. Its dependency is fundamentally about its cars and the complex politics of reducing its demand for gasoline without causing dislocation in large sectors of the U.S. economy.[1] There are medium- and long-term solutions to address this problem: advanced automotive technologies, alternative fuels, the promotion of hybrid vehicles, and the accelerated development of hydrogen technology.

As Melanie Kenderdine, Ernest Moniz, and John Holdren document, America has the technology to reduce its demand for oil and gas. It can make great gains through conservation and efficiency. Conservation is not merely a civic virtue. The country can protect its jobs and check the exodus of gas-consuming industries to other nations through measures that conserve natural gas. It can deploy these technologies both at home and abroad, bolstering the U.S. industries that invented them, and it can help slow oil and gas demand in the developing world and ease the U.S. transition to a more modern hydrogen-based economy.

Natural gas offers a future bridge from excessive oil dependence to the hydrogen-based economy, but the future is not yet here. It is clear that gas can produce hydrogen, reduce emissions, and often substitute for oil and coal. Yet the day when natural gas can serve commercially as a fuel or feedstock for transportation fuels is visible but not upon us. U.S. gas supplies today are tight, and the country has not built the infrastructure to avoid a squeeze that might set back demand. Opposition to new liquefied natural gas (LNG) infrastructure persists, and political challenges to an Alaska gas pipeline remain formidable. There is no global market for LNG yet, which could provide security of supply, but America can take steps to build one. Again, the potential for gas to replace other fuels and power hydrogen will be constrained unless policymakers find a way to bring more supply to the United States.

If America has the will to change how it uses energy, it will see significant foreign policy dividends. Along with its allies and partners, it can make common cause with forces for political and economic change, transparency, and reform. It can attract nations like China, which fear they must compete with it for energy, into a coalition seeking shared solutions for energy and economic security—based on the shared interests described by Amy Jaffe and Kenneth Medlock, and by Australia's John Ryan—in energy supply diversification, the research and deployment of energy efficient technologies, and the promotion of alternative energy. We can also use the demand for electric power as a tool for good.

But to do so, America must change the way it conceptualizes and implements its energy and foreign policy. It needs to consider how to launch a new energy security strategy.

## Toward a New Energy Security Strategy

This book was designed to provide the building blocks for a new energy security strategy: the global framework for understanding the constraints under which the United States must operate, the regional challenges it faces around the world, and a set of innovative policy responses. But America must take six steps at the broad policy level before more specific policy responses can be more widely successful:

- Lead by example.
- Pursue homeland and global security.
- Adopt a national technology strategy.
- Continue to diversify supply.
- Expand the community of consumer nations.
- Multilateralize its efforts.

### *Leading by Example*

If the United States is to be compelling in its advocacy abroad, it must deal with its pattern of energy consumption at home. Dependence on gasoline is its greatest unchecked vulnerability, and it cannot reduce this dependency unless it addresses transportation. Morse and Jaffe contend that the United States can meaningfully limit its demand for oil as a transportation fuel, not with draconian European- or Japanese-style 400 percent tax increases but with a mix of more modest taxes, incentives to use efficient low-sulfur diesel rather than gasoline, the regulation of the efficiency of sport utility vehicles, and mandates for large government fleets to be fueled by natural gas or electric power. In the short to medium terms, it can also legislate at home for higher fuel efficiency standards across the board, as well as for the promotion of hybrid technology.

For the long term, America must make a far more serious commitment to develop a carbon-free automobile. And, as Lee Hamilton suggests, the country should also finance the expansion of mass transit and "join the rest of the world in seriously combating greenhouse gas emissions"—even more timely in light of Russia's 2004 decision to ratify the Kyoto Protocol and thereby enable it to go into effect. The United States needs to take conservation, environmental protection, and efficiency seriously and make the transition from a consumption rate driven by decades of cheap gasoline and oil to one that considers the hidden costs that this dependency imposes on society. As for natural gas, Shirley Neff, Donald Juckett, and Michelle Foss warn that a price and supply crisis can be avoided, if America takes steps now to increase efficiency of consumption, access domestic supplies, and increase its ability to import LNG. But to provide this security, it must have the will to build the infrastructure to import LNG and avoid a dependence on gas analogous to its dependence on oil. To achieve a diversity of gas supply, it must be equipped to import from a variety of countries.

## *Pursuing Homeland and Global Security*

The U.S. energy infrastructure, and that of its allies and partners, is vulnerable to attack. As Daniel Yergin warns, the country must now secure the entire energy system, from the electric power grid to refineries, to LNG and chemical plants, and nuclear reactors. The lesson of September 11, 2001, is that we must take steps at home to protect the critical nodes of energy systems against sabotage and cyberattack. Significant funds will be needed to enhance intelligence, increase physical protection, and create redundancy for the most vulnerable parts of these systems. The U.S. Department of Homeland Security has only begun to scratch the surface of this problem— as Fuerth points out, large increases of resources will be needed not only at the federal but also at the local levels for those actually responsible for the security of critical installations and for damage control.

At the same time, much more needs to be done to strengthen global security, from international cooperation on energy transportation to maximum efforts to prevent the proliferation of nuclear weapons capabilities to such countries as Iran and North Korea. If peaceful uses of nuclear energy are to remain possible, we will require far more intrusive, internationally sanctioned efforts to shore up the Nuclear Non-Proliferation Treaty and the international regime of safeguards and controls, including more effective limits on uranium enrichment and plutonium reprocessing. Potential proliferators must be exposed to credible international sanctions and, at the same time, offered credible non-nuclear alternatives if they desist. Energy cooperation, or access to Western capital and markets, may also be a tool to reduce existing nuclear threats. Libya's agreement in late 2003 to dismantle its nuclear weapons program, in our view motivated by its desire to obtain relief from sanctions, represents a historic breakthrough—already clearing the way for U.S. investment to renovate its energy sector, and for Libya to rejoin the global economy. Jan Kalicki, Jonathan Elkind, and Keiichi Yokobori propose measures to engage both Iran and North Korea in cooperative regional systems, including oil transportation through the former and gas and power supply to the latter, which could become instrumental elements of a broader policy aimed at ending their nuclear weapons programs.

## Adopting a National Technology Strategy

Technology can provide a significant part of the answer to global dependence on oil and gas and a key to global change. As Kenderdine and Moniz point out, the U.S. government could invest in technology more wisely by devising technology road maps that focus on the country's most critical needs. Energy security is a public good, and it is an appropriate role of government to make additional investments to meet national security needs. At the same time, industry can and should continue to play a major role in developing new technologies that reduce U.S. energy dependence. With a public-private national technology strategy, America can make the transition more quickly to a hydrogen-based economy, and it can seek to share the burden and benefits of these investments globally, welcoming the other OECD members as well as Russia, China, India, and other nations into a collaborative energy technology initiative.

## Continuing to Diversify Supply

The United States will have no choice but to continue to import most of its energy—oil and gas—for the next two decades. In particular, as Robin West notes, Saudi Arabia will continue to be the swing supplier for the world's oil supplies—neither Russia nor any other country can play this role. America needs to manage the risks of near-term dependence because it cannot avoid them. Yergin, Morse, and Jaffe highlight the likelihood of uncertainty and disruptions in energy prices and the shocks these can impose on the global economy. With a counterpoint from Alvaro Silva-Calderón, Morse and Jaffe point out that the United States cannot be sanguine about reliance on OPEC as it faces internal pressures to preserve market share and to maximize revenues. Juckett and Foss describe the opportunities for using much more natural gas—including notably LNG—from Alaska to western Australia, and from Qatar to Russia. But to protect the diversity and security of supply, U.S. foreign policy must focus even more on non-OPEC suppliers, and it must be concerned far more with the internal governance of U.S. suppliers. As detailed in the next section, this will require the adoption of new foreign policy priorities and sustained attention to other traditional priorities.

## Expanding the Community of Consumer Nations

One of the signal achievements of the last century was the creation of the International Energy Agency (IEA) and the construction of collective emergency response mechanisms to counter the power of OPEC and defend Western economies against supply disruptions. As William Martin and Evan Harrje—as well as Morse and Jaffe, and David Goldwyn and Michelle Billig—make clear, these institutions are not organized or equipped to address today's challenges, and they omit key countries from their membership. The lesson of the twentieth century is that collective military and economic security is effective, from NATO and ANZUS to the European Union. The integration of nations into organizations that advance their common interests can help reduce conflict and foster the expansion of freedom and commerce.

We must envisage a global energy commons, where all nations with a shared interest can address together security of supply, efficiency and conservation, global climate change, technology deployment, and strategic stocks. The United States should step up its energy diplomacy in Asia, where nations are already moving to forge regional integrated solutions to energy problems. Ryan and Yokobori highlight the deep dependency of the nations of East Asia on imported oil and gas. These nations face a strategic challenge in the rapid growth of Chinese demand for energy. Ryan describes how the Asia-Pacific Economic Cooperation (APEC) forum's Energy Working Group has forged an initiative to avert competition and confrontation among Asian nations for energy. Yokobori recommends ways to integrate the power grids of China, Japan, and both North and South Korea to increase efficiency, lower power costs, and foster interdependence. Neff notes the fledgling efforts for regional cooperation in North America, through the North American Energy Working Group. But many of the leading energy producers, such as Russia, and leading consumers, such and China and India, have yet to be incorporated into serious regional energy cooperation programs. Martin and Harrje argue that it is time to find a way to integrate developing countries such as Brazil, China, India, and Russia into a cooperative arrangement with the IEA.

## Multilateralizing U.S. Efforts

America has the tools to foster new policies through existing multilateral organizations. But the United States and its partners need to use their shareholding in the World Bank and International Monetary Fund—and their membership in the Group of Eight (G-8), the OECD, APEC, the Summit of the Americas process, and the United Nations—to advance energy security policies. America has few sources of leverage over many of the countries that are critical to its energy supply. Where debt relief, trade, and infrastructure finance are tools that can promote better governance, such as in Sub-Saharan Africa—as McPherson and Hueper make clear—the United States should act with others to create powerful incentives or, as needed, new conditionality. The opportunity for America is to use these organizations to advance better governance and reform and to make support of their efforts a U.S. foreign policy priority.

## Integrating Energy and Foreign Policy

We believe that these energy concerns must be integrated into U.S. foreign policy. We do not intend for the energy tail to wag the foreign policy dog. Fundamental U.S. foreign policy goals remain unchanged—including a common defense against a growing variety of threats including terrorism, and the promotion of political, economic, and humanitarian objectives around the world. But we consider that energy is an increasingly important vehicle for advancing these and other international objectives, and that ignoring the political and economic costs of America's consumption of energy will further undermine its national security.

The positive relationship among energy, foreign policy, and national security can be visualized in terms of concentric circles (figure C.1). The core circle is defense against the physical disruption of supply, on which the U.S. economy and society depend. The next circle is strategic reserves, which guard against excessive pressures from energy suppliers and markets. The third circle is the use of energy resources to spur development, promote transparency, and help resolve conflicts. And the fourth circle is the use of energy as a tool to promote regional foreign policy objectives in a manner that reinforces—and is reinforced by—the other circles.

## Foreign Policy Challenges . . .

What are the consequences of such an integrated approach for U.S. foreign policy? We believe that they can be best understood in terms of the central challenges ahead, which we address in this section, and the foreign policy

Figure C.1. Energy, Foreign Policy, and National Security

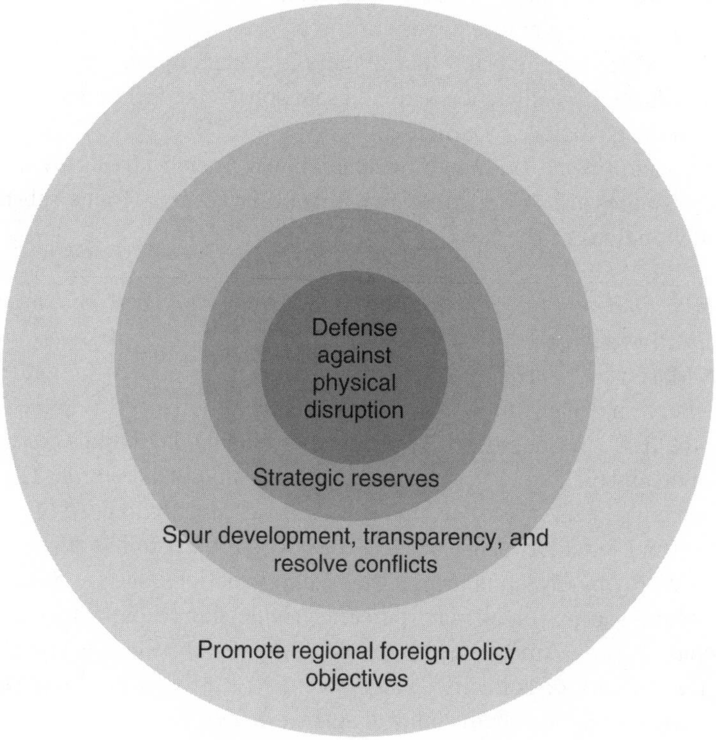

Defense
against
physical
disruption

Strategic reserves

Spur development, transparency, and
resolve conflicts

Promote regional foreign policy
objectives

responses, which we address in the next section. From an energy security perspective, America faces four major foreign policy challenges: building alliances, strengthening collective energy security, asserting its interests with energy suppliers, and addressing the rise of state control in energy.

*The first major challenge is to build alliances when energy dependency is pulling coalitions apart.* Major U.S. allies are growing more dependent on key regions for energy and economic survival. As Loyola de Palacio and Willy Olsen make clear, Europe is deeply dependent on Russian gas, and Yokobori sets forth a similar dependence by Japan on the Middle East, which is certainly also felt by China and India. On security matters, it will be increasingly difficult to muster coalitions to contain proliferation, or to repel aggression through the UN Security Council, when coalition members are competing for access to the target state's oil and gas. It was no coincidence when:

- Russia, China, and France, with potential large oil contracts in Iraq, resisted calls for "smart sanctions" or forceful inspections in the UN Security Council, long before the use of force.
- China, which had invested substantially in Sudan, resisted efforts in the UN Security Council action to use oil sanctions to compel Sudan's leaders to end the genocide in Darfur.
- Russia and France, both with substantial investment in Iran's oil and gas sector, opposed UN Security Council action to redress Iran's substantiated violations of the Nuclear Non-Proliferation Treaty.

*The second major challenge will be to strengthen and expand the system of collective energy security when forces of competition are undermining it.* As Martin and Harrje make clear, the IEA can do more to strengthen its cooperative mechanism to deal with future energy crises. But at the same time, the IEA's present members no longer dominate the world's consumption of oil and their stocks cannot fully redress a supply disruption. The major new consumers, notably China and India, are deeply in need of energy security and so far have chosen to compete to get it. China has attempted to secure supply by investing in countries facing sanctions, such as Sudan and Iran; trading arms for oil; and pursuing single-source pipelines that stir regional rivalries. America needs to find a way to draw the new consumers into the network of collective energy security, starting with an expanded IEA, rather than have them compete against it.

*The third major challenge is to assert U.S. security interests, in concert with its allies and partners, with the world's major suppliers.* The 9/11 terrorist attacks brought home the need not only to respond to such attacks but also to deal with the underlying sources of terrorism. America and its allies share fundamental interests in helping Middle Eastern societies to modernize, Eurasia to democratize and respect the rule of law, Africa and Latin America to develop in a sustainable way, and China and East Asia to extend economic growth—all in a manner that promotes security and reduces the risks of conflict.

While we therefore seek change in many sectors of U.S. foreign policy, we also seek price stability in its energy and economic policies. These two elements are often contradictory, and U.S. policymakers have failed to make the hard choice of risking short-term supply to secure long-term security and stability. America seeks higher production and more open markets from Saudi Arabia, yet it and many Saudi reformers also wish it to create more opportunities for the Saudi population and to open its society—in which they may succeed in rooting out terrorism but may also promote economic nationalism or even a more extreme backlash that may undermine the initial objectives. America seeks more access to oil in Russia and the Caspian Sea region, yet it deplores their regression on democracy and the rule of law. America seeks greater energy security from Africa, yet African leaders' progress in renouncing corruption and investing in their societies is halting at best. The United States and its allies must muster the courage to not simply protect near-term supplies but also to pilot through the Scylla and Charybdis of change.

*The fourth key challenge is to address the rise of state control in energy.* State control is not a new phenomenon in natural resources—with antecedents in the nationalizations of the 1970s and the development of the Soviet oil and gas industry. In the 1990s in particular, there was a renewed movement toward liberalizing energy markets, showing that private investment capital could bring increased prosperity to OPEC and non-OPEC nations alike. As Yergin recognizes, however, the current decade has seen the return of state control over oil resources, from Venezuela to Russia. The danger from both an economic and energy security standpoint is that state control will have an adverse impact on investment and production, with collateral damage to both economic growth and global energy supplies—a danger reflected in oil price jumps in response to strikes against Petróleos de Venezuela and, as noted by Julia Nanay, the expanding role of Gazprom and the state's takeover of Yukos assets in Russia. Conversely, it is possible to promote forms of state control that are consistent with increased private investment and development of more open societies, a reasonable policy goal while continuing to encourage a greater private-sector role over the longer term.

## . . . and Foreign Policy Responses

If these are the main foreign policy challenges, what foreign policy responses can enhance the energy security of the United States and its partners? Eight responses emerge from the discussion of these issues in this book.

*The first component of a new foreign policy strategy is both candor and respect.* U.S. leaders and policymakers have too long feared that if they publicly criticize U.S. suppliers or give voice to their concerns, they will "jeopardize the relationship." The allergy is bipartisan. The relative silence of the United States and other countries on Africa's kleptocracy, Russia's trespasses on the rule of law, and repression in the Middle East undermines reformers and engenders resentment. America and its partners need not badger or patronize to simply give voice to democratic values. Rather, they need to be able to act firmly and respectfully, but not to shy away from publicly making common cause with reformers to achieve transparency, economic opportunity, and rule-based societies—rather than seeking to impose these reforms in an arrogant and unilateralist fashion.[2]

Yet the objection is often heard that such an approach will undermine ties with precisely those countries on which America and its partners depend for energy supplies. It is highly unlikely that any nation will cease to export gas pursuant to contracts or to export oil in a globalized market to punish the United States and its partners. For one thing, it is both impractical and risky to target individual consumers. For another, most exporters need their revenues as much as the market needs their oil and gas. Even more fundamentally, this objection ignores the fact that reformist forces, which are often associated with younger generations of emerging leaders, are seeking reasonable change, and a wise policy would associate with rather than accept the suppression of these forces. In 2004 and 2005, U.S. and European support of democratically elected leaders in Ukraine as well as democratic trends in Egypt, Lebanon, and Saudi Arabia have all paid dividends. There are modest but long overdue applications of principle to public diplomacy.

*Second, America needs a foreign policy that promotes the security and stability of its suppliers.* Both the surrounding environment and the internal governance of key suppliers affect America's energy and national security. Thus, it is in the U.S. interest to help resolve regional conflicts and strengthen the capacity to counter terrorist or military threats in Eurasia and the Middle East. But internal governance should also be made a higher priority of U.S. foreign policy. If America seeks greater stability of supply from Africa, it must make anticorruption and transparency a top concern. If it wants Mexico to play an expanded role as a supplier, it must work harder on migration and integration issues, as noted by Luis Tellez, just as it encourages an appropriate role for foreign investment. If it wants to see Russia and the Caspian region grow, it must make respect for the rule of law and fair market access a top priority.[3] And if it wants to find more peace and less hostility in the Middle East, it must make the modernization of those societies and the resolution of festering conflicts a high priority as well.

*Third, the United States must prioritize expanding the umbrella of energy security to other major consumers.* Today, America has more in common on energy with China and India—just as it does with Brazil, Japan, and other

APEC countries—than it realizes. Both the United States and these other nations seek stability in the oil markets, stability in the Middle East, open access for foreign investment, and smarter ways to conserve energy. As suggested by Jaffe, Medlock, Goldwyn, and Billig, and by Bennett Johnston in his commentary, America must give China and India reason to cooperate rather than compete. Though both nations are beginning to build strategic reserves, China has made only modest progress and India is at the conceptual stage. Both nations will require billions of dollars in investment to build adequate tankage and billions more to buy adequate supplies of oil. Giving these nations access to strategic reserves, cooperating jointly on automotive and power technologies, and expanding cooperation in gas, coal, and future energy alternatives can lead to cooperation on security as well. America cannot simply wish them into an alliance. Just as the United States offered a nuclear umbrella to Japan—cementing its alliance with Japan and securing stability in Asia—so it needs to construct an energy security umbrella for developing Asia. Bold steps to this end are building a global strategic petroleum reserve to which China and India would have access, or sponsoring their membership in the IEA's emergency response system, as Morse and Jaffe, and also Martin and Haarje, suggest. Diplomatic steps include cooperative multilateral approaches through APEC, as suggested by Ryan, as well as through relations among the great powers of Northeast Asia—China, Japan, Russia, and the United States—which can make common cause on a broad agenda ranging from energy cooperation to nuclear nonproliferation.

*Fourth, America must prepare its energy defenses.* With market capacity constrained and OPEC's power projected to grow, and with producing states continuing to face tensions, the United States must be prepared for energy price volatility. It must be better prepared should democratic regime change in Iran, elections in Nigeria and Venezuela, attacks on Russian oil companies, or terrorism in the Middle East disrupt supply. As we are reminded by Goldwyn and Billig, Martin and Harrje, and Morse and Jaffe, America needs adequate strategic stocks for both itself and the global market, to counter whatever disruption may come and to deter any politically motivated effort to squeeze consumers. Cooperation on the environment, as suggested by Kevin Baumert and John Holdren, may also win America cooperation on energy and other issues. The United States needs to increase the security of its gas supply and to achieve secure redundancy for its power, fuels, and transportation infrastructure.

*Fifth, America should promote a free market in energy.* With the historic opening of U.S. markets should come the expectation of increased access to the markets of U.S. energy suppliers. The first step, as Morse and Jaffe suggest, is to make rules of open access and fair competition in the energy sector a priority for the World Trade Organization through the next round of international trade negotiations. The second, as suggested by Goldwyn and Billig, is to give preferential access in expanding America's own or new strategic energy reserves to those nations that allow market access. A third is for the United States to enforce competition where it can—as Loyola de Palacio and Gordon Shearer demonstrate that the European Union has done with Russia and North Africa as the price of entry to its market. If these steps fail, Morse and Jaffe suggest considering the use of the "monopsony wedge" of consumers to deny access to energy markets to those that deny consuming countries access to theirs—an option that may be more effective as a threat than a course of action.

*Sixth, the United States must find a way to engage the nations of the Middle East constructively, candidly, and productively.* As Sieminski and West make clear, it is simply unrealistic, at least for the next two decades, to replace the Middle East, and particularly Saudi Arabia, as a key supplier. Western countries cannot sustain long-term loss of the Kingdom's supplies without severe global economic dislocation; they have no other candidate for maintaining excess capacity for the world's oil balance. Rather, they need a new approach that recognizes the importance of Arab oil suppliers but engages them on the fundamental issue of modernizing their societies. They need to encourage reformist trends from within the region rather than seeking to impose reforms from outside. The United States cannot do this bilaterally. It needs a multilateral process that engages with reformist leaders in the region and their counterparts in other countries, both developing and developed, Islamic and non-Islamic, in a dialogue based on mutual respect and shared objectives for social, economic, and political progress. It also needs to recognize the imperative of resolving the Israeli–Palestinian dispute, not only for the sake of Israel and the Palestinians but also because this is a continuing sore in the broader relationship between the Arab world and the West.

*Seventh, America must recognize the indispensable role of government.* The United States has maintained a contradictory and false mythology when it comes to energy markets. It regularly discourages a role for government, proclaiming an allegiance to market forces. The need to avoid government interference in price signals in the market is indispensable. Price and supply regulation created unnecessary shortages in the United States of the 1960s and 1970s and does so today in the developing world. But it is irresponsible to deny to consumer governments the ability to counter market intervention by OPEC, an alliance of producer governments, or to deny market access by non-OPEC nations when OPEC states enjoy access to the United States and Western markets. Governments also have tools to deploy in constraining demand, from Europe's successful taxation of fuels, to regulatory mandates for cleaner fuels and more efficient engines, to the utilization of strategic stocks.

*Eighth and finally, America can convert energy poverty and global environmental concern into the basis for a new global partnership.* We believe that energy and the issues associated with it give the United States a powerful opportunity to regain the world's respect and support for its political and economic leadership—not just the world's fear of its military prowess. Throughout its history, the United States has built vast reserves of "soft power" by leading magnanimous efforts to transform or aid troubled societies. From Lend Lease and the Marshall Plan, to the Voice of America, Alliance for Progress, and the Peace Corps, it has made friends and strengthened alliances through its leadership. America and its partners have the opportunity to do this again, focusing on the 2 billion people with no access to electricity.

The United States should lead a global effort—incorporating the World Bank; U.S. allies and partners in the G-8 and OECD; the leading energy producers and consumers; and regional organizations in Africa, the Middle East, and Latin America—to provide universal access to electricity in this century. The goal is ambitious, and the costs would be high. Yet there are nearly 2 billion people in the world living in energy poverty. That poverty means no access to the means of development, but also no access to education, information, and modernity. Electricity will bring light, heat, and unparalleled potential for development to the rural poor, disaffected, and alienated societies that compose a large portion of the breeding ground for religious extremism, terror, drug cultivation, and regional conflict. It is a capital investment that will surely earn security dividends.

The United States can recommit itself to leading the world, rather than simply dictating to it, in modernizing global institutions. As Martin and Harrje suggest, expanding the IEA to include China and India, helping APEC to create a regional gas grid, and fostering power pools in Africa, Central America, and Eurasia through regional organizations will strengthen these economies and integrate the nations of each region into an interdependent economic unit. America's vision should be nothing less than global—and the regional energy institutions that it establishes should become at least as robust as the international financial institutions and an expanded NATO.

America can also find a new path to addressing global climate change. Whether the path is through reforming the Kyoto Protocol, as Baumert suggests, or a common technological alternative, as Martin and Haarje suggest, or some third way, the United States must reengage the world. It can find a path to rebuilding its alliances with Europe, bringing demand-restraining technologies to Asia as it adopts them at home, and creating a powerful counterweight to its fossil fuel dependency through a new path away from the long-term consequences of unchecked greenhouse gas emissions.

It will be far better for the United States to demonstrate the maturity to address these consequences at a pace it can manage economically than to hope passively for some technological miracle to rescue a deeply polluted planet two or more decades from now. It will be far better for America to lead on this issue, leveraging its support for cooperation on matters of fundamental global as well as national concern than to isolate itself and gain neither stronger alliances nor a sustainable future.

We conclude this book where we began: Energy is the lifeblood of America's security and well-being. By becoming fully integrated into foreign policy and reflected in the institutions of this new century, energy can help assure not only the United States' national security but regional and global security as well. Failure to recognize this opportunity, and to act on it, is not an option.

## Notes

1. For a bold proposal for altering transportation technologies, see Amory Lovins, E. K. Datta, O. Bustnes, J. Koomey, and N. Glasgow, *Winning the Oil Endgame* (Denver: Rocky Mountain Institute, 2004).

2. See David L. Goldwyn, "Extracting Transparency," *Georgetown Journal of International Affairs,* Winter 2004.

3. See Jan H. Kalicki and Eugene K. Lawson, eds., *Russian-Eurasian Renaissance? U.S. Trade and Investment with Russia and Eurasia* (Stanford, Calif., and Washington, D.C.: Stanford University Press and Woodrow Wilson Center Press, 2003).

# About the Contributors

**Abdullah bin Hamad Al-Attiyah** is second deputy prime minister and minister of energy and industry of the State of Qatar, and chairman and chief executive of Qatar Petroleum. He has served several times as president of the OPEC Ministerial Conference.

**Kevin A. Baumert**, a senior associate at the World Resources Institute, was the chief editor of *Building on the Kyoto Protocol: Options for Protecting the Climate* (World Resources Institute, 2002).

**Michelle Billig** has served as international affairs fellow at the Council on Foreign Relations and as international policy adviser at the U.S. Department of Energy from 1999 to 2003.

**Loyola de Palacio** has served as vice president of the European Commission and commissioner of transport and energy, with responsibility for relations with the European Parliament. She previously served as Spain's minister for agriculture, fisheries, and food.

**Jonathan Elkind** is an independent energy consultant. He served as director for Russian, Ukrainian, and Eurasian Affairs at the National Security Council from 1998 to 2001, and as special adviser to Vice President Al Gore from 1996 to 1998.

**Michelle Michot Foss** is founder and executive director of the Institute for Energy, Law, and Enterprise and assistant research professor at the University of Houston Law Center. She served previously as director of research at Simmons & Company.

**Leon Fuerth** is Research Professor of International Affairs at George Washington University, where he previously was Shapiro Professor. He served as national security adviser to Vice President Al Gore from 1993 to 2000.

**David L. Goldwyn** is president of Goldwyn International Strategies. He served as U.S. assistant secretary of energy for international affairs from 2000 to 2001, and as national security deputy to former U.S. ambassador to the United Nations Bill Richardson.

**Lee H. Hamilton** is the president and director of the Woodrow Wilson International Center for Scholars and the director of the Center on Congress at Indiana University. While a U.S. representative from Indiana from 1965 to 1999, he chaired the House committees on foreign affairs and intelligence as well as the Joint Economic Committee.

**Evan M. Harrje** is an energy policy analyst based in Washington. From 1999 to 2003, he was director of energy research at Washington Policy & Analysis, an international energy consulting firm.

**John P. Holdren** is Teresa and John Heinz Professor and director of the Program on Science, Technology, and Public Policy at the John F. Kennedy School of Government, and professor of environmental science and public policy at Harvard University.

**Paul F. Hueper** is a special adviser on global energy issues at the U.S. Department of Commerce. He has worked for several U.S. government agencies, including the Department of Energy, on technical energy, energy policy, and energy security issues.

**Amy Myers Jaffe** is the Wallace Wilson Fellow for Energy Studies at the James A. Baker III Institute for Public Policy and associate director of the Rice University Energy Program.

**J. Bennett Johnston** is a partner at Johnston & Associates and at Johnston Development Company. As a U.S. senator from Louisiana from 1972 to 1996, he served as chairman of the Senate Committee on Energy and Natural Resources.

**Donald A. Juckett** served as director of the Office of Natural Gas and Petroleum Import and Export at the U.S. Department of Energy from 1997 to

2003, and as director of the Office of Geoscience Research and other Department of Energy offices from 1988 to 1997.

**Jan H. Kalicki** is a public policy scholar at the Woodrow Wilson International Center for Scholars and also counselor for international strategy at Chevron Corporation. From 1994 to 2001, he served as White House ombudsman for the Newly Independent States of the former Soviet Union and as counselor to the U.S. Department of Commerce.

**Viktor I. Kalyuzhny** has served as the Russian Federation's minister of fuel and energy, deputy minister of foreign affairs, and special representative of the president to the Caspian.

**Melanie A. Kenderdine** is vice president of the Gas Technology Institute. She served earlier in several capacities, most recently as director of policy, at the U.S. Department of Energy from 1993 to 2001.

**William F. Martin** has been chairman of Washington Policy & Analysis, an international energy consulting firm, since 1988. From 1981 to 1988, he served in Ronald Reagan's administration as executive secretary of the National Security Council and as deputy secretary of energy.

**Charles McPherson** is senior adviser in the Oil, Gas, Mining, and Chemicals Department of the World Bank.

**Kenneth B. Medlock III** is a visiting professor of economics at Rice University and an energy consultant at the James A. Baker III Institute for Public Policy. He previously served as a corporate consultant at El Paso Energy Corporation.

**Ernest J. Moniz** is professor of physics and director of energy studies at the Laboratory for Energy and the Environment of the Massachusetts Institute of Technology. He served earlier as U.S. undersecretary of energy (1997–2001) and as associate director of the White House's Office of Science and Technology Policy (1995–97).

**Edward L. Morse** is executive adviser at Hess Energy Trading Company. From 1988 to 1999, he served as president and publisher of the Energy Intelligence Group and as deputy assistant secretary of state for international energy policy.

**Julia Nanay** is a senior director at PFC Energy, a Washington-based industry advisory firm. She has worked with PFC Energy in various capacities since 1985.

**Shirley Neff** is the president of the U.S. Association for Energy Economics, an adjunct professor at Columbia University, and the former economist for the Energy and Natural Resources Committee of the U.S. Senate.

**Willy H. Olsen** is oil and gas adviser at the INTSOK Foundation. He served earlier as senior adviser to the president and chief executive of Statoil, and as head of the editorial staff of the Oslo newspaper *Arbeiderbladet.*

**Bill Richardson** is the governor of New Mexico and previously served as U.S. secretary of energy, as permanent U.S. representative to the United Nations, and as a member of the U.S. House of Representatives.

**John Ryan** is deputy secretary of the Australian Department of Industry, Tourism, and Resources. From 1999 to 2001, he headed the Canberra office of the Allen Consulting Group.

**James R. Schlesinger** is senior adviser at Lehman Brothers and previously served as the first U.S. secretary of energy as well as secretary of defense and director of the Central Intelligence Agency.

**Gordon Shearer** is president and chief executive of HESS LNG, a joint venture of Amerada Hess Corporation and Poten & Partners. He previously served as senior commercial adviser at Poten and as chief executive of Cabot LNG Corporation.

**Adam E. Sieminski** is the director and global oil strategist at Deutsche Bank in London. From 1988 to 1997, he served as a senior energy analyst at NatWest Securities in New York.

**Alvaro Silva-Calderón** was secretary general of the Organization of Petroleum Exporting Countries from July 2002 to December 2003. He previously served as Venezuela's minister of energy and mines.

**Luis Téllez Kuenzler** is managing director at the Carlyle Group in Mexico. He served earlier as executive vice president of Grupo Desc (2001–3), as

Mexico's secretary of energy (1997–2000), and as President Ernesto Zedillo's chief of staff.

**J. Robinson (Robin) West** is the founder and chairman of PFC Energy, a Washington-based industry advisory firm. He served previously as U.S. assistant secretary of the interior (1981–83), on the White House staff, and as a deputy assistant secretary of defense for international economic affairs.

**Daniel Yergin** is chairman of Cambridge Energy Research Associates. He is the author of *The Prize: The Epic Quest for Oil, Money, and Power* (Simon & Schuster, 1991), for which he won the Pulitzer Prize, and, with Joseph Stanislaw, of *The Commanding Heights: The Battle for the World Economy* (Simon & Schuster, 2000).

**Keiichi Yokobori** is director and research adviser at the Institute of Research and Innovation in Japan and a visiting professor at Waseda University. From 1996 to 2001, he served as president of the Asia-Pacific Energy Research Centre.

# Index

*Boxes, figures, notes, and tables are indicated by b, f, n, and t.*

585